Bowditch's Coastal Navigation

Nathaniel Bowditch

NOT FOR RESALE
DISTRIBUTE THRU
BALTIMORE CITY HEALTH DEPARTMENT

ARCO PUBLISHING, INC.
219 Park Ave. South, New York, N.Y. 10003

Reprinted from AMERICAN PRACTICAL NAVIGATOR, An Epitome of Navigation.
Originally by Nathaniel Bowditch, 1977 Edition, published by Defense
Mapping Agency Hydrographic Center.

First Edition, Second Printing, 1980

Published by Arco Publishing, Inc.
219 Park Avenue South, New York, N.Y. 10003

Library of Congress Cataloging in Publication Data

Bowditch's coastal navigation.

"This . . . edition reprints fourteen pertinent chapters and selected appendices from the 1977 edition of the American practical navigator."

1. Navigation. I. Bowditch, Nathaniel, 1773–1838.
II. American practical navigator. III. Title:
Coastal navigation.

VK555.B734 1978 623.89′2 78-5232
ISBN 0-668-04460-8 (Paper Edition)

Printed in the United States of America

PREFACE

According to John Hamilton Moore in his book *The Practical Navigator*, as revised by Joseph Dessiou and published in London in 1814, "The end and business of Navigation is to instruct the mariner how to conduct a ship through the wide and pathless oceans, to the remotest parts of the world, the safest and shortest way, in passages navigable." This definition, as appearing over a century and a half ago in a manual which was to later have an important American counterpart, *The American Practical Navigator* by Nathaniel Bowditch, remains essentially valid.

Navigation today is the art or science of determining the location of a ship or aircraft. It can be regarded as an art because its application involves the exercise of special skills and fine techniques which can be perfected only by experience and careful practice. On the other hand, the subject can be regarded with equal validity as a science inasmuch as it is a branch of knowledge dealing with a body of facts and truths systematically arranged and showing the operation of general laws. Navigation has been practiced for thousands of years; however, modern methods date from the invention of the chronometer, a precision timepiece, in the eighteenth century.

Nathaniel Bowditch, near the end of the eighteenth century, discovered numerous errors in *The Practical Navigator*. Bowditch then published a corrected version with additional information. In 1802 he completely revised his earlier work, including a new method for the simplified form, his new *American Practical Navigator*.

The American Practical Navigator, Volume I, 1977 and Volume II, 1975, has been maintained continuously since it was first published in 1802. The U.S. Navy maintained "Bowditch" from 1868 until 1972, when the Defense Mapping Agency Hydrographic Center was assigned the responsibility for its publication.

The intent of the original author to provide a compendium of navigational material understandable to the mariner has been consistently followed. However, navigation is not presented as a mechanical process to be followed blindly. Rather, emphasis has been given to the fact that the aids provided by science can be used effectively to improve the art of navigation only if a well-informed person of mature judgment and experience is on hand to interpret information as it becomes available. Thus, the facts needed to perform the mechanics of navigation have been supplemented with additional material intended to help the navigator acquire perspective in meeting the various needs that arise.

This ARCO edition reprints fourteen pertinent chapters and selected appendices and tables from the 1977 edition of *The American Practical Navigator*. These are concerned with coastal navigation and piloting for yachtsmen. All references are to the 1977 edition. A portion of an ARCO NAUTICAL CHART is included for reader use with Chapter V: The Nautical Chart. We hope you will be able to practice your chart reading and simulate navigational calculations using the chart included in this book.

Readers should refer corrections, additions, and comments for improving this edition of "Bowditch" to Director, Defense Mapping Agency Hydrographic Center, Washington, D.C. 20390.

James W. Morrison
Editor and Chart Maker
Aboard the *Windsong*

CONTENTS

Last painting by Gilbert Stuart (1828). Considered by the family of Bowditch to be the best of various paintings made, although it was unfinished when the artist died.

NATHANIEL BOWDITCH

(1773–1838)

Nathaniel Bowditch was born on March 26, 1773, at Salem, Mass., fourth of the seven children of shipmaster Habakkuk Bowditch and his wife, Mary.

Since the migration of William Bowditch from England to the Colonies in the 17th century, the family had resided at Salem. Most of its sons, like those of other families in this New England seaport, had gone to sea, and many of them became shipmasters. Nathaniel Bowditch himself sailed as master on his last voyage, and two of his brothers met untimely deaths while pursuing careers at sea.

It is reported that Nathaniel Bowditch's father lost two ships at sea, and by late Revolutionary days he returned to the trade of cooper, which he had learned in his youth. This provided insufficient income to properly supply the needs of his growing family, and hunger and cold were often experienced. For many years the nearly destitute family received an annual grant of fifteen to twenty dollars from the Salem Marine Society. By the time Nathaniel had reached the age of ten, the family's poverty necessitated his leaving school and joining his father in the cooper's trade.

Nathaniel was unsuccessful as a cooper, and when he was about 12 years of age, he entered the first of two ship-chandlery firms by which he was employed. It was during the nearly ten years he was so employed that his great mind first attracted public attention. From the time he began school Bowditch had an all-consuming interest in learning, particularly mathematics. By his middle teens he was recognized in Salem as an authority on that subject. Salem being primarily a shipping town, most of the inhabitants sooner or later found their way to the ship chandler, and news of the brilliant young clerk spread until eventually it came to the attention of the learned men of his day. Impressed by his desire to educate himself, they supplied him with books that he might learn of the discoveries of other men. Since many of the best books were written by Europeans, Bowditch first taught himself their languages. French, Spanish, Latin, Greek, and German were among the two dozen or more languages and dialects he studied during his life. At the age of 16 he began the study of Newton's *Principia*, translating parts of it from the Latin. He even found an error in that classic, and though lacking the confidence to announce it at the time, he later published his findings and had them accepted.

During the Revolutionary War a privateer out of Beverly, a neighboring town to Salem, had taken as one of its prizes an English vessel which was carrying the philosophical library of a famed Irish scholar, Dr. Richard Kirwan. The books were brought to the Colonies and there bought by a group of educated Salem men who used them to found the Philosophical Library Company, reputed to have been the best library north of Philadelphia at the time. In 1791, when Bowditch was 18, two Harvard-educated ministers, Rev. John Prince and Rev. William Bentley, persuaded the Company to allow Bowditch the use of its library. Encouraged by these two men and a third—Nathan Read, an apothecary and also a Harvard man—Bowditch studied the works of the great men who had preceded him, especially the mathematicians and the astronomers. By the time he became of age, this knowledge, acquired before and after his long working hours and in his spare time, had made young Bowditch the outstanding mathematician in the Commonwealth, and perhaps in the country.

In the seafaring town of Salem, Bowditch was drawn to navigation early, learning the subject at the age of 13 from an old British sailor. A year later he began studying surveying, and in 1794 he assisted in a survey of the town. At 15 he devised an almanac reputed to have been of great accuracy. His other youthful accomplishments included the construction of a crude barometer and a sundial.

When Bowditch went to sea at the age of 21, it was as captain's writer and nominal second mate, the officer's berth being offered him because of his reputation as a scholar. Under Captain Henry Prince, the ship *Henry* sailed from Salem in the winter of 1795 on what was to be a year-long voyage to the Ile de Bourbon (now called Île de la Réunion) in the Indian Ocean.

Bowditch began his seagoing career when accurate time was not available to the average naval or merchant ship. A reliable marine chronometer had been invented some 60 years before, but the prohibitive cost, plus the long voyages without opportunity to check the error of the timepiece, made the large investment an impractical one. A system of determining longitude by "lunar distance," a method which did not require an accurate timepiece, was known, but this product of the minds of mathematicians and astronomers was so involved as to be beyond the capabilities of the uneducated seamen of that day. Consequently, ships navigated by a combination of dead reckoning and parallel sailing (a system of sailing north or south to the latitude of the destination and then east or west to the destination).

To Bowditch, the mathematical genius, computation of lunar distances was no mystery, of course, but he recognized the need for an easier method of working them in order to navigate ships more safely and efficiently. Through analysis and observation, he derived a new and simplified formula during his first trip, a formula which was to open the book of celestial navigation to all seamen.

John Hamilton Moore's *The Practical Navigator* was the leading navigational text when Bowditch first went to sea, and had been for many years. Early in his first voyage, however, the captain's writer-second mate began turning up errors in Moore's book, and before long he found it necessary to recompute some of the tables he most often used in working his sights. Bowditch recorded the errors he found, and by the end of his second voyage, made in the higher capacity of supercargo, the news of his findings in *The Practical Navigator* had reached Edmund Blunt, a publisher at Newburyport, Mass. At Blunt's request, Bowditch agreed to correct Moore's book. The first edition of *The New Practical Navigator* was published in 1799, with correction of the errors Bowditch had found to that time, and with some additional information. The following year a second edition was published with additional corrections. Bowditch eventually found more than 8,000 errors in the work, however, and it was finally decided to completely rewrite the book and to publish it under his own name. In 1802 the first edition of *The New American Practical Navigator* by Nathaniel Bowditch was published, and his vow to put nothing in the book he could not teach every member of his crew served to keep the work within the understanding of the average seaman. In addition to the improved method of determining longitude, Bowditch's book gave the ship's officer information on winds, currents, and tides; directions for surveying; statistics on marine insurance; a glossary of sea terms; instruction in mathematics; and numerous tables of navigational data. His simplified methods, easily grasped by the intelligent seaman willing to learn, paved the way for "Yankee" supremacy of the seas during the clipper ship era.

Two months before sailing for Cadiz on his third voyage, in 1798, Bowditch married Elizabeth Boardman, daughter of a shipmaster. While he was away, his wife died at the age of 18. Two years later, on October 28, 1800, he married his cousin, Mary Ingersoll, she, too, the daughter of a shipmaster. They had eight children.

Bowditch made a total of five trips to sea, over a period of about nine years, his last as master and part owner of the three-masted *Putnam*. Homeward bound from a 13-month voyage to Sumatra and the Ile de France (now called Mauritius) the *Putman* approached Salem harbor on December 25, 1803, during a thick fog without having had a celestial observation since noon on the 24th. Relying upon his dead reckoning, Bowditch conned his wooden-hulled ship to the entrance of the rocky harbor, where he had the good fortune to get a momentary glimpse of Eastern Point, Cape Ann, enough to confirm his position. The *Putnam* proceeded in, past such hazards as "Bowditch's Ledge" (named after a great-grandfather who had wrecked his ship on the rock more than a century before) and anchored safely at 1900 that evening. Word of the daring feat, performed when other masters were hove-to outside the harbor, spread along the coast and added greatly to Bowditch's reputation. He was, indeed, the "practical navigator."

His standing as a mathematician and successful shipmaster earned him a lucrative (for those times) position ashore within a matter of weeks after his last voyage. He was installed as president of a Salem fire and marine insurance company, at the age of 30, and during the 20 years he held that position the company prospered. In 1823 he left Salem to take a similar position with a Boston insurance firm, serving that company with equal success until his death.

From the time he finished the "*Navigator*" until 1814, Bowditch's mathematical and scientific pursuits consisted of studies and papers on the orbits of comets, applications of Napier's rules, magnetic variation, eclipses, calculations on tides, and the charting of Salem harbor. In that year, however, he turned to what he considered the greatest work of his life, the translation into English of *Mécanique Céleste*, by Pierre Laplace. *Mècanique Cèleste* was a summary of all the then known facts about the workings of the heavens. Bowditch translated four of the five volumes before his death, and published them at his own expense. He gave many formula derivations which Laplace had not shown, and also included further discoveries following the time of publication. His work made this information available to American astronomers and enabled them to pursue their studies on the basis of that which was already known. Continuing his style of writing for the learner, Bowditch presented his English version of *Mècanique Cèleste* in such a manner that the student of mathematics could easily trace the steps involved in reaching the most complicated conclusions.

Shortly after the publication of *The New American Practical Navigator*, Harvard College honored its author with the presentation of the honorary degree of Master of Arts, and in 1816 the college made him an honorary Doctor of Laws. From the time the Harvard graduates of Salem first assisted him in his studies, Bowditch had a great interest in that college, and in 1810 he was elected one of its Overseers, a position he held until 1826, when he was elected to the Corporation. During 1826–27 he was the leader of a small group of men who saved the school from financial disaster by forcing necessary economies on the college's reluctant president. At one time Bowditch was offered a Professorship in Mathematics at Harvard but this, as well as similar offers from West Point and the University of Virginia, he declined. In all his life he was never known to have made a public speech or to have addressed any large group of people.

Many other honors came to Bowditch in recognition of his astronomical, mathematical, and marine accomplishments. He became a member of the American Academy of Arts and Sciences, the East India Marine Society, the Royal Academy of Edinburgh, the Royal Society of London, the Royal Irish Academy, the American Philosophical Society, the Connecticut Academy of Arts and Sciences, the Boston Marine Society, the Royal Astronomical Society, the Palermo Academy of Science, and the Royal Academy of Berlin.

Nathaniel Bowditch outlived all of his brothers and sisters by nearly 30 years. Death came to him on March 16, 1838, in his sixty-fifth year. The following eulogy by the Salem Marine Society indicates the regard in which this distinguished American was held by his contemporaries:

"In his death a public, a national, a human benefactor has departed. Not this community, nor our country only, but the whole world, has reason to do honor to his memory. When the voice of Eulogy shall be still, when the tear of Sorrow shall cease to flow, no monument will be needed to keep alive his memory among men; but as long as ships shall sail, the needle point to the north, and the stars go through their wonted courses in the heavens, the name of Dr. Bowditch will be revered as of one who helped his fellow-men in a time of need, who was and is a guide to them over the pathless ocean, and of one who forwarded the great interests of mankind."

The New American Practical Navigator was revised by Nathaniel Bowditch several times after 1802 for subsequent editions of the book. After his death, Jonathan Ingersoll Bowditch, a son who made several voyages, took up the work and his name appeared on the title page from the eleventh edition through the thirty-fifth, in 1867. In 1868 the newly organized U.S. Navy Hydrographic Office bought the copyright. Revisions have been made from time to time to keep the work in step with navigational improvements. The name has been altered to the *American Practical Navigator*, but the book is still commonly known as "Bowditch." A total of more than 850,000 copies has been printed in about 70 editions during the more than a century and a half since the book was first published in 1802. It has lived because it has combined the best thoughts of each generation of navigators, who have looked to it as their final authority.

CHAPTER I

HISTORY OF NAVIGATION

Introduction

101. Background.—Navigation began with the first man. One of his first conscious acts probably was to home on some object that caught his eye, and thus **land navigation** was undoubtedly the earliest form. His first venture upon the waters may have come shortly after he observed that some objects float, and through curiosity or an attempt at self-preservation he learned that a larger object, perhaps a log, would support him. **Marine navigation** was born when he attempted to guide his craft.

The earliest marine navigation was a form of **piloting,** which came into being as man became familiar with landmarks and used them as guides. **Dead reckoning** probably came next as he sought to predict his future positions, or perhaps as he bravely ventured farther from landmarks. **Celestial navigation,** as it is known today, had to await acquisition of information regarding the motions of the heavenly bodies, although these bodies were used to steer by almost from the beginning.

102. From art to science.—Navigation is the process of directing the movements of a craft from one point to another. To do this safely is an *art*. In perhaps 6,000 years—some writers make it 8,000—man has transformed this art almost into a *science*, and navigation today is so nearly a science that the inclination is to forget that it was ever anything else. It is commonly thought that to navigate a ship one must have a chart to determine the course and distance, a compass to steer by, and a means of determining the positions of the ship during the passage. *Must* have? The word "must" betrays how dependent the modern navigator has become upon the tools now in his hands. Many of the great voyages of history—voyages that made known much of the world—were made without one or more of these "essentials."

103. Epic voyages.—History records a number of great voyages of varying navigational significance. Little or nothing is known of the navigational accomplishments of the ancient mariners, but the record of the knowledge and equipment used during later voyages serves to illustrate periodic developments in the field.

104. Pre-Christian navigation.—Down through the stream of time a number of voyages have occurred without navigational significance. Noah's experience in the ark is of little interest navigationally, except for his use of a dove to locate land. There is evidence to support the view that at least some American Indians reached these shores by sea, the earliest of several groups probably having come about 2200 BC, the approximate time that a general exodus seems to have occurred from a center in southwestern Asia. This is about the time the Tower of Babel is believed to have been built. It is noteworthy that almost every land reached by the great European explorers was already inhabited.

It is not difficult to understand how a people not accustomed to the sea might make a single great voyage without contributing anything of significance to the advancement of navigation. Not so clear, however, is the fact that the Norsemen and the Polynesians, great seafaring people, left nothing more than conflicting traditions of their methods. The reputed length of the voyages made by these people suggests more advanced navigational methods than their records indicate, although the explanation may be that they left few written accounts of any kind. Or perhaps they developed their powers of perception to such an extent that navigation to them, was a highly advanced art. In this respect their navigation may not have differed greatly from that of some birds, insects, fishes, and animals.

One of the earliest well-recorded voyages is known today through the book of observations written by Pytheas of Massalia, a Greek astronomer and navigator. Sometime between the years 350 BC and 300 BC he sailed from a Mediterranean port and followed an established trade route to England. From there he ventured north to Scotland and Thule, the legendary land of the midnight sun. He went on to explore Norwegian fiords, and rivers in northwest Germany. He may have made his way into the Baltic.

Pytheas' voyage, and others of his time, were significant in that they were the work of men who had no compasses, no sextants, no chronometers, no electronic devices such as are commonplace today. The explanation of how they did it is not what some historians have said, that before seafaring men had adequate equipment, the compass especially, they hugged the shore and sailed only by daylight in fair weather. Many undoubtedly did use this practice. But the more intrepid did not creep along the coast, venturing nothing more daring than sailing from headland to headland. They were often out of sight of land, and yet knew sufficiently well where they were and how to get home again. They were able to use the sun, the stars, and the winds without the aid of mechanical devices.

Pytheas had none of the equipment considered essential by the modern navigator—none, at least, as it is thought of today. It would be incorrect, however, to say that he had no navigational aids whatever. He was not the first to venture upon the sea, and even in his time man was the inheritor of his predecessors' knowledge.

He must have known what the mariners of his time, Phoenician and Greek, knew about navigation. There was a fair store of knowledge about the movements of the stars, for example, which all seafaring men shared. They had a practical grasp of some part of what is now called celestial navigation, for the moving celestial bodies were their compasses. Pytheas may not have been acquainted with the *Periplus* of Scylax, the earliest known sailing directions, but it is reasonable to suppose that he had similar information.

If there were sailing directions, there may well have been charts of a sort, even though no record of them exists.

Even if Pytheas and his contemporaries had sailing directions and charts, these must have been far from comprehensive, and they undoubtedly did not cover the areas north of Britain. But these early seamen knew direction by day or night if the sky was clear, and they could judge it reasonably well when the sky was overcast, using the wind and the sea. They knew the hot Libyan wind from the desert—today called the **sirocco**—and the northern wind, the **mistral.**

They could estimate distance. Their ships must have carried some means of measuring time—the sand glass was known to the ancients—and they could estimate speed by counting the strokes of the oars, a common practice from galley to modern college racing shell. Mariners who spent their lives traveling the Mediterranean knew what their ships could do, even if today it is not known what they meant by "a day's sail"—whether 35 miles, or 50, or 100.

105. Sixteenth century navigation.—Progress in the art of navigation came slowly during the early centuries of the Christian era, all but stopped during the Dark Ages, and then spurted forward when Europe entered a golden age of discovery. The circumnavigation of the globe by the expedition organized by Ferdinand Magellan, a disgraced Portuguese nobleman who sailed under the flag of Spain, was a voyage which illustrates the advances made during the 1,800 years following Pytheas.

Magellan was able to find justification for his belief that a navigable pass to the Pacific Ocean existed in high southern latitudes, in Martin Behaim's globe or chart of the world, in the globe constructed by Johann Schoner of Nuremberg in 1515, and in Leonardo da Vinci's map of the world drawn in the same year. He obtained further information for his voyage from Ruy Faleiro, an astronomer and cartographer whose charts, sailing directions, nautical tables, and instructions for use of the astrolabe and cross-staff were considered to be among the best available. Faleiro was also an advocate of the fallacious methods of determining longitude by variation.

When Magellan sailed in 1519, his equipment included sea charts, parchment skins to be made into charts en route, a terrestrial globe, wooden and metal theodolites, wooden and wood-and-bronze quadrants, compasses, magnetic needles, hour glasses and "timepieces," and a log to be towed astern.

So the 16th century navigator had crude charts of the known world, a compass to steer by, instruments with which he could determine his latitude, a log to estimate speed, certain sailing directions, and solar and traverse tables. The huge obstacle yet to be overcome was an accurate method of determining longitude.

Eighteenth century navigation.—Little is known today of the "timepieces" carried by Magellan, but surely they were not used to determine longitude. Two hundred years later, however, the chronometer began to emerge. With it, the navigator, for the first time, was able to determine his longitude accurately and fix his position at sea.

The three voyages of discovery made by James Cook of the Royal Navy in the Pacific Ocean between 1768 and 1779 may be said to mark the dawn of modern navigation. Cook's expedition had the full backing of England's scientific organizations, and he was the first captain to undertake extended explorations at sea with navigational equipment, techniques, and knowledge that might be considered modern.

On his first voyage Cook was provided with an astronomical clock, a "journeyman" clock, and a watch lent by the Astronomer Royal. With these he could determine longitude, using the long and tedious lunar distance method. On his second voyage four chronometers were provided. These instruments, added to those already possessed by the mariner, enabled Cook to navigate his vessels with a precision undreamed of by Pytheas and Magellan.

By the time Cook began his explorations, astronomers had made great contributions to navigational advancement, and the acceptance of the heliocentric theory of the universe had led to the publication of the first official nautical almanac. Charts had progressed steadily, and adequate projections were available. With increased understanding of variation, the compass had become reliable. Good schools of navigation existed, and textbooks which reduced the mathematics of navigation to the essentials had been published. Speed through the water could be determined with reasonable accuracy by the logs then in use. Most important, the first chronometers were being produced.

Twentieth century navigation.—The maiden voyage of the SS *United States* in July 1952 served to illustrate the progress made in navigation during the 175 years since Cook's voyages. Outstanding because of its record trans-Atlantic passage, the vessel is of interest navigationally in that it carried the most modern equipment then available and exemplified the fact that navigation had become nearly a science.

Each of the deck officers owned a sextant with which he could make observations more accurately than did Cook. Reliable chronometers, the product of hundreds of years of experimental work, were available to determine the time of each observation. The gyrocompass indicated true north regardless of variation and deviation.

Modern, convenient almanacs were used to obtain the coordinates of various celestial bodies, to an accuracy greater than needed. Easily used altitude and azimuth tables gave the navigator data for determining his Sumner (celestial) line of position by the method of Marcq St.-Hilaire. Accurate charts were available for the waters plied, sailing directions for coasts and ports visited, light lists giving the characteristics of the various aids to navigation along these coasts, and pilot charts and navigational texts for reference purposes.

Electronics served the navigator in a number of ways. Radio time signals and weather reports enabled him to check his chronometers and avoid foul weather. A radio direction finder was available to obtain bearings, and a radio telephone was used to communicate with persons on land and sea. The electrically operated echo sounder indicated the depth of water under the keel, radar the distances and bearings of objects within range, even in the densest fog. Using Loran, the navigator could fix the position of his ship a thousand miles and more from transmitting stations.

Piloting and Dead Reckoning

108. Background.—The history of piloting and dead reckoning extends from man's earliest use of landmarks to the latest model of the gyrocompass. In the thousands of years between, navigation by these methods has progressed from short passages along known coastlines to transoceanic voyages during which celestial observations cannot be, or are not, made.

109. Charts.—A form of sailing directions was written several hundred years before Christ. Although charts cannot be traced back that far, they may have existed during the same time. From earliest times men have undoubtedly known that it is more difficult to explain how to get to a place than it is to draw a diagram, and since the first charts known are comparatively accurate and cover large areas, it seems logical that earlier charts served as guides for the cartographers.

Undoubtedly, the first charts were not made on any "projection" (ch. III) but were simple diagrams which took no notice of the shape of the earth. In fact, these "plane" charts were used for many centuries after chart projections were avilable.

The **gnomonic projection** (art. 317) is believed to have been developed by Thales of Miletus (640–546 BC), who was chief of the Seven Wise Men of ancient Greece; founder of Greek geometry, astronomy, and philosophy; and a navigator and cartographer.

The size of the earth was measured at least as early as the third century BC, by Eratosthenes. He observed that at noon on the day of the summer solstice, a certain well at Syene (Assuan) on the tropic of Cancer was lighted throughout its depth by the light of the sun as it crossed the meridian; but that at Alexandria, about 500 miles to the north, shadows were cast by the sun at high noon. He reasoned that this was due to curvature of the earth, which must be spherical. By double measurement of the arc of the meridian between the two places in degrees and stadia, Eratosthenes determined the circumference of the earth to be 252,000 stades (art. 113).

Eratosthenes is believed to have been the first person to measure latitude, using the degree for this purpose. He constructed a 16-point wind rose, prepared a table of winds, and recognized local and prevailing winds. From his own discoveries and from information gleaned from the manuscripts of mariners, explorers, land travelers, historians, and philosophers, he wrote an outstanding description of the known world, which helped elevate geography to the status of a science.

Stereographic (art. 318) and **orthographic** (art. 319) **projections** were originated by Hipparchus in the second century BC.

Ptolemy's World Map. The Egyptian Claudius Ptolemy was a second century AD astronomer, writer, geographer, and mathematician who had no equal in astronomy until the arrival of Copernicus in the 16th century. An outstanding cartographer, for his time, Ptolemy constructed many charts and listed the latitudes and longitudes, as determined by celestial observations, of the places shown. As a geographer, however, he made his most serious mistake. Though Eratosthenes' calculations on the circumference of the earth were available to him, he took the estimate of the Stoic philosopher, Posidonius (circa 130–51 BC), who calculated the earth to be 180,000 stadia in circumference. The result was that those who accepted his work—and for many hundreds of years few thought to question it—had to deal with a concept that was far too small. In 1409 the Greek original of Ptolemy's *Cosmographia*, a book in which he declared this doctrine, was discovered and translated into Latin. It served as the basis for future cartographic work, and so it was that Columbus died convinced that he had found a shorter route to the East Indies. Not until 1669, when Jean Picard computed the circumference of the earth to be 24,500 miles, was a more accurate figure generally used.

Ptolemy's map of the world (fig. 109a) was a great achievement, however. It was the original conic projection, and on it he located some 8,000 places by latitude and longitude. It was he who fixed the convention that the top of the map is north.

Asian Charts. Through the Dark Ages some progress was made. Moslem cartographers as well as astronomers took inspiration from Ptolemy. However, they knew that Ptolemy had overestimated the length of the Mediterranean by some 20°. Charts of the Indian Ocean, bearing horizontal lines indicating parallels of latitude, and vertical lines dividing the seas according to the direction of the wind, were drawn by Persian and Arabian navigators. The prime meridian separated a windward from

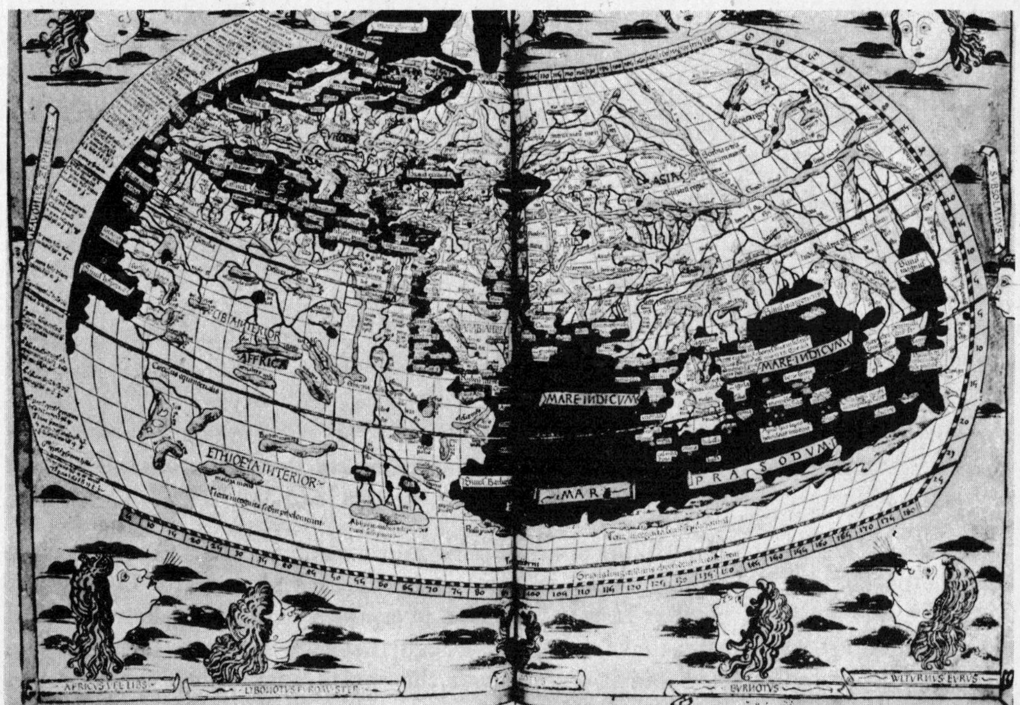

Courtesy of the Map Division of the Library of Congress.

FIGURE 109a.—The world, as envisioned by Ptolemy about AD 150. This chart was prepared in 1482 by Nicolaus Germanus for a translation of *Cosmographia*.

a leeward region and other meridians were drawn at intervals indicating "three hours sail." This information, though far from exact, was helpful to the sailing ship masters.

Portolan Charts. The mariners of Venezia (Venice), Livorno (Leghorn), and Genova (Genoa) must have had charts when they competed for Mediterranean trade before, during, and after the Crusades. Venice at one time had 300 ships, a navy of 45 galleys, and 11,000 men engaged in her maritime industry. But perhaps the rivalry was too keen for masters carelessly to leave charts lying about. At any rate, the earliest useful charts of the Middle Ages that are known today were drawn by seamen of Catalonia (now part of Spain).

The Portolan charts were constructed from the knowledge acquired by seamen during their voyages about the Mediterranean. The actual courses and dead reckoning distances between land points were used as a skeleton for the charts, and the coasts between were usually filled in from data obtained in land surveys. After the compass came into use, these charts became quite accurate. Some, for example, indicated the distance between Gibraltar and Bayrūt (Beirut) to be 3,000 Portolan miles, or 40°.5 of longitude. The actual difference of longitude is 40°.8.

These charts were distinguished by a group of long rhumb lines intersecting at a common point, surrounded by eight or 16 similar groups of shorter lines. Later *Portolanis* had a *rose dei venti* (rose of the winds), the forerunner of the compass rose, superimposed over the center (fig. 109b). They carried a scale of miles, located nearly all the known hazards to navigation, and had numerous notes of interest to the pilot. They were not marked with parallels of latitude or meridians of longitude, but present-day harbor and coastal charts trace their ancestry directly to them.

Courtesy of the Map Division of the Library of Congress.

FIGURE 109b.—A 14th-century Portolan chart.

Padrón Real. The growing habit of assembling information for charts took concrete form in the *Padrón Real.* This was the pattern, or master, map kept after 1508 by the *Casa de Contratación* at Seville. It was intended to contain everything known about the world, and it was constructed from facts brought back by mariners from voyages to newly discovered lands. From it were drawn the charts upon which the explorers of the Age of Discovery most depended.

World maps of the Middle Ages. In 1515 Leonardo da Vinci drew his famous map of the world. On it, America is represented as extending more to the east and west than to the north and south, with only a chain of islands, the largest named Florida, between it and South America. A wide stretch of ocean is shown between South America and *Terra Australis Nondum Cognita,* the mythical south-seas continent whose existence in the position shown was not disproved until 250 years later.

Ortelius' atlas *Theatrum Orbis Terra* was published at Antwerp in 1570. One of the most magnificent ever produced, it illustrates Europe, Africa, and Asia with comparative accuracy. North and South America are poorly depicted, but Magellan's Strait is shown. All land to the south of it, as well as Australia, is considered part of *Terra Australis Nondum Cognita* (fig. 109c).

Courtesy of the New York Public Library.

FIGURE 109c.—Ortelius' world map, from his atlas *Theatrum Orbis Terra*, published at Antwerp in 1570.

The Mercator projection (art. 305). For hundreds, perhaps thousands, of years cartographers drew their charts as "plane" projections, making no use of the discoveries of Ptolemy and Hipparchus. As the area of the known world increased, however, the attempt to depict that larger area on the flat surface of the plane chart brought map makers to the realization that allowance would have to be made for the curvature of the earth.

Gerardus Mercator (Latinized form of Gerhard Kremer) was a brilliant Flemish geographer who recognized the need for a better method of chart projection. In 1569 he published a world chart which he had constructed on the principle since known by his name. The theory of his work was correct, but Mercator made errors in his computation, and because he never published a complete description of the mathematics involved, mariners were deprived of the full advantages of the projection for another 30 years.

Then Edward Wright published the results of his own independent study in the matter, explaining the Mercator projection fully and providing the table of meridional parts which enabled all cartographers to make use of the principle.

Wright was a mathematician at Caius College who developed the method and table and gave them to certain navigators for testing. After these proved their usefulness, Wright decided upon publication, and in 1599 *Certaine Errors in Navigation Detected and Corrected* was printed.

The Lambert projections. Johann Heinrich Lambert, 1728–1777, self-educated son of an Alsace tailor, designed a number of map projections. Some of these are still widely used, the most renowned being the **Lambert conformal** (art. 314).

110. Sailing directions.—From earliest times there has been a demand for knowledge of what lay ahead, and this gave rise to the early development of sailing directions (art. 1301).

The *Periplus* of Scylax, written sometime between the sixth and fourth centuries BC, is the earliest known book of this type. Surprisingly similar to modern sailing directions, it provided the mariner with information on distances between ports, aids and dangers, port facilities, and other pertinent matters. The following excerpt is typical:

"Libya begins beyond the Canopic mouth of the Nile. . . . The first people in Libya are the Adrymachidae. From Thonis the voyage to Pharos, a desert island (good harbourage but no drinking water), is 150 stadia. In Pharos are many harbors. But ships water at the Marian Mere, for it is drinkable. . . . The mouth of the bay of Plinthine to Leuce Acte (the white beach) is a day and night's sail; but sailing round by the head of the bay of Plinthine is twice as long. . . ."

Parts Around the World, Pytheas' book of observations made during his epic voyage in the fourth century BC, was another early volume of sailing directions. His rough estimates of distances and descriptions of coastlines would be considered crude today, but they served as an invaluable aid to navigators who followed him into these otherwise unknown waters.

Sailing directions during the Renaissance. No particularly noteworthy improvements were made in sailing directions during the Middle Ages, but in 1490 the *Portolano Rizo* was published, the first of a series of improved design. Other early volumes of this kind appeared in France and were called "routiers"—the **rutters** of the English sailor. In 1557 the Italian pilot Battista Testa Rossa published *Brieve Compendio del Arte del Navigar*, which was designed to serve the mariner on soundings and off. It forecast the single, all-inclusive volume that was soon to come, the **Waggoner.**

About 1584 the Dutch pilot Lucas Janszoon Waghenaer published a volume of navigational principles, tables, charts, and sailing directions which served as a guide for such books for the next 200 years. In *Spieghel der Zeevaerdt* (The Mariner's Mirror), Waghenaer gave directions and charts for sailing the waters of the Low Countries and later a second volume was published covering waters of the North and Baltic seas.

These "Waggoners" met with great success and in 1588 an English translation of the original book was made by Anthony Ashley. During the next 30 years, 24 editions of the book were published in Dutch, German, Latin, and English. Other authors followed the profitable example set by Waghenaer, and American, British, and French navigators soon had "Waggoners" for most of the waters they sailed.

The success of these books and the resulting competition among authors were responsible for their eventual discontinuance. Each writer attempted to make his work more inclusive than any other (the 1780 *Atlantic Neptune* contained 257 charts of North America alone) and the result was a tremendous book difficult to handle. They were too bulky, the sailing directions were unnecessarily detailed, and the charts too large. In 1795 the British Hydrographic Department was established, and charts and sailing directions were issued separately. The latter, issued for specific waters, were returned to the form of the original *Periplus*.

Modern sailing directions. The publication of modern sailing directions by the Defense Mapping Agency Hydrographic Center is one of the achievements properly attributed to Matthew Fontaine Maury. During the two decades he headed the Depot of Charts and Instruments (renamed U. S. Naval Observatory and Hydrographical Office in 1854), Maury gathered data that led to the publication of eight volumes of sailing directions.

111. The compass.—Early in the history of navigation man noted that the pole star (it may have been *α Draconis* then) remained close to one point in the northern sky. This served as his compass. When it was not visible, he used other stars, the sun and moon, winds, clouds, and waves. The development of the magnetic compass, perhaps a thousand years ago, and the 20th century development of the gyrocompass, offer today's navigator a method of steering his course with an accuracy as great as he is capable of using.

The **magnetic compass** (art. 623) is one of the oldest of the navigator's instruments. Its origin is not known. In 203 BC, when Hannibal set sail from Italy, his pilot was said to be one *Pelorus*. Perhaps the compass was in use then; no one can say for certain that it was not. There is little to substantiate the story that the Chinese invented it, and the legend that Marco Polo introduced it into Italy in the 13th century is almost certainly false. It is sometimes stated that the Arabs brought it to Europe, but this, too, is unlikely. Probably it was known first in the west. The Norsemen of the 11th century were familiar with it, and about 1200 a compass used by mariners when the pole star was hidden was described by a French poet, Guyot de Provins.

A needle thrust through a straw and floated in water in a container comprised the earliest compass known. A 1248 writer, Hugo de Bercy, spoke of a new compass construction, the needle "now" being supported on two floats. Petrus Peregrinus de Maricourt, in his *Epistola de Magnete* of 1269, wrote of a pivoted floating compass with a lubber's line, and said that it was equipped with sights for taking bearings.

The reliability of the magnetic compass of today is a comparatively recent achievement. It was not until the 1870's that Sir William Thomson (Lord Kelvin) was able to successfully combine all of the requirements for a good dry-card compass, and mount it in a well-designed binnacle. The dry-card compass was the standard compass in the Royal Navy until 1906 when the Board of Admiralty adopted the liquid compass as the standard compass.

The **compass card,** according to tradition, originated about the beginning of the 14th century, when Flavio Gioja of Amalfi attached a sliver of lodestone or a magnetized needle to a card. But the rose on the compass card is probably older than the needle. It is the wind rose of the ancients. Primitive man naturally named directions by the winds. The prophet Jeremiah speaks of the winds from the four quarters of heaven (Jer. 49:36) and Homer named four winds—Boreas, Eurus, Notus, and Lephyrus. Aristotle is said to have suggested a circle of 12 winds, and Eratosthenes, who measured the world correctly, reduced the number to eight about 200 BC. The "Tower of Winds" at Athens, built about 100 BC, had eight sides. The Latin rose of 12 points was common on most compasses used in the Middle Ages.

Variation (art. 706) was well understood 200 years ago, and navigators made allowance for it, but earliest recognition of its existence is not known. Columbus and even the 11th century Chinese have been given credit for its discovery, but little proof can be offered for either claim.

The secular change in variation was determined by a series of magnetic observations made at Limehouse, England. In 1580 William Borough fixed the variation in that area at approximately 11°25′ east. Thirty-two years later Edmund Gunter, professor of astronomy at Gresham College, determined it to be 6°13′ east. At first it was believed that Borough had made an error in his work, but in 1633 a further decrease was found, and the earth's changing magnetic field was established.

A South Atlantic expedition was led by Edmond Halley at the close of the 17th century to gather data and to map, for the first time, lines of variation. In 1724 George Graham published his observations in proof of the diurnal change in variation. Canton determined that the change was considerably less in winter than in summer, and about 1785 the strength of the magnetic force was shown by Paul de Lamanon to vary in different places.

The existence of **deviation** (art. 709) was known to John Smith in 1627 when he wrote of the "bittacle" as being a "square box nailed together with wooden pinnes, because iron nails would attract the Compasse." But no one knew how to correct a compass for deviation until Captain Matthew Flinders, while on a voyage to Australia in HMS *Investigator* in 1801–02, discovered a method of doing so. Flinders did not understand deviation completely, but the vertical bar he erected to correct for it was part of the solution, and the **Flinders bar** (art. 720) used today is a memorial to its discoverer. Between 1839 and 1855 Sir George Airy, then Astronomer Royal, studied the matter further and developed combinations of permanent magnets and soft iron masses for adjusting the compass. The introduction, by Lord Kelvin, of short needles as compass magnets made adjustment more precise.

The gyrocompass (art. 631). The age of iron ships demanded a compass which could be relied upon to indicate true north at all times, free from disturbing forces of variation and deviation.

In 1851, at the Pantheon in Paris, Leon Foucault performed his famous pendulum experiment to demonstrate the rotation of the earth. Foucault's realization that the swinging pendulum would maintain the plane of its motion led him, the following year, to develop and name the first gyroscope, using the principle of a common toy called a "rotascope." Handicapped by the lack of a source of power to maintain the spin of his gyroscope, Foucault used a microscope to observe the indication of the earth's rotation during the short period in which his manually operated gyroscope remained in rotation. A gyrocompass was not practical until electric power became available, more than 50 years later, to maintain the spin of the gyroscope.

Elmer A. Sperry, an American, and Anschutz-Kampfe, a German, independently invented gyrocompasses during the first decade of the 20th century. Tested first in 1911 on a freighter operating off the East Coast of the United States and then on American warships, Sperry's compass was found adequate, and in the years following World War I gyrocompasses became standard equipment on all large naval and merchant ships.

Gyrocompass auxiliaries commonly used today were added later. These include gyro repeaters, to indicate the vessel's heading at various locations; gyro pilots, to steer vessels automatically; course recorders, to provide a graphic record of courses steered; gyro-magnetic compasses, to repeat headings of magnetic compasses so located as to be least affected by deviation; and others in the fields of fire control, aviation, and guided missiles.

112. The log.—Since virtually the beginning of navigation, the mariner has attempted to determine his speed in traveling from one point to another. The earliest method was probably by estimate.

The oldest speed measuring device known is the **Dutchman's log.** Originally, any object which would float was thrown overboard on the lee side, from a point well forward, and the time required for it to pass between two points on the deck was noted. The time, as determined by sand glass, was compared with the known distance along the deck between the two points to determine the speed.

Near the end of the 16th century a line was attached to the log, and as the line was paid out a sailor recited certain sentences. The length of line which was paid out during the recitation was used to determine the speed. There is record of this method having been used as recently as the early 17th century. In its final form this **chip log, ship log,** or **common log** consisted of the *log chip* (or *log ship*), *log line*, *log reel*, and *log glass*. The chip was a quadrant-shaped piece of wood weighted along its circumference to keep it upright in the water (fig. 112). The log line was made fast to the log chip by means

Courtesy of "Motor Boating & Sailing."

FIGURE 112.—The common or chip log, showing the log reel, the log line, the log chip, and the log glass.

of a bridle, in such manner that a sharp pull on the log line dislodged a wooden peg and permitted the log chip to be towed horizontally through the water, and hauled aboard. Sometimes a *stray line* was attached to the log to veer it clear of the ship's wake. In determining speed, the observer counted the knots in the log line which was paid out during a certain time. The length of line between knots and the number of seconds required for the sand to run out were changed from time to time as the accepted length of the mile was altered.

The chip log has been superseded by patent logs that register on dials. However, the common log has left its mark on modern navigation, as the use of the term **knot** to indicate a speed of one nautical mile per hour dates from this device. There is evidence to support the opinion that the expression "dead reckoning" had its origin in this same device, or perhaps in the earlier Dutchman's log. There is logic in attributing "dead" reckoning to a reckoning relative to an object "dead" in the water.

Mechanical logs first appeared about the middle of the 17th century. By the beginning of the 19th century, the forerunners of modern mechanical logs were used by some navigators, although many years were to pass before they became generally accepted.

In 1773 logs on which the distance run was recorded on dials secured to the taffrail were tested on board a British warship and found reasonably adequate, although the comparative delicateness of the mechanism led to speculation about their long-term worth. Another type in existence at the time consisted of a wheel arrangement made fast on the underside of the keel, which transmitted readings to a dial inside the vessel as the wheel rotated.

An improved log was introduced by Edward Massey in 1802. This log gave considerably greater accuracy by means of a more sensitive rotator attached by a short length of line to a geared recording instrument. The difficulty with this log was that it had to be hauled aboard to take each reading. Various improvements were made, notably by Alexander Bain in 1846 and Thomas Walker in 1861, but it was not until 1878 that a log was developed in which the rotator could be used in conjunction with a dial secured to the after rail of the ship, and although refinements and improvements have been made, the patent log used today is essentially the same as that developed in 1878.

Engine revolution counters (art. 616) had their origin with the observations of the captains of the first paddle steamers, who discovered that by counting the paddle revolutions, they could, with practice, estimate their runs in thick weather as accurately as they could by streaming the log. Later developments led to the modern revolution counter on screw-type vessels, which can be used with reasonable accuracy if the propeller is submerged and an accurate estimate of slip is made.

Pitot-static and **impeller logs** (arts. 613, 614) are mechanical developments in the field of speed measurement. Each utilizes a retractable "rodmeter" which projects through the hull of the ship into the water. In the Pitot-static log, static and dynamic pressures on the rodmeter transmit readings to the master speed indicator. In the impeller log an electrical means of transmitting speed indications is used.

113. Units of distance and depth.—The modern navigator is concerned principally with four units of linear measure: the **nautical mile,** the **fathom,** the **foot** and the **meter.** Primitive man, however, used such natural units as the width of a finger, the **span** of his hand, the length of his foot, the distance from his elbow to the tip of the middle finger (the **cubit** of biblical renown), or the **pace** (sometimes one but usually a double step) to measure short distances.

Although the **Roman mile** had a value of about 1,488 meters or about 0.9248 of our statute mile of 5,280 feet, several standards were in use among the cities of ancient Greece at the same time. The Greek stadia being variable, there is uncertainty as to the accuracy of the measurement of the earth by Eratosthenes.

The **nautical mile** bears little relation to these land measures, which were not associated with the size of the earth. With the emergence of the nautical chart, it became customary to show a scale of miles on the chart, and the accepted value of this unit varied over the centuries with the changing estimates of the size of the earth. These estimates varied widely, ranging from about 44.5 to 87.5 modern nautical miles per degree of latitude, although generally they were too small. Columbus and Magellan used the value 45.3. Actually, the earth is about 32 percent larger. The *Almagest* of Ptolemy considered 62 Roman miles equivalent to one degree, but a 1466 edition of this book contained a chart of southern Asia drawn by Nicolaus Germanus on which 60 miles were shown to a degree. Whether the change was considered a correction or an adaptation to provide a more convenient relationship between the mile and the degree is not clear, but this is the earliest known use of this ratio.

Later, when the size of the earth was determined by measurement, the relationship of 60 Roman miles of 4,858.60 U. S. feet to a degree of latitude was seen to be in error. Both possible solutions to the problem—changing the ratio of miles to a degree, or changing the length of the mile—had their supporters, and neither group was able to convince the other. As a result, the shorter mile remained as the **land** or **statute mile** (now established as 5,280 feet in the United States), and the longer **nautical mile** gradually became established at sea. The earliest known reference to it by this name occurred in 1730.

Finer instruments and new methods make increasingly more accurate determinations of the size of the earth an ever-present possibility. Hence, a unit of length defined in terms of the size of the earth is undesirable. Recognition of this led, in 1875, to a change in the definition of the **meter** from one ten-millionth of the distance from the pole to the equator of the earth to the distance between two marks (approximately 39.37 U. S. inches) on a standard platinum-iridium bar kept at the Pavillon de Breteuill at Sevres, near Paris, France, by the International Commission of Weights and Measures. In further recognition of this principle, the International Hydrographic Bureau in 1929 recommended adoption of a standard value for the nautical mile, and proposed 1,852 international meters. This International Nautical Mile of 1,852 meters exactly has been adopted by nearly all maritime nations. The U. S. Departments of Defense and Commerce adopted this value in July 1954. With the yard-meter relationship then in use, the International Nautical Mile was equivalent to 6,076.10333 feet, approximately. Using the yard-meter exact relationship of one yard equal to 0.9144 meter adopted by the United States on July 1, 1959, the International Nautical Mile is equivalent to 6,076.11549 feet, approximately. In October 1960, the Eleventh General (International) Conference on Weights and Measures redefined the meter as equal to 1,650,763.73 wavelengths of the orange-red radiation in vacuum of krypton 86.

The **meter** as a unit of depth and height on U. S. nautical charts is of recent origin. The current policy of the Defense Mapping Agency Hydrographic Center of converting new compilations of nautical and special purpose charts to the metric system was implemented on January 2, 1970.

The **fathom** as a unit of length or depth is of obscure origin, but primitive man considered it a measure of the outstretched arms, and the modern seaman still estimates the length of a line in this manner. That the unit was used in early times is indicated by reference to it in the detailed account given of the Apostle Paul's voyage to Rome, as recorded in the 27th chapter of the *Acts of the Apostles*. Posidonius reported a sounding of more than 1,000 fathoms in the second century BC. How old the unit was at that time is unknown.

114. Soundings.—Probably the most dangerous phase of navigation occurs when the vessel is "on soundings." Since man first began navigating the waters, the possibility of grounding his vessel has been a major concern, and frequent soundings have been the most highly valued safeguard against that experience. Undoubtedly used long before the Christian era, the lead line is perhaps the oldest instrument of navigation.

The lead line. The **hand lead** (art. 618), consisting of a lead weight attached to a line usually marked in fathoms, has been known since antiquity and, with the exception of the markings, is probably the same today as it was 2,000 or more years ago. The **deep sea lead,** a heavier weight with a longer line, was a natural outgrowth of the hand lead. A 1585 navigator speaks of soundings of 330 fathoms, and in 1773, in the Norwegian Sea, Captain Phipps had all the sounding lines on board spliced together to obtain a sounding of 683 fathoms. Matthew Fontaine Maury made his deep sea soundings by securing a cannon shot to a ball of strong twine. The heavy weight caused the twine to run out rapidly, and when bottom was reached, the twine was cut and the depth deduced from the amount remaining on the ball.

The sounding machine. The biggest disadvantage of the deep sea lead is that the vessel must be stopped if depths are to be measured accurately. This led to the development of the sounding machine.

Early in the 19th century a sounding machine similar to one of the earlier patent logs was invented. A wheel was secured just above the lead and the cast made in such a way that all the line required ran out freely and the lead sank directly to the bottom. The motion through the water during the descent set the wheel revolving, and this in turn caused the depth to be indicated on a dial. Ships sailing at perhaps 12 knots required 20 or 30 men to heave aboard the heavy line with its weight of 50 or more pounds after each cast. A somewhat similar device was the **buoy sounder.** The lead was passed through a buoy in which a spring catch was fitted and both were cast over the side. The lead ran freely until bottom was reached, when the catch locked, preventing further running out of the line. The whole assembly was then brought on board, the depth from the buoy to the lead being read.

The first use of the pressure principle to determine the depth of water occurred early in the 19th century when the "Self-acting Sounder" was introduced. A hollow glass tube open at its lower end contained an index which moved up in the tube as greater water pressure compressed the air inside. The index retained its highest position when hauled aboard the vessel, and its height was proportional to the depth of the water.

The British scientist, Sir William Thomson (Lord Kelvin) in 1878 perfected the sounding machine after repeated tests at sea. Prior to his invention, fibre line was used exclusively in soundings. His introduction of piano wire solved the problem of rapid descent of the lead and also that of hauling it back aboard quickly. The chemically coated glass tube which he used to determine depth was an improvement of earlier methods, and the worth of the entire machine is evidenced by the fact that it is still used in essentially the same form.

Echo sounding. Based upon the principle that sound travels through sea water at a nearly uniform rate, automatic depth-registering devices (art. 619) have been invented to indicate the depth of water under a vessel, regardless of its speed. In 1911 an account was published of an experiment performed by Alexander Behm of Kiel, who timed the echo of an underwater explosion, testing this theory. High frequency sounds in water were produced by Pierre Langevin, and in 1918 he used the principle for echo depth finding. The first practical echo sounder was developed by the United States Navy in 1922.

The actual time between emission of a sonic or ultrasonic signal and return of its echo from the bottom, the angle at which the signal is beamed downward in order that its echo will be received at another part of the vessel, and the phase difference between signal and echo have all been used in the development of the modern echo sounder.

115. Aids to navigation.—The Cushites and Libyans constructed towers along the Mediterranean coast of Egypt, and priests maintained beacon fires in them. These were the earliest known lighthouses. At Sigeum in the Troad (part of Troy) a lighthouse was built before 660 BC. One of the seven wonders of the ancient world was the lighthouse called the Pharos of Alexandria, which may have been more than 200 feet tall. It was built by Sostratus of Cnidus (Asia Minor) in the third century BC, during the reign of Ptolemy Philadelphus. The word "pharos" has since been a general term for lighthouses. Some time between 1584 and 1611 the light of Cordouan, the earliest wave-swept lighthouse, was erected at the entrance to the Gironde river in western France. An oak log fire illuminated this structure until the 18th century.

Wood or coal fires were used in the many lighthouses built along the European and British coasts in the 17th and 18th centuries. One of these, the oak pile structure erected by Henry Whiteside in 1776 to warn shipmasters of Small's Rocks, subsequently played a major role in navigational history, as it was this light which figured in the discovery of the celestial line of position by Captain Thomas Sumner some 60 years later (art. 131).

In England such structures were privately maintained by interested organizations. One of the most famous of these groups, popularly known as "Trinity House," was organized in the 16th century, perhaps earlier, when a "beaconage and buoyage" fee was levied on English vessels. This prompted the establishment of Trinity House "to make, erect, and set up beacons, marks, and signs for the sea" and to provide vessels with pilots. The organization is now in its fifth century of operation, and its chief duties are to serve as a general lighthouse and pilotage authority, and to supply pilots.

The first lightship was a small vessel with lanterns hung from its yardarms. It was stationed at the Nore in the Thames estuary, in 1732.

The pilot's profession is not much younger than that of the mariner. The Bible relates (1 Kings 9:27) that Hiram of Tyre provided pilots for King Solomon. The duties of these pilots are not specified. In the first century AD, fishermen of the

Gulf of Cambay, India, met seagoing vessels and guided them into port. It is probable that pilots were established in Delaware Bay earlier than 1756.

Seafaring people of the United States had erected lighthouses and buoys before the Revolutionary War, and in 1789 Congress passed legislation providing for federal expansion of the work. About 1767 the first buoys were placed in the Delaware River. These were logs or barrels, but about 1820 they were replaced with spar buoys. In that same year, the first lightship was established in Chesapeake Bay.

As the maritime interests of various countries grew, more and better aids to navigation were made available. In 1850 Congress prescribed the present system of coloring and numbering United States buoys (app. Y). Conformity as to shape resulted from the recommendations of the International Marine Conference of 1889. The second half of the 19th century saw the development of bell, whistle, and lighted buoys, and in 1910 the first lighted buoy in the United States utilizing high pressure acetylene apparatus was placed in service. Stationed at the entrance to Ambrose Channel in New York, it provided the basis for the high degree of perfection which has been achieved in the lighted buoy since that time. The complete buoyage system maintained by the U. S. Coast Guard today is chiefly a product of the 20th century. In 1900 there were approximately 5,000 buoys of all types in use in the United States, while today there are more than 20,000.

116. The sailings.—The various methods of mathematically determining course, distance, and position arrived at have a history almost as old as mathematics itself. Thales, Hipparchus, Napier, Wright, and others contributed the formulas that led to the tables permitting computation of course and distance by plane, traverse, parallel, middle-latitude, Mercator, and great-circle sailings.

Plane sailing (art. 810). Based upon the assumption that the surface of the earth is plane, or flat, this method was used by navigators for many centuries. The navigator solved problems by laying down his course relative to his meridian, and stepping off the distance run to the new position. This system is used with accuracy today in measuring short runs on a Mercator chart, which compensates for the convergence of the meridians, but on the plane chart, serious errors resulted. Early navigators might have obtained mathematical solutions to this problem, with no greater accuracy, but the graphical method was commonly used.

Traverse sailing (art. 810). Because sailing vessels were subject to the winds, navigators of old were seldom able to sail one course for great distances, and consequently a series of small triangles had to be solved. Equipment was designed to help seamen in maintaining their dead reckoning positions. The modern **rough log** evolved from the *log board*, hinged wooden boards that folded like a book and on which courses and distances were marked in chalk. Each day the position was determined from this data and entered in the ship's journal, today's **smooth log.**

The log board was succeeded by the **travas,** a board with lines radiating from the center in 32 compass directions. Regularly spaced along the lines were small holes into which pegs were fitted to indicate time run on the particular course. In 1627 John Smith described the travas as a "little round board full of holes upon lines like the compasse, upon which by the removing of a little sticke they (seamen) keepe an account, how many glasses (which are but halfe houres) they steare upon every point of the compasse."

These devices were of great value to the navigator in keeping a record of the courses and distances sailed, but still left him the long mathematical solutions necessary to determine the new position. In 1436 what appears to have been the first **traverse table** was prepared by Andrea Biancho. Using this table of solutions of right-angled plane triangles, the navigator was able to determine his course and distance made good after sailing a number of distances in different directions.

Parallel sailing (art. 810) was an outgrowth of the navigator's inability to determine his longitude. Not a mathematical solution in the sense that the other sailings are, it involved converting the distance sailed along a parallel (departure), as determined by dead reckoning, into longitude.

Middle-latitude sailing (art. 810). The inaccuracies involved in plane sailing led to the improved method of middle-latitude sailing early in the 17th century. A mathematician named Ralph Handson is believed to have been its inventor.

Middle-latitude sailing is based upon the assumption that the use of a parallel midway between those of departure and arrival will eliminate the errors inherent in plane sailing due to the convergence of the meridians. The assumption is reasonably accurate and although the use of Mercator sailing usually results in greater accuracy, middle-latitude sailing still serves a useful purpose.

Mercator sailing (art. 810). Included in Edward Wright's *Certaine Errors in Navigation Detected and Corrected*, of 1599, was the first published table of meridional parts which provided the basis for the most accurate of rhumb line sailings—Mercator sailing.

Great-circle sailing (art. 812). For many hundreds of years mathematicians have known that a great circle is the shortest distance between two points on the surface of a sphere, but it was not until the 19th century that navigators began to regularly make use of this information.

The first printed description of great-circle sailing appeared in Pedro Nunes' 1537 *Tratado da Sphera*. The method had previously been proposed by Sebastian Cabot in 1498, and in 1524 Verrazano sailed a great-circle course to America. But the sailing ships could not regularly expect the steady winds necessary to sail such a course, and their lack of knowledge concerning longitude, plus the necessity of stopping at islands along their routes to take supplies, made it impractical for most voyages at that time.

The gradual accumulation of knowledge concerning seasonal and prevailing winds, weather conditions, and ocean currents eventually made it possible for the navigator to plan his voyage with more assurance. Nineteenth century writers of navigational texts recommended the use of great-circle sailing, and toward the close of that century such sailing became increasingly popular, particularly in the Pacific.

117. Hydrographic offices.—The practice of recording hydrographic data was centuries old before the establishment of the first official hydrographic office, in 1720. In that year the **Depot des Cartes, Plans, Journaux et Memoirs Relatifs a la Navigation** was formed in France with the Chevalier de Luynes in charge. The Hydrographic Department of the British Admiralty, though not established until 1795, has played a major part in European hydrographic work.

The **National Ocean Survey** was originally founded when Congress, in 1807, passed a resolution authorizing a survey of the coast, harbors, outlying islands, and fishing banks of the United States. On the recommendation of the American Philosophical Society, President Jefferson appointed Ferdinand Hassler, a Swiss immigrant who had founded the Geodetic Survey of his native land, the first Director of the "Survey of the Coast." The survey was renamed "Coast Survey" in 1836.

The approaches to New York were the first sections of the coast charted, and from there the work spread northward and southward along the eastern seaboard. In 1844 the work was expanded and arrangements made to chart simultaneously the gulf and east coasts. Investigation of tidal conditions began, and in 1855 the first tables of tide predictions were published. The California gold rush gave impetus to the survey of the west coast, which began in 1850, the year California became a State. The survey ship *Washington* undertook investigations of the Gulf Stream. Coast pilots, or sailing directions, for the Atlantic coast of the United States were privately published in the first half of the 19th century, but about 1850 the Survey began accumulating data that led to federally produced coast pilots. The 1889 *Pacific Coast Pilot* was an outstanding contribution to the safety of west coast shipping.

In 1878 the survey was renamed "Coast and Geodetic Survey"; in 1970 the survey became the "National Ocean Survey."

Today the National Ocean Survey provides the mariner with the charts and coast pilots of all waters of the United States and its possessions, and tide and tidal current tables for much of the world.

Defense Mapping Agency Hydrographic Center. In 1830 the U. S. Navy established a "Depot of Charts and Instruments" in Washington, D.C. Primarily, it was to serve as a storehouse where such charts and sailing directions as were available, together with navigational instruments, could be assembled for issue to Navy ships which required them. Lieutenant L. M. Goldsborough and one assistant, Passed Midshipman R. B. Hitchcock, constituted the entire staff.

The first chart published by the Depot was produced from data obtained in a survey made by Lieutenant Charles Wilkes, who had succeeded Goldsborough in 1834, and who later earned fame as the leader of a United States exploring expedition to Antarctica.

From 1842 until 1861 Lieutenant Matthew Fontaine Maury served as Officer-in-Charge. Under his command the Depot rose to international prominence. Maury decided upon an ambitious plan to increase the mariner's knowledge of existing winds, weather, and currents. He began by making a detailed record of pertinent matter included in old log books stored at the Depot. He then inaugurated a hydrographic reporting program among shipmasters, and the thousands of answers received, along with the log book data, were first utilized to publish the *Wind and Current Chart of the North Atlantic* of 1847. The United States instigated an international conference in 1853 to interest other nations in a system of exchanging nautical information. The plan, which was Maury's, was enthusiastically adopted by other maritime nations, and is the basis upon which hydrographic offices operate today.

In 1854 the Depot was redesignated the "U. S. Naval Observatory and Hydrographical Office," and in 1866 Congress separated the two, broadly increasing the functions of the latter. The Office was authorized to carry out surveys, collect information, and print every kind of nautical chart and publication, all "for the benefit and use of navigators generally."

One of the first acts of the new Office was to purchase the copyright of *The New American Practical Navigator*. Several volumes of sailing directions had already been published. The first *Notice to Mariners* appeared in 1869. Daily broadcast of navigational warnings was inaugurated in 1907, and in 1912, following the sinking of the SS *Titanic*, Hydrographic Office action led to the establishment of the International Ice Patrol.

The development by the U. S. Navy of an improved depth finder in 1922 made possible the acquisition of additional information concerning bottom topography. During the same year aerial photography was first employed as an aid in chart making. The Hydrographic Office published the first chart for lighter-than-air craft in 1923.

In 1962 the U. S. Navy Hydrographic Office was redesignated the U. S. Naval Oceanographic Office. In 1972 certain hydrographic functions of the latter office were transferred to the Defense Mapping Agency Hydrographic Center.

The **International Hydrographic Organization** (**IHO**) was originally established in 1921 as the **International Hydrographic Bureau** (**IHB**). The present name was adopted in 1970 as a result of a revised international agreement among member nations. However, the former name, International Hydrographic Bureau, was retained for the IHO's administrative body of three Directors and a small Staff at the Organization's headquarters in Monaco.

The IHO (as did the former IHB) sets forth hydrographic standards as they are agreed upon by the member nations. All member States are urged and encouraged to follow these standards in their surveys, nautical charts, and publications. As these standards are uniformly adopted, the products of the world's hydrographic and oceanographic offices become more uniform. Much has been done in the field of standardization since the Bureau was founded.

The principal work undertaken by the IHO is:

1. to bring about a close and permanent association between national hydrographic offices;
2. to study matters relating to hydrography and allied sciences and techniques;
3. to further the exchange of nautical charts and documents between hydrographic offices of Member Governments;
4. to circulate the appropriate documents;
5. to tender guidance and advice upon request, in particular to countries engaged in setting up or expanding their hydrographic service;
6. to encourage coordination of hydrographic surveys with relevant oceanographic activities;
7. to extend and facilitate the application of oceanographic knowledge for the benefit of navigators;
8. to cooperate with international organizations and scientific institutions which have related objectives.

During the 19th century, many maritime nations established hydrographic offices to provide means for improving the navigation of naval and merchant vessels by providing nautical publications, nautical charts, and other navigational services. Nonuniformity of hydrographic procedures, charts, and publications was much in evidence. In 1889, an International Marine Conference was held at Washington, D.C., and it was proposed to establish a "permanent international commission." Similar proposals were made at the sessions of the International Congress of Navigation held at St. Petersburg in 1908 and again in 1912.

In 1919 the hydrographers of Great Britain and France cooperated in taking the necessary steps to convene an international conference of hydrographers. London was selected as the most suitable place for this conference, and on July 24, 1919, the First International Conference opened, attended by the hydrographers of 24 nations. The object of the conference was clearly stated in the invitation to attend. It read, "To consider the advisability of all maritime nations adopting similar methods in the preparation, construction, and production of their charts and all hydrographic publications; of rendering the results in the most convenient form to enable them to be readily used; of instituting a prompt system of mutual exchange of hydrographic information between all countries; and of providing an opportunity to consultations and discussions to be carried out on hydrographic subjects generally by the hydrographic experts of the world." In general, this is still the purpose of the International Hydrographic Organization. As a result of the conference, a permanent organization was formed and statutes for its operations were prepared. The International Hydrographic Bureau, now the International Hydrographic Organization, began its activities in 1921 with 18 nations as members. The Principality of Monaco was selected because of its easy communication with the rest of the world and also because of the generous offer of Prince Albert I of Monaco to provide suitable accommodations for the Bureau in the Principality. The IHO, including the three Directors and their staff, is housed in its own headquarters which were built and are maintained by the Government of Monaco.

The works of the IHO are published in both French and English and are distributed through various media. Many of the publications are available to the general public, and a discount of 30 percent is offered to naval and merchant marine officers of any of the member nations. Inquiries as to the availability of the publications should be made directly to the "International Hydrographic Bureau, Avenue President J. F. Kennedy, Monte-Carlo, Monaco."

118. Navigation manuals.—Although navigation is as old as man himself, navigation textbooks, as they are thought of today, are a product of the last several centuries. Until the end of the Dark Ages such books, or manuscripts, as were available were written by astronomers for other astronomers. The navigator was forced to make use of these, gleaning what little was directly applicable to his profession. After 1500, however, the need for books on navigation resulted in the publication of a series of manuals of increasing value to the mariner.

Sixteenth century manuals. Frequently a command of Latin was required to study navigation during the 16th century. *Regimento do estrolabio e do quadrante* (fig. 130a), which was published at Lisbon in 1509, or earlier, explained the method of finding latitude by meridian observations of the sun and the pole star, contained a traverse table for finding the longitude by dead reckoning, and listed the longitudes of a number of places. Unfortunately, the author made several errors in transcribing the declination tables published by Abraham Zacuto in 1474, and this resulted in errors being made for many years in determining latitude. Nevertheless, the nameless writer of the *Regimento* performed a great service for all mariners. His "Handbook for the Astrolabe and Quadrant"—to translate the title—had many editions and many emulators.

In 1519 Fernandez de Encisco published his *Suma de Geographia,* the first Spanish manual. The book was largely a translation of the *Regimento,* but new information was included, and revisions were printed in 1530 and 1546.

The Flemish mathematician and astronomer R. Gemma Frisius published a book on navigation in 1530. This manual, entitled *De Principiis Astronomiae,* gave an excellent description of the sphere, although the astronomy was that of Ptolemy, and discussed at length the use of the globe in navigation. Gemma gave courses in terms of the principal winds, proposed that longitude be reckoned from the Fortunate Islands (Canary Islands), and gave rules for finding the dead reckoning position by courses and distances sailed.

Tratado da Sphera, Pedro Nunes' great work, appeared in 1537. In addition to the first printed description of great-circle sailing, Nunes' book included a section on determining the latitude by two altitudes of the sun (taken when the azimuths differed by not less than 40°) and solving the problem on a globe. The method was first proposed by Gemma. *Tratado da Sphera* contained the conclusion of a study of the "plane chart" which Nunes had made. He exposed its errors, but was unable to develop a satisfactory substitute.

During the years that followed, an extensive navigational literature became available. The Spaniards Pedro de Medina and Martin Cortes published successful manuals in 1545 and 1551, respectively. Medina's *Arte de Navegar* passed through 13 editions in several languages and *Breve de la Spera y de la Arte de Navegar,* Cortes' book, was eventually translated into English and became the favorite of the British navigator. Cortes discussed the principle which Mercator used 18 years later in constructing his famous chart, and he also listed accurately the distance between meridians at all latitudes.

The first western hemisphere navigation manual was published by Diego Garcia de Palacio at Mexico City in 1587. His *Instrucion Nauthica* included a partial glossary of nautical terms and certain data on ship construction.

John Davis' *The Seaman's Secrets* of 1594 was the first of the "practical" books. Davis was a celebrated navigator who asserted that it was the purpose of his book to give "all that is necessary for sailors, not for scholars on shore." Davis' book discussed at length the navigator's instruments, and went into detail on the "sailings." He explained the method of dividing a great circle into a number of rhumb lines, and the work he had done with Edward Wright qualified him to report on the method and advantages of Mercator sailing. He endorsed the system of determining latitude by two observations of the sun and the intermediate bearing.

Although best known for the presentation of the theory of Mercator sailing, Edward Wright's *Certaine Errors in Navigation Detected and Corrected* (1599) was a sound navigation manual in its own right Particularly, he advocated correcting sights for dip, refraction, and parallax.

Later manuals. The next 200 years saw a succession of navigation manuals made available to the navigator; so many that only a few can be mentioned. Among those which enjoyed the greatest success were Blundeville's *Exercises*, John Napier's *Mirifici Logarithmorum Canonis Descriptio* (which introduced the use of logarithms at sea), the tables and rules of Edmund Gunter, *Arithmetical Navigation* by Thomas Addison, and Richard Norwood's *The Sea-mans Practice* (which gave the length of the nautical mile as 6,120 feet). Robert Dudley filled four volumes in writing the *Arcano del Mare* (1646–47) as did John Robertson with *Elements of Navigation*. Jonas and John Moore, William Jones, and several Samuel Dunns were others who contributed navigation books before Nathaniel Bowditch in America and J. W. Norie in England wrote the manuals which navigators found best suited to their needs.

Bowditch's *The New American Practical Navigator* was first published in 1802 (fig. 118), and Norie's *Epitome of Navigation* appeared the following year. Both were outstanding books which enabled the mariner of little formal education to grasp the essentials of his profession. The Englishman's book passed through 22 editions in that country before losing its popularity to Captain Lecky's famous *"Wrinkles" in Practical Navigation* of 1881. The *American Practical Navigator* is still read widely, more than a century-and-a-half after its original printing.

A number of worthy navigation manuals have appeared in recent years.

Celestial Navigation

119. Astronomy is sometimes called the oldest of sciences. The movements of the sun, moon, stars, and planets were used by the earliest men as guides in hunting, fishing, and farming. The first maps were probably of the heavens.

Babylonian priests studied celestial mechanics at a very early date, possibly as early as 3800 BC, more probably about 1500 years later. These ancient astronomers predicted lunar and solar eclipses, constructed tables of the moon's hour angle, and are believed to have invented the zodiac. The week and month as known today originated with their calendar. They grouped the stars by constellations. It is probable that they were arranged in essentially their present order as early as 2000 BC. The five planets easily identified by the unaided eye were known to the Babylonians, who were apparently the first to divide the sun's apparent motion about the earth into 24 equal parts. They published this and other astronomical data in ephemerides. There is evidence that the prophet Abraham had an excellent knowledge of astronomy.

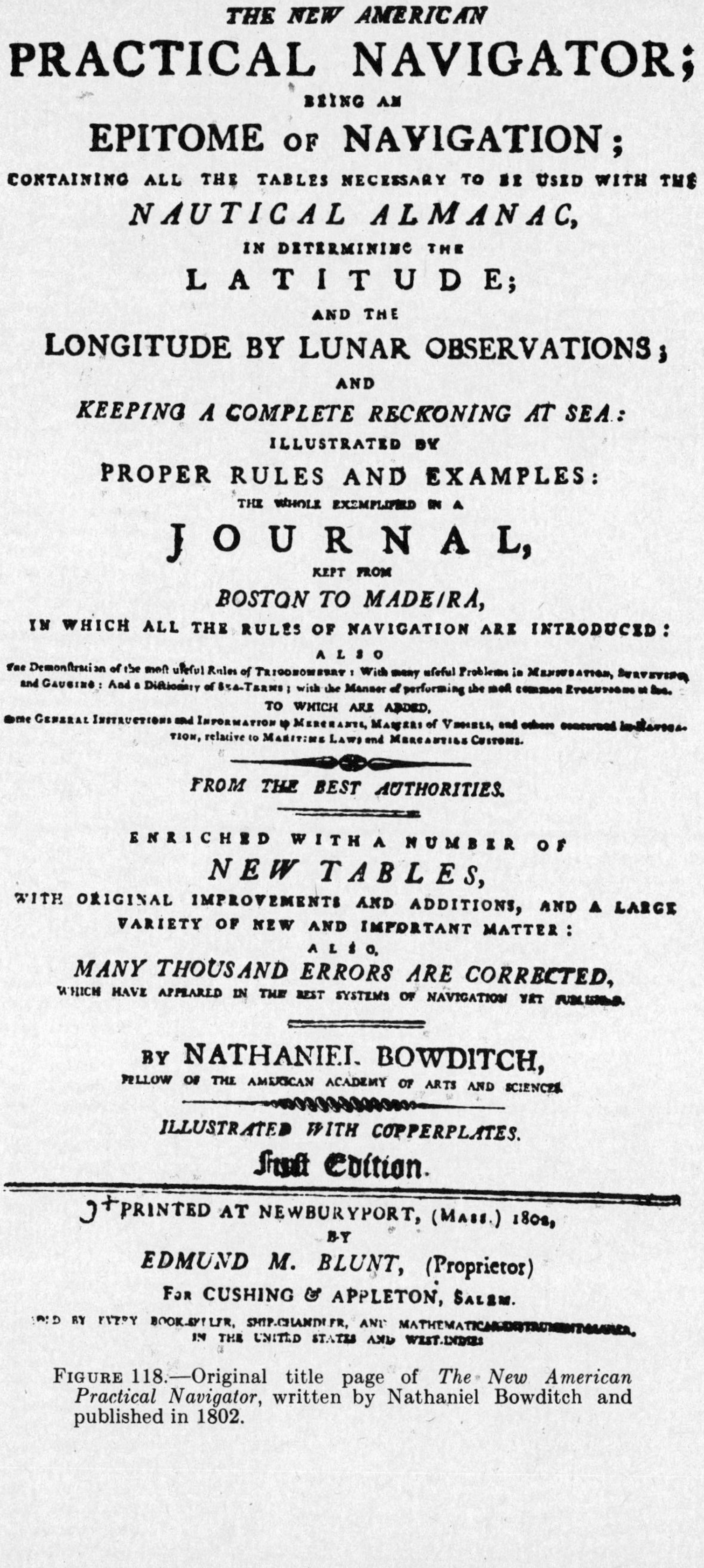

THE NEW AMERICAN

PRACTICAL NAVIGATOR;

BEING AN

EPITOME OF NAVIGATION;

CONTAINING ALL THE TABLES NECESSARY TO BE USED WITH THE

NAUTICAL ALMANAC,

IN DETERMINING THE

LATITUDE;

AND THE

LONGITUDE BY LUNAR OBSERVATIONS;

AND

KEEPING A COMPLETE RECKONING AT SEA:

ILLUSTRATED BY

PROPER RULES AND EXAMPLES:

THE WHOLE EXEMPLIFIED IN A

JOURNAL,

KEPT FROM

BOSTON TO MADEIRA,

IN WHICH ALL THE RULES OF NAVIGATION ARE INTRODUCED:

ALSO

The Demonstration of the most useful Rules of TRIGONOMETRY: With many useful Problems in MENSURATION, SURVEYING, and GAUGING: And a Dictionary of SEA-TERMS; with the Manner of performing the most common EVOLUTIONS at Sea.

TO WHICH ARE ADDED,

Some GENERAL INSTRUCTIONS and INFORMATION to MERCHANTS, MASTERS of VESSELS, and others concerned in NAVIGATION, relative to MARITIME LAWS and MERCANTILE CUSTOMS.

FROM THE BEST AUTHORITIES.

ENRICHED WITH A NUMBER OF

NEW TABLES,

WITH ORIGINAL IMPROVEMENTS AND ADDITIONS, AND A LARGE VARIETY OF NEW AND IMPORTANT MATTER:

ALSO,

MANY THOUSAND ERRORS ARE CORRECTED,

WHICH HAVE APPEARED IN THE BEST SYSTEMS OF NAVIGATION YET PUBLISHED.

BY NATHANIEL BOWDITCH,

FELLOW OF THE AMERICAN ACADEMY OF ARTS AND SCIENCES.

ILLUSTRATED WITH COPPERPLATES.

First Edition.

PRINTED AT NEWBURYPORT, (MASS.) 1802,

BY

EDMUND M. BLUNT, (Proprietor)

For CUSHING & APPLETON, SALEM.

SOLD BY EVERY BOOK-SELLER, SHIP-CHANDLER, AND MATHEMATICAL-INSTRUMENT-MAKER, IN THE UNITED STATES AND WEST-INDIES

FIGURE 118.—Original title page of *The New American Practical Navigator*, written by Nathaniel Bowditch and published in 1802.

The Chinese, too, made outstanding contributions to the science of the heavens. They may have fixed the solstices and equinoxes before 2000 BC. They had quadrants and armillary spheres, used water clocks, and observed meridian transits. These ancient Chinese determined that the sun made its annual apparent revolution about the earth in 365¼ days, and divided circles into that many parts, rather than 360. About 1100 BC the astronomer Chou Kung determined the sun's maximum declination within about 15'.

Astronomy was used by the Egyptians in fixing the dates of their religious festivals almost as early as the Babylonian studies. By 2000 BC or earlier the new year began with the heliacal rising of Sirius; that is, the first reappearance of this star in the eastern sky during morning twilight after having last been seen just after sunset in the western sky. The heliacal rising of Sirius coincided approximately with the annual Nile flood. The famous Pyramid of Cheops, which was probably built in the 17th century BC, was so constructed that the light of Sirius shone down a southerly shaft when at upper transit, and the light of the Pole Star shone down a northerly shaft at lower transit, the axes of the two shafts intersecting in the royal burial chamber. When the pyramid was constructed, *α Draconis*, not Polaris, was the Pole Star.

The Greeks learned of navigational astronomy from the Phoenicians. The earliest Greek astronomer, Thales, was of Phoenician ancestry. He is given credit for dividing the year of the western world into 365 days, and he discovered that the sun does not move uniformly between solstices. Thales is most popularly known, however, for predicting the solar eclipse of 585 BC, which ended a battle between the Medes and the Lydians. He was the first of the great men whose work during the next 700 years was the controlling force in navigation, astronomy, and cartography until the Renaissance.

120. Shape of the earth.—Advanced as the Babylonians were, they apparently considered the earth to be flat. Land surveys of about 2300 BC show a "salt water river" encircling the country (fig. 120).

But seafarers knew that the last to be seen of a ship as it disappeared over the horizon was the masthead. They recognized the longer summer days in England when they sailed to the tin mines of Cornwall, as early as 900 BC. In that "northland" the Mediterranean sailors noticed that the Pole Star was higher in the sky and the lower southern constellations were no longer visible. When Thales invented the gnomonic projection

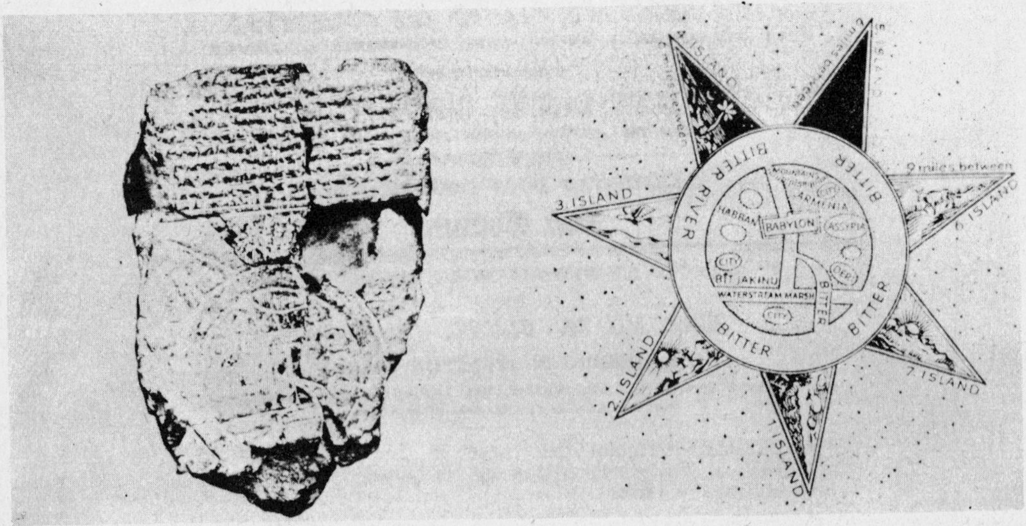

Courtesy of the Map Division of the Library of Congress.

FIGURE 120.—The original and reconstruction of a Babylonian map of about 500 BC. The Babylonians believed the earth to be a flat disk encircled by a salt water river.

about 600 BC, he must have believed the earth to be a sphere. Two centuries later Aristotle wrote that the earth's shadow on the moon during an eclipse was always circular. Archimedes (287–212 BC) used a glass celestial globe with a smaller terrestrial globe inside it. Although the average man has understood the spherical nature of the earth for only a comparatively short period, learned astronomers have accepted the fact for more than 25 centuries.

121. Celestial mechanics.—Among astronomers the principal question for 2,000 years was not the shape of the earth, but whether it or the sun was the center of the universe. A stationary earth seemed logical to the early Greeks, who calculated that daily rotation would produce a wind of several hundred miles per hour at the equator. Failing to realize that the earth's atmosphere turns with it, they considered the absence of such a wind proof that the earth was stationary.

The belief among the ancients was that all celestial bodies moved in circles about the earth. However, the planets—the "wanderers," as they were called—contradicted this theory by their irregular motion. In the fourth century BC Eudoxus of Cnidus attempted to account for this by suggesting that planets were attached to concentric spheres which rotated about the earth at varying speeds. The plan of **epicycles,** the theory of the universe which was commonly accepted for 2,000 years, was first proposed by Appolonius of Perga in the third century BC. Ptolemy accepted and amplified the plan, explaining it in his famous books, the *Almagest* and *Cosmographia*. According to Ptolemy, the planets moved at uniform speeds in small circles, the centers of which moved at uniform speeds in circles about the earth (fig. 121).

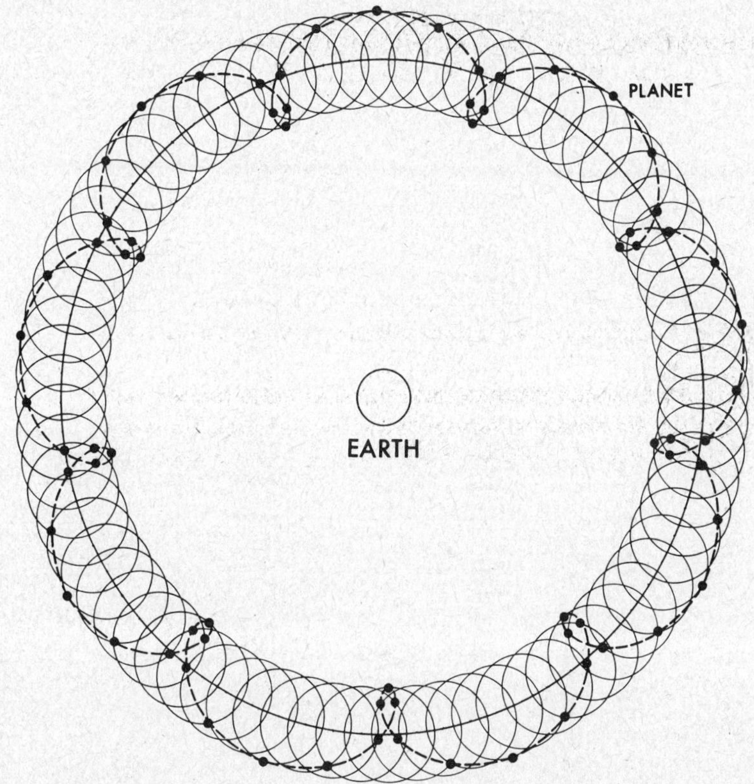

FIGURE 121.—The plan of epicycles, by which the ancients explained the retrograde motion of the planets. The planets were believed to rotate in small circles whose centers moved about the earth in a large circle.

At first the Ptolemaic theory was accepted without question, but as the years passed, forecasts based upon it proved to be inaccurate. By the time the *Alfonsine Tables* were published in the 13th century AD, a growing number of astronomers considered the Ptolemaic doctrine unacceptable. However, Purbach, Regiomontanus, Bernhard Walther of Nuremberg, and even Tycho Brahe in the latter part of the 16th century, were among those who tried to reconcile the earth-centered epicyclic plan to the observed phenomena of the heavens.

As early as the sixth century BC, a brotherhood founded by Pythagoras, a Greek philosopher, proposed that the earth was round and self-supported in space, and that it, the other planets, the sun, and the moon revolved about a central fire which they called *Hestia*, the hearth of the universe. The sun and the moon, they said, shone by reflected light from Hestia.

The central fire was never located, however, and a few hundred years later Aristarchus of Samos advanced a genuine heliocentric theory. He denied the existence of Hestia and placed the sun at the center of the universe, correctly considering it to be a star which shone by itself. The Hebrews apparently understood the correct relationship at least as early as Abraham (about 2000 BC), and the early inhabitants of the Western Hemisphere probably knew of it before the Europeans did.

The Ptolemaic theory was generally accepted until its inability to predict future positions of the planets could no longer be reconciled. Its replacement by the heliocentric theory is credited principally to Nicolaus Copernicus (or Koppernigk). After studying mathematics at the University of Cracow, Copernicus went to Bologna, where he attended the astronomical lectures of Domenicao Maria Novara, an advocate of the Pythagorean theory. Further study in Martianus Copella's *Satyricon*, which includes a discussion of the heliocentric doctrine, convinced him that the sun was truly the center of the universe.

Until the year of his death Copernicus tested his belief by continual observations, and in that year, 1543, he published *De Revolutionibus Orbium Coelestium*. In it he said that the earth rotated on its axis daily and revolved in a circle about the sun once each year. He placed the other planets in circular orbits about the sun also, recognizing that Mercury and Venus were closer than the earth, and the others farther out. He concluded that the stars were motionless in space and that the moon moved circularly about the earth. His conclusions did not become widely known until nearly a century later, when Galileo publicized them. Today, "heliocentric" and "Copernican" are synonymous terms used in describing the character of the solar system.

122. Other early discoveries.—A knowledge of the principal motions of the planets permitted reasonably accurate predictions of future positions. Other, less spectacular data, however, were being established to help round out the knowledge astronomers needed before they could produce the highly accurate almanacs known today.

More than a century before the birth of Christ, Hipparchus discovered the **precession of the equinoxes** (art. 1419) by comparing his own observations of the stars with those recorded by Timocharis and Aristyllus about 300 BC. Hipparchus cataloged more than a thousand stars, and compiled an additional list of time-keeping stars which differed in sidereal hour angle by 15° (one hour), accurate to 15′. A spherical star map, or planisphere, and a celestial globe were among the equipment he designed. However, his instruments did not permit measurements of such precision that stellar parallax could be detected, and, consequently, he advocated the geocentric theory of the universe.

Three centuries later Ptolemy examined and confirmed Hipparchus' discovery of precession. He published a catalog in which he arranged the stars by constellations and gave the magnitude, declination, and right ascension (art. 1426) of each. Following Hipparchus, Ptolemy determined longitudes by eclipses. In the *Almagest* he included the plane and spherical trigonometry tables which Hipparchus had developed, mathematical tables, and an explanation of the circumstances upon which the equation of time (art. 1809) depends.

The next thousand years saw little progress in the science of astronomy. Alexandria continued as a center of learning for several hundred years after Ptolemy, but succeeding astronomers at the observatory confined their work to comments on his great books. The long twilight of the Dark Ages had begun.

Alexandria was captured and destroyed by the Arabs in AD 640, and for the next 500 years Moslems exerted the primary influence in astronomy. Observatories were erected at Baghdād and Damascus during the ninth century. Ibn Yunis' observatory near Cairo gathered the data for the Hakimite tables in the 11th century. Earlier, the Spanish, under Moorish tutelage, set up schools of astronomy at Cordova and Toledo.

123. Modern astronomy may be said to date from Copernicus, although it was not until the invention of the telescope, about 1608, that precise measurement of the positions and motions of celestial bodies was possible.

Galileo Galilei, an Italian, made outstanding contributions to the cause of astronomy, and these served as a basis for the work of later men, particularly Isaac Newton. He discovered Jupiter's satellites, providing additional opportunities for determining longitude on land. He maintained that it is natural for motion to be uniform and in a straight line and that a force is required only when direction or speed is changing. Galileo's support of the heliocentric theory, his use and improvement of the telescope, and particularly the clarity and completeness of his records provided firm footing for succeeding astronomers.

Early in the 17th century, before the invention of the telescope, Tycho Brahe found that planet Mars to be in a position differing by as much as 8′ from that required by the geocentric theory. When the telescope became available, astronomers learned that the apparent diameter of the sun varied during the year, indicating that the earth's distance from the sun varies, and that its orbit is not circular.

Johannes Kepler, a German who had succeeded Brahe and who was attempting to account for his 8′ discrepancy, published in 1609 two of astronomy's most important doctrines, the **law of equal areas,** and the **law of elliptical orbits.** Nine years later he announced his third law, relating the periods of revolution of any two planets to their respective distances from the sun (art. 1407).

Kepler's discoveries provided a mathematical basis by which more accurate tables of astronomical data were computed for the maritime explorers of the age. His realization that the sun is the controlling power of the system and that the orbital planes of the planets pass through its center almost led him to the discovery of the law of gravitation.

Sir Isaac Newton reduced Kepler's conclusions to the **universal law of gravitation** (art. 1407) when he published his three laws of motions in 1687. Because the planets exert forces one upon the other, their orbits do not agree exactly with Kepler's laws. Newton's work compensated for this and, as a result, the astronomer was able to forecast with greater accuracy the positions of the celestial bodies. The navigator benefited through more exact tables of astronomical data.

Between the years 1764 and 1784, the Frenchmen Lagrange and Laplace conclusively proved the solar system's mechanical stability. Early in the 19th century, Nathaniel Bowditch translated and commented upon Laplace's *Mécanique Céleste*, bringing it up-to-date. Prior to their work this stability had been questioned due to apparent inconsistencies in the motions of some of the planets. After their demonstrations, men were convinced and could turn to other important work necessary to refine and improve the navigator's almanac.

But there were real, as well as apparent, irregularities of motion which could not be explained by the law of gravitation alone. By this law the planets describe ellipses about the sun, and these orbits are repeated indefinitely, except as the other planets influence the orbits of each by their own gravitational pull. Urbain Leverrier, one-time Director of the Paris Observatory, found that the line of apsides of Mercury was advancing 43″ per century faster than it should, according to the law of gravitation and the positions of other known planets. In an attempt to compensate for the resulting errors in the predicted positions of the planet, he suggested that there must be a mass of circulating matter between the sun and Mercury. No such circulating matter has been found, however, and Leverrier's discovery is attributed to a shortcoming of Newton's law, as explained by Albert Einstein.

In Einstein's hands, Leverrier's 43″ became a fact as powerful as Brahe's 8′ had been in the hands of Kepler. Early in the 20th century, Einstein announced the general theory of relativity. He stated that for the planets to revolve about the sun is natural, and gravitational force is unnecessary for this, and he asserted that there need be no circulating matter to account for the motion of the perihelion of Mercury as this, too, is in the natural order of things. Calculated from his theory, the correction to the previously computed motion of the perihelion in 100 years is 42″.9.

Prior to Einstein's work, other discoveries had helped round out man's knowledge of the universe.

Aberration (art. 1417), discovered by James Bradley about 1726, accounted for the apparent shifting of the stars throughout the year, due to the combined orbital speed of the earth and the speed of light. Twenty years later Bradley described the periodic wobbling of the earth's axis, called **nutation** (art. 1417), and its effect upon precession of the equinoxes.

Meanwhile, in 1718 Edmond Halley, England's second Astronomer Royal, detected a motion of the stars, other than that caused by precession, that led him to conclude that they, too, were moving. By studying the works of the Alexandrian astronomers, he found that some of the most prominent stars had changed their positions by as much as 32′. Jacques Cassini gave Halley's discovery further support when he found, a few years later, that the declination of Arcturus had changed 5′ in the 100 years since Brahe made his observations. This **proper motion** (art. 1414) is motion in addition to that caused by precession, nutation, and aberration.

Sir William Herschel, the great astronomer who discovered the planet Uranus in 1781, proved that the solar system is moving toward the constellation *Hercules*. As early as 1828 Herschel advocated the establishment of a standard time system. Neptune was discovered in 1846 after its position had been predicted by the Frenchman Urbain Leverrier. Based upon the work of Percival Lowell, an American, Pluto was identified in 1930. Uranus, Neptune, and Pluto are of little concern to the navigator.

A more recent discovery may well have greater navigational significance. This is the existence of sources of electromagnetic energy in the sky in the form of **radio stars** (art. 1414). The sun has been found to transmit energy of radio frequency, and instruments have been built which are capable of tracking it across the sky regardless of weather conditions.

124. Sextant.—Prior to the development of the magnetic compass, the navigator used the heavenly bodies chiefly as guides by which to steer. The compass, however, led to more frequent long voyages on the open sea, and the need for a vertical-angle measuring device which could be used for determining altitude, so that latitude could be found.

Probably the first such device used at sea was the **common quadrant,** the simplest form of all such instruments. Made of wood, it was a fourth part of a circle, held vertical by means of a plumb bob. An observation made with this instrument at sea was a two- or three-man job. This device was probably used ashore for centuries before it went to sea, although its earliest use by the mariner is unknown.

Invented perhaps by Apollonius of Perga in the third century BC, the **astrolabe** (fig. 124a)—from the Greek for *star* and *to take*—had been made portable by the Arabs possibly as early as AD 700. It was in the hands of Christian pilots by the end of the 13th century, often as an elaborate and beautiful creation wrought of precious metals. Some astrolabes could be used as **star finders** by fitting an engraved plate to one side. Large astrolabes were among the chief instruments of 15th and 16th century observatories, but the value of this instrument at sea was limited.

The principle of the astrolabe was similar to that of the common quadrant, but the astrolabe consisted of a metal disk, graduated in degrees, to which a movable sight vane was attached. In using the astrolabe, which may be likened to a pelorus held on its side, the navigator adjusted the sight vane until it was in line with the star, and

Courtesy of the John Carter Brown Library, Brown University.

FIGURE 124a.—An ancient astrolabe, one of the earliest kinds of altitude-measuring instruments.

then read the zenith distance from the scale. As with the common quadrant, the vertical was established by plumb bob.

Three men were needed to make an observation with the astrolabe (one held the instrument by a ring at its top, another aligned the sight vane with the body, a third made the reading) and even then the least rolling or pitching of a vessel caused large acceleration errors in observations. Therefore, navigators were forced to abandon the plumb bob and make the horizon their reference.

The **cross-staff** (fig. 124b) was the first instrument which utilized the visible horizon in making celestial observations. The instrument consisted of a long, wooden shaft upon which one of several cross-pieces was mounted perpendicularly. The cross-pieces were of various lengths, the one being used depending upon the angle to be measured. The navigator fitted the appropriate cross-piece on the shaft and, holding one end of the shaft beside his eye, adjusted the cross until its lower end was in line with the horizon and its upper end with the body. The shaft was calibrated to indicate the altitude of the body observed.

In using the cross-staff, the navigator was forced to look at the horizon and the celestial body at the same time. In 1590 John Davis, author of *The Seaman's Secrets*, invented the **backstaff** (fig. 124c) or **sea quadrant.** He was one of the few practical seamen (Davis Strait is named for him, in honor of his attempt to find the Northwest Passage) to invent a navigational device. The backstaff marked a long advance and was particularly popular among American colonial navigators.

In using this instrument, the navigator turned his back to the sun and aligned its shadow with the horizon. The backstaff had two arcs, and the sum of the values shown on each was the zenith distance of the sun. Later, this instrument was fitted with a mirror to permit observations of bodies other than the sun.

Another instrument developed about the same time was the **nocturnal** (fig. 124d). Its purpose was to provide the mariner with the appropriate correction to be made to the altitude of Polaris to determine latitude. By sighting on Polaris through the hole

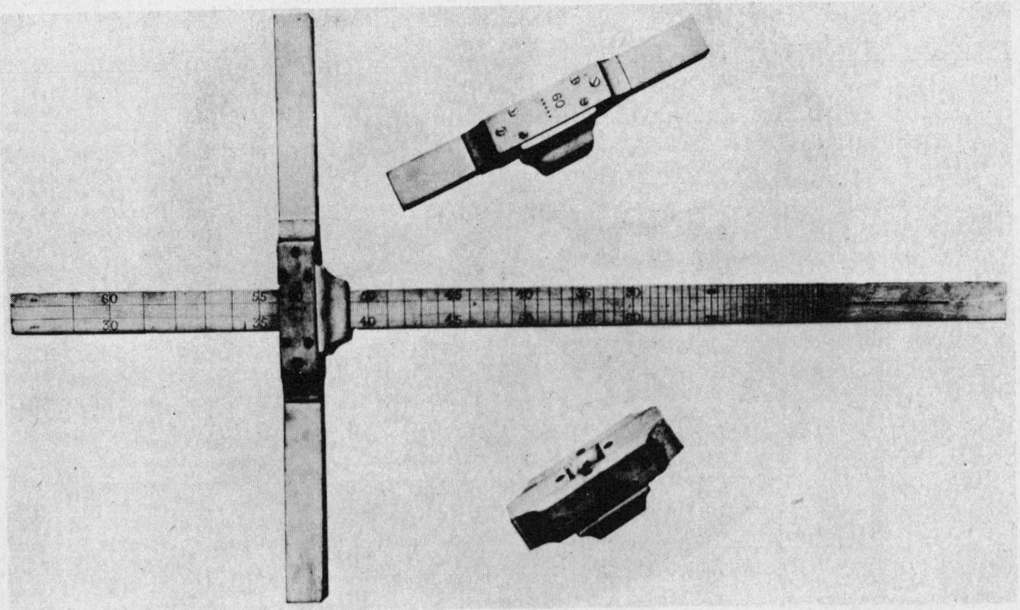

Courtesy of Peabody Museum of Salem.

FIGURE 124b.—The cross-staff, the first instrument to utilize the visible horizon in making celestial observations.

in the center of the instrument and adjusting the movable arm so that it pointed at Kochab, the navigator could read the correction from the instrument. Most nocturnals had an additional outer disk graduated for the months and days of the year and by adjusting this the navigator could also determine solar time.

Tycho Brahe designed several instruments with arcs of 60°, having one fixed sight and another movable one. He called the instruments **sextants** and the name is now commonly applied to all altitude-measuring devices used by the navigator.

Courtesy of Peabody Museum of Salem.

FIGURE 124c.—The backstaff, or sea quadrant, a favorite instrument of American colonial navigators.

British Crown copyright. Science Museum, London, England.

FIGURE 124d.—The nocturnal, an instrument used to determine latitude by an observation of Polaris.

In 1700, Sir Isaac Newton sent to Edmond Halley, the Astronomer Royal, a description of a device having double-reflecting mirrors, the principle of the modern marine sextant. However, this was not made public until after somewhat similar instruments had been made in 1730 by the Englishman John Hadley, and the American Thomas Godfrey.

The original instrument constructed by Hadley was, in fact, an *octant*, but due to the double-reflection principle it measured angles up to one-fourth of a circle, or 90°. Godfrey's instrument is reported to have been a *quadrant*, and so could measure angles through 180°. The two men received equal awards from England's Royal Society, as their work was considered to be a case of simultaneous independent invention, although Hadley probably preceded Godfrey by a few months in the actual construction of his sextant.

In the next few years both instruments were successfully tested at sea, but 20 years or more passed before the navigator gave up his backstaff or sea quadrant for the new device. In 1733 Hadley attached a spirit level to a quadrant, and with it was able to measure altitudes without reference to the horizon. Some years later the first bubble sextant (art. 1513) was developed.

Pierre Vernier, in 1631, had attached to the limb of a quadrant a second, smaller graduated arc, thereby permitting angles to be measured more accurately, and this device was incorporated in all later angle-measuring instruments.

The sextant has remained practically unchanged since its invention more than two centuries ago. The only notable improvements have been the addition of an endless tangent screw and a micrometer drum, both having been added during the 20th century.

125. Determining latitude.—The ability to determine longitude at sea is comparatively modern, but latitude has been available for thousands of years.

Meridian transit of the sun. Long before the Christian era, astronomers had determined the sun's declination for each day of the year, and prepared tables listing the data. This was a comparatively simple matter, for the zenith distance obtained by use of a shadow cast by the sun on the day of the winter solstice could be subtracted from that obtained on the day of the summer solstice to determine the range of the sun's declination, about 47°. Half of this is the sun's maximum declination, which could then be applied to the zenith distance recorded on either day to determine the latitude of the place. Daily observations thereafter enabled the ancient astronomers to construct reasonably accurate declination tables.

Such tables were available long before the average navigator was ready to use them, but certainly by the 15th century experienced seamen were determining their latitude at sea to within one or two degrees. In his 1594 *The Seaman's Secrets*, Davis made use of his experience in high latitudes to explain the method of determining latitude by lower transit observations of the sun.

Ex-meridian observation of the sun. The possibility of overcast skies at the one time each day when the navigator could get a reliable observation for latitude led to the development of the "ex-meridian" sight. Another method, involving two sights taken with a considerable time interval between, had previously been known, but the mathematics were so involved that it is doubtful that many seamen made use of it.

There are two methods by which ex-meridian observations can be solved. The direct process was the more accurate, although it required a trigonometrical solution. By the latter part of the 19th century, tables were introduced which made the method of reduction to the meridian more practical and, when occasion demands such an observation, this is the method generally used today. However, with the development of line of position methods and the modern inspection table, ex-meridian observations have lost much of their popularity.

Latitude by Polaris. First use of the Pole Star to determine latitude is not known, but many centuries ago seamen who used it as a guide by which to steer were known to comment upon its change of altitude as they sailed north or south.

By Columbus' time some navigators were using Polaris to determine latitude, and with the invention of the nocturnal late in the 16th century, providing corrections to the observed altitude, the method came into more general use. The development of the chronometer in the 18th century permitted exact corrections, and this made determination of latitude by Polaris a common practice. Even today, more than a century after discovery of the celestial line of position, the method is still in use. The modern inspection table has eliminated the need for meridian observations as a special method for determining latitude. Perhaps when the almanacs and sight reduction tables make the same provision for solution of Polaris sights as they do for any other navigational star, this last of the special methods will cease to be used for general navigation. But customs die slowly, and one as well established as that of position finding in terms of separate latitude and longitude observations—instead of lines of position—is not likely to disappear completely for many years to come.

126. The search for a method of "discovering" longitude at sea.—A statement once quite common was, "The navigator always knows his latitude." A more accurate statement would have been, "The navigator never knows his longitude." In 1594 Davis wrote: "Now there be some that are very inquisitive to have a way to get the longitude, but that is too tedious for seamen, since it requireth the deep knowledge of astronomy, wherefore I would not have any man think that the longitude is to be found at sea by any instrument, so let no seamen trouble themselves with any such rule, but let them keep a perfect account and reckoning of the way of their ship." In speaking of conditions of his day, he was correct, for it was not until the 19th century that the average navigator was able to determine his longitude with accuracy.

Parallel sailing. Without knowledge of his longitude, the navigator of old found it necessary on an ocean crossing to sail northward or southward to the latitude of his destination, and then to follow that parallel of latitude until the destination was reached, even though this might take him far out of his way. Because of this practice, parallel sailing was an important part of the navigator's store of knowledge. The method was a crude one, however, and the time of landfall was often in error by a matter of days, and, in extreme cases, even weeks.

Eclipses. Almost as early as the rotation of the earth was established, astronomers recognized that longitude could be determined by comparing local time with that at the reference meridian. The problem was the determination of time at the reference meridian.

One of the first methods proposed was that of observing the disappearance of Jupiter's satellites as they were eclipsed by their planet. This method, originally proposed by Galileo for use on land, required the ability to observe and identify the satellites by using a powerful telescope, knowledge of the times at which the eclipses would take place, and the skill to keep the instrument directed at the bodies while aboard a small vessel on the high seas. Although used in isolated cases for many years, the method was not satisfactory at sea, due largely to the difficulty of observation (some authorities recommended use of a telescope as long as 18 or 19 feet) and the lack of sufficiently accurate predictions.

Variation of the compass was seriously considered as a method of determining longitude for 200 years or more. Faleiro, Magellan's advisor, believed it could be so utilized, and, until development of the chronometer, work was carried on to perfect the theory. Although there is no simple relationship between variation and longitude, those who advocated the method felt certain that research and investigation would eventually provide the answer. Many others were convinced that such a solution did not exist. In 1676, Henry Bond published *The Longitude Found,* in which he stated that the latitude of a place and its variation could be referred to the prime meridian to determine longitude. Two years later Peter Blackborrow rebutted with *The Longitude Not Found.*

Variation was put to good use in determining the nearness to land by shipmasters familiar with the waters they plied, but as the solution to the longitude problem it was a failure, and with the improvement of lunar distance methods and the invention of the chronometer, interest in the method waned. If it had been possible to provide the mariner with an accurate chart of variation, and to keep it up-to-date, a means of establishing an approximate line of position in areas where the gradient is large would have resulted; in many cases this would have established longitude if latitude were known.

Lunar distances. The first method widely used at sea to determine longitude with some accuracy was that of lunar distances (art. 131), by which the navigator determined GMT by noting the position of the relatively fast-moving moon among the stars. Both Regiomontanus, in 1472, and John Werner, in 1514, have been credited with being the first to propose the use of the lunar distance method. At least one source states that Amerigo Vespucci, in 1497, determined longitude using the moon's position relative to that of another body. One of the principal reasons for establishing the Royal Observatory at Greenwich was to conduct the observations necessary to provide more accurate predictions of the future positions of the moon. Astronomers, including the Astronomers Royal, favored this method, and half a century after the invention of the chronometer it was still being perfected. In 1802 Nathaniel Bowditch simplified the method and its explanation, thus eliminating much of the mystery surrounding it and making it understandable to the average mariner. By using Bowditch's method, the navigator was able to head more or less directly toward his destination, rather than travel the many additional miles often required in "running down the latitude" and then using parallel sailing. An explanation of the lunar distance method, and tables for its use, were carried in the *American Practical Navigator* until 1914.

The Board of Longitude. The lunar distance method, using the data and equipment available early in the 18th century, was far from satisfactory. Ships, cargoes, and lives were lost because of inaccurately determined longitudes. During the Age of Discovery, Spain and Holland posted rewards for solution to the problem, but in vain. When 2,000 men were lost as a squadron of British men-of-war ran aground on a foggy night in 1707, officers of the Royal Navy and Merchant Navy petitioned Parliament for action. As a result, the Board of Longitude was established in 1714, empowered to reward the person who could solve the problem of "discovering" longitude at sea. A voyage to the West Indies and back was to be the test of proposed methods which were deemed worthy. The discoverer of a system which could determine the longitude within 1° by the end of the voyage was to receive £10,000; within 40′, £15,000; and within 30′, £20,000. These would be handsome sums today. In the 18th century they were fortunes.

127. Evolution of the chronometer.—Many and varied were the solutions proposed for finding longitude, and as the different methods were found unsatisfactory, it became increasingly apparent that the problem was one of keeping the time of the prime meridian. But the development of a device that would keep accurate time during a long voyage seemed to most men to be beyond the realm of possibility. Astronomers were flatly opposed to the idea and felt that the problem was properly theirs. There is even some evidence to indicate that the astronomers of the Board of Longitude made unfair tests of chronometers submitted to them.

Christian Huygens (1629–95), a Dutch scientist and mathematician, made a number of contributions of great value in the field of astronomy, but his most memorable work, to the navigator, was his attempt at constructing a prefect timepiece. It was probably Galileo who first suggested using a pendulum in keeping time. Huygens realized that an error would result from the use of a simple pendulum, however, and he devised one in which the bob hung from a double cord that passed between two plates in such a way that it traced a cycloidal path.

In 1660 Huygens built his first chronometer. The instrument utilized his cycloidal pendulum, actuated by a spring. To compensate for rolling and pitching, Huygens mounted the clock in gimbals. Two years later the instrument was tested at sea, with promising results. The loss of tension in the spring as it ran down was the major weakness in this clock. Huygens compensated for this by attaching oppositely tapered cones and a chain to the spring. A 1665 sea test of the new timepiece showed greater accuracy, but still not enough for determination of longitude. In 1674 he constructed a chronometer with a special balance and long balance-spring. Although it was the best marine timepiece then known, Huygens' last clock was also unsuited for use at sea due to the error caused by temperature changes.

John Harrison was a carpenter's son, born in Yorkshire in 1693. He followed his father's trade during his youth, but soon became interested in the repair and construction of clocks. At the age of 20 he completed his first timekeeper, a pendulum-type clock with wooden wheels and pinions. Harrison's gridiron pendulum, one which maintained its length despite temperature changes, was designed about 1720, and contained alternate iron and brass rods to eliminate distortion. Until the time that metal alloys having small coefficients of temperature expansion were developed, Harrison's invention was the type pendulum used by almost all clockmakers.

By 1728 Harrison felt ready to take his pendulum, an escapement he had invented, and plans for his own marine timepiece before the Board of Longitude. In London, however, George Graham, a famous clockmaker, advised him to first construct the timekeeper. Harrison did, and in 1735 he submitted his No. 1 chronometer (fig. 127). The Board authorized a sea trial aboard HMS *Centurion.* The following year, that vessel sailed for Lisbon with Harrison's clock on board, and upon her return, the error was found to be three minutes of longitude, a performance which astounded members of the Board. But the chronometer was awkward and heavy, being enclosed in glass and weighing some 65 pounds, and the Board voted to give Harrison only £500, to be used in producing a more practical timepiece.

During the next few years he constructed two other chronometers, which were stronger and less complicated, although there is no record of their being tested by the Board of Longitude. Harrison continued to devote his life to the construction of an accurate clock to be used in determining longitude, and finally, as he approached old age, he developed his No. 4. Again he went before the Board, and again a test was arranged. In November of 1761, HMS *Deptford* sailed for Jamaica with No. 4 aboard, in the custody of Harrison's son, William. On arrival, after a passage lasting two months, the watch was only nine seconds slow (2¼ minutes of longitude). In January of 1762 it was placed aboard HMS *Merlin* for the return voyage to England. When the *Merlin* anchored in English waters in April of that year, the total error shown by the chronometer was 1 minute, 54.5 seconds. This is equal to less than a half degree of longitude, or less than the minimum error prescribed by the Board for the largest prize. Harrison applied for the full £20,000, but the Board, led by the Astronomer Royal, allowed him only a fourth of that, and insisted on another test.

William Harrison sailed again with No. 4 for Barbados in March of 1764, and throughout the almost four-months-long voyage the chronometer showed an error of

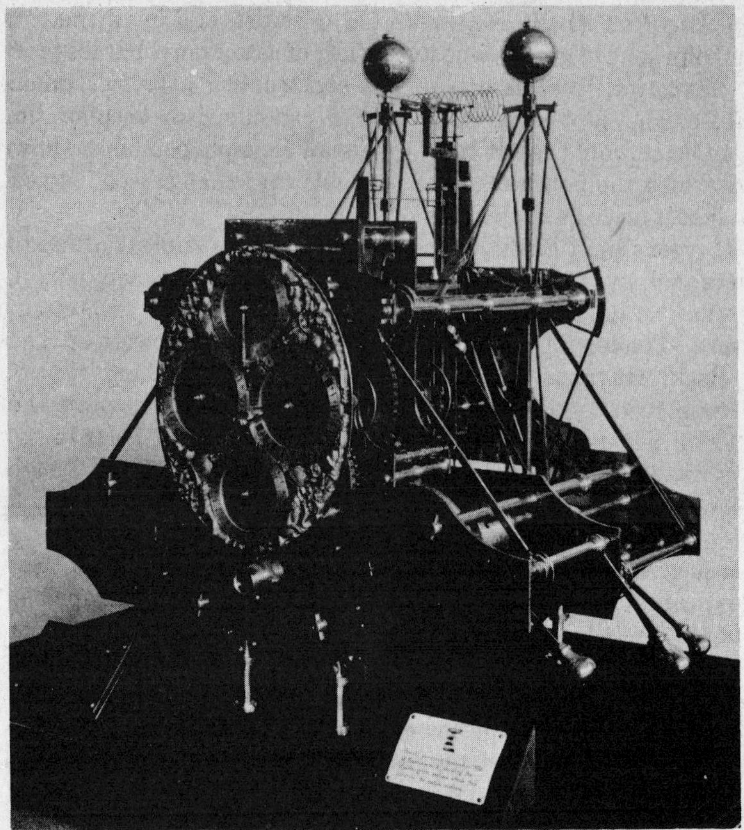

British Crown copyright. From the original in the National Maritime Museum, London, England. Reproduced by permission of the Admiralty.

FIGURE 127.—Harrison's No. 1 chronometer. The first of four timekeepers constructed by Harrison, this clock weighs 65 pounds.

only 54 seconds, or 13.5 minutes of longitude. The astronomers of the Board reluctantly joined in a unanimous declaration that Harrison's timepiece had exceeded all expectations, but they still would not pay him the full reward. An additional £5,000 were paid on the condition that plans be submitted for the construction of similar chronometers. Even when this was done, the Board delayed payment further by having one of its members construct a timepiece from the plans. Not until 1773, Harrison's 80th year, was the rest of the reward paid, and only then because of intervention by the king himself.

Pierre LeRoy, a great French clockmaker, constructed a chronometer in 1766 which has since been the basis for all such instruments. LeRoy's several inventions made his chronometer a timepiece which has been described as a "masterpiece of simplicity, combined with efficiency." Others to contribute to the art of watchmaking included Ferdinand Berthoud of France and Thomas Mudge of England, each of whom developed new escapements. The balance wheel was improved by John Arnold, who invented the escapement acting in one direction only, substantially that used today. Acting independently, Thomas Earnshaw invented a similar escapement. He built the first reliable chronometer at a relatively low price. The chronometer the Board of Longitude had made from Harrison's plans cost £450; Earnshaw's cost £45.

Timepieces designed to provide the navigator with information other than time were popular a century or more ago. One showed the times of high and low water, the state of the tide at any time, and the phases of the moon; another gave the equation of time and the apparent motions of the stars and planets; a third offered the position of the sun and both mean and sidereal times. But the chronometers produced by LeRoy and Earnshaw were the ones of greatest value to the navigator; they gave him a simple and reliable method of determining his longitude.

Time signals, which permit the mariner at sea to check the error in his chronometer, are essentially a 20th century development. Telegraphic time signals were inaugurated in the United States at the end of the Civil War, and enabled ships to check their chronometers in port by **time ball** signals. Previously, the Navy's "standard" chronometer had been carried from port to port to allow such comparison. In their most advanced form, time balls were dropped by telegraphic action. In 1904 the first official "wireless" transmission of time signals began from a naval station at Navesink, N.J. These were low-power signals which could be heard for a distance of about 50 miles. Five years later the range had been doubled, and, as other nations began sending time signals, the navigator was soon able to check his chronometer around the world.

The search for longitude was ended.

128. Establishment of the prime meridian.—Until the beginning of the 19th century, there was little uniformity among cartographers as to the meridian from which longitude was measured. The navigator was not particularly concerned, as he could not determine his longitude, anyway.

Ptolemy, in the second century AD, had measured longitude eastward from a reference meridian two degrees west of the Canary Islands. In 1493 Pope Alexander VI drew a line in the Atlantic west of the Azores to divide the territories of Spain and Portugal, and for many years this meridian was used by chart makers of the two countries. In 1570 the Dutch cartographer Ortelius used the easternmost of the Cape Verde Islands. John Davis, in his 1594 *The Seaman's Secrets*, said the Isle of Fez in the Canaries was used because there the variation was zero. Mariners paid little attention, however, and often reckoned their longitude from several different capes and ports during a voyage, depending upon their last reliable fix.

The meridian of London was used as early as 1676, and over the years its popularity grew as England's maritime interests increased. The system of measuring longitude both east and west through 180° may have first appeared in the middle of the 18th century. Toward the end of that century, as the Greenwich Observatory increased in prominence, English map makers began using the meridian of that observatory as a reference. The publication by the Observatory of the first British *Nautical Almanac* in 1767 further entrenched Greenwich as the prime meridian. A later and unsuccessful attempt was made in 1810 to establish Washington as the prime meridian for American navigators and cartographers. At an international conference held in Washington in 1884 the meridian of Greenwich was officially established, by the 25 nations in attendance, as the prime meridian. Today all maritime nations have designated the Greenwich meridian the prime meridian, except in a few cases where local references are used for certain harbor charts.

129. Astronomical observatories.—Thousands of years before the birth of Christ, crude observatories existed, and astronomers constructed primitive tables which were the forerunners of modern almanacs. The famous observatory at Alexandria, the first "true" observatory, was constructed in the third century BC, but the Egyptians, as well as the Babylonians and Chinese, had already studied the heavens for many centuries. The **armillary sphere** (fig. 129a) was the principal instrument used by the early astronomers. It consisted of a skeleton sphere with several movable rings which could be adjusted to indicate the orbits of the various celestial bodies. One source attributes the invention of the armillary sphere to Eratosthenes in the third century

BC; another says the Chinese knew it 2,000 years earlier, as well as the water clock and a form of astrolabe. The Alexandrian observatory was the seat of astronomical learning in the western world for several centuries, and there Hipparchus discovered the precession of the equinoxes, and Ptolemy did the work which led to his *Almagest*.

Astronomical study did not cease entirely during the Dark Ages. The Arabians erected observatories at Baghdād and Damascus in the ninth century AD, and observatories in Cairo and northwestern Persia followed. The Moors brought the astronomical knowledge of the Arabs into Spain, and the *Toledan Tables* of 1080 resulted from an awakening of scientific interest that brought about the establishment of schools of astronomy at Cordova and Toledo in the tenth century.

The great voyages of western discovery began early in the 15th century, and chief among those who recognized the need for greater precision in navigation was Prince Henry "The Navigator" of Portugal. About 1420 he had an observatory constructed at Sagres, on the southern tip of Portugal, so that more accurate information might be available to his captains. Henry's hydrographic expeditions added to the geographical knowledge of the mariner, and he was responsible for the simplification of many navigational instruments.

The Sagres observatory was rudimentary, however, and not until 1472 was the first complete observatory built in Europe. In that year Bernard Walther, a wealthy astronomer, constructed the Nuremberg Observatory, and placed Regiomontanus in charge. Regiomontanus, born Johann Müller, contributed a wealth of astronomical data of the greatest importance to the navigator.

The observatory at Cassel, built in 1561, had a revolving dome and an instrument capable of measuring altitude and azimuth at the same time. Tycho Brahe's Uraniburgum Observatory, located on the Danish island Hveen, was opened in 1576, and the results of his observations contributed greatly to the navigator's knowledge. Prior to the discovery of the telescope, the astronomer could increase the accuracy of his observations only by using larger instruments. Brahe used a quadrant with a radius of 19 feet, with which he could measure altitudes to 0.′6, an unprecedented degree of precision at that time. He also had an instrument with which he could determine altitude and azimuth simultaneously (fig. 129b). After Brahe, Kepler made use of the observatory and his predecessor's records in determining the laws which bear his name.

The **telescope,** the modern astronomer's most important tool, was invented by Hans Lippershey about 1608. Galileo heard of Lippershey's invention, and soon improved upon it. In 1610 he discovered the four great moons of Jupiter, which led to the "longitude by eclipse" method successfully used ashore for many years and experimented with at sea. With the 32-power telescope he eventually built, Galileo was able to observe clearly the motions of sun spots, by which he proved that the sun rotates on its axis. In Paris, in 1671, the French National Observatory was established.

Greenwich Royal Observatory. England had no early privately supported observatories such as those on the continent. The need for navigational advancement was ignored by Henry VIII and Elizabeth I, but in 1675 Charles II, at the urging of John Flamsteed, Jonas Moore, Le Sieur de Saint-Pierre, and Christopher Wren, established the Greenwich Royal Observatory. Charles limited construction costs to £500, and appointed Flamsteed the first Astronomer Royal, at an annual salary of £100. The equipment available in the early years of the observatory consisted of two clocks, a "sextant" of seven-foot radius, a quadrant of three-foot radius, two telescopes, and the star catalog published almost a century before by Tycho Brahe. Thirteen years passed before Flamsteed had an instrument with which he could determine his latitude accurately. In 1690 a transit instrument equipped with a telescope and vernier was invented by Romer, and he later added a vertical circle to the device. This enabled the astronomer to

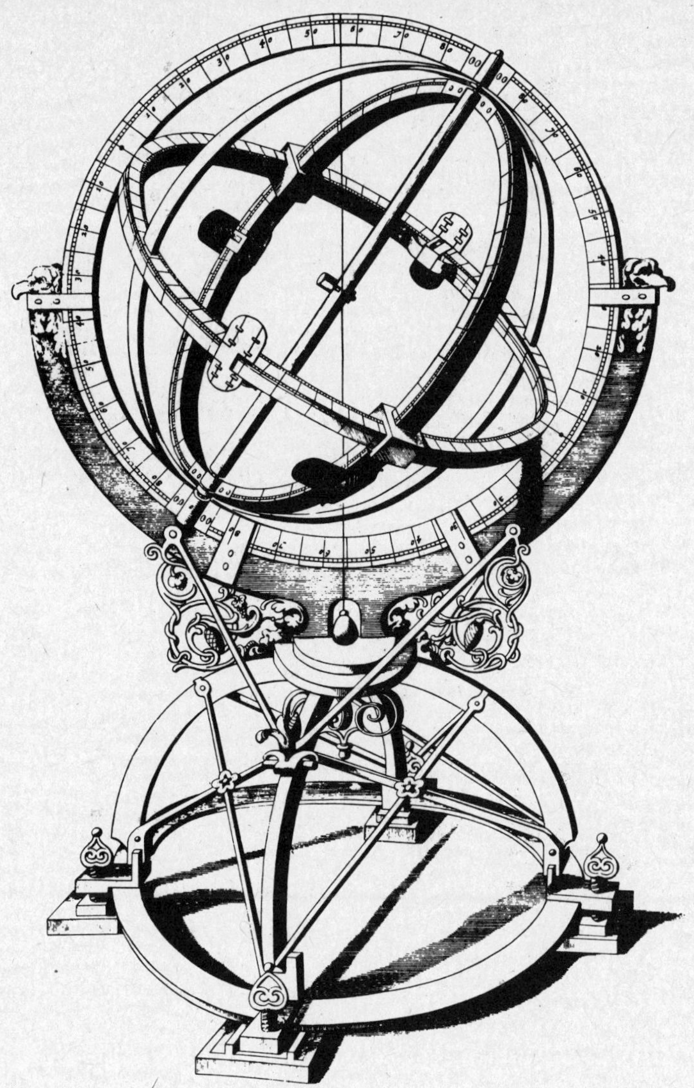

Courtesy of the Map Division of the Library of Congress.

FIGURE 129a.—An armillary sphere, one of the most important instruments of the ancient astronomers.

determine declination and right ascension at the same time. One of these instruments was added to the equipment at Greenwich in 1721, replacing the huge quadrant previously used. The development and perfection of the chronometer in the next hundred years added further to the accuracy of observations.

Other national observatories were constructed in the years that followed; at Berlin in 1705, St. Petersburg in 1725, Palermo in 1790, Cape of Good Hope in 1820, Parramatta in New South Wales in 1822, and Sydney in 1855.

U. S. Naval Observatory. The first observatory in the United States is said to have been built in 1831–1832 at Chapel Hill, N.C. The Depot of Charts and Instruments, established in 1830, was the agency from which the U. S. Navy Hydrographic Office and the Naval Observatory evolved 36 years later. Under Lieutenant Charles Wilkes, the second Officer-in-Charge, the Depot about 1835 installed a small transit instrument for rating chronometers. The Mallory Act of 1842 provided for the estab-

Courtesy of the Map Division of the Library of Congress.

FIGURE 129b.—A reproduction of Brahe's pelorus. This instrument was used to determine altitude and azimuth simultaneously.

ishment of a permanent observatory, and the director was authorized to purchase all such supplies as were necessary to continue astronomical study. The observatory was completed in 1844 and the results of its first observations were published two years later. Congress established the Naval Observatory as a separate agency in 1866. In 1873 a refracting telescope with a 26-inch aperture, then the world's largest, was installed. The observatory, located at Washington, D.C., has occupied its present site since 1893.

The **Mount Wilson Observatory** of the Carnegie Institution of Washington was built in 1904–05. The observatory's 100-inch reflector telescope opened wider the view of the heavens, and enabled astronomers to study the movements of celestial bodies with greater accuracy than ever before. But a still finer tool was needed, and in 1934 the 200-inch reflector for the **Palomar Mountain Observatory** was cast. The six-million-dollar observatory was built by the Rockefeller General Education Board for the California Institute of Technology, which also operates the Mount Wilson Observatory. The 200-inch telescope makes it possible to see individual stars 20,000,000 light-years away and galaxies at least 1,600,000,000 light-years away.

As with earlier instruments, the telescope has about reached the limit of practical size. Present efforts are being directed toward application of the electron microscope to the telescope, to increase the range of present instruments.

130. Almanacs.—From the beginning, astronomers have undoubtedly recorded the results of their observations. Tables computed from such results have been known for centuries. The work of Hipparchus, in the second century BC, and Ptolemy, in his famous *Almagest*, are examples. Then the *Toledan Tables* appeared in AD 1080, and the *Alfonsine Tables* in 1252. Even with these later tables, however, few copies were made, for printing had not yet been invented, and those that were available were kept in the hands of astronomers. Not until the 15th century were the first almanacs printed and made available to the navigator. In Vienna, in 1457, George Purbach issued the first almanac. Fifteen years later the Nuremberg Observatory, under Regiomontanus, issued the first of the ephemerides it published until 1506. These tables gave the great maritime explorers of the age the most accurate information available. In 1474 Abraham Zacuto introduced his *Almanach Perpetuum* (fig. 130a) which contained tables of the sun's declination in the most useful form yet available to the mariner. *Tabulae Prutenicae*, the first tables to be calculated on Copernican principles, were published by Erasmus Reinhold in 1551 and gave the mariner a clearer picture of celestial movements than anything previously available. The work of Brahe and Kepler at the Uraniburgum Observatory provided the basis for the publication of the *Rudolphine Tables* in 1627.

Still, the information contained in these books was intended primarily for the use of the astronomer, and the navigator carried the various tables only that he might make use of the portions applicable to his work. The first official almanac, *Connaissance des Temps*, was issued by the French National Observatory in 1696. The French Observatory rose to its greatest prominence during the 20 years that Urbain Leverrier held the position of director.

In 1767 the British *Nautical Almanac* was first published. Nevil Maskelyne was then Astronomer Royal, and he provided the navigator with the best information available. The book contained tables of the sun's declination, and corrections to the observed altitude of Polaris. The moon's position relative to other celestial bodies was included at 12-hour intervals, and lunar distance tables gave the angular distance between the moon and certain other bodies at three-hour intervals.

For almost a hundred years the British *Nautical Almanac* was the one used by American navigators, but in 1852 the Depot of Charts and Instruments published the first *American Ephemeris and Nautical Almanac*, for the year 1855.

Early American almanacs were distinguished by their excessive detail in some cases and shortage of data of importance to the navigator in others. Declination was given to the nearest $0''.1$ and the equation of time to the nearest $0^s.01$. Most figures were given only for noon at Greenwich, and a tedious interpolation was involved in converting the information to that at a given time at the longitude of the observer. Lunar distances were given at three-hour intervals. Few star data were listed (fig. 130b).

Since 1858 the *American Nautical Almanac* has been printed without the ephemeris section, that part of value chiefly to astronomers. Until 1908 the positions of the brighter stars were given only for January 1st, and in relation to the meridian of Washington. Beginning in that year, the apparent places of 55 major stars were given for the first of each month. In 1912, the tables of lunar distances were omitted. In 1919, sunrise and sunset tables were added.

One of the greatest inconveniences involved in using the old almanacs was the astronomical day, which began at noon of the civil day of the same date. This system was abolished in 1925, and the United States adopted the expression "civil time" to designate time by the new system. Greenwich hour angle was first published for the moon in the *Lunar Ephemeris for Aviators* for the last four months of 1929. This

KL Março tem dias .xxxi. ha lũa .xxx. ho. dia .xij. hõs e no .xij.

		Di: Domes	Lugar. sol Pisces	Declinaçã: Graã	Decl.: Minu.
d	Adrian martyr e simplici	1	20	3	59
e	Donado martyr e basilci	2	21	3	35
f	Marcimino martyr pẽça	3	12	3	11
g	Lucio papa e martyre	4	23	2	48
A	Sam focas martyre.	5	24	2	24
b	Victor e victorino marti	6	25	2	0
c	Thome d'aquino confessor	7	26	1	36
d	Appollonio martyre.	8	72	1	12
e	Os q̃rẽta martyres.	9	28	0	48
f	Alexandre e gaio martyr	10	29	0	24
g	Quarenta mil martyres	11	1 ♈	0	0
A	Sam gregorio papa e co	12	2	0	24
b	Sam leãdre bispo bispo	13	3	0	48
c	Leeo papa e martyrr e do	14	4	1	12
d	longinus martyr.	15	5	1	36
e	Gertrudis virgem e mart	16	6	2	0
f	Patricio bispo e confesso	17	6	2	24
g	Anselmo bispo e douctor	18	7	2	48
A	Joseph d nossa senhora	19	8	3	11
b	Cuthberto confessor	20	9	3	35
c	Beento abade fundador	21	10	3	59
d	Paulo bispo e confessor	22	11	4	22
e	Pigmete preste e martyr	23	12	4	46
f	Theodoro psbi Dia d jejũ	24	13	5	9
g	Anunciacã de nossa senhora	25	14	5	33
A	Sam castorio martyre	26	15	5	56
b	Joam yrmitam confessor	27	16	6	19
c	Marcello papa e gronoan	28	17	6	43
d	Quirino martyr eustalio e	29	18	7	6
e	Sam segundo martyre·	30	19	7	29
f	Felice pappa e babina vi	31	20	7	51.

Courtesy of the John Carter Brown Library, Brown University.

FIGURE 130a.—An excerpt from the Portuguese *Regimento do estrolabio e do quadrante* of about 1509, giving the sun's declination and other data based upon Zacuto's calculations for the month of March. The first day of spring, the 11th by the Julian calendar then in use, is marked by the symbol of Aries, the ram (♈).

publication became a supplement to the *Nautical Almanac* in 1931, and for 1932 the two were merged.

The *Air Almanac*, designed by Captain P. V. H. Weems, USN (Ret.), was published for 1933, giving Greenwich hour angle for all bodies included. For 1934 this information was given in the *Nautical Almanac*, and the *Air Almanac* was discontinued. The first British air almanac was published for the last quarter of 1937, and modified for 1939 with features followed closely in the first *American Air Almanac*, for 1941. In 1950 a revised *Nautical Almanac* appeared, patterned after the popular *American Air Almanac*. Starting with the 1953 edition, the British and American air almanacs were combined in a single publication. In that year the United States reverted to the expression "mean time" in place of "civil time." In 1958, the British and American nautical almanacs were combined, and in 1960, the name was standardized.

131. The navigational triangle.—It is customary for modern navigators to reduce their celestial observations by solving the triangle whose points are the elevated pole, the celestial body, and the zenith of the observer. The sides of this triangle are the polar distance of the body (codeclination), its zenith distance (coaltitude), and the polar distance of the zenith (colatitude of the observer).

Lunar distances. A spherical triangle was first used at sea in solving lunar distance problems. Simultaneous or nearly simultaneous observations were made of the altitudes

FIXED STARS, 1855.

MEAN PLACES OF 100 PRINCIPAL FIXED STARS, FOR JANUARY 1, 1855.					
Star's Name.	Mag.	Right Ascension.	An. Variation.	Declination.	An. Variation.
		h. m. s.	s.	° ′ ″	″
α Andromedæ .	2	0 0 53.97	+ 3.087	+28 17 23.3	+19.93
γ Pegasi (*Algenib*)	3.2	0 5 46.37	3.085	+14 22 38.1	20.05
β Hydri . . .	3	0 18 3.62	3.292	—78 4 23.1	20.23
α Cassiopeæ .	var.	0 32 18.36	3.356	+55 44 29.2	19.83
β Ceti . . .	2	0 36 18.45	3.016	—18 47 0.1	19.86
α Urs. Min. (*Polaris*)	2	1 6 29.82	+18.117	+88 32 11.3	+19.23
θ^1 Ceti . . .	3	1 16 46.57	3.000	— 8 55 58.6	18.74
α Eridani (*Achernar*)	1	1 32 18.42	2.238	—57 58 28.2	18.59
α Arietis . . .	2	1 59 0.44	3.365	+22 46 28.4	17.29
γ Ceti . . .	3.4	2 35 47.42	3.102	2 37 19.4	15.44
α Ceti . . .	2.3	2 54 42.21	+ 3.129	+ 3 31 4.7	+14.40
α Persei . .	2	3 13 59.52	4.243	49 20 26.8	13.25
η Tauri . . .	3	3 38 52.31	3.553	+23 39 11.0	11.54
γ^1 Eridani . .	3	3 51 15.91	2.796	—13 55 26.7	10.59
α Tauri (*Aldebaran*)	1	4 27 36.26	3.436	+16 12 49.4	7.72
α Aurigæ (*Capella*) .	1	5 5 59.03	+ 4.423	+45 50 41.8	+ 4.27
β Orionis (*Rigel*)	1	5 7 34.23	2.884	— 8 22 22.5	4.54
β Tauri . .	2	5 17 7.72	3.791	+28 28 48.3	3.55
δ Orionis . .	2	5 24 36.06	3.066	— 0 24 37.8	3.05
α Leporis . .	3	5 26 20.19	2.648	—17 55 46.0	2.94
ε Orionis . .	2	5 28 51.43	+ 3.044	— 1 17 54.6	+ 2.71
α Columbæ . .	2	5 34 24.05	2.177	—34 9 13.3	2.23
α Orionis . .	var.	5 47 19.35	3.249	+ 7 22 32.6	+ 1.11
μ Geminorum .	3	6 14 11.30	3.636	+22 34 59.9	— 1.37
α Argus (*Canopus*) .	1	6 20 44.13	1.330	—52 37 4.7	— 1.81
51 (Hev.) Cephei .	5	6 31 6.10	+30.650	+87 15 7.9	— 2.80
α Canis Maj. (*Sirius*)	1	6 38 45.60	2.646	—16 31 12.8	4.52
ε Canis Majoris . .	2.1	6 52 55.69	2.360	—28 46 40.3	4.58
δ Geminorum .	3.4	7 11 27.65	3.597	+22 14 41.7	6.16
α^2 Geminor. (*Castor*)	2.1	7 25 20.49	3.841	32 12 6.2	7.37
α Can. Min. (*Procyon*)	1	7 31 42.52	+ 3.145	+ 5 35 35.7	— 8.79
β Geminor. (*Pollux*)	1.2	7 36 26.23	3.681	+28 22 19.9	8.26
15 Argus . . .	3	8 1 22.22	2.557	—23 53 20.5	10.06
ε Hydræ . .	3.4	8 39 5.74	3.189	+ 6 56 52.2	12.86
ι Ursæ Majoris . .	3	8 49 15.44	4.123	+48 36 26.7	13.78
ι Argus . .	2	9 13 12.52	+ 1.602	—58 40 3.3	—14.91
α Hydræ . . .	2	9 20 27.65	2.951	— 8 1 56.8	15.36
θ Ursæ Majoris .	3	9 23 7.85	4.048	+52 20 6.3	16.13
ε Leonis . . .	3	9 37 36.82	3.424	24 26 22.0	16.34
α Leonis (*Regulus*)	1.2	10 0 38.72	3.205	+12 40 26.4	17.40
η Argus . .	2	10 39 26.75	+ 2.306	—58 55 21.5	—18.74

FIGURE 130b.—Star data from the 1855 *Nautical Almanac.* The annual corrections in declination and right ascension can be used to obtain reasonably correct values today.

of the moon and the sun or a star near the ecliptic, and the angular distance between the moon and the other body. The zenith of the observer and the two celestial bodies formed the vertices of the triangle, whose sides were the two coaltitudes and the angular distance between the bodies. By means of a mathematical calculation the navigator "cleared" this distance of the effects of refraction and parallax applicable to each altitude, and other errors. The corrected value was then used as an argument for entering the almanac, which gave the true lunar distance from the sun and several stars at three-hour intervals.

Previously, the navigator had set his watch or checked its error and rate, which could be relied upon for short periods, with the local mean time determined by celestial observations. The local mean time of the watch, properly corrected, applied to the Greenwich mean time obtained from the lunar distance observation, gave the longitude.

The mathematics involved was tedious, and few mariners were capable of solving the triangle until Nathaniel Bowditch published his simplified method in 1802 in *The*

New American Practical Navigator. Chronometers were reliable by that time, but their high cost prevented their general use aboard the majority of naval and merchant ships. Using Bowditch's method, however, most navigators, for the first time, could determine their longitude, and so eliminate the need for parallel sailing and the lost time associated with it. The popularity of the lunar distance method is indicated by the fact that tables for its solution were carried in the *American Nautical Almanac* until the second decade of the 20th century.

The determination of latitude was considered a separate problem, usually solved by means of a meridian altitude or an observation of Polaris.

The time sight. The theory of the time sight had been known to mathematicians since the dawn of spherical trigonometry, but not until the chronometer was developed could it be used by mariners.

The time sight made use of the modern navigational triangle. The codeclination, or polar distance, of the body could be determined from the almanac. The zenith distance (coaltitude) was determined by observation. If the colatitude were known, three sides of the triangle were available. From these the meridian angle was computed. The comparison of this with the Greenwich hour angle from the almanac yielded the longitude.

The time sight was mathematically sound, but the navigator was not always aware that the longitude determined was only as accurate as the latitude, and together they merely formed a point on what is known today as a line of position. If the observed body was on the prime vertical, the line of position ran north and south and a small error in latitude generally had little effect on the longitude. But when the body was close to the meridian, a small error in latitude produced a large error in longitude.

The line of position by celestial observation (art. 1703) was unknown until discovered in 1837 by 30-year-old Captain Thomas H. Sumner, a Harvard graduate and son of a United States Congressman from Massachusetts. The discovery of the "Sumner line," as it is sometimes called, was considered by Maury "the commencement of a new era in practical navigation." In Sumner's own words, the discovery took place in this manner:

"Having sailed from Charleston, S.C., 25th November, 1837, bound to Greenock, a series of heavy gales from the Westward promised a quick passage; after passing the Azores, the wind prevailed from the Southward, with thick weather; after passing Longitude 21° W., no observation was had until near the land; but soundings were had not far, as was supposed, from the edge of the Bank. The weather was now more boisterous, and very thick; and the wind still Southerly; arriving about midnight, 17th December, within 40 miles, by dead reckoning, of Tusker light; the wind hauled S.E., true, making the Irish coast a lee shore; the ship was then kept close to the wind, and several tacks made to preserve her position as nearly as possible until daylight; when nothing being in sight, she was kept on E.N.E. under short sail, with heavy gales; at about 10 A.M. an altitude of the sun was observed, and the Chronometer time noted; but, having run so far without any observation, it was plain the Latitude by dead reckoning was liable to error, and could not be entirely relied on.

"Using, however, this Latitude, in finding the Longitude by Chronometer, it was found to put the ship 15′ of Longitude, E. from her position by dead reckoning; which in Latitude 52° N. is 9 nautical miles; this seemed to agree tolerably well with the dead reckoning; but feeling doubtful of the Latitude, the observation was tried with a Latitude 10′ further N., finding this placed the ship E.N.E. 27 *nautical* miles, of the former position, it was tried again with a Latitude 20′ N. of the dead reckoning; this also placed the ship still further E.N.E., and still 27 *nautical miles* further; these three positions were then seen to lie in the direction of *Small's light*. It then at once appeared that the observed altitude must have happened at *all the three* points, and at *Small's light*, and at the ship, at the *same instant of time;* and it followed, that Small's light must bear E.N.E., if the Chronometer was right. Having been convinced of this truth, the ship was kept on her course, E.N.E., the wind being still S.E., and in less than an hour, Small's light was made bearing E.N.E. ½ E., and close aboard."

In 1843 Sumner published his book, *A New and Accurate Method of Finding a Ship's Position at Sea by Projection on Mercator's Chart*, which met with great acclaim. In it he proposed that a single time sight be solved twice, as he had done (fig. 131), using latitudes somewhat greater and somewhat less than that arrived at by dead reckoning, and joining the two positions obtained to form the line of position. It is significant that Sumner was able to introduce this revolutionary principle without seriously upsetting the method by which mariners had been navigating for years. Perhaps he realized that a better method could be derived, but almost certainly navigators would not have accepted the line of position so readily had he recommended that they abandon altogether the familiar time sight.

The Sumner method required the solution of two time sights to obtain each line of position. Many older navigators preferred not to draw the lines on their charts, but to fix their position mathematically by a method which Sumner had also devised and included in his book. This was a tedious procedure, but a popular one. Lecky recommended the method, and it was still in use early in the 20th century.

The alternative to working two time sights in the Sumner method was to determine the azimuth of the body and to draw a line perpendicular to it through the point obtained by working a single time sight. Several decades after the appearance of Sumner's book, this method was made available to navigators through the publication of accurate azimuth tables, and the system was widely used until comparatively recent times. The 1943 edition of the *American Practical Navigator* included examples of its use. The two-minute azimuth tables still found on many ships were designed principally for this purpose. The mathematical solution for azimuth was not at first a part of the time sight.

132. Modern methods of celestial navigation.—Sumner gave the mariner the line of position; St.-Hilaire the altitude difference or intercept method. Others who followed these men applied their principles to provide the navigator with rapid means for determining his position. The new navigational methods developed by these men, although based upon work done earlier, are largely a product of the 20th century.

Four hundred years ago Pedro Nunes used a globe to obtain a fix by two altitudes of the sun, and the azimuth angles. Fifty years later Robert Hues determined his latitude on a globe by using two observations and the time interval between them. G. W. Littlehales, of the U. S. Navy Hydrographic Office, advocated using a stereographic projection to obtain computed altitude and azimuth in his *Altitude, Azimuth, and Geographical Position*, published in 1906.

Various graphic and mechanical methods have also been proposed. Of these, only one, the *Star Altitude Curves* of Captain P. V. H. Weems, USN (Ret.), has had wide usage, almost entirely among aviators. During World War II, some aircraft were fitted with a device called an "astrograph," which projected star altitude curves from film upon a special plotting sheet. The curves could be moved to allow for the earth's rotation. When they were properly oriented, part of the line of position could be traced on the plotting sheet. More generally, however, the navigational triangle has been solved mathematically or by the use of tables.

Spherical trigonometry is the basis for solving every navigational triangle, and until about 80 years ago the navigator had no choice but to completely solve each triangle himself. The cosine formula is a fundamental spherical trigonometry formula

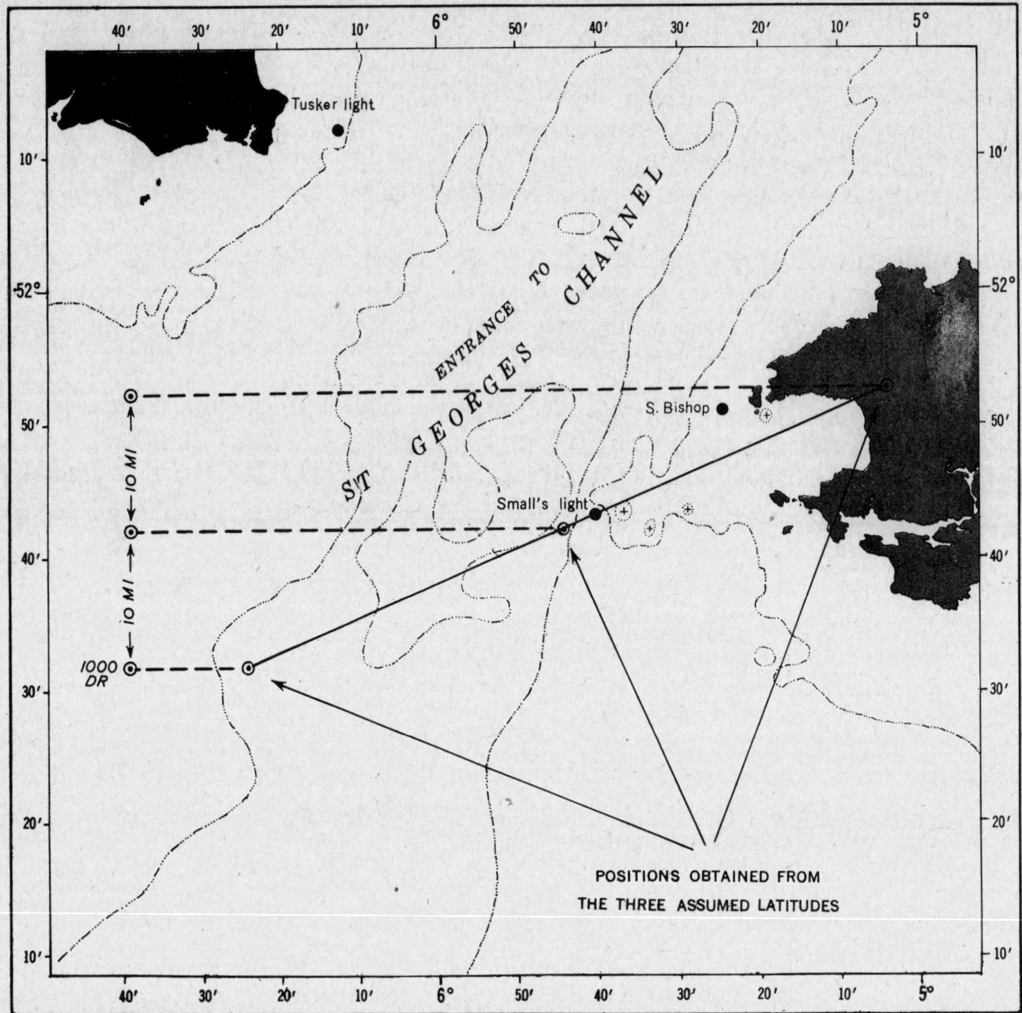

FIGURE 131.—The first celestial line of position, obtained by Captain Thomas Sumner in 1837.

by which the navigational triangle can be conveniently solved. This formula was commonly used in lunar distance solutions when they were first introduced, but, because ambiguous results are obtained when the azimuth is close to 90° or 270°, mathematicians turned to the haversine, which has the advantage of increasing numerically from 0° to 180°. The **cosine-haversine formula** (art. 2109) was used by navigators until recent years.

Toward the end of the 19th century the "short" methods began to appear. About 1875, A. C. Johnson of the British Royal Navy published his book *On Finding the Latitude and Longitude in Cloudy Weather*. No plotting was involved in Johnson's method, but he made use of the principle that a single time sight be worked, rather than the two that Sumner proposed, and the line of position drawn through the point thus determined.

In 1879 Percy L. H. Davis, of the British Nautical Almanac Office, and Captain J. E. Davis collaborated on a *Sun's True Bearing or Azimuth Table*, which enabled the navigator to lay down a line of position using a computed azimuth. *Chronometer Tables*, published by Percy Davis 20 years later, covered latitudes up to 50° and gave local hour angle values for selected altitudes to one minute of arc. In 1905 his *Requisite*

Tables were issued, enabling the mariner to "solve spherical triangles with three variable errors."

These were the first of a large number of "short" solutions which followed the work of Marcq St.-Hilaire. Generally, they consist of adaptations of the formulas of spherical trigonometry, and tables of logarithms in a convenient arrangement. It is customary for such methods to divide the navigational triangle into two right spherical triangles by dropping a perpendicular from one vertex to the side opposite. In some methods, partial solutions are made and the results tabulated. Aquino and Braga of Brazil; Ball, Comrie, Davis, and Smart of England; Bertin, Hugon, and Souillagouet of France; Fuss of Germany; Ogura and Yonemura of Japan; Blackburne of New Zealand; Pinto of Portugal; Garcia of Spain; and Ageton, Driesonstok, Gingrich, Rust, and Weems of the United States are but a few of those providing such solutions. Although "inspection tables" have largely superseded them, many of these "short" methods are still in use, kept alive largely by the compactness of their tables and the universality of their application. They are an intermediate step between the tedious earlier solutions and the fast tabulated ones, and they encouraged the navigator to work to a practical precision. The earlier custom of working to a precision not justified by the accuracy of the information used created a false sense of security in the mind of some navigators, especially those of little experience.

A book of tabulated solutions, from which an answer can be extracted by inspection, is not a new idea. Lord Kelvin, generally considered the father of modern navigational methods, expressed interest in such a method. However, solution of the many thousands of triangles involved would have made the project too costly if done by hand. Electronic computers have provided a practical means of preparing tables. In 1936 the first published volume of Pub. No. 214 was made available, and later Pub. No. 249 was provided for air navigators. British Admiralty editions of both these sets of tables have been published. Editions of Pub. No. 214 have also been published by the Instituto Hidrographico de la Marina, Cadiz, Spain, and by the Istituto Idrografico della Marina, Genova, Italy.

Electronics and Navigation

133. Electricity.—Twenty-five hundred years ago Thales of Miletus commented on basic electrical phenomena, but more than two millenniums passed before men first approached an understanding of electricity and the uses to which it could be put.

Until about 1682 the only known method of creating electricity was by rubbing glass with silk or amber with wool. Then Otto von Guericke of Magdeburg invented an "electric machine" and made possible the creation of electricity for experimental work. The Leyden jar, the electrical condenser (or machine) commonly used today, had its origin in 1745 when its principle was accidentally discovered independently by P. van Musschenbroek, of the University of Leyden, and von Kleist.

Stephen Gray, about 1729, demonstrated the difference between conductors and non-conductors, or insulators, and ten years later Hawkesbee and DuFay, working independently, each discovered the positive and negative qualities of electricity.

In the middle of the 18th century Sir William Watson of England, developer of the Leyden jar in essentially its present form, sent electricity more than two miles by wire. Whether Watson was aware of the tremendous possibilities his experiment demonstrated is not known. Twenty-five years later, about 1774, Lesage devised what is believed to have been the first method of electrical communication. He had a separate wire for each letter of the alphabet and momentarily charged the appropriate wire to send each letter.

A German scholar, Francis Aepinus (1728–1802), was the first to recognize the reciprocal relationship of electricity and magnetism. In 1837 Karl Gauss and Wilhelm Weber collaborated in inventing a reflecting galvanometer for use in telegraphic work, which was the forerunner of the galvanometer at one time employed in submarine signaling. Michael Faraday (1791–1867), in a lifetime of experimental work, contributed most of what is known today in the field of electromagnetic induction. In 1864 James Clerk Maxwell of Edinburgh made public his electromagnetic theory of light. Many consider it the greatest single advancement in man's knowledge of electricity.

134. Electronics.—In 1887 Heinrich Hertz provided the proof of Maxwell's theory by producing electromagnetic waves and showing that they could be reflected. A decade later Joseph J. Thomson discovered the electron and so provided the basis for the development of the vacuum tube by Fleming and DeForest. In 1899 R. A. Fessenden pointed out that directional reception of radio signals was possible if a single coil or frame aerial was used as the receiving antenna. In 1895 Guglielmo Marconi transmitted a "wireless" message a distance of about one mile. By 1901 he was able to communicate between stations more than 2,000 miles apart. The following year Arthur Edwin Kennelly and Oliver Heaviside introduced the theory of an ionized layer in the atmosphere and its ability to reflect radio waves. Pulse ranging had its origin in 1925 when Gregory Breit and Merle A. Tuve used this principle to measure the height of the ionosphere.

135. Application of electronics to navigation.—Perhaps the first application of electronics to navigation was the transmission of radio **time signals** (art. 1826) in 1904, thus permitting the mariner to check his chronometer at sea. Telegraphic time signals had been sent since 1865, providing a means of checking the chronometer in various ports.

Next, radio broadcasts providing navigational warnings, begun in 1907 by the U. S. Navy Hydrographic Office, helped increase the safety of navigation at sea.

By the latter part of World War I the directional properties of a loop antenna were successfully utilized in the **radio direction finder** (art. 4201). The first radiobeacon was installed in 1921.

Early 20th century experiments by Behm and Langevin led to the development, by the U. S. Navy, of the first practical **echo sounder** (art. 619) in 1922.

As early as 1904, Christian Hulsmeyer, a German engineer, obtained patents in several countries on a proposed method of utilizing the reflection of radio waves as an obstacle detector and a navigational aid to ships. Apparently, the device was never constructed. In 1922 Marconi said, "It seems to me that it should be possible to design apparatus by means of which a ship could radiate or project a divergent beam of these rays (electromagnetic waves) in any desired direction, which rays if coming across a metallic object, such as another ship, would be reflected back to a receiver screened from the local transmitter on the sending ship, and thereby immediately reveal the presence and bearing of the other ship in fog or thick weather."

In the same year of 1922 two scientists, Dr. A. Hoyt Taylor and Leo C. Young, testing a communication system at the Naval Aircraft Radio Laboratory at Anacostia, D.C., noted fluctuations in the signals when ships passed between stations on opposite sides of the Potomac River. Although the potential value of the discovery was recognized, work on its exploitation did not begin until March 1934, when Young suggested to Dr. Robert M. Page, an assistant, that this might bear further investigation. By December, Page had constructed a pulse-signal device that determined the positions of aircraft. This was the first **radar** (art. 4301). In the spring of 1935 the British, unaware of American efforts, began work in this field, and developed radar independently. In 1937 the USS *Leary* tested the first seagoing radar. In 1940 United States and British scientists combined their efforts, resulting in more rapid progress. The British revealed the principle of the multicavity magnetron developed by J. T. Randall and H. A. H. Boot at the University of Birmingham in 1939. This magnetron made microwave radar practical. Probably no scientific or industrial development in history expanded so rapidly in all phases—research, development, design, production, trials, and training—and on such a scale. In 1945, at the close of hostilities of World War II, radar was made available for commercial use.

136. Development of hyperbolic radio aids.—The work on television and cosmic-ray counting devices in the decade prior to World War II provided the electronic techniques needed for the practical development of radio aids to navigation based upon the time of transmission of radio signals. Because the frequency stability of oscillators used in those early days was very poor—about a million times less than is available in 1975—it was obvious that only the *difference* in transmission times of two or more signals from different places could be measured. But this quantity would become useful only if the various signals could be kept in close synchronism by some control mechanism. Using this method, with the assumption of a constant velocity of propagation, it was clear that two signals would define a family of hyperbolic lines of position having the transmitting antennas as foci, and signals from either three or four different stations would establish a position fix.

It was also obvious, since the velocity of light is about 300 meters or nearly 1000 feet per microsecond, that time-difference measurements would have to be made within a very few microseconds if positional accuracy comparable to other methods of navigation were to be achieved. This precision generally exceeded that attained in ionospheric pulse-sounding techniques available at the time, but not by a very substantial margin. The only potentially difficult problem was the irregular variations of transmission times of most radio signals. These variations could be reduced or practically eliminated only by operating at very high frequencies where line-of-sight transmission could be achieved without interference from waves reflected from the ionosphere. It was natural, therefore, that the first operational hyperbolic radio aid was arranged to use these principles in the very high frequency part of the radio spectrum.

This first aid to navigation of the new kind was the British **Gee** system, proposed by Robert J. Dippy in 1937 and brought into operation by a team headed by Dippy in early 1942. This system was designed in accordance with the principles given above. Gee operated with a pulse length of about 5 microseconds at frequencies from 30 to 80 megahertz with separations between transmitters of the order of 100 miles. For high-flying aircraft the system could be used at distances up to 350 or 400 miles. Even though it was heavily jammed over western Europe, Gee was of the greatest importance to the night flying of the Bomber Command of the Royal Air Force, as it made return to bases in the British Isles relatively easy and accurate even under very poor flying conditions.

In 1940 the Microwave Committee of the U. S. National Defense Research Committee was assigned a project to develop a long-range, precision aircraft navigation system. Operational specifications for the system included an accuracy of about 1,000 feet at a range of 200 miles. To meet these requirements it was planned to use synchronized pairs of pulse-type transmitting stations separated by distances of several hundred miles. Transmitters radiating a peak power of about 1½ megawatts in the 30 to 40 megahertz band were contemplated. Except for instrumentation, the system would have been very similar to Gee.

The original system concepts used groundwave signals only. However during the course of system developments, measurements were made of the timing stability of pulsed radio waves having frequencies of from about 2 to 8 megahertz received via reflections from the ionosphere. Contrary to what was generally believed at the time, the stability of the signal reflected from the E-layer of the ionosphere was found to be quite good. Computations based on these measurements indicated that a long-range system using a combination of groundwaves and skywaves would provide a fixed accuracy of better than 5 miles at a range of 1,500 miles. The possibilities of a navigational system with this range and accuracy were so great that the original concept was abandoned and all efforts were concentrated toward this new goal. The revised project was assigned to the Radiation Laboratory of the Massachusetts Institute of Technology in the summer of 1941. Experimental transmitting stations were located at U. S. Coast Guard facilities near Montauk Point, New York, and Fenwick Island, Delaware.

In January 1942 the first skywave accuracy tests were made; a radio-frequency band was selected. Trials in moving vehicles were undertaken in June. By October 1942 a four-station chain was inaugurated for extended field trials by the U. S. Navy. About 40 receiver-indicators were installed in naval vessels during the next 4 or 5 months. Data were rapidly taken that defined the necessary skywave correction to reduce nighttime E-layer signals to the equivalent groundwave readings given on the charts.

On January 1, 1943, the administration of the new Loran program was assigned to the U. S. Navy. The U. S. Coast Guard and the Royal Canadian Navy were assigned responsibility for operation of the transmitting stations. The Loran system became fully operational in the spring of 1943 when charts for the four-station North Atlantic chain became available. The first chain comprised the two test stations at Montauk Point and Fenwick Island plus two new stations at Baccaro and Deming, Nova Scotia. The Fenwick station was first moved to Bodie Island, North Carolina, and later to Cape Hatteras, North Carolina. The Montauk Point station was moved to Nantucket Island. Installations in the Aleutians and the South Pacific soon followed.

This first version of Loran which operated on channels in the 1800 to 2000 kilohertz band was originally called **Standard Loran** to distinguish it from other experimental versions then being evaluated. Standard Loran later became known as **Loran-A.**

The most successful variation of Standard Loran during World War II was known as **Skywave Synchronized** (SS) **Loran.** This SS Loran operated at 2 megahertz, but, as its name implies, the stations maintained synchronization by using skywaves rather than the groundwave. This system was usable only during nighttime because of radio propagation conditions. SS Loran was first tested on the night of April 10, 1943, between Fenwick Island, Delaware, and Bonavista, Newfoundland, 1,100 miles away. Observations at the Radiation Laboratory, Cambridge, Massachusetts, revealed a line of position probable error of about 0.5 mile. This demonstrated the important fact that the errors of a few microseconds in the skywave transmission would not prevent position fixing to a useful accuracy when a sufficiency long baseline could be used. By the fall of 1943 two SS Loran pairs were in operation with transmitting stations at East Brewster, Massachusetts, Gooseberry Falls, Montana, Montauk Point, New York and Key West, Florida. Extensive evaluation flights by U. S. and Allied Forces revealed an average position-fixing error of 1 to 2 miles.

In the early spring of 1944, the four SS Loran stations in the U. S. were dismantled, and the equipment was installed in Europe and North Africa. Stations were located in Scotland, Tunisia, Algeria, and Libya. This system became operational in October 1944 and was used extensively for night bombing operations. The combination of very long baselines (approximately 950 miles) and favorable baseline orientation provided nighttime service over a large part of Europe with an accuracy of 1 to 2 miles. SS Loran systems were also operated successfully in Southeast Asia. Lack of daytime coverage was the major limitation of SS Loran.

Skywave Long Baseline Loran was tested by the U. S. Coast Guard shortly after World War II. This system was similar to SS Loran but operated at 10.585 megahertz during the day and at 2 megahertz during the night for synchronization purposes. In order to provide normal 2 megahertz service, transmitters were operated at 2 megahertz during the day as well as at night, being controlled by the synchronization on 10.585 megahertz in daytime.

Preliminary tests were conducted between Chatham, Massachusetts, and Fernandina, Florida, in May 1944. These tests were followed by additional tests between Hobe Sound, Florida, and Point Chinato, Puerto Rico, in December 1945 and January 1946. Results of these tests demonstrated the basic concepts to be sound, but the difficulty in obtaining a suitable frequency allocation ended development.

It was recognized early that a low frequency Loran system would provide improved accuracy and greatly extended navigational coverage during the day and night with fewer transmitting stations. The first experimental low frequency Loran system, operating at 180 kilohertz and called **LF Loran,** was placed in operation in 1945 with transmitting stations at Cape Cod, Massachusetts, Cape Fear, North Carolina, and Key Largo, Florida. Monitor stations for overwater observations were installed at Bermuda, the Azores, Puerto Rico, and Trinidad. Overland signals were observed at monitor stations in Ohio, Minnesota, and aboard specially equipped aircraft.

The LF Loran system was basically an extension of the techniques of 2 megahertz Loran to the lower frequency. However, the LF stations operated in synchronized triplets instead of pairs, and the individual radio-frequency cycles of the master and slave pulses were displayed on the user's receiver-indicator. The receivers were designed to provide for visual matching of pulse and cycles. A rough match was made first using the envelopes of the two pulses, as in standard Loran, and then a fine measurement was made by matching selected radio-frequency cycles within each pulse.

In 1946 all equipment installed in the experimental east coast LF Loran system was transferred to northwest Canada where it served the requirements of special Arctic maneuvers in the area. Upon completion of the maneuvers, a joint Canadian-United States project was initiated to evaluate the system. Nine fixed-monitor stations and a number of specially equipped aircraft were placed in operation and comprehensive tests were made over a period of months. These operational tests, together with results of the east coast tests, showed that the LF Loran system could operate with substantially longer baselines than was feasible with the 2 megahertz system and that a 24-hour service coverage over land would be of the order of two-thirds of that of sea water as opposed to the almost negligible overland coverage provided by 2 megahertz Loran. The accuracy achieved was equivalent to an average line of position error of 160 feet at 750 miles. Beyond 750 miles, accuracy deteriorated rapidly due to skywave interference.

However, operators found that they could not select the correct pair of cycles more than 75 percent of the time without prior knowledge of the correct pulse envelope delay. The resulting positional ambiguities were operationally unacceptable; the system was judged unsatisfactory for general purpose navigation. Work was begun in 1946 on the development of cycle-identification and phase-measuring techniques to correct these positional ambiguities. This work by government and industry culminated in the field tests of a low frequency, cycle matching Loran system called **Cyclan.** This name was derived from **Cycle** matching Lor**an**.

Cyclan was the first fully automatic Loran system. The cyclic ambiguity problem was solved through the use of pulse transmissions on two frequencies 20 kilohertz apart. At first 180 and 200 kilohertz were used, followed by operation on 160 and 180 kilohertz. Slope matching on the first 50 microseconds of the pulse was followed by cycle matching within the pulse envelope for precise determination of arrival time-differences. Incorrect cycle matching at one frequency was readily apparent by an obvious mismatch at the second frequency utilized. Cyclan coverage was limited to the groundwave region and, depending on local noise, gave a range of about 1,000 to 1,500 miles. Operational tests with Cyclan were complicated by serious interference problems involving broadcast stations and aeronautical radiobeacons on adjacent frequencies. The tests did show, however, that the radio-frequency cycle identification problem could be solved. Significant progress was also made in instrumentation. It became necessary to seek another solution when the 1947 Atlantic City Radio Conference designated the 90 to 110 kilohertz band (20 kilohertz bandwidth) for the development of long range navigational systems; Cyclan required a total bandwidth of approximately 40 kilohertz.

Navaglobe was an early system investigated as a potential low frequency system operating within the 90 to 110 kilohertz band. Work on this system started in 1945. The directional characteristics were obtained from a configuration of three vertical antennas placed at the corners of an equilateral triangle. The antennas were excited alternately in pairs so that three overlapping figure-eight patterns were obtained. Measurement of the relative amplitudes of the received signals determined the navigator's bearing from the transmitting station. Cross bearings were required to establish position. To obtain range information, parallel development of a distance measuring system called **Facom** was carried out. This system also operated in the 90 to 110 kilohertz band. Coarse distance data were developed by comparing the phase of a low frequency modulating tone on a local oscillator with the phase of a similar tone on the continuous wave signal from the Facom ground station. Fine distance measurements were made on the radio frequency cycles in the carrier.

Navarho, the combined Navaglobe-Facom system, was extensively evaluated during 1957. The project was discontinued because the overall system performance was unsatisfactory.

Navarho was the first system to attempt the distance-difference measurement from observation of the change of phase of the received signal relative to a very stable, locally generated reference signal of the same frequency. To obtain useful navigational accuracy the frequencies of the transmitted signals and of the receiver's reference signals had to be synchronized with an accuracy of a part in a billion or better. One of the first commercial cesium beam frequency standards was used to control the frequency of the signals radiated from three towers at Camden, New York. Although the airborne crystal oscillators were awkward to operate, requiring close attention to attain the necessary stability, the results of numerous flights out to ranges of 2,000 miles demonstrated acceptable range and accuracy in the distance measurement; the bearing measurements at long range, however, were relatively poor.

In 1952 work began under government contract on a long range, automatic, ground-reference tactical bombing system known as **Cytac**. A pulsed, hyperbolic navigation system operating in the 90 to 110 kilohertz band was an integral part of the Cytac system. Equipment development was completed in 1955, and three transmitting stations were constructed at Forestport, New York; Carolina Beach, North Carolina; and Carrabelle, Florida. Tests with the navigational component of the system throughout 1956 showed that automotic instrumentation could solve the radio frequency cycle identification problem and could measure time-difference in a hyperbolic system with an average error of a few tenths of a microsecond. The coverage area extended from the Atlantic Ocean to the Mississippi River, and from the Great Lakes to the Gulf of Mexico. Monitor stations installed at widely separated locations collected data during a year of testing. The results of the tests demonstrated that the system was not only capable of a high degree of precision but also that the laws controlling its accuracy were sufficiently well known to permit sound predictions of accuracy prior to installation. For operational reasons, the Cytac concept was abandoned. Its use as a navigational aid was immediately apparent.

In 1957 an operational requirement for a highly accurate long range maritime radionavigation aid was developed. The stated accuracy and range requirements were considerably in excess of the capabilities of existing Loran-A equipment. On the basis of the results of the Cytac tests, it was believed that this requirement could be satisfied by implementing the Cytac concepts as well as some of the Cytac equipment. Consequently, equipment from stations at Forestport, New York, and Carrabelle, Florida, was transferred to Martha's Vineyard, Massachusetts, and Jupiter, Florida, respectively. These stations operating in conjunction with the existing station at Carolina Beach, North Carolina, were placed in operation in 1957. The U. S. Coast Guard in accordance with the U. S. Federal Laws assumed responsibility for operation of the stations in August 1958. Comprehensive tests by both ships and aircraft showed that the original concepts were sound. The new system, designated **Loran-C,** was at that time placed in operational status.

Following the closing of the Radiation Laboratory at the Massachusetts Institute of Technology, a small group of the scientists moved to the Cruft Laboratory of Harvard University, intending to apply some of the new techniques the war had brought forward to various investigations of radio wave propagation. A theoretical study was made of the stability of the phase of a modulated signal that might be expected under the conditions of interference between modes of propagation in long-distance ionospheric transmission. This study indicated that a relatively long-period modulation might be measureable with nearly the accuracy that had been achieved in the LF Loran trials. Refinement of this concept led to the proposal in 1947 of a system called **Radux.**

This new system was to be very similar to LF Loran, except that the arrival times would be measured in terms of the phase of 200 Hertz modulation instead of the time of a pulse having a duration of about 300 microseconds. Because a 200 Hertz modulation could be radiated from a good low frequency antenna at a frequency as low as 40 or 50 kilohertz, it was hoped that a 1,000-mile baseline could be used and that useful service could be provided as far as 3,000 miles. However, little was known about propagational characteristics in this frequency region.

After 2 to 3 years of study of the proposal, the U. S. Navy assigned the Navy Electronics Laboratory (NEL) the task of making the necessary tests to develop Radux as an aid to navigation. With the advice of an informal steering committee, representing several naval technical bureaus and laboratories and commercial contractors, NEL proceeded to build and install transmitters where suitable antennas could be found, initially in Hawaii and San Diego, and to procure and operate receivers. This work occupied nearly the entire decade of the 1950's. The results were very much like those of the work of the Radiation Laboratory on LF Loran; the range and accuracy were less than desired.

Going back to 1953, Dr. Louis Essen of the National Physical Laboratory (NPL) in Teddington, England, who had designed by far the best crystal oscillator then available (the Essen ring) and who was developing the first practical cesium frequency standard, visited Harvard University. He called attention to the fact that the British Post Office transmitter at Rugby had begun transmitting a standard frequency of 60 kilohertz. This transmission was made for only 1 hour per day, but it was derived from an Essen ring oscillator and the frequency was accurately monitored by both the Post Office and NPL. The group at Harvard University immediately began observing this transmission, and made the pleasing discovery that the frequency could be measured to a part in 10^{10} during the 1-hour transmission. This accuracy exceeded by a factor of 10^2 to 10^3 that available through high-frequency transmission of standard frequencies. This link from Rugby to Cambridge, Massachusetts became for a time the primary intercomparison mechanism between the British and American systems of standard time, which differed greatly in those days. The first international intercomparison of cesium-controlled clocks was made in the same way.

The Rugby (GBR) frequency was stabilized in 1954. This started an era in which the frequencies of most VLF transmissions have been stabilized so that they can be used for frequency intercomparisons and for new kinds of propagational research. It was soon found that daily measurement yielded an accuracy of about 2 parts in 10^{11} in frequency, even at distances of thousands of miles.

The Radux work was being done under conditions of military classification. These new VLF discoveries were therefore published only through their bearing on frequency comparison. In April, 1955, however, a letter report to the Office of Naval Research and verbal and other communications with the Naval Laboratories recommended extension of the navigational efforts to the very low frequencies; in particular to those below 14 kilohertz, where circuit bandwidths are so low that the frequencies are not of general interest for communication.

It had been found that the accuracy of Radux, while inadequate to resolve cyclic ambiguities at 40 kilohertz (periods of 25 microseconds), would resolve the four times larger phase ambiguities at a frequency of 10 kilohertz. A composite system was therefore proposed which could operate as Radux, probably at 40 kilohertz, while coherent bursts of 10 kilohertz carrier, radiated from the same antenna at different times, would permit measurements of much greater precision but with 8-mile ambiguities resolvable, at least in theory, by measurements of the 200 Hertz modulation of Radux. This composite system was called **Radux-Omega,** and was investigated for a few years. It rapidly became obvious that this marriage was an unfortunate one, because the useful range of the 10 kilohertz component greatly exceeded that of Radux, while the relatively short baselines of Radux spoiled the geometrical accuracy of the Omega (10 kilohertz) component at long distances, and kept the ultimate accuracy far less than it might otherwise be.

One of the primary reasons for the suggestion of such a low modulation frequency as 200 Hertz was to guard against the cyclic ambiguities that are a feature of any phase measuring system. When measuring at 200 Hertz in a hyperbolic system, any possible ambiguities would be separated by 400 miles or more and could be disregarded as an operational problem.

During the decade beginning in 1950, forces were at work that made the design of Radux less attractive than it had seemed in 1947. The most obvious change was a general increase in the desired accuracy of a navigational aid. When Loran was developed the only standard of excellence in the deep-water environment was celestial navigation, with perhaps 3 nautical miles as a typical error. Loran, especially Loran-C and a number of short-distance aids, gave navigators a desire for higher accuracy. Two other factors became important: (1) a general improvement in dead reckoning, including the inertial systems, and (2) a very great increase in the reliability of electronic devices. The first of these made the recovery of a lost cycle count much more probable, while the second made the loss of a count itself a relatively unlikely event.

The overall result of these external forces was to reduce by a large factor the fear of lane ambiguity. It therefore became possible to think of satisfying the need for accuracy beyond that of Radux by using a much more ambiguous system, with real hope that the possibility of ambiguities would not become a serious operational defect.

These considerations gradually led to the abandoning of Radux, leaving Omega to stand by itself. During the hybrid period, enough data had been taken to confirm the phenomenal range available at VLF, with timing errors that did not increase markedly with increasing distance. It was also realized that long baselines are especially effective on a spherical earth. For example, with a baseline subtending 60 degrees of arc the divergence of the hyperbolic lines of position is limited to a factor of two, instead of increasing infinitely as it does with a baseline negligibly long in comparison with the curvature of the earth. And, of course, if a pair can link the opposite ends of a diameter of the earth there is no divergence at all, and a measurement accuracy of 12 microseconds in time-difference corresponds to a positional accuracy of a nautical mile, anywhere on earth.

The Omega experiments began with the pair linking Hawaii and California, operating at first at 12.5 kilohertz, although experiments were rapidly extended throughout the 9 to 15 kilohertz region, and even higher at times. One of the earliest experiments gave an exciting and convincing demonstration of the merits of VLF cycle matching. Commander Lyle C. Read, USN, who was the Radux Program Officer at the Navy Electronics Laboratory, was traversing the baseline with an early Omega receiver on a naval vessel, essentially counting the number of wavelengths between Hawaii and California as a check on the then somewhat nebulous ideas about phase velocity at very low frequencies. Fortunately, the ship got a little ahead of schedule and Commander Read was able to induce the captain to make a standard 360° turn midway in the passage. Although only a single pair was being tracked, the double amplitude of the sinusoidal variation on the phase record gave the diameter of the ship's turning circle within 50 yards.

This and many other demonstrations of the sensitivity of the Omega technique accelerated the decision to concentrate on VLF because of its range and potential accuracy, and to accept the best that could be done to solve the ambiguity problem.

From this point, the work went rapidly for a time. A station in the Panama Canal Zone was borrowed from Naval Communications, and one in Wales from the British Post Office. With these, and San Diego and Hawaii, the network was large enough to permit monitoring from Alaska to South America and from Hawaii to Europe. Early ideas of the velocity of propagation and of its variation with time of day were refined (a process that is still being carried forward) and innumerable trials and demonstrations were conducted.

By 1966 Omega signals were being transmitted on a regular basis from stations located in New York, Hawaii, Trinidad, and Norway. But since these stations utilized existing facilities and developmental equipment, none of these stations was capable of transmitting the power required for an operational system. However, signals were being transmitted full time from a four station complex providing the vital ingredients necessary to further system development.

By 1976 seven of the eight stations of the fully implemented system were in normal operation. The developmental station at Trinidad remained in operation pending implementation of the South Pacific station.

Other developments include Decca, a short to medium range hyperbolic system, which was first used under the code name "QM" during the landings in Normandy in 1944. Another World War II development was the rotating electronic beam utilized in the German navigation system called sonne, later further perfected by the British under the name Consol.

In the late 1950's the Decca Navigator Company Ltd., developed an experimental VLF radionavigation system known as **Delrac,** a name derived from **De**cca **l**ong-**r**ange **a**rea **c**overage. In principle, this system was similar to Omega.

137. Development of satellite navigation.—**The Navy Navigation Satellite System (NAVSAT)** was developed within the Navy to fulfill a requirement established by the Chief of Naval Operations for an accurate worldwide navigation system for all naval surface vessels, aircraft, and submarines. The system was conceived and developed by the Applied Physics Laboratory of The Johns Hopkins University under Navy contract.

The underlying concept that led to development of the system dates back to 1957 and the first launch of an artificial satellite into orbit—Russia's **Sputnik I.** Dr. William H. Guier and Dr. George C. Wieffenbach at the Applied Physics Laboratory of the Johns Hopkins University were monitoring the famous "beeps" transmitted by the passing satellite. They plotted the received signals at precise intervals, and noticed that a characteristic doppler curve emerged. Since celestial bodies followed fixed orbits, they reasoned that this curve could be used to describe the satellite orbit. Later, they demonstrated that they could determine all of the orbital parameters for a passing satellite by doppler observation of a single pass from a single fixed station. The doppler shift apparent while receiving a transmission from a passing satellite was proven to be an effective measuring device for establishing the satellite orbit.

Dr. Frank T. McClure, also of the Applied Physics Laboratory concluded inversely that if the satellite-orbit were known, doppler shift measurement could be used to determine one's position on earth—thereby suggesting a new method for navigation—a more precise method than any yet known, available anywhere on earth without regard for weather conditions. His studies earned for him the first National Aeronautics and Space Administration award for important contributions to space study development.

In 1958, on the strength of Dr. McClure's studies, the Applied Physics Laboratory proposed to the Bureau of Naval Weapons that possibilities be explored for establishing a satellite doppler navigation system. The Chief of Naval Operations set forth requirements for such a system to provide accurate all-weather worldwide navigation, recommending to the Advanced Research Projects Agency that funds be made available for the purpose. Although this was only one of a number of proposals to utilize satellites for navigation, it was accepted, and, until 1960, all work on the system was performed by the Navy with that Agency's backing. An experimental satellite that failed to achieve orbit in September 1959 indicated the feasibility of tracking by doppler; the first successful launching of a prototype system satellite in April 1960 demonstrated its operational usefulness for navigation.

138. Development of inertial navigation.—The first inertial navigation system was developed in 1942 for use in the V–2 missile by the Peenmunde group under the leadership of Dr. Wernher von Braun. This system used two 2-degree-of-freedom gyroscopes and an integrating accelerometer to determine the missile velocity. By the end of World War II, the Peenmunde group had developed a stable platform with three single-degree-of-freedom gyroscopes and an integrating accelerometer.

Following World War II inertial navigation development in the United States was conducted by four groups, one sponsored by the Army and three by the Air Force. The Army group included the Peenmunde group under Dr. Wernher von Braun. This group later became the inertial group for the National Aeronautics and Space Administration. The Air Force-sponsored groups were Northrup Aircraft, Autonetics Division of North American Aviation, and the Massachusetts Institute of Technology Instrumentation Laboratory, which was later to become The Charles Stark Draper Laboratory.

At first the systems developed for the Air Force were combinations of stellar and inertial systems. As the state-of-the-art improved, purely inertial systems were designed.

During this development the principal proponent of purely inertial systems was Dr. Charles Stark Draper of the Massachusetts Institute of Technology.

The Autonetics Division of North American Aviation ingeniously adapted one of its systems for shipboard use. In 1958 this system was used to navigate the USS *Nautilus* under the ice to the North Pole.

The development of purely inertial systems for air and marine applications proceeded along parallel lines. Missile and space applications followed.

The development of the **Ship Inertial Navigation System** (**SINS**) began in 1951 and was completed in 1954. The initial system test on the highway provided realistic operating conditions under close monitoring and control. The results of the shipboard test of SINS in 1955 indicated that it provided what was needed for the fleet ballistic missile submarine.

Conclusion

139. Navigation has come a long way, but there is no evidence that it is nearing the end of its development. Progress will continue as long as man remains unsatisfied with the means at his disposal.

References

Collinder, Per. *A History of Marine Navigation.* Tr. Maurice Michael. New York, St. Martin's, 1955.

Hewson, J. B. *A History of the Practice of Navigation.* Glasgow, Brown, 1951.

May, W. E. *A History of Marine Navigation.* Oxfordshire, G. T. Foulis and Company Limited, 1973.

Petze, C. L., Jr. *The Evolution of Celestial Navigation.* Vol. 26, Ideal Series. New York, Motor Boating, 1948.

Pierce, J. A., and R. H. Woodward. "The Development of Long-Range Hyperbolic Navigation in the United States." Harvard University, Cambridge, Massachusetts, Office of Naval Research Technical Report No. 620, February 1971.

Stewart, J. Q., and N. L. Pierce. "The History of Navigation." *Marine and Air Navigation* (Boston, Ginn, 1944). Chap. 29.

Taylor, E. G. R. *The Mathematical Practitioners of Tudor and Stuart England.* London, Cambridge University Press, 1955.

Taylor, E. G. R. *The Haven-Finding Art.* London, Hollis and Carter, 1956.

Taylor, E. G. R. *The Geometrical Seaman.* London, Hollis and Carter, 1962.

Waters, D. W. *The Art of Navigation in England in Elizabethan and Early Stuart Times.* New Haven, Yale University Press, 1958.

Wroth, L. C. *Some American Contributions to the Art of Navigation,* 1519–1802. Providence, John Carter Brown Library, 1947.

In addition, articles pertaining to the history of navigation are frequently carried in certain periodicals, including:

The American Neptune. (Salem)

The Journal of Navigation. (London)

The Nautical Magazine. (Glasgow)

NAVIGATION: *Journal of the Institute of Navigation.*

NAVIGATION: *Revue Technique de Navigation Maritime,* Aerienne *et Spatiale.* (Paris)

United States Naval Institute Proceedings. (Annapolis)

CHAPTER II

BASIC DEFINITIONS

201. Navigation is the process of directing the movements of a craft, expeditiously and safely, from one point to another. The word *navigate* is from the Latin *navigatus*, the past participle of the verb *navigere*, which is derived from the words *navis*, meaning "ship," and *agere*, meaning "to move" or "to direct." Navigation of water craft is called **marine navigation** to distinguish it from navigation of aircraft, called **air navigation.** Navigation of a vessel on the surface is sometimes called **surface navigation** to distinguish it from **underwater navigation** of a submerged vessel. Navigation of vehicles across land or ice is called **land navigation.** The expression **lifeboat navigation** is used to refer to navigation of lifeboats or life rafts, generally involving rather crude methods. The expression **polar navigation** refers to navigation in the regions near the geographical poles of the earth, where special techniques are employed.

The principal divisions of navigation are as follows:

Dead reckoning is the determination of position by advancing a known position for courses and distances. A position so determined is called a **dead reckoning position.** It is generally accepted that the course *steered* and the speed *through the water* should be used, but the expression is also used to refer to the determination of position by use of the course and speed expected to be made good over the ground, thus making an estimated allowance for disturbing elements such as current and wind. A position so determined is better called an **estimated position.** The expression "dead reckoning" probably originated from use of the Dutchman's log a buoyant object thrown overboard, to determine the speed of the vessel relative to the object, which was assumed to be *dead* in the water. Apparently, the expression **deduced reckoning** was used when allowance was made for current and wind. It was often shortened to *ded reckoning* and the similarity of this expression to *dead reckoning* was undoubtedly the source of the confusion that is still associated with these expressions.

Piloting (or **pilotage**) is navigation involving frequent or continuous determination of position or a line of position relative to geographic points, and usually requiring need for close attention to the vessel's draft with respect to the depth of water. It is practiced in the vicinity of land, dangers, etc., and requires good judgment and almost constant attention and alertness on the part of the navigator. **Celestial navigation** is navigation using information obtained from celestial bodies.

Radionavigation is navigation using radio waves for determination of position or of a line of position. Radar navigation and satellite navigation are parts of the radionavigation division. **Radar navigation** involves the use of radio waves, usually in the centimeter band, to determine the distance and direction of an object reflecting the waves to the sender. **Satellite navigation** involves the use of artificial earth satellites for determination of position.

The term **electronic navigation** is used to refer to navigation involving the use of electronics in any way. Thus, the term includes the use of the gyrocompass for steering and the echo sounder when piloting. Because of the wide use of electronics in navigation equipment, the term electronic navigation has limited value as a term for a division of navigation.

Electronics is the science and technology relating to the emission, flow, and effects of electrons in a vacuum or through a semiconductor, and to systems using devices in which this action takes place.

202. The earth is approximately an **oblate spheroid** (a sphere flattened at the poles). For many navigational purposes, the earth is assumed to be a sphere without intolerable error.

The **axis of rotation** or **polar axis** of the earth is the line connecting the North Pole and the South Pole.

203. Circles of the earth.—**A great circle** is the line of intersection of a sphere and a plane through the center of the sphere (fig. 203a). This is the largest circle that can be drawn on a sphere. The shortest line on the surface of a sphere between two points on that surface is part of a great circle. On the spheroidal earth the shortest line is called a **geodesic.** A great circle is a near enough approximation to a geodesic for most problems of navigation.

A **small circle** is the line of intersection of a sphere and a plane which does not pass through the center of the sphere (fig. 203a).

A **meridian** is a great circle through the geographical poles of the earth. Hence, all meridians meet at the poles, and their planes intersect each other in a line, the **polar axis** (fig. 203b). The term **meridian** is usually applied to the **upper branch** only, that half from pole to pole which passes through a given point. The other half is called the **lower branch.**

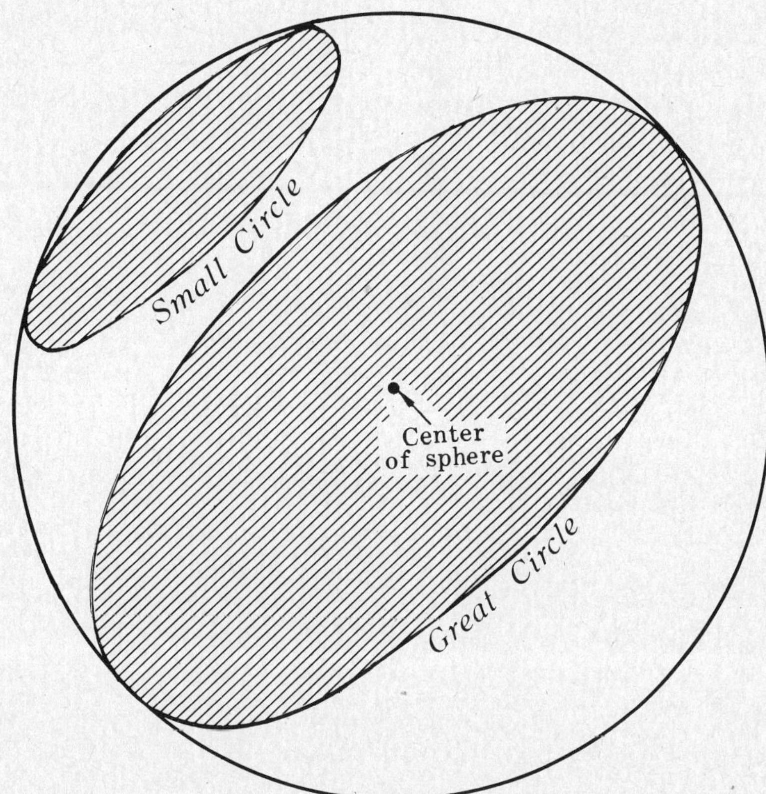

FIGURE 203a.—Great and small circles.

The **prime meridian** is that meridian used as the origin for measurement of longitude (fig. 203c). The prime meridian used almost universally is that through the original position of the British Royal Observatory at Greenwich, near London.

The **equator** is the terrestrial great circle whose plane is perpendicular to the polar axis (fig. 203d). It is midway between the poles.

A **parallel** or **parallel of latitude** is a circle on the surface of the earth, parallel to the plane of the equator (fig. 203e). It connects all points of equal latitude. The equator, a great circle, is a limiting case connecting points of 0° latitude. The poles, single points at latitude 90°, are the other limiting case. All other parallels are small circles.

204. Position on the earth.—A position on the surface of the earth (except at either of the poles) may be defined by two magnitudes called **coordinates.** Those customarily used are *latitude* and *longitude*. A position may also be expressed in relation to known geographical positions.

Latitude (L, lat.) is angular distance from the equator, measured northward or southward along a meridian from 0° at the equator to 90° at the poles (fig. 203c). It is designated *north* (N) or *south* (S) to indicate the direction of measurement.

The **difference of latitude (*l*, D. Lat.)** between two places is the angular length of arc of any meridian between their parallels (fig. 203c). It is the numerical difference of the latitudes if the places are on the same side of the equator, and the sum if they are on opposite sides. It may be designated *north* (N) or *south* (S) when appropriate.

The **middle** or **mid latitude (Lm)** between two places on the same side of the equator is half the sum of their latitudes. Mid latitude is labeled N or S to indicate whether it is north or south of the equator. The expression is occasionally used with

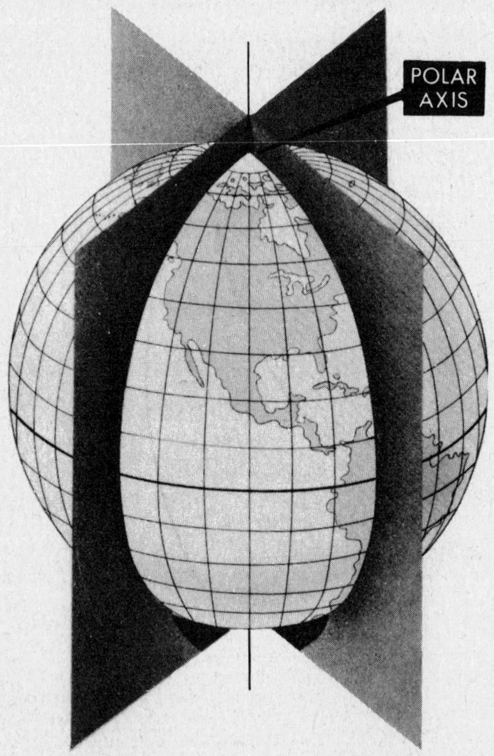

FIGURE 203b.—The planes of the meridians meet at the polar axis.

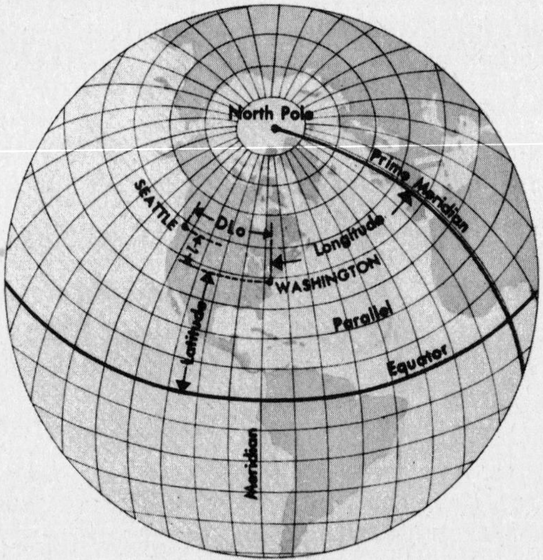

FIGURE 203c.—Circles and coordinates of the earth. All parallels except the equator are small circles; the equator and meridians are great circles.

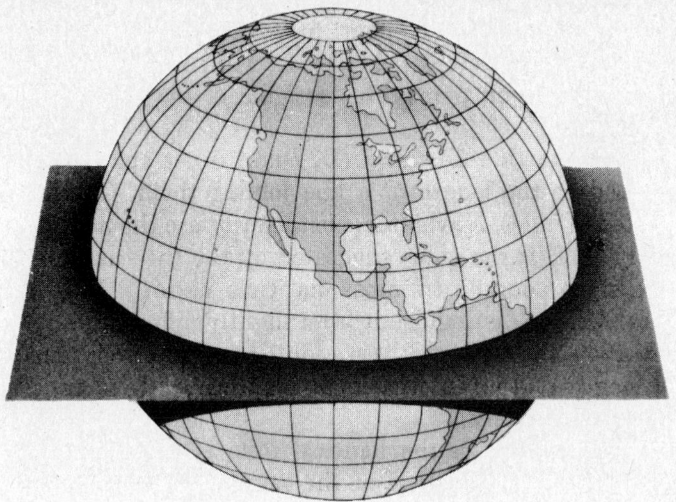

FIGURE 203d.—The equator is a great circle midway between the poles.

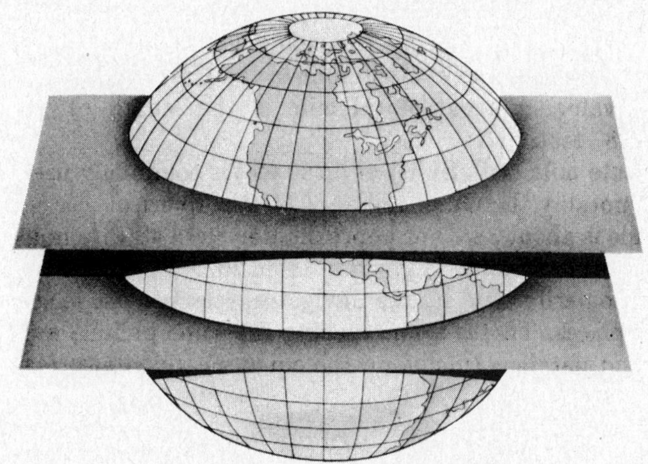

FIGURE 203e.—A parallel of latitude is parallel to the equator.

reference to two places on opposite sides of the equator, when it is equal to half the *difference* between the two latitudes, and takes the name of the place farthest from the equator. However, this usage is misleading, as it lacks the significance usually associated with the expression. When the places are on opposite sides of the equator, two mid latitudes are generally used, the average of each latitude and 0°.

Longitude (λ, long.) is the arc of a parallel or the angle at the pole between the prime meridian and the meridian of a point on the earth, measured eastward or westward from the prime meridian through 180° (fig. 203c). It is designated *east* (E) or *west* (W) to indicate the direction of measurement.

The **difference of longitude (DLo)** between two places is the shorter arc of the parallel or the smaller angle at the pole between the meridians of the two places (fig. 203c). If both places are on the same side (east or west) of Greenwich, DLo is the numerical difference of the longitudes of the two places; if on opposite sides, DLo is the numerical sum unless this exceeds 180°, when it is 360° minus the sum. The distance between two meridians at any parallel of latitude, expressed in distance units, usually nautical miles, is called **departure (p, Dep.)**. It represents distance made good to the east or west as a craft proceeds from one point to another. Its numerical value between any two meridians decreases with increased latitude, while DLo is numerically the same at any latitude. Either DLo or p may be designated *east* (E) or *west* (W) when appropriate.

205. Distance on the earth.—**Distance (D, Dist.)** is the spatial separation of two points, and is expressed as the length of a line joining them. On the surface of the earth it is usually stated in miles. Navigators customarily use the **nautical mile (mi., M)** of 1852 meters exactly. This is the value suggested by the International Hydrographic Bureau in 1929, and since adopted by most maritime nations. It is often called the **International Nautical Mile** to distinguish it from slightly different values used by some countries. On July 1, 1959, the United States adopted the exact relationship of 1 yard= 0.9144 meter. The length of the International Nautical Mile is consequently equal to 6,076.11549 feet (approximately).

For most navigational purposes the nautical mile is considered the length of 1 minute of latitude, or of any great circle of the earth, regardless of location. On the Clarke spheroid of 1866, used for mapping North America, the length of 1 minute of latitude varies from about 6,046 feet at the equator to approximately 6,108 feet at the poles. The length of 1 minute of a great circle of a sphere having an area equal to that of the earth, as represented by this spheroid, is 6,080.2 United States feet. This was the standard value of the nautical mile in the United States prior to adoption of the international value. A **geographical mile** is the length of 1 minute of the equator, or about 6,087 feet.

The **land** or **statute mile (mi., St M)** of 5,280 feet is commonly used for navigation on rivers and lakes, notably the Great Lakes of North America.

The nautical mile is about 38/33 or approximately 1.15 statute miles. A conversion table for nautical and statute miles is given in table 20.

Distance, as customarily used by the navigator, refers to the length of the **rhumb line** connecting two places. This is a line making the same oblique angle with all meridians. Meridians and parallels (including the equator) which also maintain constant

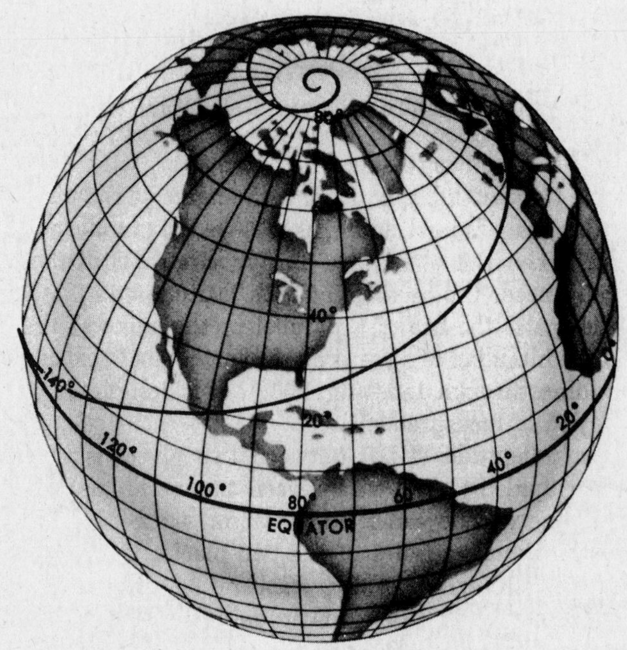

FIGURE 205.—A rhumb line or loxodrome.

true directions, may be considered special cases of the rhumb line. Any other rhumb line spirals toward the pole, forming a **loxodromic curve** or **loxodrome** (fig. 205). Distance along the great circle connecting two points is customarily designated **great-circle distance.**

206. Speed (S) is rate of motion, or distance per unit of time.

A **knot (kn.)**, the unit of speed commonly used in navigation, is a rate of one nautical mile per hour. The expression "knots per hour" refers to acceleration, not speed.

The expression **speed of advance** (**SOA**) is used to indicate the speed intended to be made along the track (art. 207), and **speed over ground** (**SOG**) the speed along the path actually followed. **Speed made good** (**SMG**) is the speed along the course made good.

207. Direction on the earth.—Direction is the position of one point relative to another, without reference to the distance between them. In navigation, direction is customarily expressed as the angular difference in degrees from a reference direction, usually north or the ship's head. Compass directions (east, south by west, etc.) or points (of 11¼° or 1/32 of a circle) are seldom used by modern navigators for precise directions.

Course (**C, Cn**) is the horizontal direction in which a vessel is steered or intended to be steered, expressed as angular distance from north, usually from 000° at north, clockwise through 360°. Strictly, the term applies to direction *through the water*, not the direction intended to be made good *over the ground.* The course is often designated as **true, magnetic, compass,** or **grid** as the reference direction is true, magnetic, compass, or grid north, respectively. **Course made good** (**CMG**) is the single resultant direction from the point of departure to point of arrival at any given time. Sometimes the expression **course of advance** (**COA**) is used to indicate the direction intended to be made good over the ground, and **course over ground** (**COG**) the direction of the path actually followed, usually a somewhat irregular line. **Course line** is a line extending in the direction of a course.

In making computations it is sometimes convenient to express a course as an angle from *either* north or south, through 90° or 180°. In this case it is designated **course angle** (**C**) and should be properly labeled to indicate the origin (prefix) and direction of measurement (suffix). Thus, C N35°E=Cn 035° (000°+35°), C N155°W =Cn 205° (360°−155°), C S47°E=Cn 133° (180°−47°). But Cn 260° may be either C N100°W or C S80°W, depending upon the conditions of the problem.

The symbol C is always used for *course angle,* and is usually used for *course* where there is little or no possibility of confusion.

Track (**TR**) is the intended or desired horizontal direction of travel with respect to the earth and also the path of intended travel. The terms **intended track** and **trackline** are also used to indicate the path of intended travel (fig. 207a). The path actually followed is usually a somewhat irregular line. The track consists of one or a series of course lines from the point of departure to the destination, along which it is intended the vessel will proceed. A great circle which a vessel intends to follow approximately is called a **great-circle track.**

Heading (**Hdg., SH**) is the direction in which a vessel is pointed, expressed as angular distance from north, usually from 000° at north, clockwise through 360°. *Heading* should not be confused with *course. Heading* is a constantly changing value as a vessel oscillates or yaws back and forth across the course due to the effects of sea, wind, and steering error.

Bearing (**B, Brg.**) is the direction of one terrestrial point from another, expressed as angular distance from a reference direction, usually from 000° at the reference direction, clockwise through 360°. When measured through 90° or 180° from *either* north or south, it is called **bearing angle** (**B**), which bears the same relationship to

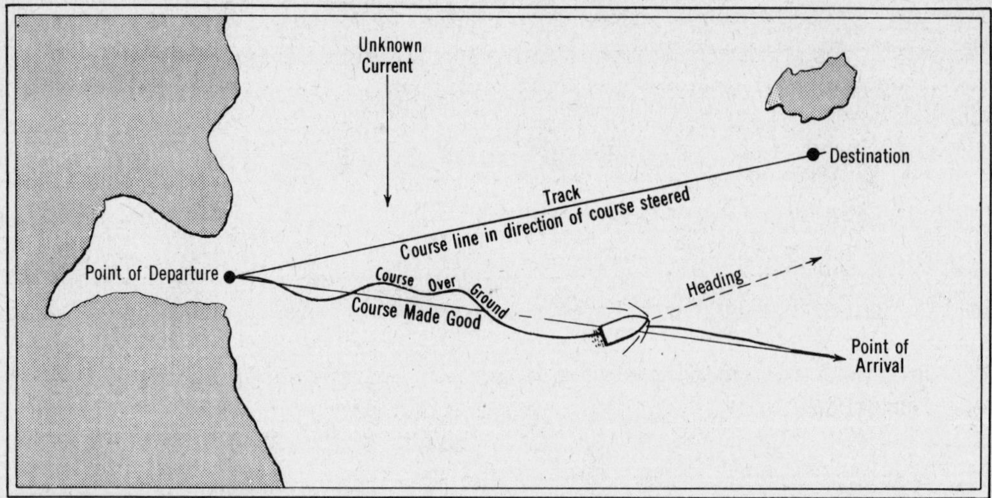

FIGURE 207a.—Course line, track, course over ground, course made good, and heading.

bearing as *course angle* does to *course*. *Bearing* and *azimuth* are sometimes used interchangeably, but the latter is better reserved exclusively for reference to horizontal direction of a point on the celestial sphere from a point on the earth.

A relative bearing is one relative to the heading, or to the vessel itself. It is usually measured from 000° at the heading, clockwise through 360°. However, it is sometimes conveniently measured right or left from 0° at the ship's head through 180°. This is particularly true when using table 7. Older methods, such as indicating the number of degrees or points from some part of the vessel (10° forward of the starboard beam, two points on the port quarter, etc.) are seldom used by modern navigators to indicate precise directions, except for bearings dead ahead or astern, or broad on the bow, beam, or quarter.

To convert a relative bearing to a bearing from north (fig. 207b), express the relative bearing in terms of the 0°–360° system and add the heading:

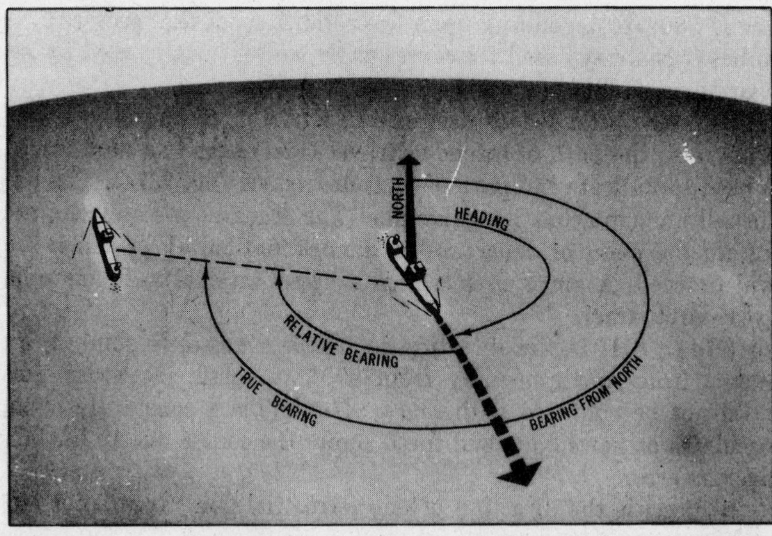

FIGURE 207b.—Relative bearing.

$$\text{True Bearing} = \text{Relative Bearing} + \text{True Heading}.$$

Thus, if another vessel bears 127° relative from a ship whose heading is 150°, the bearing from north is 127°+150°=277°. If the total exceeds 360°, subtract this amount. To convert a bearing from north to a relative bearing, subtract the heading:

$$\text{Relative Bearing} = \text{True Bearing} - \text{True Heading}.$$

Thus, a lightship which bears 241° from north bears 241°−137°=104° relative from a ship whose heading is 137°. If the heading is larger than the true bearing, add 360° to the true bearing before subtracting.

CHAPTER III

CHART PROJECTIONS

General

301. The navigator's chart.—A **map** is a conventional representation, usually on a plane surface, of all or part of the physical features of the earth's surface or any part of it. A **chart** is such a representation intended primarily for navigation. A **nautical** or **marine chart** is one intended primarily for marine navigation. It generally shows depths of water (by soundings and sometimes also by depth curves), aids to navigation, dangers, and the outline of adjacent land and such land features as are useful to the navigator.

Chart making presents the problem of representing the surface of a spheroid upon a plane surface. The surface of a sphere or spheroid is said to be **undevelopable** because no part of it can be flattened without distortion. A **map projection** or **chart projection** is a method of representing all or part of the surface of a sphere or spheroid upon a plane surface. The process is one of transferring points on the surface of the sphere or spheroid onto a plane, or onto a **developable** surface (one that can be flattened to form a plane) such as a cylinder or cone. If points on the surface of the sphere or spheroid are projected from a single point (including infinity), the projection is said to be **perspective** or **geometric.** Most map projections are not perspective.

302. Selecting a projection.—Each projection has distinctive features which make it preferable for certain uses, no one projection being best for all conditions. These distinctive features are most apparent on charts of large areas. As the area becomes smaller, the differences between various projections become less noticeable until on the largest scale chart, such as of a harbor, all projections become practically identical. Some of the desirable properties are:

1. *True shape* of physical features.
2. *Correct angular relationship.* A projection with this characteristic is said to be **conformal** or **orthomorphic.**
3. *Equal area,* or the representation of areas in their correct relative proportions.
4. *Constant scale* values for measuring distances.
5. *Great circles* represented as straight lines.
6. *Rhumb lines* represented as straight lines.

It is possible to preserve any one and sometimes more than one property in any one projection, but it is impossible to preserve all of them. For instance, a projection cannot be both conformal and equal area, nor can both great circles and rhumb lines be represented as straight lines.

303. Types of projection.—Projections are usually classified primarily as to the type of developable surface to which the spherical or spheroidal surface is transferred. They are sometimes further classified as to whether the projection (but not necessarily the charts made by it) is centered on the equator (**equatorial**), a pole (**polar**), or some point or line between (**oblique**). The name of a projection often indicates its type and sometimes, in addition, its principal feature.

The projection used most frequently by mariners is commonly called **Mercator,** after its inventor (art. 109). Classified according to type this is an **equatorial cylindri-**

cal orthomorphic projection, the cylinder conceived as being tangent along the equator. A similar projection based upon a cylinder tangent along a meridian is called **transverse Mercator** or **transverse cylindrical orthomorphic.** It is sometimes called **inverse Mercator** or **inverse cylindrical orthomorphic.** If the cylinder is tangent along a great circle other than the equator or a meridian, the projection is called **oblique Mercator** or **oblique cylindrical orthomorphic.**

In a **simple conic** projection points on the surface of the earth are conceived as transferred to a tangent cone. In a **Lambert conformal** projection the cone intersects the earth (a **secant** cone) at two small circles. In a **polyconic** projection, a series of tangent cones is used.

An **azimuthal** or **zenithal** projection is one in which points on the earth are transferred directly to a plane. If the origin of the projecting rays is the center of the earth, a **gnomonic** projection results; if it is the point opposite the plane's point of tangency, a **stereographic** projection; and if at infinity (the projecting lines being parallel to each other), an **orthographic** projection (fig. 303). The gnomonic, stereographic, and orthographic are perspective projections. In an **azimuthal equidistant** projection, which is not perspective, the scale of distances is constant along any radial line from the point of tangency.

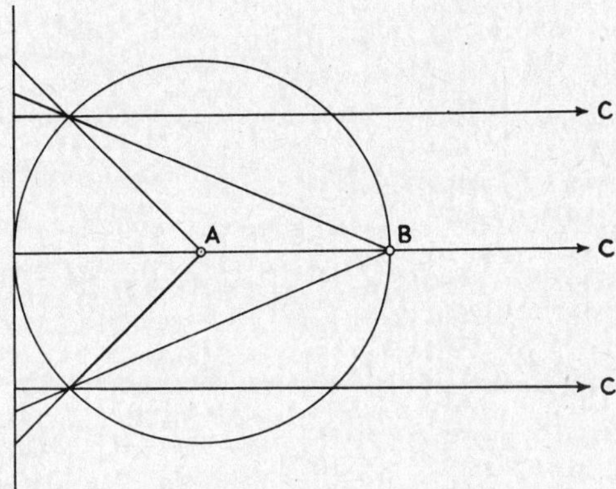

FIGURE 303.—Azimuthal projections: *A*, gnomonic; *B*, stereographic; *C* (at infinity), orthographic.

Cylindrical and plane projections can be considered special cases of conical projections with the heights infinity and zero, respectively.

A **graticule** is the network of latitude and longitude lines laid out in accordance with the principles of any projection.

Cylindrical Projections

304. Features.—If a cylinder is placed around the earth, tangent along the equator, and the planes of the meridians are extended, they intersect the cylinder in a number of vertical lines (fig. 304). These lines, all being vertical, are parallel, or everywhere equidistant from each other, unlike the terrestrial meridians, which become closer together as the latitude increases. On the earth the parallels of latitude are perpendicular to the meridians, forming circles of progressively smaller diameter as the latitude increases. On the cylinder they are shown perpendicular to the projected meridians, but because a cylinder is everywhere of the same diameter, the projected parallels are all the same size.

If the cylinder is cut along a vertical line (a meridian) and spread out flat, the meridians appear as equally spaced, vertical lines, and the parallels as horizontal

FIGURE 304.—A cylindrical projection.

lines. The spacing of the parallels relative to each other differs in the various types of cylindrical projections.

The cylinder may be tangent along some great circle other than the equator, forming an oblique or transverse cylindrical projection, on which the pattern of latitude and longitude lines appears quite different, since the line of tangency and the equator no longer coincide.

305. Mercator projection.—The only cylindrical projection widely used for navigation is the **Mercator** or **equatorial cylindrical orthomorphic,** named for its inventor Gerhard Kremer (Mercator), a Flemish geographer. It is not perspective and the parallels cannot be located by geometrical projection, the spacing being derived mathematically. The use of a tangent cylinder to explain the development of the projection has been used, but the relationship of the terrestrial latitude and longitude lines to those on the cylinder is often carried beyond justification, resulting in misleading statements and illustrations.

The distinguishing feature of the Mercator projection (fig. 305) among cylindrical projections is that both the meridians and parallels are expanded at the same ratio with increased latitude. The expansion is equal to the secant of the latitude, with a small correction for the ellipticity of the earth. Since the secant of 90° is infinity, the projection cannot include the poles. Expansion is the same in all directions and angles are correctly shown, the projection being conformal. Rhumb lines appear as straight lines, the directions of which can be measured directly on the chart. Distances can also be measured directly, to practical accuracy, but not by a single distance scale over the entire chart, unless the spread of latitude is small. The latitude scale is customarily used for measuring distances, the expansion of the scale being the same as that of distances at the same latitude. Great circles, except meridians and the equator, appear as curved lines concave to the equator (fig. 310a). Small areas appear in their correct shape but of increased size unless they are near the equator. Plotting of positions by latitude and longitude is done by means of rectangular coordinates, as on any cylindrical projection.

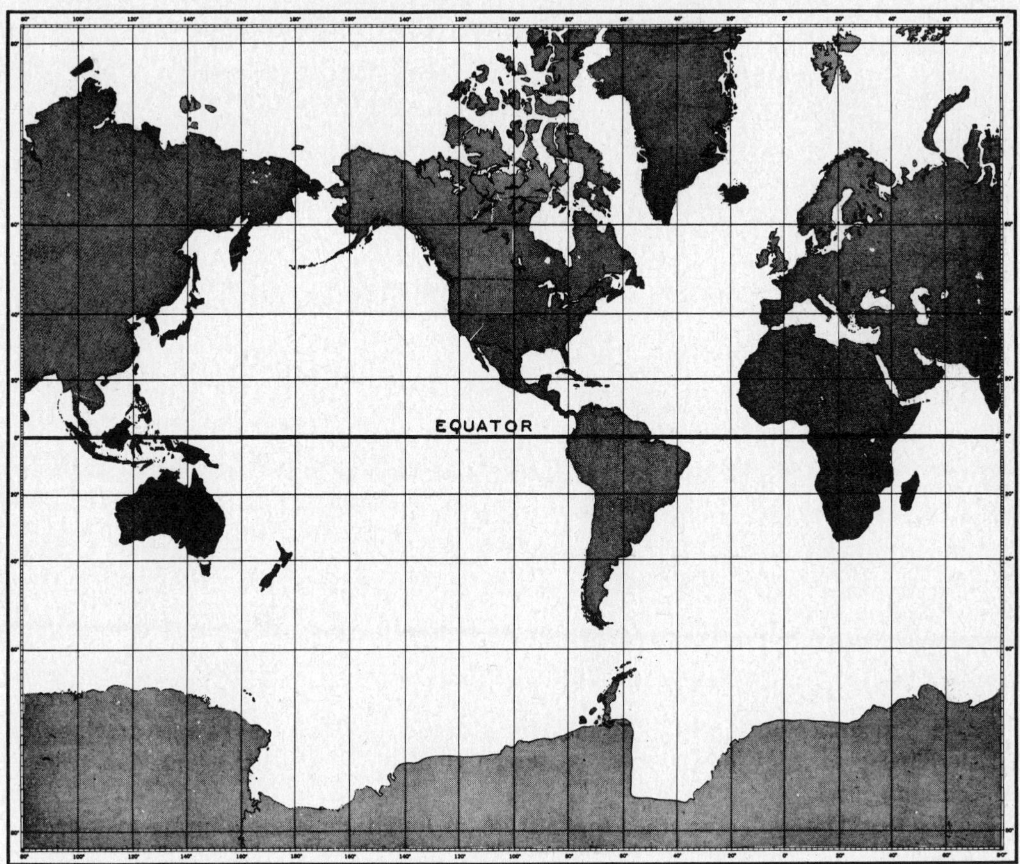

FIGURE 305.—A Mercator map of the world.

306. Meridional parts.—At the equator a degree of longitude is approximately equal in length to a degree of latitude. As the distance from the equator increases, degrees of latitude remain approximately the same (not exactly because the earth is not quite a sphere), while degrees of longitude become progressively shorter. Since degrees of longitude appear everywhere the same length in the Mercator projection, it is necessary to increase the length of the meridians if the expansion is to be equal in all directions. Thus, to maintain the correct proportions between degrees of latitude and degrees of longitude, the former are shown progressively longer as the distance from the equator increases (fig. 305).

The length of the meridian, as thus increased between the equator and any given latitude, expressed in minutes of the equator as a unit, constitutes the number of **meridional parts (M)** corresponding to that latitude. Meridional parts, given in table 5 for every minute of latitude from the equator to the pole, afford facilities for constructing a Mercator chart and for solving problems in Mercator sailing. These values are for the Clarke spheroid of 1866. The formula for meridional parts, given in the explanation to table 5, is derived from an integral representing the exact relationship.

307. Mercator chart construction.—To construct a Mercator chart, first select the scale and then proceed as follows:

Draw a series of vertical lines to represent the meridians, spacing them in accordance with the scale selected. Thus, if 1° (60′) of longitude is to be shown as one inch, each meridional part will be 1/60 or 0.01667 inch in length. The distance, in inches, of any parallel from the equator is then determined by dividing its meridional parts by 60 or multiplying them by 0.01667.

If the equator is not to be included, the **meridional difference** (**m**) is used. This is the difference between the meridional parts of the various latitudes and that of the lowest parallel (the one nearest the equator) to be shown. Distances so determined are measured from the lowest parallel.

It is often desired to show a minimum area on a chart of limited size, to the largest possible scale. The scale is then dictated by the limitations.

When the graticule has been completed, the features to be shown are located by means of the latitude and longitude scales.

Example.—A Mercator chart is to be constructed at the maximum scale on a sheet of paper 35 × 46 inches, with a minimum two-inch margin outside the **neatline** limiting the charted area. The minimum area to be covered is lat. 44°–50° north and long. 56°–68° west.

Solution.—*Step one:* Determine which dimension to place horizontal. From table 5 the meridional difference is:

$$\begin{array}{lr} M_{50°} & 3456.6 \\ M_{44°} & \underline{2929.6} \\ m & 527.0 \end{array}$$

The chart is to cover at least 12° (68°−56°) of longitude. The longitude is therefore to cover a distance of 12×60=720 meridional parts. Since there are a greater number of meridional parts of longitude to be shown than of latitude, the long dimension is placed horizontal.

Step two: Determine whether the latitude or longitude is the limiting scale factor. The number of inches available for latitude coverage is 31 (35 inches minus a two-inch margin top and bottom). If 527 meridional parts are to be shown in 31 inches, each meridional part will be $\frac{31}{527}=0.05882$ inch. There are 46−4=42 inches available for longitude, and therefore the length of each meridional part will be $\frac{42}{720}=0.05833$ inch. Thus, the longitude is the limiting scale factor, for all of the desired area could not be shown in the available space if the larger scale were to be used. Using the smaller scale, it is found that 30.74 inches (0.05833×527) will be needed to show the desired latitude coverage. The top and bottom margins can be increased slightly, or additional latitude coverage can be shown. If it is desired to include the additional coverage, the amount can be determined by dividing the available space, 31 inches, by the scale, 0.05833. This is 531.5 meridional parts, or 4.5 more than the minimum. By inspection of table 5, it is seen that the latitude can be extended either 3′.3 below 44° or 2′.9 above 50°. Suppose it is decided that the margin will be increased slightly and only the desired minimum coverage shown.

Step three: Determine the spacing of the meridians and parallels. Meridians 1° or 60′ apart will be placed 60×0.05833=3.50 inches apart. Next, determine each degree of latitude separately. First, compute the meridional difference between the lowest parallel and the various parallels to be shown:

$M_{45°}$	3013.5	$M_{46°}$	3098.8	$M_{47°}$	3185.7	$M_{48°}$	3274.2	$M_{49°}$	3364.5	$M_{50°}$	3456.6
$M_{44°}$	2929.6	$M_{44°}$	2929.6	$M_{44°}$	2929.6	$M_{44°}$	2929.6	$M_{44°}$	2929.6	$M_{44°}$	2929.6
m	83.9	m	169.2	m	256.1	m	344.6	m	434.9	m	527.0

Next, determine the distance of each parallel from that of L 44°N by multiplying its meridional difference by the scale, 0.05833:

L 44° to L 45°=0.05833× 83.9= 4.89 in.
L 44° to L 46°=0.05833×169.2= 9.87 in.
L 44° to L 47°=0.05833×256.1=14.94 in.
L 44° to L 48°=0.05833×344.6=20.10 in.
L 44° to L 49°=0.05833×434.9=25.37 in.
L 44° to L 50°=0.05833×527.0=30.74 in.

Step four: Draw the graticule. Draw a horizontal line 2.13 inches $\left(\frac{35-30.74}{2}\right)$ from the bottom. This is the lower neatline. Label it "44°N." Draw the right-hand neatline two inches from the edge. Label it "56°W." Along the lower parallel measure off distances in units of 3.50 inches from λ 56°W at the right to λ 68°W at the left. Through the points thus located draw vertical lines to represent the meridians. Along any meridian measure upward from the horizontal line a series of distances as

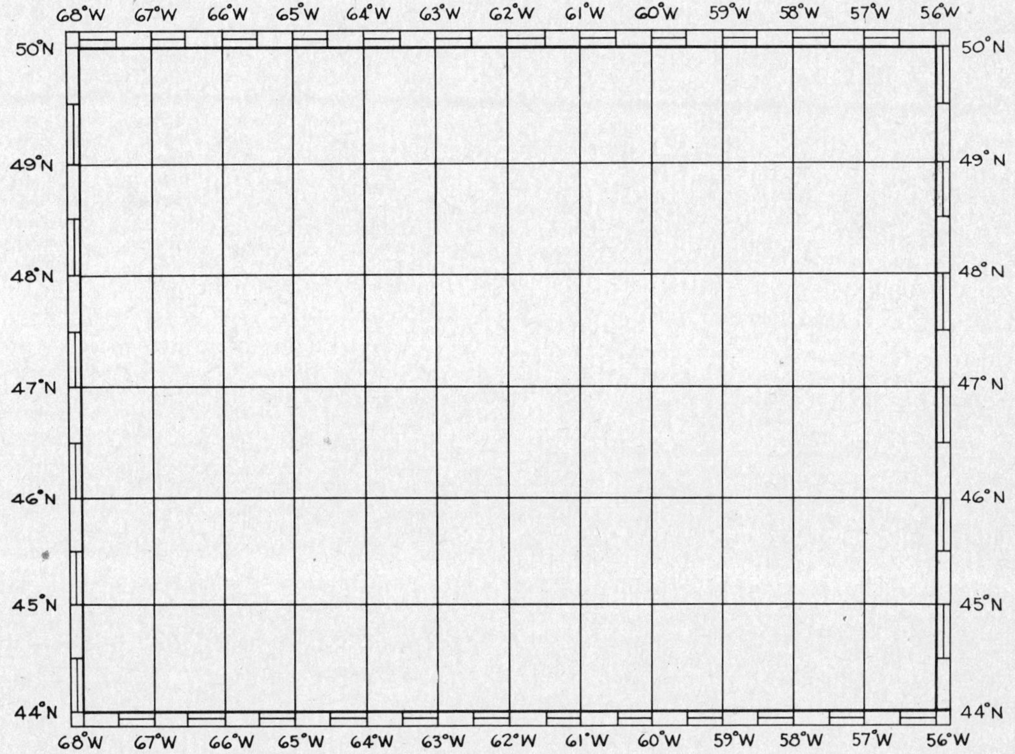

Figure 307.—The graticule of a Mercator chart from L 44°N to L 50°N and from λ 56°W to λ 68°W.

determined by the calculations above. Through these points draw horizontal lines to represent the parallels. Label the meridians and parallels as shown in figure 307.

Step five: Mark off the latitude and longitude scales around the neatline. The scales can be graduated in units as small as desired. Determine the longitude scale by dividing the degrees into equal parts. Establish the latitude scale by computing each subdivision of a degree in the same manner as described above for whole degrees. In low latitudes degrees of latitude can be divided into equal parts without serious loss of accuracy.

Step six: Fill in the desired detail.

In *south* latitude the distance between consecutive parallels increases toward the *south.* The top parallel is drawn first and distances measured downward from it. Latitude labels increase toward the *south* (down).

In *east* longitude the longitude labels increase toward the *east* (right).

308. Transverse and oblique Mercator projections.—If Mercator principles are used to construct a chart, but with the cylinder tangent along a meridian, a **transverse Mercator** or **transverse cylindrical orthomorphic** projection results. The word "inverse" is sometimes used in place of "transverse" with the same meaning. If the cylinder is tangent at some great circle other than the equator or a meridian (fig. 308a), the projection is called **oblique Mercator** or **oblique cylindrical orthomorphic.** These projections utilize a **fictitious graticule** similar to but offset from the familiar network of meridians and parallels (fig. 308b). The tangent great circle is the **fictitious equator.**

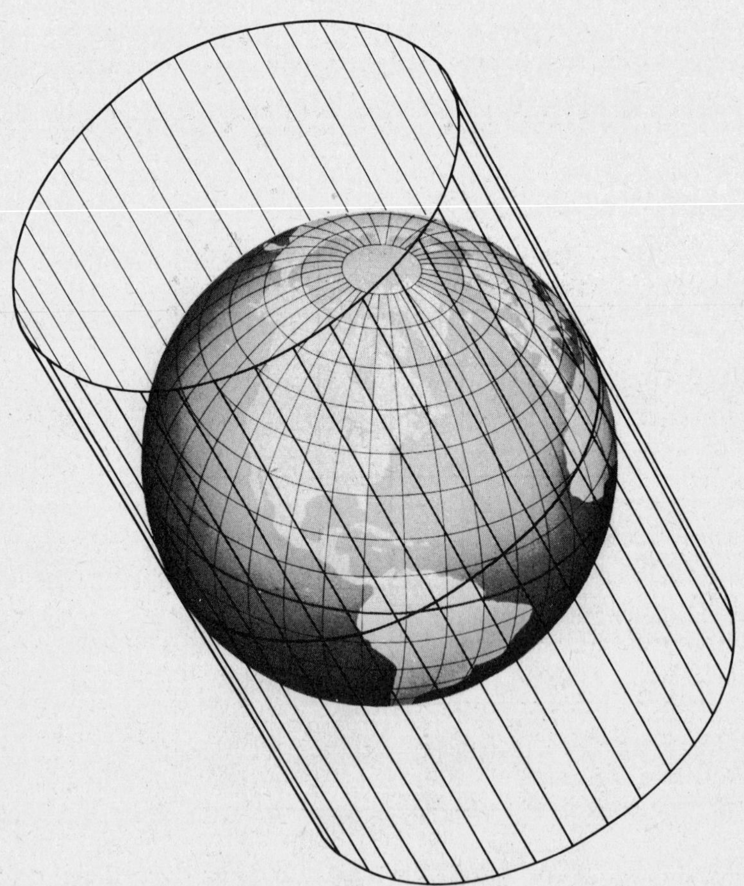

FIGURE 308a.—An oblique Mercator projection.

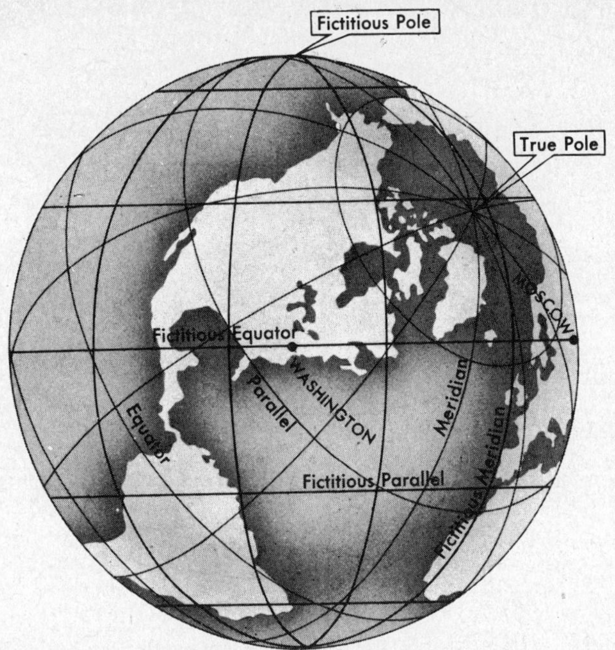

FIGURE 308b.—The fictitious graticule of an oblique Mercator projection.

Ninety degrees from it are two **fictitious poles.** A group of great circles through these poles and perpendicular to the tangent great circle are the **fictitious meridians,** while a series of circles parallel to the plane of the tangent great circle form the **fictitious parallels.**

The actual meridians and parallels appear as curved lines (figs. 309, 310b, and 322).

A straight line on the transverse or oblique Mercator projection makes the same angle with all fictitious meridians, but not with the terrestrial meridians. It is therefore a **fictitious rhumb line.** Near the tangent great circle a straight line closely approximates a great circle. It is in this area that the chart is most useful.

The **Universal Transverse Mercator (UTM) grid** is a military grid superimposed upon a transverse Mercator graticule, or the representation of these grid lines upon any graticule.

This grid system and these projections are often used for large-scale (harbor) nautical charts and military charts.

309. Transverse Mercator projection.—A special case of the Mercator projection in which the cylinder is tangent along a meridian is called a **transverse (inverse) Mercator** or **transverse (inverse) cylindrical orthomorphic** projection. Since the area of minimum distortion is near a meridian, this projection is useful for charts covering a large band of latitude and extending a relatively short distance on each side of the tangent meridian (fig. 309) or for charts of the polar regions (fig. 322). It is sometimes used for star charts showing the evening sky at various seasons of the year.

310. Oblique Mercator projection.—The Mercator projection in which the cylinder is tangent along a great circle other than the equator or a meridian is called an **oblique Mercator** or **oblique cylindrical orthomorphic** projection. This projection is used principally where it is desired to depict an area in the near vicinity of an oblique great circle, as, for instance, along the great-circle route between two important, widely

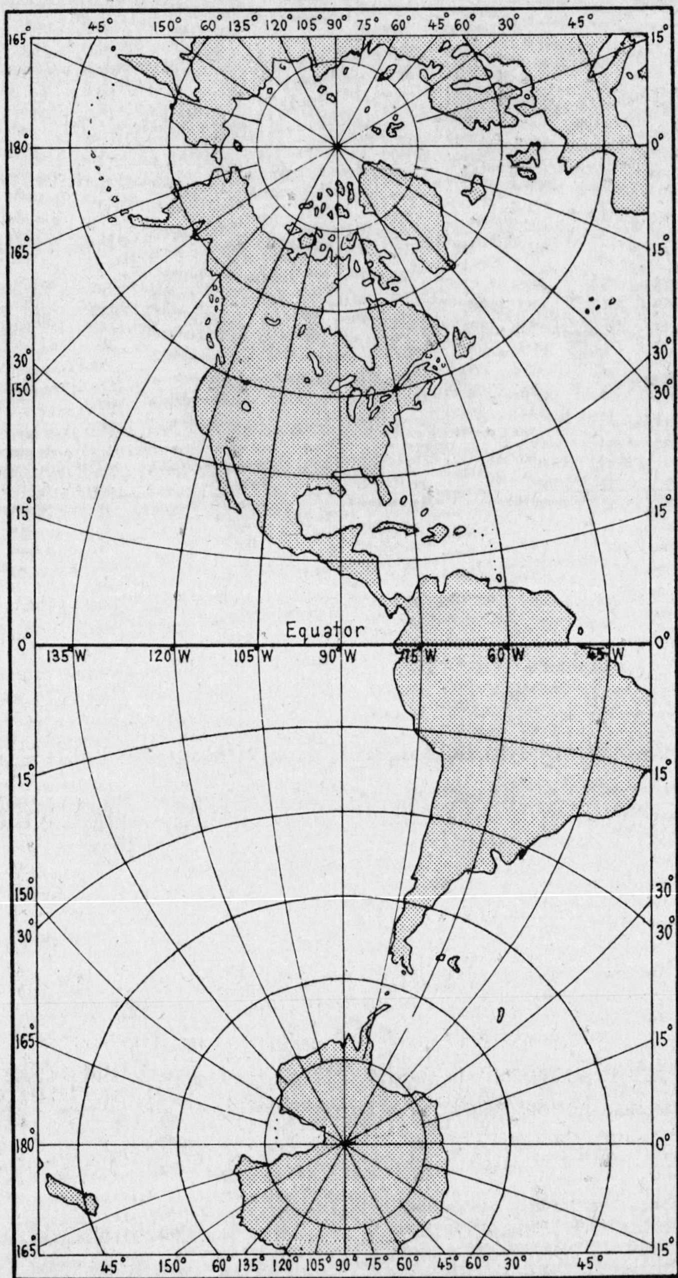

FIGURE 309.—A transverse Mercator map of the western hemisphere.

separated centers. Figure 310a is a Mercator map showing Washington and Moscow and the great circle joining them. Figure 310b is an oblique Mercator map with the great circle between these two centers as the tangent great circle or fictitious equator (as in fig. 308b). The limits of the chart of figure 310b are indicated in figure 310a. Note the large variation in scale as the latitude changes.

311. Rectangular projection.—A cylindrical projection similar to the Mercator but with uniform spacing of the parallels is called a **rectangular** projection (fig. 311). It is convenient for graphically depicting information where distortion is not important. The principal navigational use of this projection is for the star chart of the *Air Almanac*

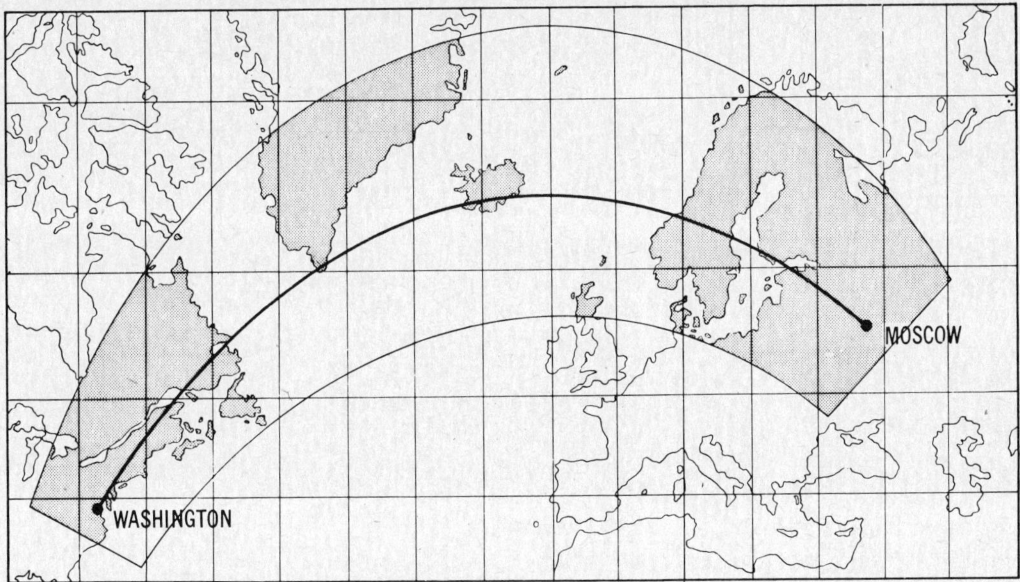

FIGURE 310a.—The great circle between Washington and Moscow as it appears on a Mercator map. See figures 308b and 310b.

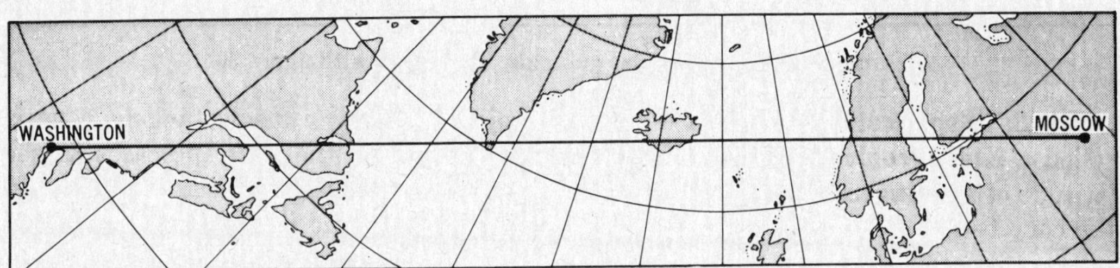

FIGURE 310b.—An oblique Mercator map based upon a cylinder tangent along the great circle through Washington and Moscow. The map includes an area 500 miles on each side of the great circle. The limits of this map are indicated on the Mercator map of figure 310a.

where positions of stars are plotted by rectangular coordinates representing declination (ordinate) and sidereal hour angle (abscissa). Since the meridians are parallel, the parallels of latitude (including the equator and the poles) are all represented by lines of equal length.

Conic Projections

312. Features.—A conic projection is produced by transferring points from the surface of the earth to a cone or series of cones which are then cut along an element and spread out flat to form the chart. If the axis of the cone coincides with the axis of the earth, the usual situation, the parallels appear as arcs of circles and the meridians as either straight or curved lines converging toward the nearer pole. Excessive distortion is usually avoided by limiting the area covered to that part of the cone near the surface of the earth. A parallel along which there is no distortion is called a **standard parallel.** Neither the **transverse conic** projection, in which the axis of the cone is in the equatorial plane, nor the **oblique conic** projection, in which the axis of the cone is oblique to the plane of the equator, are ordinarily used for navigation, their chief use being for illustrative maps.

The appearance and features of conic projections are varied by using cones tangent at various parallels, using a secant (intersecting) cone, or by using a series of cones.

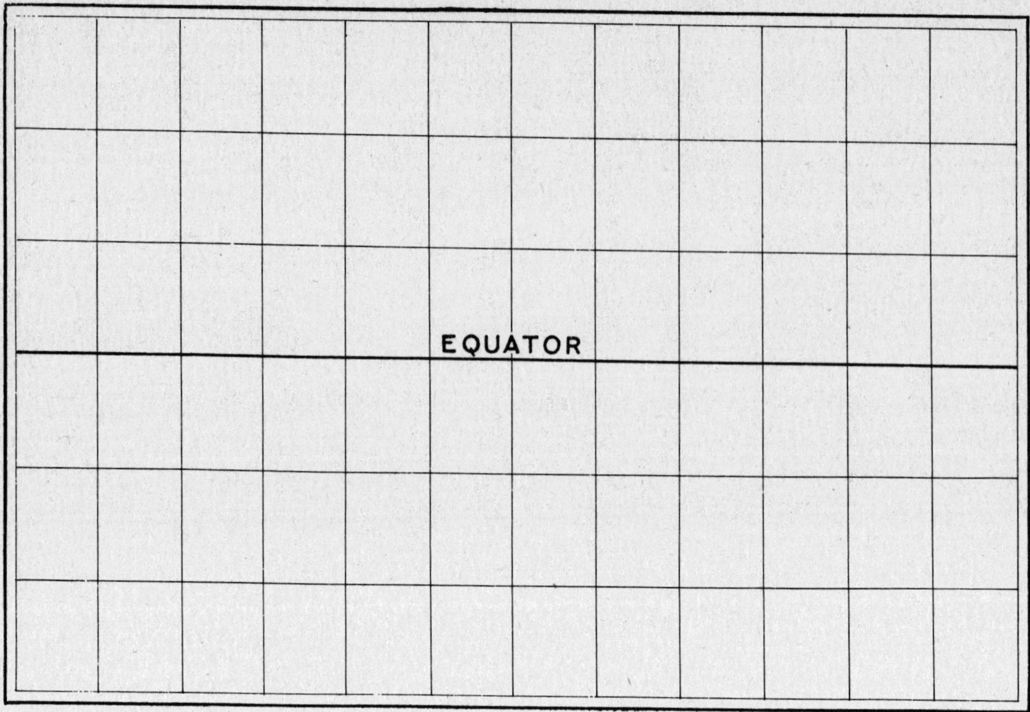

FIGURE 311.—A rectangular graticule. Compare with figure 305.

313. Simple conic projection.—A conic projection using a single tangent cone is called a **simple conic** projection (fig. 313a). The height of the cone increases as the latitude of the tangent parallel decreases. At the equator the height reaches infinity and the cone becomes a cylinder. At the pole its height is zero and it becomes a plane. As in the Mercator projection, the simple conic projection is not perspective, as only the meridians are projected geometrically, each becoming an element of the cone. When this is spread out flat to form a map, the meridians appear as straight lines converging at the apex of the cone. The standard parallel, or that at which the cone is tangent to the earth, appears as the arc of a circle with its center at the apex of the cone, or the

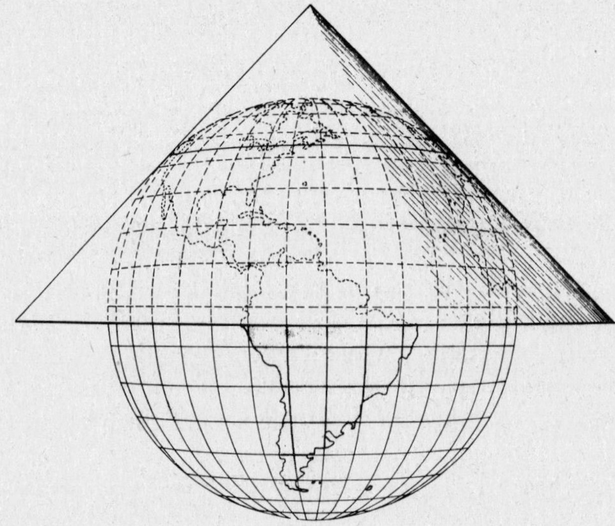

FIGURE 313a.—A simple conic projection.

common point of intersection of all the meridians. The other parallels are concentric circles, the distance along any meridian between consecutive parallels being in correct relation to the distance on the earth, and hence derived mathematically. The pole is represented by a circle (fig. 313b). The scale is correct along any meridian and along the standard parallel. All other parallels are too great in length, the error increasing with increased distance from the standard parallel. Since the scale is not the same in all directions about every point, the projection is not conformal, its principal disadvantage for navigation. Neither is it an equal-area projection.

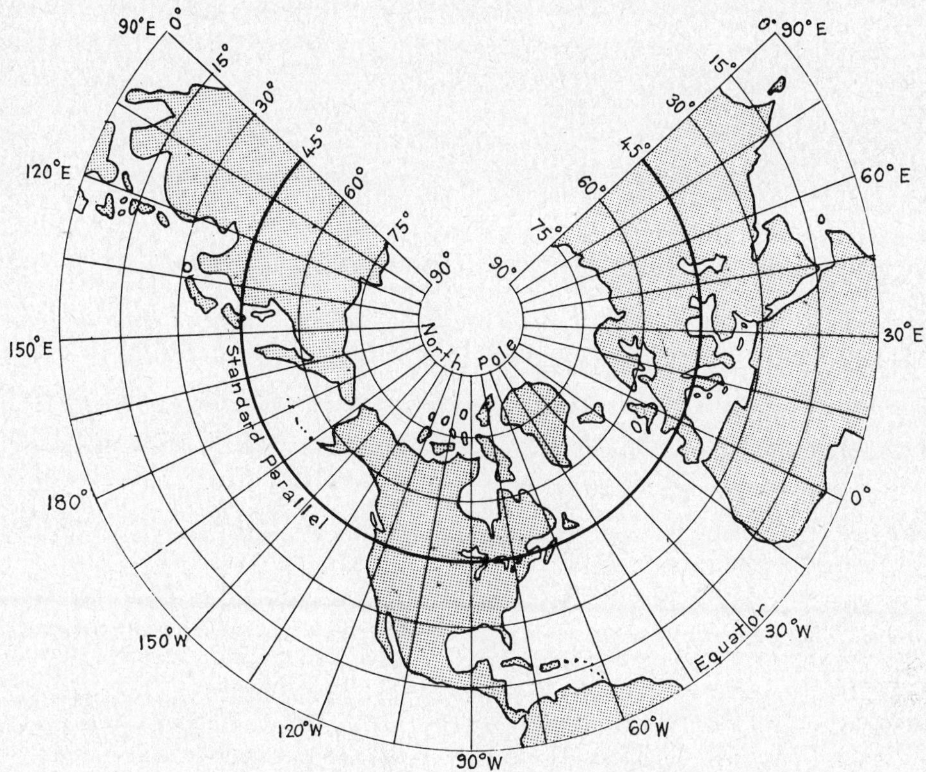

FIGURE 313b.—A simple conic map of the northern hemisphere.

Since the scale is correct along the standard parallel and varies uniformly on each side, with comparatively little distortion near the standard parallel, this projection is useful for mapping an area covering a large spread of longitude and a comparatively narrow band of latitude. It was developed by Claudius Ptolemy in the second century after Christ to map just such an area, the Mediterranean.

314. Lambert conformal projection.—The useful latitude range of the simple conic projection can be increased by using a secant cone intersecting the earth at two standard parallels (fig. 314). The area between the two standard parallels is compressed, and that beyond is expanded. Such a projection is called a **secant conic** or **conic projection with two standard parallels.**

If, in such a projection, the spacing of the parallels is altered so that the distortion is the same along them as along the meridians, the projection becomes conformal. This is known as the **Lambert conformal** projection, after its eighteenth century Alsatian inventor, Johann Heinrich Lambert. It is the most widely used conic projection for navigation, though its use is more common among aviators than mariners. Its appearance is very much the same as that of the simple conic projection. If the chart is not

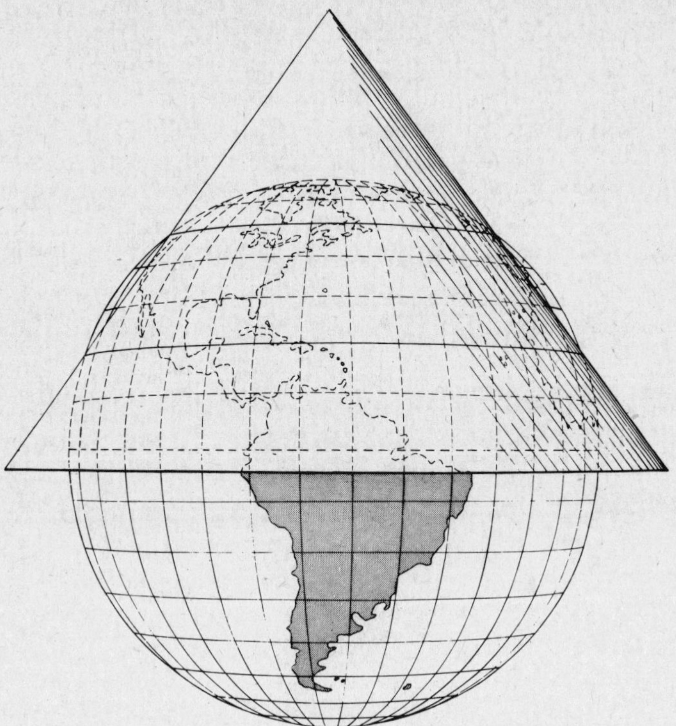

FIGURE 314.—A secant cone for a conic projection with two standard parallels.

carried far beyond the standard parallels, and if these are not a great distance apart, the distortion over the entire chart is small. A straight line on this projection so nearly approximates a great circle that the two can be considered identical for many purposes of navigation. Radio bearings, from signals which are considered to travel great circles, can be plotted on this projection without the correction needed when they are plotted on a Mercator chart. This feature, gained without sacrificing conformality, has made this projection popular for aeronautical charts, since aircaft make wide use of radio aids to navigation. It has made little progress in replacing the Mercator projection for marine navigation, except in high latitudes. In a slightly modified form this projection has been used for polar charts (art. 321).

315. Polyconic projection.—The latitude limitations of the secant conic projection can be essentially eliminated by the use of a series of cones, resulting in a **polyconic** projection. In this projection each parallel is the base of a tangent cone (fig. 315a). At the edges of the chart the area between parallels is expanded to eliminate gaps. The scale is correct along any parallel and along the central meridian of the projection. Along other meridians the scale increases with increased difference of longitude from the central meridian. Parallels appear as nonconcentric circles and meridians as curved lines converging toward the pole and concave to the central meridian.

The polyconic projection is widely used in atlases, particularly for areas of large range in latitude and reasonably large range in longitude, as for a continent such as North America (fig. 315b). However, since it is not conformal, this projection is not customarily used in navigation, except for **boat sheets** used in hydrographic surveying.

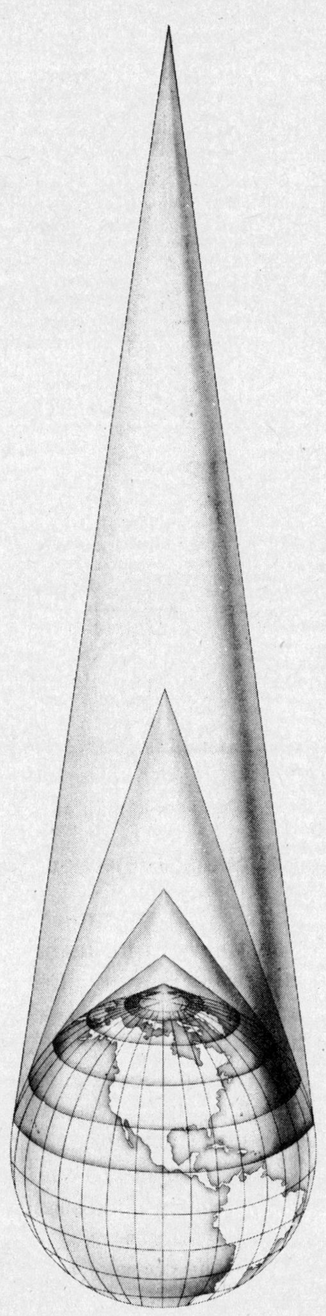

FIGURE 315a.—A polyconic projection.

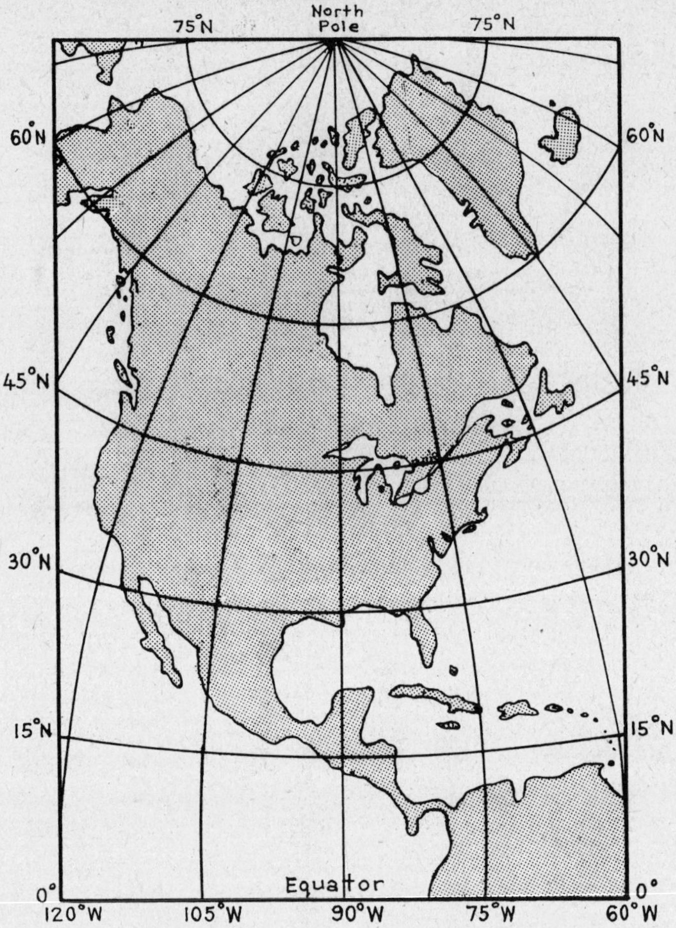

FIGURE 315b.—A polyconic map of North America.

Azimuthal Projections

316. Features.—If points on the earth are projected directly to a plane surface, a map is formed at once, without cutting and flattening, or "developing." This can be considered a special case of a conic projection in which the cone has zero height.

The simplest case of the azimuthal projection is one in which the plane is tangent at one of the poles. The meridians are straight lines intersecting at the pole, and the parallels are concentric circles with their common center at the pole. Their spacing depends upon the method of transferring points from the earth to the plane.

If the plane is tangent at some point other than a pole, straight lines through the point of tangency are great circles, and concentric circles with their common center at the point of tangency connect points of equal distance from that point. Distortion, which is zero at the point of tangency, increases along any great circle through this point. Along any circle whose center is the point of tangency, the distortion is constant. The bearing of any point from the point of tangency is correctly represented. It is for this reason that these projections are called **azimuthal.** They are also called **zenithal.** Several of the common azimuthal projections are prespective.

317. Gnomonic projection.—If a plane is tangent to the earth, and points are projected geometrically from the center of the earth, the result is a **gnomonic** projection (fig. 317a). This is probably the oldest of the projections, believed to have been devel-

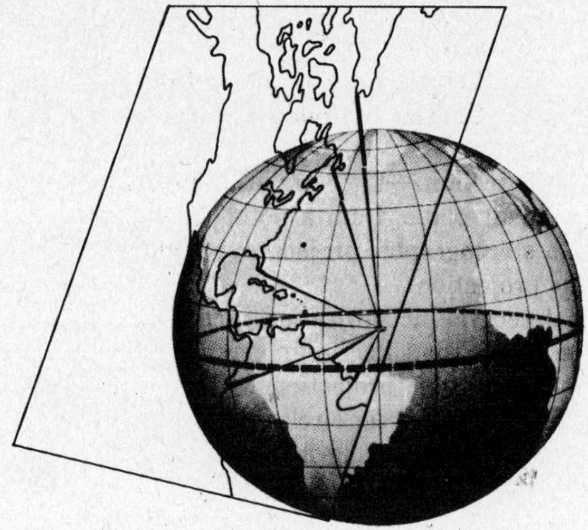

FIGURE 317a.—An oblique gnomonic projection.

oped by Thales about 600 BC. Since the projection is perspective, it can be demonstrated by placing a light at the center of a transparent terrestrial globe and holding a flat surface tangent to the sphere.

For the oblique case the meridians appear as straight lines converging toward the nearer pole. The parallels, except the equator, appear as curves (fig. 317b). As in all azimuthal projections, bearings from the point of tangency are correctly represented. The distance scale, however, changes rapidly. The projection is neither conformal nor equal area. Distortion is so great that shapes, as well as distances and areas, are very poorly represented, except near the point of tangency.

The usefulness of the projection rests upon the one feature that *any* great circle appears on the map as a straight line. This is apparent when it is realized that a great circle is the line of intersection of a sphere and a plane through the center of the sphere, this center being the origin of the projecting rays for the map. This plane intersects any other nonparallel plane, including the tangent plane, in a straight line. It is this one useful feature that gives charts made on this projection the common name **great-circle charts.**

Gnomonic charts published by the Defense Mapping Agency Hydrographic Center bear instructions for determining direction and distance on the charts. The principal

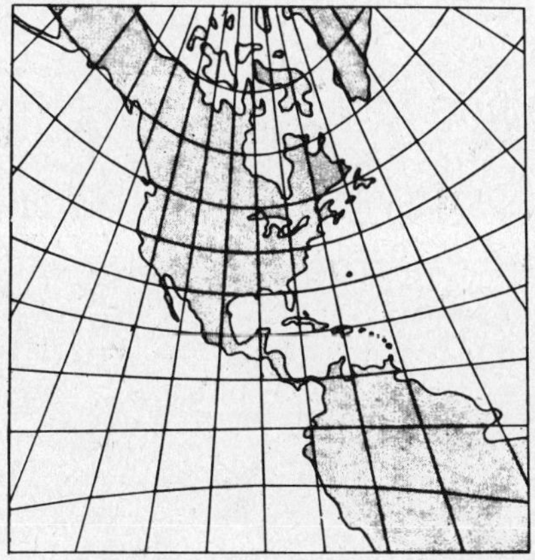

FIGURE 317b.—A gnomonic map with point of tangency at latitude 30° N, longitude 90° W.

navigational use of such charts is for plotting the great-circle track between points, for planning purposes. Points along the track are then transferred, by latitude and longitude, to the navigational chart, usually one on the Mercator projection. The great circle is then followed approximately by following the rhumb line from one point to the next (art. 813).

318. Stereographic projection.—If points on the surface of the earth are projected geometrically onto a tangent plane, from a point on the surface of the earth opposite the point of tangency, a **stereographic** projection results (fig. 318a). It is also called an **azimuthal orthomorphic** projection.

The scale of the stereographic projection increases with distance from the point of tangency, but more slowly than in the gnomonic projection. An entire hemisphere can be shown on the stereographic projection without excessive distortion (fig. 318b). As in other azimuthal projections, great circles through the point of tangency appear as straight lines. All other circles, including meridians and parallels, appear as circles or arcs of circles.

The principal navigational use of the stereographic projection is for charts of the polar regions and devices for mechanical or graphical solution of the navigational triangle.

319. Orthographic projection.—If terrestrial points are projected geometrically from infinity (projecting lines parallel) to a tangent plane, an **orthographic** projection results (fig. 319a). This projection is neither conformal nor equal area and has no advantages as a map projection. Its principal navigational use is in the field of navigational astronomy, where it is useful for illustrating or graphically solving the navigational triangle and for illustrating celestial coordinates. If the plane is tangent at a point on the equator, the usual case, the parallels (including the equator) appear as straight lines and the meridians as ellipses, except that the meridian through the point of tangency appears as a straight line and the one 90° away as a circle (fig. 319b).

320. Azimuthal equidistant projection.—An azimuthal projection in which the distance scale along any great circle through the point of tangency is constant is called an **azimuthal equidistant** projection. If a pole is the point of tangency, the meridians appear as straight radial lines and the parallels as concentric circles, equally spaced.

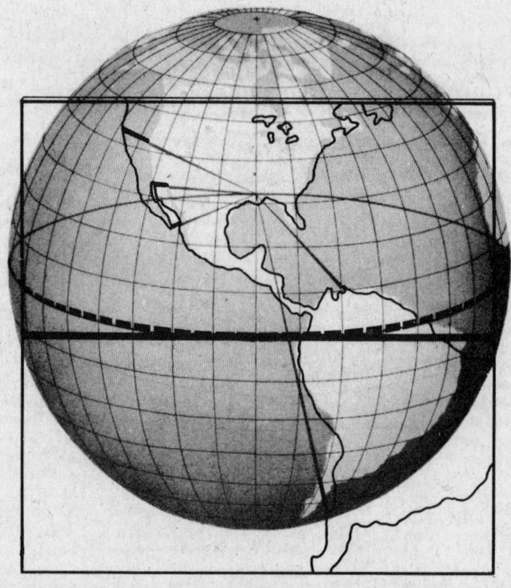

FIGURE 318a.—An equatorial stereographic projection.

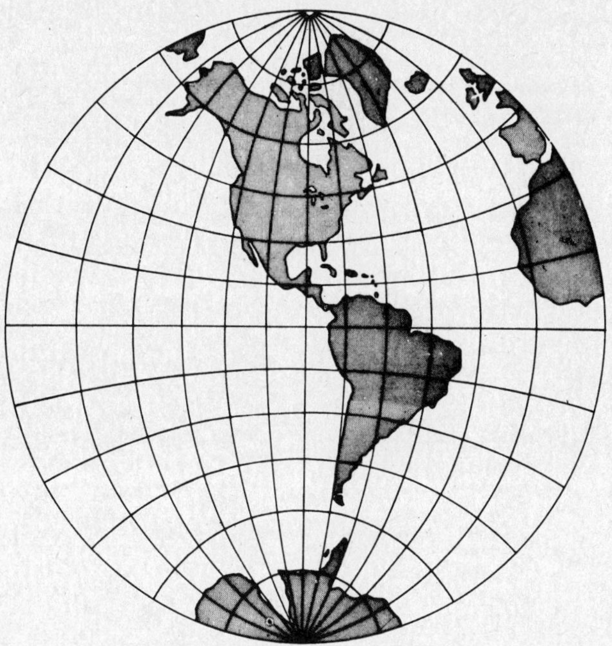

FIGURE 318b.—A stereographic map of the western hemisphere.

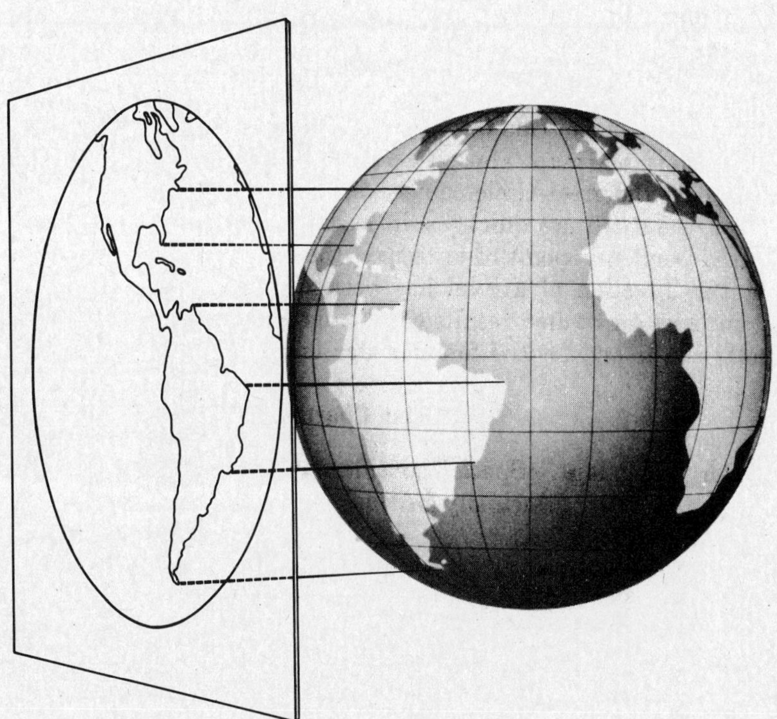

FIGURE 319a.—An equatorial orthographic projection.

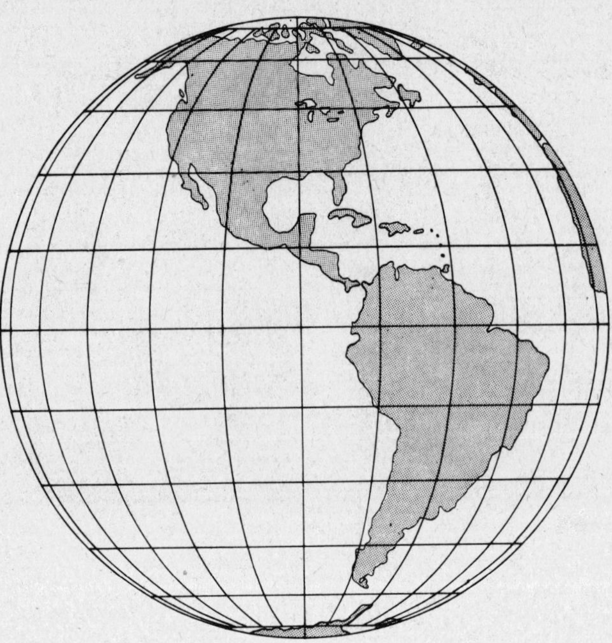

FIGURE 319b.—An orthographic map of the western hemisphere.

If the plane is tangent at some point other than a pole, the concentric circles represent distance from the point of tangency. In this case meridians and parallels appear as curves. The projection can be used to portray the entire earth, the point 180° from the point of tangency appearing as the largest of the concentric circles. The projection is neither conformal nor equal area, nor is it perspective. Near the point of tangency the distortion is small, but it increases with distance until shapes near the opposite side of the earth are unrecognizable (fig. 320).

The projection is useful because it combines the three features of being azimuthal, having a constant distance scale from the point of tangency, and permitting the entire earth to be shown on one map. Thus, if an important harbor or airport is selected as the point of tangency, the great-circle course, distance, and track from that point to any other point on the earth are quickly and accurately determined. For communication work at a fixed point, the point of tangency, the path of an incoming signal is at once apparent if the direction of arrival has been determined. The direction to train a directional antenna for desired results can be determined easily. The projection is also used for polar charts and for the familiar star finder and identifier, No. 2102-D (art. 2210).

Polar Charts

321. Polar projections.—Special consideration is given to the selection of projections for polar charts, principally because the familiar projections become special cases with unique features.

In the case of cylindrical projections in which the axis of the cylinder is parallel to the polar axis of the earth, distortion becomes excessive and the scale changes rapidly. Such projections cannot be carried to the poles. However, both the transverse and oblique Mercator projections are used.

Conic projections with their axes parallel to the earth's polar axis are limited in their usefulness for polar charts because parallels of latitude extending through a full 360° of longitude appear as arcs of circles rather than full circles. This is because a

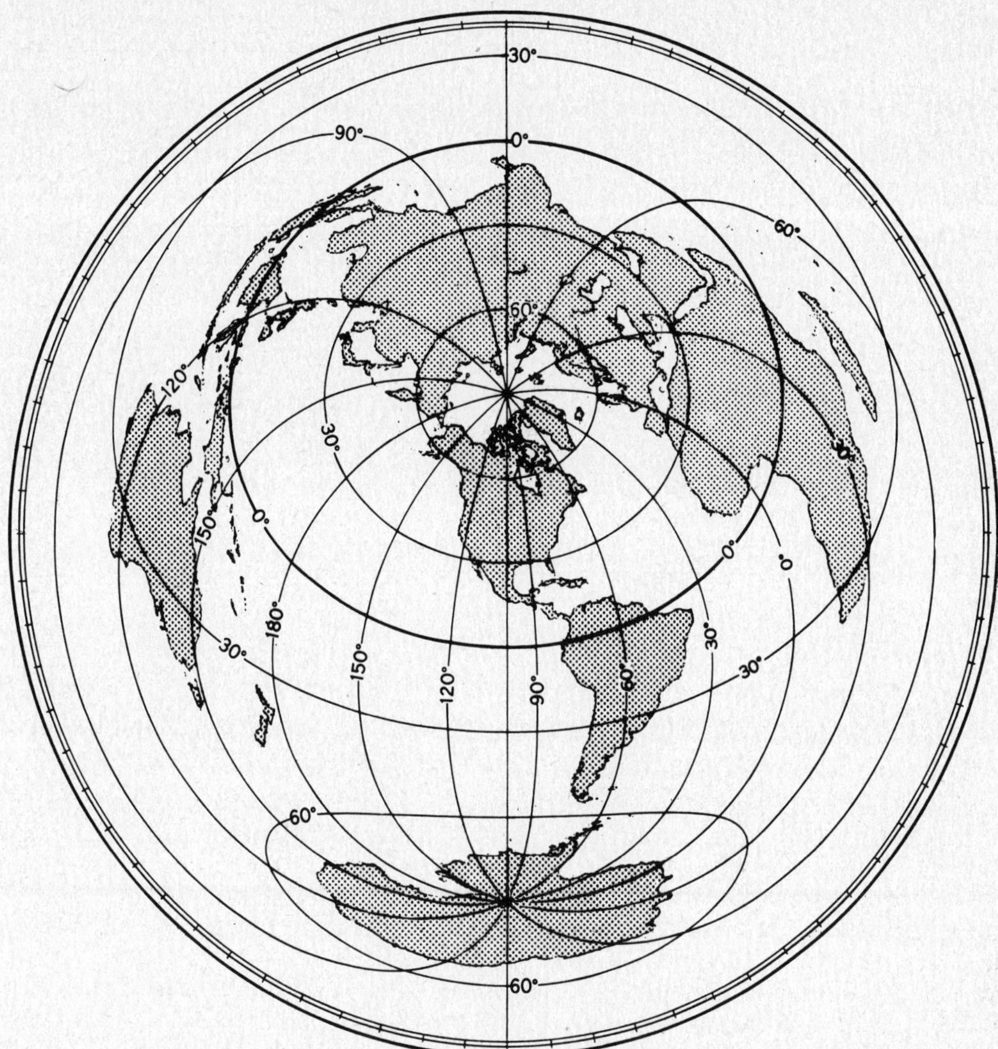

Figure 320.—An azimuthal equidistant map of the world with the point of tangency at latitude 40° N, longitude 100° W.

cone, when cut along an element and flattened, does not extend through a full 360° without stretching or resuming its former conical shape. The usefulness of such projections is also limited by the fact that the pole appears as an arc of a circle instead of a point. However, by using a parallel very near the pole as the higher standard parallel, a conic projection with two standard parallels can be made which requires little stretching to complete the circles of the parallels and eliminate that of the pole. Such a projection, called the **modified Lambert conformal** or **Ney's** projection, is useful for polar charts. It is particularly acceptable to those accustomed to using the ordinary Lambert conformal charts in lower latitudes.

Azimuthal projections are in their simplest form when tangent at a pole, since the meridians are straight lines intersecting at the pole, and parallels are concentric circles with their common center at the pole. Within a few degrees of latitude of the pole they all look essentially alike, but as the distance becomes greater, the spacing of the parallels becomes distinctive in each projection. In the polar azimuthal equidistant it is uniform; in the polar stereographic it increases with distance from the pole until

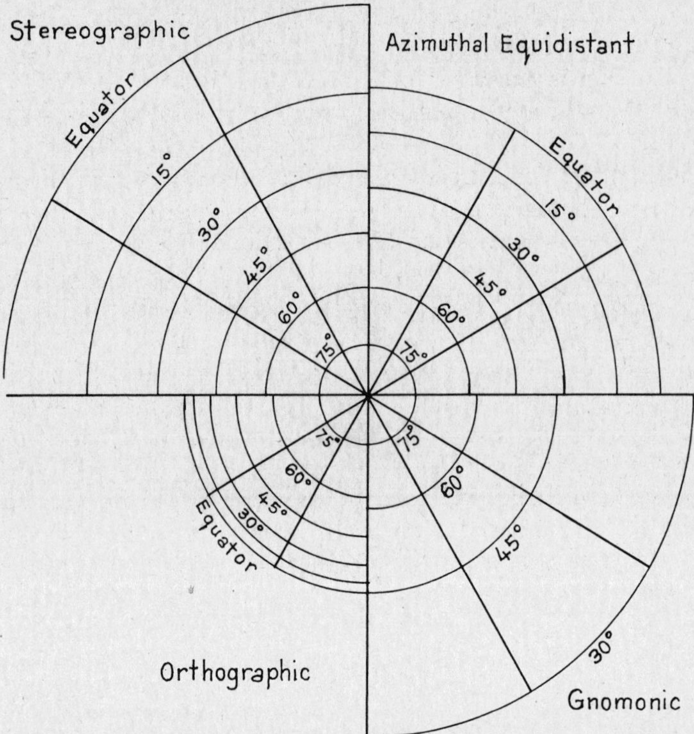

FIGURE 321.—Expansion of polar azimuthal projections.

the equator is shown at a distance from the pole equal to twice the length of the radius of the earth, or about 27% too much; in the polar gnomonic the increase is considerably greater, becoming infinity at the equator; in the polar orthographic it decreases with distance from the pole (fig. 321). All of these but the last are used for polar charts.

322. Selection of a polar projection.—The principal considerations in the choice of a suitable projection for polar navigation are:

1. *Conformality*. It is desirable that angles be correctly represented so that plotting can be done directly on the chart, without annoying corrections.
2. *Great-circle representation*. Since great circles are more useful than rhumb lines in high latitudes, it is desirable that great circles be represented by straight lines.
3. *Scale variation*. Constant scale over an entire chart is desirable.
4. *Meridian representation*. Straight meridians are desirable for convenience and accuracy of plotting, and for grid navigation.
5. *Limits of utility*. Wide limits are desirable to reduce to a minimum the number of projections needed. The ideal would be a single projection for world coverage.

The projections commonly used for polar charts are the transverse Mercator, modified Lambert conformal, gnomonic, stereographic, and azimuthal equidistant. Near the pole there is little to choose between them. Within the limits of practical navigation all are essentially conformal and on all a great circle is nearly a straight line.

As the distance from the pole increases, however, the distinctive features of each projection become a consideration. The transverse Mercator is conformal and its type of distortion is familiar to one accustomed to using a Mercator chart. Distances can be measured in the same manner as on any Mercator chart. The tangent meridian and all straight lines perpendicular to it are great circles. All other great circles, including the meridians, are curves. The departure of a great circle from a straight line becomes a maximum at the outer edges parallel to the tangent meridian, where the straight lines are nearer the pole than the arcs of great circles between the same points. A slight inconvenience in measurement of angles may result from the curvature of the meridians (fig. 322). The projection is excellent for a narrow band along the tangent meridian and for use with automatic navigation equipment generating transverse latitude and transverse longitude.

The modified Lambert conformal projection is virtually conformal over its entire extent, and the amount of its scale distortion is comparatively little if it is carried only to about 25° or 30° from the pole. Beyond this, the distortion increases rapidly. A great circle is very nearly a straight line anywhere on the chart. Distances and directions can be measured directly on the chart in the same manner as on a Lambert conformal chart. However, for highly accurate work this projection is not suitable, for it is not strictly conformal, and great circles are not exactly straight lines.

The polar gnomonic projection is the one polar projection on which great circles are exactly straight lines. The excessive distortion and lack of conformality of this projection make it unsuitable for ordinary navigation.

The polar stereographic projection is conformal over its entire extent, and a great circle differs but little from a straight line. The scale distortion is not excessive for a considerable distance from the pole, but is greater than that of the modified Lambert conformal projection.

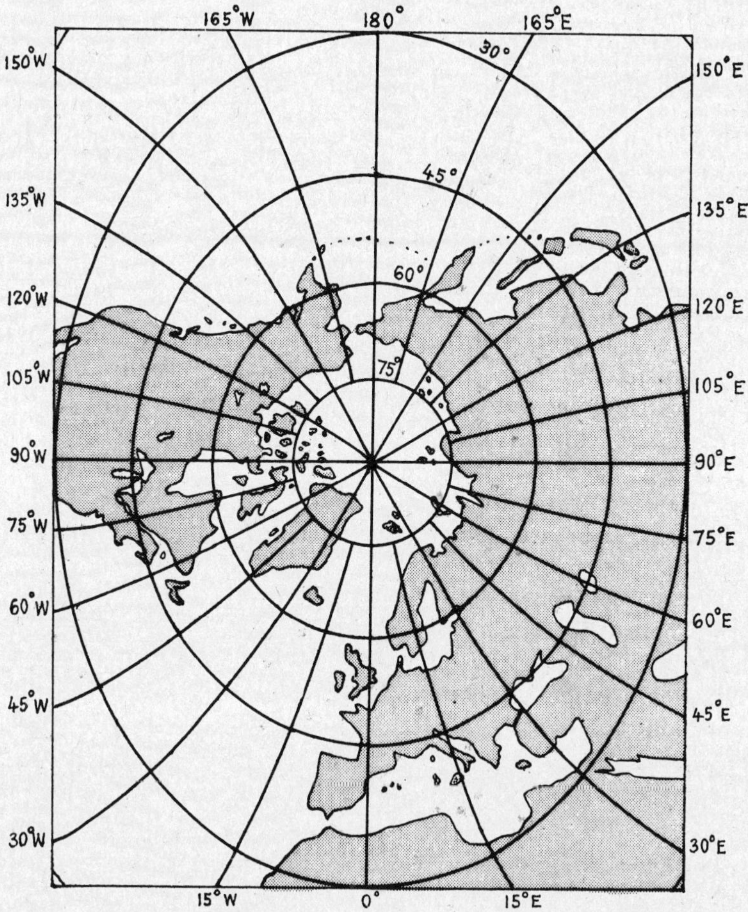

FIGURE 322.—A polar transverse Mercator map with the cylinder tangent at the 90° E-90° W meridian.

The polar azimuthal equidistant projection is useful for showing a large area such as a hemisphere, because there is no expansion along the meridians. However, the projection is not conformal, and distances cannot be measured accurately in any but a north-south direction. Great circles other than the meridians differ somewhat from straight lines. The equator is a circle centered at the pole.

The three projections most commonly used for charts for ordinary navigation near the poles are the transverse Mercator, modified Lambert conformal, and the polar stereographic. When a directional gyro is used as a directional reference, the track of the craft is approximately a great circle. A desirable chart is one on which a great circle is represented as a straight line with a constant scale and with angles correctly represented. These requirements are not met entirely by any single projection, but they are approximated by both the modified Lambert conformal and the polar stereographic. The scale is more nearly constant on the former, but the projection is not strictly conformal. The polar stereographic is conformal, and its maximum scale variation can be reduced by using a plane which intersects the earth at some parallel intermediate between the pole and the lowest parallel, so that that portion within this standard parallel is compressed, and that portion outside is expanded.

The selection of a suitable projection for use in polar regions, as in other areas, depends upon the requirements, which establish relative importance of the various features. For a relatively small area, any of several projections is suitable. For a large area, however, the choice is more critical. If grid directions are to be used, it is important that all units in related operations use charts on the same projection, with the same standard parallels, so that a single grid direction exists between any two points. Nuclear powered submarine operations under the polar icecap have increased the need for grid directions in marine navigation.

Plotting Sheets

323. Definition and use.—A **position plotting sheet** is a plotting sheet designed primarily for plotting the dead reckoning and lines of position obtained from celestial observations or radio aids to navigation. It has the latitude and longitude graticule, and it may have one or more *compass roses* (art. 516) for measuring direction, but little or no additional information. The meridians are usually unlabeled by the publisher so the plotting sheet can be used for any longitude.

Plotting sheets are less expensive to produce than charts and are equally suitable or superior for some purposes. They are used primarily when land, visual aids to navigation, and depth of water are not important.

Any projection can be used for constructing a plotting sheet, but that used for the navigator's charts is customarily employed also for his plotting sheets.

324. Small area plotting sheets.—A Mercator plotting sheet can be constructed by the method explained in article 307. For a relatively small area a good approximation can be more quickly constructed by the navigator by either of two alternative methods based upon a graphical solution of the secant of the latitude, which approximates the expansion.

First method (**fig. 324a**). *Step one.* Draw a series of equally spaced, vertical lines at any spacing desired. These are the meridians; label them at any desired interval, as 1′, 2′, 5′, 10′, 30′, 1°, etc.

Step two. Through the center of the sheet draw a horizontal line to represent the parallel of the mid latitude of the area to be covered, and label it.

Step three. Through any convenient point, such as the intersection of the central meridian and the parallel of the mid latitude, draw a line making an angle with the *horizontal* equal to the mid latitude. In figure 324a this angle is 35°.

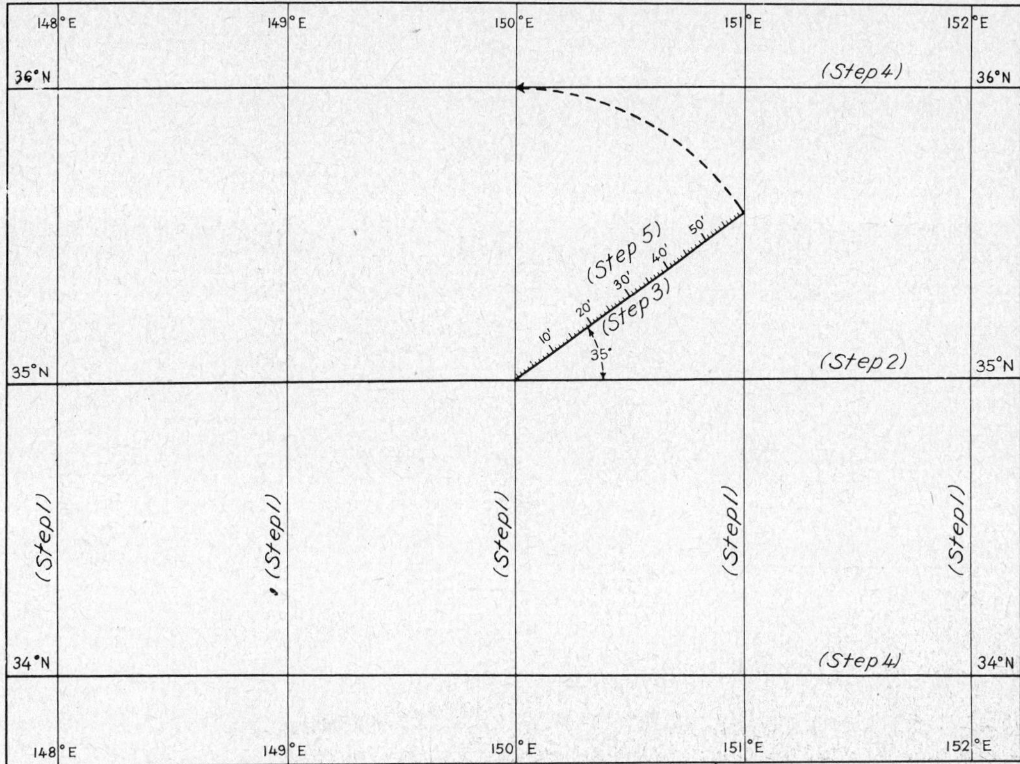

FIGURE 324a.—Small area plotting sheet with selected longitude scale.

Step four. Draw in and label additional parallels. The length of the oblique line between consecutive meridians is the perpendicular distance between consecutive parallels, as shown by the broken arc. The number of minutes of arc between consecutive parallels thus drawn is the same as that between the meridians shown.

Step five. Graduate the oblique line into convenient units. If 1′ is selected, this scale serves as both a latitude and mile scale. It can also be used as a longitude scale by measuring horizontally from a meridian instead of obliquely along the line.

Second method (fig. 324b). *Step one.* At the center of the sheet draw a circle with a radius equal to 1° (or any other convenient unit) of latitude at the desired scale. If a sheet with a compass rose is available, as in figure 324b, the compass rose can be used as the circle and will prove useful for measuring directions. It need not limit the scale of the chart, as an additional concentric circle can be drawn and desired graduations extended to it.

Step two. Draw horizontal lines through the center of the circle and tangent at the top and bottom. These are parallels of latitude; label them accordingly, at the selected interval (as every 1°, 30′, etc.).

Step three. Through the center of the circle draw a line making an angle with the *horizontal* equal to the mid latitude. In figure 324b this angle is 40°.

Step four. Draw in and label the meridians. The first is a vertical line through the center of the circle. The second is a vertical line through the intersection of the oblique line and the circle. Additional meridians are drawn the same distance apart as the first two.

Step five. Graduate the oblique line into convenient units. If 1′ is selected, this scale serves as a latitude and mile scale. It can also be used as a longitude scale by measuring horizontally from a meridian instead of obliquely along the line.

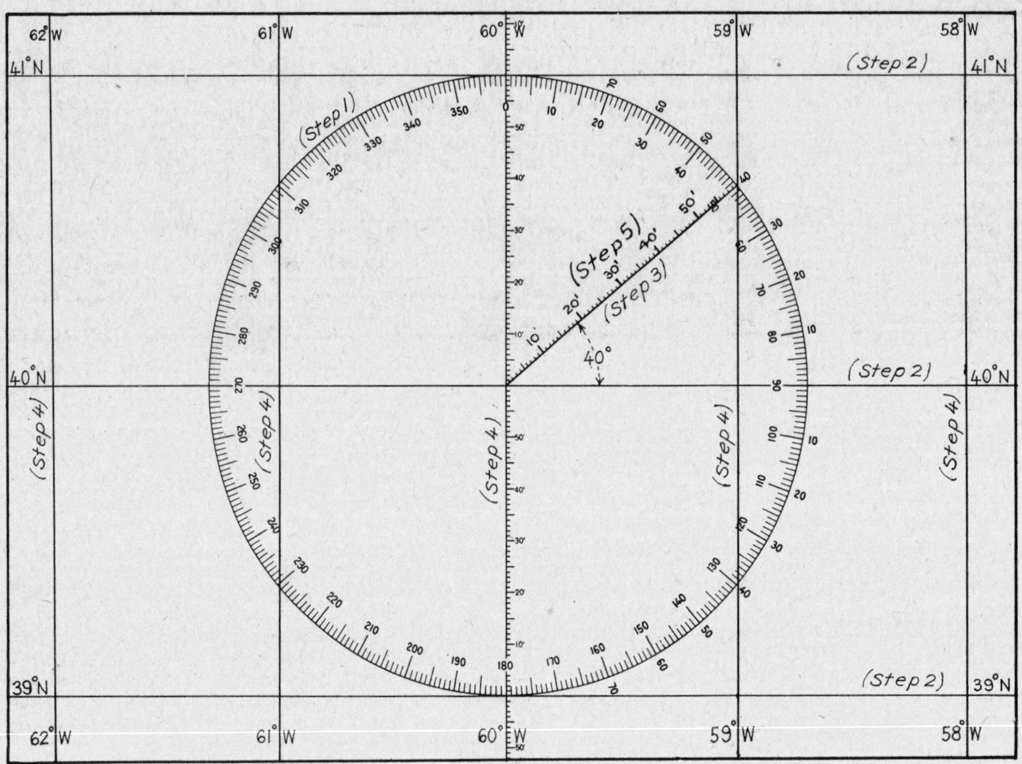

FIGURE 324b.—Small area plotting sheet with selected latitude scale.

The same end result is produced by either method. The first method, starting with the selection of the longitude scale, is particularly useful when the longitude limits of the plotting sheet determine the scale. When the latitude coverage is more important, the second method may be preferable. If a standard size is desired, part of the sheet can be printed in advance, forming what is called a **universal plotting sheet.** This is done by the Defense Mapping Agency Hydrographic Center. In either method a central compass rose might be printed. In the first method the meridians may be shown at the desired interval and the mid parallel may be printed and graduated in units of longitude. In using the sheet it is necessary only to label the meridians and draw the oblique line and from it determine the interval and draw in and label additional parallels. If the central meridian is graduated, the oblique line need not be. In the second method the parallels may be shown at the desired interval, and the central meridian may be printed and graduated in units of latitude. In using the sheet it is necessary only to label the parallels, draw the oblique line and from it determine the interval and draw in and label additional meridians. If the central meridian is graduated, as shown in figure 324b, the oblique line need not be.

Both methods use a constant relationship of latitude to longitude over the entire sheet and both fail to allow for the ellipticity of the earth. For practical navigation these are not important considerations for a small area. If a larger area is to be shown or if more precise results are desired, the method of article 307 should be used.

Grids

325. Purpose and definition of grid.—No system has been devised for showing the surface of the earth *on a flat surface,* without distortion. Moreover, the appearance of any portion of the surface varies with the projection and, in many cases, with the location of the portion with respect to the point or line of tangency. For some purposes (particularly military) it is desirable to be able to identify a location or area by rectangular coordinates, using numbers or letters, or a combination of numbers and letters, without the necessity of indicating the units used or assigning a name (north, south, east, or west), thus reducing the possibility of a mistake. This is accomplished by means of a **grid.** In its usual form this consists of two series of lines which are mutually perpendicular *on the chart,* with suitable designators.

326. Types of grids.—A grid may use the rectangular graticule of the Mercator projection, or a set of arbitrary lines on a particular projection. The most widely used system of the first is called the **World Geographic Referencing System (Georef).** It is merely a method of designating latitude and longitude by a system of letters and numbers instead of by angular measure, and therefore is not strictly a grid, except on a Mercator projection. It is particularly useful for operations extending over a wide area. Examples of the second type of grid are the **Universal Transverse Merctor (UTM) grid,** the **Universal Polar Stereographic (UPS) grid,** and the **Temporary Geographic Grid (TGG).** Since these systems are used primarily by military forces, they are sometimes called **military grids.**

References

Chamberlin, Wellman. *The Round Earth on Flat Paper.* Washington, National Geographic Society, 1947.

Deetz, C. H., and O. S. Adams. *Elements of Map Projection.* 5th ed. U. S. Coast and Geodetic Survey Special Publication No. 68. Washington, U. S. Govt. Print. Off., 1945.

Greenhood, David. *Down to Earth: Mapping for Everybody.* New York, Holiday House, 1944.

Hinks, A. R. *Map Projections.* 2nd ed. London, Cambridge University Press, 1921.

Jameson, A. H., and M. T. M. Ormsby. *Mathematical Geography.* Vol. I, *Elementary Surveying and Map Projection.* London, Pitman, [1942?].

Jervis, W. W. *The World in Maps.* New York, Oxford, 1937.

Mainwaring, James. *An Introduction to the Study of Map Projection.* London, Macmillan, 1942.

Raisz, Erwin. *General Cartography.* New York, McGraw-Hill, 1938.

Steers, J. A. *An Introduction to the Study of Map Projections.* Rev. ed. London, U. of London Press, 1929.

CHAPTER IV

VISUAL AND AUDIBLE AIDS TO NAVIGATION

401. Introduction.—The term **aid to navigation**, as used herein, means any device external to a vessel intended to be of assistance to a navigator in his determination of position or safe course, or to provide him with a warning to dangers or obstructions to navigation. This term includes lighthouses, beacons, lightships, sound signals, buoys, marine radiobeacons, racons, and the medium and long range radionavigation systems. The discussion of the various aids to navigation in this chapter is limited to the visual and audible aids established in the navigable waters of the United States and its possessions.

Aids to navigation are placed at various points along the coast and navigable waterways as markers and guides to mark safe water and to provide navigators with means to determine their position with relation to the land and to hidden dangers. Within the bounds of actual necessity, each aid is designed to be seen or heard so that it provides the necessary system coverage to enable safe transit of a waterway.

As all aids to navigation serve the same general purpose, structural differences, such as those between an unlighted buoy and a lightship, are solely for the purpose of meeting the conditions and requirements of the particular location at which the aid is established.

The maintenance of marine aids to navigation is a function of the United States Coast Guard. This responsibility includes the maintenance of lighthouses, lightships, radiobeacons, racons, Loran, sound signals, buoys, and beacons upon all navigable waters of the United States and its possessions, including the Atlantic and Pacific coasts of the continental United States, the Great Lakes, the Mississippi River and its tributaries, Puerto Rico, the U.S. Virgin Islands, the Hawaiian Islands, Alaska, Trust Territory of the Pacific Islands, and such other places where aids to navigation are required to serve the needs of the armed forces.

Lights on Fixed Structures

402. Lights on fixed structures vary from the tallest lighthouse on the coast, flashing with an intensity of millions of candlepower, to a simple battery-powered lantern on a wooden pile in a small creek. Being in fixed positions enabling accurate charting, lights provide navigators with reliable means to determine their positions with relation to land and hidden dangers during daylight and darkness. The structures are often distinctively colored to facilitate their observation during daylight.

A **major light** is a light of high intensity and reliability exhibited from a fixed structure or on a marine site (except range lights). Major lights include primary seacoast lights and secondary lights. **Primary seacoast lights** are those major lights established for the purpose of making landfalls and coastwise passages from headland to headland. **Secondary lights** are those major lights, other than primary seacoast lights, established at harbor entrances and other locations where high intensity and reliability are required. Major lights are usually located at manned or monitored automated stations.

A **minor light** is an automatic unmanned (unwatched) light on a fixed structure showing usually low to moderate intensity. Minor lights are established in harbors, along channels, rivers, and isolated locations. They usually have the same numbering, coloring, and light and sound characteristics as the lateral system of buoyage (art. 411).

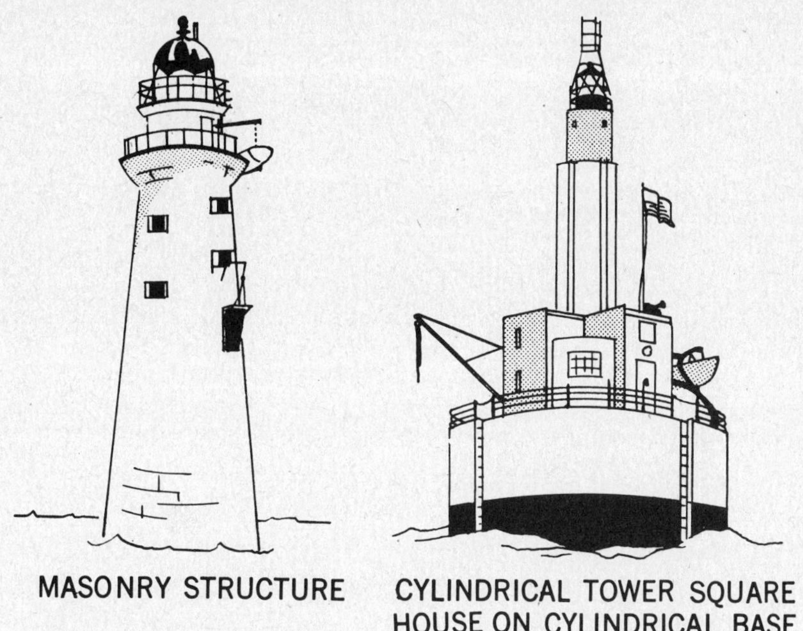

FIGURE 402a.—Typical light structures.

Lighthouses (fig. 402a), all of which exhibit major lights, are placed where they will be of most use: on prominent headlands, at entrances, on isolated dangers, or at other points where it is necessary that mariners be warned or guided. Their principal purpose is to support a light at a considerable height above the water. In many instances, sound signals, radiobeacon equipment, and operating personnel are housed in separate buildings located near the tower. Such a group of facilities is called a **light station.**

Many of the lighthouses which were originally tended by resident keepers are now operated automatically. There are also many automatic lights on smaller structures maintained through periodic visits of Coast Guard cutters or of attendants in charge of a group of such aids. The introduction of new automatic apparatus means that the relative importance of lights cannot be judged on the basis of whether or not they have resident keepers.

FIGURE 402b.—Typical offshore light station.

Offshore light stations and large navigational buoys (art. 408) are replacing lightships (art. 407) where practicable. The offshore light stations in U. S. waters, such as the one shown in figure 402b have helicopter landing surfaces. In the 1975 *Light List*, the CHESAPEAKE LIGHT station is described as a blue tower on a white square superstructure on four black piles. "CHESAPEAKE" is on sides; the piles are floodlighted sunset to sunrise.

Range lights (fig. 402c) are pairs of lights so located as to form a range in line with the center of channels or entrance to a harbor. The rear light is higher than the front light and a considerable distance in back of it, thus enabling the mariner to use the range by keeping the lights in line as he progresses up the channel. Range lights are sometimes used during daylight hours through the use of high intensity lights. Otherwise, the range light structures are equipped with daymarks (art. 412) for ordinary daytime use.

Range lights are usually white, red, or green, and display various characteristics to differentiate them from surrounding lights.

FIGURE 402c.—Range lights.

A **directional light** is a single light which projects a beam of high intensity, separate color, or special characteristic in a given direction. It has limited use for those cases where a two-light range may not be practicable or necessary, and for special applications. The directional light is essentially a narrow sector light with or without adjacent sectors which give information as to the direction of and relative displacement from the narrow sector.

Aeronautical lights, which are lights of high intensity, may be the first lights observed at night from vessels approaching the coast. Those situated near the coast are accordingly listed in the *List of Lights* (art. 1301) in order that the navigator may be able to obtain more complete information concerning their description. These lights are not listed in the U. S. Coast Guard *Light List*.

Aeronautical lights are placed in geographic sequence in the body of the text of the *List of Lights* along with lights for marine navigation. It should be borne in mind, however, that these lights are not designed or maintained for marine navigation, and that they are *subject to changes of which neither lighthouse authorities nor the marine navigator may receive prompt notification.*

Bridges across navigable waters of the United States are generally marked with red, green, and white lights for nighttime navigation. Red lights mark piers and other parts of the bridge. Red lights are also used on drawbridges to show when they are in the closed position. Green lights are used to mark the centerline of navigable channels through fixed bridges. The preferred channel, if there are two or more channels through the bridge, is marked by three white lights in a vertical line above the green light.

Green lights are also used on drawbridges to show when they are in the open position. Because of the variety of drawbridges, the position of the green lights on the bridge will vary according to the type of structure. Navigational lights on bridges are prescribed by regulation.

Bridges infrequently used may be unlighted. In unusual cases the type and method of lighting may be different than normally found.

Drawbridges required to be operated for passage of vessels operate upon sound and light signals given by the vessel and acknowledged by the bridge. These signals are prescribed by regulation.

In addition to lighting, certain bridges may be equipped with sound signals and radar reflectors where unusual geographic or weather conditions require them.

Light Characteristics

403. Characteristics.—Lights are given distinctive characteristics so that one light may be distinguished from another navigational light or from the general background of shore lights or as a means of conveying certain definite information. This distinctiveness may be obtained by giving each light a distinctive sequence of light and dark intervals, having lights that burn steadily and others that flash or occult, or by giving each light a distinctive color, or color sequence. In the light lists, the dark intervals are referred to as **eclipses.** An **occulting light** is a light totally eclipsed at regular intervals, the duration of light always being greater than the duration of darkness. A **flashing light** is a light which flashes at regular intervals, the duration of light always being less than the duration of darkness. An **equal interval light** is a light which flashes at regular intervals, the duration of light always being equal to the duration of darkness. This light is also called an **isophase light.**

404. Light phase characteristics (fig. 404) are the distinctive sequences of light and dark intervals or distinctive sequences in the variations of the luminous intensity of a light. The light phase characteristics of lights which change color do not differ from those of lights which do not change color. A continuous steady light which shows periodic color change is described as an **alternating light.** The alternating characteristic is also used with other light phase characteristics as shown in figure 404.

A *Light List* entry for an **alternating fixed and flashing light** may be given as:

Alt. F.W., F.R. and Fl. R.
90^s (F.W., 59^s, F.R., 14^s,
Fl. R. 3^s (high intensity),
F.R. 14^s).

With each 90^s period the light is first fixed white for 59^s, then fixed red for 14^s, then there is a flash of brilliant red for 3^s, and finally the light is fixed red for 14^s.

A *Light List* entry for a **group flashing light** may be given as:

Gp. Fl. W., 15^s
0.2^s fl., 3.0^s ec.
0.2^s fl., 11.6^s ec.
2 flashes.

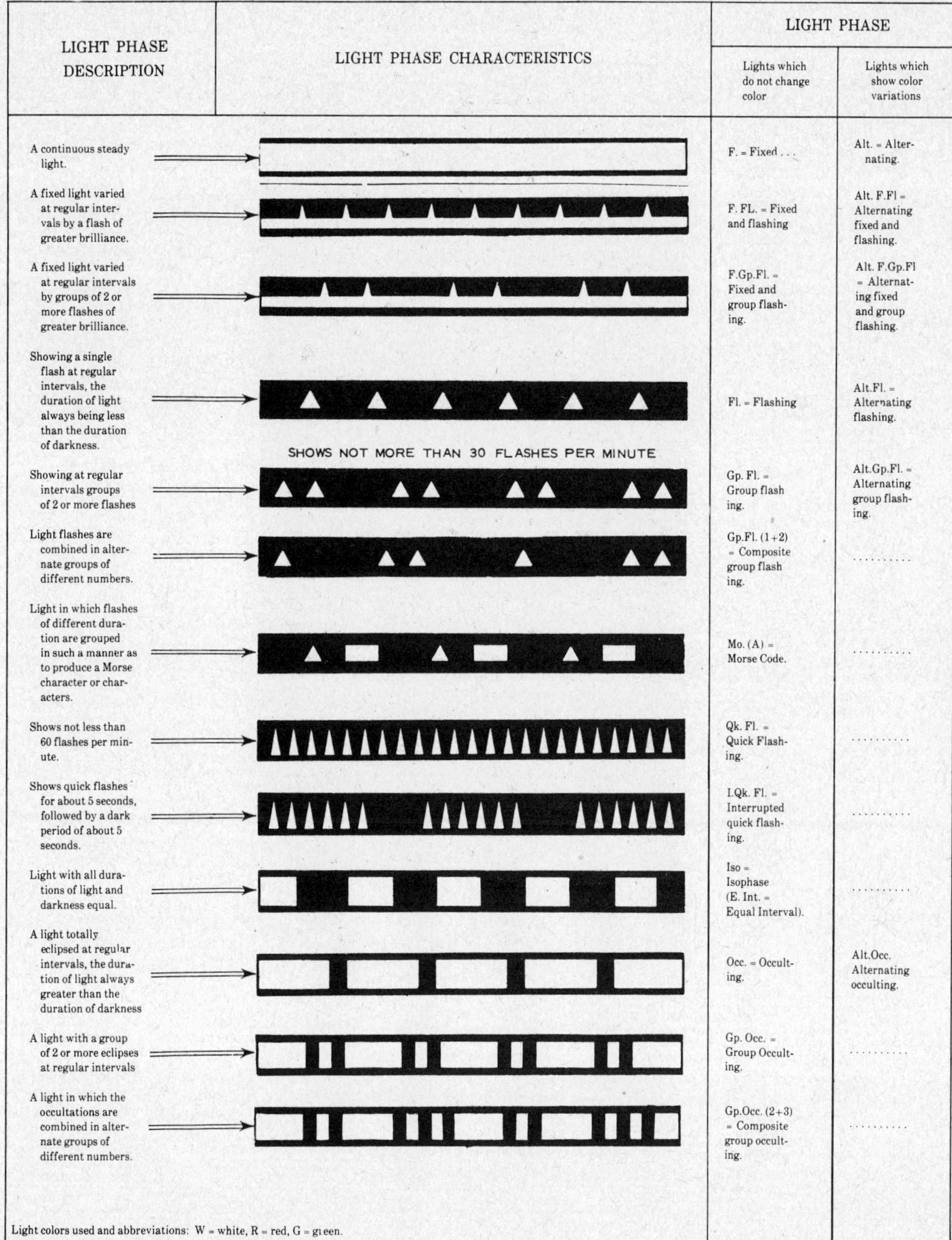

LIGHT PHASE DESCRIPTION	LIGHT PHASE CHARACTERISTICS	LIGHT PHASE	
		Lights which do not change color	Lights which show color variations
A continuous steady light.		F. = Fixed . . .	Alt. = Alternating.
A fixed light varied at regular intervals by a flash of greater brilliance.		F. FL. = Fixed and flashing	Alt. F.Fl = Alternating fixed and flashing.
A fixed light varied at regular intervals by groups of 2 or more flashes of greater brilliance.		F.Gp.Fl. = Fixed and group flashing.	Alt. F.Gp.Fl = Alternating fixed and group flashing.
Showing a single flash at regular intervals, the duration of light always being less than the duration of darkness.	SHOWS NOT MORE THAN 30 FLASHES PER MINUTE	Fl. = Flashing	Alt.Fl. = Alternating flashing.
Showing at regular intervals groups of 2 or more flashes		Gp. Fl. = Group flashing.	Alt.Gp.Fl. = Alternating group flashing.
Light flashes are combined in alternate groups of different numbers.		Gp.Fl. (1+2) = Composite group flashing.	....
Light in which flashes of different duration are grouped in such a manner as to produce a Morse character or characters.		Mo. (A) = Morse Code.	....
Shows not less than 60 flashes per minute.		Qk. Fl. = Quick Flashing.	....
Shows quick flashes for about 5 seconds, followed by a dark period of about 5 seconds.		I.Qk. Fl. = Interrupted quick flashing.	....
Light with all durations of light and darkness equal.		Iso = Isophase (E. Int. = Equal Interval).	....
A light totally eclipsed at regular intervals, the duration of light always greater than the duration of darkness		Occ. = Occulting.	Alt.Occ. Alternating occulting.
A light with a group of 2 or more eclipses at regular intervals		Gp. Occ. = Group Occulting.	....
A light in which the occultations are combined in alternate groups of different numbers.		Gp.Occ. (2+3) = Composite group occulting.	....

Light colors used and abbreviations: W = white, R = red, G = green.

FIGURE 404.—Light phase characteristics.

Within each 15^s period, there is first a white flash of $0^s.2$ duration, the light is eclipsed (extinguished) for 3^s, then there is a white flash of $0^s.2$ duration, and then the light is eclipsed for $11^s.6$ before the sequence begins again.

A *Light List* entry for a **composite group flashing light** may be given as:

Gp. Fl.W. (1+2), 15^s
0.2^s fl., 5.8^s ec.
0.2^s fl., 2.8^s ec.
0.2^s fl., 5.8^s ec.
3 flashes.

Within each 15^s period, there is first a white flash of $0^s.2$ duration, the light is eclipsed for $5^s.8$, then there is a white flash of $0^s.2$ duration, the light is eclipsed for $2^s.8$, and then there is a $0^s.2$ duration white flash followed by a $5^s.8$ eclipse. Thus, the first group consists of a single flash; the second group consists of two flashes. This is indicated by the (1+2) notation.

Most lighted aids to navigation are automatically extinguished during daylight hours by switches activated by daylight. These switches are not of equal sensitivity. Therefore, all lights do not come on or go off at the same time. Mariners should take this fact into account when identifying aids to navigation during twilight periods when some lighted aids are on while others are not.

405. Sectors of colored glass or plastic are placed in the lanterns of certain lights to mark shoals or to warn mariners off the nearby land. Lights so equipped show one color from most directions and a different color or colors over definite arcs of the horizon as indicated in the light lists and upon the charts. A sector changes the color of a light, when viewed from certain directions, but not the characteristic. For example, a flashing white light having a red sector, when viewed from within the sector, will appear flashing red.

Sectors may be but a few degrees in width, marking an isolated rock or shoal, or of such width as to extend from the direction of the deep water toward shore. Bearings referring to sectors are expressed in degrees as observed from a vessel toward the light.

In the majority of cases, water areas covered by red sectors should be avoided, the exact extent of the danger being determined from an examination of the charts. In some cases a narrow sector may mark the best water across a shoal. A narrow sector may also mark a turning point in a channel.

The transition from one color to the other is not abrupt, but changes through an arc of uncertainty of about 2° or less, which depends upon the optical design of the components of the lighting apparatus.

406. Factors affecting visual range and apparent characteristics.—The condition of the atmosphere has a considerable effect upon the distance at which lights can be seen. Sometimes lights are obscured by fog, haze, dust, smoke, or precipitation which may be present at the light or between it and the observer, but not at the observer and possibly unknown to him. On the other hand, refraction may often cause a light to be seen farther than under ordinary circumstances. A light of low intensity will be easily obscured by unfavorable conditions of the atmosphere and less dependence can be placed on its being seen. For this reason, the intensity of a light should always be considered when expecting to sight it in thick weather. Haze and distance may reduce the apparent duration of the flash of a flashing light. In some conditions of the atmosphere white lights may have a reddish hue. In clear weather green lights may have a whitish hue.

It should be remembered that lights placed at great elevations are more frequently obscured by clouds, mist, and fog than those near sea level.

In regions where ice conditions prevail in the winter, the lantern panes of unattended lights may become covered with ice or snow, which will greatly reduce the luminous ranges of the lights and may also cause lights to appear of different color.

The increasing use of brilliant shore lights for advertising, illuminating bridges, and other purposes, may cause navigational lights, particularly those in densely inhabited areas, to be outshone and difficult to distinguish from the background lighting. Mariners are requested by the U. S. Coast Guard to report such cases as outlined above in order that steps may be taken to attempt to improve the conditions.

The "loom" of a powerful light is often seen beyond the geographic range of the light. The loom may sometimes appear sufficiently sharp to obtain a bearing.

At short distances, some *of the brighter* flashing lights may show a faint continuous light between flashes.

It should be borne in mind that, when attempting to sight a light at night, the geographic range is considerably increased from aloft. By noting a star immediately over the light an accurate compass bearing may be indirectly obtained on the light from the navigating bridge although the light is not yet visible from that level.

The distance of an observer from a light cannot be estimated by its apparent intensity. *Always check the characteristics of lights* in order that powerful lights visible in the distance shall not be mistaken for nearby lights showing similar characteristics at lower intensity (such as those on lighted buoys).

If lights are not sighted within a reasonable time after prediction, a dangerous situation may exist requiring prompt resolution or action to insure the safety of the vessel.

The apparent characteristic of a complex light may change with the distance of the observer. For example, a light which actually displays a characteristic of fixed white varied by flashes of alternating white and red (the phases having a decreasing range of detection in the order: flashing white, flashing red, fixed white) may, when first sighted in clear weather, show as a simple flashing white light. As the vessel draws nearer, the red flash will become visible and the characteristic will apparently be alternating flashing white and red. Later, the fixed white light will be seen between the flashes and the true characteristic of the light finally recognized—fixed white, alternating flashing white and red (F.W.Alt.Fl. W. and R.).

There is always the possibility of a light being extinguished. In the case of unattended lights, this condition might not be immediately detected and corrected. The mariner should immediately report this condition. During periods of armed conflict, certain lights may be deliberately extinguished without notice if the situation warrants such action.

Lightships and Large Navigational Buoys

407. Lightships serve the same purposes as lighthouses, being equipped with lights, sound signals, and radiobeacons. They take the form of ships only because they are placed at points where it has been impracticable to build lighthouses. Lightships mark the entrances to important harbors or estuaries and dangerous shoals lying in much frequented waters. They also serve as leading marks for both transocean and coastwise traffic. The two lightships in United States waters are painted red with the name of the station in white on both sides. Superstructures are white; masts, lantern galleries, ventilators, and stacks are painted buff. Relief lightships are painted the same as the regular station ships, with the word "RELIEF" in white letters on the sides.

By night a lightship displays a characteristic masthead light and a less brilliant light on the forestay. The forestay indicates the direction in which the vessel is headed, and hence the direction of the current (or wind), since lightships head into the wind or current. By day a lightship displays the International Code signal of the station when requested, or if an approaching vessel does not seem to recognize it.

It should be borne in mind that most lightships are anchored to a very long scope of chain and, as a result, the radius of their swinging circle is considerable. The chart symbol represents the approximate location of the anchor. Furthermore, under certain conditions of wind and current, they are subject to sudden and unexpected sheers which are certain to hazard a vessel attempting to pass close aboard.

During extremely heavy weather and due to their exposed locations, lightships may be carried off station without the knowledge and despite the best efforts of their crews. The mariner should, therefore, not implicitly rely on a lightship maintaining its precisely charted position during and immediately following severe storms. A lightship known to be off station will secure her light, sound signal, and radiobeacon and fly the International Code signal "LO" signifying "I am not in my correct position."

Station buoys, often called **watch buoys,** are sometimes moored near lightships to mark the approximate station should the lightship be carried away or temporarily

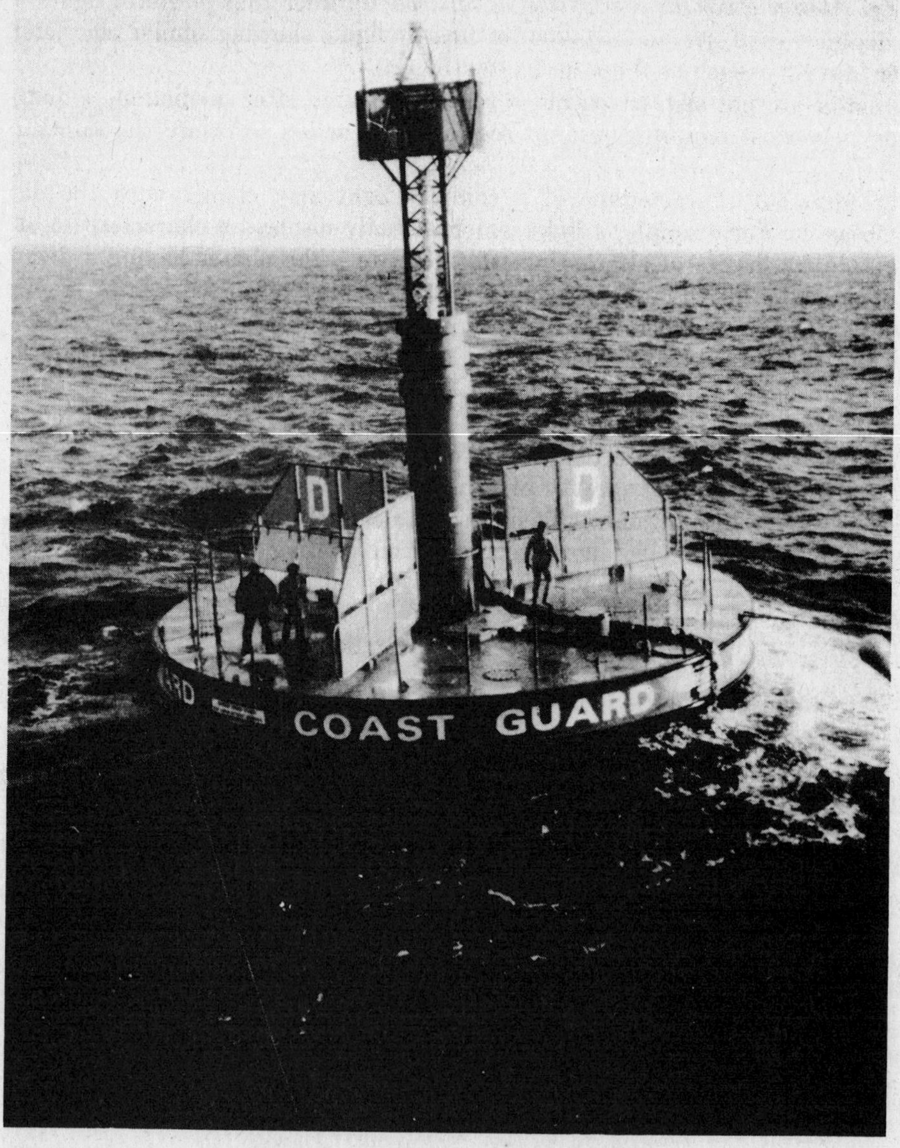

FIGURE 408.—Large navigational buoy.

removed and to give the crew an indication of dragging. Since these buoys are always unlighted and, in some cases, moored as much as a mile from the lightship, the danger of a closely passing vessel colliding with them is always present—particularly so during darkness or periods of reduced visibility.

Experience shows that lightships and offshore light stations cannot be safely used as leading marks to be passed close aboard, but should always be left broad off the course, whenever searoom permits.

408. Large navigational buoys and offshore light stations are replacing lightships where practicable. These 40-foot diameter buoys (fig. 408) may show secondary lights (art. 402) from heights of about 36 feet above the water. In addition to the light, these buoys may mount a radiobeacon and provide sound signals. A station buoy (art. 407) may be moored nearby.

Buoyage and Beaconage

409. Buoys are used to delineate channels, indicate shoals, mark obstructions, and warn the mariner of dangers where the use of fixed aids for such purposes would be uneconomical or impracticable. By their color, shape, number, and light or sound characteristics, buoys provide indications to the mariner as to how he may avoid navigational hazards.

There are many different sizes and types of buoys to meet the wide range of environmental conditions and user requirements. The principle types of buoys used by the United States are lighted, lighted sound, unlighted sound, and unlighted. Some examples of these types are illustrated in figure 409a.

A **lighted buoy** consists of a floating hull with a tower on which a lantern is mounted. Batteries to power the light are contained in special pockets in the buoy hull. To keep the buoy in an upright stable position a large counterweight (fig. 409b) sometimes is extended from a tube attached to the base of the hull below the water surface. The radar reflector, on those buoys so equipped, forms a part of the buoy tower.

Lighted sound buoys have the same general configuration as lighted buoys but are equipped with either a gong, bell, whistle, or electronic horn. Bells and gongs on buoys are sounded by tappers that hang from the tower and swing as the buoys roll in the sea. Bell buoys produce sound of only one tone; gong buoys produce several tones.

Whistle buoys make a loud moaning sound caused by the rising and falling motions of the buoy in the sea. A sound buoy equipped with an electronic horn will produce a pure tone at regular intervals and will operate continually regardless of the sea state.

Unlighted sound buoys have the same general appearance as lighted buoys (except for old whistle buoys) but are not equipped with any light apparatus.

Unlighted buoys have either a can or nun shape. **Can buoys** have a cylindrical shape whereas **nun buoys** have a conical shape usually located on top of a cylindrical shape. Since these buoys are unlighted there is no requirement for battery pockets, and the hull of the buoy forms part of the shape.

Buoys are *floating aids* and therefore require moorings to hold them in position. Typically the mooring consists of chain and a large concrete sinker (fig. 409c). Because buoys are subjected to waves, wind, tides, and other conditions, the moorings must be deployed in lengths greater than the water depth. The scope of chain can be as much as 5 times the depth of water or more but normally will be about 3 times the water depth. For this reason the buoy can be expected to swing in a circle as the current, wind, and wave conditions change.

410. Fallibility of buoys.—It is *imprudent* for a navigator to rely on floating aids to navigation to always maintain their charted positions and to constantly and unerringly display their advertised characteristics.

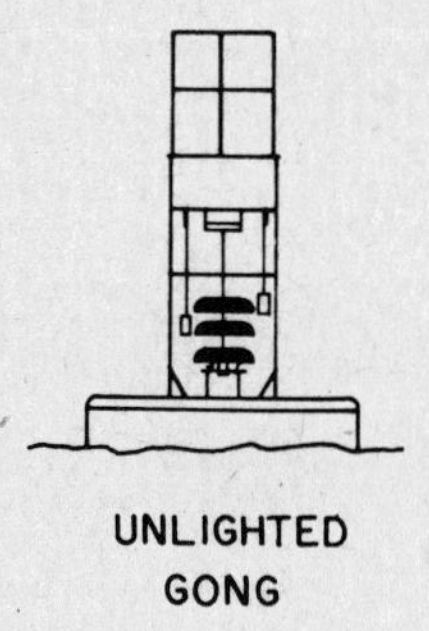

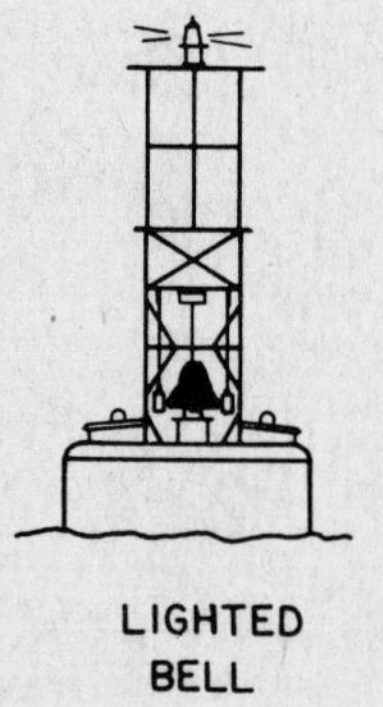

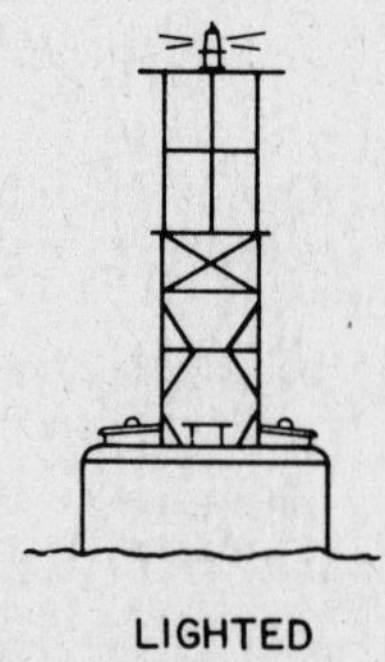

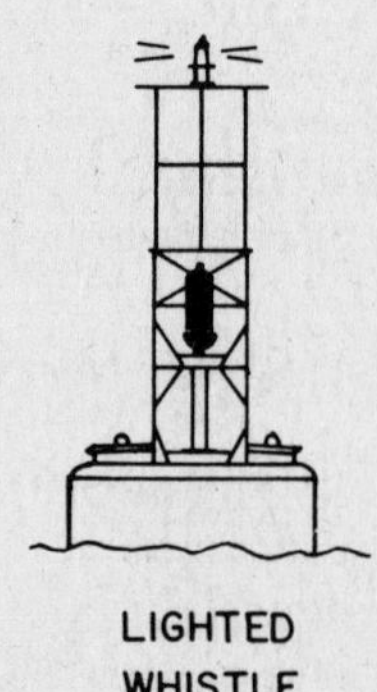

FIGURE 409a.—Principal types of buoys in U. S. waters.

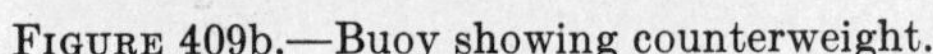
FIGURE 409b.—Buoy showing counterweight.

FIGURE 409c.—Sinkers used to anchor bouys.

The buoy symbol shown on charts indicates the approximate position of the buoy body and the sinker which secures the buoy to the seabed. The approximate position is used because of practical limitations in placing and keeping buoys and their sinkers in exact geographical locations. These limitations include, but are not limited to, inherent inaccuracies in position fixing methods, prevailing atmospheric and sea conditions, the slope of and the material making up the seabed, the fact that buoys are moored to sinkers with more chain than the water depth, and the fact that the positions of the buoys and the sinkers are not under continuous surveillance but are normally checked only during periodic maintenance visits which often occur more than a year apart. The position of the buoy can be expected to shift inside and outside the area shown by the the chart symbol due to the forces of nature. The mariner is also cautioned that buoys are liable to be missing, shifted, overturned, etc. Lighted buoys may be extinguished or sound signals may not function because of ice, running ice, natural causes, collisions, or other accidents.

For these reasons, a prudent mariner must not rely completely upon the position or operation of buoys, but will also navigate using bearings of charted features, structures, and aids to navigation on shore. Further a vessel attempting to pass too close always risks a collision with a yawing buoy or with the obstruction which the buoy marks.

The concept that a wreck buoy always occupies a position directly over the wreck it is intended to mark is erroneous. Buoys must be placed in position by a vessel. It is usually physically impossible for these vessels to maneuver directly over a wreck to place the sinker without incurring serious underwater damage. For this reason, a wreck buoy is usually placed on the seaward or channelward side of a wreck, the proximity thereto being governed by existing conditions. To avoid confusion in some situations, two buoys may be used to mark the wreck. Both may not be located on the seaward or channelward side of the wreck, but the wreck will lie between them. Obviously, the mariner should not attempt to pass between buoys so placed.

Sunken wrecks are not always static. They are sometimes moved away from their buoys by severe sea conditions or other causes. Just as shoals may shift away from the buoys placed to mark them, wrecks may shift away from wreck buoys.

All buoys should, therefore, be regarded as warnings, guides, or aids but not as infallible navigation marks, especially those located in exposed positions. Whenever possible, a mariner should navigate by bearings or angles of reliable and identifiable fixed charted features or landmarks and by soundings rather than by sole reliance on buoys.

411. Buoyage systems.—Most maritime countries use either a **lateral system** of buoyage or the **cardinal system,** or both. In the lateral system, used on all navigable waters of the United States, the coloring, shape, numbering, and lighting of buoys indicate the direction to a danger relative to the course which should be followed. In the cardinal system the coloring, shape, and lighting of buoys indicate the cardinal direction to a danger relative to the buoy itself. The color, shape, lights, and numbers of buoys in the lateral system as used by the United States are determined relative to a direction *from* seaward. Along the *coasts* of the United States, the *clockwise* direction around the country is arbitrarily considered to be the direction "from seaward." Proceeding in a westerly and northerly direction on the Great Lakes (except Lake Michigan), and in a southerly direction on Lake Michigan, is proceeding "from seaward." On the Intracoastal Waterway proceeding in a general southerly direction along the Atlantic coast, and in a general westerly direction along the gulf coast, is considered as proceeding "from seaward." On the Mississippi and Ohio Rivers and their tributaries the aids to navigation characteristics are determined as proceeding from sea toward the head of navigation although local terminology describes "left bank" and "right bank" as proceeding with the flow of the river. Some countries using the lateral system have methods of coloring their buoys and lights opposite to that of the United States.

In United States waters the following distinctive system of identification is used:

Red nun buoys mark the *right* side of channels for an inbound vessel and obstructions which should be kept to starboard. They have *even* numbers which increase from seaward.

Black can buoys mark the *left* side of channels for an inbound vessel and obstructions which should be kept to port. They have *odd* numbers which increase from seaward.

Red and black horizontally banded buoys mark junctions and bifurcations of channels or wrecks or obstructions that can be passed on either side. The color (red or black) of the top band and the shape (nun or can) indicate the side on which the buoy should be passed by a vessel proceeding along the primary channel. If the topmost band is black, the primary channel will be followed by keeping the buoy on the port hand of an *inbound* vessel. If the topmost band is red, the primary channel will be followed by keeping the buoy on the starboard hand of an *inbound* vessel. It may not be possible for an *outbound* vessel to pass on either side of these buoys; the navigational chart should always be consulted to determine how these buoys should be passed by an outbound vessel.

Black and white vertically striped buoys mark the fairway or midchannel and should be passed close aboard. These mid-channel or fairway buoys can have any shape.

Lighted buoys, *spar* buoys, and *sound* buoys are not differentiated by shape to indicate the side on which they should be passed. No special significance is attached to the shapes of these buoys, their purpose being indicated only by the coloring, numbering, or light characteristics.

All *solid red* and *solid black* buoys are numbered, the red buoys bearing even numbers and the black buoys bearing odd numbers, the numbers for each increasing from seaward. The numbers are kept in approximate sequence on both sides of the channel by omitting numbers where required. Buoys of other colors are not numbered; however, a buoy of any other color may be lettered for the purpose of identification.

Lights. Red lights are used only on red buoys and buoys with a red band at the top, green lights are used only on black buoys and buoys with a black band at the top. White lights are used without any color significance. Lights on red or black buoys are always regularly flashing or regularly occulting. Quick flashing lights are used when a light of distinct cautionary significance is desired, as at a sharp turn or constriction in the channel. Interrupted quick flashing lights are used on red and black horizontally banded buoys. White Morse A flashing lights are used on midchannel buoys.

Special purpose buoys. White buoys mark anchorages. Yellow buoys mark quarantine anchorages. White buoys with green tops are used in dredging and survey operations. Black and white horizontally banded buoys mark fish net areas. Yellow and black vertically striped buoys mark seadromes. White and international orange banded, either horizontally or vertically, are used for special purposes to which neither the lateral system colors nor the other special purpose colors apply. The shape of special purpose buoys has no significance. They are not numbered but may be lettered. They may display any color light except red or green. Only fixed, occulting, or Slow-Flash A characteristics are used.

Wreck buoys are generally placed on the seaward or channel side, as near the wreck as conditions permit. To avoid confusion in some situations, two buoys may be used to mark the wreck. The possibility of the wreck having shifted position due to sea action since the buoy was placed should not be overlooked.

Station buoys are placed close to some lightships and important buoys to mark the approximate position of the station. Such buoys are colored and numbered the same as the regular aid, lightship station buoys having the letters "LS" above the initials of the station. If a station is marked with an additional station buoy, and the two buoys are not found close together, it is an indication that at least one of the buoys has moved. However, it is not an indication as to which buoy has moved.

Minor lights and daybeacons (art. 412) used to mark the sides of channels are given numbers and characteristics in accordance with the lateral system of buoyage.

Certain aids to navigation are fitted with light reflecting material (reflectors) to assist in their location in darkness. The colors of such reflectors have the same lateral significance as the color of lights.

Certain aids to navigation may be fitted with, or have incorporated in their design, radar reflectors designed to enhance their ability to reflect radar energy. In general, these reflectors will materially improve the aids for use by vessels equipped with radar.

412. Beacons are fixed aids to navigation placed on shore or on marine sites. If unlighted, the beacon is referred to as a **daybeacon.** A daybeacon is identified by its color and the color, shape, and number of its daymark. The simplest form of daybeacon consists of a single pile with a daymark affixed at or near its top (fig. 412).

Daybeacons may be used instead of range lights (art. 402) to form a **range** (art. 1005).

Daymarks serve to make aids to navigation readily visible and easily identifiable against daylight viewing backgrounds. For example, the distinctive color pattern and shape of a lighthouse aid identification during the daytime as does the color and shape of a buoy. The size of the daymark that is required to make the aid conspicuous depends upon how far the aid must be seen. On those structures which do not by themselves present an adequate viewing area to be seen at the required distance, the

FIGURE 412.—Daybeacon.

aid is made more visible by affixing a daymark to the structure. These daymarks have a distinctive shape and color depending upon the purpose of the aid. Most daymarks also display numbers or letters so that the daymark can be more readily identified as a particular aid. The numbers and letters, as well as portions of most daymarks (and portions of unlighted buoys) are made to be retro-reflective to enhance their illumination by the mariner.

Increasing amounts of information are conveyed by a daymark as the mariner approaches. At the detection distance, the daymark will convey only the information of its existence; it will be just detectable from its background. At the recognition distance, the daymark can be recognized as an aid to navigation. At this distance the distinctive shape or color pattern is recognizable. At the identification distance, when the number or letter can be read, the daymark can be identified as a particular aid.

The detection, recognition, and identification distances vary widely for any particular daymark depending upon the viewing conditions. This is an inherent limitation of any visual signal but is especially true for passive visual signals which utilize the sun as the source for their signal energy. The reflectivity of the daymark surface varies with the angle of the sun relative to the daymark. This causes the luminance of the daymark to vary. The detection, recognition, and identification distances depend upon the relative difference between the luminance of the daymark and that of the background, the position of the sun relative to the observer, and the meteorological visibility.

Beginning in 1975, a revised system of daymarks is gradually being implemented in the United States. The significant changes include the following:

1. On port side daymarks, green is used in lieu of the colors black or white; green numbers and letters are used.

2. On starboard side daymarks, red numbers and letters are used in lieu of white numbers and letters.

3. On ICW daymarks (art. 415), a yellow horizontal reflective strip is used in lieu of a yellow reflective border as the marking.

4. On junction daymarks, green is used in lieu of black in the color pattern.

Sound Signals

413. Sound signals.—Most lighthouses, light platforms, and lightships and some minor light structures and buoys are equipped with sound-producing instruments to aid the mariner in periods of low visibility.

Charts and light lists of the particular area should be consulted for positive identification. Caution: buoys fitted with a bell, gong, or whistle and actuated by wave motion may produce no sound when the sea is calm. Their positive identification is not always possible.

Any sound-producing instrument operated in time of fog from a definite point shown on the charts, such as a lighthouse, lightship, or buoy, serves as a useful fog signal. To be effective as an aid to navigation, a mariner must be able to identify it and to know from what point it is sounded.

At all lighthouses and lightships equipped with sound signals, these signals are operated by mechanical or electrical means and are sounded during periods of low visibility, providing the desirable feature of positive identification.

The characteristics of mechanized signals are varied blasts and silent periods. A definite time is required for each signal to perform a complete cycle of changes. Where the number of blasts and the total time for a signal to complete a cycle is not sufficient for positive identification, reference may be made to details in the *Light List* regarding the exact length of each blast and silent interval. The various types of sound signals also differ in tone, and this facilitates recognition of the respective stations.

Diaphones produce sound by means of a slotted piston moved back and forth by compressed air. Blasts may consist of two tones of different pitch, in which case the first part of the blast is high and the last of a low pitch. These alternate-pitch signals are called "two-tone."

Diaphragm horns produce sound by means of a disc diaphragm vibrated by compressed air or electricity. Duplex or triplex horn units of differing pitch produce a chime signal.

Sirens produce sound by means of either a disc or a cup-shaped rotor actuated by compressed air, steam, or electricity.

Whistles produce sound by compressed air emitted through a circumferential slot into a cylindrical bell chamber.

Bells are sounded by means of a hammer actuated by a descending weight, compressed gas or electricity.

414. Limitations of sound signals.—Sound signals depend upon the transmission of sound through air. As aids to navigation, they have limitations that should be considered. Sound travels through the air in a variable and frequently unpredictable manner.

It has been clearly established that:

1. Sound signals are heard at greatly varying distances and that the distance at which a sound signal can be heard may vary with the bearing of the signal and may be different on occasion.

2. Under certain conditions of the atmosphere, when a sound signal has a combination high and low tone, it is not unusual for one of the tones to be inaudible. In the case of sirens, which produce a varying tone, portions of the blast may not be heard.

3. There are occasionally areas close to the signal in which it is wholly inaudible. This is particularly true when the sound signal is screened by intervening land or other obstruction, or the signal is on a high cliff.

4. A fog may exist a short distance from a station and not be observable from it, so that the signal may not be in operation.

5. Some sound signals cannot be started at a moment's notice.

6. Even though a sound signal may not be heard from the deck or bridge of a ship when the engines are in motion, it may be heard when the ship is stopped, or from a quiet position. Sometimes it may be heard from aloft though not on deck.

7. The loudness of the sound emitted by a sound signal may be greater at a distance than in the immediate proximity.

All these considerations point to the necessity for the utmost caution when navigating near land in a fog. Mariners are therefore warned that sound signals can never be implicitly relied upon, and that the practice of taking soundings of the depth of water should never be neglected. Particular attention should be given to placing lookouts in positions in which the noises in the ship are least likely to interfere with hearing a sound signal. Sound signals are valuable as warnings but the mariner should not place implicit reliance upon them in navigating his vessel. They should be considered solely as warning devices.

Emergency sound signals are sounded at some of the light and fog signal stations when the main and stand-by sound signal is inoperative. Some of these emergency sound signals are of a different type and characteristic than the main sound signal. The characteristics of the emergency sound signals are listed in the *Light List*.

The mariner must not assume:

1. That he is out of ordinary hearing distance because he fails to hear the sound signal.

2. That, because he hears a sound signal faintly, he is at a great distance from it.

3. That he is near to it because he hears the sound plainly.

4. That the distance from and the intensity of a sound on any one occasion is a guide to him for any future occasion.

5. That the sound signal is not sounding because he does not hear it, even when in close proximity.

6. That the sound signal is in the direction the sound appears to come from.

415. Intracoastal Waterway aids to navigation.—The Intracoastal Waterway (ICW) runs parallel to the Atlantic and gulf coasts from Manasquan Inlet on the New Jersey shore to the Mexican border. Aids marking these waters have some portion of them marked with yellow as shown in Chart No. 1. Otherwise, the coloring and numbering of buoys and beacons follow the same system as that in other U. S. waterways.

In order that vessels may readily follow the Intracoastal Waterway route where it coincides with another marked waterway such as an important river, special markings are employed. These special markings are applied to the buoys or other aids which already mark the river or waterway for other traffic. These aids are then referred to as "Dual Purpose" aids. The marks consist of a yellow square or a yellow triangle, placed on a conspicuous part of the dual purpose aid. The yellow square, in outline similar to a can buoy, indicates that the aid on which it is placed should be kept on the left hand when following the Intracoastal Waterway down the coast. The yellow triangle has the same meaning as a nun; it should be kept on the right side. Where such dual purpose marking is employed, the mariner following the Intracoastal Waterway disregards the color and shape of the aid on which the mark is placed, being guided solely by the shape of the yellow mark.

416. Mississippi River system.—Aids to navigation on the Mississippi River and its tributaries in the Second Coast Guard District and parts of the Eighth Coast Guard District generally conform to the lateral system of buoyage. The following differences are significant:

1. Buoys are not numbered.

2. The numbers on lights and daybeacons do not have lateral significance; they indicate the mileage from a designated point downstream, normally the river mouth.

3. Flashing lights on the left side proceeding upstream show single green or white flashes while those on the right side show double (group flashing) red or white flashes.

4. "Crossing daymarks" are used to indicate where the channel crosses from one side of the river to the other.

417. The Uniform State Waterway Marking System (**USWMS**) was developed jointly by the U. S. Coast Guard and state boating administrators to assist the small craft operator in those state waters marked by participating states. The USWMS consists of two categories of aids to navigation. One is a system of aids to navigation, generally compatible with the Federal lateral system of buoyage, to supplement the federal system in state waters. The other is a system of regulatory markers to warn the small craft operator of dangers or to provide general information and directions.

On a well-defined channel, including a river or other relatively narrow, natural or improved waterway, solid colored red and black buoys are established in pairs (called "gates"), one on each side of the navigable channel which they mark, and opposite to each other to inform the user that the channel lies between the buoys and that he should pass between the buoys. The buoy which marks the left side of the channel viewed looking upstream or toward the head of navigation is colored all black; the buoy which marks the right side of the channel is colored all red.

On an irregularly-defined channel, solid colored buoys may be staggered on alternate sides of the channel but spaced at sufficiently close intervals to inform the user that the channel lies between the buoys and that he should pass between the buoys.

When there is no well-defined channel or when a body of water is obstructed by objects whose nature or location is such that the obstruction can be approached by a vessel from more than one direction, aids to navigation having cardinal meaning may be used. The aids conforming to the cardinal system consist of three distinctly colored buoys:

1. A white buoy with a red top is used to indicate to a vessel operator that he must pass to the south or west of the buoy.

2. A white buoy with a black top is used to indicate to a vessel operator that he must pass to the north or east of the buoy.

3. A buoy showing alternate vertical red and white stripes is used to indicate to a vessel operator that an obstruction to navigation extends from the nearest shore to the buoy and that he must not pass between the buoy and the nearest shore.

The shape of buoys has no significance in the USWMS.

Regulatory buoys are colored white with international orange horizontal bands completely around the buoy circumference. One band is at the top of the buoy with a second band just above the waterline of the buoy so that both orange bands are clearly visible from approaching vessels.

Geometric shapes are placed on the white portion of the buoy body and are colored international orange. The authorized geometric shapes and meanings associated with them are as follows:

1. A vertical open faced diamond shape means danger.

2. A vertical open faced diamond shape having a cross centered in the diamond means that vessels are excluded from the marked area.

3. A circular shape means that vessels in the marked area are subject to certain operating restrictions.

4. A square or rectangular shape indicates that directions or information is contained inside.

Regulatory markers consist of square and rectangular shaped signs displayed from a fixed structure. Each sign is white with an international orange border. Geometric shapes with the same meanings as those displayed on buoys are centered on the sign boards. The geometric shape displayed on a regulatory marker is intended to convey specific meaning to a vessel operator—whether or not he should stay well clear of the marker or may safely approach the marker in order to read any wording on the marker.

418. Private aids to navigation are those aids not established and maintained by the U. S. Coast Guard. Private aids include those established by other federal agencies with prior U. S. Coast Guard approval, those aids to navigation on marine structures or other works which the owners are legally obligated to establish, maintain, and operate as prescribed by the U. S. Coast Guard, and those aids which are merely desired, for one reason or another, by the individual, corporation, state or local government, or other body that has established the aid with U. S. Coast Guard approval.

Before any private aid to navigation consisting of a fixed structure is placed in the navigable waters of the United States, authorization to erect such structure shall first be obtained from the District Engineer, U. S. Army Corps of Engineers, in whose district the aid will be located.

Private aids to navigation are similar to the aids established and maintained by the U. S. Coast Guard, but are specially designated on the chart and *Light List*.

Although private aids to navigation are inspected periodically by the U. S. Coast Guard, the mariner should exercise special caution when using them for general navigation.

419. Protection by law.—All aids to navigation, including private aids, are protected by law (14 USC 83). The *Code of Federal Regulations* (33 CFR 70) refers.

It is unlawful to take possession of or make use of for any purpose, or build upon, alter, deface, destroy, move, injure, obstruct by fastening vessels thereto or otherwise, or in any manner whatever impair the usefulness of any aid to navigation established and maintained by the United States or with approval of the U. S. Coast Guard.

Whenever any vessel collides with an aid to navigation established and maintained by the United States or any private aid established or maintained in accordance with 33 CFR 64, 67, or 68, or is connected with any such collision, it shall be the duty of the person in charge of such vessel to report the accident to the nearest Officer in Charge, Office of Marine Inspection, U. S. Coast Guard.

CHAPTER V

THE NAUTICAL CHART

General Information

501. Introduction.—A nautical chart is a conventional graphic representation, on a plane surface, of a navigable portion of the surface of the earth. It shows the depth of water by numerous soundings, and sometimes by soundings and depth contours, the shoreline of adjacent land, topographic features that may serve as landmarks, aids to navigation, dangers, and other information of interest to navigators. It is designed as a work sheet on which courses may be plotted, and positions ascertained. It assists the navigator in avoiding dangers and arriving safely at his destination. The nautical chart is one of the most essential and reliable aids available to the navigator.

502. Projections.—Nearly all nautical charts used for ordinary purposes of navigation are constructed on the Mercator projection (art. 305). Large-scale harbor charts are sometimes constructed on the transverse Mercator projection. Charts for special purposes, such as great-circle sailing or polar navigation, are on appropriate projections; great-circle sailing charts are usually on the gnomonic projection (art. 317); polar charts are often on the polar stereographic projection (art. 318). The principal projections, with their navigational uses, are discussed in chapter III.

503. Scale.—The *scale* of a chart is the ratio of a given distance on the chart to the actual distance which it represents on the earth. It may be expressed in various ways. The most common are:

A simple ratio or fraction known as the **representative fraction.** For example, 1:80,000 or $\frac{1}{80,000}$ means that one unit (such as an inch) on the chart represents 80,000 of the same unit on the surface of the earth. This scale is sometimes called the **natural** or **fractional scale.**

A statement of that distance on the earth shown in one unit (usually an inch) on the chart, or vice versa. For example, "30 miles to the inch" means that 1 inch on the chart represents 30 miles of the earth's surface. Similarly, "2 inches to a mile" indicates that 2 inches on the chart represent 1 mile on the earth. This is sometimes called the **numerical scale.**

Graphic scale. A line or bar may be drawn at a convenient place on the chart and subdivided into nautical miles, yards, etc. All charts vary somewhat in scale from point to point, and in some projections the scale is not the same in all directions about a single point. A single subdivided line or bar for use over an entire chart is shown only when the chart is of such scale and projection that the scale varies a negligible amount over the chart, usually one of about 1:75,000 or larger. Since 1 minute of latitude is very nearly equal to 1 nautical mile, the latitude scale serves as an approximate graphical scale. On most nautical charts the east and west borders are subdivided to facilitate distance measurements.

On a Mercator chart the scale varies with the latitude. This is noticeable on a chart covering a relatively large distance in a north-south direction. On such a chart the scale at the latitude in question should be used for measuring distances.

Of the various methods of indicating scale, the graphical method is normally available in some form on the chart. In addition, the scale is customarily stated on charts on which the scale does not change appreciably over the chart.

The ways of expressing the scale of a chart are readily interchangeable. For instance, in a nautical mile there are about 6,076.11549 feet or $6{,}076.11549 \times 12 = 72{,}913.39$ inches. If the natural scale of a chart is 1:80,000, one inch of the chart represents 80,000 inches of the earth, or a little more than a mile. To find the exact amount, divide the scale by the number of inches in a mile, or $\frac{80{,}000}{72{,}913.39} = 1.097$. Thus, a scale of 1:80,000 is the same as a scale of 1.097 (or approximately 1.1) miles to an inch. Stated another way, there are $\frac{72{,}913.39}{80{,}000} = 0.911$ (approximately 0.9) inch to a mile. Similarly, if the scale is 60 nautical miles to an inch, the representative fraction is 1: (60 × 72, 913.39) = 1:4,374,803. Table 9 provides the scale equivalents.

A chart covering a relatively large area is called a *small-scale* chart and one covering a relatively small area is called a *large-scale* chart. Since the terms are relative, there is no sharp division between the two. Thus, a chart of scale 1:100,000 is large scale when compared with a chart of 1:1,000,000 but small scale when compared with one of 1:25,000.

504. Chart classification by scale.—Charts are constructed on many different scales, ranging from about 1:2,500 to 1:14,000,000 (and even smaller for some world charts). Small-scale charts covering large areas are used for planning and for offshore navigation. Charts of larger scale, covering smaller areas, should be used as the vessel approaches pilot waters. Several methods of classifying charts according to scale are in use in various nations. The following classifications of nautical charts are those used by the National Ocean Survey:

Sailing charts are the smallest scale charts used for planning, fixing position at sea, and for plotting the dead reckoning while proceeding on a long voyage. The scale is generally smaller than 1:600,000. The shoreline and topography are generalized and only offshore soundings, the principal navigational lights, outer buoys, and landmarks visible at considerable distances are shown.

General charts are intended for coastwise navigation outside of outlying reefs and shoals. The scales range from about 1:150,000 to 1:600,000.

Coast charts are intended for inshore coastwise navigation where the course may lie inside outlying reefs and shoals, for entering or leaving bays and harbors of considerable width, and for navigating large inland waterways. The scales range from about 1:50,000 to 1:150,000 (see Arco Nautical Chart).

Harbor charts are intended for navigation and anchorage in harbors and small waterways. The scale is generally larger than 1:50,000.

In the classification system used by the Defense Mapping Agency Hydrographic Center, the sailing charts are incorporated in the general charts classification (smaller than about 1:150,000); those coast charts especially useful for approaching more confined waters (bays, harbors) are classified as **approach charts.**

505. Accuracy.—The accuracy of a chart depends upon:

1. *Thoroughness and up-to-dateness of the survey and other navigational information.* Some estimate of the accuracy of the survey can be formed by an examination of the source notes given in the title of the chart. If the chart is based upon very old surveys, it should be used with caution. Many of the earlier surveys were made under conditions

that were not conducive to great accuracy. It is safest to question every chart based upon surveys of doubtful accuracy.

The number of soundings and their spacing is some indication of the completeness of the survey. Only a small fraction of the soundings taken in a thorough survey are shown on the chart, but sparse or unevenly distributed soundings indicate that the survey was probably not made in detail. Large or irregular blank areas, or absence of depth contours (commonly called **depth curves**), generally indicate lack of soundings in the area. If the water surrounding such a blank area is deep, there is generally considerable depth in the blank; conversely, shallow water surrounding such an area indicates the strong possibility of shoal water. If neighboring areas abound in rocks or are particularly uneven, the blank area should be regarded with additional suspicion. However, it should be kept in mind that relatively few soundings are shown when there is a large number of depth contours or where the bottom is flat or gently and evenly sloping. Additional soundings are shown when they are helpful in indicating the uneven character of a rough bottom (figs. 505a and 505b).

Even a detailed survey may fail to locate every rock or pinnacle, and in waters where their existence is suspected, the best methods for determining their presence are wire drag surveys. Areas that have been dragged may be indicated on the chart and a note added to show the effective depth at which the drag was operated.

Changes in the contour of the bottom are relatively rapid in areas where there are strong currents or heavy surf, particularly when the bottom is composed principally of soft mud or sand. The entrances to bar harbors are especially to be regarded with suspicion. Similarly, there is sometimes a strong tendency for dredged channels to shoal, especially if they are surrounded by sand or mud, and cross currents exist. Notes are sometimes shown on the chart when the bottom contours are known to change rapidly. However, the absence of such a note should not be regarded as evidence that rapid change does not occur.

Changes in aids to navigation, structures, etc., are more easily determined, and charts are generally corrected in this regard to the date of printing. However, there is always the possibility of a change having occurred since the chart was printed. All issues of *Notice to Mariners* printed after that date (art. 506) should be checked to insure accuracy in this respect.

2. *Suitability of the scale for the design and intended navigational use.* The same detail cannot be shown on a small-scale chart as on one of a larger scale. On small-scale charts detailed information, including minor aids to navigation, is omitted or generalized in the areas covered by larger scale charts. Therefore, it is good practice to use the largest scale chart available when in the vicinity of shoals or other dangers.

3. *Presentation and adequacy of data.* The amount and kind of detail to be shown, and the method of presentation, are continually under study by charting agencies. Development of a new navigational aid may render many previous charts inadequate. An example is radar. Many of the charts produced before radar became available lack the detail needed for reliable identification of targets.

Part of the responsibility for the continuing accuracy of charts lies with the user. If charts are to remain reliable, they must be corrected as indicated by the *Notice to Mariners*. In addition, the user's reports of errors and changes and his suggestions often are useful to the publishing agencies in correcting and improving their charts. Navigators and maritime activities have contributed much to the reliability and usefulness of the modern nautical chart. If a chart becomes wet, the expansion and subsequent shrinkage when the chart dries are likely to cause distortion.

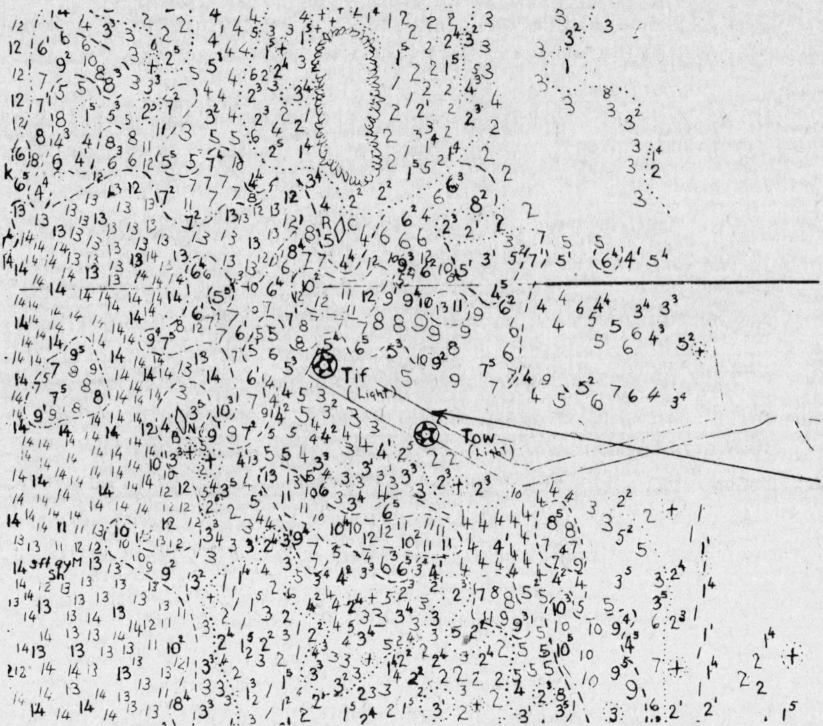

FIGURE 505a.—Part of a boat sheet, showing the soundings obtained in a survey.

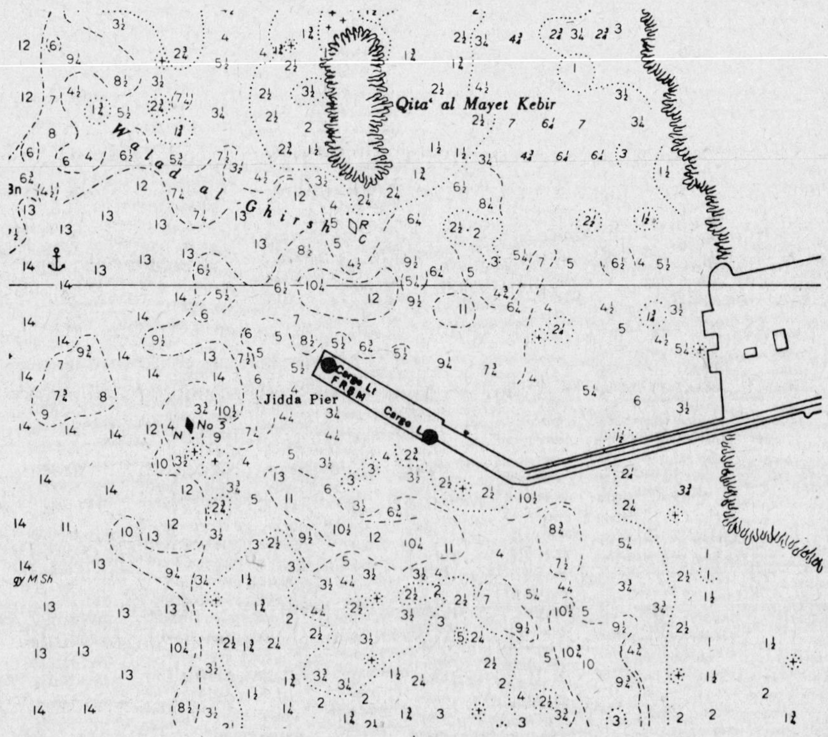

FIGURE 505b.—Part of a nautical chart made from the boat sheet of figure 505a. Compare the number of soundings in the two figures.

506. Dates on charts.—The system of dates now used on charts published by the Defense Mapping Agency Hydrographic Center and the National Ocean Survey is as follows:

First edition. The original date of issue of a new chart is shown at the top center margin, thus:

1st Ed., Sept. 1950

New edition. A new edition is made when, at the time of printing, the corrections are too numerous or too extensive to be reported in *Notice to Mariners*, making previous printings obsolete. The date of the first edition is retained at the top margin. At the lower left-hand corner it is replaced by the number and date of the new edition. The latter date is the same as that of the latest *Notice to Mariners* to which the chart has been corrected, thus:

5th Ed., July 11, 1970

Revised print. A revised print published by the National Ocean Survey may contain corrections which have been published in *Notice to Mariners* but does not supersede a current edition. The date of the revision is shown to the right of the edition date, thus:

5th Ed., July 11, 1970; Revised 4/12/75.

Reprint. A reprint is initiated by a low stock situation and is a reprint of the chart with a limited number of corrections from *Notice to Mariners.* The magnetic variation data on a reprint published by the Defense Mapping Agency Hydrographic Center is updated to the latest epoch at the time of printing.

Chart Reading

507. Chart symbols.—Much of the information contained on charts is shown by conventional symbols which make no attempt at accuracy in scale or detail, but are shown at the correct location and make possible the showing of a large amount of information without congestion or confusion. The standard symbols and abbreviations which have been approved for use on regular nautical charts published by the United States of America are shown in Chart No. 1, *Nautical Chart Symbols and Abbreviations*. A knowledge of the meanings of these symbols is essential to a full understanding of charts. The Arco Nautical Chart included herewith shows some of these symbols.

Most of the symbols and abbreviations shown in Chart No. 1 are in agreement with those recommended by the International Hydrographic Organization (IHO). Symbol and abbreviation status is indicated by alphanumeric style differences in the first column of Chart No. 1. The status is explained in the general remarks section of Chart No. 1.

The symbols and abbreviations on any given chart may differ somewhat from those shown in Chart No. 1 because of a change in the standards since printing of the chart or because the chart was published by an agency having a different set of standards.

508. Lettering.—Certain standards regarding lettering have been adopted, except on charts made from reproducibles furnished by foreign nations.

Vertical type is used for features which are dry at high water and not affected by movement of the water, except for heights above water.

Slanting type is used for water, underwater, and floating features, except soundings.

The type of lettering used may be the only means of determining whether a feature may be visible at high tide. For instance, a rock might bear the title "_________Rock" whether or not it extends above the surface. If the name is given in vertical letters, the rock constitutes a small islet; if in slanting type, the rock constitutes a reef.

509. The shoreline shown on nautical charts represents the line of contact between the land and a selected water elevation. In areas affected by tidal fluctuations, this line of contact is usually the mean high-water line. In confined coastal waters of diminished tidal influence, a mean water level line may be used. The shoreline of interior waters (rivers, lakes) is usually a line representing a specified elevation above a selected datum. A shoreline is symbolized by a heavy line. A broken line indicates that the charted position is approximate only. The nature of the shore may be indicated, as shown by the symbols in part A of Chart No. 1.

Where the low-water line differs considerably from the high-water line, the low-water line may be indicated by dots in the case of mud, sand, gravel, or stones, with the kind of material indicated, and by a characteristic symbol in the case of rock or coral. The area alternately covered and uncovered may be shown by a tint which is usually a combination of the land tint and a blue water tint.

The apparent shoreline is used on charts to show the outer edge of marine vegetation where that limit would reasonably appear as the shoreline to the mariner, or where it prevents the shoreline from being clearly defined. The apparent shoreline is symbolized by a light line. The inner edge is marked by a broken line when no other symbol (such as a cliff, levee, etc.) furnishes such a limit. The area between inner and outer limits may be given the combined land-water tint or the land tint.

510. Water areas.—Soundings or depths of water are shown in several ways. Individual soundings are shown by numbers. These do not follow the general rule for lettering. They may be either vertical or slanting, or both may be used on the same chart to distinguish between the data based upon different surveys, different datums, smaller scale charts, or furnished by different authorities.

The unit of measurement used for soundings on each chart is shown in large block letters at the top and bottom of the chart. When the unit of measurement is meters or meters and decimeters, SOUNDINGS IN METERS is shown. When soundings in fathoms or fathoms and fractions are used, SOUNDINGS IN FATHOMS is shown, and when the soundings are in fathoms and feet, SOUNDINGS IN FATHOMS AND FEET is shown.

A depth conversion scale is placed outside the neatline on the chart for use in converting charted depths to feet, meters, or fathoms.

"No bottom" soundings are indicated by a number with a line over the top and a dot over the line, thus: $\dot{\overline{45}}$. This indicates that the spot was sounded to the depth indicated without reaching the bottom. Areas which have been wire dragged (fig. 510a) are shown by a broken limiting line, and the clear effective depth is indicated, with a characteristic symbol under the numbers.

On charts of the Defense Mapping Agency Hydrographic Center, a purple tint is shown within the limits of the swept area unless such tinting would result in excessive use of purple, in which case a green tint is shown within the limits of the swept area.

The soundings are supplemented by a series of *depth contours* (fig. 510b) connecting points of equal depth. These lines present a graphic indication of the configuration of the bottom. The types of lines used for various depths are shown in part R of Chart No. 1. On some charts depth contours are shown in solid lines, the depth represented by each being shown by numbers placed in breaks in the lines, as with land contours. Solid line depth contours are derived from intensively developed hydrographic surveys.

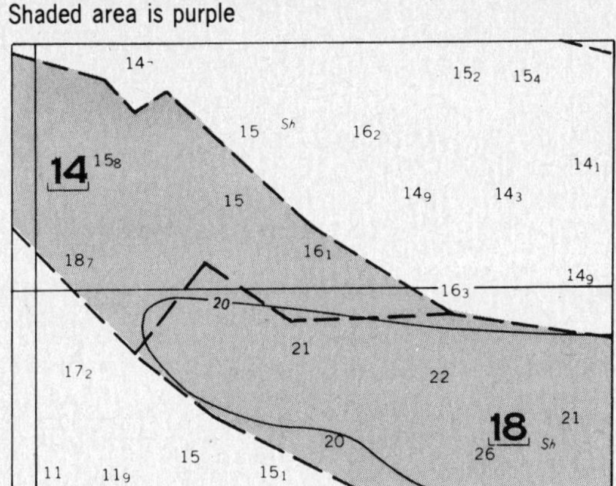

FIGURE 510a.—Swept area.

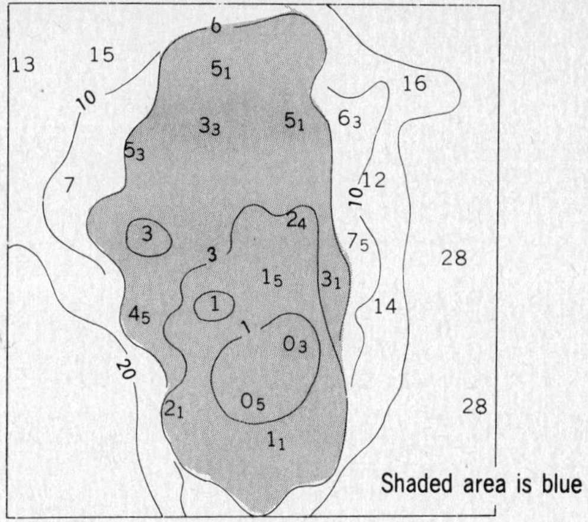

FIGURE 510b.—Depth contours.

A broken or indefinite contour is substituted for a solid depth contour whenever the reliability of the contour is questionable. Depth contours are labeled with numerals in the unit of measurement of the soundings. This type chart, presenting a more detailed indication of the bottom configuration with fewer numerical soundings, is particularly useful to the vessel equipped with an echo sounder permitting continuous determination of a profile of the bottom. Such a chart, to be reliable, can be made only for areas which have been surveyed in great detail.

Areas which uncover at low tide are tinted as indicated in article 509. Those areas out to a given depth often are given a blue tint, and occasionally a lighter blue is carried to some greater depth. On older charts the one-, two-, and three-fathom curves have stippled edges. Charts designed to give maximum emphasis to the configuration of the bottom show depths, beyond the 100-fathom curve, over the entire chart by depth contours similar to the contours shown on land areas to indicate graduations in height. These are called *bottom contour* or *bathymetric* charts.

The side limits of dredged channels are indicated by broken lines. The *project depth* and the date of dredging, if known, are shown by a statement in or along the channel. The possibility of silting should be considered. Local authorities should be consulted for the *controlling depth*.

The chart scale is generally too small to permit all soundings to be shown. In the selection of soundings to be shown, *least* depths are generally chosen first and a sounding pattern worked out to provide safety, a practical presentation of the bottom configuration, and a neat appearance. Depths greater than those indicated may be found close to charted depths, but steep changes in depth are given every consideration in sounding selection. Also, the state of the tide affects the depth at any given moment. An isolated shoal sounding should be approached with caution, or avoided, unless it is known that the area has been wire dragged, for there is always the possibility that a depth less than the least shown may have escaped detection. Also, the shoal area near a coast little frequented by vessels is sometimes not surveyed with the same thoroughness as other areas. Such areas and those where rocks, coral, etc., are known to exist should be entered with caution, or avoided.

The substance forming the bottom is shown by abbreviations. The meaning of some of the less-well-known terms is given below:

Ooze is a soft, slimy, organic sediment composed principally of shells or other hard parts of minute organisms.

Marl is a crumbling, earthy deposit, particularly one of clay mixed with sand, lime, decomposed shells, etc. A layer of marl may become quite compact.

Shingle consists of small, rounded, waterworn stones. It is similar to gravel but with the average size of stone generally larger.

Schist is crystalline rock of a finely laminated nature.

Madrepore is a stony coral which often forms an important building material for reefs.

Lava is rock in the fluid state, or such material after it has solidified. It is formed at very high temperature and issues from the earth through volcanoes.

Pumice is cooled volcanic glass with a great number of minute cavities caused by the expulsion of water vapor at high temperature, resulting in a very light material.

Tufa is a porous rocky deposit sometimes formed in streams and in the ocean near the mouths of rivers.

Scoria (plural *scoriae*) is rough, cinderlike lava.

Sea tangle is any of several species of seaweed, especially those of large size.

Spicules are the small skeletons of various marine animals such as sponges.

Foraminifera (plural) are small marine animals with hard shells of from one to many chambers.

Globigerina is a very small marine animal of the foraminifera order, with a chambered shell, or the shell of such an animal. In large areas of the ocean the calcareous shells of these animals are very numerous, being the principal constituent of a soft mud or **globigerina ooze,** forming part of the ocean bed.

Diatom is a microscopic animal with external skeletons of silica, often found in both fresh and salt water. Part of the ocean bed is composed of a sedimentary ooze consisting principally of large collections of the skeletal remains of diatoms.

Radiolaria (plural) are minute sea animals with a siliceous outer shell. The skeletons of these animals are very numerous, especially in the tropics.

Pteropod is a small marine animal with or without a shell and having two thin, winglike feet. These animals are often so numerous they cover the surface of the sea for miles. In some areas their shells cover the bottom.

Polyzoa (plural) are very small marine animals which reproduce by budding, many generations often being permanently connected by branchlike structures.

Cirripeda (plural) are barnacles and certain other parasitic marine animals.

Fucus is a coarse seaweed growing attached to rocks.

Matte is a dense, twisted growth of a sea plant such as grass.

"Calcareous" is an adjective meaning "containing or composed of calcium or one of its compounds."

511. Chart sounding datum.—*Depths.* All depths indicated on charts are reckoned from some selected level of water, called the *chart sounding datum.* On charts made from surveys conducted by the United States the chart datum is selected with regard to the tides of the region, so that depths might be shown in their least favorable aspect. On charts based upon those of other nations the datum is that of the original authority. When it is known, the datum used is stated on the chart. In some cases where the chart is based upon old surveys, particularly in areas where the range of tide is not great, the actual chart datum may not be known.

For National Ocean Survey charts of the Atlantic and gulf coasts of the United States and Puerto Rico the chart datum is *mean low water.* For charts of the Pacific coast of the United States, including Alaska, it is *mean lower low water.* Most Defense Mapping Agency Hydrographic Center charts are based upon *mean low water, mean lower low water*, or *mean low water springs*. The chart datum for charts published by other countries varies greatly, but is usually lower than mean low water. On charts of the Baltic Sea, Black Sea, the Great Lakes, and other areas where tidal effects are small or without significance, the datum adopted is an arbitrary height approximating the mean water level.

The chart datum of the largest-scale charts of an area is generally the same as the reference level from which height of tide is tabulated in the tide tables.

The height of a chart datum is usually only an approximation of the actual mean value specified, for determination of the actual mean height usually requires a longer series of tidal observations than is available to the cartographer, and the height changes somewhat over a period of time.

Since the chart datum is generally a computed mean or average height at some state of the tide, the depth of water at any particular moment may be less than shown on the chart. For example, if the chart datum is *mean lower low water*, the depth of water at *lower low water* will be less than the charted depth about as often as it is greater. A lower depth is indicated in the tide tables by a minus sign (−).

Heights. The shoreline shown on charts is the high-water line, generally the level of mean high water. The heights of lights, rocks, islets, etc., are generally reckoned from this level. However, heights of islands, especially those at some distance from the coast, are often taken from sources other than hydrographic surveys, and may be reckoned from some other level, often mean sea level. The plane of reference for topographic detail is frequently not stated on the chart.

Since heights are usually reckoned from high water and depths from some form of low water, the reference levels are seldom the same. This is generally of little practical significance, but it might be of interest under some conditions, particularly where the range of tide is large.

512. Dangers are shown by appropriate symbols.

A rock that uncovers at mean high water may be shown as an islet. If an isolated, offlying rock is known to uncover at the chart datum but to be covered at high water, the appropriate symbol is shown and the height above the chart datum, if known, is usually given, either by statement such as "*Uncov 2 ft*" or by the figure indicating the number of feet above the chart datum underlined and usually enclosed in parentheses, thus: ($\underline{2}$). This is illustrated in figure 512a. A rock which does not uncover is shown by the appropriate symbol. If it is considered a danger to surface vessels, the symbol is enclosed by a dotted curve for emphasis.

A distinctive symbol is used to show a detached coral reef which uncovers at the chart datum. For a coral or rocky reef which is submerged at chart datum, the sunken rock symbol or an appropriate statement is used, enclosed by a dotted or broken line if the limits have been determined.

Several different symbols are used for wrecks, depending upon the nature of the wreck or scale of the chart. The usual symbol for a visible wreck is shown in figure 512b. A sunken wreck with less than 11 fathoms of water over it is considered dangerous and its symbol is surrounded by a dotted curve. The safe clearance depth found over a wreck is indicated by a standard sounding number placed at the wreck, (fig. 512c). If this depth is determined by a wire drag, the sounding is underscored by the wire drag symbol (art. 510). An unsurveyed wreck over which the exact depth is unknown, but is considered to have a safe clearance to the depth shown is depicted as shown in figure 512c.

Tide rips, eddies, and kelp are shown by symbol or lettering.

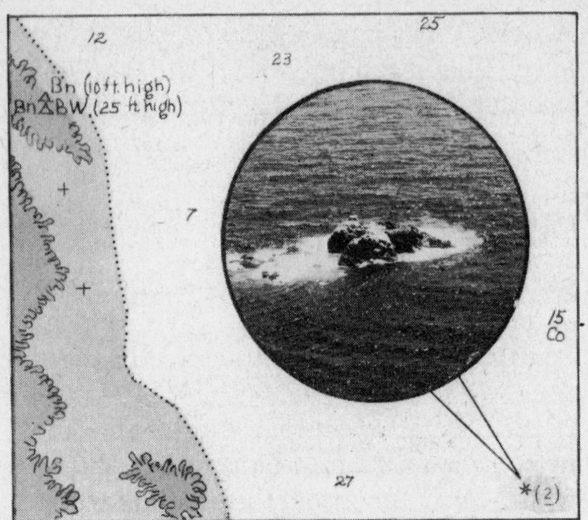

FIGURE 512a.—A rock awash.

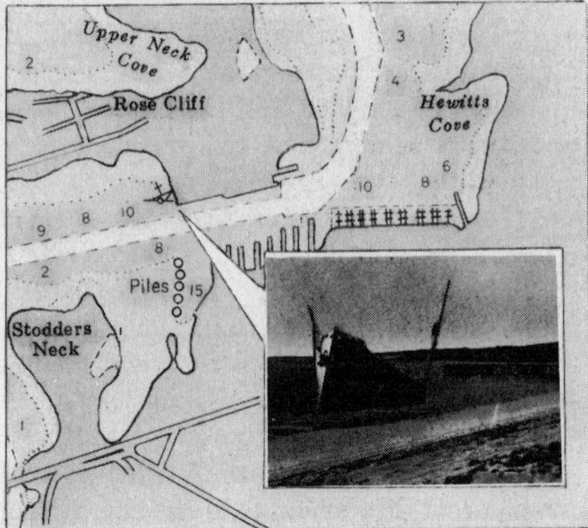

FIGURE 512b.—A visible wreck.

Piles, dolphins (clusters of piles), snags, stumps, etc., are shown by small circles and a label identifying the type of obstruction. If such dangers are submerged, the letters "Subm" precede the label.

Fish stakes and traps are shown when known to be permanent or hazardous to navigation.

The importance of knowing the chart symbols for dangers to navigation cannot be emphasized strongly enough. Most dangers are emphasized with a blue tint and dotted line surrounding the danger. Some of the danger symbols are shown in figure 512c.

513. Aids to navigation are shown by symbol, as given in Chart. No 1, usually supplemented by abbreviations and sometimes by additional descriptive text. In order to render the symbols conspicuous it is necessary to show them in greatly exaggerated size relative to the scale of the chart. It is therefore important that the navigator know which part of the symbol represents the actual position of the aid. For floating aids (lightships and buoys), the position part of the symbol marks the approximate location of the anchor or sinker, the aid swinging in an orbit around this approximate position.

The principal charted aids to navigation are lighthouses, other lights on fixed structures, beacons, lightships, radiobeacons, and buoys. The number of aids shown and the amount of information concerning them varies with the scale of the chart. Unless otherwise indicated, lights which do not alternate in color are white, and alternating lights are red and white. Light lists give complete navigational information concerning them.

Lighthouses and *other lights on fixed structures* are shown as black dots surrounded by nautical purple disks or as black dots with purple flare symbols. The center of the black dot is the position of the light.

On large-scale charts the characteristics of lights are shown in the following order:

Characteristic	*Example*	*Meaning*
1. Character	Gp Fl	group flashing
2. Color	R	red
3. Period	(2) 10 sec	two flashes every 10 seconds
4. Height	160 ft	160 feet
5. Range	19M	19 nautical miles (See article 1307)
6. Number	"6"	light number 6

The legend for this light would appear on the chart:

Gp Fl R (2) 10 sec 160 ft 19 M "6"

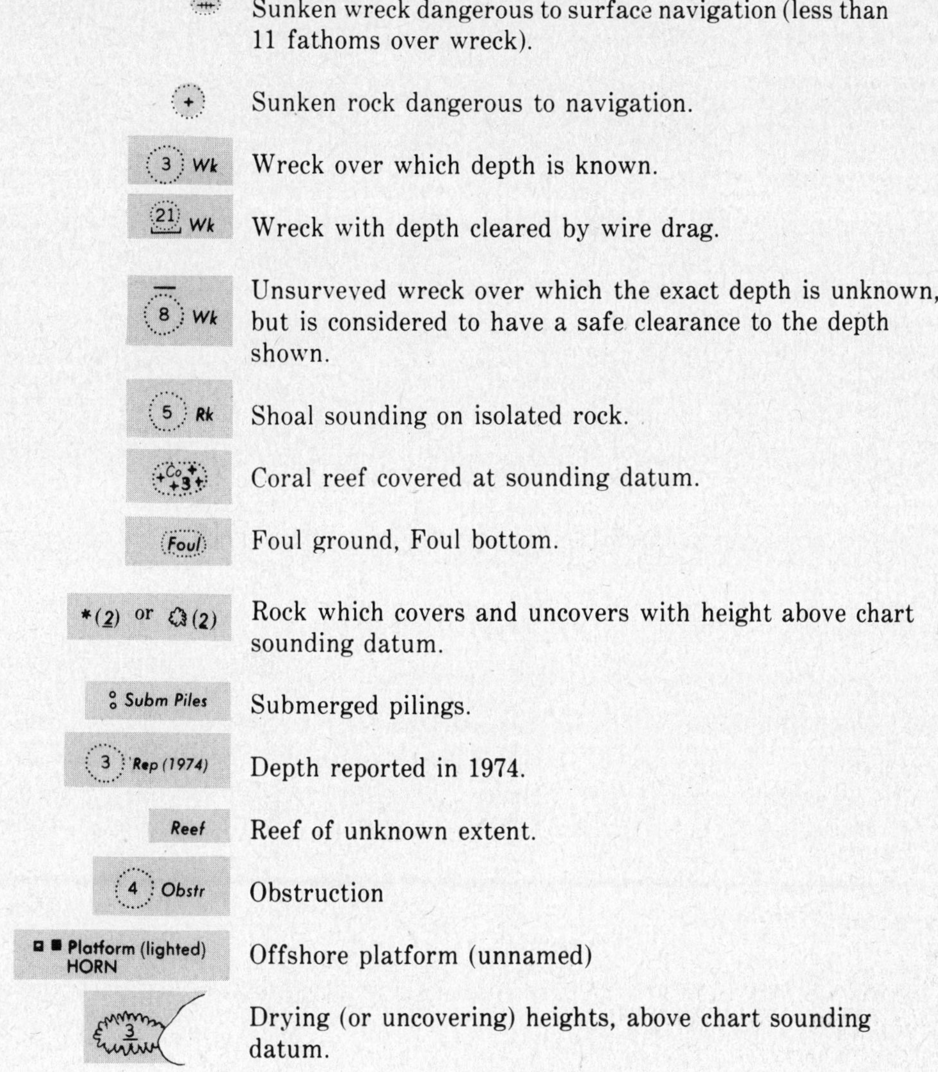

Sunken wreck dangerous to surface navigation (less than 11 fathoms over wreck).
Sunken rock dangerous to navigation.
3 Wk
Wreck over which depth is known.
21 Wk
Wreck with depth cleared by wire drag.
8 Wk
Unsurveyed wreck over which the exact depth is unknown, but is considered to have a safe clearance to the depth shown.
5 Rk
Shoal sounding on isolated rock.
Co 3
Coral reef covered at sounding datum.
Foul
Foul ground, Foul bottom.
*(2) or (2)
Rock which covers and uncovers with height above chart sounding datum.
Subm Piles
Submerged pilings.
3 Rep (1974)
Depth reported in 1974.
Reef
Reef of unknown extent.
4 Obstr
Obstruction
Platform (lighted) HORN
Offshore platform (unnamed)
3
Drying (or uncovering) heights, above chart sounding datum.

FIGURE 512c.—Danger symbols.

On older charts this form is varied slightly. As the chart scale becomes smaller the six items listed above are omitted in the following order: first, height; second, period (seconds); third, number (of flashes, etc.) in group; fourth, light number; fifth, visibility. Names of unnumbered lights are shown when space permits.

Daybeacons (unlighted beacons) are shown as depicted in Chart No. 1. When daybeacons are shown by small triangles, the center of the triangle marks the position of the aid. Except on Intracoastal Waterway charts and charts of state waterways the abbreviation Bn is shown beside the symbol, with the appropriate abbreviation for color if known. For black beacons the triangle is solid black and there is no color abbreviation. All beacon abbreviations are in vertical lettering, as appropriate for fixed aids (fig. 513a).

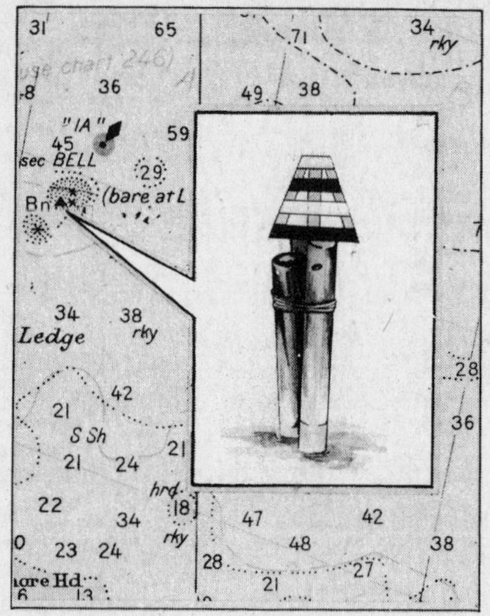

FIGURE 513a.—A daybeacon.

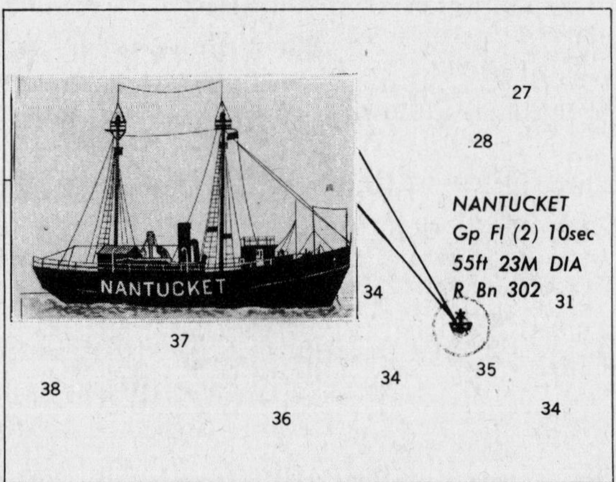

FIGURE 513b.—A lightship with a radiobeacon.

Lightships are shown by ship symbol, the center of the small circle at the base of the symbol indicating the approximate position of the lightship's anchor. The circle is overprinted by a small purple disk as shown in figure 513b or a purple flare emanating from the top of the symbol. As a floating aid, the light characteristics and the name of the lightship are given in leaning letters.

Radiobeacons are indicated on the chart by a small purple circle, as shown in figure 513b, accompanied by the appropriate abbreviation to indicate whether an ordinary radiobeacon (R Bn) or a radar beacon (Racon). The same symbol is used for a radio direction finder station with the abbreviation "RDF" and a coast radar station with the abbreviation Ra. Other radio stations are indicated by a small black circle with a dot in the center, or a smaller circle without a dot, and the appropriate abbreviation. In every case the center of the circle marks the position of the aid.

Buoys, except mooring buoys, are usually shown by a diamond-shaped symbol and a small dot or small circle in conjunction with one of its points (at one of its acute angles). The dot or small circle indicates the approximate position of the buoy's sinker. **A mooring buoy is shown by a distinctive symbol. The small circle interrupting the symbol's base line indicates the approximate position of the sinker.**

A black buoy is shown by a solid black diamond symbol, without abbreviation. For all other buoys, color is indicated by an abbreviation, or in full by a note on the chart. In addition, the diamond-shaped symbols of red buoys often are colored purple. A buoy symbol with a line connecting the side points (shorter axis), half of the symbol being purple or open and the other half black, indicates horizontal bands. A line connecting the upper and lower points (longer axis) represents vertical stripes. Two lines connecting the opposite *sides* of the symbol indicate a checkered buoy.

There is no significance to the angle at which the diamond-shape appears on the chart. The symbol is placed so as to avoid interference with other features of the chart.

Lighted buoys are indicated by a purple flare emanating from the buoy symbol or by a small purple disk centered on the dot or small circle indicating the approximate position of the buoy's sinker, as shown in figure 513c.

Abbreviations for light characteristics, type and color of buoy, number of the buoy, and any other pertinent information given near the symbol are in slanting letters. The

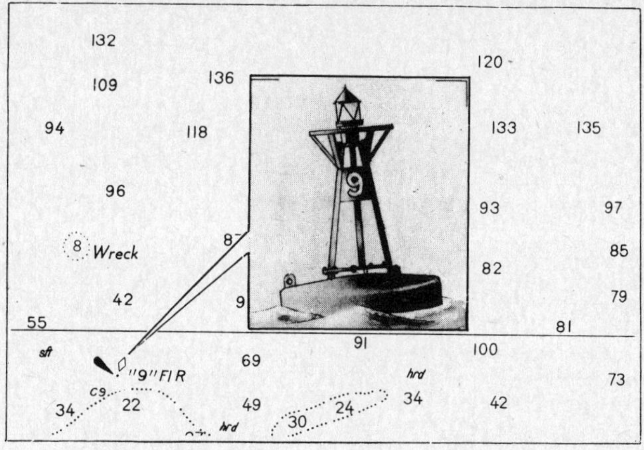

FIGURE 513c.—A lighted buoy.

letter *C*, *N*, or *S*, indicates a can, nun. or spar, respectively (art. 409). The words "bell," "gong," and "whistle," are shown as *BELL*, *GONG*, and *WHIS*, respectively. The number or letter designation of the buoy is given in quotation marks on National Ocean Survey charts. On other charts they may be given without quotation marks or punctuation, thus: No 1, No 2, etc.

Station buoys are not shown on small-scale charts, but are given on some large-scale charts.

Aeronautical lights included in the light lists are shown by the lighthouse symbol, accompanied by the abbreviation "AERO." The completeness to which the characteristics are shown depends principally upon the effective range of other navigational lights in the vicinity, and the usefulness of the light for marine navigation.

Ranges are indicated by a broken or solid line. The solid line, which indicates that part of the range intended for navigation, may be broken at irregular intervals to avoid being drawn through soundings. That part of the range line drawn only to guide the eye to the objects to be kept in range is broken at regular intervals. If the direction is given, it is expressed in degrees clockwise from true north.

Sound signal apparatus is indicated by the appropriate word in capital letters (*HORN*, *BELL*, *GONG*, etc.) or an abbreviation indicating the type of sound. Sound signals of all types other than submarine sound signals are represented by three arcs of concentric circles within an angle of 45°, orientated and placed as necessary for clarity. The letters "DFS" indicate a **distance finding station** having synchronized sound and radio signals. The location of a sound signal which does not accompany a visual aid, either lighted or unlighted, is shown by a small circle and the appropriate word in vertical block letters.

Private aids, when shown, are marked "Priv maintd." Some privately maintained unlighted aids are indicated by a small circle accompanied by the word "Marker," or a larger circle with a dot in the center and the word "MARKER." The center of the circle indicates the position of the aid. A privately maintained lighted aid has the light symbol and is accompanied by the characteristics and the usual indication of its private nature. Private aids should be used with caution.

A *light sector* is the sector or area bounded by two radii and the arc of a circle in which a light is visible or in which it has a distinctive color different from that of adjoining sectors. The limiting radii are indicated on the chart by dotted lines.

Colors of the sectors are indicated by words spelled out if space permits, or by abbreviation (W, R, etc.) if it does not.

Limits of light sectors and arcs of visibility *as observed from a vessel* are given in the light lists, in clockwise order.

514. Land areas.—The amount of detail shown on the land areas of nautical charts depends upon the scale and the intended purpose of the chart.

Relief is shown by contours and form lines.

Contours are lines connecting points of equal elevation. The heights represented by the contours are indicated in slanting figures at suitable places along the lines. Heights are usually expressed in feet (or in meters with means for conversion to feet). The interval between contours is uniform over any one chart, except that certain intermediate contours are sometimes shown by broken line. When contours are broken, their locations are approximate.

Form lines are approximations of contours used for the purpose of indicating relative elevations. They are used in areas where accurate information is not available in sufficient detail to permit exact location of contours. Elevations of individual form lines are not indicated on the chart.

Spot elevations are generally given only for summits or for tops of conspicuous landmarks. The heights of spot elevations and contours are given with reference to mean high water when this information is available.

When there is insufficient space to show the heights of islets or rocks, they are indicated by slanting figures enclosed in parentheses in the water area nearby.

Cities and roads. Cities are shown in a generalized pattern that approximates their extent and shape. Street names are generally not charted except those along the waterfront on the largest scale charts. In general, only the main arteries and thoroughfares or major coastal highways are shown on smaller scale charts. Occasionally, highway numbers are given. When shown, trails are indicated by a light broken line. Buildings along the waterfront or individual ones back from the waterfront but of special interest to the mariner are shown on large-scale charts. Special symbols are used for certain kinds of buildings. Both single and double track railroads are indicated by a single line with cross marks. In general, city electric railways are not charted. A fence or sewer extending into the water is shown by a broken line, usually labeled. Airports are shown on small-scale charts by symbol and on large-scale charts by shape and extent of runways. Breakwaters and jetties are shown by single or double lines depending upon the scale of the chart. A submerged portion and the limits of the submerged base are shown by broken lines.

515. Landmarks are shown by symbols. A large circle with a dot at its center is used for selected landmarks that have been accurately located. Capital letters are used to identify the landmark: HOUSE, FLAGPOLE, STACK, sometimes followed by "(conspic)."
accurately located. Capital letters are used to identify the landmark: HOUSE, FLAGPOLE, STACK, sometimes followed by "(conspic)."

A small circle without a dot is used for landmarks not accurately located. Capital and lower case letters are used to identify the landmark: Mon, Cup, Dome. The abbreviation "PA," for position approximate, is used when necessary as a safety feature.

When only one object of a group is charted, its name is followed by a descriptive legend in parenthesis, including the number of objects in the group, for example (TALLEST OF FOUR) or (NORTHEAST OF THREE).

Some of the accompanying labels on a chart are interpreted as follows:

Building or **house.** One of these terms, as appropriate, is used when the entire structure is the landmark, rather than an individual feature of it.

A **spire** is a slender pointed structure extending above a building. It is seldom less than two-thirds of the entire height of the structure, and its lines are rarely broken by stages or other features. The term is not applied to a short pyramid-shaped structure rising from a tower or belfry.

A **cupola** (kū′pō·lȧ) is a small dome-shaped tower or turret rising from a building (fig. 515).

A **dome** is a large, rounded, hemispherical structure rising above a building, or a roof of the same shape. A prominent example is that of the Capitol of the United States, in Washington, D.C.

A **chimney** is a relatively small, upright structure projecting above a building for the conveyance of smoke.

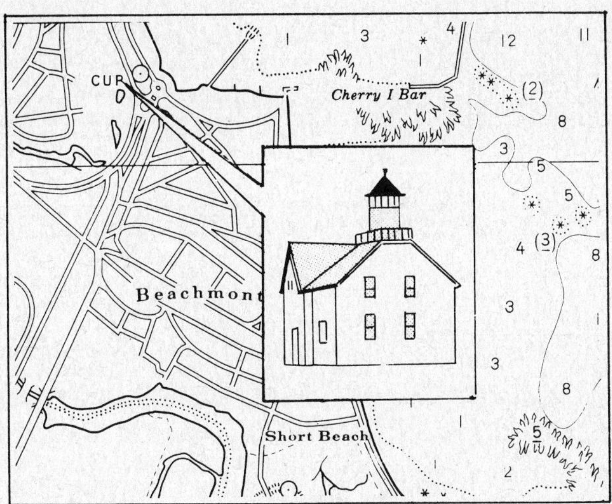

FIGURE 515.—A cupola.

A **stack** is a tall smokestack or chimney. The term is used when the stack is more prominent as a landmark than accompanying buildings.

A **flagpole** is a single staff from which flags are displayed. The term is used when the pole is not attached to a building.

The term **flagstaff** is used for a flagpole rising from a building.

A **flag tower** is a scaffold-like tower from which flags are displayed.

A **radio tower** is a tall pole or structure for elevating radio antennas.

A **radio mast** is a relatively short pole or slender structure for elevating radio antennas, usually found in groups.

A **tower** is any structure with its base on the ground and high in proportion to its base, or that part of a structure higher than the rest, but having essentially vertical sides for the greater part of its height.

A **lookout station** or **watch tower** is a tower surmounted by a small house from which a watch is kept regularly.

A **water tower** is a structure enclosing a tank or standpipe so that the presence of the tank or standpipe may not be apparent.

A **standpipe** is a tall cylindrical structure, in a waterworks system, the height of which is several times the diameter.

The term **tank** is used for a water tank elevated high above the ground by a tall skeleton framework.

The expression **gas tank** or **oil tank** is used for the distinctive structures described by these words.

516. Miscellaneous.—*Measured mile.* A measured nautical mile indicated on a chart is accurate to within six feet of the correct length. Most measurements in the United States were made before 1959, when the United States adopted the International Nautical Mile. The new value is within six feet of the previous standard length of 6,080.20 feet, adjustments not having been made. If the measured distance differs from the standard value by more than six feet, the actual measured distance is stated and the words "measured mile" are omitted.

Periods after abbreviations in water areas are omitted, as these might be mistaken for rocks. However, a lower case *i* or *j* is dotted.

Courses shown on charts are given in true directions, to the nearset minute of arc.

Bearings shown are in true directions *toward* (not from) the objects.

Commercial radio broadcasting stations are shown on charts when they are of value to the mariner either for obtaining radio bearings or as landmarks.

Rules of the road. Lines of demarcation between the areas in which international and inland rules apply are shown only when they cannot be adequately described in notes on the chart.

Compass roses are placed at convenient locations on Mercator charts to facilitate the plotting of bearings and courses. The outer circle is graduated in degrees with zero at true north. The inner circle is graduated in points and degrees with the arrow indicating magnetic north.

Magnetic information. On many charts magnetic variation is given to the nearest 15′ by notes in the centers of compass roses; the annual change is given to the nearest 1′ to permit correction of the given value at a later date. When this is done, the magnetic information is updated when a new edition is issued. The current practice of the Defense Mapping Agency Hydrographic Center is to give the magnetic variation to the nearest 1′, but the magnetic information on new editions is only updated to conform with the latest epoch (1975.0, 1980.0, etc.). Whenever a chart is reprinted, the magnetic information is updated to the latest epoch. On other charts the variation is given by a series of **isogonic lines** connecting points of equal variation, usually a separate line being given for each degree of variation. The line of zero variation is called the **agonic line.** Many plans and insets show neither compass roses nor isogonic lines, but indicate magnetic information by note. A local magnetic disturbance of sufficient force to cause noticeable deflection of the magnetic compass, called **local attraction,** is indicated by a note on the chart.

Currents are sometimes shown on charts by means of arrows giving the directions, and figures giving the speeds. The information thus given refers to the usual or average conditions, sometimes based upon very few observations. It is not safe to assume that conditions at any given time will not differ considerably from those shown.

Longitudes are reckoned eastward and westward from the meridian of Greenwich, England, unless otherwise stated.

Notes on charts should be read with care, as they may give important information not graphically presented. Several types of notes are used. Those in the margin give such information as the chart number and (sometimes) publication and edition notes, identification of adjoining charts, etc. Notes in connection with the chart title include such information as scale, sources of charted data, tidal information, the unit in which soundings are given, cautions, etc. Another class of notes is that given in proximity to the detail to which it refers. Examples of this type of note are those referring to local magnetic disturbance, controlling depths of channels, measured miles, dangers, dumping grounds, anchorages, etc.

Overlapping charts constructed on different horizontal geodetic datums (app. X) may carry the following note:

CAUTION

Differences in latitude and longitude may exist between this and other charts of the area; therefore, the transfer of positions from one chart to another should be done by bearings and distances from common features.

Horizontal geodetic datum shifts may be given to provide the corrections necessary to shift to a different datum. It is the practice of the Defense Mapping Agency Hydrographic Center to provide, if plottable, the corrections to new charts and new editions of charts that are necessary to shift the geodetic datum to the World Geodetic System.

Anchorage areas are shown within purple broken lines and labeled as such. Anchorage berths are shown as purple circles with the number or letter assigned to the berth inscribed within the circle. Caution notes are sometimes shown when there are specific anchoring regulations.

Spoil areas are shown within short broken black lines. The area is tinted blue (National Ocean Survey charts only) and labeled SPOIL AREA.

Firing and bombing practice areas in the United States territorial and adjacent waters are shown on National Ocean Survey charts and Defense Mapping Agency Hydrographic Center charts of the same area and comparable scale. Danger areas established for short periods of time are not charted, but are announced locally. Danger areas in effect for longer periods are published in the *Notice to Mariners*. Any aid to navigation established to mark a danger area or a fixed or floating target is shown on charts.

Traffic separation schemes show routes to increase safety of navigation, particularly in areas of high density shipping. Traffic separation schemes are shown on standard nautical charts of scale 1:600,000 and larger and are printed in purple. The arrows printed on charts to indicate tracks are intended to give the general direction of traffic only, ships need not set their courses strictly by the arrows. At points where several recommended routes meet, circular or triangular separation zones with traffic direction arrows are shown.

Recommended tracklines, portrayed in black, are used to indicate suggested courses through particular passages and are selected according to their value for oceangoing ships.

A *logarithmic time-speed-distance nomogram* with an explanation of its application is shown on harbor charts at scales of 1:40,000 and larger.

Tidal boxes (fig. 516a) are shown on charts of scales 1:75,000 and larger.

TIDAL INFORMATION

Place	Position		Height above datum of soundings			
			Mean High Water		Mean Low Water	
	N. Lat.	E. Long.	Higher	Lower	Lower	Higher
			meters	meters	meters	meters
Olongapo.......	14°49′	120°17′	...0.9....	... 0.4...	...0.0....	.. 0.3....

FIGURE 516a.—Tidal box.

Tabulations of controlling depths (fig. 516b) are shown on National Ocean Survey harbor charts.

NANTUCKET HARBOR Tabulated from surveys by the Corps of Engineers - report of June 1972 and surveys of Nov. 1971							
Controlling depths in channels entering from seaward in feet at Mean Low Water					Project Dimensions		
Name of Channel	Left outside quarter	Middle half of channel	Right outside quarter	Date of Survey	Width (feet)	Length (naut. miles)	Depth M.L.W. (feet)
Entrance Channel	11.1	15.0	15.0	11-71	300	1.2	15
Note.-The Corps of Engineers should be consulted for changing conditions subsequent to the above.							

FIGURE 516b.—Tabulations of controlling depths.

Title. The chart title may be at any convenient location, usually in some area not important to navigation. It is composed of several distinctive parts as shown in figure 516c.

Reproductions of Foreign Charts

517. Modified facsimile charts are modified reproductions of foreign charts produced in accordance with bilateral agreements. Such agreements serve to provide the mariner with more up-to-date charts. *Chart No. 1, Nautical Chart Symbols and Abbreviations,* is available from the Defense Mapping Agency Hydrographic Center, Washington, D.C.

Modified facsimile charts published by the Defense Mapping Agency Hydrographic Center are, in general, reproduced with minimal changes. Such changes may include all or part of the following:

1. The original name of the chart is removed and replaced by an anglicized version.
2. English language equivalents of names and terms on the original chart are printed in a suitable glossary on the reproduction, as appropriate.
3. All hydrographic information, except bottom characteristics, is shown as depicted on the original chart.
4. Bottom characteristics are shown as depicted in Chart No. 1.
5. The unit of measurement used for soundings is shown in block letters outside the upper and lower neatlines.
6. A scale for converting charted depth to feet, meters, or fathoms is added.
7. A blue tint is shown from a significant depth curve to the shoreline.
8. A blue tint is added to all dangers enclosed by a dotted danger curve.
9. A blue tint is added to dangerous wrecks, foul areas, obstructions, rocks awash, sunken rocks, and swept wrecks.
10. Aids to navigation, landmarks, and special area symbols and abbreviations on the original chart are changed to conform with Chart No. 1.
11. Caution notes are shown in purple and enclosed in a box.
12. Restricted, danger, and prohibited areas are usually outlined in purple and labeled "RESTRICTED AREA," "DANGER AREA," etc.
13. Traffic separation schemes are shown in purple.
14. A note on traffic separation schemes, printed in purple, is added to the chart.
15. Wire dragged (swept) areas are shown in purple or green.
16. If plottable, suitable corrections are provided to shift the horizontal datum to the World Geodetic System (1972).

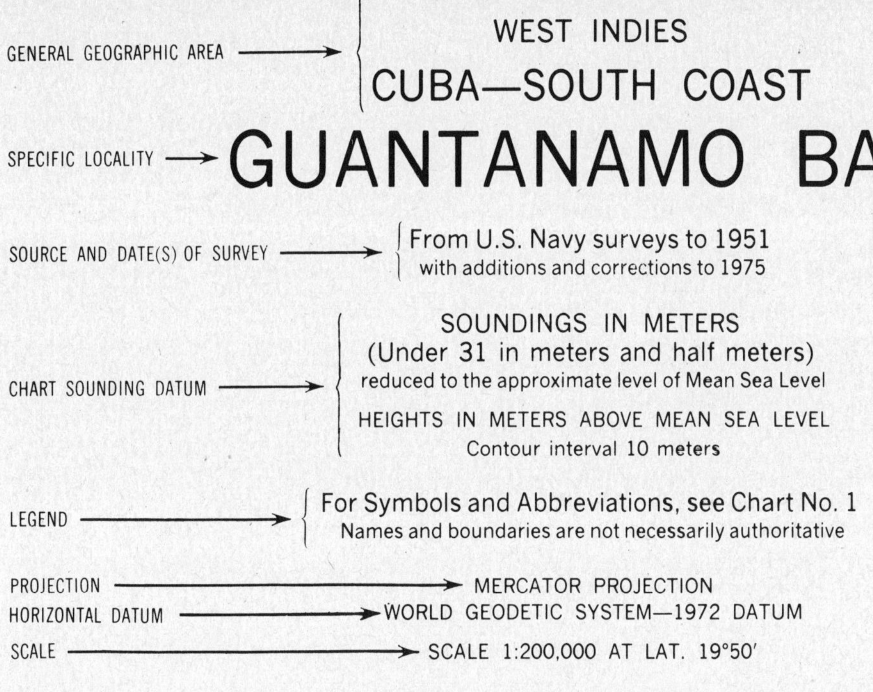

FIGURE 516c.—A chart title.

518. International charts.—The need for mariners and chartmakers to understand and use nautical charts of different nations became increasingly apparent during the late 19th and 20th centuries as the maritime nations of the world developed their own establishments for the compilation and publication of nautical charts from hydrographic surveys. There followed a growing awareness that international standardization of symbols and presentation was desirable, which led to twenty-two maritime nations sending their representatives to a Hydrographic Conference in London in 1919. That conference resulted in the establishment of the International Hydrographic Bureau (IHB) in Monaco in 1921, where the seat of the International Hydrographic Organization (IHO), with a membership of over forty States remains today.

Recognizing that there was considerable duplication of effort by various Member States when each was charting the same parts of the ocean, and being conscious of the significant level of standardization in chart symbolization which had been reached, a move was made by the IHO in 1967 to introduce the first international chart. A Committee of representatives from six Member States was organized which reported in 1970. The Committee drew up plans and specifications for two series of international charts of the oceans on scales 1:10,000,000 and 1:3,500,000, respectively. The limits of each of some 83 of these charts, giving worldwide small scale navigational cover, were agreed, and responsibility for compiling each of these has subsequently been accepted by Member States' Hydrographic Offices.

Once a Member State publishes an international chart, reproduction material is made available to any other Member State which may wish to print the chart for its own purposes.

By 1974 twenty-one of these international charts had been published by 12 Member States, while four Member States had availed themselves of the right to reprint. This encouraging beginning to a new era of international hydrographic cooperation has led to the establishment of a committee to study the problems involved in extending the concept to larger scale charts.

International charts can be identified by the letters INT before the chart number and the International Hydrographic Organization seal in addition to what other seals may appear on the chart.

Chart Numbering System

519. Chart numbering system.—The numbering of nautical charts produced and issued by the Defense Mapping Agency Hydrographic Center and the National Ocean Survey is based on a system in which numbers are assigned in accordance with the scale range and geographical area of coverage of a chart. With the exception of certain charts produced for military use only, one- to five-digit numbers are used. And with the exception of one-digit numbers, the first digit identifies the area; the number of digits establishes the scale range (fig. 519a). The *one-digit numbers* are used for products in the chart system which are not actually charts, such as Chart No. 1, *Nautical Chart Symbols and Abbreviations*, chart 5, *National Flags and Ensigns*, and foreign symbols and abbreviations sheets for military use.

Two- and three-digit numbers are assigned to those small-scale charts which depict the major portion of an ocean basin or a large area, with the first digit identifying the ocean basin (fig. 519b). Two-digit numbers are used for charts of scale 1:9,000,000 and smaller. Three-digit numbers are used for charts of scale 1:2,000,000 to 1:9,000,000.

Due to the limited sizes of certain ocean basins, no charts for navigational use at scales of 1:9,000,000 and smaller are published to cover these basins. The otherwise unused two-digit numbers (30 to 49 and 70 to 79) are assigned to special world charts, such as chart 33, *Horizontal Intensity of the Earth's Magnetic Field*, chart 42, *Magnetic Variation*, and chart 76, *Standard Time Zone Chart of the World.*

One exception to the scale range criteria for three-digit numbers is the use of three-digit numbers for a series of position plotting sheets which are of larger scale than 1:2,000,000 because they have application in ocean basins and can be used in all longitudes.

Number of Digits	Scale
1	No Scale
2	1:9,000,000 and smaller.
3	1:2,000,000 to 1:9,000,000.
4	Nonnavigational and special purpose.
5	1:2,000,000 and larger.

FIGURE 519a.—Scales ranges for number of digits in chart number.

Four-digit numbers are used for nonnavigational and special purpose charts, such as chart 5090, *Maneuvering Board*, chart 5101, *Gnomonic Plotting Chart North Atlantic*, and chart 7707, *Omega Plotting Chart.*

Five-digit numbers are assigned to those charts of scale 1:2,000,000 and larger that cover portions of the coastline rather than significant portions of ocean basins. These charts are based on the regions of the nautical chart index (fig. 519c).

The first of the five digits indicates the region; the second digit indicates the subregion; the last three digits indicate the geographical sequence of the chart within

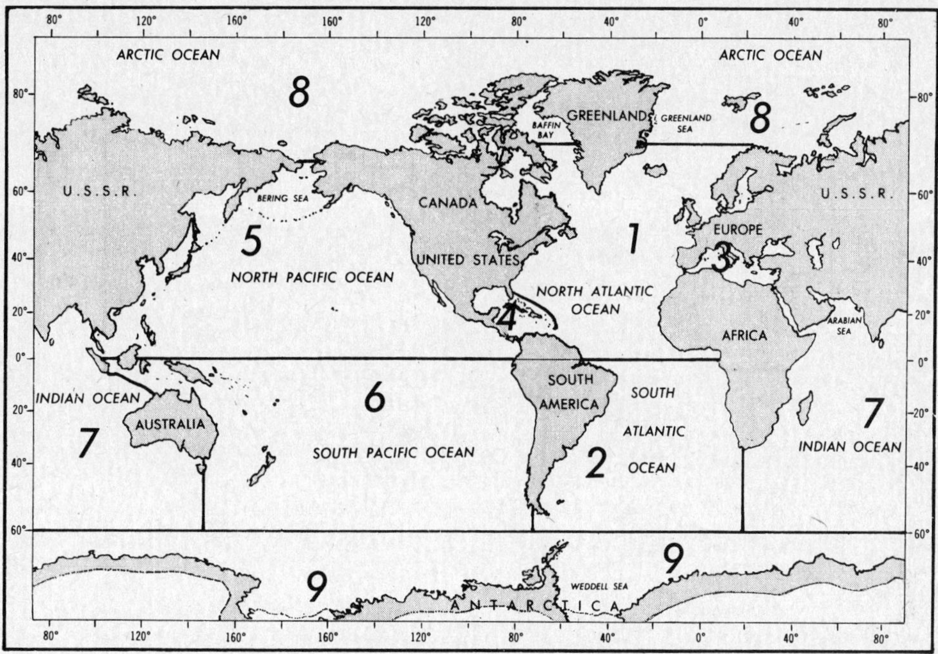

FIGURE 519b.—Ocean basins.

the subregion. Many numbers have been left unused in order that future charts may be placed in their proper geographical sequence as they are produced.

In order to establish a logical numbering system within the geographical subregions (for the 1:2,000,000 and larger-scale charts), a worldwide skeleton framework of coastal charts was laid out at a scale 1:250,000. This skeleton series was used as basic coverage for the numbering except in areas where a coordinated series at about this scale already existed. An example of an exception is the coast of Norway were a coordinated series of 1:200,000 coast charts is in existence. Within each region, the geographical subregions are numbered counterclockwise around the continents, and within each subregion the basic (1:250,000 skeleton) series also is numbered counterclockwise around the continents. The skeleton coverage is assigned generally every 20th digit, except that the first 40 numbers in each subregion are reserved for smaller-scale coverage. Charts with scales larger than the skeleton coverage are assigned one of the 19 numbers following the number assigned to the skeleton sheet within which it falls. Thus, charts on the west coast of the Iberian Peninsula and the northwest coast of Africa are numbered as shown in figure 519d.

As shown in figure 519d, five-digit numbers are assigned to the charts produced by other hydrographic offices. This numbering system is applied to foreign charts so that they can be filed in logical sequence with the charts produced by the Defense Mapping Agency Hydrographic Center and the National Ocean Survey.

Exceptions to the numbering system to satisfy military needs are as follows:

1. Bottom contour and non-submarine contact charts at a scale larger than 1:2,000,000 do not portray portions of a coastline but chart parts of the ocean basins. In view of the characteristics of these charts, they are identified with an alphabetical character plus four digits. The letter *B* denotes bottom contour charts with or without Loran-A. The letter *C* denotes bottom contour charts with Loran-C information.

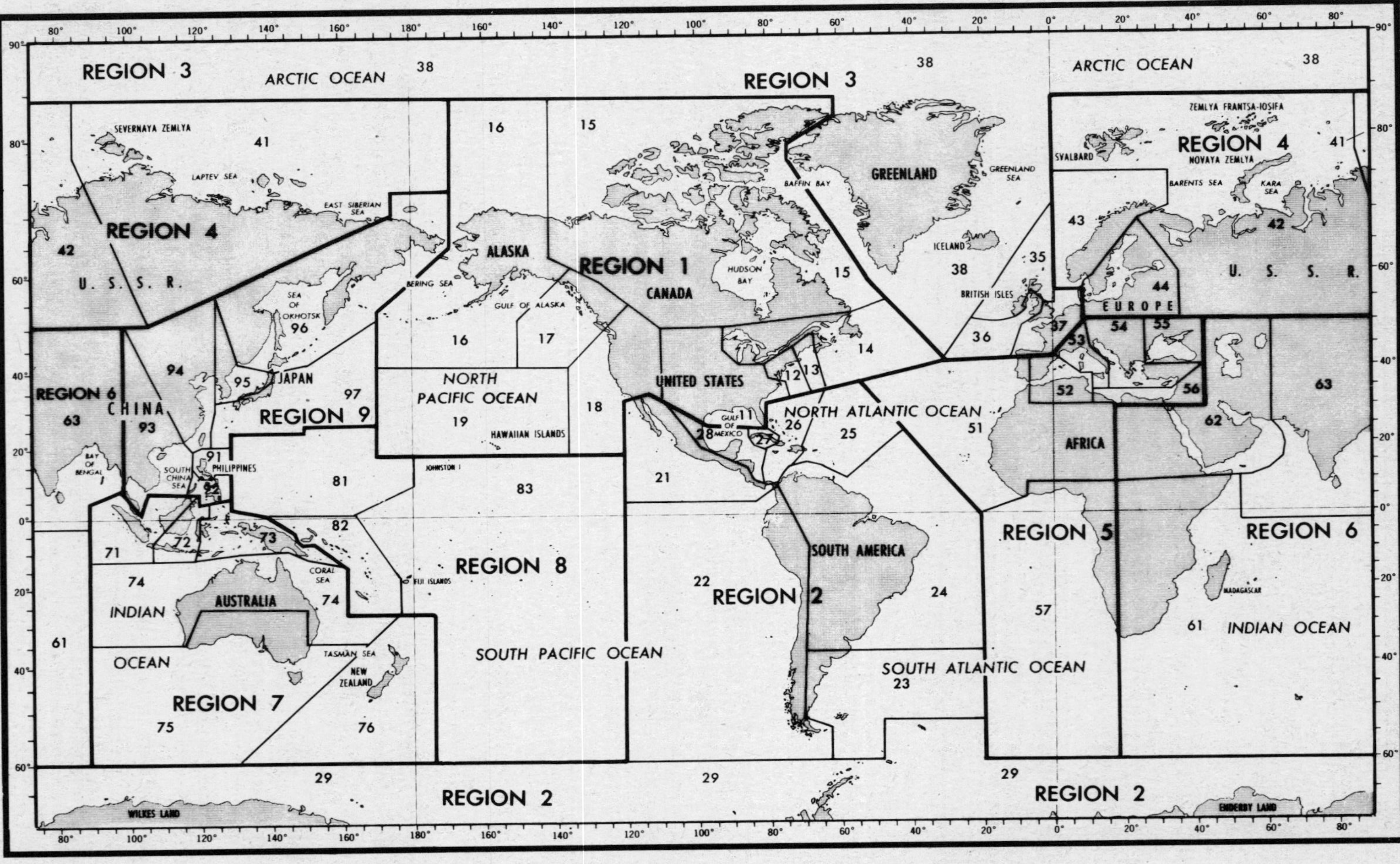

FIGURE 519c.—Regions and subregions of the nautical chart index.

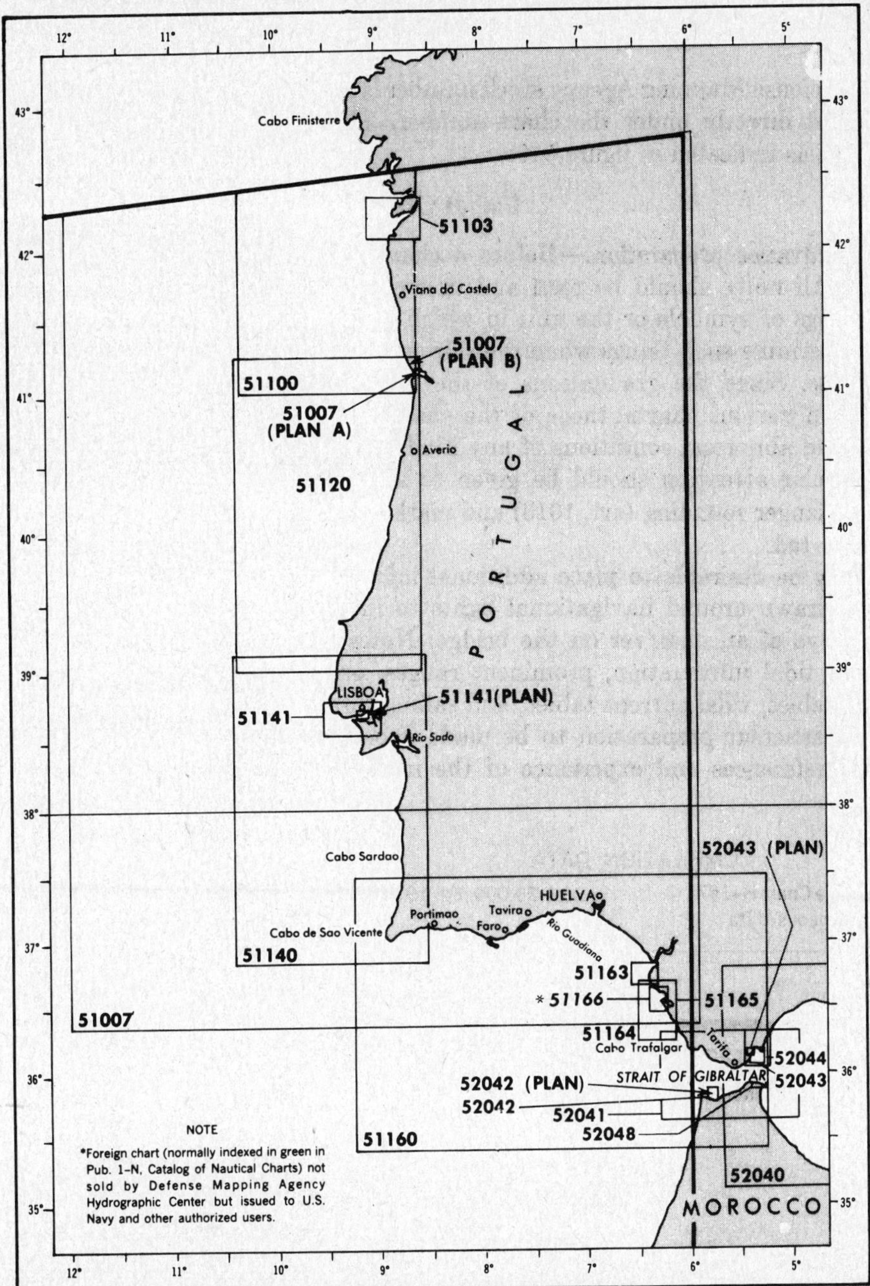

FIGURE 519d.—Area of subregion 51 illustrating the numerical sequence of larger-scale charts along a coast.

The letter *N* denotes non-submarine contact charts containing Loran-C, and the letter *D* denotes bottom contour charts with Omega information. The first two digits of these charts describe the longitude band and the last two digits the latitude band, which in itself is a logical system.

2. Combat charts at a scale of 1:50,000, which would otherwise be assigned five-digit numbers, are assigned four digits separated by a letter of the alphabet. The first two digits indicate the region and subregion; the third character is a letter of the alpha-

bet; the last two digits indicate the geographical sequence of the chart within the subregion.

The Defense Mapping Agency stock number is shown in the lower right-hand corner of the chart directly under the chart number. The letters and numbers have chart significance as indicated in figure 519e.

Use of Charts

520. Advance preparation.—Before a chart is to be used, it should be studied carefully. All notes should be read and understood. There should be no question of the meanings of symbols or the unit in which depths are given, for there may not be time to determine such things when the ship is underway, particularly if an emergency should arise. Since the graduations of the latitude and longitude scales differ considerably on various charts, those of the chart to be used should be noted carefully. Dangers and abnormal conditions of any kind should be noted.

Particular attention should be given to soundings. It is good practice to select a realistic danger sounding (art. 1013) and mark this prominently with a colored pencil other than red.

It may be desirable to place additional information on the chart. Arcs of circles might be drawn around navigational lights to indicate the limit of visibility at the height of eye of an observer on the bridge. Notes regarding the appearance of light structures, tidal information, prominent ranges, or other information from the light lists, tide tables, tidal current tables, and sailing directions might prove helpful.

The particular preparation to be made depends upon the requirements and the personal preferences and experience of the individual navigator. The specific infor-

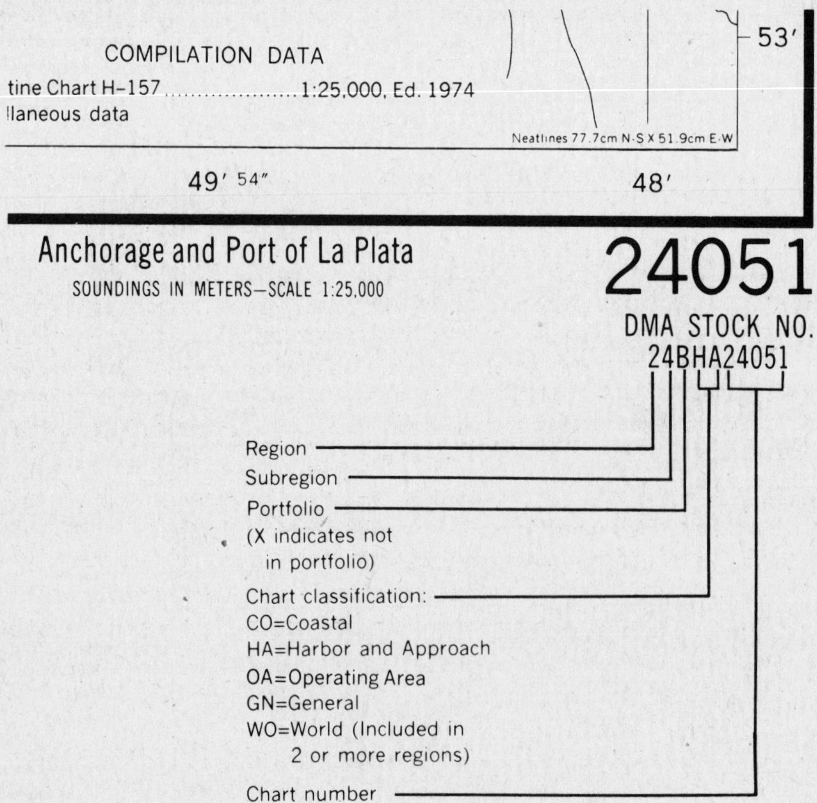

FIGURE 519e.—Defense Mapping Agency stock number.

mation selected is not important. But it *is* important that the navigator familiarize himself with his chart so that in an emergency the information needed will be available and there will be no question of its meaning.

521. Maintaining charts.—The print date in the lower left-hand corner of the chart is the date of the latest *Notice to Mariners* used to update the chart. Responsibility for maintaining it after this date lies with the user. *An uncorrected chart is a menace.* The various issues of *Notice to Mariners* subsequent to the print date contain all the information needed for maintaining charts. The more urgent items are also given in advance in the *Daily Memorandum* or by radio broadcast. A convenient way of keeping a record of the *Notice to Mariners* corrections made to each chart on hand is by means of the 5x8–inch *Chart/Publication Correction Record Card* (DMAHC 8660/9).

Periodically the Defense Mapping Agency Hydrographic Center publishes a *Summary of Corrections* containing previously published *Notice to Mariners* corrections.

When a new edition of a chart is published, it should be obtained and the old one retired from use. The very fact that a new edition has been prepared generally indicates that there have been changes that cannot adequately be shown by hand correction.

522. Use and stowage of charts.—Charts are among the most important aids of the navigator, and should be treated as such. When in use they should be spread out flat on a suitable chart table or desk, and properly secured to prevent loss or damage. Every effort should be made to keep charts dry, for a wet chart stretches and may not return to the original dimensions after drying. The distortion thus introduced may cause inaccurate results when measurements are made on the chart.

Permanent corrections to charts should be made in ink so that they will not be inadvertently erased. All other lines should be drawn lightly in pencil so that they can be easily erased without removing permanent information or otherwise damaging the chart. To avoid possible confusion, lines should be drawn no longer than necessary, and adequately labeled. When a voyage is completed, the charts should be carefully and thoroughly erased unless there has been an unusual incident such as a grounding or collision, when they should be preserved without change, as they will undoubtedly be requested by the investigating authority. After a chart has been erased, it should be inspected carefully for possible damage and for incompletely erased or overlooked marks that might prove confusing when the chart is next used.

When not in use charts should be stowed flat in their proper drawers or portfolios, with a minimum of folding. The stowed charts should be properly indexed so that any desired one can be found when needed. In removing or replacing a chart, care should be exercised to avoid damage to it or other charts.

A chart that is given proper care in use and stowage can have a long and useful life.

523. Chart lighting.—In the use of charts it is important that adequate lighting be provided. However, the light on the bridge of a ship underway at night should be such as to cause the least interference with the darkness-adaptation of the eyes of bridge personnel who watch for navigational lights, running lights, dangers, etc. Experiments by the Department of the Navy have indicated that red light is least disturbing to eyes which have been adapted to maximum vision during darkness. In some instances red lights, filters, or goggles have been provided on the bridges or in chartrooms of vessels. However, the use of such light seriously affects the appearance of a chart. Red, orange, and buff disappear. Other colors may appear changed. This has led to the substitution of nautical purple for red and orange, and gray for buff on some charts. However, before a chart is used in any light except white, a preliminary test should be made and the effect noted carefully. If a glass or plastic top is provided for the chart table or desk, a dim white light *below* the chart may provide sufficient illumination to permit chart reading, without objectionable disturbance of night vision.

524. Use of small-craft charts.—Although the small-craft charts published by the National Ocean Survey are designed primarily for boatmen, these charts at scales of 1:80,000 and larger are in some cases the only charts available of inland waters transited by large vessels. In other cases the small-craft charts may provide a better presentation of navigational hazards than the standard nautical chart because of scale and detail. *Therefore, it behooves navigators of large vessels transiting inland waters not to ignore the small-craft charts.*

CHAPTER VI

INSTRUMENTS FOR PILOTING AND DEAD RECKONING

Introduction

601. Kinds of instruments.—The word "instrument" has several meanings, at least two of which apply to navigation: (1) an implement or tool, and (2) a device by which the present value of a quantity is measured. Thus, a straightedge and a mechanical log are both instruments, the first serving as a tool, and the second as a measuring device. This chapter is concerned with the navigational instruments used for plotting, and those for measuring distance or speed, depth, and direction. These quantities are the basic data in dead reckoning (ch. VIII) and piloting (ch. X).

In addition to the instruments discussed, several others are important to the navigator. Binoculars are helpful in observing landmarks. A flashlight has many uses, the principal one being to illuminate the scales of instruments when they are to be read at night. Erasers should be soft, and pencils should not be so hard that they damage the surface of the chart. The navigator's chart is discussed in chapter V.

Plotting Instruments

602. Dividers and compasses.—**Dividers,** or "pair of dividers," is an instrument originally used for dividing a line into equal segments. The instrument consists essentially of two hinged legs with pointed ends which can be separated to any distance from zero to the maximum imposed by physical limitations. The setting is retained either by friction at the hinge, as in the usual navigational dividers, or by means of a screw acting against a spring.

If one of the legs carries a pencil or ruling pen, the instrument is called **compasses.** The two legs may be attached to a bar of metal or wood instead of being hinged, thus permitting greater separation of the points. Such an instrument is called **beam compasses** or **beam dividers.**

The principal use of dividers in navigation is to measure or transfer distances on a chart, as described in article 804. Compasses are used for drawing distance circles or any plotting requiring an arc of a circle.

The friction at the hinge of most dividers and compasses can be varied, and should be adjusted so that the instrument can be manipulated easily with one hand, but will retain the separation of the points in normal handling. A drop of oil on the hinge may be required occasionally. The points should be sharp, and should have equal length, permitting them to be brought close together for the measurement of very short distances.

For navigation, it is desirable to have dividers and compasses with comparatively long legs, to provide adequate range for most requirements. It is desirable to learn to manipulate dividers or compasses with one hand.

603. Parallel rulers are an instrument for transferring a line parallel to itself. In its most common form it consists of two parallel bars or rulers, connected in such a manner that when one is held in place on a flat surface, the other can be moved, remaining parallel to its original direction. Firm pressure is required on one ruler while the other is being moved, to prevent slippage. The principal use of parallel rulers in navigation is to transfer the direction of a charted line to a compass rose, and vice versa.

The edges of the rulers should be truly straight; and in the case of double-edged rulers, should be parallel to each other in order that either edge can be used. Parallelism can be tested by comparison of all edges with the same straight line, as a meridian or parallel of a Mercator chart. The linkage can be tested for looseness and lack of parallelism by "walking" the rulers between parallel lines on opposite sides of the chart and back again.

Some metal parallel rulers have a protractor engraved on the upper surface to permit orientation of the ruler at any convenient meridian.

In one type of instrument, parallelism during transfer is obtained by supporting a single ruler on two knurled rollers. Both rollers have the same diameter, and the motion of one is transmitted to the other by an axle having a cover which provides a convenient handle. This type of ruler is convenient and accurate, and is less likely to slip than the linked double-ruler type. However, care is necessary to prevent its rolling off the chart table when the vessel is rolling or pitching.

Directions can also be transferred by means of two triangles such as are used in drafting, or by one triangle and a straightedge. One edge of a triangle is aligned in the desired direction and the triangle is then moved along a straightedge held firmly against one of its other edges until the first edge is at the desired place on the chart. Some triangles have protractors (art. 604) engraved on them to assist in transferring lines. Such a triangle becomes a form of plotter (art. 605).

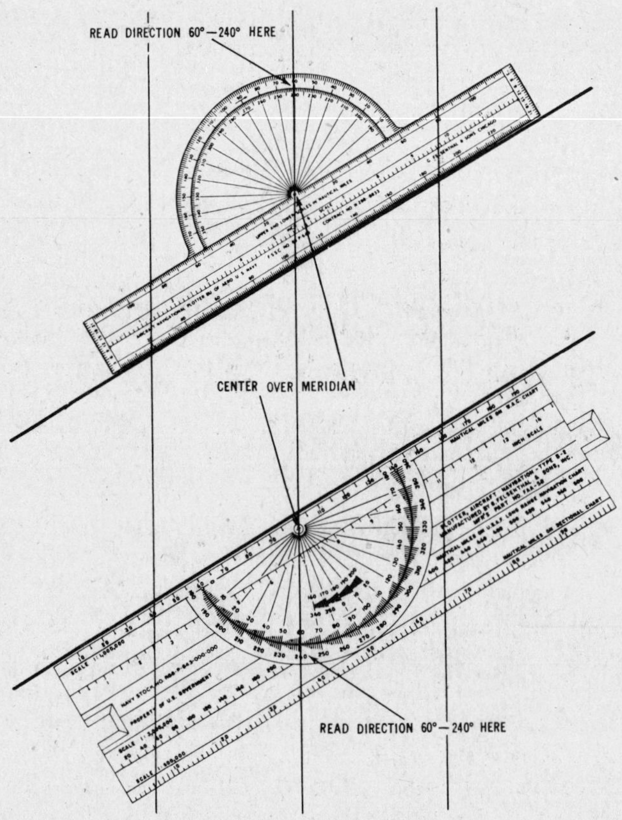

FIGURE 605.—Two plotters having no movable parts.

604. Protractor.—A **protractor** is a device for measuring angles on a chart or other surface. It consists essentially of a graduated arc, usually of 180°, on suitable material such as metal or plastic.

A **three-arm protractor** consists essentially of a circular protractor with three radial arms attached. This instrument is discussed in greater detail in article 1102.

605. Plotters.—The increased popularity of graphical methods in practical navigation during recent decades has resulted in the development of a wide variety of devices to facilitate plotting. In its most common form, such a device consists essentially of a protractor combined with a straightedge. There are two general types, one having no movable parts, and the other having a pivot at the center of the arc of the protractor, to permit rotation of the straightedge around the protractor. Examples of the fixed type are illustrated in figure 605. Those shown were designed for air navigation, but are applicable to many processes of marine navigation. The direction of the straightedge is controlled by placing the center of the protractor arc and the desired scale graduation on the same reference line. If the reference line is a meridian, the directions shown by the straightedge are true geographic directions. If, as in some processes of celestial navigation, it is desired to plot a line perpendicular to another line, the direction may be measured from a parallel of latitude or its equivalent, instead of adding or subtracting 90° from the value and measuring from a meridian. Some fixed-type plotters have auxiliary scales labeled to indicate true direction if a parallel is used as the reference.

Most plotters also provide linear distance scales, as shown in figure 605. In the movable-arm type of plotter, a protractor is aligned with a meridian, and the movable arm is rotated until it is in the desired direction.

606. Drafting machine.—If a chart table of sufficient size is available, a **drafting machine** (fig. 606) is probably the most desirable plotting instrument. The straightedge of this instrument can be clamped so as to retain its direction during movement over the entire plotting area. Straightedges of various lengths and linear scales are interchangeable. Some models make provision for mounting two straightedges perpendicular to each other. However, for most purposes of navigation, the perpendicular is more conveniently obtained by the use of a triangle with a single straightedge. The movable protractor also retains its orientation, and can be adjusted to conform to the compass rose of a chart secured in any position on the chart table. Directions of the straightedge can then be read or set on the protractor without reference to charted compass roses. Use of the clamped protractor requires that charted meridians be straight and parallel, as on a Mercator chart (art. 305). Its use is restricted with projections such as the Lambert conformal (art. 314), on which meridians converge.

When a drafting machine is used, the chart or plotting sheet is first secured to the chart table. The straightedge is aligned with a meridian (or parallel) and clamped in position. The protractor is then adjusted so that 000° and 180° (090° and 270° if a parallel is used) are at the ruler indices, and clamped. With this setting, any subsequent position of the ruler is indicated as a true direction. If the protractor is offset by the amount of the compass error (ch. VII), true directions can be plotted by setting the straightedge at the compass direction on the protractor, without need for applying compass error arithmetically. However, it is generally preferable to keep it set to true directions.

If accurate results are to be obtained, the anchor base must be rigidly fastened to the chart table. This should be checked from time to time, as the base may be loosened by vibration or normal use. The pivots in the anchor base should be firm without binding. The endless belts of the parallel motion mechanism should be taut if rigidity of the ruler is to be preserved. Provision is usually made for adjusting each of the

FIGURE 606.—Drafting machine.

various rulers to uniformity of alignment so that any other ruler can be substituted without changing the setting. As with parallel rulers, the device can be checked for parallelism by means of meridians or parallels on opposite sides of a Mercator chart.

Distance and Speed Measurement

607. Units of measurement.—Mariners generally measure horizontal distances in nautical miles (art. 205), but occasionally in yards or feet. Feet, meters, and fathoms are used for measuring depth of water, and feet or meters for measuring height above water. Nations which have adopted the metric system use meters in place of yards, feet, and fathoms, and for some purposes they use kilometers in place of nautical miles.

Speed is customarily expressed in knots (art. 206), or for some purposes, in kilometers per hour, or yards or feet per minute. For short distances, a nautical mile can be considered equal to 2,000 yards or 6,000 feet. This is a useful relationship because $\frac{6{,}000 \text{ feet}}{60 \text{ minutes}} = 100$ feet per minute. Thus, speed in knots is equal approximately to hundreds of feet per minute or, hundreds of yards per 3-minute interval.

608. Distance, speed, and time are related by the formula

$$\text{distance} = \text{speed} \times \text{time}.$$

Therefore, if any two of the three quantities are known, the third can be found. The units, of course, must be consistent. Thus, if speed is measured in knots, and time in hours, the answer is in nautical miles. Similarly, if distance is measured in yards, and time in minutes, the answer is in yards per minute.

Table 7 is a speed, time, and distance table which supplies one of the three values if the other two are known. It is intended primarily for use in finding the distance steamed in a given time at a known speed. Table 6 is for use in determining speed by measuring the time needed to steam exactly one mile.

The solution of problems involving distance, speed, and time can easily be accomplished by means of a slide rule. If the index of scale *C* is set opposite speed in knots on scale *D*, the distance in nautical miles appears on scale *D* opposite time in hours on scale *C*. If 60 of scale *C* is set opposite speed in knots on scale *D*, the distance covered in any number of *minutes* is shown on scale *D* opposite the minutes on scale *C*. Several circular slide rules particularly adapted for solution of distance, speed, and time problems have been devised. One of these, called the "Nautical Slide Rule," is shown in figure 608.

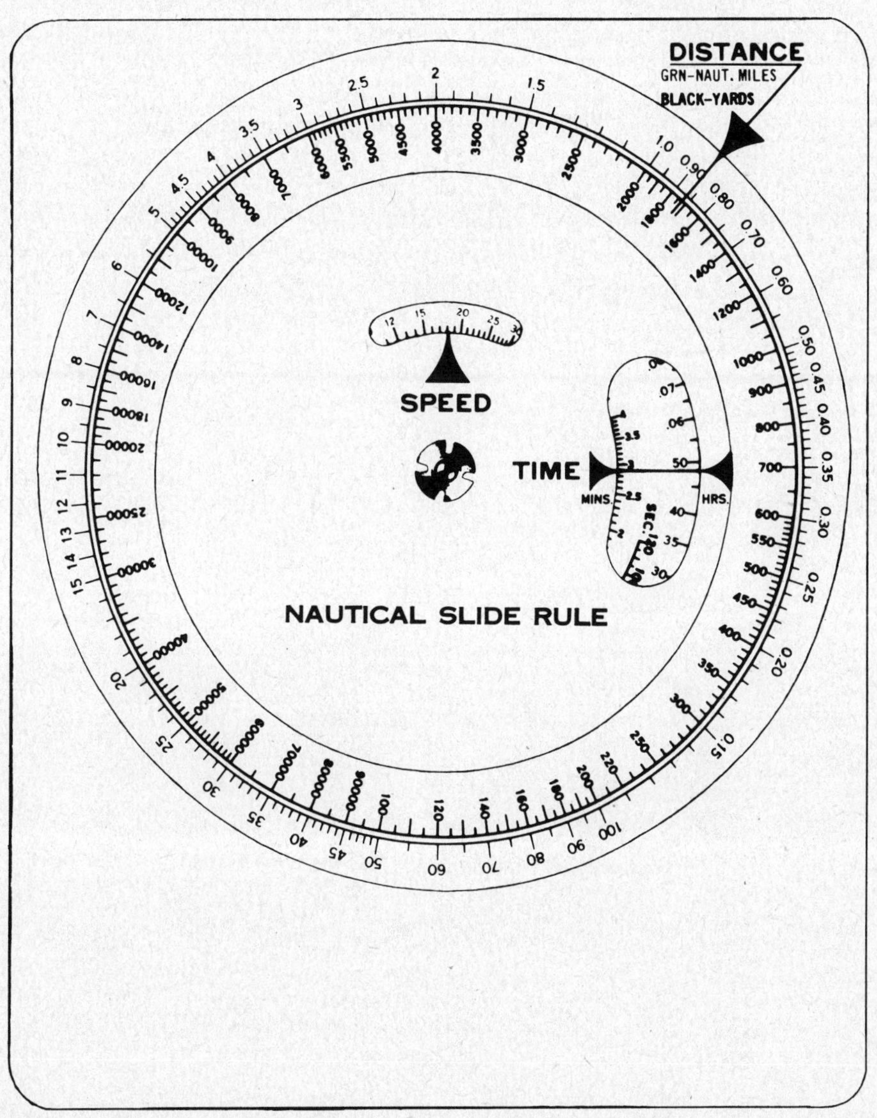

FIGURE 608.—The Nautical Slide Rule.

609. Measurement of distance to an object can be made in a variety of ways, as by radar, sextant angle, range finder, or by several indirect methods. Another method used principally for measuring distance between ships in formation, but useful in measuring other distances, is by means of a small, hand-held instrument called a **stadimeter.**

Two types of stadimeters are illustrated in figure 609a. Both the Brandon or sextant type and the Fisk type operate on the principle used in table 6:

In a plane right triangle, *ABC*, having opposite sides *a*, *b*, and *c*,

$$\tan A = \frac{a}{b}, \text{ and } b = a \cot A.$$

This is applied to the stadimeter as shown in figure 609b. The height of the object is set on the height scale of the instrument, and the measured subtended angle is expressed in yards on the distance (range) scale. To measure the angle, one directs the line of sight through the instrument to the water line of the object observed, and adjusts the range index until the reflection of the top of the object is seen in coincidence with the water line. If the readings are not within the scale of the instrument, some fraction or multiple of the height can be used and a corresponding adjustment made to the answer. Thus, if *half* the height is set on the instrument, the distance indicated is *half* the correct value.

Since the observer's eye is not at the water level, a right angle is not necessarily formed between the line of sight and the top of the observed object. However, the resulting error is so small that it can be neglected under ordinary circumstances.

The aspect of a ship observed should be considered in stadimeter ranges. Thus, little error is introduced if the observer is broad on the beam of the other vessel, as in figure 609b, but less accuracy is obtained if the other vessel presents an end-on view, unless the water line directly below the masthead is correctly estimated.

FIGURE 609a.—Stadimeters. Brandon (sextant) type at left; Fisk type at right.

A stadimeter can be used to indicate that a *change* in distance has occurred, even when the height of the object is not known. Similar indication of a change in distance can be obtained by a sextant (art. 1005), or the actual distance can be determined by the measured angle and table 6 if the height is known.

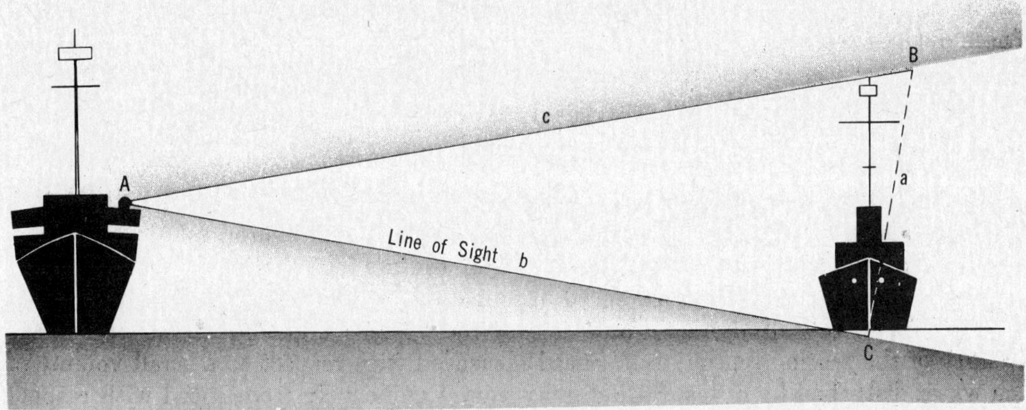

FIGURE 609b.—Geometry of a stadimeter measurement. The distance $b=a \cot A$.

610. Measurement of distance traveled may be made directly, or the distance can be determined indirectly by means of the speed and time, using the relationship given in article 608.

One of the simplest mechanical distance-measuring devices is the **taffrail log,** consisting of (1) a *rotator* which turns like a screw propeller when it is towed through the water; (2) a braided *log line,* up to 100 fathoms in length, which tows the rotator and transmits its rotation to an indicator on the vessel; and (3) a dial and pointer mechanism which registers the distance traveled through the water. In some installations, the readings of the register are transferred electrically to a dial on or near the bridge.

The taffrail log is usually streamed from the ship's quarter, although it may be carried at the end of a short boom extending outboard from the vessel. The log line should be sufficiently long, and attached in such position, that the rotator is clear of the disturbed water of the wake of the vessel; otherwise an error is introduced. Errors may also be introduced by a head or following sea; by mechanical wear or damage, such as a bent fin; or by fouling of the rotator, as by seaweed or refuse.

An accurately calibrated taffrail log in good working order provides information of sufficient reliability for most purposes of navigation. Its readings should be checked at various speeds by towing it over a known distance in an area free from currents. Usually, the average of several runs, preferably in opposite directions, is more accurate than a single one. If an error is found, it is expressed as a percentage and applied to later readings. The calibration should be checked from time to time.

Although a taffrail log is included in the equipment carried by many oceangoing vessels, the convenience and reliability of other methods of determining distance or speed have reduced the dependence formerly placed upon this instrument.

611. Measurement of speed.—Speed can be determined indirectly by means of distance and time, or it can be measured directly. All instruments now in common use for measuring speed determine rate of motion *through the water.* This is done (1) by electromagnetic induction, (2) by differential pressure or measurement of the water pressure due solely to the forward motion of the vessel, (3) by measuring the resistance to the motion of the vessel, (4) by means of a small screw propeller having a speed of rotation proportional to the speed of the vessel, and (5) by determining the relationship between vessel speed and speed of rotation of its screw or screws. Instruments for measuring speed, like those for measuring distance, are called **logs.**

Before the development of modern logs, speed was determined in a number of ways. Perhaps the most common primitive device is the **chip log** (art. 112), although a

ground log (a weight, with line attached, which was thrown overboard and rested on the bottom in shallow water) and a **Dutchman's log** (art. 112) have also been used. These devices are rarely used by modern navigators.

Speed over the bottom can be determined: (1) by direct measurement as by doppler sonar speed log and sensing accelerations; (2) by measuring on the chart or plotting sheet the distance made good between fixes, and dividing this by the time; or (3) by finding the vector sum of velocity through the water and velocity of the current.

612. Problems of water-speed measurement.—Speed measured relative to water is not a stable well-defined quantity because of the motion of the water itself. Most speed logs now used to measure speed through the water measure speed relative to water within the hydrodynamic influence of the vessel's hull and in the immediate vicinity of the motion sensor itself. Speed measured with respect to a small volume of the water disturbed by a vessel's hull may vary significantly from speed with respect to a nearby volume of water. In addition, the motions of a vessel, such as yaw and pitch, introduce variations in the speed over ground. These speed variations combined with sensor response characteristics can generate appreciable errors in the speed measurement. Many of the uncertainties and errors in the measurement of a vessel's speed are functions of the ocean environment and of the characteristics of the vessel carrying the speed sensor. These causes of measurement uncertainty limit the ultimate accuracy of a speed log installation irrespective of the accuracy of the instrumentation itself.

The **potential flow field** represents the changes in the water velocity and pressure distributions caused by the shape, size, and orientation to the flow of the vessel carrying the speed sensor. As water changes its flow direction to pass around the underwater body of a vessel of a given configuration, the resulting accelerations and decelerations generate water velocities near the hull that are significantly different from the velocity of water relative to the vessel far from the influence of the vessel's hull.

Since each hull configuration experiences different local velocities, each system (hull and sensor) must be calibrated to remove the *system errors* inherent in the combination of hull and sensor. The usefulness of measured-mile calibrations in calibrating out system errors is limited by the water depth. Many of the available measured-mile courses are too shallow for accurate calibration. The viscosity of the water results in a friction **boundary layer** or layer of water carried along with the hull. The thickness of this boundary layer varies from fractions of inches at the bow to the order of feet near the stern. In this layer, the water velocity changes from zero at the hull to a value within several percent of free-stream velocity at the outer edge of the boundary layer. As a consequence, sensing elements usually have to extend beyond the boundary layer.

Appendages, such as sonar domes, create wakes that cause error in speed sensors located downstream. For optimum operation, speed sensors should not be mounted near wakes of appendages. However, it is not always possible to place a sensor entirely out of the wake of an appendage and the resulting error must be accepted.

Shallow water effect is a particular aspect of the potential-flow problem that occurs when a vessel is in shallow water. The closeness of the bottom changes the potential-flow velocity distribution by restricting the region in which the water can flow around the hull, causing an increase in the speed reading of a bottom-mounted sensor. The speed problem is compounded because shallow water increases the drag of a vessel causing a decrease of actual speed. It is possible that the speed-reading error coupled with the actual speed decrease may result in no change in indicated speed, while, in fact, the vessel has actually slowed. The precise effects of shallow water on the speed reading are difficult to determine for any specific vessel, and there is no rule of thumb that is applicable to all types and sizes of hulls.

The speed sensor is usually rigidly attached to and undergoes the motions of the vessel carrying it. The vessel may be considered a rigid body with six degrees of freedom, three translation degrees of the vessel's center of gravity and three rotational degrees about the center of gravity. The speed sensor or sensing region is seldom located at the vessel's center of gravity; therefore, the sensor undergoes additional linear displacements proportional to the distance from the center of gravity and the rotation rate.

Average motion errors result from static or dynamic orientation difference from the designed sensor orientation. Speed sensors are usually orientated to measure the water velocity component parallel to the longitudinal axis of the vessel. Neglecting the effects of vessel trim on the water flow near the hull, a change in the static trim from the design trim could reduce the sensed velocity by the cosine of the trim angle through the geometric effects alone. Also, the vessel is normally pitching, yawing, and rolling. The instantaneous pitch and yaw angles cause similar cosine function reductions because the vessel's actual velocity vector is not parallel to the longitudinal axis, and the sensor signal is always reduced by these effects. A more significant error results when the vessel has a drift component due to wind. The speed sensor will not measure this leeway. Most of the average motion errors are quite small (less than a few tenths of 1 percent) and can be neglected. Leeway due to wind may be several knots and cannot be neglected if accurate velocity sensing is required.

Oscillatory errors are the differences between the instantaneous speed reading and the vessel's speed caused by its motion. The oscillatory errors tend to average out over a period of several minutes but may cause appreciable errors in applications requiring a continuous speed input. While almost all of the vessel's motions affect the instantaneous speed reading, the primary cause of the oscillatory error is the pitching motion. For example, for a vessel pitching with an amplitude of only 2½ degrees and a period of 5 seconds with the sensor mounted 10 feet below the center of gravity, the oscillatory error is $\pm 1/3$ knot.

Maneuvering errors are those speed-sensing errors caused by controlled motions of the vessel. For example, when a vessel turns, a drift angle is developed between the heading and the actual water velocity vector at the sensor. The speed sensor only measures the longitudinal velocity component, and the speed is reduced by the cosine of the drift angle at the sensor.

Variability is one of the primary characteristics of water movement in the ocean. This allows prediction of only average values, with the possibility that at any particular time the actual current may be quite different in both direction and magnitude. For example, in the Gulf Stream off Florida, there is 72 percent probability that the current will be toward the northeast with a strength greater than 2 knots. However, there is a 4 percent probability of no current, and a 7 percent probability that the current will be toward the southwest with a strength of 2/3 to 1 knot. In the Sargasso Sea there is almost equal probability of any current direction with magnitudes of 1/3 to 2/3 knot. Thus, it becomes obvious that in correcting for current, average values can be predicted, but large errors are possible unless currents can be accurately measured.

613. The electromagnetic underwater log, commonly called the **EM log,** consists essentially of a rodmeter, sea valve, indicator-transmitter, and remote control unit (fig. 613a). The rodmeter is a strut of streamlined cross section. A sensing device near its tip develops a signal voltage proportional to the speed of the water past it. Of the two general types of rodmeters, one is fixed hull mounted and the other is retractable through a sea valve. The sea valve is mounted in the hull of the vessel and provides a watertight support through which the retractable rodmeter protrudes. It also seals

FIGURE 613a.—Components of electromagnetic underwater log.

the vessel's hull when the rodmeter is removed. The indicator-transmitter houses all moving parts of the equipment and performs the following functions: (1) It indicates the vessel's speed in knots on a dial, (2) it operates synchro transmitters to generate corresponding synchro signals for transmission of speed signals to receivers, (3) it registers on a counter the distance in nautical miles that the vessel has traveled through the water, and (4) it develops a synchro signal representing distance for transmission to receivers. The remote control unit may be used to set speed into the indicator-transmitter. In this mode the underwater log is being used as a **dummy log.**

The fixed rodmeter is designed for submarines, mounts on the exterior of the hull, and does not require a sea valve. The hull penetration is small since only the connector end of the rodmeter passes into the hull. There may be two or three rods installed, depending on the submarine. One is usually mounted topside. A fixed rodmeter has also been developed for use on surface vessels.

The principle of the electromagnetic log is that any conductor will produce a voltage when it is moved across a magnetic field or when a magnetic field is moved with respect to the conductor. Figure 613b illustrates this in elementary form. Note that the direction of the field, the direction of motion, and the direction of the induced voltage are all at right angles to each other. If the magnetic field remains constant, the magnitude of the voltage will be proportional to the speed of movement in the direction indicated.

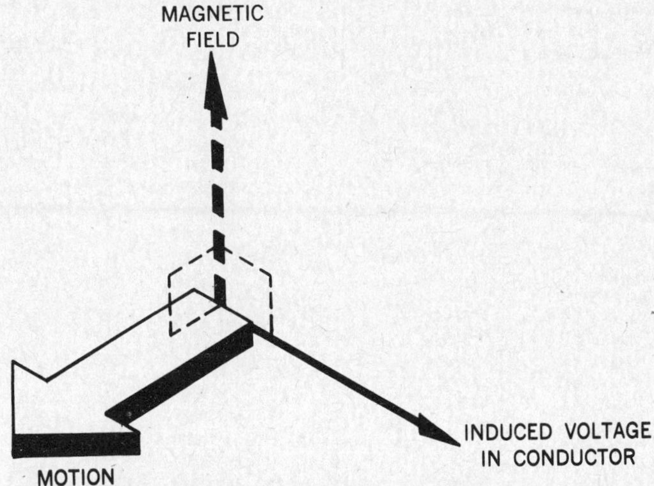

FIGURE 613b.—Voltage induced by relative movement between magnetic field and conductor.

In the electromagnetic log system, a magnetic field produced by a coil in the sensing unit at the outer end of the rodmeter is set up in the water in which the vessel is floating. The sensing unit's outer surface is an insulating layer or boot, except for two Monel (nickel-copper alloy) buttons, one on each side of the rodmeter. As shown in the inset at the upper left of figure 613c, the horizontal plane in which the buttons are located is in the water. The axis of the coil in the sensing unit is perpendicular to this plane, and so are its magnetic flux lines where they cut the plane. If the vessel is moving in the direction indicated by the white arrow, the flux lines cut the water in this plane and induce a voltage in it. Since the plane is cut by the insulating boot of the rodmeter, the induced voltage, sometimes called electromotive force (emf), appears at the buttons in the boot.

A better understanding of this effect can be obtained by comparing the inset of figure 613c with the main part of the figure. The main part shows the coil, its flux field, and one possible symmetrical "water circuit" (the broken white line from button to button) in which the voltage is induced. The inset shows the plane in which the "water circuit" (one of the many that are possible) exists.

The voltage induced by the vessel's motion is in general proportional to the rodmeter's speed with respect to the water. The induced voltage is affected by the flow characteristics of the water past the rodmeter (whether laminar (smooth) or turbulent). The sensor and electronics are designed so that no significant current is drawn from the induced voltage and normal variations of water conductivity do not affect the sensor accuracy.

The vessel's motion other than forward speed, such as pitch and roll, will also produce output signals from the rodmeter.

In order to accurately measure the precise speed signal generated by the sensing unit, most electromagnetic log systems employ a "null-balance" type of electronic voltmeter. For systems currently in naval service, this voltmeter employs an electromechanical servo and dial indicator system such as the one illustrated in figure 613d. Newer systems use all electronic instrumentation and have digital displays. Typical system characteristics include: (1) sensor output signal of 325 microvolts per knot;

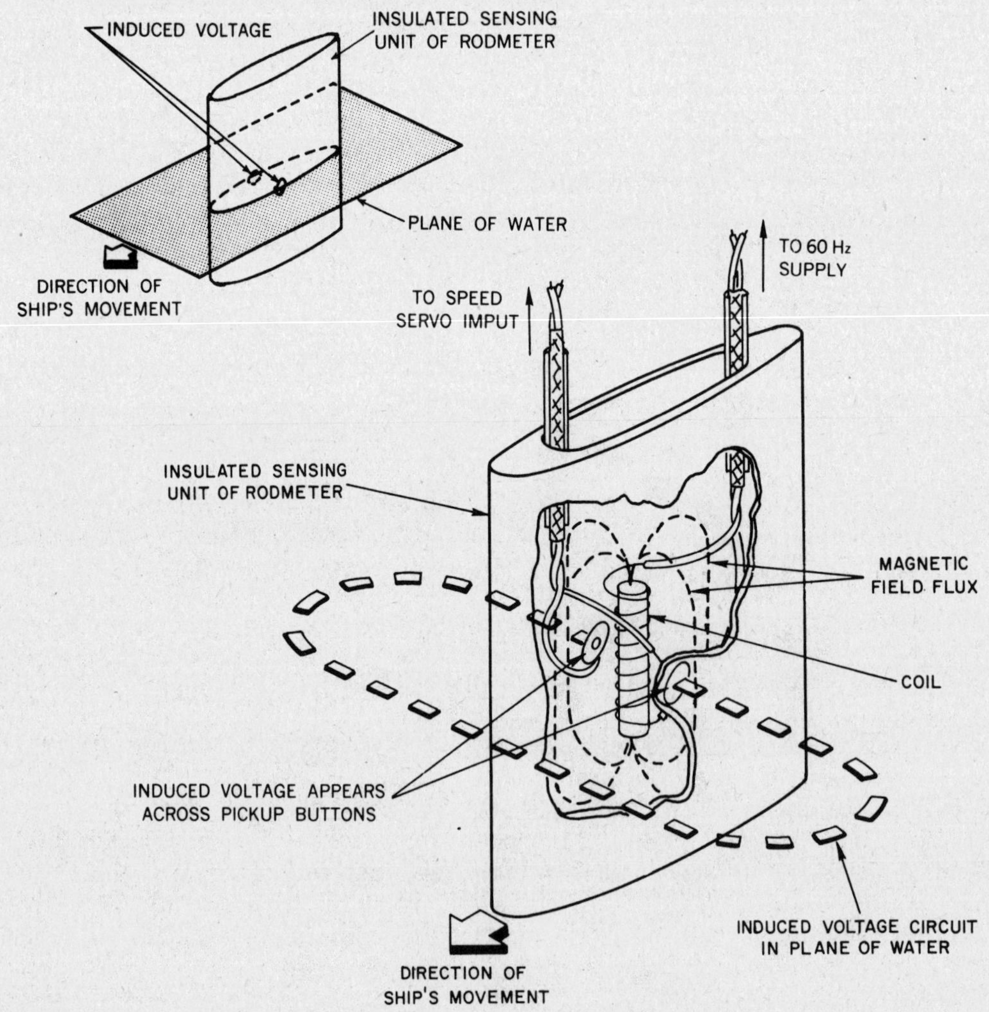

FIGURE 613c.—Sensing principle of electromagnetic log.

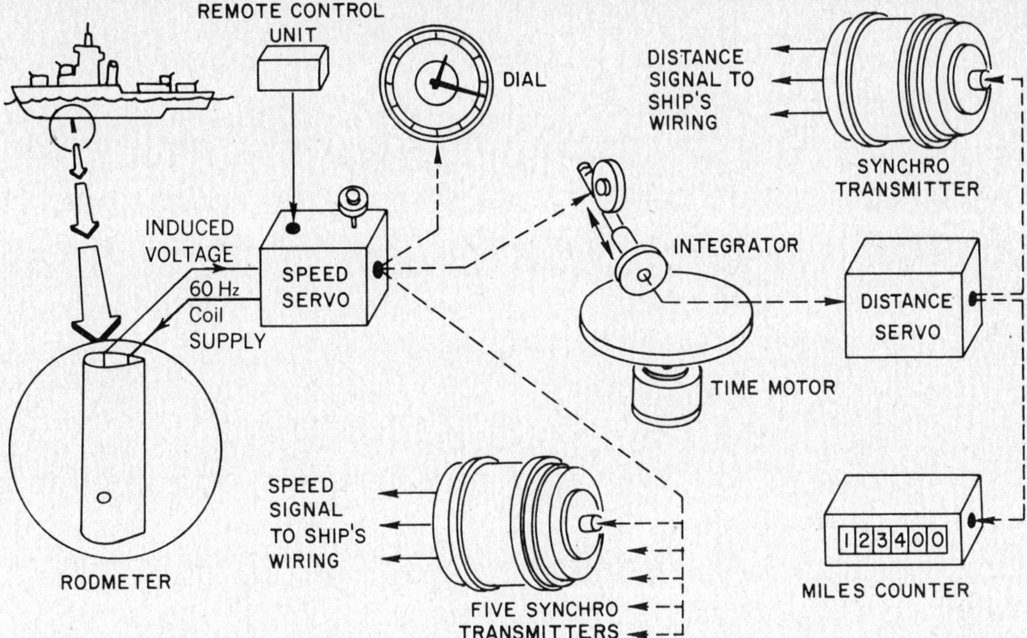

FIGURE 613d.—Electromagnetic log speed measuring system.

(2) instrument speed accuracy of 0.05 knot; (3) sensitivity to speed changes of 0.01 knot; (4) instrument distance accuracy of better than 1 percent of water distance traveled; and (5) capability to compensate for different hull flow characteristics. Several commercial electromagnetic logs provide slightly less precision.

614. Speed measurement by dynamic water pressure.—When an object is moving through a fluid such as water or air, its forward side is exposed to a *dynamic* pressure which is proportional to the speed at which the object is moving, in addition to the *static* pressure due to depth and density of the fluid above the object. Therefore, if dynamic pressure can be measured, this principle can be used for determining speed.

One of the most widely used means of measuring dynamic pressure is by a **Pitot tube.** This device consists of a tube having an opening on its forward side or end. If the tube is stationary in the water, this opening is subject to static pressure only. But when the tube is in motion, the pressure at the opening is the sum of static and dynamic pressures. This is called **Pitot pressure** or **total pressure.** The Pitot tube is surrounded by an outer tube which has openings along its athwartship sides. Whether the tube is stationary or in motion, these openings are subject to static pressure only.

In the **Pitot-static log** the Pitot tube is in the form of a vertical "rodmeter" which extends through and is supported by a sea valve in the the vessel's bottom. The tube extends 24 to 30 inches below the bottom of the vessel, into water relatively undisturbed by motion of the hull. The two pressures, Pitot and static, are led to separate bellows attached to opposite ends of a centrally pivoted lever. This lever is electrically connected to a mechanism which controls the speed of a pump. When the vessel is dead in the water, the pressures are equal, and the pump is stopped. When the ship is moving, the pump speed is regulated so that the pressures in the two bellows are equalized. Thus, the pump speed is proportional to the ship speed.

Various less accurate instruments have been devised for determining speed by measuring water pressure due to forward motion of the vessel. These are relatively simple, inexpensive instruments intended primarily for use by small craft. One instrument, the **force log,** has a strut which the water pressure forces aft against a calibrated spring. A flexible hydraulic cable transmits the motion to a speed indicator. The force log is probably the oldest of the speed logs used today. The principle of this log is that the resistance (drag) force on a drag strut is proportional to the square of the vessel's speed. Another instrument uses a small scoop attached to the hull of the vessel. The pressure of the water scooped up is transmitted by tubing to the speed indicator, which is essentially a pressure gage graduated in knots. A third type measures the drag of a small towed object. The accuracy of such devices depends to a large extent upon the refinements of design, manufacture, installation, maintenance, and calibration.

615. Impeller log.—The impeller log may be a hull-mounted or a towed log. The impeller (propeller) rotates as it moves through the water. The number of its revolutions is proportional to the distance traveled through the water, and its speed of rotation is proportional to the vessel's speed. These logs usually employ a magnetic-induction type of pulse frequency generator so that no physical contact, other than bearing surface, is required between the rotor and the body of the instrument. This design permits the use of simple and accurate instrumentation. The characteristic curve of output frequency versus speed for this log is quite linear, except at very low speeds. The nonlinear curve at low speeds is the result of bearing drag on the otherwise freely rotating impeller.

616. Speed by engine revolution counter.—The number of turns of a propeller shaft is proportional to the distance traveled. If the element of time is added, speed can be determined. If the screw were advancing through a solid substance, the distance it would advance in one revolution would be the **pitch** of the screw. Thus, if a propeller having a pitch of ten feet turns at 200 revolutions per minute, it advances 2,000 feet in one minute, equivalent to a speed of 19.75 knots. It does not do so in water because of **slip,** the difference between the distance it would advance in a solid substance and actual distance traveled, expressed as a percentage of the former. For example, if slip is 18 percent, both the ship's speed and distance covered are reduced by this percentage. Thus, instead of 19.75 knots, the speed is only $19.75 \times 0.82 = 16.2$ knots.

Slip depends upon the type and speed of rotation of the propeller, the type of ship, the condition of loading and ship's bottom, the state of the sea and the ship's course relative to it, and the apparent wind. Despite the many variables, slip can be determined with sufficient accuracy for practical navigation. This is usually accomplished by steaming a known distance and noting the time of passage. The speed corresponding to the number of revolutions being used can then be determined by means of the formula of article 608, in the form

$$\text{speed} = \frac{\text{distance}}{\text{time}}$$

or by reference to table 6 (if the distance is exactly one mile). Thus, speed can be determined directly, without computing slip, and a table or curve of ship speed for various engine revolution speeds can be made. Any suitable distance can be used, but a distance of one nautical mile has been measured at various convenient locations. Each such **measured mile** is suitably marked on the beach, and shown on the chart, with the course to steer.

This method of determining speed is widely used in the merchant marine. By means of an **engine revolution counter** the number of revolutions during any suitable time interval can be measured. If a **tachometer** is available, the *rate* of shaft revolution is determined, usually in revolutions per minute. For best results, allowance should be made for condition of the bottom, draft and trim of the vessel, and the state of the sea.

Depth Measurement

617. Importance.—Accurate knowledge of the depth of water under a vessel is of such navigational importance that there is a legal requirement that American merchant vessels of 500 gross tons or more engaged in ocean and coastwise service "shall be fitted with an efficient mechanical deep-sea sounding apparatus in addition to the deep-sea hand leads."

618. The lead (lĕd) is a device consisting of a suitably marked line having a weight attached to one of its ends. It is used for measuring depth of water. Although the lead is probably the oldest of all navigational aids, it is still a highly useful device, particularly in periods of reduced visibility. Although its greatest service is generally in the shoal water near the shore, it sometimes can provide valuable information when the vessel is out of sight of land.

Two types of lead are in common use, the **hand lead,** weighing from 7 to 14 pounds and having a line marked to about 25 fathoms; and the **deep-sea (dipsey) lead,** weighing from 30 to 100 pounds and having a line marked to 100 fathoms or more in length. The markings commonly used on lead lines are as follows:

Distance from lead in fathons	*Marking*	*Distance from lead in fathoms*	*Marking*
2	two strips of leather	20	short line with two knots
3	three strips of leather	25	short line with one knot
5	white rag (usually cotton)	30	short line with three knots
7	red rag (usually wool)	35	short line with one knot
10	leather with hole	40	short line with four knots
13	same as three fathoms	45	short line with one knot
15	same as five fathoms	50	short line with five knots
17	same as seven fathoms		etc.

Fathoms marked on the lead line are called **marks.** The intermediate whole fathoms are called **deeps.** In reporting depths it is customary to use these terms, as "by the mark five," "deep six," etc. The only fractions of a fathom usually reported are halves and quarters, the customary expressions being "and a half, eight," "less a quarter, four," etc. A practice sometimes followed is to place distinctive markings on the hand lead line at each foot near the critical depths of the vessel with which it is to be used. The markings should be placed on the lead line when it is wet, and the accuracy of the marking should be checked from time to time to detect any changes in the length of the line. The distance from the hand of the leadsman to the surface of the water under various conditions of loading should be determined so that correct allowance can be made when the marking nearest the surface cannot be observed.

The lead itself has a recess in its bottom. If this recess is filled with tallow or other suitable substance, a sample of the bottom can sometimes be obtained. This information can prove helpful in establishing the position of the vessel. If tallow is not available, some other substance can be used. Soap is suitable if it is replaced from time to time. When the recess is filled for obtaining a sample, the lead is said to be **armed** with the substance used.

619. Echo sounder.—Most soundings are made by means of an **echo sounder.** In this instrument a pulse of electrical energy is converted periodically to sound energy and transmitted downward by a transducer. When the energy strikes the bottom (or any other object having acoustic properties different from those of water), a portion is reflected back to the transducer as an echo. This energy is reconverted to electrical energy for presentation. Because the speed of sound in water is nearly constant, the amount of time which elapses between the transmission of a pulse and the reception of its echo is a measure of the distance traveled, or in this case, depth.

Depth information is presented in either of two ways; namely, an indicator consisting of a cathode-ray tube or a recorder which records depth on calibrated paper.

There are many forms of echo sounder. A typical installation (fig. 619a) consists essentially of a receiver-transmitter, transducer, and interconnecting cables. The receiver-transmitter includes all components and subassemblies of the system, except the transducer and interconnecting cables. The recorder performs the function of recording depth versus time on a paper roll visible through a window in the cabinet's front door. When the recorder is used, it keys the transmitter at a predetermined rate. The cathode-ray tube indicator, mounted below the recorder, indicates depth on a cathode-ray tube; a calibrated circular dial overlays the cathode-ray tube providing a means for reading the depth through an opening in the cabinet's front door. When the indicator is used, it keys the transmitter at a predetermined rate. The transducer converts the electrical energy to sound energy, transmits the sound into the water, receives returned echoes, and converts the returned energy to electrical energy.

When the recorder of the typical installation (fig. 619a) is energized by placing the depth range switch in one of the three recorder positions (600 feet, 600 fathoms, 6000 fathoms), a specially treated recording paper, held between two rollers, is moved at a uniform speed horizontally in front of a grounded plate. At the same time a stylus assembly is moved at a uniform speed vertically across the face of the paper. The rate of movement depends on the range selected, and is so fixed that one of the two stylii appears at the top of the recording paper (0 depth) when the transmitter is keyed and reaches the bottom of the paper at the same time as an echo would be received from the maximum depth of the selected depth range.

The recording paper is marked by the application of a voltage between the stylus and the grounded plate when the echo is received.

In the same installation, depth indication on the 100 feet and 100 fathom scales is given on the face of a cathode-ray tube by radial modulation of a circular sweep. The illuminated trace follows a circular course at a constant angular velocity. The time to complete one revolution is the time required for an echo to return from 100 feet or 100 fathoms at the assumed speed of sound in water. The transmitted pulse and the returned echoes cause radial modulations. Beams of light thus appear behind a calibrated screen covering the indicator tube face, one at position zero (transmitted pulse) and the others at positions corresponding to the echoes (fig. 619b).

The transmitter is keyed mechanically by the recorder or electronically by the cathode-ray tube indicator circuit, depending on the depth range scale in use. Keying may be automatic or manual.

The operator must observe certain precautions in his use of this typical installation. He must change depth range scales when conditions warrant. For example, a depth of 300 feet can be recorded on the 6000-fathom scale, better on the 600-fathom scale, but best on the 600-foot scale. If a range is selected which is less than the water depth, the echo will return either after the stylus that keyed the transmitter has left the paper (resulting in no indication) or after the other stylus has reached the paper (resulting in a false indication). Similarly, if an indicator range is selected which is less than the water depth, the result will be no indication or a false indication.

Examples of how false echoes can be produced follow. Suppose the water depth beneath the vessel is 1,300 feet and the 600-foot recorder scale is in use. Refer to figure 619c. Stylus A marks the paper at zero and travels downward while stylus B travels upward. Stylus B must travel a distance corresponding to 1,200 feet before it appears

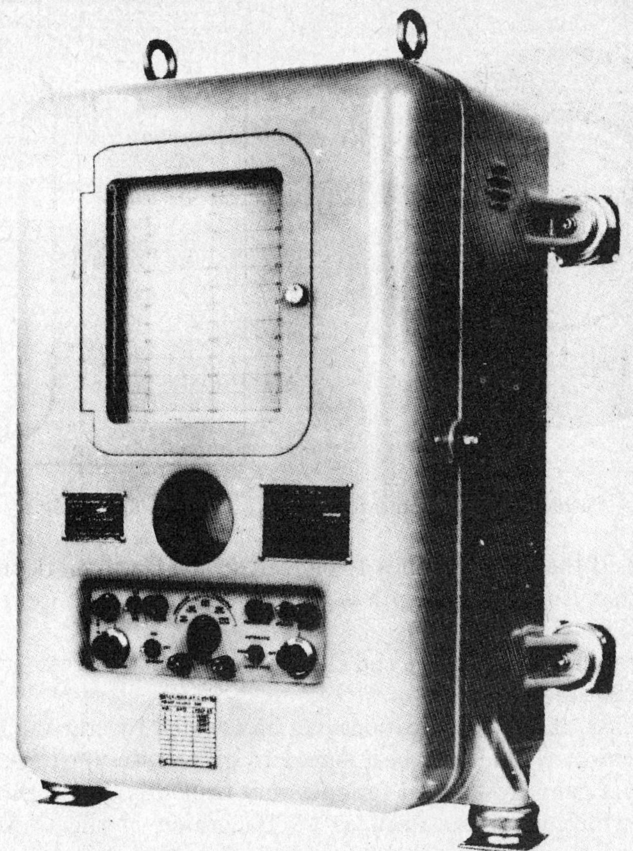
SONAR RECEIVER-TRANSMITTER

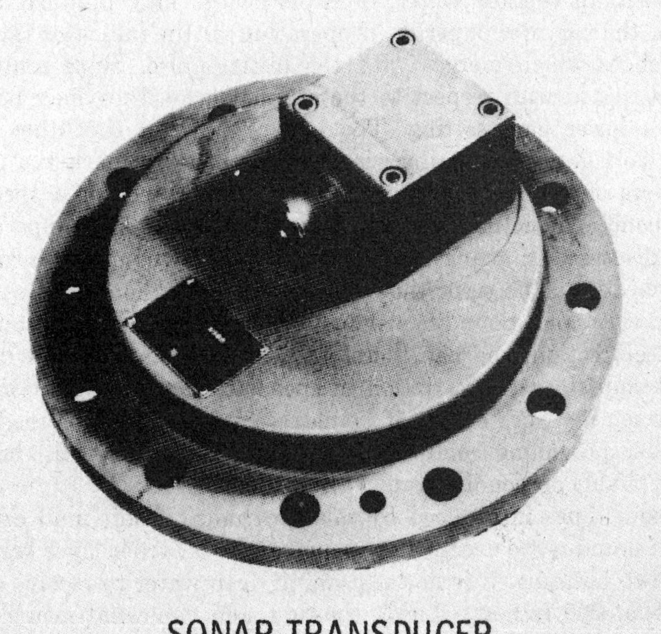
SONAR TRANSDUCER

FIGURE 619a.—Echo sounder.

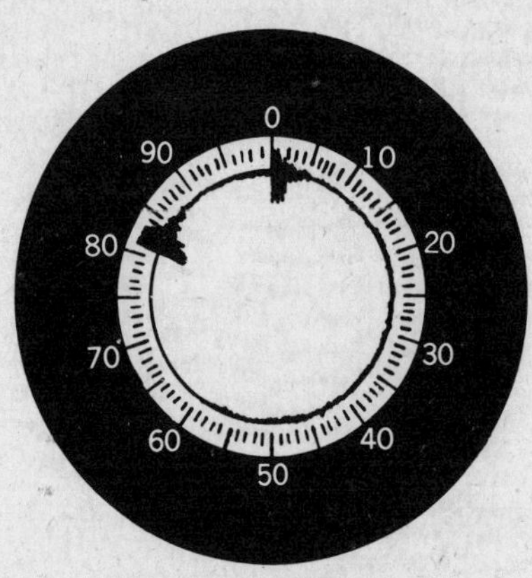

FIGURE 619b.—Cathode-ray tube indicator.

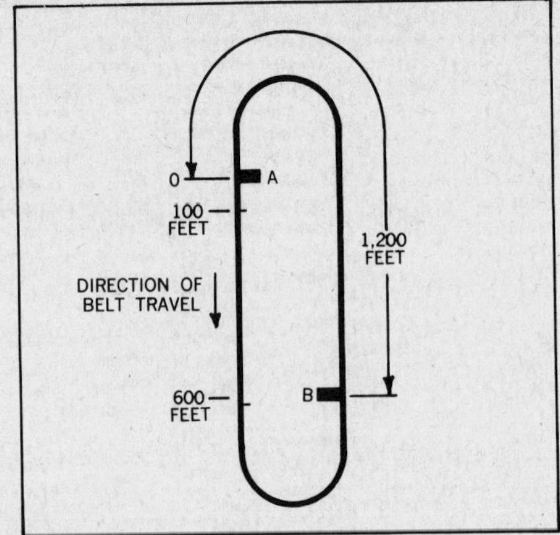

FIGURE 619c.—Side view of stylus belt.

at the zero line. If the water depth is 1,300 feet, stylus B will mark the paper at 100 feet. It is obvious that if the water depth is from 600 to 1,200 feet, no echo will appear on the paper.

If the water depth is 120 feet and the 100-foot indicator scale is in use, a false echo will appear at 20 feet.

In either case, the false indications can be avoided by starting on the highest scale and then switching to the scale best suited to give optimum presentation.

The receiver gain must be set for optimum response. Too high a gain will result in reverberation which manifests itself as an elongation of the transmitted pulse. Too high a gain may also result in multiple echoes. Multiple echoes are caused by the returning echo striking the vessel's keel or the water surface, reflecting back to the bottom, and again returning to the transducer. Very often, several of these multiple echoes can be seen. In shallow water, multiple echoes may produce a straight line the full length of the recorder paper or, if operating on the indicator ranges, produce a solid mass of echoes which merges with the initial pulse. Since multiple echoes are considerably attenuated with respect to the original echo, they may be eliminated by operating with a lower gain setting. Too low a gain, on the other hand, will not develop enough voltage from an otherwise suitable echo to mark the paper.

Echo sounders of American manufacture are calibrated for a speed of sound of 4,800 feet per second. The actual speed varies primarily with the temperature, pressure, and salinity, but in the ocean is nearly always faster than the speed of calibration. The error thus introduced is on the side of safety unless the water is fresh or very cold. Soundings shown on charts are those obtained by an echo sounder without correction, and can therefore be compared directly with the readings obtained aboard ship since the variation in speed from mean conditions is not great. Only in precise scientific work should it be necessary to correct the reading for actual sound speed under prevailing conditions. Accurate adjustment can be made only if information is available on conditions at various depths.

Errors are sometimes introduced by false bottoms. If soft mud covers the ocean floor, some of the sound-wave energy may penetrate to a harder layer beneath, resulting in indication of two bottoms. It is not unusual in deep water to receive a strong return at a depth of about 200 fathoms during the day, and somewhat nearer the surface at night. This is called the **phantom bottom** or **deep scattering layer.** It is believed to be due to large numbers of tiny marine animals. Schools of fish return an echo sufficiently strong to make the echo sounder a valuable aid to commercial fishermen.

In modern equipment the sound waves, whether sonic or ultrasonic, are produced electrically by means of a **transducer,** a device for converting electrical energy to sound waves, or vice versa. The transducer utilizes either the piezo-electric properties of quartz or the magnetostriction properties of nickel and its alloys.

Early models produced sound signals by striking the ship's hull with a mechanical hammer in the forward part of the vessel. The echo was received by a microphone in the after part of the vessel, depth being determined by the angle at which the signal returned.

Direction Measurement

620. Reference directions.—A horizontal direction is generally expressed as an angle between a line extending in some **reference direction** and a line extending in the given direction. The angle is numerically equal to the difference between the two directions, called the **angular distance** from the reference direction. Unless the reference direction is stated or otherwise understood, the intended direction is in doubt. Thus, to a navigator, direction 135° is southeast. To an astronomer or surveyor, it may be northwest.

A number of reference directions are used in navigation. If a direction is stated in three figures, without designation of reference direction, it is generally understood that the direction is related to true (geographical) north. When grid navigation is being used, particularly when in the high latitudes, grid north is generally used as the reference direction. The reference direction for magnetic directions is magnetic north, and that for compass directions is compass north. For relative bearings it is the heading of the ship. For amplitudes, the reference direction is east or west, usually 090° or 270° true, but magnetic, compass, or even grid east or west may be used. In maneuvering situations, the heading of another vessel might be used as the reference direction.

The primary function of an instrument used for measuring direction is to determine the reference direction. This having been done, other directions can be indicated by a compass rose oriented in the reference direction. North is established by some form of compass. A compass rose is attached to the north-seeking element so that other directions can be determined directly. However, if one always keeps in mind that the primary function of the instrument is to indicate a reference direction, he should be able to avoid some of the mistakes commonly made in the application of compass errors.

621. Desirable characteristics of a navigational compass.—To adequately serve its purpose, a navigational compass needs to have certain characteristics to permit it to meet requirements of accuracy, reliability, and convenience.

The most important characteristic is accuracy. No other quality, however important or to whatever extent it may be possessed, compensates for the lack of accuracy. This does not mean that the compass need be without error, but that such errors as it may possess can be readily determined. Provisions should be made for removing deviation or reducing it to a minimum (ch. VII). If accurate horizontal directions are to be determined, the compass needs to be provided with some type of compass rose maintained in a horizontal position. Adequate sighting equipment is needed if bearings are to be observed, and an index is needed to mark the forward direction parallel to the keel if heading is to be measured. Accurate readings cannot be expected from a compass that **hunts** (oscillates) excessively. A characteristic closely related to accuracy is precision. The amount of precision required varies somewhat with the use and depends as much upon the steadiness of the compass and its design as upon its inherent qualities.

A compass is reliable when its operation is not often interrupted; when its indications are relatively free from unknown or unsuspected disturbances; when it is little affected by extremes of temperature, moisture, vibration, or the shock of gunfire; and when it is not so sensitive that large errors are introduced by ordinary changes in conditions or equipment near the compass.

The value of a compass is dependent somewhat upon the convenience with which it can be used. Accuracy, too, may be involved. Thus, a compass should not be installed in such a position that one must be in an unnatural or uncomfortable position to use it. A compass intended for use in obtaining bearings is of reduced value if it is installed at a location that does not permit an unobstructed view in most directions. The compass graduations and index should be clean, adequately lighted if the instrument is to be used at night, and clearly marked.

622. Kinds of compasses.—The compasses commonly used by the mariner are (1) *magnetic* and (2) *gyroscopic*. The magnetic compass tends to align itself with the magnetic lines of force of the earth, while the gyrocompass seeks the true (geographic) meridian. The word "compass" is also applied to instruments which do not continuously indicate some form of north. Thus, the free gyro (art. 630) tends to remain approximately aligned with any great circle to which it is set.

A compass may be designated to indicate its principal use, as a **standard, steering,** or **boat compass.** The compass designated as standard is usually a magnetic compass installed in an exposed position having an unobstructed view in most directions, permitting accurate determination of error. Preferably, it is located at a magnetically favorable position near the bridge. Before the development of a reliable gyrocompass, the standard compass was used for navigation of the vessel and for determining the error of the steering compass.

Although the modern, reliable gyrocompass has largely superseded the magnetic compass for most purposes, directional information is so important to a vessel that the availability of a second method is considered justified. It is wise to understand both types, keep a record of errors and the performance of all compasses, and to compare the indications of magnetic and gyrocompasses at frequent intervals, as every half hour when underway.

623. Magnetic compasses.—If a small magnet is pivoted at its center of gravity in such manner that it is free to turn and dip, it will tend to align itself with the magnetic field of the earth (art. 706). It thus provides a directional reference and becomes a simple compass. However, such a compass would not be adequate for use aboard ship. For this purpose a compass should have a stronger directive element than that provided by a single, pivoted magnet, should have provision for measuring various directions, should have some means of damping the oscillations of the directive element, should be approximately horizontal, and should have some means of neutralizing local magnetic influences.

In a mariner's compass, several magnets are mounted parallel to each other. To them is attached a **compass card** having a compass rose to indicate various directions (art. 624). Both magnets and compass card are enclosed in a bowl having a glass top through which the card can be seen. The bowl is weighted at the bottom and is suspended in gimbals in such manner that it remains nearly horizontal as the vessel rolls and pitches. In nearly all modern compasses the bowl is filled with a liquid that supplies a buoyant force almost equal to the force of gravity acting upon the directive element and card. This reduces the friction on the pivot (a metal point in a jeweled bearing), and provides a means of damping the oscillations of the compass card. The card is mounted in such manner as to remain in an essentially horizontal position. A mark called a **lubber's line** is placed on the inner surface of the bowl, adjacent to the compass card, to indicate the forward direction parallel to the keel when the bowl is correctly installed. The gimbals used for mounting the compass bowl are attached to a stand called a **binnacle,** which in most installations is permanently and rigidly attached to the deck of the vessel, usually on its longitudinal center line. Most binnacles provide means for neutralization of local magnetic influences due to magnetism within the vessel. A cover or "hood" is provided to protect the compass from the elements, dust, etc.

Directional information is of such importance that selection and installation of a suitable compass should be made carefully, seeking such guidance as may be needed. In the U. S. Navy this is covered by systems command directives. For merchant vessels and yachts, one would do well to consult a dependable compass adjustor before selecting and installing a compass or making any alteration in the vicinity of the compass. Common errors are the use of a compass designed for a different type craft (as an aircraft compass in a boat), permitting chrome plating of a binnacle by someone who does not know how to do this without creating a magnetic field, authorizing electric welding of steel near the compass, improper installation of magnetic equipment or electric appliances near the compass, allowing short circuits to occur in the vicinity of the compass, etc.

After the compass has been selected and installed, proper adjustment and compensation (ch. VII) are important, and future care of the instrument should not be neglected. It should be checked and overhauled at regular intervals, and any indication of malfunctioning or deterioration, however slight, should not be overlooked. Discoloration of the liquid or the presence of a bubble, for instance, indicates a condition that should be investigated and corrected at once. If it becomes necessary to add liquid, one should be certain that he has the correct substance, and should attempt to determine the source of the leak. Except as a temporary expedient, this is best done by a professional. Some compasses should be protected from prolonged exposure to sunlight, to prevent discoloration of the card and liquid.

624. The compass card is composed of light, nonmagnetic material. In nearly all modern compasses the card is graduated in 360°, increasing clockwise from north through east, south, and west. An older system still used somewhat is to graduate the card through 90° in each quadrant, increasing from both north and south. Some compass cards are graduated in "points," usually in addition to the degree graduations. There are 32 **points of the compass,** 11¼° apart. The four **cardinal points** are north, east, south, and west. Midway between these are four **intercardinal points** at northeast, southeast, southwest, and northwest. These eight points are the only ones appearing on the cards of compasses used by the U. S. Navy. The eight points between cardinal and intercardinal points are named for the two directions between which they lie, the cardinal name being given first, as north northeast, east northeast, east southeast, etc. The remaining 16 points are named for the nearest cardinal or intercardinal point "by" the next cardinal point in the direction of measurement, as north by east, northeast by north, etc. Smaller graduations are provided by dividing each point into four "quarter points," thus producing 128 graduations altogether. There are several systems of naming the quarter points. That used in the U. S. Navy when quarter points were used is given in table. 2.

The naming of the various graduations of the compass card in order is called **boxing the compass,** an important attainment by the student mariner of earlier generations. The point system of indicating relative bearings (art. 1004) survived long after degrees became almost universally used for compass and true directions. Except for the cardinal and intercardinal points, and occasionally the two-point graduations, all of which are used to indicate directions generally (as "northwest winds," meaning winds from a general northwesterly direction), the point system has become largely historical.

625. The U. S. Navy 7½-inch compass has a liquid-filled bowl in which a 7½-inch aluminum card is pivoted. There is provision for either one or two pairs of magnets, symmetrically placed. The card and magnet assembly is provided with a central float or air chamber to reduce the weight on the pivot to between 60 and 90 grains (0.14 and 0.21 oz.) at 60°F when the correct compass fluid is used. Older compasses use a fluid consisting of 45 percent ethyl alcohol and 55 percent distilled water. Newer compasses use a highly refined petroleum distillate similar to varsol. Use of this oil increases the stability and efficiency of the compass. A hollow cone extends into the underside of the float. The bottom of this cone is open. The pointed top has a jewel bearing of synthetic sapphire. The card-float-magnet assembly rests on an osmium-iridium tipped pivot at the jewel center. This pivot extends upward from the bottom of the bowl. This compass is illustrated in figure 625.

The compass bowl is made of cast bronze, and has a tightly gasketed glass top cover to prevent leakage of the liquid. A bellows-type expansion chamber is provided to allow for changes in volume of the liquid as the temperature changes. The top rim or bezel of the bowl is accurately machined so that an azimuth or bearing circle can be placed over it. The compass is equipped with a gimbal ring for keeping the compass level when mounted in a binnacle. In addition to providing support for the compass, the binnacle has provision for housing the correctors used to partially neutralize local magnetic effects within the vessel.

626. The U. S. Navy 5-inch compass is lighter in weight and requires less space than the 7½-inch compass. This U. S. Navy No. 3 compass has a brass compass card with photo-etched perforations which permit underlighting with red light to meet darkness adaptation requirements. When such a card is used with both transmitted and reflected light in all combinations, there is a "twilight zone" in which the intensity of the

FIGURE 625.—U. S. Navy 7½-inch compass.

Courtesy of John E. Hand & Sons Company.

FIGURE 626a.—Binnacle for U. S. Navy 5-inch magnetic compass.

light transmitted through the perforations is equal to that of the reflected light from the surrounding area. In the U. S. Navy No. 3 compass this problem is overcome by the installation of a shaded lamp inside the binnacle hood. The light from this lamp is directed at the lubber's line and adjacent compass card area. This light enables daylight viewing of the compass card. The red illumination is required only when practically complete darkness prevails.

In addition to providing support for the compass, the binnacle illustrated in figure 626a has provision for housing the correctors used to partially neutralize local magnetic effects within the vessel. The correctors consist of a tube assembly with heeling magnet, quadrantal correctors, fixed fore-and-aft and athwartship permanent magnetic correctors, and permanent magnet correctors rotatable about fore-and-aft and athwartship axes.

The fixed permanent magnets are in the form of wire magnet bundles of up to seven magnets each and are contained in three magnet tubes as shown in figure 626a. The athwartship tube is fixed to the after side of the binnacle. One fore-and-aft tube is on the port side of the binnacle; the other is on the starboard side.

The fixed fore-and-aft and athwartship magnets are used to obtain a "coarse" correction; the rotatable correctors are used to obtain a "fine" correction. Normally the coarse correction reduces the deviation from its original value to about 5°, the fine correction reduces the deviation to its residual value.

Except for the heeling magnet the various correctors are shown in schematic form in figure 626b. When the rotatable magnets on either axis lie in a plane parallel to the plane of the compass card, the associated magnetic field has no effect on the compass card magnets. This magnetic field is shown schematically in figure 626c for

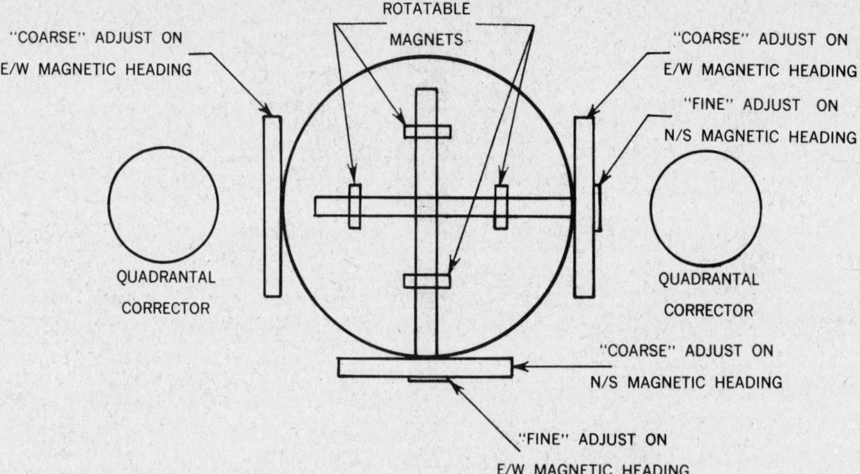

FIGURE 626b.—Correcting system of U. S. Navy 5-inch magnetic compass.

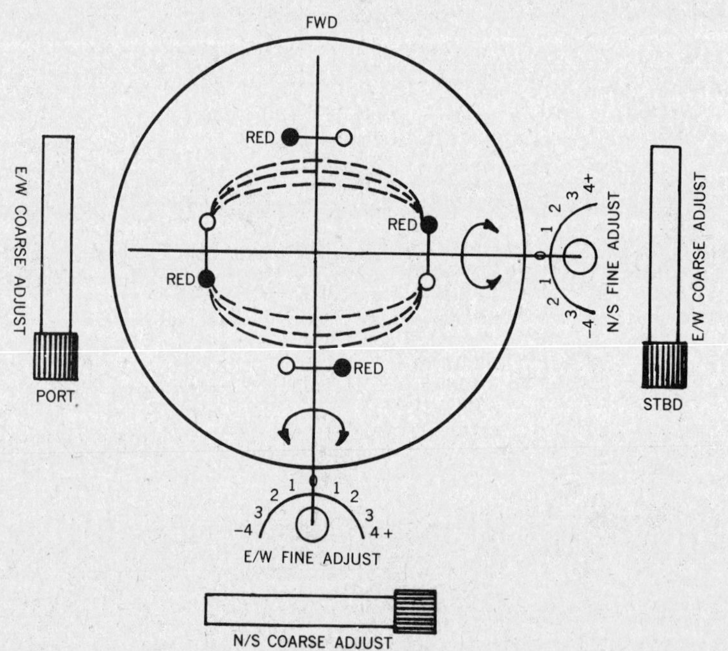

FIGURE 626c.—Coarse and fine adjustments of U. S. Navy 5-inch magnetic compass.

the magnets rotatable about the athwartship axis. When the rotatable magnets are inclined to the plane of the compass card, the effect on the compass card magnets varies with the sine function of the angle of inclination, the maximum effect being when the plane of the rotatable magnets is inclined 90° to the plane of the compass card.

Figure 626d illustrates the fine adjustment control used to rotate the magnets. The fine adjustment should be limited to approximately the last 5° of deviation correction or to the range in which the sine function is more nearly linear.

627. Other magnetic compasses.—The U. S. Navy No. 5 magnetic boat compass (fig. 627a) is a top reading, flat glass topped unit. The 3-inch compass card is made of sheet aluminum and incorporates an annular float to obtain a degree of buoyancy

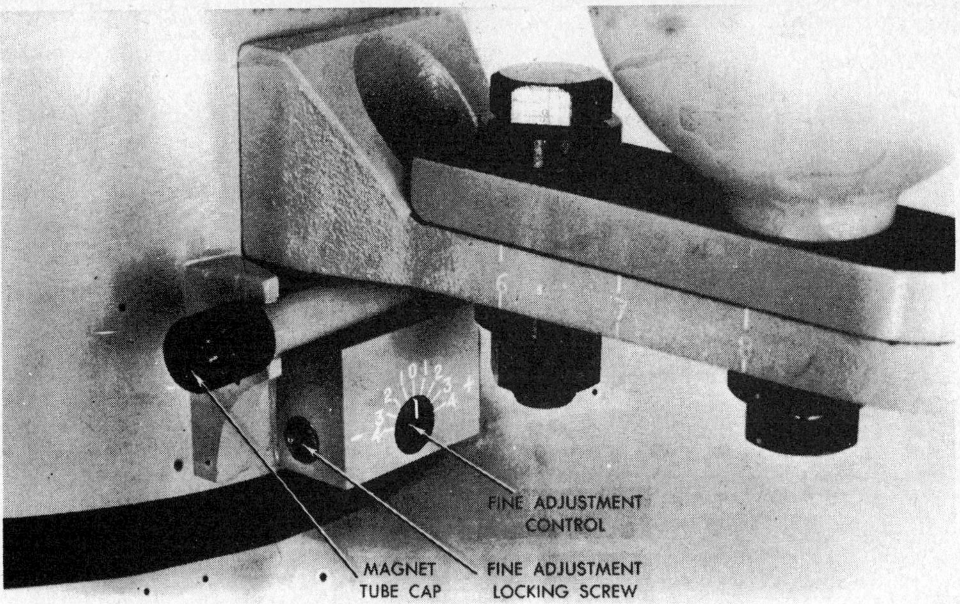

Courtesy of John E. Hand & Sons Company.

FIGURE 626d.—Fine adjustment control.

in the Varsol compass fluid. The card is supported on a jewel post without the use of gimbals. The compass bowl employs a bellows expansion chamber which permits volumetric changes of the compass fluid without bubble formation.

The correctors consist of quadrantal correctors, fore-and-aft and athwartship permanent magnet correctors.

A wide variety of magnetic compasses are used in merchant ships and yachts. The basic principles of operation of all magnetic compasses are the same, the various types differing only in details of construction. A feature which is widely used in commercial compasses is a hemispherical top (fig. 627b) which provides magnification of the graduations.

Reflection binnacles providing a periscopic readout in the wheelhouse enable mounting of the compass where it is usually less subject to the vessel's magnetic field and the installed electrical and electronic equipment than a wheelhouse installation. Location on the flying bridge also serves to facilitate compass adjustment and bearing observations.

628. Magnetic compass limitations.—Because of its essential simplicity, a magnetic compass does not easily become totally inoperative. Being independent of any power supply or other service, a magnetic compass may survive major damage to its ship without losing its utility. Small boat compasses often remain serviceable under the most rigorous conditions.

Despite its great reliability, however, a magnetic compass is subject to some limitations. Since it responds to *any* magnetic field, it is affected by any change in the local magnetic situation. Hence, the undetected presence or change of position of magnetic material near the compass may introduce an unknown error. Thus, an error might be introduced by a steel wrench or paint can left near the compass, or by a change in position of a steel boom or gun in the vicinity of the compass. Even such small amounts of magnetic material as might be included in a pocketknife or steel keys are sufficient to affect the compass if brought as close as they are when on the person of an individual standing by a compass. Nylon clothing may also introduce error in a magnetic compass. As distance from the compass increases, the strength of the mag-

FIGURE 627a.—U. S. Navy No. 5 magnetic boat compass.

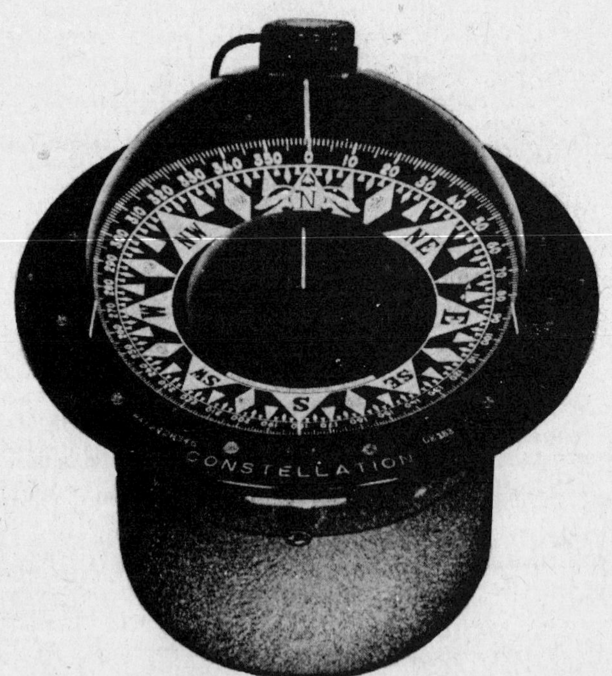

Caurtesy of Danforth Division of The Eastern Company, a Connecticut Corporation.

FIGURE 627b.—A compass with a hemispherical top.

netic field needed to introduce an error increases. A cargo of large amounts of iron or steel may be sufficient to affect the compass. The compass may also be affected by changes of the magnetic characteristics of the vessel itself. Such changes may occur during a protracted docking period, during a long sea voyage on substantially the same course, when repairs or changes of equipment are made, if the ship sustains heavy shock as by gunfire or riding out a heavy sea, if the vessel is struck by lightning, or if a short circuit occurs near the compass.

The directive force acting upon a magnetic compass is the horizontal component of the earth's magnetic field. This component is strongest at or near the magnetic equator, decreasing to zero at the magnetic poles (ch. VII). Near the magnetic poles, therefore, the magnetic compass is useless, and in a wider area its indications are of questionable reliability. The magnetic field of the earth has a number of local anomalies due to the presence of magnetic material within the earth. During magnetic storms it may be altered considerably. Changes in the magnetic field surrounding a vessel, due either to changes of the field itself or to change of position of the vessel within the field, affect the magnetism of the vessel and the correctors used to neutralize this effect, with a possible disturbance of the balance set up between them.

For these and other reasons, frequent determination of compass error is necessary for safe navigation. Methods of determining and correcting compass error are discussed in chapter VII.

629. Magnetic compass accessories.—Compass heading is indicated by the lubber's line. Compass bearings may be measured by sighting across the compass, bringing the object and the vertical axis of the compass in line. Accuracy in making this alignment is increased by the use of a device to direct the line of sight across the center of the compass. Perhaps the simplest device of this kind is a **bearing bar,** consisting of two vertical **sighting vanes** mounted at opposite ends of a horizontal bar having a small pivot which fits into a hole drilled part way through the glass cover of the compass, at its center. The "near" vane (nearer the eye of the observer) has a very thin, open, vertical slot through which the line of sight is directed; the "far" vane has a thin, vertical wire or thread mounted on a suitable frame. The bar is rotated until the object is in line with the two vanes. The bearing is the reading of the compass in line with the vanes, on the far side from the observer. If a reflecting surface is pivoted to the far vane to permit observation of the azimuth of a celestial body, the device is called an **azimuth instrument.** Bearing bars and azimuth instruments are usually used only with smaller compasses, and never with an after-reading compass (art. 627).

Larger compasses or repeaters (art. 643) are usually provided with a **bearing circle** or **azimuth circle** (fig. 629). These devices take a variety of forms, but consist essentially of two parts: (1) a pair of sighting vanes attached to a ring which fits snugly over the compass, and (2) a mirror to reflect the compass graduation into the line of sight. The use of these devices is similar to that of the bearing bar and azimuth instrument. The azimuth circle has a pivoted reflecting surface attached to the far vane, to permit observation of celestial bodies. In most cases it also has a reflecting mirror and prism mounted on opposite sides of the ring, midway between the vanes. The prism is covered with opaque material except for a thin, vertical slot at its center. The surface of the mirror is curved so that reflection of sunlight falling upon it is in the form of a slender vertical line (at the distance of the prism) of about the same width as the slot. When the azimuth circle is adjusted so that this line of light falls upon the slot, a thin, bright line appears on the compass card graduations at the bearing of the sun. Most bearing and azimuth circles are provided with reverse compass rose graduations to permit reading of relative bearings or azimuths (by the vanes) at a mark on top of the compass bowl, in line with the lubber's line; bubbles for indicating the level position during observation; means for adjusting the snugness of the fit over the compass bowl; and handles for turning the device.

If a bearing or azimuth circle does not fit snugly over the compass bowl, an error might be introduced. Inaccuracy may also result from tilting of the reflecting surface

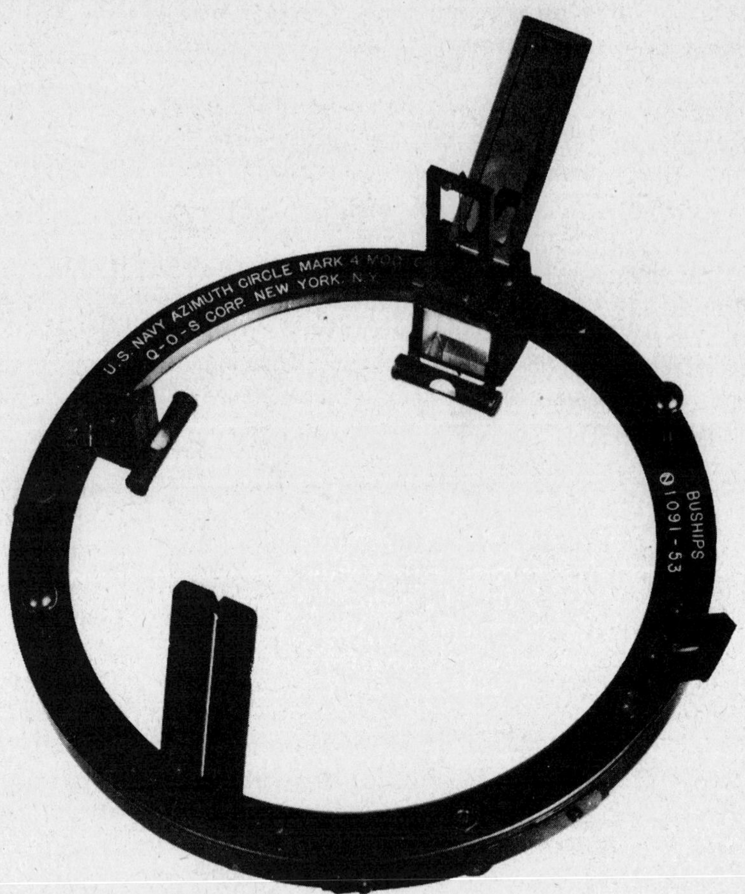

FIGURE 629.—An azimuth circle.

of an **azimuth** circle with respect to the vertical plane through the line of sight. This can be checked by comparing an azimuth of the sun observed by means of the prism with one observed with the sighting vanes (with suitable protection being provided for the eyes). If the prism attachment is not available, a check can be made by comparing observed (compass) azimuths at different altitudes with computed (true) values at the time of observation. If both observed and computed azimuths are correct, the difference between them will be constant (if the compass error remains constant throughout the observation).

None of the bearing or azimuth instruments described above can be used with a compass not designed for it, as one having a hemispherical top, or an after-reading compass.

Some modern magnetic compasses are provided with electrical pick-offs of sufficient sensitivity that the instrument can be used to control such devices as remote indicators, automatic steering equipment, course recorders, and dead reckoning equipment without disturbing the reliability of the compass. However, these devices are more commonly controlled by a gyrocompass and hence are considered later in the chapter, after a discussion of this type compass.

630. The gyroscope.—Leon Foucault, a French physicist, first demonstrated the rotation of the earth by means of a pendulum. However, the pendulum was not entirely acceptable as proof of rotation because it required the earth's gravity for operation. In 1852, he gave the name **gyroscope** to a toy top which had been known for a quarter of a century as a "rotascope." By means of the gyroscope, Foucault illustrated the earth's rotation without the use of gravity.

A conventional gyroscope consists of a comparatively massive, wheel-like rotor balanced in gimbals which permit rotation in any direction about three mutually perpendicular axes through the center of gravity. The three axes are called the **spin axis,** the **horizontal axis,** and the **vertical axis,** as shown in figure 630a.

Since the rapidly spinning rotor is balanced at its center of gravity, it is in a state of neutral rotational equilibrium. If the gimbal bearings were completely frictionless, the spin axis would retain its direction in space despite any motion applied to the system as a whole, as by the rotation of the earth. This property is called **gyroscopic inertia.** Thus, if the spin axis were directed toward a star, the axis would continue to point toward the star during its apparent motion across the sky. To an observer on the earth, the spin axis would appear to change direction as the earth rotated eastward.

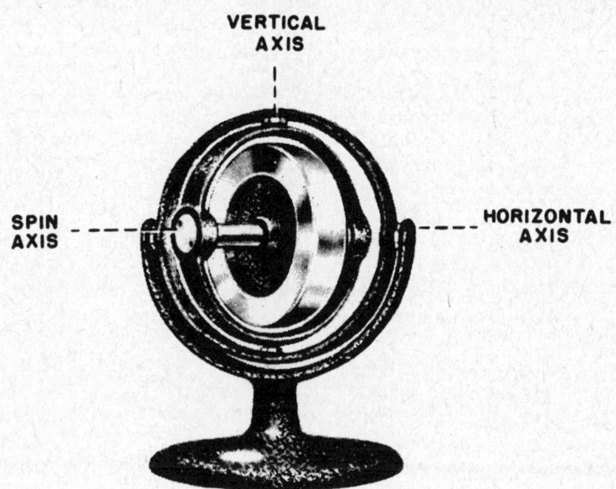

FIGURE 630a.—Gyroscope.

FIGURE 630b.—Demonstration of gyroscopic inertia.

This phenomenon, also known as **rigidity in space,** can be demonstrated by slowly tilting the base of the gyroscope as shown in figure 630b. If the gyroscope rotor is stationary, bearing friction will cause the rotor to tilt as the base is tilted. If the rotor is spinning, the rotor maintains the original plane of rotation as the gyroscope is tilted. It will continue to maintain the original plane of rotation no matter how much the gyroscope is tilted, as long as it continues to spin with sufficient velocity. Although bearing friction still affects the gyroscope, it affects it to a lesser degree than when the rotor was stationary.

Gyroscopic inertia depends upon angular velocity, mass, and the radius at which the mass is concentrated. For a given mass, maximum effect is obtained, therefore, from a mass rotating at high speed with the principal part of the mass concentrated near the periphery of the wheel.

Gyroscopic precession is that property of a gyroscope exhibited when a force is applied which tends to change the *direction* in space of the spin axis. The motion resulting from such a force is not in line with the force, as might be expected, but *perpendicular* to it. Precession can be demonstrated by applying a torque to the spinning gyroscope about its horizontal axis. This is done by applying a force at point A as illustrated in figure 630c. The gyroscope instead of turning about the horizontal axis as it would if it were not spinning, turns or precesses about its vertical axis. The direction of precession is such that it appears as though a force applied to the rotor at A is, instead,

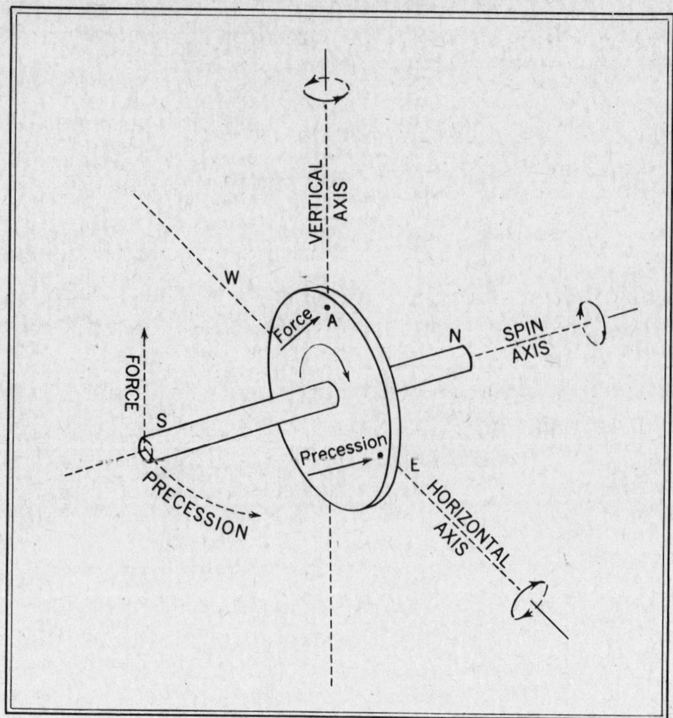

FIGURE 630c.—Axes of a gyroscope, and the direction of precession.

applied at a point 90° away in the direction of spin from point A. Similarly, if a torque is applied about the vertical axis, the gyroscope will precess about its horizontal axis in a direction such that it appears as though the force is applied at a point 90° away in the direction of spin from the point where the force is applied on the rotor.

A **torque** is defined as that which effects or tends to effect rotation or torsion and which is measured by the product of the applied force and the perpendicular distance from the line of action of the force to the axis of rotation. It is obvious that a force acting through or parallel to an axis cannot produce any turning effect about that axis. In a gyroscope the three axes about which rotation is possible all intersect at the center of gravity of the entire system (excluding the supporting frame). A force, therefore, acting through the center of gravity acts through all the axes and cannot exert torque about any axis. But a force acting at any other point will produce a torque about one or more axes.

Precession can be caused only by a force attempting to tilt or turn the spin axis about one of the other axes. So, a force through the center of gravity of a gyroscope (or force of translation) cannot cause the gyroscope to precess, but can only cause it to move as a whole in the direction of the force, with its axle always pointing in the same direction and the plane in which the rotor is spinning always parallel to its original plane of spin.

A torque about the spin axis of a gyroscope does not attempt to change the plane in which the rotor is spinning, so it cannot cause precession. The only effect such a torque can have on the rotor is to increase or decrease its speed.

Any torque about either the horizontal or vertical axis of a gyroscope will cause it to precess about an axis at right angles to that about which the torque acts. This precession will continue as long as the torque acts, but will cease when the torque is removed. If the plane in which the torque is acting remains unchanged, the gyroscope will precess until the plane of the spin of the rotor is in the plane of the torque. When this position is reached, the torque will be about the spin axis and can cause no further precession. If, however, the plane in which the torque acts moves at the same rate and in the same direction as the precession it causes, the precession will be continuous.

The rotor of the conventional gyroscope previously described has three degrees of freedom: (1) freedom to spin on its axle, (2) freedom to tilt about its horizontal axis, and (3) freedom to turn about its vertical axis. These three degrees of freedom permit the rotor to assume any position with respect to the supporting frame. This gyroscope is called a **free gyroscope**.

The term **degree-of-freedom** refers to the number of orthogonal axes about which the spin axis is free to rotate, the spin axis not being counted in one convention.

The reason for gyroscopic precession may be explained simply by considering what happens to a single particle on the rim of the gyroscope wheel as shown in figure 630d. Assume that the wheel is spinning in the direction of arrow *R*. Also assume that a force *F* is applied against the wheel at point *B* on the particular particle *P*, which happens to be at the position shown at any particular instant.

Force *F* exerts a force upon this small particle along the vector *BL* and therefore accelerates it in that direction. During a short interval of time, the acceleration will give the particle a component of velocity *BL*. This velocity vector and the velocity of the particle along the vector *BJ*, due to rotation of the wheel, have as a resultant the vector *BK*, different in direction from *BJ*. This is equivalent to a rotation about axis, *YY*. Therefore, the effect of a torque acting about the *XX* axis is to cause a rotation of the gyroscope wheel about the *YY* axis. This rotation about the *YY* axis is gyroscopic precession.

If the gyroscope, or **gyro** as it is commonly called, is mounted at the equator with its spin axis pointing east and west, figure 630e illustrates how it would appear from a point in space beyond the South Pole. From the observation point in space, the earth is seen turning from west to east at a rate of 15° per hour carrying the gyro with it. However, the spin axis of the gyro, because of gyroscopic inertia, remains in rigid space just as it did when the base was tilted in figure 630b. To an observer on earth the same gyro appears to rotate about its horizontal axis with an angular velocity equal but opposite in direction to the rate of rotation of the earth. This effect, commonly referred to as **horizontal earth rate,** is equal to the rate of rotation of the earth (**earth rate**) times the cosine function of the latitude. It is therefore zero at the poles and increases to earth rate at the equator.

Similarly, if the gyro is mounted at the North or South Pole with its spin axis horizontal, as shown in figure 630f, the gyro will appear to rotate about its vertical axis. This effect is commonly referred to as **vertical earth rate.** At points between the poles and the equator, the gyro appears to turn partly about the horizontal axis and partly about the vertical axis as shown in figure 630g, because it is affected by both horizontal and vertical earth rates.

In general, horizontal earth rate causes the spin axis of the gyro to appear to tilt about its horizontal axis; vertical earth rate causes the gyro to appear to rotate about its vertical axis. The apparent motion of stars can be used as a convenient reminder of the effect of the earth's rotation on a **free gyro.** Being rigid in space, the spin axis remains pointing at the same fixed star as the earth rotates. Thus, the spin axis describes a circle about Polaris in a counterclockwise direction as the earth rotates.

With reference to space the direction of the spin axis of the free gyro remains the same as the earth rotates. With respect to the earth, however, the spin axis rotates as just described. It is this rotation with respect to the earth which makes it possible to apply the force of gravity so as to convert the free gyro into a north-seeking gyrocompass.

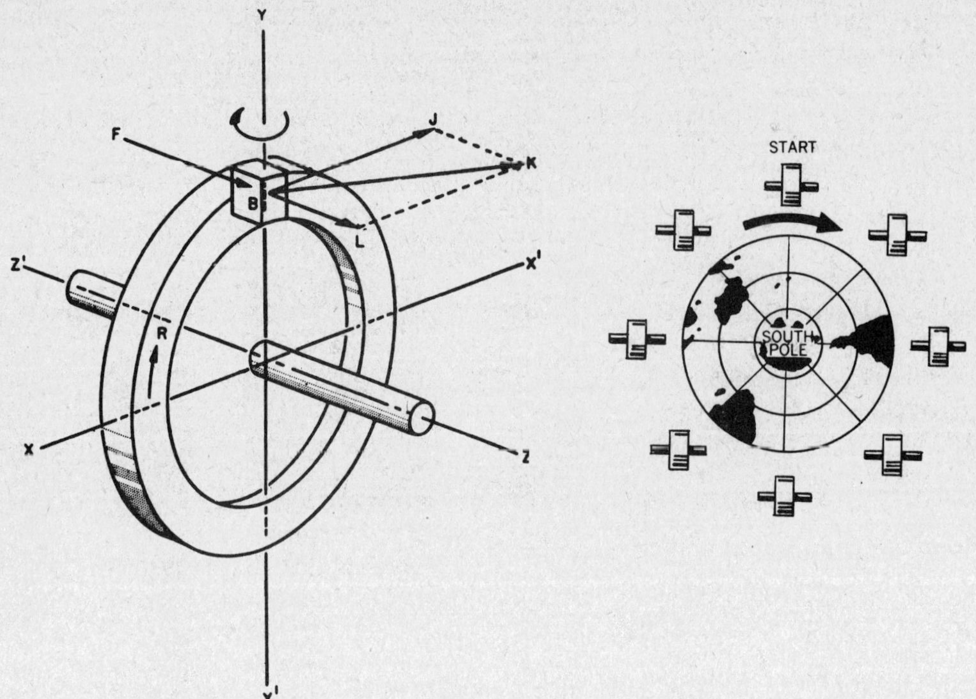

FIGURE 630d.—Forces causing precession of gyroscope rotor.

FIGURE 630e.—Demonstration of horizontal earth rate of gyro.

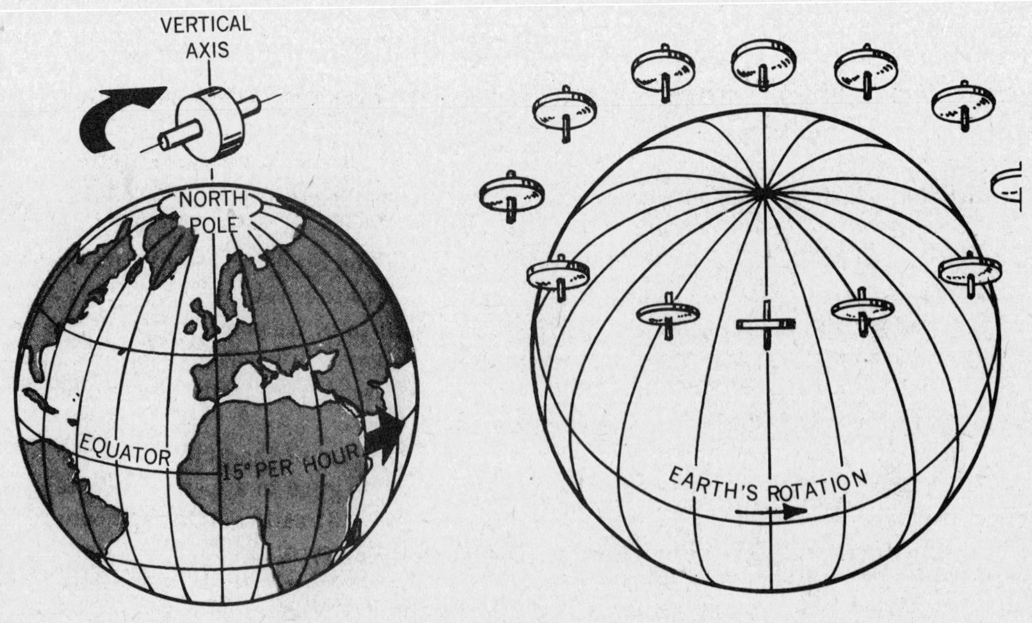

FIGURE 630f.—Demonstration of vertical earth rate of gyro.

FIGURE 630g.—Combined effects of horizontal and vertical earth rates.

631. The gyrocompass depends upon four natural phenomena for its operation. It is only the methods whereby these phenomena are utilized that distinguish one type of gyrocompass from another. Of the four natural phenomena, two are inherent properties of the gyroscope, namely gyroscopic inertia and gyroscopic precession; the other two are the earth's rotation and gravity.

Before a free gyro can be converted into a gyrocompass, the mounting structure must be changed slightly. As shown in figure 631a, the rotor is mounted in a sphere (**gyrosphere**) and the sphere is supported in what is called the **vertical ring.** The sphere and vertical ring are, in turn, mounted in a base called the **phantom.** Means are provided for the vertical ring and phantom to follow the gyro as it turns about its vertical axis.

With no further additions, the gyro shown in figure 631a will, neglecting friction, maintain its direction in space so long as no outside forces are exerted on it. To make the gyro into a gyrocompass, the gyro has to be made *to seek and maintain true north.* Since north is the direction represented by a horizontal line in the plane of the meridian, some means have to be provided to: (1) make the gyro spin axis seek the meridian plane, (2) make the spin axis horizontal, and (3) make it maintain its position once reached.

The first step in making a gyro a gyrocompass is to make the gyro seek the meridian. To do this, a weight W is added to the bottom of the vertical ring, as shown in figure 631b. This causes the vertical ring to be pendulous about the horizontal axis.

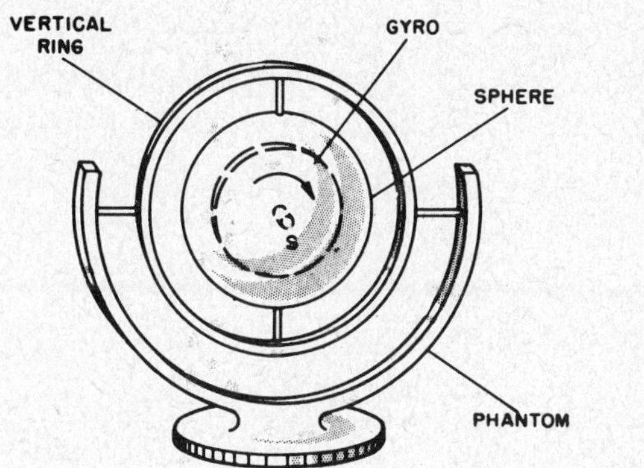

FIGURE 631a.—Modified model gyroscope.

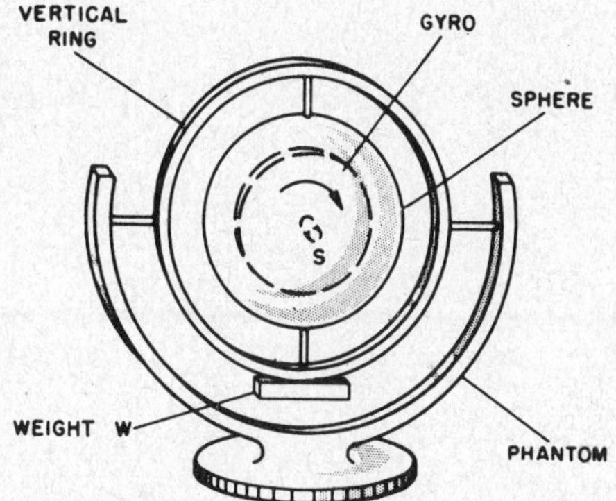

FIGURE 631b.—Making the free gyro seek north by the addition of a weight to the vertical ring.

If as at A of figure 631c the gyro is at the *equator*, the spin axis is horizontal pointing east-west, and the rotor is spinning clockwise as viewed from the west, the rotor and vertical ring are vertical and no torque is created by the added weight. At this point both properties of the gyroscope, gyroscopic inertia and precession, are brought into play. As the earth rotates, the spin axis and, therefore, the vertical ring become inclined to the horizontal as shown at B. The weight W is raised against the pull of gravity and consequently causes a torque about the horizontal axis of the gyro. This torque causes precession about the vertical axis in the direction indicated at C. The spin axis then has moved out of its original east-west direction.

As the end of the spin axis which was first pointing east (which will now be referred to as the north end) continues to rise, the torque on the gyro caused by the weight becomes greater since the moment arm through which the weight acts gets longer due to the greater tilt. Since the speed of precession is closely proportional to the tilt, the gyro turns about its vertical axis as shown at D at an increasing speed until the axis is on the meridian.

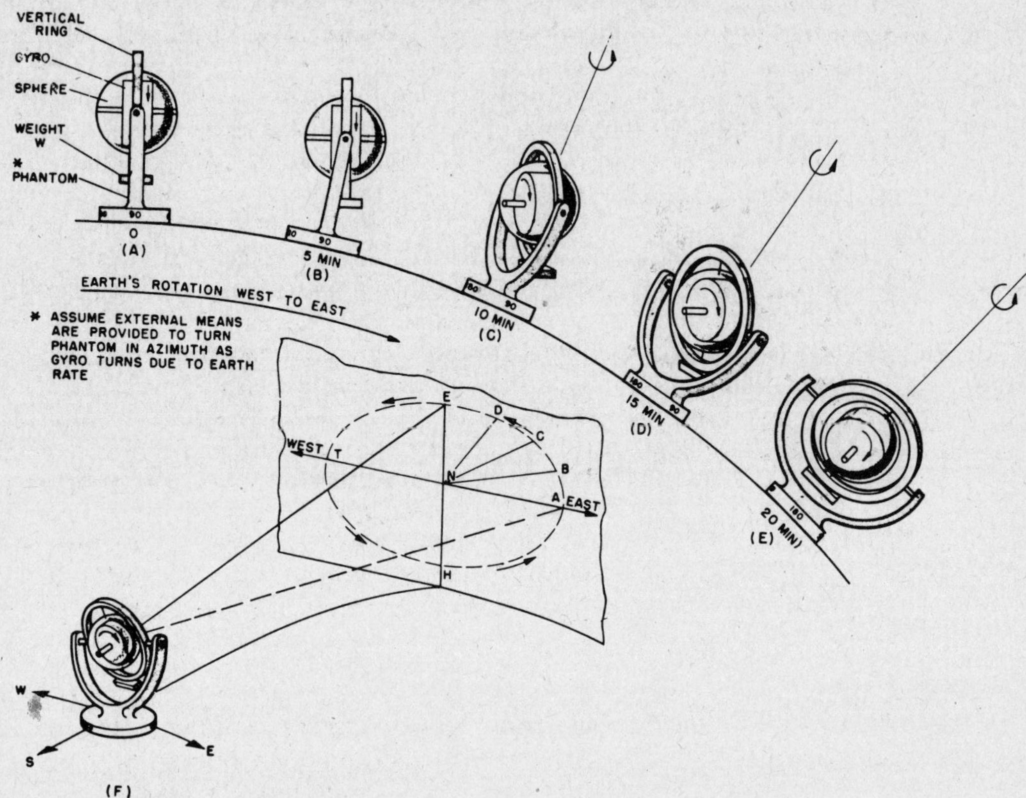

FIGURE 631c.—Effect of pendulous weight and earth's rotation on gyro.

At the meridian, the tilt, the torque caused by the weight, and speed of precession are all at a maximum. It should be noted here that it is the righting couple applied to the tilted axis by the pendulous weight which causes the compass to precess past the meridian, the kinetic energy of precession having negligible effect. After the north end of the spin axis crosses the meridian the higher (north) end of the tilted axle is to the west of the meridian. As a result, referring back to figure 630e, the earth's rotation reduces the tilt. As the tilt becomes less, the speed of precession in azimuth decreases. Finally the spin axis becomes horizontal and precession to the west stops; the weight on the vertical ring causes no torque about the horizontal axis since its force acts in the same plane as the gyro rotor and vertical ring. At this point, the axle has precessed as far west of the meridian as it was to the east originally.

As the earth continues to rotate, the north end of the spin axis starts to dip. The weight W is raised on the opposite side of the horizontal axis in the opposite direction carrying the spin axis back across the meridian to its original position. At this point, the cycle is repeated and will go on indefinitely. The oscillation about the meridian may be clearly understood by referring to F in figure 631c which shows the movement of the end of the spin axis projected on a vertical plane. The ellipse is the result of a displacement of the spin axis only a few degrees from the meridian. If the spin axis were pointing east-west at the beginning of the cycle as shown at A in figure 631c, precession would take place through 180 degrees in each direction, and at one extreme the axle would point east, at the other, west, In any case, the gyro never comes to rest since there is no force tending to restore the spin axis to the horizontal position until it has passed the meridian.

The ratio of the movement about the horizontal axis (caused by apparent rotation) to the precessional movement about the vertical axis caused by the swing of the weight determines the shape of the ellipse. If the weight is increased, the speed of precession will increase and the ellipse will be flatter. If the weight is decreased, the speed of precession will decrease and the ellipse would, theoretically, be almost circular. The time, in minutes, required for one complete oscillation, is called the period of oscillation. For any given wheel and speed at a certain point on the earth, the period will be nearly the same regardless of the angle through which the wheel oscillates. The period can be changed by changing the amount of weight on the bottom of the vertical ring.

With such a gyroscope modified by hanging a weight on the vertical ring, the first requirement to make a gyroscope into a gyrocompass, that of making the spin axis seek the meridian, has been fulfilled. However, some means must be provided for damping these oscillations so the gyro wheel will quickly come to rest with its spin axis level in the north-south position.

To damp the oscillations of the spin axis about the meridian a small weight W_1 is added to the sphere in which the rotor is housed. This weight is placed on the east side of the sphere in a position shown in figure 631d. With the spin axis level, the torque produced by gravity acting upon the weight W_1 is restrained by the vertical axis bearings. When the spin axis tilts due to earth rate, the vertical axis is no longer vertical; the force of gravity, however, still pulls straight down on the weight. This allows the torque to act about the vertical axis.

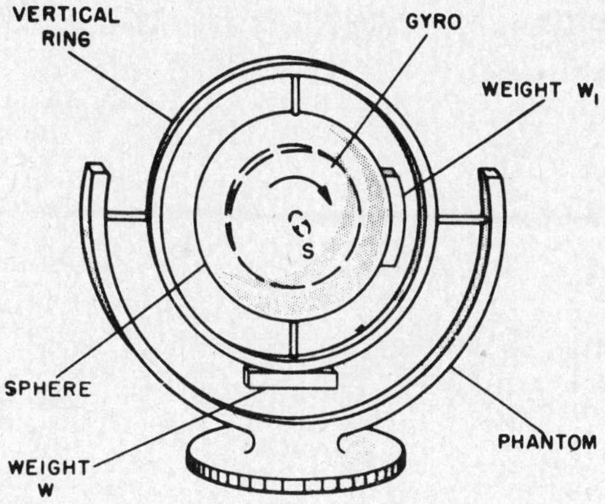

FIGURE 631d.—Modified model gyroscope with weights on the vertical ring and sphere.

Now, with both weights, the spin axis will begin to tilt due to earth rate and as soon as it tilts, the spin axis precesses toward the meridian and downward toward the level position. As a result of the leveling action of weight W_1, the spin axis is not tilted up as much when it reaches the meridian as it was with only weight W. Since the spin axis is not tilted as much, the torque produced by weight W is not as great. Therefore, the spin axis will not precess as far to the west of the meridian as it was east of the meridian when it was started.

After reaching a point where the spin axis is level and as far west of the meridian as it is going due to the action of weight W, earth rate is still causing the spin axis to tilt downward. As a result, the forces due to the weights are reversed and torques are created which precess the gyro to the east and up. The same action takes place in the reverse direction. The gyro is not precessed as far to the east as it was to the west. Thus, the added weight W_1 causes the ellipse to be reduced each successive oscillation;

the north end of the gyro axle will follow a spiral path as shown in figure 631e instead of an elliptical path as previously.

A careful consideration of the action of the two weights will make it apparent that the only position of rest that the gyro can find will be with the spin axis horizontal and on the meridian. The period of the compass can be changed by varying the weight *W* With a given period the speed with which it settles to a level position can be changed by varying the weight W_1.

With the second modification to the model gyroscope (adding a weight to the sphere in which the gyro is housed), the second requirement to make a gyroscope into a gyrocompass, that of making the spin axis horizontal, has been fulfilled. However, when this modified gyroscope is moved, accelerations on the weights, because they are pendulous, will cause torques on the gyroscope. Also any change in latitude from the equator will result in false indications. The model gyroscope, as so far modified, does not fulfill the third requirement, that of *maintaining* the level position in the plane of the meridian once reached. Therefore, some means must be provided to eliminate the effect of unbalanced weights hanging on the modified gyroscope; means must be provided to compensate for false indications resulting from change in latitude from the equator.

Practical gyrocompasses employ both pendulous and nonpendulous gyroscopes. In addition these compasses have means of compensating for influences that might introduce errors into their indications.

One method of utilizing precession to cause the gyroscope of a practical gyrocompass to seek north is illustrated in figure 631f. Two reservoirs connected by a tube are attached to the bottom of the case enclosing the gryo rotor, with one reservoir north of the rotor and the other south of it. The reservoirs are filled with mercury to such a level that the weight below the spin axis is equal to the weight above it, so that the gyroscope is nonpendulous. The system of reservoirs and connecting tubes is called a **mercury ballistic.** In practice, there are usually four symmetrically placed reservoirs.

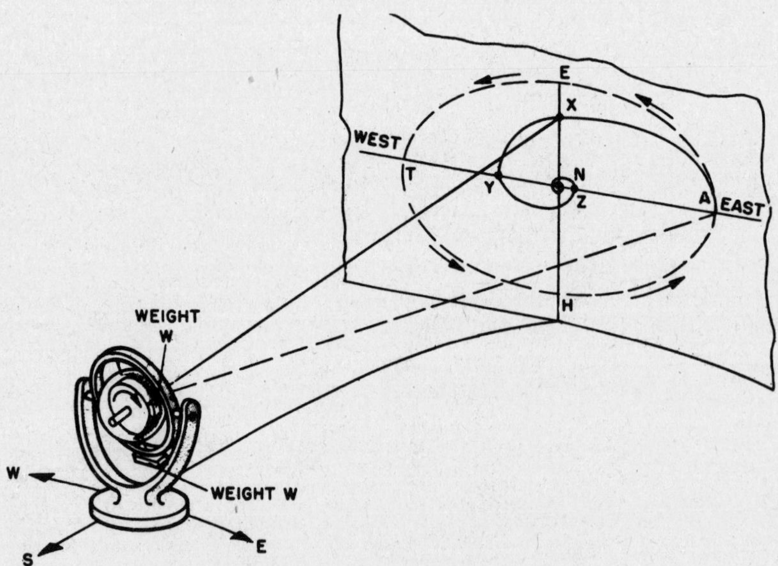

FIGURE 631e.—Settling on the meridian.

Suppose that the spin axis is horizontal but is directed to the eastward of north. As the earth rotates eastward on its axis, the spin axis tends to maintain its direction in space; that is, it appears to follow a point, such as a star rising in the northeastern sky.

With respect to the earth, the north reservoir rises and some of the mercury flows under the force of gravity into the south reservoir. The south side becomes heavier than the north side, and a force is applied to the bottom of the rotor case at point *A*. If the gyro rotor is spinning in the direction shown, the north end of the spin axis precesses slowly to the westward, following an elliptical path. When it reaches the meridian, upward tilt reaches a maximum. Precession continues, so that the axis is carried past the meridian and commences to sink as the earth continues to rotate. When the sinking has continued to the point where the axis is horizontal again, the excess mercury has returned to the north reservoir and precession stops. As sinking continues, due to continued rotation of the earth, an excess of mercury accumulates in the north reservoir, thus reversing the direction of precession and causing the spin axis to return slowly to its original position with respect to the earth, following the path shown at the right of figure 631f. One circuit of the ellipse requires about 84 minutes.

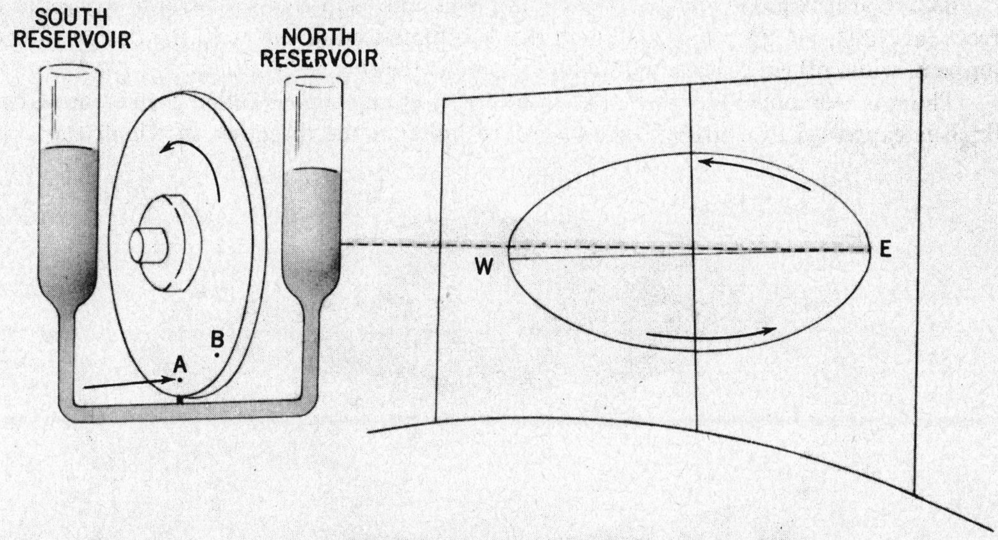

FIGURE 631f.—The mercury ballistic (left) and the elliptical path (right) of the axis of spin without damping.

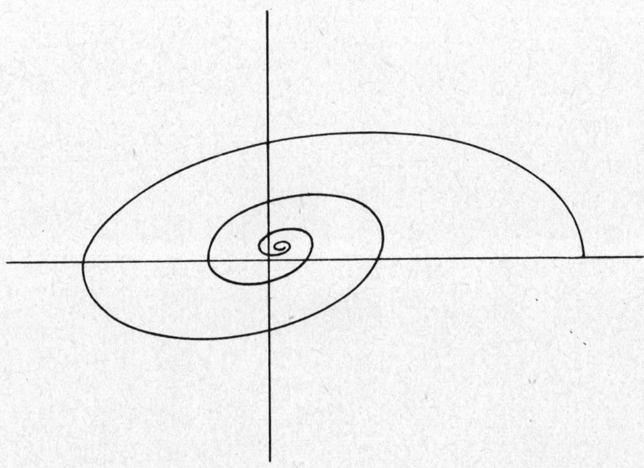

FIGURE 631g.—Spiral path of the axis of spin with damping.

The elliptical path is symmetrical with respect to the meridian, and, neglecting friction, would be retraced indefinitely, unless some method of damping the oscillation were found. One method is by offsetting the point of application of the force from the mercury ballistic. Thus, if the force is applied not in the vertical plane, but at a point to the eastward of it, as at *B* in figure 631f, the resulting precession causes the spin axis to trace a spiral path as shown in figure 631g, and eventually to settle near the meridian. The gyroscope is now north-seeking. The gyrocompass shown in figure 631h uses this method to seek north.

Another method of damping the oscillations caused by the rotation of the earth is to reduce the precessing force of a pendulous gyro as the spin axis approaches the meridian. One way of accomplishing this is to cause oil to flow from one damping tank to another in such a manner as to counteract some of the tendency of an offset pendulous weight to cause precession. Oscillations are completely damped out in approximately one and one-half swings.

632. Gyrocompass errors.—Gyrocompasses are subject to several systematic errors. Some of these can be eliminated or offset in the design of the compass, while others require manual adjustment for their correction.

The total combined error (the resultant error) at any time is called **gyro error (GE)**, which is expressed in degrees east or west to indicate the direction in which the axis

Courtesy of Sperry Marine Systems.

FIGURE 631h.—The Mark 14 Mod 2 Gyrocompass.

of the compass is offset from true north. If the gyro error is east, the readings are too low; and if it is west, they are too high. Thus, if GE is 1° W, 1° is subtracted from all readings of the compass, either headings or bearings, to determine the equivalent true directions. One degree is added to all true directions to determine the equivalent gyro directions. The gyro error of modern compasses is generally small. However, significant errors can be introduced in several ways, and it is good practice to compare the gyro heading with the magnetic heading at frequent intervals (as every half hour and after each change of course) and to check the accuracy of the gyrocompass by celestial observation or landmarks from time to time (as every morning and afternoon when means are available).

The errors generally associated with the gyrocompass are speed error, tangent latitude error, ballistic deflection error, ballistic damping error, quadrantal error, and gimballing error. In addition, gyrocompasses are subject to the errors common to directional instruments, such as those introduced by inaccurate graduation of the compass rose or incorrectly located lubber's line. Error may also be introduced, of course, by malfunctioning of the compass.

633. Speed error.—The north-seeking tendency of a gyrocompass depends upon the fact that north is at right angles to the west-to-east direction in which the earth's rotation carries the compass. If the gyrocompass is carried over the earth in some direction other than west to east, it will seek a settling position at right angles to that direction, whatever it may be.

A gyrocompass on the earth's surface is carried from west to east only when it is stationary with respect to the earth's surface, or when it is moving east or west. If the vessel in which the compass is installed is moving in other than an east or west direction the compass is, in effect, being carried in a direction which is a little to the north or south of exactly east. It will then seek a settling position which is at right angles to this direction, and will settle on a line at a small angle off true north.

This error, known as **speed error** and sometimes called **speed-course-latitude error,** is westerly if any component of the vessel's course is north, and easterly if south. Its magnitude depends upon the speed, course, and latitude of the vessel. Refer to figure 633a. If a vessel is at anchor at any point *A*, it is being carried eastward by rotation of the earth at the rate of 902.46 minutes of longitude per hour (with respect to the stars). In terms of knots, this is equal to 902.46 times the cosine of the latitude, approximately. Because of the ellipticity of the earth, the actual value is a little more than this in low latitudes, and a little less in high latitudes. The actual value at any latitude can be found by multiplying the length of a degree of longitude at that latitude by $\frac{902.46}{60}=15.041$.

This eastward motion due to rotation of the earth is shown in figure 633a by the vector *AB*. The north-south axis of the gyrocompass settles in a direction 90° from the direction of motion. Therefore, if the vessel is stationary with respect to the earth, 0° on the compass card coincides with a true meridian, and no error is introduced. This is also true if the vessel is moving due east or due west. In this case the speed of the ship over the surface of the earth is added to or subtracted from the motion due to rotation of the earth, but the direction of motion is unchanged (unless the speed of the vessel is greater than the rotational speed of the earth, and in the opposite direction). The only effect, therefore, is to strengthen or weaken the directive force, usually by a small amount.

If the vessel is on course north or south, as shown by the vector *AC* in figure 633a, the motion in space is tilted toward the north or south of due east. In this case, it is the

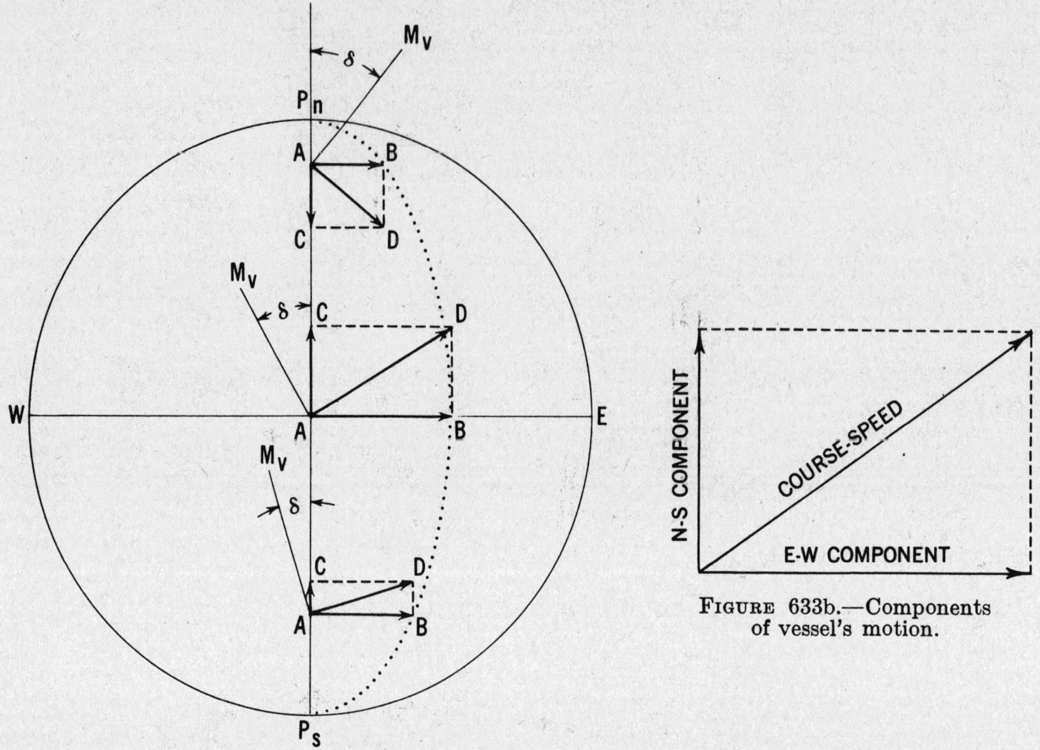

FIGURE 633a.—Speed error.

FIGURE 633b.—Components of vessel's motion.

vector sum of the motion due to rotation of the earth and the velocity of the vessel over the surface of the earth, or *AD* in figure 633a. Since *AD* is not due east, the perpendicular to it does not lie in the true meridian, but at some angle δ to it, along AM_v. Since the axis of the gyro lies along AM_v, the "virtual meridian," the angle is the error introduced by the motion of the vessel along its track. Since *AD* is perpendicular to AM_v, and *AB* is perpendicular to *AC*, angle *BAD* is equal to angle δ. Therefore, the angle δ can be found by the formula

$$\tan \delta = \frac{AC}{AB}.$$

Since *AC* is the speed of the vessel and *AB* is 902.46 cos L, approximately, the formula can be written

$$\tan \delta = \frac{S}{902.46 \cos L}$$

where S is the speed and L the latitude of the vessel.

If the course of the vessel is not a cardinal direction, the resultant is still the vector sum of two speed vectors, and can be found graphically or by computation. One method is to resolve the vessel's speed vector into two components, as shown in figure 633b, obtaining the N–S component along the true meridian, and the E–W component in the direction of rotation of the earth. The N–S component is equal to S cos C, and the E–W component to S sin C, where C is the true course angle. The total N–S motion is then S cos C. The total easterly motion is that due to rotation of the earth plus or minus the E–W component of the ship's speed across the surface of the earth, or 902.46 cos L±S sin C, approximately. The term S sin C is positive

(+) for easterly courses and negative (−) for westerly courses. The formula for finding δ now becomes

$$\tan \delta = \frac{S \cos C}{902.46 \cos L \pm S \sin C} \text{(approximately)}.$$

At ship speeds in latitudes less than 70°, the term S sin C is much smaller than 902.46 cos L and has so little effect upon the answer that it can be ignored. The angle δ is small enough that its tangent can be considered the angle itself (expressed in radians). That is, a tangent to a circle can be considered of the same length as an arc of the circle over a short distance from the point of tangency. Therefore, the formula for δ can be written

$$\delta = \frac{57.3 \text{ S} \cos C}{902.46 \cos L}$$

or

$$\delta = 0.0635 \text{ S} \cos C \sec L.$$

As shown in this formula, the speed error δ is affected by the three variables, speed, course, and latitude. If the course has a northerly component, the error is westerly; and if it has a southerly component, the error is easterly.

Example.—A ship at latitude 30°N is steaming on true course 045°, at a speed of 20 knots.

Required.—Speed error.

Solution.—

0.0635	log	8. 80277
S 20 kn.	log	1. 30103
C N45°E	*l* cos	9. 84949
L 30°N	*l* sec	10. 06247
δ 1°.04W	log	10. 01576

Answer.—δ 1°.04W.

In some gyrocompasses this error is corrected mechanically. Speed and latitude are set in by hand, and the cosine of the course is introduced automatically by means of a "cosine cam" running in an eccentric groove on the underside of the azimuth gear. In some compasses these corrections combine to offset the lubber's line by the correct amount. Small changes in speed or latitude have relatively little effect upon the result. Therefore, in normal operations, infrequent changes are sufficient for satisfactory results. If no provision is made for mechanically applying this correction, a table or curves can be used to indicate the correction to be applied mathematically to readings of the compass. These are made up from the formula given above, and are entered with the speed, course, and latitude (art. 639).

634. Tangent latitude error applies only to those gyrocompasses in which damping is accomplished by offsetting the point of application of the force from a mercury ballistic (art. 631). It can be found from the equation

$$\alpha = r \tan L$$

in which α is the damping error, r is the angle between the vertical through the spin axis of the gyro rotor and a line through this axis and the point of application of the force from the mercury ballistic (1°.7 for Sperry compasses), and L is the latitude. The error is easterly in north latitude and westerly in south latitude.

Example.—A gyrocompass having a value of r of 1°.7 is at latitude 50°N.

Required.—The tangent latitude error.

Solution.—

$$\alpha = r \tan L$$
$$= 1°.7 \times 1.1918$$
$$= 2°.03E$$

Answer.—$\alpha = 2°.03E$.

As in the case of speed error, provision is made in most compasses (to which it applies) for correcting this error. An auxiliary latitude-correction scale is provided for this purpose. In some compasses this offsets the lubber's line. In others, it alters the position of a small weight attached to the casing near one end of the axle. The first method is preferable because it is unaffected by changes of gyro speed of rotation.

If this error is not corrected mechanically, it can be combined algebraically with speed error and a single set of tables or graphs made up. This is a method sometimes used in polar regions, beyond the scale of the latitude corrections (art. 639).

635. Ballistic deflection error.—When the north-south component of the speed changes, an accelerating force acts upon the compass, causing a surge of mercury from one part of the system to another, or a deflection (along the meridian) of the mass of a pendulous compass. In either case, this is called **ballistic deflection.** It results in a precessing force which introduces a temporary **ballistic deflection error** in the readings of the compass unless it is corrected.

A change of course or speed also results in a change in the speed error, and unless the correcting mechanism responds promptly to this change, a temporary error from this source is also introduced. The sign of this error is opposite that of the ballistic deflection, and so the two tend to cancel each other. If they are of equal magnitude and equal duration, the cancellation is complete and the compass responds immediately and automatically to changes of speed error. This can be accomplished by designing the compass so that

$$\frac{B}{H} = 0.0211 \sec L.$$

in which B is the pendulous moment of a pendulous compass and the couple per unit angle applied by a mercury ballistic, H is the angular momentum of the gyro rotor, and L is the latitude.

Gyrocompasses using the fluid ballistic are often designed so that the ratio $\frac{B}{H}$ is correct for some particular latitude (as 41° or 45°) and accept the small residual error that is temporarily present at other latitudes. This is satisfactory for vessels which remain within relatively narrow limits of latitude, or which are seldom subjected to large accelerating forces. However, where these conditions are not met, provision is made for varying the ratio with latitude. In a compass having a mercury ballistic, this is customarily accomplished by moving the mercury reservoirs radially toward or away from the center of the compass, thus altering the value of B. In a pendulous gyro, the value of H is changed by altering the rotational speed of the gyro.

When the ratio $\frac{B}{H}$ is as given in the equation above, the period of oscillation about the vertical axis is given by the equation

$$T = \frac{\pi}{30}\sqrt{\frac{R}{g}}$$

in which T is the period in minutes, R is the radius of the earth in feet (approximately 20,900,000) and g is the acceleration due to gravity (approximately 32.2 feet per second). Substituting in the formula,

$$T=0.1047\sqrt{\frac{20,900,000}{32.2}}$$

$$=84 \text{ minutes (approximately).}$$

This is sometimes stated as the period of a pendulum having a radius equal to the radius of the earth, since the equation for a short pendulum is the same as that given above with l (length) being substituted for R. More accurately, it is the period of a pendulum of infinite length with its bottom at the surface of the earth, or the largest period that a simple pendulum can have when acting under the gravitational force of the earth. When a device is adjusted so as to have this period it is said to be "Schuler tuned," after Max Schuler, a German scientist who discovered the relationship. It is because of this tuning of the gyrocompass that one oscillation occurs in about 84 minutes, and that the maximum effect of certain disturbing forces occurs about 21 minutes (one-fourth cycle) after application of the force.

636. Ballistic damping error is a temporary oscillatory error of a gyrocompass introduced during changes of course or speed as a result of the means used to damp the oscillations of the spin axis.

During a change of course or speed the fluid in the ballistic of the nonpendulous compass or in the damping tanks of the pendulous compass (art. 631) is accelerated. As shown in figure 636, during the turn from the westerly to the northerly direction the centrifugal force acting on the mercury causes an excess of mercury to accumulate in the south tanks of the ballistic at *A*. Because of the offset connection of the mercury ballistic, the excess mercury in the south tanks exerts a torque about the vertical axis in addition to the one being exerted about the horizontal axis during the turn. This torque about the vertical axis produces a downward tilt of the north end of the gyro axle at *B* as a result of precession. This tilt of the gyro axle causes an oscillation of the spin axis to start as the centrifugal force diminishes to zero at *C*. This oscillation on a compass with a damped period of about 84 minutes becomes a maximum at *D*, 21 minutes after the change of course is completed, and ends in about 2 hours.

The liquid in the damping tanks of the pendulous compass is subjected to the same centrifugal force on change of course. An excess of liquid collects in one tank. This action causes a torque and consequent movement of the spin axis from the meridian.

The ballistic damping error is eliminated in the nonpendulous compass by automatically moving the point of application of the mercury ballistic from the offset position to the true vertical axis of the gyro whenever rates of change of course or speed exceed certain limits. Moving the point of application of the mercury ballistic to the true vertical axis eliminates the torque about this axis caused by the centrifugal force and prevents the compass from going through a damped oscillation.

In the pendulous gyrocompass, the ballistic damping error is eliminated by automatically closing a valve in the pipe line between the damping tanks whenever rates of change of course or speed exceed certain limits.

637. Quadrantal error.—If a body mounted in gimbals is not suitably balanced, a disturbing force causes it to swing from side to side. A swinging body tends to rotate so that its long axis of weight is in the plane of the swing. The rolling of a vessel introduces the force needed to start a gyrocompass swinging. The effect reaches a maximum on intercardinal headings, midway between the two horizontal axes of the compass,

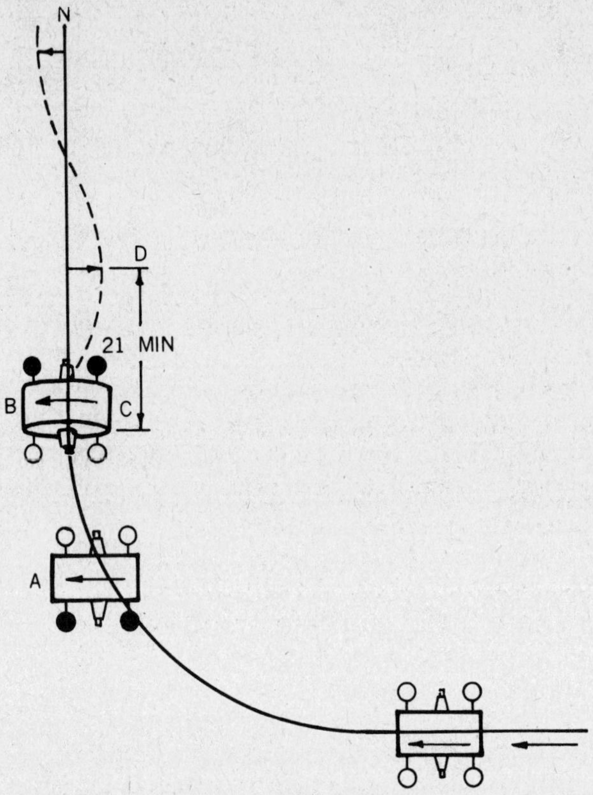

FIGURE 636.—Ballistic damping error.

and changes direction of error in consecutive quadrants. This is called **quadrantal error,** or sometimes **intercardinal rolling error.** It is corrected by the addition of weights to balance the compass so that the weight is the same in all directions from the center. Without a long axis of weight, there is no tendency to rotate during a swing.

A second cause of quadrantal error is more difficult to eliminate. As a vessel rolls, the apparent vertical is displaced first to one side and then to the other, due to the accelerations involved. The vertical axis of the gyrocompass tends to align itself with the apparent vertical. If the vessel is on a northerly or southerly course, the pivot of the compass is displaced from the vertical, resulting in a precession first to one side, then to the other. The effect is negligible and would be exactly balanced if successive rolls on opposite sides were equal. On an easterly or westerly heading, the pivot remains under the gyro axle, but the dynamic effect of the roll, acting upon the damping mechanism, introduces a precessing force which causes an error. However, the period is short and the error is in opposite directions on opposite rolls, so the effect is negligible. On noncardinal headings, both effects are present, and the relationship is such that the error is in the same direction regardless of the direction of roll. Thus, a persistent error is introduced, which changes direction in successive quadrants. This error is generally eliminated by the use of a second gyroscope. In some compasses, this is in the form of a small gyroscope called a **floating ballistic** which stabilizes the point of application of the mercury ballistic with respect to the true vertical as the vessel rolls. In others, two gyroscopes are used for the directive element and these are so installed that they tend to precess in opposite directions. Thus, they neutralize each other.

Another way of eliminating this error is to design the mercury ballistic system so that the surge of liquid due to north-south component of the roll is diminished in amount and delayed so that it is about a quarter of a cycle out of phase with the roll.

638. Gimballing error is that due to tilt of the compass rose. Directions are measured in the horizontal plane. If the compass card is tilted, the projection of its outer rim into the horizontal is an ellipse, and the graduations are not equally spaced with respect to a circle. This error applies to all instruments making use of a compass rose that can be tilted. For normal angles of tilt, this error is small and can be neglected. For accurate results, readings should be made when the card is horizontal. This error applies to the reading of the compass *or its repeaters* (art. 643), rather than to the compass itself. If the compass and its repeaters are installed so that the outer gimbals are in the longitudinal axis of the vessel, this error is minimized.

639. Use of the gyrocompass in polar regions. If means are not available for determining an equivalent setting or correction, a correction graph can be constructed. Ballistic deflection error, quadrantal error, and gimballing error are temporary or corrected in the design of the compass, and so can be ignored. Speed error and tangent latitude error (if it applies to the particular compass involved) can be combined into a single table or curve of corrections, using the formulas of articles 633 and 634. In high latitudes the east-west component of the vessel's speed is significant, and the error may be too large to consider its tangent equal to the angle itself expressed in radians. Therefore the applicable formulas are:

$$\tan \delta = \frac{\mathrm{S} \cos \mathrm{C}}{902.46 \cos \mathrm{L} \pm \mathrm{S} \sin \mathrm{C}} \qquad (1)$$

$$\alpha = \mathrm{r} \tan \mathrm{L}. \qquad (2)$$

The only approximation remaining is the use of 902.46, which varies slightly with latitude. The error thus introduced is not significant. The U. S. Navy gyrocompass error curves for latitude 80° are shown in figure 639. From the intersection of the appropriate speed curve and the radial line representing the *true* course (interpolating if necessary) a horizontal line is drawn to the vertical line through the origin, where the correction is indicated. To construct the curve for speed 35 knots, proceed as follows:

1. Compute the speed error, δ, for true courses at intervals of perhaps 30°. As an example, the error for course 210° (C S30°W) is:

$$\tan \delta = \frac{35 \times 0.86603}{902.46 \times 0.17365 - 35 \times 0.50000}$$

$$= 0.21773.$$

$$\delta = 12^{\circ}.3\mathrm{E}.$$

The error is easterly because the course has a southerly component (art. 633).

2. Compute the tangent latitude error. The curves of figure 639 are for a value of r of 1°.7:

$$\alpha = 1^{\circ}.7 \times 5.6713 = 9^{\circ}.6\mathrm{E}.$$

In northern latitudes tangent latitude error is easterly.

3. Combine δ and α algebraically to obtain gyro error (GE):

TC °	δ °	α °	*GE* °
000	12.6W	9.6E	3.0W
030	9.9W	9.6E	0.3W
060	5.3W	9.6E	4.3E
090	0.0	9.6E	9.6E
120	5.3E	9.6E	14.9E
150	9.9E	9.6E	19.5E
180	12.6E	9.6E	22.2E
210	12.3E	9.6E	21.9E
240	7.9E	9.6E	17.5E
270	0.0	9.6E	9.6E
300	7.9W	9.6E	1.7E
330	12.3W	9.6E	2.7W

4. To draw the curve, select a convenient origin and label this with the value of α. Draw a vertical line through the origin and mark off a convenient scale such that all values of δ can be shown both above and below the origin. The zero on this scale is at point α units above the origin (below in the Southern Hemisphere). Label the scale according to GE. Through the origin draw various radial lines at any convenient interval to represent true courses. For each computed course draw a horizontal construction line from the GE on the central scale to the appropriate radial line. The intersection of each pair of lines is one point on the curve. Connect all such points with a smooth curve, and erase the construction lines. If a straightedge or graph paper is used, the construction lines need not be drawn.

It is good practice to draw the curve for the highest speed first, to be sure that succeeding curves will fit on the paper. From such curves the gyro courses corresponding to various true courses can be determined and the radial lines labeled with these values for converting gyro directions to true directions.

The curves described in this article are for use *when all correctors are set on zero*, or if no provision is made for mechanically correcting for speed and damping errors. If the compass does not have a mercury ballistic, the tangent latitude error is omitted from the calculations and curves.

640. Desirable characteristics of the gyrocompass.—Since a gyrocompass is not affected by a magnetic field, it is not subject to magnetic compass errors (ch. VII), nor is it useless near the earth's magnetic poles. If an error is present, it is the same on all headings, and no table of corrections is needed. The directive force is sufficiently strong to permit directional pick-off for use in remote-indicating repeaters, automatic steering, dead reckoning and fire-control equipment, course recorders, etc.

641. Undesirable characteristics of the gyrocompass.—A gyrocompass is dependent upon a source of suitable electric power.

If operation of the compass is interrupted long enough to permit uncertainty in its indications, a considerable period (as much as four hours for some gyrocompasses) may be needed for it to settle on the meridian after it reaches operating speed. This period can be reduced by orienting the compass in the proper direction before it is started. If this is not practicable, the settling period can be hastened by leveling the compass when it reaches the meridian (one-fourth of a cycle or 21 minutes after starting at maximum deflection) or by leveling *and* precessing the gyro to the approximate meridian after its direction and rate of precession are observed for several minutes. Either process may need to be repeated several times and followed by a settling period.

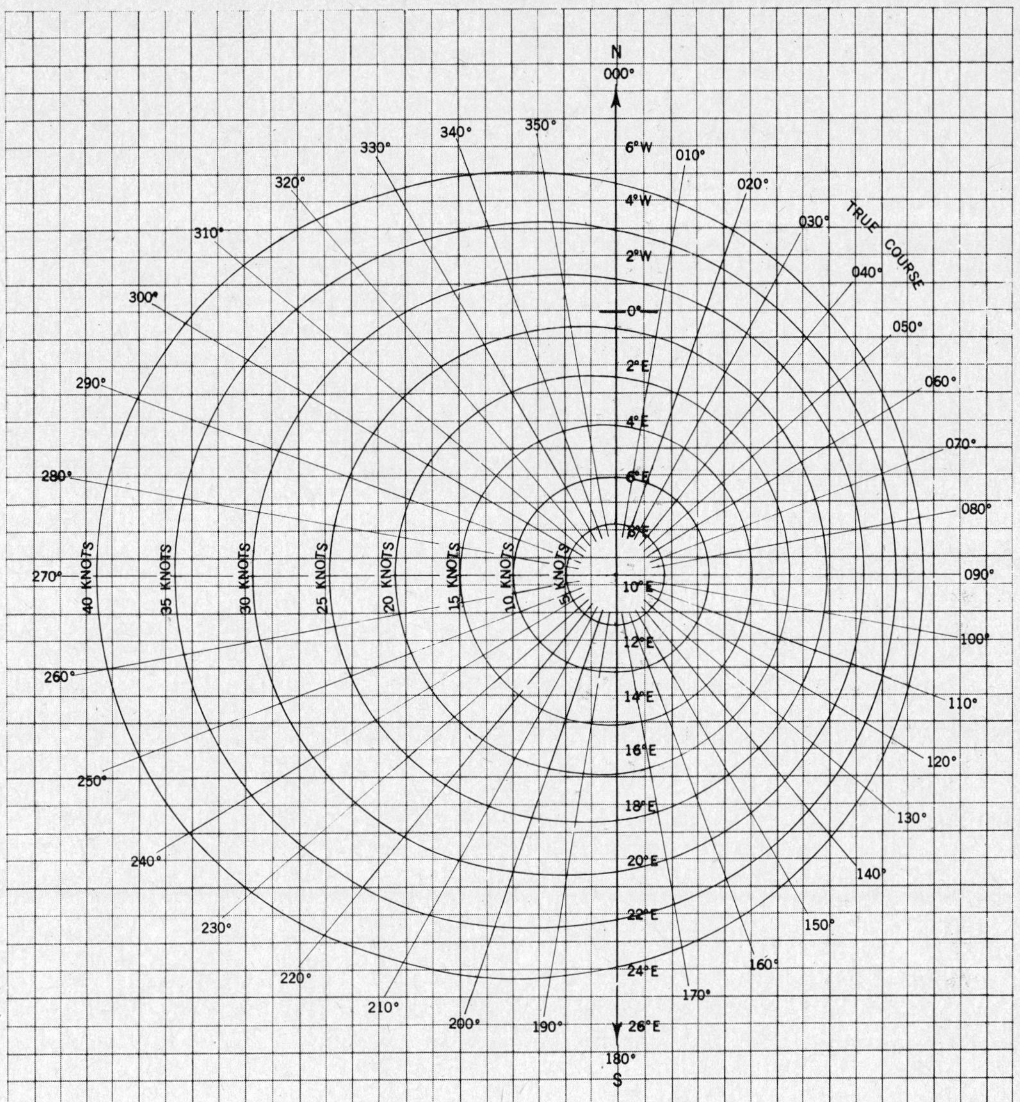

FIGURE 639.—Gyrocompass error curves for latitude 80°.

The gyrocompass is subject to certain errors requiring applications of corrections, either manually or automatically (art. 632).

The compass is an intricate mechanism of many parts. Thus, it requires some maintenance. In heavy seas a gyrocompass may become unreliable unless certain features are included in the design—features which are generally omitted from the sm all, simpler compasses.

The directive force of a gyrocompass decreases with latitude, being maximum at the equator and zero at the geographical poles.

642. Gyrocompass models.—The Mark 19 Gyrocompass System (fig. 642a) consists of four components: the master compass, the control cabinet, the compass failure annunciator, and the solid state power supply.

The two main elements of the master compass (fig. 642b) are the compass element and the supporting element. The compass element includes the sensitive element (meridian and slave gyros), the phantom or follower element, and the gimbal. The supporting

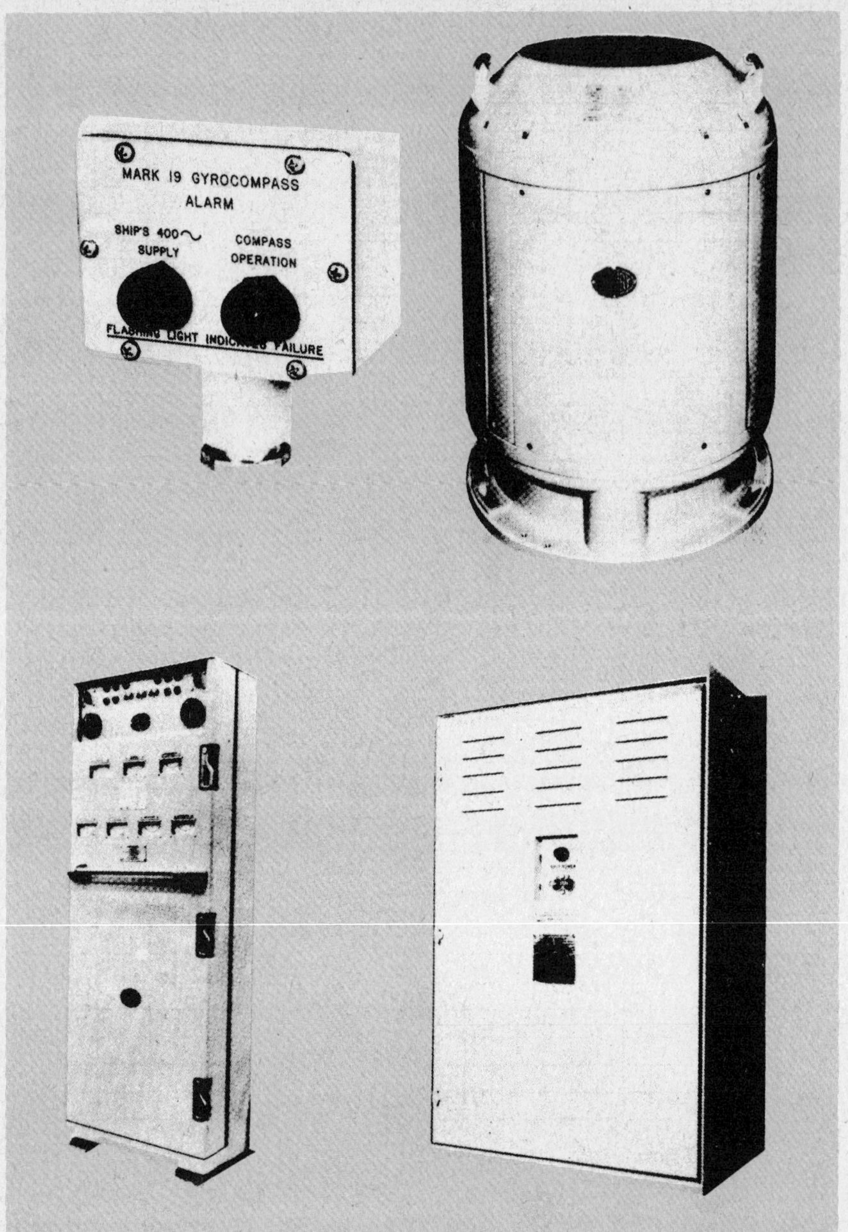

FIGURE 642a.—Mark 19 Gyrocompass System.

element includes the frame and binnacle which provide a shock-mount support for the compass element.

The control cabinet contains all controls and indicators necessary for the operation of the equipment.

The compass failure annunciator contains two indicator lights to indicate a malfunction of the compass system or failure of the vessel's 400 Hertz power supply.

The solid state power supply provides the power necessary for operation of the master compass, control cabinet, compass failure annunciator, and charging batteries used as emergency power. All other gyrocompass system components must be energized from ship power. In the event of loss of ship power, the solid state supply will continue

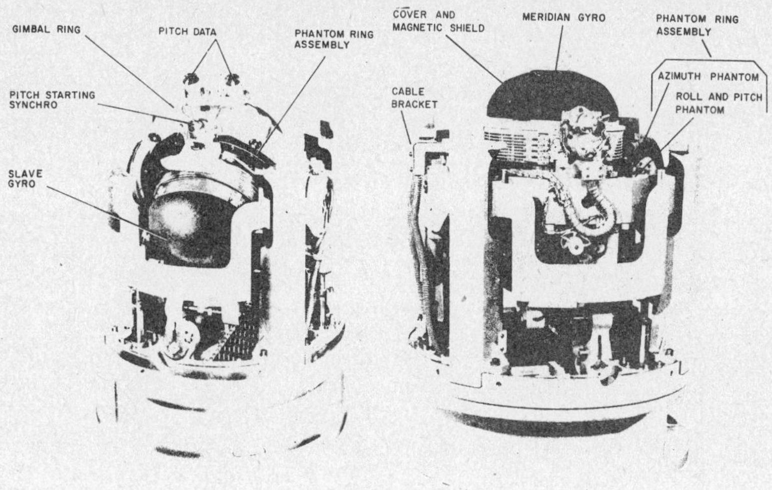

FIGURE 642b.—Mark 19 master compass.

to operate from the batteries until the ship's line is restored or the batteries are discharged.

Fluid suspension of the sensitive element provides high shock tolerance and greatly reduces the effect of accelerations. At running temperature, the specific gravity of the gyrosphere is the same as that of the oil in which it is immersed. Since the gyrosphere is in neutral buoyancy, it exerts no load on the vertical bearings which, therefore, serve only as guides for the sphere.

The Mark 19 Gyrocompass has four modes of operation. The normal mode provides optimum performance up to latitude 75°. The fast settle mode provides accelerated settling of the compass upon starting. The high latitude mode provides optimum performance from latitude 75° to about latitude 86°. The directional gyro mode enables operation of the compass as a free gyro with the spin axis oriented to grid north (art. 2510).

The Mark 19 Gyrocompass consists basically of two gyros (fig. 642c) placed with their spin axes mutually perpendicular in the horizontal plane. The spin axis of one gyro is directed along a north-south line, and the spin axis of the second is slaved to the first along an approximate east-west line. The north-seeking or meridian gyro and the slave gyro are mounted one above the other in a supporting ring. This ring is made to follow the gyros in heading and tilt by azimuth, roll, and pitch servos. These servos also drive the synchro transmitters which serve to supply output data.

The meridian gyro is essentially a gyrocompass. It furnishes indications of heading as well as tilt about the east-west axis. The slave gyro is essentially a free gyro and furnishes only an indication of tilt about the north-south axis. Thus, the Mark 19 Gyrocompass provides heading, roll, and pitch data.

In the meridian gyro of the Mark 19 Gyrocompass, the tilt is detected by a gravity reference attached to the vertical ring in such a way that it is parallel to the gyro axle. This device (electrolytic level) is a special level which transmits an electrical signal with magnitude and sense according to tilt. Since the gravity reference and axle are parallel and rigidly fixed with respect to one another, the signal emitted by the gravity reference is a measure of the gyro axle tilt about the east-west axis. In the more recent modifications of the gyrocompass, higher accuracy is obtained through the use of linear accelerometers instead of electrolytic levels to sense the direction of gravity.

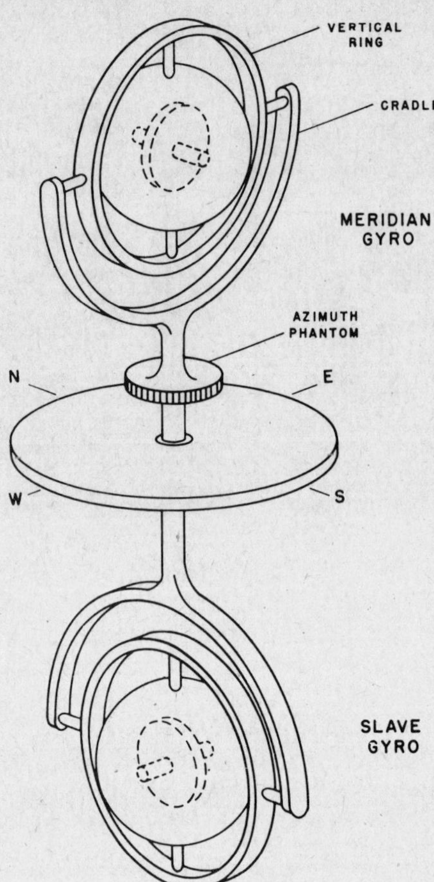

FIGURE 642c.—Simplified diagram of the Mark 19 compass element.

The tilt signal, after amplification, is applied to the control fields of electrical torquers, as shown in figure 642d, which cause torques about the vertical and horizontal axes. The torquers located about the horizontal axis are known as the azimuth torquers. They apply a torque about the horizontal axis proportional to the amount of tilt of the spin axis and cause the gyro to precess in azimuth. The effect of this torque is the same as making the gyro pendulous by attaching a heavy weight to the bottom of the vertical ring. When one end of the axis is tilted up, the resulting torque about the horizontal axis precesses the gyro in azimuth, i.e., about its vertical axis.

The leveling torquer, located about the vertical axis of the gyro, applies a torque about the vertical axis proportional to tilt and causes the gyro to precess about the horizontal axis to reduce the tilt to zero. The effect of this torque is the same as attaching a weight to the east side of the sphere (art. 631). When one end of the gyro axle is tilted up, the resulting torque about the vertical axis precesses the high end down. Thus, the effect of these two torques is to continually precess the axis to the meridian and make it level.

The Technical Manual for the Mark 19 Gyrocompass should be referred to for an explanation of the means used to control the compass.

The **Mark 27 Gyrocompass** (fig. 642e) consisting of two major components—the master compass unit and the compass electronics unit—is designed for both military and commercial, small to medium class vessels. The equipment is powered by an internal 400 Hz solid state supply (inverter) operating from a 24 volt DC battery source or

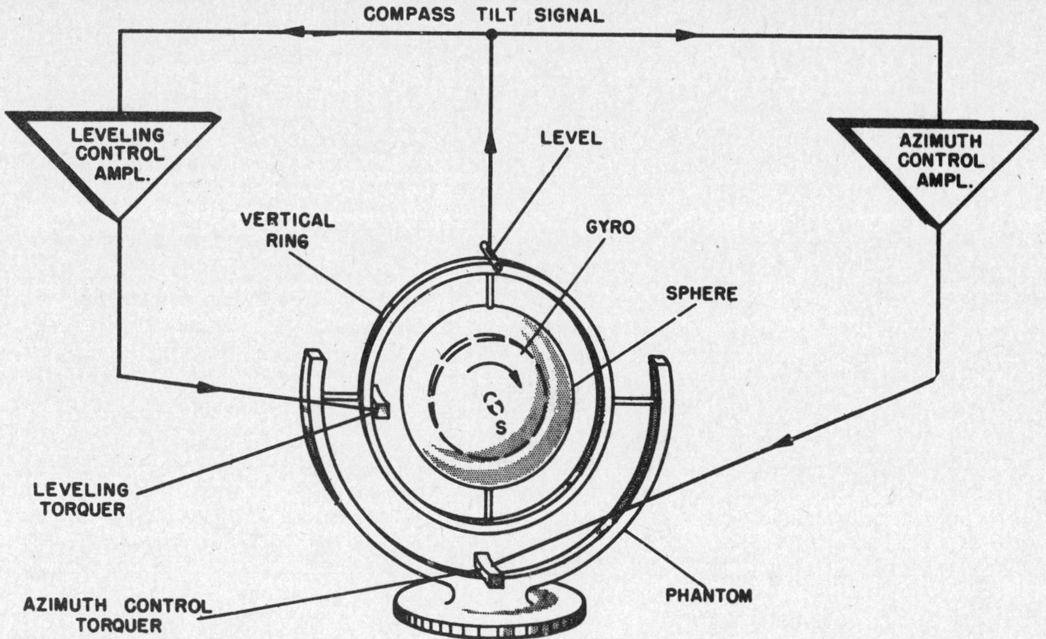

FIGURE 642d.—Simplified diagram of electrical azimuth and leveling controls for meridian gyro.

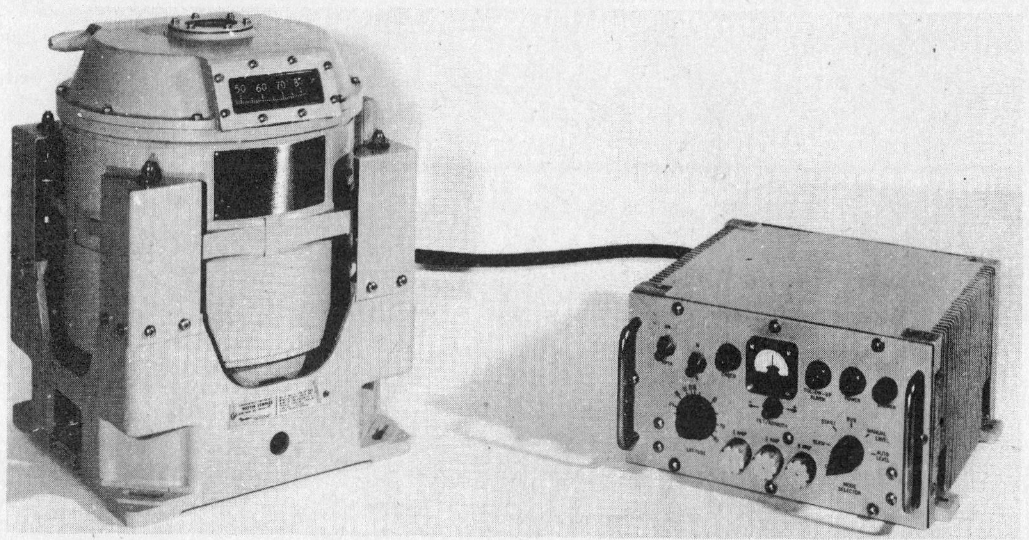

Courtesy of Sperry Marine Systems.

FIGURE 642e.—Mark 27 Gyrocompass System.

from an external 115 volt 60 to 400 Hz converter (rectifier) unit. The master compass unit is an oil-filled sealed unit containing the sensitive element, fluid ballistic, and the supporting gimbals and servo drive. The compass electronics unit contains the compass controls, supporting solid state electronics, and a solid state power supply. A direct-reading heading indication dial on the master compass has red illumination for night viewing. The master compass can be provided with various types of electrical transducers for transmission of the heading data to remote repeaters. The internal static power supply has the capability to power either two step repeaters or two servo synchro repeaters. Additional repeaters can be accomodated with externally supplied power. The master compass unit can be mounted on top of the compass electronics unit, or in a remote location.

Fluid suspension of the sensitive element provides high shock tolerance and greatly reduces the effect of accelerations. The sensitive element can be caged when not in use to prevent damage. The manually operated caging element is on top of the master compass.

A fluid ballistic (art. 631) provides the gravitational torques to make the gyro seek north. This ballistic consists of two interconnected brass tanks, partially filled with a 20 centistoke silicone fluid. The small bore of the tubing connecting the tanks retards the free flow of fluid between the tanks. Because of the time it takes for the fluid to flow, the disturbing effects of ship maneuvers and roll and pitch motion are minimized.

To compensate for the effect of changes in vertical earth rate due to change of latitude, a manual latitude dial and a North/South switch is incorporated on the control unit for producing an electrical torque on the gyrosphere. The switch and dial should be properly positioned by the operator.

The **Mark 227 Gyrocompass** (fig. 642f) utilizes the basic Mark 27 design in a configuration designed primarily for large commercial and auxiliary naval vessels. The master compass, which is identical to the Mark 27 master compass except for mounting facilities, is mounted in gimbals atop a deck-mounted console. All of the controls, except for the caging control, power supplies, and repeater switches (for up to

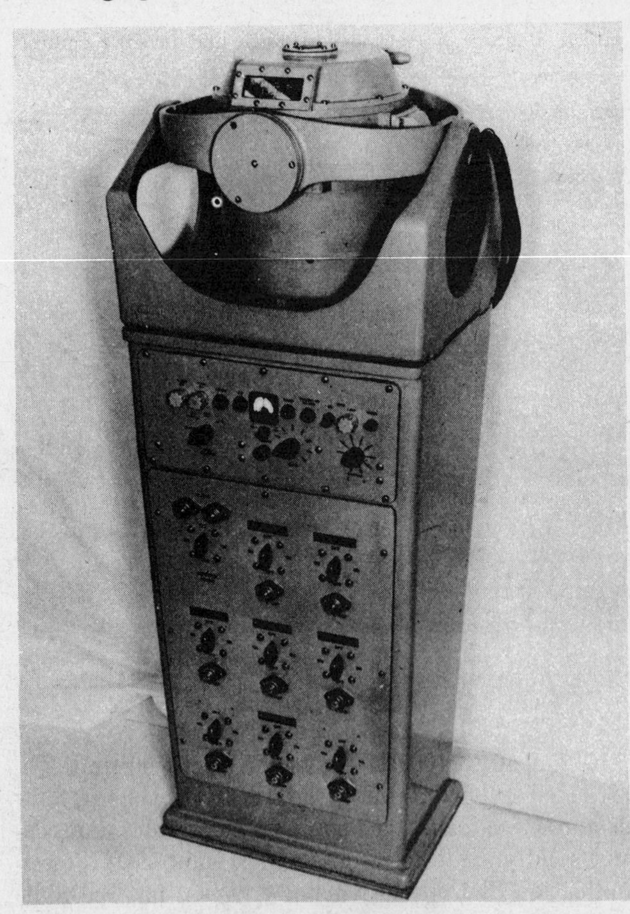

Courtesy of Sperry Marine Systems.

FIGURE 642f.—Mark 227 Gyrocompass System.

8 repeaters) are contained in the console. Standard units are equipped with a step transmitter and auxiliary equipment to power 8 step repeaters. Synchros, either 60 or 400 Hz, can be added to supply single or single and 36-speed data. Input power to this unit is 115 volt 60 to 400 Hz. Speed correction has been added and is set with a front panel knob. The additional gimbals enable transmission of azimuth data free of error due to deck tilt.

643. Gyrocompass repeaters.—A gyrocompass is customarily located at a favorable position below decks, and its indications transmitted electrically to various positions throughout the vessel. Each repeater consists of a compass rose on a suitable card so mounted that the direction of the ship's head is indicated at a lubber's line. Although the repeater may be mounted in any position, including vertically on a bulkhead, it is generally placed in gimbals in a bowl, similar to the mounting of a compass, which it resembles (fig. 643). This is true particularly of repeaters used for obtaining bearings. A gyro repeater used primarily to indicate the gyro heading is sometimes called a **ship's course indicator.**

Gyrocompass indications are also used in automatic steering devices, direction-stabilized radarscopes, wind indicators, fire control equipment, etc.

A compass used to control other equipment, particularly repeaters, is sometimes called a **master compass.** In the case of a gyrocompass, it is usually called a **master**

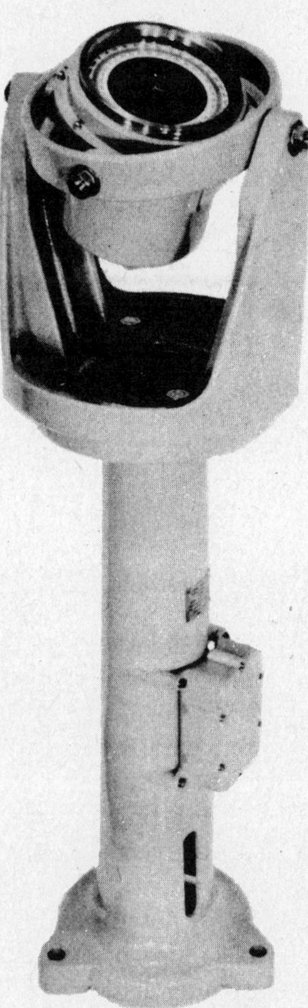

Courtesy of Ahrendt Instrument Co.

FIGURE 643.—A gyro repeater used as a ship's course indicator (Mark 2 Mod 5).

gyrocompass. It is good practice to check all repeaters periodically with the master compass to insure continued synchronization.

644. Gyro repeater accessories.—The bearing circle and azimuth circle (art. 629) are also used with the gyro repeater for bearing and azimuth observations. A **telescopic alidade** (fig. 644) may also be provided for bearing observations from repeaters. The telescopic alidade is basically similar to the bearing circle, except that it is fitted with a telescope instead of sighting vanes. The telescope of the telescopic alidade shown in figure 644 is mounted on a ring that fits on the gyro repeater. The erecting telescope is fitted with crosshair, level vial, polarizing light filter, and internal focusing. The optical system projects the image of approximately 25° of the compass card together with a view of the level vial onto the optical axis of the telescope. By this means, both the observed object and its bearing can be viewed at the same time through the eyepiece.

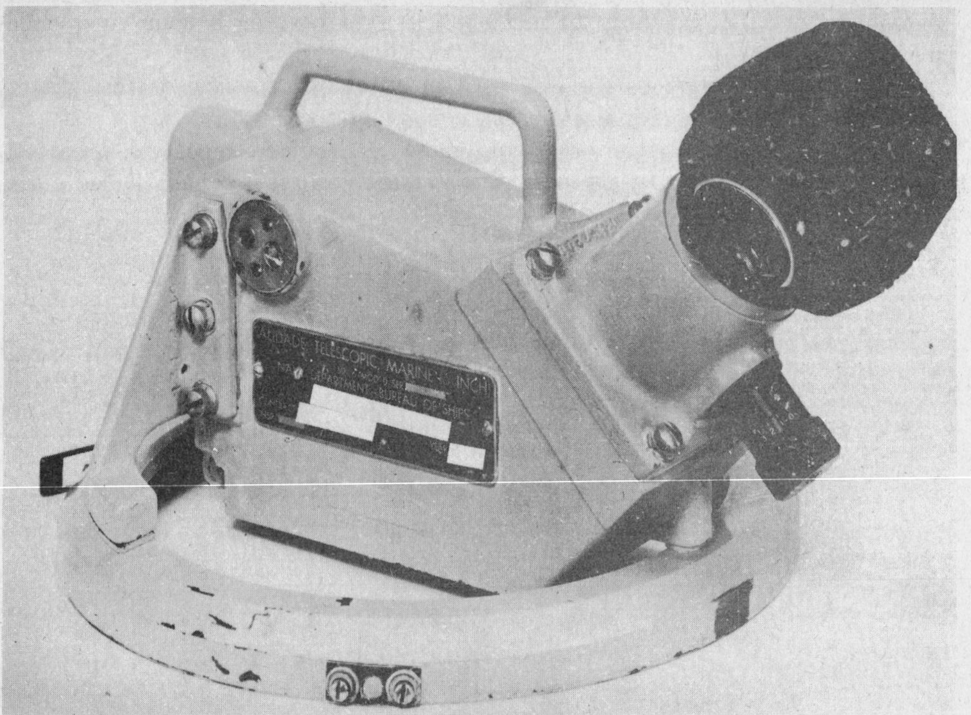

FIGURE 644.—Telescopic alidade.

645. Pelorus.—Although it is desirable to have a compass, a compass repeater, or an alidade for obtaining bearings, satisfactory results can be obtained by means of an inexpensive device known as a **pelorus** (fig 645). In appearance and use this device resembles a compass or compass repeater, with sighting vanes or a sighting telescope attached, but it has no directive properties. That is, it remains at any *relative* direction to which it is set. It is generally used by setting 000° at the lubber's line. Relative bearings are then observed. They can be converted to bearings true, magnetic, grid, etc., by *adding* the appropriate heading. The direct use of relative bearings is sometimes of value. A pelorus is useful, for instance, in determining the moment at which an aid to navigation is broad on the beam. It is also useful in measuring pairs of relative bearings for use with table 7 or for determining distance off and distance abeam without a table.

If the true heading is set at the lubber's line, true bearings are observed directly. Similarly, compass bearings can be observed if the compass heading is set at the lub-

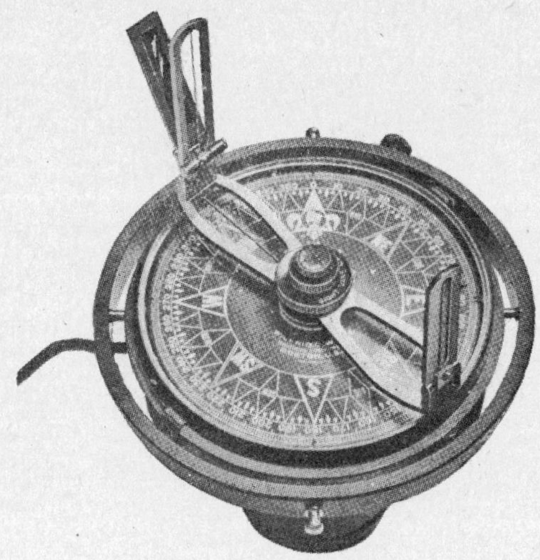

FIGURE 645.—A pelorus.

ber's line, etc. However, the vessel must be on the heading to which the pelorus is set if accurate results are to be obtained, or else a correction must be applied to the observed results. Perhaps the easiest way of avoiding error is to have the steersman indicate when the vessel is on course. This is usually done by calling out "mark, mark, mark" as long as the vessel is within a specified fraction of a degree of the desired heading. The observer, who is watching a distant object across the pelorus, selects an instant when the vessel is steady and is on course. An alternative method is to have the observer call out "mark" when the relative bearing is steady, and the steersman note the heading. If the compass is swinging at the moment of observation, the observation should be rejected. The number of degrees between the desired and actual headings is *added* if the vessel is to the *right* of the course, and *subtracted* if to the *left*. Thus, if the course is 060° and the heading is 062° at the moment of observation, a correction of 2° is added to the bearing.

Each observer should determine for himself the technique that produces the most reliable results.

646. Course recorder.—A continuous graphical record of the headings of a vessel can be obtained by means of a **course recorder** (fig. 646). In its usual form, paper with both heading and time graduations is slowly wound from one drum to another, its speed being controlled by a spring-powered clockwork mechanism. A pen is in contact with the paper, tracing a line to indicate the heading at each moment. The pen is attached to an arm controlled by indications from a compass, usually the master gyrocompass.

647. Dead reckoning equipment.—The primary navigational functions of **dead reckoning equipment** (**DRE**) are to (1) provide continuous indications of the vessel's present latitude and longitude, and (2) provide a graphical record of the vessel's dead reckoning track. In addition, most types of dead reckoning equipment provide means for tracking one or more other craft, to obtain a graphical record of the other craft's course and speed. This equipment is generally installed only on warships.

Dead reckoning equipment consists in general of four components: (1) an analyzer; (2) latitude and longitude indicator dials; (3) a desk-size unit called a **dead reckoning tracer** (**DRT**); and (4) a glass plotting surface over the dead reckoning tracer.

The analyzer receives directional signals from the vessel's gyrocompass, and distance signals from the underwater log. The course and distance data are transformed

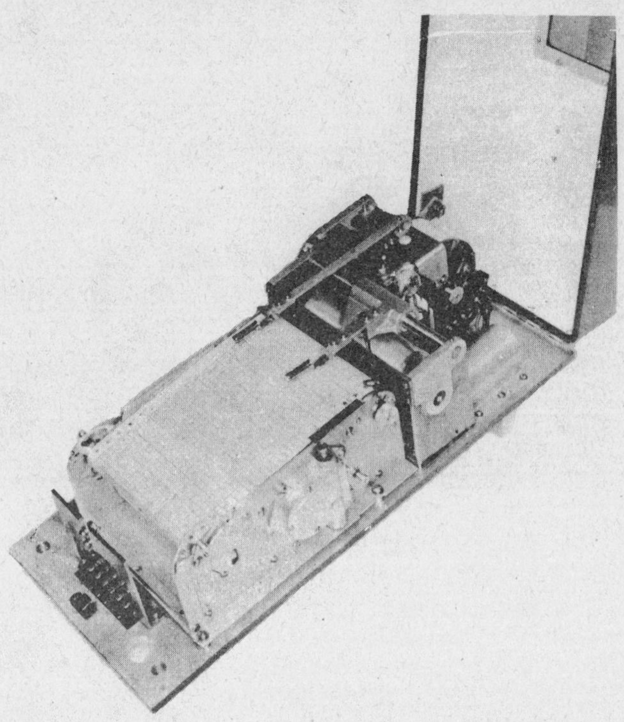

Courtesy of Sperry Marine Systems.

FIGURE 646.—A course recorder.

automatically to electrical signals proportional to the north-south and east-west components of the vessel's movement. These distance signals are transmitted to the latitude and longitude indicators, changing their readings by the correct amount to indicate the new latitude and the new longitude in degrees and minutes. Since the number of miles in the north-south component of distance traveled is nearly equal to the change in latitude expressed in minutes, the latitude indicator is fed directly. Departure (art. 204) is automatically tranformed to difference of longitude before being registered on the longitude indicator dials. If the indicator dials are correctly set to latitude and longitude, they continuously show subsequent dead reckoning positions of the vessel.

The north-south and east-west component signals from the analyzer are also transmitted to the DRT (fig. 647), where they control the motion of a pencil which moves across a chart or plotting sheet attached to the DRT base. The pencil draws a line which conforms to the maneuvers of the vessel. The mechanism can be set to plot the track at any scale from ¼ mile per inch (1/10 mile on some) to 16 miles per inch. A clock-controlled contact lifts the pencil from the paper for 15 seconds of each minute and for a longer period each 10 minutes, thus providing automatic time measurement. The pencil carriage can be moved manually to any part of the chart for initial setting and the direction of travel can be adjusted so that the chart can be placed with any cardinal direction "up."

The cover of the DRT is a sheet of glass to which a plotting sheet or blank paper can be fastened. An electric lamp on the top of the pencil carriage throws a spot of light through the paper directly over the carriage, thus providing a moving reference scaled to the course and speed of the vessel. If the position of the spot of light is marked periodically on the paper, a second record of the vessel's track is obtained. However,

FIGURE 647.—A dead reckoning tracer. *Courtesy of Ahrendt Instrument Co.*

the principal use of this sheet is for plotting successive positions of another craft, using the spot of light as the origin. A polar grid centered on the light may be projected onto the paper to facilitate measurement. The course of the other vessel can be measured directly from the plot, and its speed can be determined by means of the time needed to travel any distance measured on the plot. This process is called **tracking.** If the ranges and bearings are plotted from a fixed point, *relative* movement is determined, a practice commonly followed in connection with radar.

While dead reckoning equipment is a great convenience, particularly when changes of course or speed are numerous, its indications should be checked by graphical plot on the chart or plotting sheet. Reliable dead reckoning is too important to be left entirely to mechanical equipment without an independent check.

CHAPTER VII

COMPASS ERROR

Magnetism

701. Theory of magnetism.—The fact that iron can be magnetized (given the ability to attract other iron) has been known for thousands of years, but the explanation of this phenomenon has awaited the recently acquired knowledge of atomic structure. According to present theory, the magnetic field around a current-carrying wire and the magnetism of a permanent **magnet** are the same phenomenon—fields created by moving electrical charges. This occurs whether the charge is moving along a wire, flowing with the magma of the earth's core, encircling the earth at high altitude as a stream of charged particles, or rotating around the nucleus of an atom.

It has been shown that microscopically small regions, called **domains,** exist in iron and other ferromagnetic substances. In each domain the fields created by electrons spinning around their atomic nuclei are parallel to each other, causing the domain to be magnetized to saturation. In a piece of unmagnetized iron, the directions of the various domains are arranged in a random manner with respect to each other. If the substance is placed in a weak magnetic field, the domains rotate somewhat toward the direction of that field. Those domains which are more nearly parallel to the field increase in size at the expense of the more non parallel ones. If the field is made sufficiently strong, entire domains rotate suddenly by angles of as much as 90° or 180° so as to become parallel to that "crystal axis" which is most nearly parallel to the direction of the field. If the strength of the field is increased to a certain value depending upon individual conditions, all of the domains rotate into parallelism with the field, and the iron itself is said to be magnetically **saturated.** If the field is removed, the domains have a tendency to rotate more or less rapidly to a more natural direction parallel to some crystal axis, and more slowly to random directions under the influence of thermal agitation.

Magnetism which is present only when the material is under the influence of an external field is called **induced magnetism.** That which remains after the magnetizing force is removed is called **residual magnetism.** That which is retained for long periods without appreciable reduction, unless the material is subjected to a demagnetizing force, is called **permanent magnetism.**

Certain substances respond readily to a magnetic field. These **magnetic materials** are principally those composed largely of iron, although nickel and cobalt also exhibit magnetic properties. The best magnets are made of an alloy composed mostly of iron, nickel, and cobalt. Aluminum and some copper may be added. Platinum and silver, properly alloyed with other material, make excellent magnets, but for ordinary purposes the increased expense is not justified by the improvement in performance. Permanent magnets occur in nature in the form of **lodestone,** a form of magnetite (an oxide of iron) possessing magnetic properties. A piece of this material constitutes a **natural magnet.**

702. Hard and soft iron.—In some alloys of iron, the crystals can be so arranged and internally stressed that the domains remain parallel to each other indefinitely, and the metal thus becomes a **permanent magnet.** Such alloys are used for the magnets of a compass. In other kinds of iron, the domains reorient themselves rapidly to conform to the direction of a changing external field, and soon take random directions if the field is removed. A ferromagnetic substance which retains much of its magnetism in the absence of an external field, is said to have high **remanence** or **retentivity.** The strength of a reverse field (one of opposite polarity) required to reduce the magnetism of a magnet to zero is called the **coercivity** or **coercive force** of the magnet. Hence, a compass magnet should have high remanence in order to be strong, and high coercivity so that stray fields will not materially affect it. For convenience, iron is called "hard" if it has high remanence, and "soft" if it has low remanence. **Permeability** (μ) is the ratio of the strength of the magnetic field inside the metal (B) to the strength of the external field (H), or $\mu=\frac{B}{H}$.

703. Lines of force.—The direction of a magnetic field is usually represented by lines, called **lines of force.** Relative intensity in different parts of a magnetic field is indicated by the spacing of the lines of force, a strong field having the lines close together. If a piece of unmagnetized iron is placed in a magnetic field, the lines of force tend to crowd into the iron, following its long axis, and the field is stronger in the vicinity of the iron, somewhat as shown in figure 703a. If the iron becomes permanently magnetized and is removed from this field, the lines of force around the iron follow paths about as shown in figure 703b.

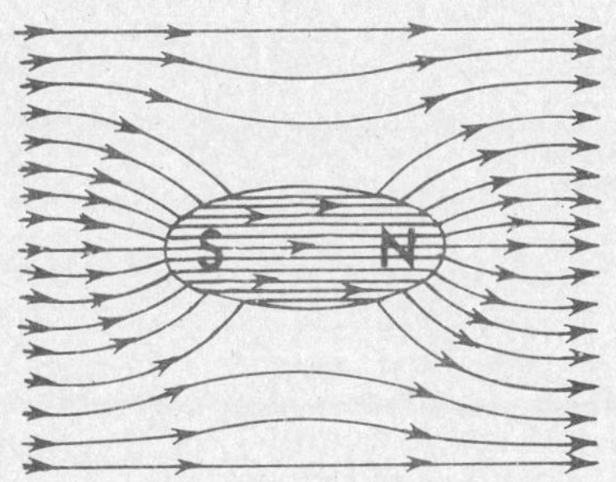

FIGURE 703a.—Lines of force crowd into ferromagnetic material placed in a magnetic field.

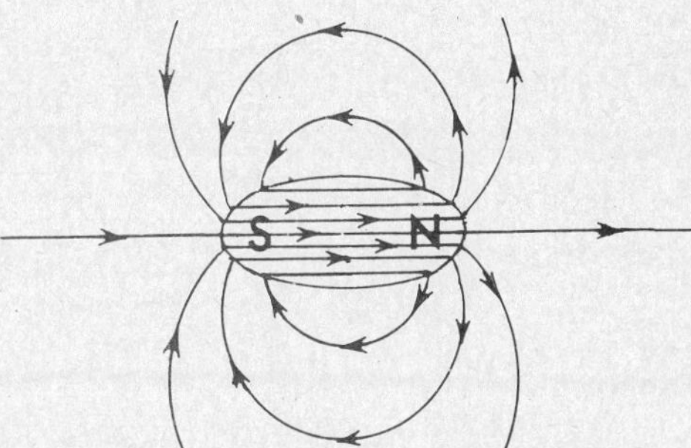

FIGURE 703b.—Field of a permanent magnet.

704. Magnetic poles.—The region in which the lines of force enter the iron is called the **south pole,** and the region in which they leave the iron is called the **north pole.** Thus, the lines of force are directed from south to north within the magnet, and from north to south in the external field. Every magnet has a north pole and a south pole. If a magnet is cut into two pieces, each becomes a magnet with a north pole and south pole. A single pole cannot exist independently. If two magnets are brought close together, *unlike poles attract each other and like poles repel.* Thus, a north pole attracts a south pole but repels another north pole.

The earth itself has a magnetic field (art. 706), with its magnetic poles being some distance from the geographical poles. If a permanent bar magnet is supported so that it can turn freely, both horizontally and vertically, it aligns itself with the magnetic field of the earth, which at most places is in a general north-south direction and inclined to the horizontal. Since the north pole of the magnet points in a northerly direction, the earth's magnetic pole in the Northern Hemisphere has *south* magnetism. Nevertheless, it is called the **north magnetic pole** because of its geographical location. For a similar reason, the pole in the Southern Hemisphere, although it has north magnetism, is called the **south magnetic pole.** To avoid confusion, north magnetism is usually called "red," and south magnetism, "blue." The red (north) pole of a magnet is usually painted red, and in some cases the south (blue) pole is painted blue. The north magnetic pole of the earth is a blue pole, and the south magnetic pole is a red pole.

705. The magnetism of soft iron, in which remanence is low, depends upon the position of the iron with respect to an external field. It is strongest if the long axis is parallel to the lines of force, and decreases to a minimum if the material is rotated so that the long axis is perpendicular to the lines of force. Figure 705 shows three positions of a bar magnet with respect to a magnetic field. At position *X* the pole at the upper end of the bar is red and relatively strong. As the bar is rotated toward position *Y*, the upper end remains red, but its strength decreases. At position *Y*, no pole is apparent at either end, but a red pole extends along the entire left side of the bar, and a blue pole along the right side. Poles are strongest when concentrated into a small area. Hence, when spread over an entire side, as at position *Y*, they are relatively weak. At position *Z*, the upper end is blue.

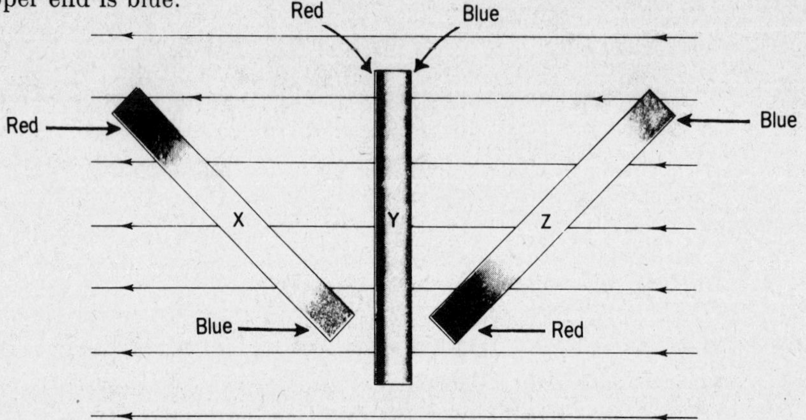

FIGURE 705.—The polarity of a soft iron bar in a magnetic field.

The change in polarity as a bar of soft iron is rotated in a magnetic field can easily be demonstrated. If a bar of soft iron is placed vertical in northern magnetic latitudes (as in any part of the United States), the north (red) end of a compass magnet brought near it will be attracted by the upper end of the bar, and repelled by the lower end. If the bar is inverted, so that its ends are interchanged, the upper end (which as the lower end previously repelled the compass needle) will attract the north end of the needle, and the lower end will repel it. Thus, the polarity of the rod is reversed, *either* end having blue magnetism if it is at the top. This changing polarity of soft iron in the earth's field is a major factor affecting the magnetic compasses of a steel vessel.

706. Terrestrial magnetism.—The earth itself can be considered to be a gigantic magnet. Although man has known for many centuries that the earth has a magnetic field, the origin of the magnetism is not completely understood. Nevertheless, the horizontal component of this field is a valuable reference in navigation, for it provides the directive force for the magnetic compass, which indicates the ship's heading *in relation to the horizontal component of this field.*

The world-wide pattern of the earth's magnetism is roughly like that which would result from a short, powerful, bar magnet near the earth's center, as shown in figure 706. The geographical poles are at the top and bottom, and the magnetic poles are offset somewhat from them. This representation, however, is greatly simplified. The actual field is more complex, and requires measurement of its strength and direction at many places (art. 707) before it can be defined accurately enough to be of practical use to the navigator. Not only are the magnetic poles offset from the geographical poles, but the magnetic poles themselves are not 180° apart and, in general, a magnetic compass aligned with the lines of force does not point toward either magnetic pole. In 1975, the north magnetic pole was located at latitude 76°.1N, longitude 100°.0W, approximately, to the northward of Prince of Wales Island; and the south magnetic pole was at latitude 65°.8S, longitude 139°.4E, approximately, off the coast of the northeastern part of Wilkes Land. However, the magnetic poles are not stationary. The entire magnetic field of the earth, including the magnetic poles, undergoes a small daily or **diurnal change,** and a very slow, progressive **secular change.** In addition, temporary sporadic changes occur from time to time during magnetic storms. During a severe storm, variation may change as much as 5°, or more. However, such disturbances are never so rapid as to cause noticeable deflection of the compass card, and in most navigable waters the change is so little that it is not significant in practical navigation. Even when there is no temporary disturbance, the earth's field is considerably more intricate than indicated by an isomagnetic chart (art. 708). Natural magnetic irregularities occurring over relatively small areas are called **magnetic anomalies** by the magneticians, but the navigator generally refers to these phenomena as **local disturbances.** Notes warning of such disturbances are shown on charts. In addition, artificial disturbances may be quite severe when a vessel is in close proximity to other vessels, piers, machinery, electric currents, etc.

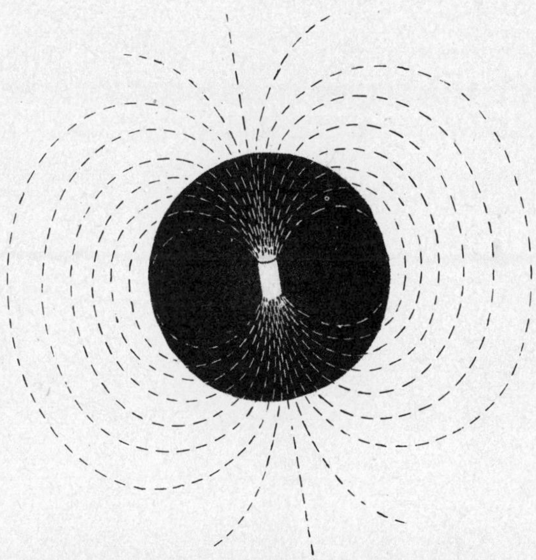

FIGURE 706.—The magnetic field of the earth.

The elements of the earth's field are as follows:

Total intensity (**F**) is the strength of the field at any point, measured in a direction parallel to the field. Intensity is sometimes measured in **oersteds,** one oersted being equal to a force of one dyne acting on a unit pole. The range of intensity of the earth's field is about 0.25 to 0.70 oersted. For convenience in geomagnetic surveying, a small unit is used, called the **gamma.** One oersted equals 100,000 gammas, so that the range of intensity of the earth's field is about 25,000 to 70,000 gammas.

Horizontal intensity (**H**) is the horizontal component of the total intensity. At the **magnetic equator,** which corresponds roughly with the geographic equator, the field is parallel to the surface of the earth, and the horizontal intensity is the same as total intensity. At the magnetic poles of the earth, the field is vertical and there is no horizontal component. The direction of the horizontal component at any place defines the **magnetic meridian** at that place. This component provides the desired directive force of a magnetic compass.

North component (X) is the horizontal intensity's component along a geographic (true) meridian.

East component (Y) is the horizontal intensity's component perpendicular to the north component.

Vertical intensity (Z) is the vertical component of the total intensity. It is zero at the magnetic equator. At the magnetic poles it is the same as the total intensity. While the vertical intensity has no direct effect upon the direction indicated by a magnetic compass, it does induce magnetic fields in vertical soft iron, and these may affect the compass.

Variation (V, Var.), called **declination** (D) by magneticians, is the angle between the geographic and magnetic meridians at any place. The expression **magnetic variation** is used when it is necessary to distinguish this from other forms of variation. This element is measured in angular units and named east or west to indicate the side of true north on which the (magnetic) northerly part of the magnetic meridian lies. For computational purposes, easterly variation is sometimes designated positive (+), and westerly variation negative (−). **Grid variation** (GV) or **grivation** is the angle between the grid and magnetic meridians at any place, measured and named in a manner similar to variation.

Magnetic dip (I), called **inclination** (I) by magneticians, is the vertical angle, expressed in angular units, between the horizontal at any point and a line of force through that point. The **magnetic latitude** of a place is the angle having a tangent equal to half that of the magnetic dip of the place.

At a distance of several hundred miles above the earth's surface, the magnetic field surrounding the earth is believed to be uniform, as it appears in figure 706, and centered around two **geomagnetic poles.** These do not coincide with either the magnetic poles (art. 704) or the geographical poles. However, they are 180° apart, the north geomagnetic pole being at latitude 78°.5N, longitude 69°W (near Etah, Greenland) and the south geomagnetic pole being at latitude 78°.5S, longitude 111°E. The great circles through these poles are called **geomagnetic meridians.** That geomagnetic meridian passing through the south geographical pole is the origin for measurement of **geomagnetic longitude,** which is measured eastward through 360°. The complement of the arc of a geomagnetic meridian from the nearer geomagnetic pole to a place is called the **geomagnetic latitude.** When the sun is over the upper branch of the geomagnetic meridian of a place, it is **geomagnetic noon** there, and when it is over the lower branch of the geomagnetic meridian, it is **geomagnetic midnight.** The angle between the lower branch of the geomagnetic meridian of a place and the geomagnetic meridian over which the sun is located is called **geomagnetic time.** The diurnal change is related to geomagnetic time. The auroral zones are centered on the geomagnetic poles.

707. Measurement of the earth's magnetic field is made continuously at about 70 permanent **magnetic observatories** throughout the world. In addition, large numbers of temporary stations are occupied for short periods to add to man's knowledge of the earth's field. In the past, measurements at sea have been made by means of nonmagnetic ships constructed especially for this purpose. However, this is a slow and expensive method, and quite inadequate to survey properly the 71 percent of the earth's surface covered with water. Since World War II, a satisfactory **airborne magnetometer** has been developed by the U. S. Navy. By means of this instrument, continuous readings can be recorded automatically during long overwater flights.

708. Isomagnetic charts showing lines of equality of some magnetic element are published by the Defense Mapping Agency Hydrographic Center. The magnetic data are compiled by the United States Geological Survey with the assistance of the National Oceanic and Atmospheric Administration and in collaboration with the U. S. Naval Oceanographic Office. The three charts of each element consist of one on the Mercator projection (art. 305) covering most of the world, and one on a polar projection (azimuthal equidistant (art. 320) or stereographic) for each of the two polar areas. All charts now included in the series are published at intervals of 10 years, showing the values for the beginning of each year ending in five. Charts showing variation are also published for the years ending in zero (1950, 1960, etc.).

The isomagnetic chart of most concern to a navigator is chart 42, *Magnetic Variation*, a simplified version of which is shown in figure 708a. The lines connecting points of equal magnetic variation are called **isogonic lines.** *These are not magnetic meridians (lines of force).* The line connecting points of zero variation is called the **agonic line.** Variation is also shown on nautical charts. Those of relatively small scale generally show isogonic lines. Those of scale larger than 1:100,000 generally give the information in the form of statements inside compass roses placed at various places on the chart, and sometimes, also, by a **magnetic compass rose** within the true compass rose and offset from it by the amount of the variation. By means of this arrangement, true directions can be plotted without arithmetically applying variation to magnetic directions, or magnetic directions can be read directly from the chart. The magnetic compass rose is generally graduated in both degrees and points. Variation is given to the nearest 15′, and the annual change to the nearest 1′. However, since the rate of change is not constant, a very old chart should not be used, even though it has been corrected for all changes shown in *Notices to Mariners*.

Another isomagnetic chart of value to the mariners is chart 30, *Magnetic Inclination or Dip*, figure 708b. Lines connecting points of equal magnetic dip are called **isoclinal lines.** The line connecting points of zero dip is called the **magnetic equator.**

Other isomagnetic charts are chart 33, showing horizontal intensity in gammas (art. 706); chart 36, showing vertical intensity in gammas; and chart 39, showing total intensity in gammas. Lines connecting points of equal intensity on any of these charts are called **isodynamic lines.**

Other isomagnetic charts show (1) magnetic inclination in north and south polar areas; (2) horizontal intensity, including horizontal intensity in north and south polar areas; (3) vertical intensity, including vertical intensity in north and south polar areas; (4) total intensity, including total intensity in north and south polar areas; (5) magnetic variation in north and south polar areas; and (6) magnetic grid variation.

All of the isomagnetic charts also show **isopors,** in a distinctive color, connecting points of equal **annual change** of the element at the epoch of the chart.

The charts are as accurate as can be made with available information, except that the lines are smoothed somewhat, rather than depicting every small irregularity. The larger irregularities are reflected in the information shown on nautical charts, but local disturbance is indicated by warning notes at appropriate places. In areas where measurements of the magnetic field have not been made for a long period, the previous information is altered in accordance with the best information available on secular change, with some adjustment to provide continuous smooth curves. When information is thus carried forward for many years, errors may be introduced, particularly in areas where the rate of change is large and variable. Magneticians have not detected a recognizable worldwide pattern in secular change, such as would occur if it were due only to shifting of the positions of the magnetic poles. Rather, these shifts are part of the general complex, little-understood secular change.

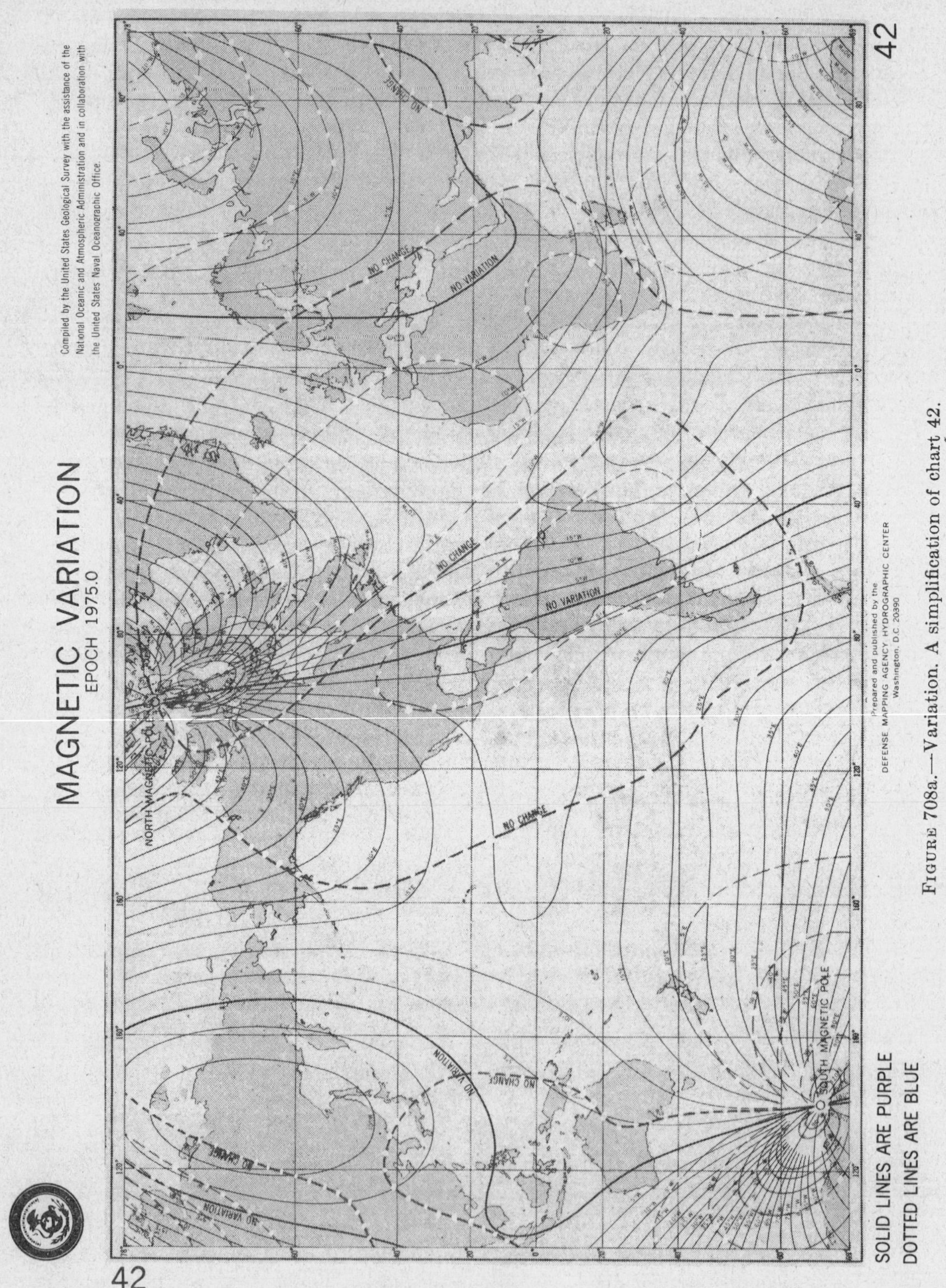

FIGURE 708a.—Variation. A simplification of chart 42.

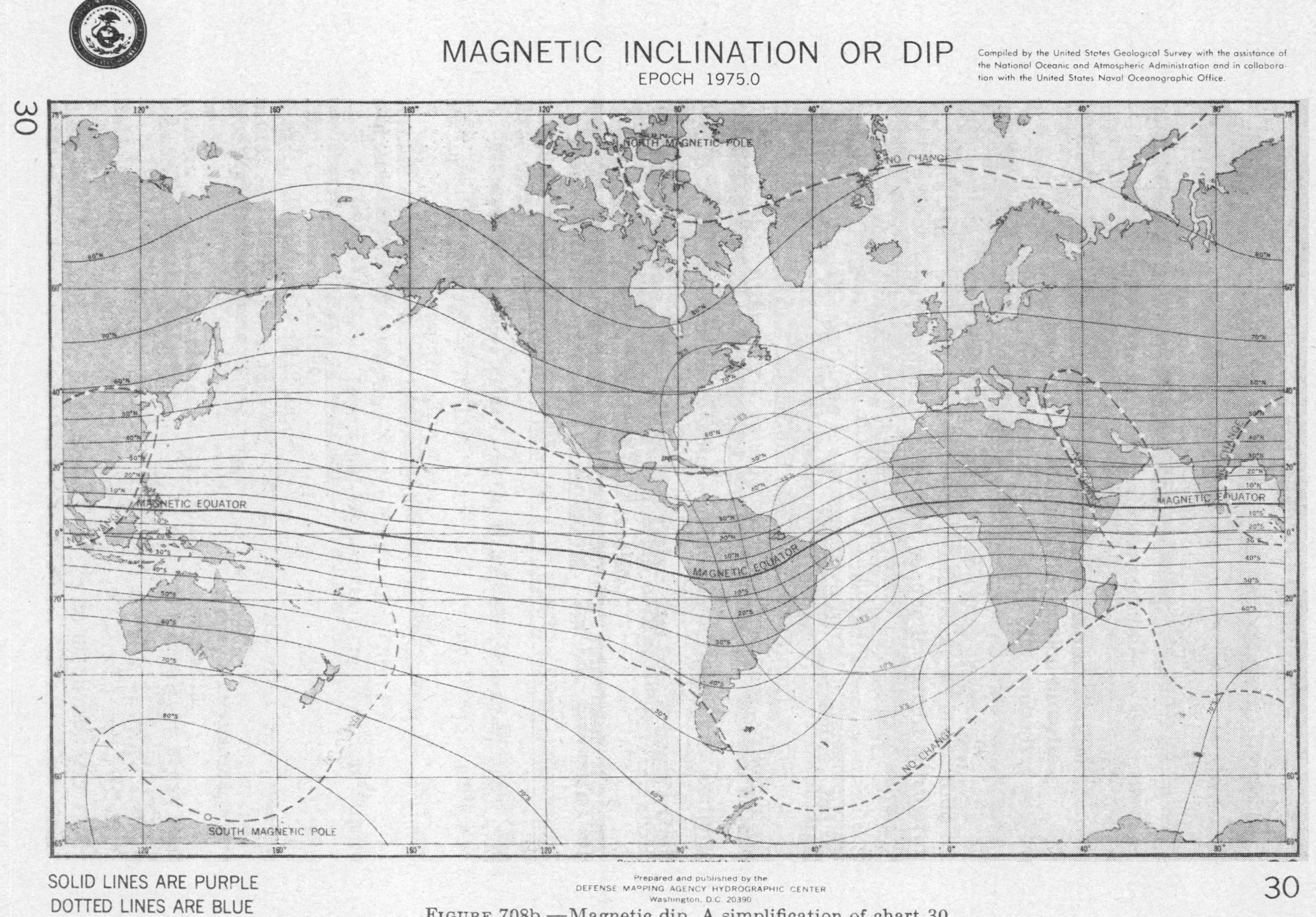

FIGURE 708b.—Magnetic dip. A simplification of chart 30.

The Compass Error

709. Magnetic compass error.—Directions relative to the northerly direction along a geographic meridian are **true.** In this case, true north is the **reference direction.** If a compass card is horizontal and oriented so that a straight line from its center to 000° points to true north, any direction measured by the card is a true direction and has no error (assuming there is no calibration or observational error). If the card remains horizontal but is rotated so that it points in any other direction, the amount of the rotation is the **compass error.** Stated differently, compass error is the angular difference between true north and **compass north** (the direction north as indicated by a magnetic compass). It is named east or west to indicate the side of true north on which compass north lies.

If a magnetic compass is influenced by no other magnetic field than that of the earth, and there is no instrumental error, its magnets are aligned with the magnetic meridian at the compass, and 000° of the compass card coincides with **magnetic north.** All directions indicated by the card are **magnetic.** As stated in article 706, the angle between geographic and magnetic meridians is called **variation** (**V** or **Var.**). Therefore, if a compass is aligned with the magnetic meridian, compass error and variation are the same.

When a compass is mounted in a vessel, it is generally subjected to various magnetic influences other than that of the earth. These arise largely from induced magnetism in metal decks, bulkheads, masts, stacks, boat davits, guns, etc., and from electromagnetic fields associated with direct current in electrical circuits. Some metal in the vicinity of the compass may have acquired permanent magnetism. The actual magnetic field at the compass is the vector sum, or resultant of all individual fields at that point. Since the direction of this resultant field is generally not the same as that of the earth's field alone, the compass magnets do not lie directly in the magnetic meridian, but in a direction that makes an angle with it. This angle is called **deviation** (**D** or **Dev.**). Thus, deviation is the angular difference between magnetic north and compass north. It is expressed in angular units and named east or west to indicate the side of magnetic north on which compass north lies. Thus, deviation is the error of the compass in pointing to magnetic north, and all directions measured with compass north as the reference direction are **compass directions.** Since variation and deviation may each be either east or west, the effect of deviation may be to either increase or decrease the error due to variation alone. The algebraic sum of variation and deviation is the total compass error.

For computational purposes (art. 727), deviation and compass error, like variation, may be designated positive (+) if east and negative (−) if west.

Variation changes with location, as indicated in figure 708a. Deviation depends upon the magnetic latitude and also upon the individual vessel, its trim and loading, whether it is pitching or rolling, the heading (orientation of the vessel with respect to the earth's magnetic field), and the location of the compass within the vessel. Therefore, deviation is not published on charts.

710. Deviation table.—In practice aboard ship, the deviation is reduced to a minimum, as explained later in this chapter. The remaining value, called **residual deviation,** is determined on various headings and recorded in some form of **deviation table.** Figure 710 shows both sides of the form used by the United States Navy. This table is entered with the magnetic heading, and the deviation on that heading is determined from the tabulation, separate columns being given for degaussing (DG) off and on (art. 740). If the deviation is not more than about 2° on any heading, satisfactory results may be obtained by entering the values at intervals of 45° only.

MAGNETIC COMPASS TABLE NAVSEA RPT. 3530-2
NAVSEA 3120/4 (REV. 6-72) (FRONT) *(Formerly NAVSHIPS 1104)*
S/N 0105-601-9521

U.S.S. ______ NO. ______ *(BB, CL, DD, etc.)*

[X] PILOT HOUSE [ ] SECONDARY CONNING STATION [ ] OTHER ______

BINNACLE TYPE [X] NAVY ST'D [ ] OTHER ______

COMPASS 7-1/2" MAKE C.G. Conn SERIAL NO. 8560

TYPE CC COILS "K" DATE 9 September 1975

READ INSTRUCTIONS ON BACK BEFORE STARTING ADJUSTMENT

SHIPS HEAD MAGNETIC	DEVIATIONS		SHIPS HEAD MAGNETIC	DEVIATIONS	
	DG OFF	DG ON		DG OFF	DG ON
0	0.5E	0.5E	180	0.5W	0.0
15	1.0E	1.0E	195	1.0W	0.5W
30	1.5E	1.5E	210	1.0W	1.0W
45	2.0E	1.5E	225	1.5W	1.5W
60	2.0E	2.0E	240	2.0W	2.0W
75	2.5E	2.5E	255	2.0W	2.5W
90	2.5E	3.0E	270	1.5W	2.0W
105	2.0E	2.5E	285	1.0W	1.5W
120	1.5E	2.0E	300	1.0W	1.0W
135	1.5E	1.5E	315	0.5W	0.5W
150	1.0E	1.0E	330	0.5W	0.5W
165	0.0	0.5E	345	0.0	0.0

DEVIATIONS DETERMINED BY: [ ] SUN'S AZIMUTH [X] GYRO [ ] SHORE BEARINGS

B 6 MAGNETS RED [ ] FORE [X] AFT AT 12" FROM COMPASS CARD

C 4 MAGNETS RED [ ] PORT [X] STBD AT 6" FROM COMPASS CARD

D 2-7" [X] SPHERES [ ] CYLS AT 12" [X] ATHWARTSHIP [ ] SLEWED -° [ ] CLOCKWISE [ ] CTR. CLOCKWISE

HEELING MAGNET: [ ] RED UP [X] BLUE UP 6" FROM COMPASS CARD FLINDERS BAR: [X] FORE [ ] AFT 12"

[X] LAT 18°00'N [ ] H 0.385 [X] LONG 120°00'E [ ] Z 0.151

SIGNED *(Adjuster or Navigator)* APPROVED *(Commanding)*

VERTICAL INDUCTION DATA
(Fill out completely before adjusting)

RECORD DEVIATION ON AT LEAST TWO ADJACENT CARDINAL HEADINGS
BEFORE STATING ADJUSTMENT: N 8 W; E 0; S 4 E; W 9 E.

RECORD BELOW INFORMATION FROM LAST NAVSHIPS 3120/4 DEVIATION TABLE:
DATE 5 December 1974 [ ] LAT 32 53N [ ] LONG 117 18W [ ] H .260 [ ] Z .420

12" FLINDERS BAR [X] FORWARD [ ] AFT DEVIATIONS N 2.5W E 7E; S 6.5E W 5W.

RECORD HERE DATA ON RECENT OVERHAULS, GUNFIRE, STRUCTURAL CHANGES, FLASHING, DEPERMING, WITH DATES AND EFFECT ON MAGNETIC COMPASSES:

Shipyard overhaul:
3 Oct - 2 Dec 1974
Depermed at Norfolk, Va.:
3 Dec 1974

PERFORMANCE DATA

COMPASS AT SEA: [ ] UNSTEADY [X] STEADY
COMPASS ACTION: [ ] SLOW [X] SATISFACTORY
NORMAL DEVIATIONS: [X] CHANGE [ ] REMAIN RELIABLE
DEGAUSSED DEVIATIONS: [X] VARY [ ] DO NOT VARY

REMARKS

INSTRUCTIONS

1. This form shall be filled out by the Navigator for each magnetic compass as set forth in Chapter 9240 of NAVAL SHIPS TECHNICAL MANUAL.
2. When a swing for deviations is made, the deviations should be recorded both with degaussing coils off and with degaussing coils energized at the proper currents for heading and magnetic zone.
3. Each time this form is filled out after a swing for deviations, a copy shall be submitted to: Naval Ship Engineering Center Hyattsville, Maryland 20782. A letter of transmittal is not required.
4. When choice of box is given, check applicable box.
5. Before adjusting, fill in section on "Vertical Induction Data" above.

NAVSEA 3120/4 (REV. 6-72) (REVERSE) C-24855

FIGURE 710.—Deviation table.

If the deviation is small, no appreciable error is introduced by entering the table with either magnetic or compass heading. If the deviation on some headings is large, the desirable action is to reduce it, but if this is not practicable, a separate deviation table for compass heading entry may be useful. This may be made by applying the tabulated deviation to each entry value of magnetic heading, to find the corresponding compass heading, and then interpolating between these to find the value of deviation at each 15° compass heading. Another method is to plot the values on cross-section paper and select the desired values graphically.

A nomogram especially designed for interconversion of magnetic and compass headings is called a **Napier diagram,** having been devised by James Robert Napier (1821–79). It consists of a dotted, vertical centerline graduated from 000° to 360° (usually in two parallel parts of 180° each), with two series of crosslines making angles of 60° with the dotted vertical line and with each other. If magnetic headings are used, deviation is measured along a solid crossline; and if compass headings are used, deviation is measured along a dotted crossline. A deviation curve is drawn through the various points. To convert a magnetic heading to a compass heading, one finds the magnetic heading on the vertical centerline, moves parallel to a solid crossline until the curve is reached, and returns to the centerline by moving parallel to a dotted line. The compass heading is the value at the point of return. The reverse process is used for converting a compass heading to a magnetic heading. This nomogram is of particular value where the deviation is large and changing rapidly. It is now possible, however, to reduce deviation to such small values that the Napier diagram has lost much of its appeal and is seldom used.

Another solution is to make a deviation table with one column for magnetic heading, a second column for deviation, and a third for compass heading. Still another solution, most popular among yachtsmen, is to center a compass rose inside a larger one so that an open space is between them, and a radial line would connect points of the same graduation on both roses. Each magnetic heading for which deviation has been determined is located on the outer rose, and a straight line is drawn from this point to the corresponding compass heading on the inner rose.

A variation of this method is to draw two parallel lines a short distance apart, and graduate each from 0 to 360 so that a perpendicular between the two lines connects points of the same graduation. Straight lines are drawn from magnetic directions on one line to the corresponding compass directions on the other. If the lines are horizontal and the upper one represents magnetic directions, the slope of the line indicates the direction of the deviation. That is, for westerly deviation the upper part of the connecting line is left (west) of the bottom part, and for easterly deviation it is right.

An important point to remember regarding deviation is that it varies with the *heading*. Therefore, a deviation table is *never* entered with a bearing (art. 1004). If the deviation table converts directly from one type heading to another, deviation is found by taking the difference between the two values. On the compass rose or straight-line type, the deviation can be written alongside the connecting line, and the intermediate values determined by estimate. If one has trouble determining whether to add or subtract deviation when bearings are involved, he has only to note which heading, magnetic or compass, is larger. The same relationship holds between the two values of bearing.

The deviation table should be protected from damage due to handling or weather, and placed in a position where it will always be available when needed. A method commonly used is to mount it on a board, cover it with shellac or varnish, and attach it to the binnacle. Another method is to post it under glass near the compass. It is good practice for the navigator to keep a second copy available at a convenient place for his use.

711. Applying variation and deviation.—As indicated in article 709, a single direction may have any of several numerical values depending upon the reference direction used. One should keep clearly in mind the relationship between the various expressions of a direction. Thus, true and magnetic directions differ by the variation, magnetic and compass directions differ by the deviation, and true and compass directions differ by the compass error. Other relationships are also useful. Thus, grid and magnetic directions differ by the grid variation or grivation, and true and relative directions differ by the true heading. The use of variation and deviation is considered here. Other relationships are discussed elsewhere in this volume.

If variation or deviation is easterly, the compass card is rotated in a clockwise direction. This brings smaller numbers opposite the lubber's line. Conversely, if either error is westerly, the rotation is counterclockwise and larger numbers are brought opposite the lubber's line. Thus, if the heading is 090° true (fig. 711, A) and variation is 6°E, the magnetic heading is 090°−6°=084° (fig. 711, B). If the deviation on this heading is 2°W, the compass heading is 084°+2°=086° (fig. 711, C). Also, compass error is 6°E−2°W=4°E, and compass heading is 090°−4°=086°. If compass error is easterly, the compass reads too low (in comparison with true directions), and if it is westerly, the reading is too high. Many rules-of-thumb have been devised as an aid to the memory, and any which assist in applying compass errors in the right direction are of value. However, one may forget the rule or its method of application, or may wish to have an independent check. If he understands the explanation given above, he can determine the correct sign without further information. The same rules apply to the use of gyro error. Since variation and deviation are compass errors, the process of removing either from an indication of a direction (converting compass to magnetic or magnetic to true) is often called **correcting.** Conversion in the opposite direction (inserting errors) is then called **uncorrecting.**

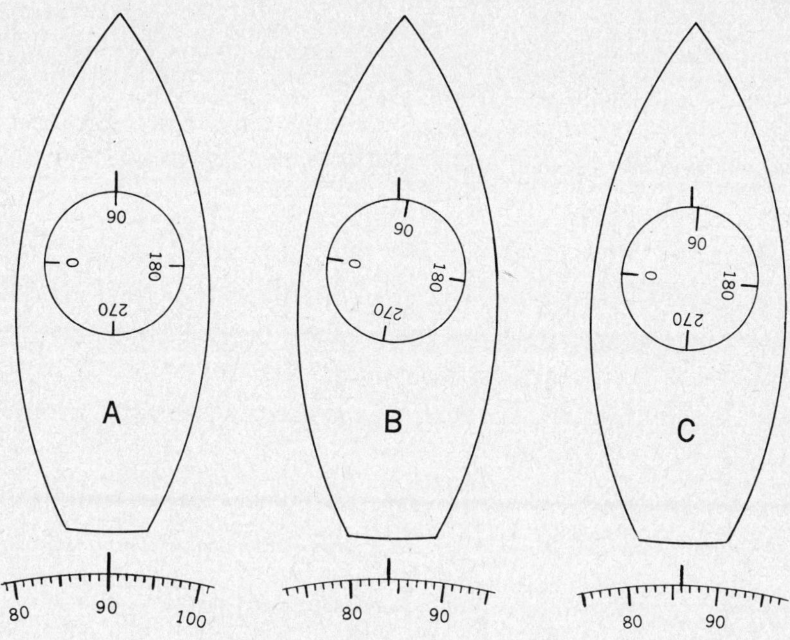

FIGURE 711.—Effect of variation and deviation on the compass card.

Example.—A vessel is on course 215° true in an area where the variation is 7°W. The deviation is as shown in figure 710. Degaussing is off. The gyro error (GE) is 1°E. A lighthouse bears 306°5 by magnetic compass.

Required.—(1) Magnetic heading (MH).
(2) Deviation.
(3) Compass heading (CH).
(4) Compass error.
(5) Gyro heading.
(6) Magnetic bearing of the lighthouse.
(7) True bearing of the lighthouse.
(8) Relative bearing (art. 904) of the lighthouse.

Solution.—

TH 215°
V 7°W
(1) MH 222°
(2) D 1°5W
(3) CH 223°5

The deviation is taken from the deviation table (fig. 710), to the nearest half degree.
(4) Compass error is 7°W+1°.5W=8°.5W.

	TH	215°
	GE	1°E
(5)	H_{pgc}	214°
	CB	306°.5
	D	1°.5W
(6)	MB	305°
	V	7°W
(7)	TB	298°

(8) RB=TB−TH=298°−215°=083°.

Answers.—(1) MH 222°, (2) D 1°.5W, (3) CH 223°.5, (4) CE 8°.5W, (5) H_{pgc} 214°, (6) MB 305°, (7) TB 298°, (8) RB 083°.

Deviation and its Reduction

712. Magnetism of a steel vessel.—The materials of which a vessel is constructed are not, in general, selected for their magnetic properties. As a result, many degrees of permeability, remanence, and coercivity (art. 702) exist within its structure. Detailed analysis of the complex field existing at a magnetic compass is a specialized study not ordinarily required of the navigator. However, a general knowledge of the basic principles involved is of value to the navigator in helping him understand better the behavior of his magnetic compasses.

For most purposes, a vessel can be considered to be composed of two types of material: "hard iron" and "soft iron."

"Hard iron" is all material having some degree of permanent magnetism. This magnetism is acquired largely during construction of the vessel, when the rearrangement of the domains (art. 701) is facilitated by the bending, riveting, welding, and other violent mechanical processes. Since a vessel remains on a constant magnetic heading while it is on the building ways, a field of permanent magnetism becomes established, the positions of the poles being dependent largely upon the orientation of the hull with respect to the magnetic field of the earth. If a vessel is constructed on a heading of magnetic north, at a place where the magnetic dip is 70°N (the approximate value at the midpoint of the east coast of the United States), its field of permanent magnetism is about as shown at the left of figure 712. The upper and stern portions are magnetically blue, while the lower and forward portions are magnetically red. If the vessel is built on a heading of magnetic east, the starboard and upper portions are blue, and the port and lower portions are red, as shown by the stern view at the right of figure 712. If the heading is magnetic northeast, the upper, starboard, and stern portions are blue, and the lower, port, and forward portions red. The red and blue portions for any given vessel can be visualized by drawing a sketch similar to that of figure 712, with the correct orientation.

The "permanent" magnetism thus acquired during construction is less permanent than that of a permanent magnet such as one of those used in a compass, and is modified somewhat after launching, particularly if the vessel remains on another heading for a considerable time during fitting out. The change is especially rapid during the first few days after launching, when the domains of the softer iron become reoriented. At this stage, deviation due to permanent magnetism may change several degrees. Further changes in the vessel's permanent magnetism may occur during long periods of being

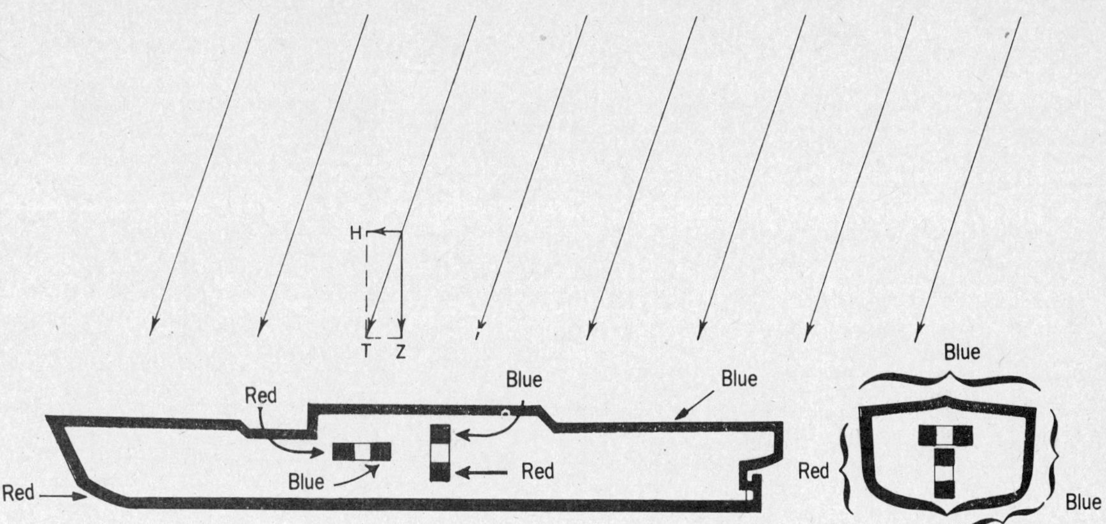

FIGURE 712.—Permanent magnetism of a vessel built on heading magnetic north (left) and magnetic east (right) at a place where the magnetic dip is 70° N.

moored on a constant heading, or during a run of several days on nearly the same heading. This change is gradual and affects the strength, but usually not the polarity, of the magnetic field. The permanent field may be changed quickly, in polarity as well as in strength, if the vessel grounds, collides with another vessel, is struck by lightning, undergoes magnetic treatment (art. 742), fires its guns, or is struck by shells or bombs, etc.

The effect that the permanent magnetism of hard iron has upon a compass depends upon the position and strength of the poles relative to the compass. When the poles are in line with the north-south axis of the compass card, the only effect is to strengthen or weaken the directive force of the compass. When the compass heading is approximately 90° away, so that the poles are east and west of the compass, the deviating effect is maximum. The direction of the deviation is the same as that of the blue pole with respect to the compass.

"Soft iron" is all that material in which induced magnetism (art. 701) is present. With respect to its effect upon the magnetic compass, it is classed as either vertical or horizontal. Unlike hard iron, its magnetic field changes quickly as its orientation with respect to the earth's field changes. It also changes as the strength of the earth's field changes. For some purposes induced magnetism can be treated as if it were concentrated in two bars of soft iron, one vertical and the other horizontal. The polarity depends upon the position of the vessel relative to the earth's magnetic field, and the strength depends upon the strength of the vertical and horizontal components of the earth's field. This is illustrated in figure 712. In north magnetic latitude the bottom of the vertical rod has red magnetism and the top has blue magnetism. In south magnetic latitude these are reversed. In both north and south magnetic latitudes the magnetic north end of the horizontal bar has red magnetism, and the magnetic south end has blue magnetism. Thus, whatever the position of the rod, that part in the direction of magnetic north has red magnetism, and that part in the direction of magnetic south has blue magnetism. That is, each end has magnetism opposite to that of the magnetic pole indicated by the direction in which it is pointed.

The effect upon a magnetic compass of the induced magnetism in soft iron depends upon the strength and direction of the field relative to the compass. The cumulative effect of the induced magnetism in vertical soft iron is generally on the centerline of the vessel (if of conventional construction), and for a compass located forward, as on the bridge, is aft of the compass. In magnetic north latitude the effect is generally that of a blue pole at the level of the compass card. In magnetic south latitude the pole is red. On a heading of compass north or south the pole is in line with the magnets of a centerline compass and serves only to strengthen or weaken the directive force. On a heading of compass east or west the pole is perpendicular to the north-south axis of the compass card, and the deviating force is greatest.

For a compass located on the centerline of a vessel of conventional construction, the horizontal soft iron close enough to have appreciable effect upon the compass is arranged in a more-or-less symmetrical manner with respect to the compass. Thus, on any cardinal compass heading, the fore-and-aft and athwartship horizontal soft iron is either in line with the compass magnets or equally and similarly arranged on both sides. No error is introduced by such symmetrical horizontal soft iron because the iron north and south of the compass magnets serves only to strengthen or weaken the directive force, and that east and west of the compass sets up an equal and opposite field on each side. On intercardinal headings, the poles of the induced magnetism are offset and a maximum deviating force occurs. That part of horizontal soft iron which is not symmetrically arranged with respect to the compass—the asymmetrical soft iron—produces deviation which is maximum on the cardinal headings and zero on the intercardinal headings (by compass). This type of deviation is particularly great in a compass not mounted on the centerline of the vessel. It may also produce deviation which is constant on all headings.

In wooden-hulled vessels such as certain yachts and small fishing vessels, one or more of these types of magnetism may be weak or entirely missing, but this does not justify the omission of any part of the correction procedure.

As far as its effect upon the compass is concerned, the magnetic field at a centerline compass located forward on a vessel of conventional construction, and on an even keel, is essentially the same as that which would result from four sources: (1) the earth's magnetism; (2) a single blue pole the location and strength of which depends upon the magnetic history of the vessel; (3) a single pole which is blue in north magnetic latitude and red in south magnetic latitude, is on the centerline aft of the compass, and increases in strength with higher magnetic latitude; and (4) a single blue pole on the starboard side for easterly headings and on the port side for westerly headings, being of zero strength on a heading of north or south and decreasing in strength with increased magnetic latitudes. The single pole concept assumes that the effect of one pole predominates. The locations of the poles depend partly upon the position of the compass to which they apply. The actual field surrounding any magnetic compass may be considerably more complex than indicated.

713. Compass adjustment.—There are at least two possible solutions to the problem of compass error. The error can be permitted to remain, and the various directions interconverted by means of variation and deviation, or compass error, as explained in article 711; or the error can be removed. In practice, a combination of both of these methods is used.

Variation depends upon location of the vessel, and the navigator has no control over it. Provision could be made for offsetting the lubber's line, but this would not be effective in correcting magnetic compass bearings, and this practice is not generally followed. Variation does not affect the operation of the compass itself, and so is not objectionable from this standpoint.

Deviation is undesirable because it is more troublesome to apply, and the magnetic field which causes it partly neutralizes the directive force acting upon the compass, causing it to be unsteady and sluggish. As the vessel rolls and pitches, or as it changes magnetic latitude, the magnetic field changes, producing a corresponding change in the deviation of an unadjusted compass.

Deviation is eliminated, as nearly as practicable, by introducing at the compass a magnetic field that is equal in magnitude and opposite in polarity to that of the vessel. This process is called **compass adjustment,** or sometimes **compass compensation,** although the latter designation is now more generally applied to the process of neutralizing the effect due to degaussing of the vessel (art. 745).

In general, the introduced field is of the same kind of magnetism as well as of the same intensity as those of the field causing deviation. That is, permanent magnets are used to neutralize permanent magnetism, and soft iron to neutralize induced magnetism, so that the adjustment remains effective with changes of heading and magnetic latitude. A relatively small mass of iron near the compass introduces a field equal to that of a much larger mass at a distance.

When a compass is properly adjusted, its remaining or **residual deviation** is small and practically constant at various magnetic latitudes, the directive force is as strong as is obtainable on all headings, and the compass returns quickly from deflections and is comparatively steady as the vessel rolls and pitches.

714. Effect of latitude.—As indicated in article 706, the magnetic field of the earth is horizontal at the magnetic equator, and vertical at the magnetic poles, the change occurring gradually as a vessel proceeds away from the magnetic equator. At any place the relative strength of the horizontal and vertical components depends upon the magnetic dip. The directive force of a magnetic compass, provided by the horizontal component of the earth's magnetic field, is maximum on or near the magnetic equator and gradually decreases to zero at the magnetic poles. Within a certain area surrounding each magnetic pole the directive force is so weak that the compass is unreliable.

Deviation changes with a change of the relative strength of either the deviating force or the directive force. Thus, with *either* an increase in deviating force or a decrease in directive force, the deviation increases. However, if both the deviating and directive forces change by the same proportion, and with the same sign, there is no change in deviation. Also, if a deviating force is neutralized by an equal and opposite force *of the same kind,* there is no change of deviation with a change of magnetic latitude.

Permanent magnetism is the same at any latitude. If the permanent magnetism of the vessel is neutralized by properly placed permanent magnets of the correct strength, a change of magnetic latitude can be made without introduction of deviation. But if residual deviation due to permanent magnetism is present, it increases with a change to higher latitude. The deviating force remains unchanged while the directive force decreases, resulting in an increase in the relative strength of the deviating force.

As magnetic latitude increases, the vertical component of the earth's magnetic field becomes stronger, increasing the amount of induced magnetism in vertical soft iron. At the same time the directive force of the compass decreases. Both effects result in increased deviation unless the deviating force is neutralized by induced magnetism in vertical soft iron.

As magnetic latitude increases, the induced magnetism in the horizontal soft iron decreases in the same proportion as the decrease in the directive force of the compass, since both are produced by the horizontal component of the earth's magnetic field. Therefore, any deviation due to this cause is the same at any latitude.

715. Parameters.—Compass adjustment might be accomplished by locating the pole of each magnetic field, and establishing another pole of opposite polarity and equal intensity at the same place, or of less intensity and nearer to the compass; or a pole of opposite polarity and suitable intensity might be established at the correct distance on the opposite side of the compass. Thus, a blue pole east of a compass attracts the red northern ends of the compass magnets and repels the blue southern ends. Both effects cause rotation of the compass magnets and the attached compass card in a clockwise direction, producing easterly deviation. Either a red pole east of a compass, or a blue pole west of it, causes westerly deviation. If there are two fields of opposite polarity, one will tend to neutralize the other. If the intensities of the two fields are equal at the compass, one will cancel the other, and no deviation occurs.

Because of the complexities of the magnetic field of a vessel, and the fact that each individual field making up the total is present continuously, the process of isolating individual poles would be a difficult and time-consuming one. Fortunately, this is unnecessary. The vessel's field is resolved into certain specified components. Each of these components, regardless of its origin or the number of individual fields contributing to it, can be neutralized separately. Each component is called a **parameter,** and the various parameters are designated by letter, as follows:

Permanent magnetism. **Parameter *P*** is the fore-and-aft component. It is positive (+) if it is the equivalent of a blue pole forward of the compass, and negative (−) if red.

Parameter *Q* is the athwartship component. It is positive if it is the equivalent of a blue pole to starboard.

Parameter *R* is the vertical component. It is positive if it is the equivalent of a blue pole below the compass.

Induced magnetism has nine parameters, each the equivalent of that produced by a slender rod of soft iron. Each *end* of a rod is positive if it is forward, to starboard, or below the compass. Each rod is positive if both ends are positive or if both ends are negative, and negative if the two ends are of opposite sign. The rods are as follows:

a, b, c—one end level with the compass and in its fore-and-aft axis, either forward or aft. It is an *a* rod if it extends fore-and-aft, a *b* rod if athwartships, and a *c* rod if vertical.

d, e, f—one end level with the compass and in its athwartships axis, either to starboard or to port. It is a *d* rod if it extends fore-and-aft, an *e* rod if athwartships, and an *f* rod if vertical.

g, h, k—one end in the vertical axis of the compass, either above it or below it. It is a *g* rod if it extends fore-and-aft, an *h* rod if athwartships, and a *k* rod if vertical.

716. Coefficients.—Deviation which is easterly throughout approximately 180° of heading and westerly throughout the remainder is called **semicircular deviation,** indicating that its sign remains unchanged throughout a semicircle. Deviation caused by permanent magnetism and that caused by induced magnetism in vertical soft iron are semicircular. Deviation which changes sign in each quadrant, being easterly in two opposite quadrants and westerly in the other two, is called **quadrantal deviation.** It is caused by induced magnetism in horizontal soft iron. The types of deviation resulting from the various parameters are called coefficients. There are six, as follows:

Coefficient *A* is constant on all headings. If its cause is magnetic, as from an asymmetrical combination of parameters, it is a "true" constant. If its cause is mechanical, as from an incorrectly placed lubber's line, or mathematical, as from an error in computation of magnetic azimuth, it is an "apparent" constant.

Coefficient *B* is semicircular deviation which is proportional to the sine of the compass heading. It is maximum on compass headings east or west, and zero on compass headings north or south. Coefficient *B* is caused by permanent magnetism, and also by induced magnetism in asymmetrical vertical soft iron.

Coefficient *C* is semicircular deviation which is proportional to the cosine of the compass heading. It is maximum on compass headings north or south, and zero on compass headings east or west. Coefficient *C* is caused by permanent magnetism or by induced magnetism in asymmetrical vertical soft iron athwartship of the compass.

Coefficient *D* is quadrantal deviation which is proportional to the sine of twice the compass heading. It is maximum on intercardinal compass headings, and zero on cardinal compass headings. Coefficient *D* is caused by induced magnetism in horizontal soft iron which is symmetrical with respect to the compass.

Coefficient *E* is quadrantal deviation which is proportional to the cosine of twice the compass heading. It is maximum on cardinal compass headings, and zero on intercardinal compass headings. Coefficient *E* is caused by induced magnetism in horizontal soft iron which is asymmetrical with respect to the compass.

Coefficient *J* is the change of deviation for a heel of 1° while the vessel is on compass heading 000°

The determination and use of the approximate coefficients in the analysis of compass deviation are discussed in article 727. The force components producing these coefficients are called **exact coefficients.** They are designated by the corresponding upper case German letters. The exact coefficients are now little used in practical navigation. They are fully discussed in various books on compass adjustment.

717. Effect of compass location.—The location of a magnetic compass greatly influences the amount and type of deviation, as well as the adjustment. Thus, if a compass is on the centerline, forward, the effective pole of vertical soft iron is aft of it; but if the compass is on the afterpart of the vessel, the effective pole is forward. If the compass is not on the centerline, as the steering compass of an aircraft carrier, the magnetic field of the vessel is not symmetrical with respect to the compass. If a compass is located in a steel pilot house, the surrounding metal acts as a shield and reduces the strength of the magnetic field of the earth. This is of particular significance in high magnetic latitudes, where the directive force is weak.

Many factors influence the selection of a position for the compass. The most important consideration is the use to be made of it. A steering compass is of little use unless it is located so that it can be seen by the steersman. A compass to be used for emergency steering should be at the emergency steering station. A compass to be used for observing bearings or azimuths, or a standard compass to be used for checking other compasses, should be located so as to have a clear view in most directions.

However, some choice is possible. A compass should not be placed off the centerline if it can be placed on the centerline and still serve its purpose. It should not be placed near iron or steel equipment that will frequently be moved, if this can be avoided. Thus, a location near a gun, boat davit, or boat crane is not desirable. The immediate vicinity should be kept free from sources of deviation—particularly those of a changing nature—if this can be done. That is, no source of magnetism, other than the structure of the vessel, should be permitted within a radius of several feet of the magnetic compass. Some sources which might be overlooked are electric wires carrying direct current; magnetic instruments, searchlights, windshield wipers, electronic equipment, or motors; steel control rods, gears, or supports associated with the steering apparatus; fire extinguishers, gas detectors, etc.; and metal coat hangers, flashlights, keys, pocketknives, metal cap devices, or nylon clothing. The effect of some items such as an ammeter or electric windshield wiper varies considerably at different times. If direct current is used to light the compass, the wires should be twisted.

A magnetic compass cannot be expected to give reliable service unless it is properly installed and protected from disturbing magnetic influences.

718. The binnacle.—The compass is housed in a **binnacle.** This may vary from a simple wooden box to an elaborate device of bronze or other nonmagnetic material. Most binnacles provide means for housing or supporting the various objects used for compass adjustment, as well as the equipment for compensating for deviation caused by degaussing. The standard binnacle for the U. S. Navy 7½-inch compass is shown in

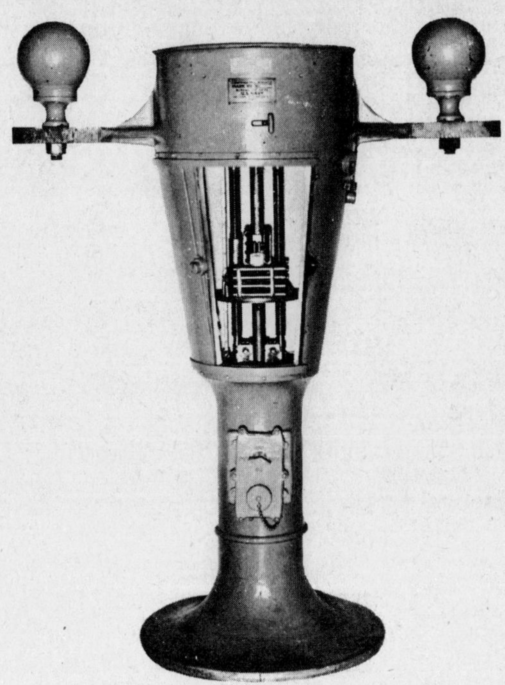

FIGURE 718.—The standard binnacle for a U. S. Navy 7½-inch compass.

figure 718. The trays for holding the fore-and-aft and athwartship magnets (art. 719), and the tube for the heeling magnet (art. 724), can be seen through the open door.

719. Adjustment for deviation due to permanent magnetism.—Permanent magnetism can be considered concentrated in a single pole, the position of which depends upon the magnetic heading upon which the vessel was constructed, and the subsequent magnetic history of the vessel. Figure 719a indicates the condition if the permanent magnetism can be considered concentrated in a single blue pole which is directly south of the compass when the vessel is headed magnetic northeast. The only effect on this heading is to weaken the directive force. No deviation is produced because the pole is in line with the compass magnets. On heading magnetic southwest, the pole is also in line with the compass magnets and there is no deviation, but the directive force is strengthened. On any other heading, the pole is not in line with the compass magnets, and deviation occurs, being in the same direction as that of the blue pole from the compass, since the blue pole attracts the red northerly ends of the compass magnets and repels the blue southerly ends. The maximum effect occurs when the *compass* heading is approximately 90° from that of zero deviation. In figure 719a the headings shown on the compass card are the magnetic headings of the vessel. Their offset from the lubber's line shows the direction and relative magnitude of deviation.

If there were no other magnetism in the vessel, the poles might easily be located and neutralized by placing a magnet in such a position that a field of permanent magnetism but opposite polarity would occur at the compass. Although this method of adjustment has been used, it has not proven entirely satisfactory.

The usual method is to adjust for the fore-and-aft (parameter P) and athwartship (parameter Q) components separately. These are shown in figure 719b. The vertical parameter R does not produce deviation while the vessel is on an even keel. Its effect when the vessel heels is discussed in article 724. Thus, the effect of a single blue pole at the position shown in figure 719a is the same as that which would be produced by two

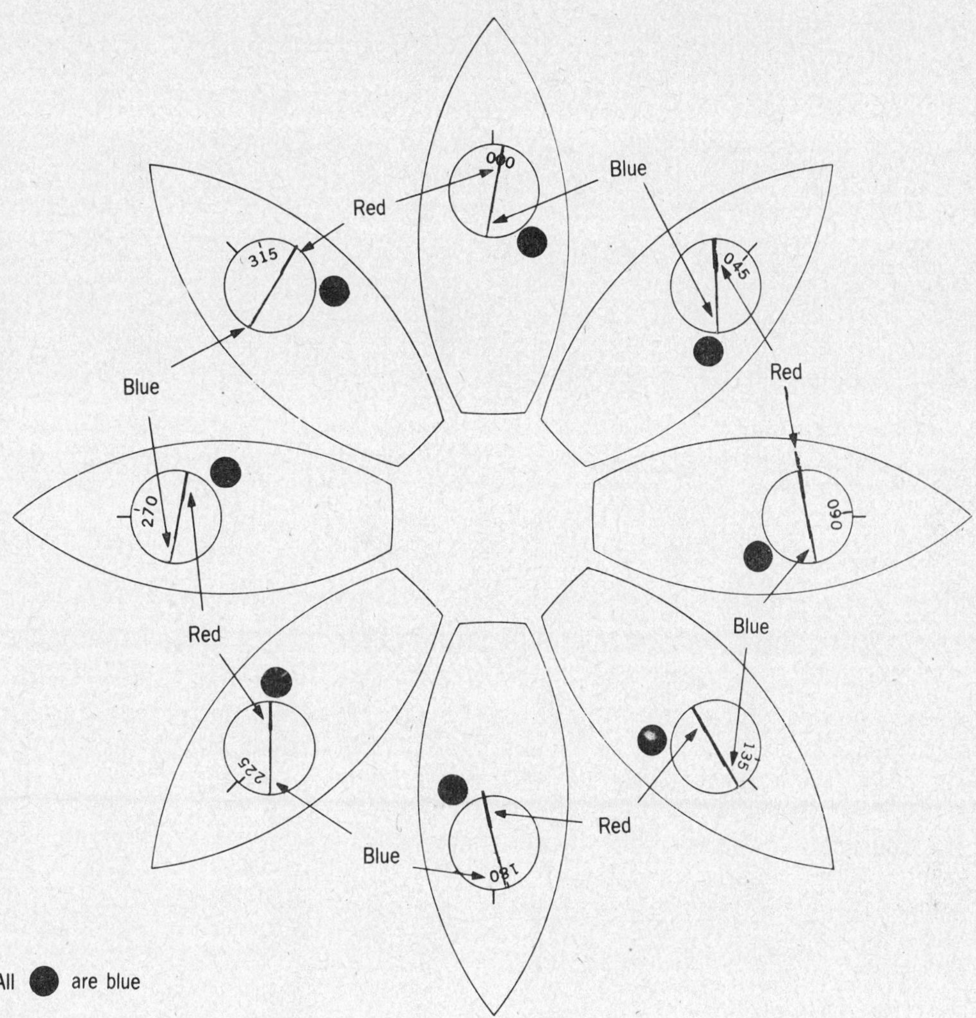

FIGURE 719a.—Deviation due to permanent magnetism if the resultant field is that of a blue pole on the starboard quarter of the vessel.

weaker poles as shown in figure 719b. On heading east or west by the compass, parameter Q does not produce deviation directly. However, on easterly headings it does weaken the directive force due to the earth's magnetic field and therefore the deviating force of parameter P (causing deviation coefficient B) is relatively stronger and has a greater deviating effect. On a westerly heading the directive force would be strengthened, with a corresponding decrease in the B coefficient of deviation. By weakening the directive force on easterly headings, parameter Q also makes the compass sluggish on these headings. In high latitudes, where the horizontal component of the earth's magnetic field is weak, the compass may lose its directivity at a greater distance from the magnetic pole. Nearer the pole, it might point in the opposite direction.

Many binnacles provide a group of several small tubes or "trays" extending in a fore-and-aft direction below the compass. One or more permanent magnets can be inserted in these trays, and the whole assembly moved up or down to vary the effect

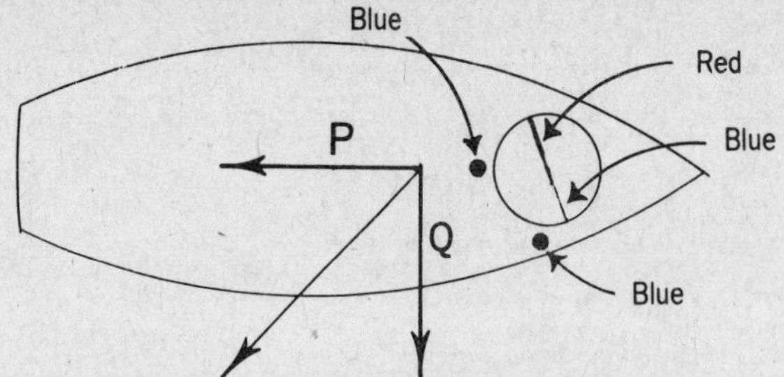

FIGURE 719b.—The horizontal component of the permanent field of figure 719a resolved into its components, parameters *P* and *Q*.

upon the compass. Figure 719c shows the situation if a single magnet is placed with its red end aft. The field at the compass is in the opposite direction of that of parameter *P*, and if it is of equal strength, the effect of this parameter is eliminated.

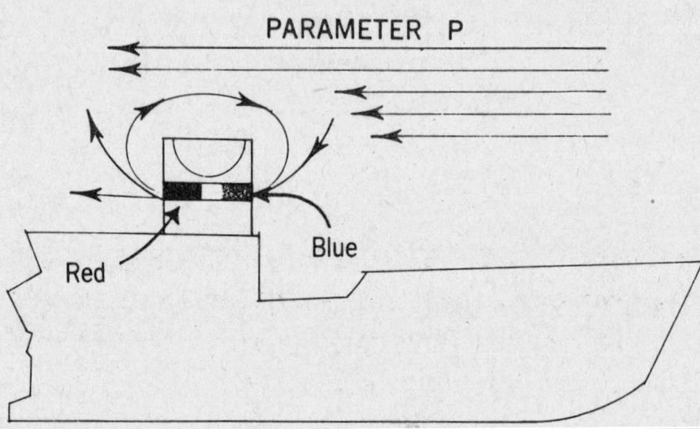

FIGURE 719c.— The field of permanent magnet below the compass and opposing parameter *P* of figure 719b.

If now the vessel is headed north or south by the compass, the only pole remaining is that due to parameter *Q* (causing deviation coefficient *C*), as shown in figure 719d. A set of trays in an athwartship direction below the compass permits insertion of one or more permanent magnets to neutralize the remaining permanent magnetism. The effect of inserting a single magnet with red end to starboard is shown in figure 719e. With both components removed, the field at the compass is completely neutralized.

Both the fore-and-aft (*B*) and athwartship (*C*) trays are in pairs with an equal number of trays on each side of the vertical axis of the compass. In each set of trays it is generally desirable to use an *even* number of magnets equally distributed on each side, to produce a symmetrical field at the compass. However, under some conditions, maximum reduction of deviation occurs with an *odd* number of magnets, particularly when two magnets at maximum distance from the compass overcorrect. If there is a choice, a greater number of magnets at a distance is preferable to a lesser number close to the compass.

With each parameter, the trays to use are those which are approximately perpendicular to the compass magnets. The magnets are placed so that the red ends will be on that side of the compass corresponding to the deviation. Thus, if deviation is easterly, the magnets should be placed so that the red ends will be east of the compass (forward if the heading is east, and to starboard if the heading is north). However, if the wrong end is inserted in the trays, the fact will be immediately apparent because the compass card will rotate in the wrong direction. If the binnacle is not constructed to receive appropriate corrector magnets, these might be secured to some supporting surface near the compass.

During adjustment, the unused magnets should be kept far enough from the compass so that they will not affect it.

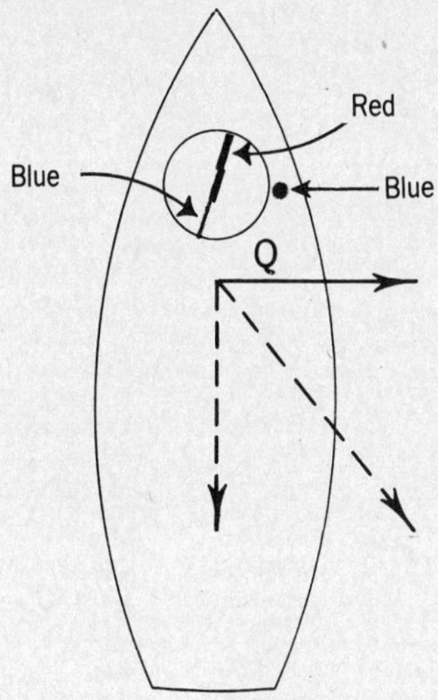

FIGURE 719d.—The permanent field of figure 719a after neutralization of parameter P.

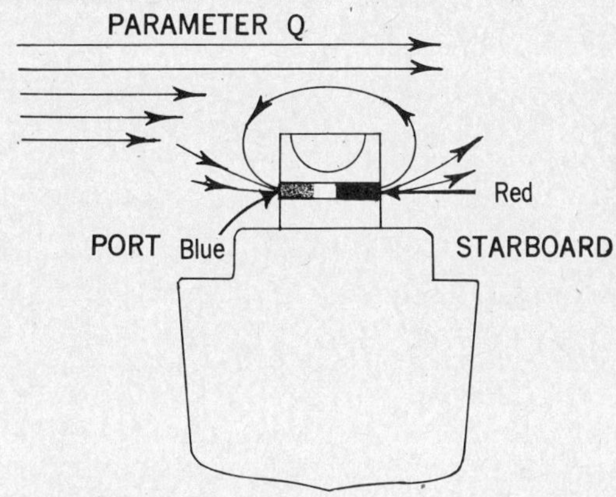

FIGURE 719e.—The field of a permanent magnet below the compass and opposing parameter Q of figure 719b.

720. Adjustment for deviation due to induced magnetism in vertical soft iron.— Figure 720 shows the effect upon the compass of a single blue pole on the centerline of the vessel, aft of the compass. This is a typical situation for induced magnetism in vertical soft iron, for a centerline compass located in the forward part of a vessel in magnetic north latitude. On heading north by compass there is no deviating force, but the directive force is weakened. In high northern latitudes, where this pole becomes strong and the directive force becomes weak, magnetism of this type, if not neutralized, can cause the compass to be unreliable in a much larger area than if the force is neutralized. On a heading of south by compass there is no deviation, but the directive force is strengthened. On headings with an easterly component the deviation is westerly, and on headings with a westerly component the deviation is easterly. In each case the maximum occurs when the vessel is on compass heading approximately east or west. Thus, the deviation due to induced magnetism in vertical soft iron is semicircular, coefficient B. In figure 720 the headings shown on the compass card are the magnetic headings of the vessel. Their offset from the lubber's line shows the direction and relative magnitude of deviation.

The deviating force due to induced magnetism in vertical soft iron is neutralized by placing a bar of soft iron in a vertical position on the opposite side of the compass from the effective pole due to the field of the vessel. This piece of metal is called a **Flinders bar,** after Captain Matthew Flinders, RN (1774–1814), an English navigator and explorer who is generally given credit for discovering both the effect and method of adjustment (art. 111). Today, most binnacles for large ships provide a tube for insertion of a Flinders bar. The bar consists of various lengths of soft iron placed end to end; with the remainder of the tube being filled with spacers of nonmagnetic material, usually wood, brass, or aluminum. The standard Flinders bar is two inches in diameter and is divided into six sections, one each of 12, 6, 3, and 1½ inches, and two of ¾ inch. This permits use of any multiple of ¾ inch to 24 inches. All the iron pieces should be above the spacers in the tube, without a gap between pieces, the largest piece

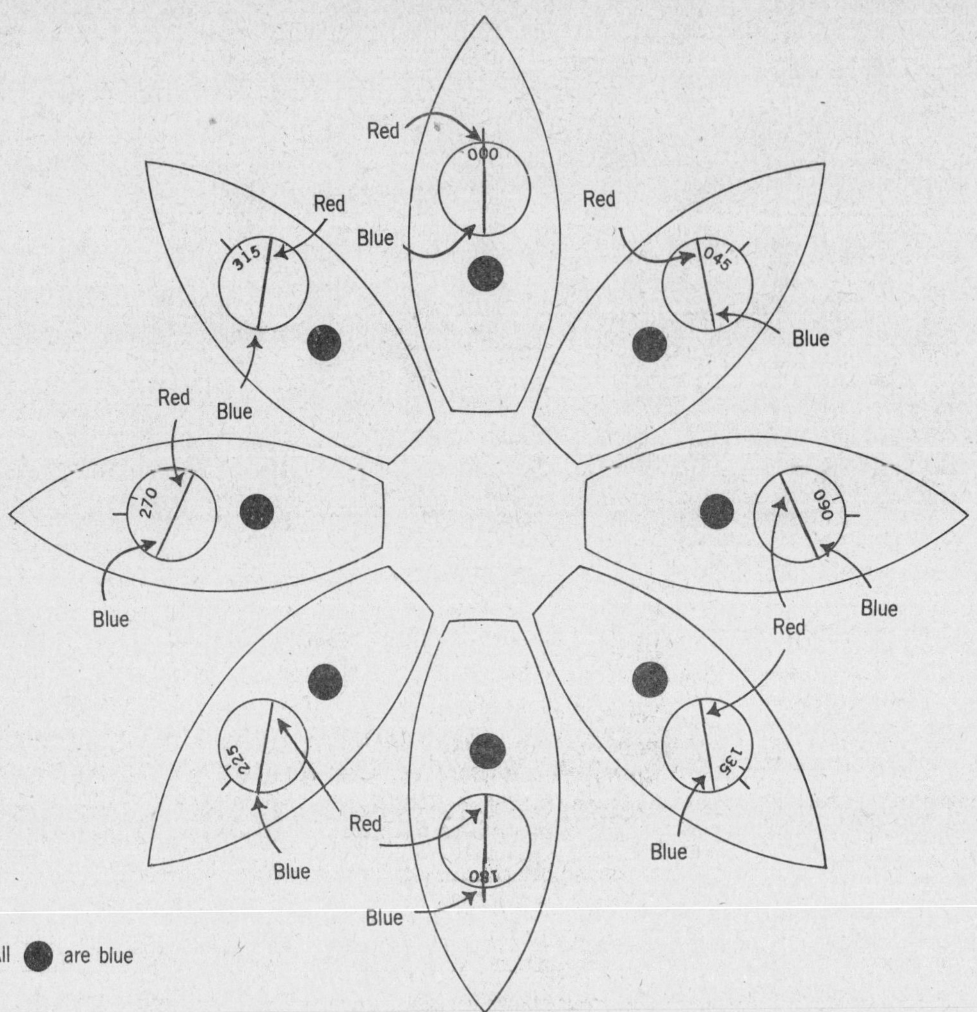

FIGURE 720.—Deviation due to induced magnetism in vertical soft iron if the resultant field is that of a blue pole on the center line aft of the compass.

being on top. The upper end is then about two inches above the level of the compass card. For short lengths, one or more spacers should be omitted so that about $\frac{1}{12}$ of the length of the bar is above the level of the compass card.

The various pieces should be inserted in the tube carefully. If they are dropped, they may acquire some permanent magnetism. This reduces their effectiveness for the purpose intended. Each piece should be tested from time to time to determine whether or not it has acquired permanent magnetism. This can be done by holding it vertical with one end east or west of the compass and very near the compass magnets, noting the reading of the compass, and then inverting the piece so that the ends are interchanged. If the reading differs, permanent magnetism has been acquired by the iron rod. The temporary change of reading while the rod is being inverted should be ignored. In making the test, one should be careful to place the rod in the same position relative to the compass before and after inversion. On an easterly or westerly heading the Flinders bar holder can be used. A small amount of permanent magnetism can be removed by holding the rod approximately parallel to the lines of force of the earth's field, with the blue pole of the rod toward the north, and tapping one end of the rod gently with a hammer. Several alternate tests and treatments may be needed to make the rod magnetically neutral. If this process is not effective in removing the permanent magnetism, the rod should be heated to a dull red and allowed to cool slowly.

An older type Flinders bar, rarely encountered with modern compasses, consists of a number of slender rods of equal length, the *number* of rods being varied rather than the length of a single rod. Another old system consists of using a single rod of fixed length, and varying its distance from the compass.

721. Determination of Flinders bar length.—As indicated in articles 719 and 720, coefficient B magnetism may be introduced both by permanent magnetism of the vessel and by induced magnetism in asymmetrical vertical soft iron. A problem thus arises as to what part of the deviation on headings magnetic east and west is due to each cause. If the vessel remains on an even keel at about the same magnetic latitude, adjustment can be made without this knowledge. However, satisfactory performance under all conditions requires separate adjustment for each cause.

There are several possible solutions to this problem. The two sources can be separated by use of the fact that a change of magnetic latitude affects them differently. On the magnetic equator there is no vertical component of the earth's magnetic field, and consequently no induced magnetism in vertical soft iron. Therefore, if the compass is adjusted on the magnetic equator, all coefficient B deviation is due to permanent magnetism, and is removed by the fore-and-aft magnets. After a considerable change of magnetic latitude, the deviation on a heading of magnetic east or west is again measured. By means of the curves of figure 721, A, the required amount of standard two-inch Flinders bar is determined. Accurate results will be obtained only if the vessel is magnetically the same at both latitudes. That is, a structural change, an alteration in the number or position of magnets or other devices used in the adjustment, magnetic treatment, etc., invalidates the measurement. After the required amount of Flinders bar has been inserted, some deviation may be present due to mutual induction among the various devices used for adjustment. This should be removed by means of the permanent magnets. Once the correct amount of Flinders bar has been installed, no change should be needed unless there is a substantial change in the amount or location of vertical soft iron, or unless the compass is relocated.

This method is not always practical. If the correct length and location of Flinders bar for another vessel of similar construction and compass location have been determined previously, the same length can be used for the compass being adjusted. If a large change in magnetic latitude can be made without appreciable change of deviation on headings east and west, the amount of Flinders bar is correct. If the deviation changes, readjustment is needed. By studying the structure of the vessel, an experienced compass adjuster may be able to make a reasonably accurate estimate of the length to use.

In the absence of enough reliable information to permit a reasonably accurate determination of the correct length, the Flinders bar may be omitted entirely, and the deviation on east and west headings removed by means of the fore-and-aft permanent magnets. This is common practice for yachts, fishing vessels, and even for some coastal vessels which do not change magnetic latitude more than a few degrees.

The correct length of Flinders bar can be determined by figure 721, B, if reliable data are available on the deviation occurring on magnetic east or west headings at two widely separated magnetic latitudes. The constant K is determined by computation, using the formula

$$K=\lambda\frac{\mathrm{H_2}\tan \mathrm{d_2}-\mathrm{H_1}\tan \mathrm{d_1}}{\mathrm{Z_2}-\mathrm{Z_1}}$$

in which

K=a constant proportional to the required length of Flinders bar.

λ=shielding factor, or the proportion of the earth's field effective at the compass. Generally, it varies from about 0.7 to 1.0, averaging about 0.9 for compasses in exposed positions, and 0.8 for those surrounded by metal deck houses.

H_1=horizontal intensity of earth's magnetic field at place of first deviation reading.

H_2=horizontal intensity of earth's magnetic field at place of second deviation reading.

d_1=total deviation on heading magnetic east or west at place of first deviation reading.

d_2=total deviation on heading magnetic east or west at place of second deviation reading.

Z_1=vertical intensity of earth's magnetic field at place of first deviation reading.

Z_2=vertical intensity of earth's magnetic field at place of second deviation reading.

The unit of intensity is the oersted.

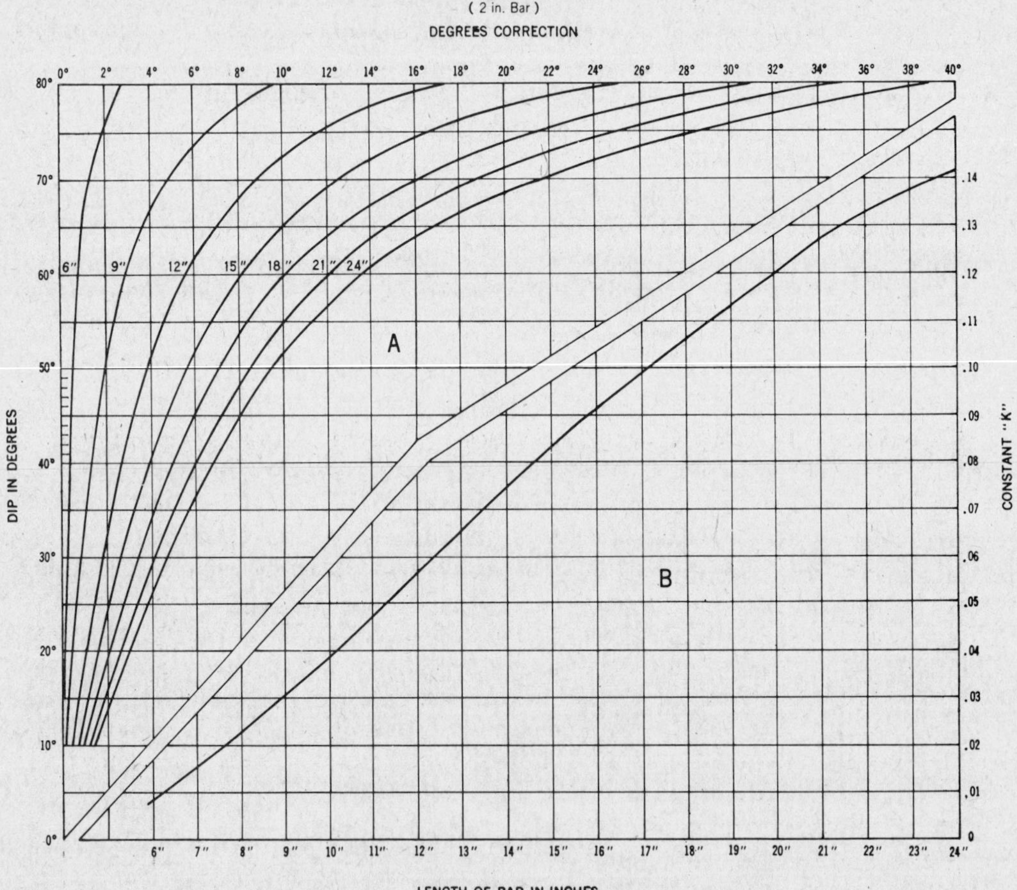

FIGURE 721.—Flinders bar curves: A, if deviation due to induced magnetism in vertical soft iron is known; B, if coefficient K is known.

The values of horizontal and vertical intensity (H and Z) can be obtained from charts 33 and 36, respectively, by dividing the values in gammas (art. 706) as shown on the charts by 100,000.

The constant K represents a mass of vertical soft iron (the c rod) causing deviation. From the intersection of the curve of figure 721, B, and a horizontal line through the value of constant K, draw a vertical line to the bottom scale, which shows the required length of Flinders bar.

If some length of Flinders bar was in place when the two deviation readings were made, enter the graph of figure 721, B, with this length and determine the corresponding value of K. Call this K_2 and that obtained by computation K_1. Algebraically add K_1 and K_2 to determine the value of K to use for finding the total length of Flinders bar required. If the Flinders bar is forward of the compass, K_2 is negative (−), and if aft of the compass, K_2 is positive (+). In the computation of K_2, both Z_1 and Z_2 are positive in north magnetic latitude and negative in south magnetic latitude. Also, d_1 and d_2 are positive if deviation is east on magnetic heading east in north latitude or magnetic heading west in south latitude. If *either* the heading or direction of the deviation is reversed, the sign of d_1 or d_2 is negative. If both are reversed, the sign is positive. If the value of K is negative, the Flinders bar should be installed forward of the compass, and if positive, it should be installed aft.

Example.—The deviation of a magnetic compass of a ship on heading magnetic east is 1°E in an area where H is 0.170 and Z is 0.539. It is 9°E in an area where H is 0.311 and Z is 0.260. The shielding factor is 0.8.

Required.—The correct length of Flinders bar if (1) no Flinders bar is in place during observations, (2) six inches of Flinders bar is in place forward of the compass during observations.

Solution.—

$$(1)\quad K_1=0.8\left(\frac{0.311\times0.15838-0.170\times0.01746}{0.260-0.539}\right)$$

$$=(-)\ 0.133$$

$$K_2=0$$

$$K=K_1+K_2=(-)\ 0.133$$

From figure 721, B, the correct amount of Flinders bar is 22 inches. Since the amount used must be a multiple of ¾ inch, the amount to use is 21¾ inches. Since K is negative, the bar should be installed forward of the compass.

(2) From figure 721, B, the value of K_2 corresponding to six inches of Flinders bar is 0.009. The value is negative because the bar is forward of the compass. Therefore, $K_1+K_2=(-)0.133+(-)0.009=(-)0.142$. From figure 721, B, the *total* amount of Flinders bar required is 24 inches, which should be installed forward of the compass.

Answers.—(1) 21¾ inches of Flinders bar installed forward of the compass, (2) 24 inches of Flinders bar installed forward of the compass.

When the length of Flinders bar is determined in this way, accurate results can be expected only if the vessel is magnetically unchanged between deviation readings.

Lord Kelvin suggested the following rule for improving the adjustment for coefficient B if no better method is available:

Remove the deviation observed on magnetic east or west headings by means of fore-and-aft B *magnets when the vessel has arrived at places of weaker vertical magnetic field, and by means of Flinders bar when it has arrived at places of stronger vertical magnetic field, whether in the Northern or Southern Hemisphere.*

After a number of applications of this rule following alternate passage from weaker to stronger fields and then stronger to weaker fields, the amount of Flinders bar should be very nearly correct.

722. Adjustment for deviation due to induced magnetism in symmetrical horizontal soft iron.—That part of horizontal soft iron which is symmetrically arranged with respect to the compass can be considered equivalent to two rods extending through the compass, one in a fore-and-aft direction ($-a$ rod) and the other in an athwartship direction ($-e$ rod). The deviation caused by both of these rods is quadrantal, but of opposite sign. If both rods were equally effective in causing deviation, they would cancel each other and no deviation would result on any heading. In most vessels, however, the athwartships iron dominates, and deviation due to all horizontal soft iron can generally be considered to be that which would result from a single (−) e rod. In figure 722a the deviation resulting from such a rod is shown for various magnetic

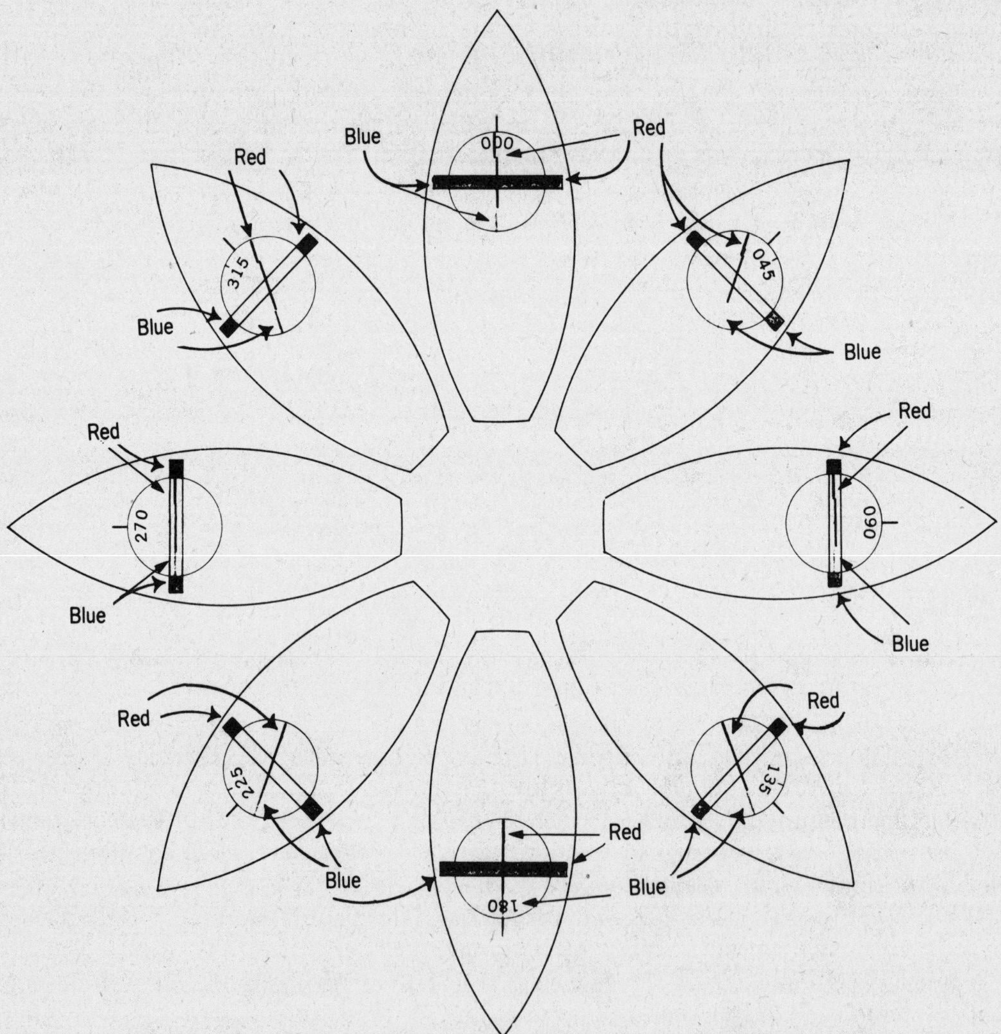

FIGURE 722a.—Deviation caused by induced magnetism in symmetrical horizontal soft iron.

headings in any latitude. There is no deviation on any cardinal heading, but the directive force is weakened on heading magnetic east or west. The maximum deviation occurs on intercardinal headings by compass, being easterly in the northeast and southwest quadrants, and westerly in the other two quadrants. This is coefficient D deviation. In figure 722a the headings shown on the compass card are the magnetic headings of the vessel. Their offset from the lubber's line shows the direction and relative magnitude of deviation.

The field causing this deviation is neutralized by installing two masses of soft iron abeam of the compass, on opposite sides and equidistant from its center. Such iron is usually in the form of hollow spheres or cylinders, called **quadrantal correctors.** These can be moved in or out in an athwartship direction along brackets on the sides of the binnacle.

Quadrantal correctors act as (+) *e* parameters which neutralize the (−) *e* parameter of the athwartships iron. As shown in figure 722b, the portion of the corrected adjacent

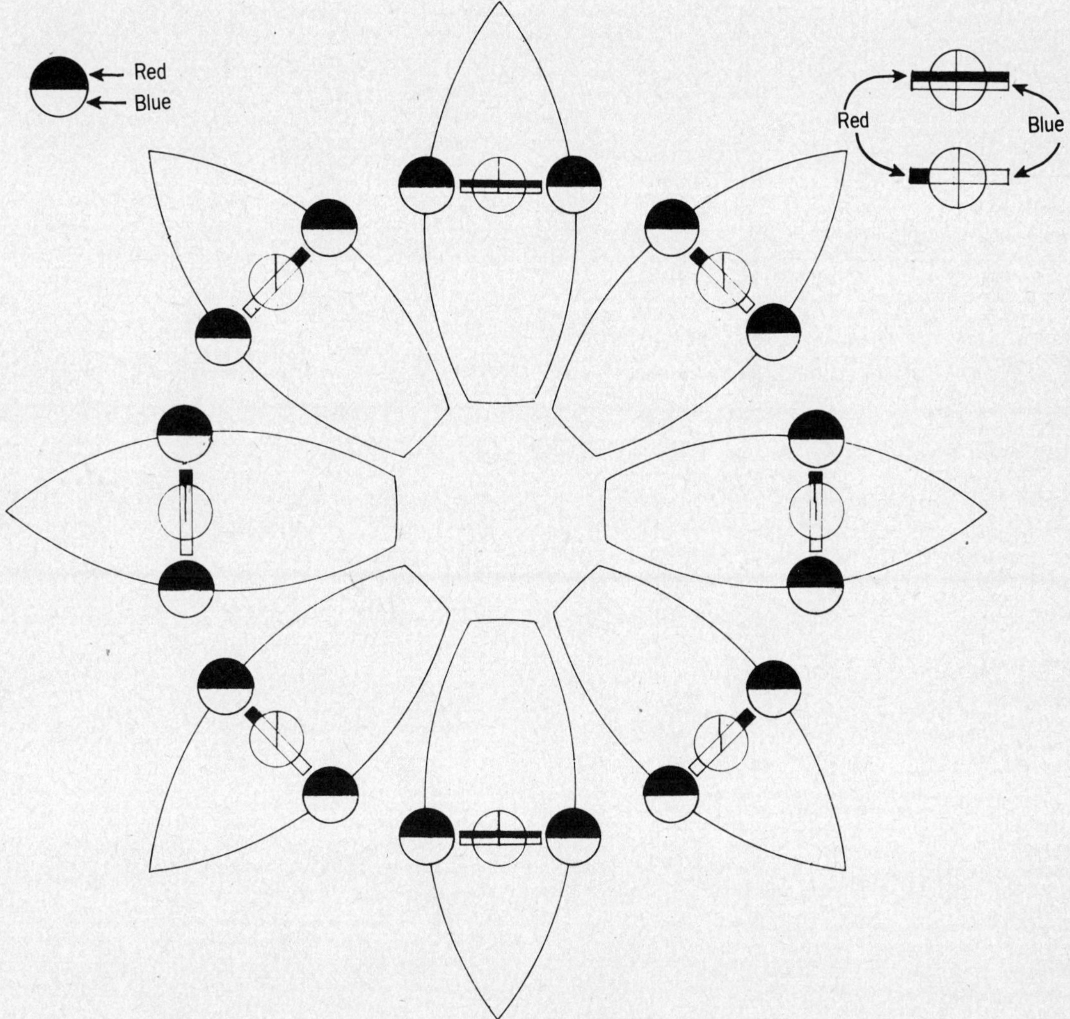

FIGURE 722b.—Adjustment for symmetrical horizontal soft iron.

to the compass is always of opposite polarity to the deflecting force. The amount of the correction can be adjusted by moving the correctors toward or away from the compass card. If the inboard limit of travel is reached without fully removing the deviation, larger correctors are needed. If overcorrection occurs at the outboard limit, smaller correctors are needed. A single corrector can be used, but this produces an unbalanced field which is less desirable than a balanced one. In general, large correctors at a greater distance are preferable to small correctors close up because there is less mutual induction between the correctors if they are widely separated. In the rare case when quadrantal deviation is *westerly* on heading northeast (coefficient D is negative, the fore-and-aft horizontal soft iron predominating), the quadrantal correctors should be mounted fore-and-aft on the binnacle.

Figure 722c shows the approximate amount of deviation correction to be expected from correctors of various sizes, shapes and distance from the center of a standard U. S. Navy 7½-inch compass. The data apply to either the athwartships or fore-and-aft position.

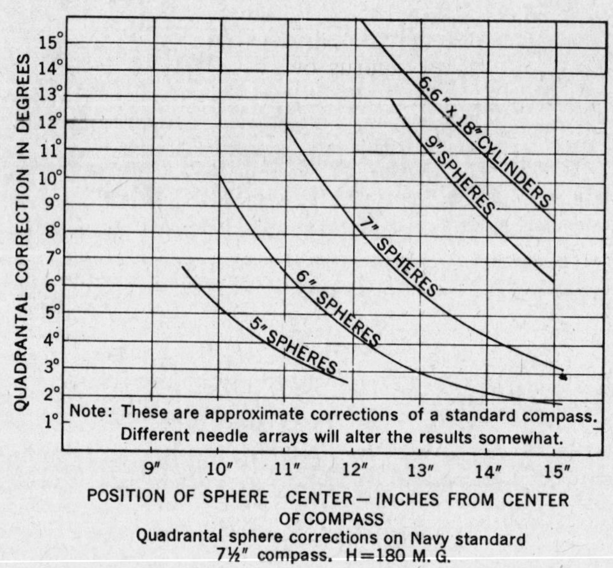

FIGURE 722c.—Effect of various quadrantal correctors.

Like the Flinders bar (art. 720), the quadrantal correctors should be handled carefully, and checked from time to time to see if they have acquired permanent magnetism. The test can be made by rotating each corrector through 180° without altering its distance from the center. If the compass heading changes, the correctors have acquired permanent magnetism which can be removed by tapping with a hammer when the blue pole is toward the north, or by removing the spheres, heating them to a dull red, and permitting them to cool slowly.

723. Adjustment for deviation due to induced magnetism in asymmetrical horizontal soft iron.—If the horizontal soft iron is not arranged symmetrically with respect to the compass, resulting in an effective pole which is on neither the fore-and-aft nor athwartships axis through the compass, quadrantal deviation with its maximum values on cardinal headings (coefficient E) results. Constant deviation (coefficient A) may also be used by this arrangement. Either coefficient E or A is due to a combination of parameters.

For a centerline compass on a ship of conventional construction, any deviation due to induced magnetism in asymmetrical horizontal soft iron is small, and many installations make no provision for neutralizing the effect. However, some binnacles are provided with a pair of ***E*-links,** which are bars that can be attached to the side brackets to permit the quadrantal correctors to be slewed somewhat with respect to the compass. When this has been done, the horizontal axis through the correctors and the compass makes an angle with the athwartship axis of the compass.

After a compass has been adjusted, any remaining constant deviation due to magnetic coefficient *A* is likely to be very small. If such deviation exists, its cause is likely to be chiefly mechanical. If a compass is used primarily for determining the heading (as a steering compass), all constant deviation can be removed by realignment of the binnacle so as to rotate the lubber's line by the required amount. However, if a compass is to be used for observing bearings or azimuths, only the mechanical *A*-error should be removed in this manner. This is because such readings are taken on the face of the card itself, and are therefore not affected by misalignment of the lubber's line. The two components of constant deviation can be separated in the following manner: **measure the deviation found on various headings by means of bearings or azimuths.** This includes only magnetic coefficient *A*. Then measure the deviation on various headings by means of the lubber's line, comparing the heading by compass with the magnetic heading determined by pelorus or gyrocompass. This includes the combined effect of magnetic and mechanical coefficient *A* deviation. The difference between the two values is the mechanical coefficient *A*. For a properly adjusted compass the magnetic coefficient *A* deviation is so small that provision is not made for its removal.

724. Heeling error.—All of the effects discussed previously refer to a vessel on an even keel. When the vessel heels, conditions are altered. Deviation which now appears or the *change* of deviation from that when the vessel was on an even keel, is called **heeling error.** For a constant angle of heel and a steady heading, this error remains essentially unchanged. However, it tends to increase as the heel becomes greater, and to reverse sign as the heel changes from one side to another. Therefore, if a vessel is rolling or pitching, the compass tends to oscillate. This increases the difficulty of reading the compass.

The cause of heeling error is the displacement of the permanent and induced magnetic fields with respect to the compass. Figure 724 shows a vessel heeled to star-

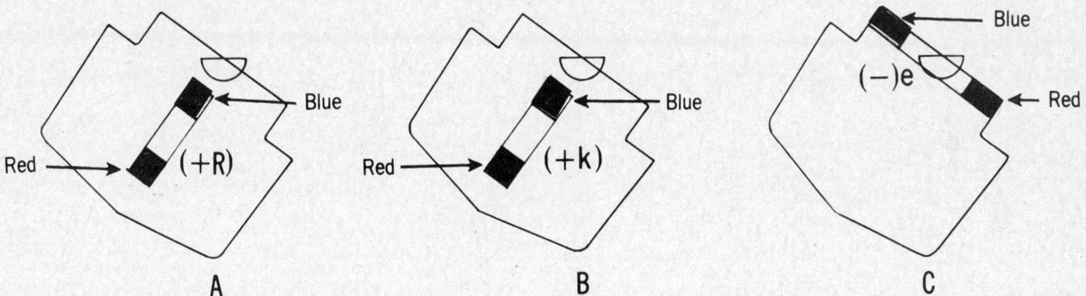

FIGURE 724.—Effect of heel.

board on heading magnetic north or south, in north magnetic latitude. The vessel was constructed in north magnetic latitude. On an even keel the vertical parameter *R* of permanent magnetism for a centrally located compass is directly below the compass, with the blue pole nearer the compass. When the vessel is heeled as shown at *A*, the blue pole is to port of the compass, causing deviation toward that side. A vertical rod of soft iron below the compass (parameter *k*) exerts a similar influence, as shown at *B*. An athwartship horizontal rod through the compass has no deviating effect while the vessel is on an even keel, but when it heels as shown in figure 724, the vertical component of the earth's field causes the port end to acquire a blue pole and the starboard end a red pole (parameter *e*), as shown at *C*. Each of the three causes shown in figure 724 results in a blue pole being established on the port or high side of the vessel. This causes the red north ends of the compass magnets to be attracted to this side. If the heading is magnetic north, the deviation is westerly, and if magnetic south, it is easterly. This effect is offset somewhat by the changed magnetic field surrounding the quadrantal correctors. On heading magnetic east or west, these components have no deviating effect, but the directive force of the compass is strengthened or weakened. When the vessel pitches, the effects described for north-south and east-west headings are reversed. On a heading other than a cardinal direction (magnetic) the effect is some combination of the two. The magnetic situation varies not only with the heading, but also with the magnetic latitude and the magnetic history of the vessel.

Although heeling error is due in part to permanent magnetism and in part to induced magnetism, the induced magnetism generally exerts the greater influence. The most effective method of neutralizing this effect would be to attack each parameter separately. This would require the placement of soft iron *above* the compass. Since this would not be a convenient arrangement, the condition is improved by placing a vertical permanent magnet, called a **heeling magnet,** centrally *below* the compass, and adjusting its height until the error is minimized. In north magnetic latitude, the red end is placed uppermost in most installations. As the vessel proceeds to lower magnetic latitudes, parameter R becomes less effective in producing deviation because of the stronger directive force due to the horizontal component of the earth's magnetic field. Parameters k and e become weaker because of decreased intensity of the vertical component of the earth's field, and the strengthening of the horizontal component also reduces their effect. Therefore, the heeling magnet requires readjustment as the magnetic latitude changes. As the vessel approaches the magnetic equator, the heeling magnet should be lowered. After the vessel crosses the magnetic equator, it may be necessary to invert the heeling magnets, so that the opposite end is uppermost. A change in the setting of the heeling magnet may introduce deviation on headings of compass east or west because of altered induction between the heeling magnet and the Flinders bar. This should be removed by means of the fore-and-aft (B) magnets in the trays below the compass.

If adjustment for heeling error is made when the vessel is tied up or at anchor, it is best done by listing the vessel on a northerly or southerly heading, and adjusting the heeling magnet until the reading of the compass is restored to what it was before the vessel heeled. If the adjustment is made at sea, the vessel should be placed on a heading of compass north or south. If there is little rolling, the vessel can be listed and the compass reading restored, as at dockside. If the vessel rolls moderately on this heading, the heeling magnet should be placed at that height at which oscillation of the compass card is minimum. If the setting for minimum oscillation is different on north and south headings, the mean position should be used. Any yawing of the vessel should be considered when reading the compass under rolling conditions.

The approximate position of the heeling magnet can be determined by means of an instrument known as a **heeling adjuster** or a **vertical force instrument,** a form of **dip needle.** This consists of a small magnet balanced about a horizontal axis by means of a small adjustable weight. A scale indicates the distance of the weight from the axis. The instrument is taken ashore and balanced at a place where the earth's field is undisturbed, the magnet being in a magnetic north-south direction, approximately. The instrument is then taken aboard ship, the compass removed from its binnacle, and the heeling adjuster installed in its place. The weight is set to a distance equal to the distance determined ashore, multiplied by λ, the shielding factor (art. 721). The heeling magnet is then moved up or down until the magnet of the instrument is level. This should be approximately the correct setting. This method is used principally when the listing of a vessel is difficult or impractical.

725. Soft iron correctors and nearby magnets.—The soft iron correctors used in compass adjustment are near enough to the compass magnets and the magnets used in compass adjustment to be influenced by them.

The Flinders bar acquires a certain amount of induced magnetism from the fields of the heeling magnet and the fore-and-aft (*B*) corrector magnets. The approximate amount of deviation caused by induced magnetism from the heeling magnet of a 7½-inch compass when H=0.165 is shown in figure 725. Because of such induced mag-

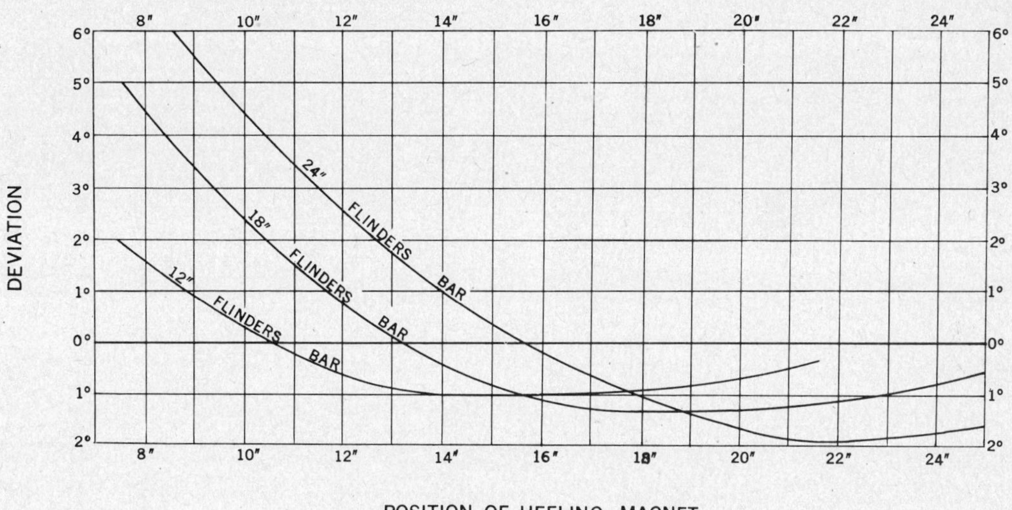

FIGURE 725.—Deviation due to inductive effect of heeling magnet on Flinders bar.

netism, the "drop-in" method of determining the amount of Flinders bar is not accurate By this method, Flinders bar lengths are added until the compass reading changes by the required amount. Better adjustment is achieved by using the required amount of Flinders bar and removing any remaining deviation on east-west headings by means of the fore-and-aft magnets. The principal reason that it is preferable to use a larger number of magnets at a distance from the compass than a smaller number near it, is that the former arrangement produces less induced magnetism in the Flinders bar and quadrantal correctors. If the Flinders bar length is changed, the deviation on headings of magnetic east and west should be checked, and any needed adjustment made by means of fore-and-aft magnets. When all correctors have been put in place, their positions relative to each other are constant. Therefore, the Flinders bar acts as a permanent magnet, and the resulting deviation is semicircular (coefficient *B*). The Flinders bar may also introduce a small amount of quadrantal deviation (coefficient *D*), its action being somewhat like that of a quadrantal corrector placed in the fore-and-aft axis of the compass.

The quadrantal correctors acquire induced magnetism from the fields of the fore-and-aft (*B*) magnets, the athwartship (*C*) magnets, and the compass magnets. The magnetism acquired from the *B* and *C* magnets is semicircular (coefficient *B* from the *B* magnets, and coefficient *C* from the *C* magnets), and that acquired from the field of the compass magnets is quadrantal (coefficient *D*). The semicircular deviation is minimized by keeping the *B* and *C* magnets as far away from the quadrantal correctors as practicable, and any deviation that does exist is removed by means of these magnets. The quadrantal deviation is removed by means of the quadrantal correctors themselves. The compass magnets of most modern compasses have little effect upon the quadrantal correctors.

Because of the interaction between the various correctors, it is good practice to insert the required amount of Flinders bar, and to install the quadrantal correctors and heeling magnet at their approximate positions before adjusting the compass. If a radical change is subsequently made in any of these adjustments, the settings of the *B* and *C* magnets should be checked and altered if necessary.

Analysis of Deviation

726. Nature and purpose of analysis.—An analysis consists of determining the approximate value of each of the six coefficients, and studying the results. The purpose of the analysis is to give the compass adjuster an understanding of the magnetic properties of the vessel. This provides the basis for the approximate placement of the various correctors, and suggests possibilities for further refinement in the adjustment. Without an analysis, compass adjustment is a more-or-less mechanical process. Fewer mistakes are likely to be made by the person who understands the nature of the magnetic field he seeks to neutralize.

727. The analysis.—The first step in an analysis is to record the deviation on each cardinal and intercardinal heading *by the compass to be analyzed.* For the purpose of analysis, easterly deviation is considered positive (+), and westerly deviation negative (−). Approximate values of the various coefficients are:

Coefficient A—mean of deviation on all headings.

Coefficient B—mean of deviation on headings 090° and 270°, with sign at 270° reversed.

Coefficient C—mean of deviation on headings 000° and 180°, with sign at 180° reversed.

Coefficient D—mean of deviation on intercardinal headings, with signs at headings 135° and 315° reversed.

Coefficient E—mean of deviation on cardinal headings, with signs at 090° and 270° reversed.

Coefficient J—change of deviation for a heel of 1° while the vessel heads 000° by compass. It is considered *positive* if the north end of the compass card is drawn toward the *low* side, and *negative* if toward the *high* side.

Example.—A magnetic compass which has not been adjusted has deviation on cardinal and intercardinal compass headings as follows:

Compass heading	*Deviation*	*Compass heading*	*Deviation*
000°	1°.5W	180°	8°.0E
045°	34°.0E	225°	1°.5W
090°	31°.0E	270°	29°.0W
135°	13°.5E	315°	36°.0W

On heading compass north the deviation is 13°.5W when the vessel heels 10° to starboard.

Required.—The approximate value of each coefficient.

Solution.—

$$A=\frac{-1°.5+34°.0+31°.0+13°.5+8°.0-1°.5-29°.0-36°.0}{8}=(+)2°.3$$

$$B=\frac{31°.0+29°.0}{2}=(+)30°.0$$

$$C=\frac{-1°.5-8°.0}{2}=(-)4°.8$$

$$D=\frac{34^\circ.0-13^\circ.5-1^\circ.5+36^\circ.0}{4}=(+)13^\circ.8$$

$$E=\frac{-1^\circ.5-31^\circ.0+8^\circ.0+29^\circ.0}{4}=(+)1^\circ.1$$

$$J=\frac{-13^\circ.5+1^\circ.5}{10}=(-)1^\circ.2$$

Answers.—A (+) 2°.3, B (+) 30°.0, C (−) 4°.8, D (+) 13°.8, E (+) 1°.1, J (−) 1°.2.

On any compass heading (CH) the deviation (d) from each coefficient acting alone is:

Coefficient A: $d_A=A$
Coefficient B: $d_B=B \sin \text{CH}$
Coefficient C: $d_C=C \cos \text{CH}$
Coefficient D: $d_D=D \sin 2\text{CH}$
Coefficient E: $d_E=E \cos 2\text{CH}$
Coefficient J: $d_J=J \cos \text{CH}$.

For a vessel on an even keel, the total deviation on any compass heading is the algebraic sum of the deviation due to each of the first five coefficients:

$$d=d_A+d_B+d_C+d_D+d_E=A+B \sin \text{CH}+C \cos \text{CH}+D \sin 2\text{CH}+E \cos 2\text{CH}.$$

For the compass of the example given above, the deviation due to each component, and the total, on various headings is:

CH	*A*	*B*	*C*	*D*	*E*	d
°	°	°	°	°	°	°
000	+2.3	0.0	−4.8	0.0	+1.1	−1.4
015	+2.3	+7.8	−4.6	+6.9	+1.0	+13.4
030	+2.3	+15.0	−4.2	+12.0	+0.6	+25.7
045	+2.3	+21.2	−3.4	+13.8	0.0	+33.9
060	+2.3	+26.0	−2.4	+12.0	−0.6	+37.3
075	+2.3	+29.0	−1.2	+6.9	−1.0	+36.0
090	+2.3	+30.0	0.0	0.0	−1.1	+31.2
105	+2.3	+29.0	+1.2	−6.9	−1.0	+24.6
120	+2.3	+26.0	+2.4	−12.0	−0.6	+18.1
135	+2.3	+21.2	+3.4	−13.8	0.0	+13.1
150	+2.3	+15.0	+4.2	−12.0	+0.6	+10.1
165	+2.3	+7.8	+4.6	−6.9	+1.0	+8.8
180	+2.3	0.0	+4.8	0.0	+1.1	+8.2
195	+2.3	−7.8	+4.6	+6.9	+1.0	+7.0
210	+2.3	−15.0	+4.2	+12.0	+0.6	+4.1
225	+2.3	−21.2	+3.4	+13.8	0.0	−1.7
240	+2.3	−26.0	+2.4	+12.0	−0.6	−9.9
255	+2.3	−29.0	+1.2	+6.9	−1.0	−19.6
270	+2.3	−30.0	0.0	0.0	−1.1	−28.8
285	+2.3	−29.0	−1.2	−6.9	−1.0	−35.8
300	+2.3	−26.0	−2.4	−12.0	−0.6	−38.7
315	+2.3	−21.2	−3.4	−13.8	0.0	−36.1
330	+2.3	−15.0	−4.2	−12.0	+0.6	−28.3
345	+2.3	−7.8	−4.6	−6.9	+1.0	−16.0

The various components and the total deviation are shown in graphical form in figure 727. Since the various coefficients are only approximated by the method given above, the curve of total deviation found in this way should not be expected to coincide exactly with a curve drawn from values found by measurement on the various headings.

The *shapes* of the curves of figure 727 are typical of those of an unadjusted compass of a large steel ship. However, an analysis of the results indicates the following:

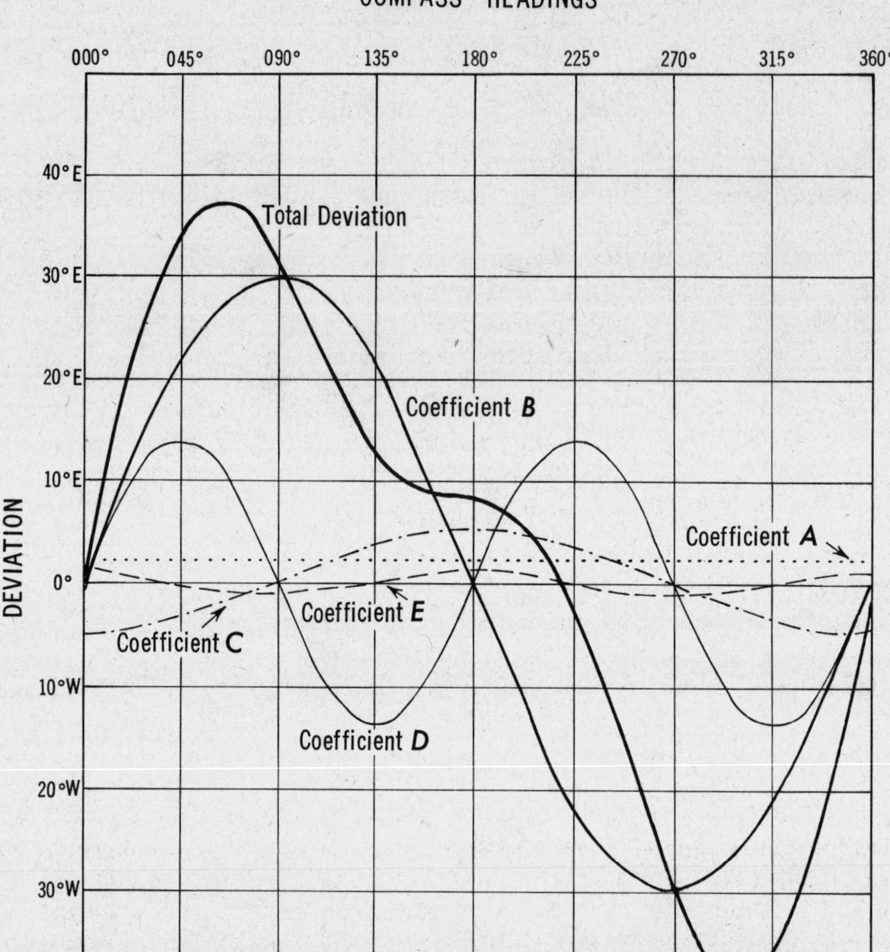

FIGURE 727.—Coefficients and total deviation of an unadjusted magnetic compass.

Coefficient *A* is normally negligible. The presence of more than 2° of constant error indicates an abnormal condition which should be discovered and corrected. If the vessel has been in service for some time without major structural change, and no misalignment of the lubber's line of the compass or the pelorus or gyrocompass used for measuring deviation has been noted previously, it is probable that a mistake has been made in determining the azimuth or bearing used for establishing deviation.

Coefficient *E* is normally negligible for a compass located on the centerline of the vessel. This vessel has an excessive amount, which should be corrected by slewing the quadrantal correctors, using an *E*-link.

Since deviation is east on heading 090° and west on 000°, it is probable that the blue pole of the vessel's permanent field is on the port bow.

The compass being unadjusted, no Flinders bar is in place, and the large *B* deviation on heading 090° is a combination of deviation from induced magnetism in vertical soft iron and that due to the permanent magnetism of the vessel. Since the deviation on heading 270° is nearly the same as that on 090°, but of opposite sign, adjustment on one of these headings should result in nearly correct adjustment on the other. Since some B and C deviation occurs on intercardinal headings, while no D deviation occurs on cardinal headings, adjustment for B and C should be made before that for final D adjustment.

A second analysis made after adjustment may reveal possibilities for further refinement in the adjustment.

If heeling error is measured on any heading other than compass north or south, the value of coefficient J can be found by means of the formula:

$$\mathrm{d} = J \cos \mathrm{CH}$$

converted to

$$J = \frac{\mathrm{d}}{\cos \mathrm{CH}}$$

or

$$J = \mathrm{d} \sec \mathrm{CH}.$$

If HE is the total observed change of deviation (heeling error), and i is the angle of heel in degrees (for relatively small angles), the formula becomes

$$J = \frac{\mathrm{HE} \sec \mathrm{CH}}{i}.$$

If heeling error is sought, the formula becomes

$$\mathrm{HE} = Ji \cos \mathrm{CH}.$$

Adjustment Procedure

728. Preliminary steps.—Efficient and accurate adjustment is preceded by certain preliminary steps best made while a vessel is moored or at anchor.

The magnetic environment of the compass should be carefully inspected. Stray magnetic influences such as those caused by tools, direct current electric appliances, personal equipment (such as keys, pocketknives, or steel belt buckles), nylon clothing etc., should be eliminated. Permanently installed equipment of magnetic material (such as cargo booms, boat davits, cranes, or guns) should be placed in the positions they normally occupy at sea. The degaussing coils should be secured by the reversing process (art. 743) if this has not already been done.

The compass itself should be checked carefully for bubbles, and to be sure it is centered on the vertical axis of the binnacle. If it is, and the vessel is on an even keel, there is no change of reading as the heeling magnet is raised and lowered in its tube. An adjustment should be made to the gimbal rings if the compass is off center. There should be no play in the position of the compass once it is centered.

The lubber's line, too, should be checked to be sure it is in line with the longitudinal axis of the vessel. This can be done by sighting on the jackstaff if the compass is on the centerline. If it is not, a batten might be erected at a distance from the centerline equal to the distance from the center of the compass to the centerline. Another way is to determine the distance from the compass to the centerline and from this point to the jackstaff. The first distance divided by the second is the natural tangent of the angle at the compass between the line of sight to the jackstaff and the line of sight through the lubber's line. If the compass is in an exposed position where bearings can be taken, and the true heading is known, the observed relative bearing of a distant object can be compared with that obtained by careful measurement on the chart. If the vessel is at anchor or underway, the method explained in article 723 can be used.

If a pelorus or gyrocompass or repeater is to be used in determining deviation of the compass, its lubber's line should be checked in the same manner, or by comparing a relative bearing of a distant object taken by two instruments, the lubber's line of one having previously been checked. If a gyrocompass is to be used, it is checked to see that it is synchronized with a repeater. With accurate synchronization, any error in one will also be present in the other. The speed and latitude adjustments of the gyrocompass should be checked carefully.

All devices to be used in the adjustment should be checked to see that they are on hand and in good condition. The trays for *B* and *C* permanent magnets, the quadrantal correctors, and heeling magnet should be checked for freedom of motion. The Flinders bar and quadrantal correctors should be checked for permanent magnetism. The correct amount of Flinders bar should be placed in its tube. The quadrantal correctors should be placed in their approximate positions, being centered if no better information is available. The heeling magnet is generally placed with the red end uppermost in north magnetic latitude, and the blue end uppermost in south magnetic latitude. If no better information is available, the heeling magnet should be placed near the bottom of the tube.

Plans for the actual adjustment should be made carefully. A suitable time and location should be selected. If landmarks are to be used, suitable ones should be selected to provide the information desired. Areas of heavy traffic should be avoided. If azimuths of the sun are to be used, a time should be selected when the sun will not be too high in the sky for suitable observation. A curve of magnetic azimuths (art. 731) should be made, and just before adjustment begins a comparing watch should be checked and set, if possible, to correct time. Local variation should be checked carefully, and corrected for date, if necessary. Any necessary recording and work forms should be made up. Each person to participate in the adjustment should be instructed regarding the general plan and his specific duties.

729. Underway procedure.—When everything is in order and the vessel has arrived at its adjusting area, final adjustment can begin. Trim should be normal, and the vessel free from list, so that no heeling error is present.

All adjustment headings should be *magnetic*. Compass headings can be used, but this results in a slight turn being required every time an adjustment is altered. Also, the coefficients are not completely separated unless the vessel is on magnetic headings.

Turns to each new heading should be made slowly, swinging slightly beyond the desired heading before steadying on it. If steering is by gyro, the gyro error should be checked on each heading if time and facilities permit. The vessel should remain on each heading for at least two minutes before the deviation is determined or an adjustment made, to permit the compass card to come to rest and the magnetic condition of the vessel to become settled. If observations are made before the vessel's magnetism becomes settled, the reading will be incorrect by an amount called the **Gaussin error.**

Adjustments should be carried out in the correct order, as follows:

1. Steady on magnetic heading 090° (or 270°) and adjust the fore-and-aft permanent magnets until the compass heading coincides with the magnetic heading, thus removing all coefficient *B* on this heading. Use magnets in pairs, from the bottom up, with the trays at the lowest point of travel. When overcorrection occurs, remove the two highest magnets and raise the trays until all deviation has been removed. If two magnets overcorrect, use a single magnet. It is not necessary to determine in ad-

vance which direction the red ends should occupy, for a mistake will be immediately apparent by an *increase* in the deviation.

2. Steady on magnetic heading 180° (or 000°) and adjust the athwartship permanent magnets until the compass heading coincides with the magnetic heading, thus removing all coefficient *C* on this heading. Use the same technique as in step 1.

3. Steady on magnetic heading 270° (090° if 270° was used in step 1) and remove *half* the deviation with the fore-and-aft magnets.

4. Steady on magnetic heading 000° (180° if 000° was used in step 2) and remove *half* the deviation with the athwartship magnets.

5. Steady on any intercardinal magnetic heading and adjust the position of the quadrantal correctors until the compass heading coincides with the magnetic heading, thus removing all coefficient *D* on this heading. Leave the quadrantal correctors at equal distances from the compass.

6. Steady on either intercardinal magnetic heading 90° from that used in step 5 and remove *half* the deviation by adjusting the positions of the quadrantal correctors, leaving them at equal distances from the compass.

7. Secure all correctors in their final positions and record their number, size, positions, and orientation, as appropriate, on the bottom of the deviation table form (if a standard form such as that shown in fig. 710 is used).

8. **Swing ship** for residual deviation. That is, determine the remaining deviation on a number of headings at approximately equal intervals. Every 15° is preferable, but if the maximum deviation is small, every 45° (cardinal and intercardinal headings) may suffice.

9. If the vessel has degaussing, energize the degaussing coils and repeat the swing.

10. Make a deviation table (art. 710) for each condition (degaussing off and on), giving values for headings at 15° intervals if the maximum deviation is large (more than about 2°), or at 45° intervals if the maximum deviation is small. Record values to the nearest half degree.

If preferred, the adjustment may be started on a north or south heading, thus reversing steps 1 and 2 and also 3 and 4.

With patience and skill, the readings can be made at exact headings. However, if some of the headings are off slightly during the swing, this need not invalidate the results. The exact headings should be recorded, and the deviation determined for these values. The results can then be plotted on cross-section paper with the deviation being one coordinate and the heading the other. The deviation at each heading to be recorded can then be read from the curve. This is good practice even when readings are made at exact headings, for if any large errors have been made, the fact will be immediately apparent. Also, such a curve may be of assistance in making an analysis. If a reason cannot be found for any marked irregularity in the curve, readings might be made again at the headings involved.

The deviation of all compasses aboard the vessel can be determined from a single swing if the heading by each compass is recorded at the moment the magnetic direction is noted. If deviation of one compass is determined by means of a magnetic bearing or azimuth (arts. 733–735), the readings of this compass can then be used to establish the magnetic headings for determining the deviation of each other compass (art. 732).

Compass adjustment is best made when the sea is relatively smooth, so that steady headings can be steered, and heeling error is absent. The setting of the heeling magnet can be checked later, preferably at the next time that the vessel is on a north or south heading and rolling moderately.

An analysis of deviation can be made either before or after adjustment. If this reveals an excessive amount of *A* (constant) deviation, the source of the error should be found and corrected (art. 723), if mechanical or mathematical. If an appreciable amount of *E* deviation is present, *E*-links should be used and the spheres slewed. This is particularly to be anticipated for compasses which are not on the centerline.

The procedure outlined above is for initial adjustment aboard a new or radically modified vessel. Deviation on the heading being used for navigation should be checked from time to time and any important differences from the values shown on the deviation table should be investigated. At sea, it is good practice to compare the magnetic and gyrocompasses at intervals not exceeding half an hour. The error of one or both of these compasses should be checked twice a day when means are available. In pilot waters deviation checks should be made as convenient opportunities present themselves.

Whenever there is reason to question the accuracy of the deviation table, the ship should be swung at the first opportunity and a new table made up if there are significant changes in the old one. Suitable occasions for swinging ship would be after a deviation check indicates a significant error or after any event that might result in changes in the magnetic field of the vessel (art. 712). Intervals of swing should not exceed three months even when there is no reason to question the accuracy of the deviation table.

If a swing indicates the presence of large maximum deviation, the compass should be readjusted. Unless there is reason to change it, the Flinders bar length should remain the same. Other adjustments are altered as needed, none of the correctors being removed at the beginning of adjustment. Whenever the vessel crosses the magnetic equator, the opportunity should be used to check the deviation on magnetic headings east and west. Any adjustment needed should be made by means of the fore-and-aft (*B*) magnets. Upon crossing the magnetic equator, the heeling magnet should be inverted.

The Flinders bar and quadrantal correctors should be checked for permanent magnetism at intervals of about a year, or more often if such magnetism is suspected.

Finding the Deviation

730. Placing a vessel on a desired magnetic heading.—As indicated in article 729 compass adjustment is best made with the vessel on *magnetic* headings. The compass being adjusted cannot be used for placing the vessel on a desired magnetic heading because its deviation is unknown, and is subject to change during the process of adjustment. A number of methods are available, including use of (1) another magnetic compass of known deviation, (2) a gyrocompass, (3) bearing of a distant object, and (4) azimuth of a celestial body.

Magnetic compass. The deviation at the desired magnetic heading is determined from the deviation table for that compass, and applied to the magnetic heading to determine the equivalent compass heading.

Example 1.—It is desired to place a vessel on magnetic heading east, using the standard compass. The deviation table for this compass is shown in figure 710. Degaussing is off.

Required.—Heading per standard compass (psc).

Solution.—From figure 710 the deviation on heading 090° magnetic with degaussing off is found to be 2°5E. Therefore, the equivalent compass heading is 090°−2°5= 087°5.

Answer.—H_{psc} 087°5.

Gyrocompass. The variation is applied to the desired magnetic heading, to determine the equivalent true heading. Any gyro error is then applied to determine the equivalent gyro heading. This is the method commonly used by vessels equipped with a reliable gyrocompass.

Example 2.—It is desired to place a vessel on magnetic heading north, using the gyrocompass. The variation in this area is 6°W, and the gyro error is 1°E.

Required.—Heading per gyrocompass (pgc).

Solution.—The equivalent true heading is $000°-6°=354°$. The gyro heading is $354°-1°=353°$.

Answer.—H_{pgc} 353°.

Bearing of distant object. If a vessel remains within a small area during compass adjustment, the bearing of a distant object is essentially constant. The required distance of the object in miles is found by multiplying the cotangent of the maximum tolerable error by the *radius* in miles of the maneuvering circle. Thus, if the maximum error that can be tolerated is 0°5 (cotangent 114.6), and the vessel can be maneuvered within 200 yards (0.1 mile) of a fixed position such as a buoy, the object selected should be at least $114.6\times0.1=11.5$ miles away. The 200-yard limit is within radial lines centered at the distant object and tangent to a circle having a radius of 200 yards and its center at the center of the maneuvering area. Thus, a vessel has considerable maneuvering space along the line of sight, but very limited room across this line. However, it is not necessary that the vessel *stay* within the required area, but only that it be there when readings are made. Thus, if the center of the area is marked by a buoy, the vessel might steady on each heading while still some distance away, and note the required readings as the buoy is passed. In this way, a small radius may be practical even for a large vessel.

The object selected should be conspicuous and should have a clearly defined feature of small visible width upon which to observe bearings. The object having been selected, its true bearing from the center of the maneuvering area should be measured on the chart. To this, the variation *at the center of the maneuvering area* should be applied to determine the equivalent magnetic bearing. The desired magnetic heading should be set at the lubber's line of the pelorus, and the far vane set at the magnetic bearing of the distant object. The vessel should then be maneuvered until the object is in line with the vanes.

Example 3.—It is desired to place a vessel on magnetic heading northeast in an area where the variation is 4°E. The true bearing of a distant object is 219°.

Required.—The setting of the pelorus.

Solution.—Set 045° at the lubber's line, and set the far vane at $219°-4°=215°$.

If preferred, 000° can be set at the lubber's line, and the far vane at the relative bearing, 170° (magnetic bearing minus desired magnetic heading). If a gyro repeater or a magnetic compass is used instead of a pelorus, the true (or magnetic) bearing should be converted to the equivalent gyro (or compass) bearing.

If the distant object selected is not charted, or the position of the vessel is not known accurately, the approximate magnetic bearing of the object can be determined by measuring its *compass* bearing on each cardinal and intercardinal compass heading, and finding the mean of these readings. The value so determined will be incorrect by the amount of any constant deviation (coefficient A).

Example 4.—The compass bearings of a distant object are as shown below.

Required.—The magnetic bearing of the object, assuming no constant deviation (coefficient A).

Solution.—

CH	*CB*
°	°
000	324.8
045	320.7
090	312.6
135	306.8
180	304.9
225	310.8
270	316.2
315	320.0
sum	2516.8
mean	314.6

Answer.—MB 314°6.

Azimuth of celestial body. The true azimuth of the celestial body selected should be computed (art. 719, vol. II) for the time of observation. The magnetic variation should then be applied to determine the equivalent magnetic azimuth. The desired magnetic heading should then be set at the lubber's line of the pelorus, and the far vane set at the magnetic azimuth of the celestial body. The vessel should then be maneuvered until the body is in line with the vanes.

Example 5.—It is desired to place a vessel on magnetic heading west in an area where the variation is 17°W, and at a time when the computed true azimuth of the sun is 098°.

Required.—The setting of the pelorus.

Solution.—Set 270° at the lubber's line, and set the far vane at 098°+17°=115°.

If preferred, 000° can be set at the lubber's line, and the far vane at the relative azimuth (magnetic azimuth minus desired magnetic heading). If a gyro repeater or a magnetic compass is used instead of a pelorus, the true (or magnetic) azimuth should be converted to the equivalent gyro (or compass) azimuth.

731. Curve of magnetic azimuths.—During the course of compass adjustment and swinging ship, a magnetic direction is needed many times, either to place the vessel on desired magnetic headings or to determine the deviation of the compass being adjusted. If a celestial body is used to provide the magnetic reference, the azimuth is continually changing as the earth rotates on its axis. Frequent and numerous computations can be avoided by preparing, in advance, a table or **curve of magnetic azimuths.** True azimuths at frequent intervals are computed. The variation at the center of the maneuvering area is then applied to determine the equivalent magnetic azimuths These are plotted on cross-section paper, with time as the other argument, using any convenient scale. A curve is then faired through the points.

Points at intervals of half an hour (with a minimum of three) are usually sufficient unless the body is near the celestial meridian and relatively high in the sky, when additional points are needed. If the body *crosses* the celestial meridian, the direction of curvature of the line reverses.

Unless extreme accuracy is required, the Greenwich hour angle and declination can be determined for the approximate midtime, the same value of declination used for all computations, and the Greenwich hour angle considered to increase 15° per hour.

An illustration of a curve of magnetic azimuths of the sun is shown in figure 731. This curve is for the period 0700–0900 zone time on May 31, 1975, at latitude 23°09'.5N, longitude 82°24'.1W. The variation in this area is 2°47'E. At the midtime, the meridian

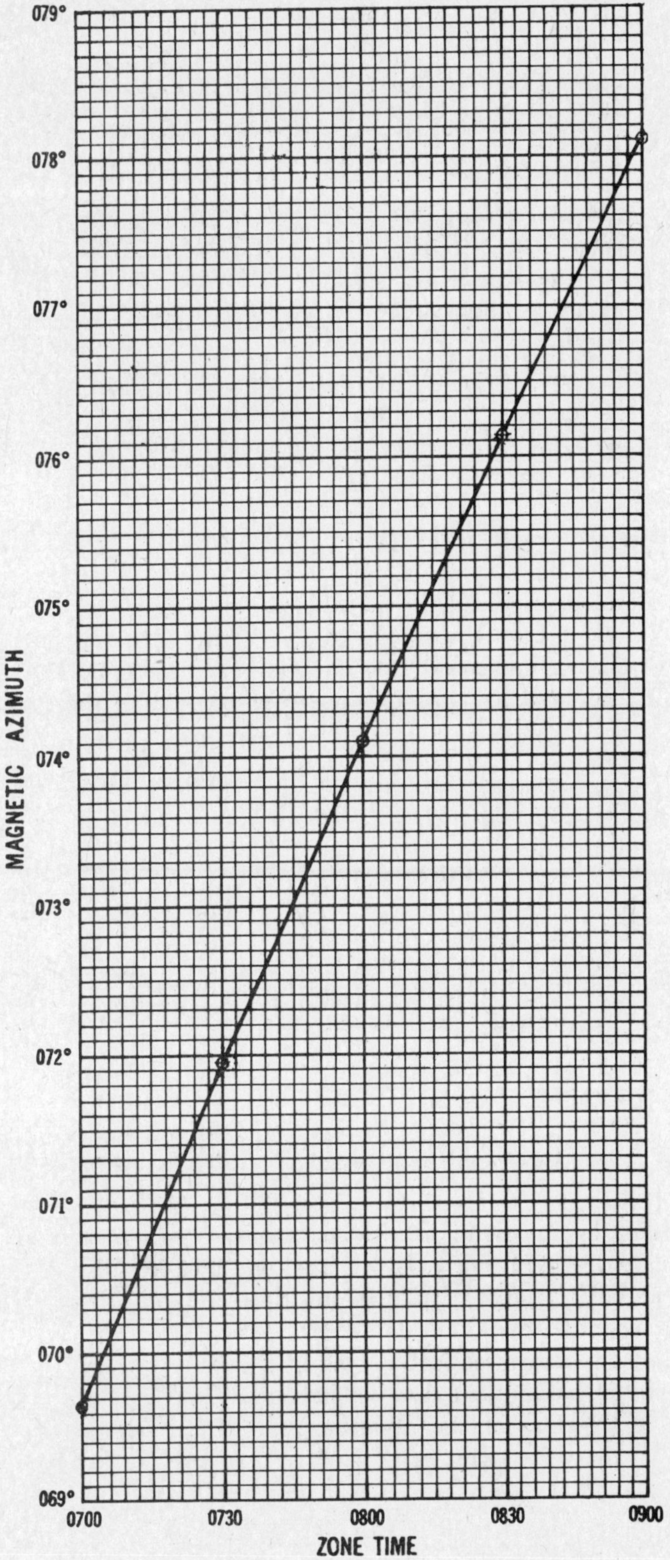

FIGURE 731.—Curve of magnetic azimuths.

angle of the sun is 66°47′.2E, and the declination is 21°52′.3N. Azimuths were computed by Pub. No. 260 at half-hour intervals, as follows:

Zone time	*Meridian angle*	*Declination*	*Latitude*	*Magnetic azimuth*
	° ′ h m	°	°	° ′
0700	81 47.1E(5 27.1E)	21.9N	23.2N	069 39
0730	74 17.1E(4 57.1E)	21.9N	23.2N	071 57
0800	66 47.2E(4 27.1E)	21.9N	23.2N	074 06
0830	59 17.2E(3 57.1E)	21.9N	23.2N	076 08
0900	51 47.2E(3 27.1E)	21.9N	23.2N	078 07

This curve was constructed on the assumption that the vessel would remain in approximately the same location during the period of adjustment and swing. If the position changes materially, this should be considered in the computation.

732. Deviation by magnetic headings.—If the vessel is placed on a magnetic heading by any of the methods of article 730, compass deviation on that heading is the difference between the magnetic heading and the compass heading. If the compass heading is less than the magnetic heading, deviation is easterly, if the compass heading is greater than the magnetic heading, deviation is westerly.

Example.—A vessel is being maneuvered to determine the deviation of the magnetic steering compass on cardinal and intercardinal headings. The gyrocompass, which has an error of 0°.5W, is used for placing the vessel on each of the magnetic headings. Variation in the area is 27°.5E.

Required.—Deviation on each magnetic heading, using the compass headings given below:

Solution.—

MH	*V*	*TH*	*GE*	*Hpgc*	*CH*	*Dev.*
°	°	°	°	°	°	°
000	27.5E	027.5	0.5W	028	000.3	0.3W
045	27.5E	072.5	0.5W	073	046.1	1.1W
090	27.5E	117.5	0.5W	118	093.6	3.6W
135	27.5E	162.5	0.5W	163	136.7	1.7W
180	27.5E	207.5	0.5W	208	179.6	0.4E
225	27.5E	252.5	0.5W	253	223.8	1.2E
270	27.5E	297.5	0.5W	298	266.5	3.5E
315	27.5E	342.5	0.5W	343	313.2	1.8E

733. Deviation by magnetic bearing or azimuth.—Deviation can be found by comparing a magnetic bearing or azimuth with one measured by compass. The magnetic direction can be obtained as explained in articles 730–731. If the compass direction is less than the magnetic direction, deviation is easterly; if the compass direction is greater than the magnetic direction, deviation is westerly. This method is used for determining deviation on a given *compass* heading. The equivalent magnetic heading can be determined by applying the deviation thus determined. If this method is used for swinging ship, the values can be plotted as explained in article 729. For a well-adjusted compass, the deviation may be so small that the compass headings can be considered magnetic headings, without introducing significant errors.

Example.—The standard compass of a vessel has been adjusted, and the vessel is to be swung for residual deviation during the period and for the place for which the curve of magnetic azimuths of figure 731 has been constructed.

Required.—Find the deviation on each heading given below, at the times indicated.
Solution.—

CH °	Time h m s	CZn °	MZn °	Deviation °
000	7 35 20	073.2	072.4	0.8W
045	7 41 12	074.0	072.8	1.2W
090	7 50 15	074.2	073.4	0.8W
135	7 57 36	074.0	073.9	0.1W
180	8 04 44	073.7	074.4	0.7E
225	8 10 10	073.5	074.8	1.3E
270	8 16 33	074.3	075.2	0.9E
315	8 24 51	075.8	075.7	0.1W

The magnetic azimuth (MZn) is determined from figure 731, and the deviation from compass azimuth (CZn) and magnetic azimuth.

734. Deviation by a range is a special case of deviation by magnetic bearing. Two objects appearing in line, one behind the other, constitute a **range.** Range markers are established in many places to mark important channels, the extremities of measured miles, etc. In addition, numerous good ranges occur naturally, as when a lighthouse is in line with a tank, or a tower with a chimney. The true direction of such a range can be determined by measurement on the chart, and variation applied to determine the equivalent magnetic direction. In the case of a natural range, the objects should preferably be at least an inch apart as they appear on the chart, to minimize any plotting errors.

A range is superior to the bearing of a single object because it provides a critical indication of when the vessel is in the correct position to take a reading. The vessel crosses the range on various compass headings. At each crossing, the compass bearing of the range is observed, and also the compass heading. It is well to use two ranges nearly 90° apart, if available, because of the difficulty of crossing at small angles.

Example.—A vessel maneuvering to adjust its compass in the Lower Bay of New York Harbor finds the true direction of the range between West Bank Light and Coney Island Light to be 032°. The variation in this area is 11°.2 W. The vessel steams across the range on various compass headings, noting the compass direction of the range at the times of crossing, as shown below.

Required.—The deviation on each compass heading indicated.

Solution.—The magnetic bearing on the range is 032°+11°.2=043°.2.

CH °	MB Range °	CB Range °	Deviation °
000	043.2	032.9	10.3E
045	043.2	023.7	19.5E
090	043.2	031.9	11.3E
135	043.2	044.2	1.0W
180	043.2	048.5	5.3W
225	043.2	051.0	7.8W
270	043.2	055.6	12.4W
315	043.2	049.8	6.6W

The analysis of these results (art. 727) indicates a constant error of 1°.0E. The mean compass bearing is 042°.2, differing from the correct magnetic bearing by the amount of constant error.

Ranges are widely used to check the deviation on the heading in use as a vessel proceeds through pilot waters. In this manner several checks can be made without advance preparation as a vessel enters or leaves port.

735. Deviation by reciprocal bearings.—Another method of using magnetic bearings is by means of a compass on the beach. This method is particularly useful when no suitable distant object or range is available, or where it may not be practical to remain close to a given bearing line.

A reliable compass is taken ashore to a location which is free from magnetic disturbance. If the location is not marked by a conspicuous object, such as a beacon, flagpole, prominent tree, etc., a temporary marker should be erected. A staff with a flag or bunting should be adequate. The marker should be of sufficient size and nature to be conspicuous at the vessel. At suitable visual or radio signals from the vessel, bearings are observed simultaneously aboard the vessel and ashore. The bearings of the vessel observed by the shore compass are magnetic. The reciprocals of these can be considered magnetic bearings of the shore station from the vessel. The bearings measured aboard the vessel are compass bearings. The difference is deviation. To avoid confusion in the sequence of bearings, the time of each bearing is recorded. Timepieces should be synchronized before the start of observations.

Example.—Simultaneous bearings are observed by a shore compass and the standard compass aboard a vessel, as shown below.

Required.—The deviation of the standard compass on each heading.

Solution.—

CH	*Time*	*MB of vessel*	*MB of shore position*	*CB of shore position*	*Deviation*
°		°	°	°	°
000	1112	307	127	137	10W
045	1120	309	129	131	2W
090	1126	312	132	130	2E
135	1018	296	116	113	3E
180	1029	295	115	109	6E
225	1039	288	108	096	12E
270	1052	288	108	113	5W
315	1104	289	109	115	6W
		mean	118	118	

The analysis of these results indicates no constant deviation. This is further indicated by the fact that the means of the bearings aboard and ashore are equal.

Adjustment by Deflector

736. Principles involved.—As indicated in article 713, the magnetic field of a vessel causes deviation of a magnetic compass, and also alters its directive force, strengthening it on some headings and weakening it on others. *The purpose of compass adjustment is to neutralize the effect of the vessel's magnetic field on the compass. If this is done completely, all deviation is removed, and the directive force is the same on all headings.* The usual procedure, described earlier in this chapter, is to adjust by reducing or eliminating the deviation. By the deflector method, the various correctors are adjusted until the directive force is the same on all cardinal headings. Deviation is then a minimum.

The *relative* directive force on various headings is determined by means of an instrument called a **deflector.** Actual measurement is of the setting of the instrument when the compass card has been rotated or "deflected" through 90° under certain standard conditions. The units are arbitrary "deflector units" which are used only for comparison with readings on other headings.

The deflector method provides a quick adjustment with only four headings being needed, without need for bearings, azimuths, or comparison with other compasses. It is easy to use. However, it is not as thorough as the method described in article 729, and should not be used when the usual method is available. The deflector method makes no provision for determination of coefficient A (art. 716), the amount of Flinders bar needed, the setting of the heeling magnet, or the residual deviation. Coefficient E can be determined, but is usually ignored. The method has never been popular in the United States. It offers little or no advantage for a vessel equipped with a reliable gyrocompass.

737. Adjustment by deflector.—The preliminary steps of adjustment are the same as indicated in article 728, omitting those relating to peloruses and other compasses. Preparations having been completed, the adjustment should be carried out as follows:

1. Steady on heading 000° (or 180°) *by the compass being adjusted.* Note the heading by another compass and keep the vessel on this heading, steering by means of the second compass. Put the deflector in place over the first compass, and deflect the compass card 90°. Record the reading on the deflector scale, and remove the deflector.

2. Steady on heading 090° (or 270°) by the compass being adjusted, and follow the procedure of step 1.

3. Steady on heading 180° (000° if 180° was used in step 1) by the compass being adjusted, and determine the deflector reading by the procedure of step 1. Leave the deflector in place and set it to the mean of the readings on headings 000° and 180°. Adjust the fore-and-aft permanent magnets until the deflection is 90°. This corrects for coefficient B, and the deflector readings on compass headings 000° and 180° should now be the same. Remove the deflector.

4. Steady on heading 270° (090° if 270° was used in step 2)by the compass being adjusted, and determine the deflector reading by the procedure of step 1. Leave the deflector in place and set it to the mean of the readings on headings 090° and 270°. Adjust the athwartship permanent magnets until the deflection is 90°. This corrects for coefficient C, and the deflector readings on compass headings 090° and 180° should now be the same.

5. Without changing the heading, set the deflector to the mean of the N–S and E–W means. Adjust the quadrantal correctors until the deflection is 90°. This corrects for coefficient D, and the deflector readings on all cardinal headings should be the same. Remove the deflector.

Adjustment is now complete. It can be checked by repeating the five steps, a procedure which is particularly recommended if the difference between deflector readings on opposite headings is more than ten units. If means are available, and time permits, the vessel should be swung for residual deviation. If preferred, a heading of east or west can be used, reversing steps 1 and 2 and also steps 3 and 4.

This method is particularly useful when a quick adjustment is needed following some change that affects the magnetic environment of the compass.

738. The Kelvin deflector was developed in Great Britain by Sir William Thomson (Lord Kelvin). It consists essentially of two permanent magnets hinged like a pair of dividers, with opposite poles at the hinge. The magnets are mounted vertically over the center of the compass, with the hinged end on top. The separation of the lower ends can be varied by means of a screw. The amount of separation, indicated by a scale and vernier drums, is the reading used in the adjustment.

The deflecting force increases as the separation becomes greater. When the deflector is in place over the compass, the blue pole is in line with the north (red) end of the compass magnets, as indicated by a pointer. As the deflecting magnets are rotated around the vertical axis of the instrument, the compass card rotates in the same direction, but at a slower rate. The separation is adjusted until the rotation of the instrument is 170° when the deflection of the compass card is 90°. These are the standard conditions under which readings are made.

The Kelvin type deflector provides adjustment to an accuracy of 2° to 3°.

739. The De Colong deflector was developed in Russia and provides an accuracy of 0°5 to 1°0. Essentially, this instrument consists of two horizontal magnets which are perpendicular to each other. The small magnet is held in a fixed position close to the compass card. The large magnet is mounted in a small tray which can be moved up and down along a vertical spindle mounted over the center of the compass. The red end of this magnet is placed toward the north. When it is positioned so that the directive force is exactly neutralized, the small magnet causes the compass card to be deflected 90°. The height of the large magnet is the deflector reading, the scale being on the vertical spindle, and the index on the movable tray.

Provision is made for mounting the large magnet vertically, to measure the vertical force of the magnetic field at the compass. A separate scale is provided for this purpose. Additional magnets are generally provided for use near the magnetic equator, where the vertical intensity is very small.

In practice, a separate deflector is provided for each compass, and they are not interchangeable. By the addition of an auxiliary scale, the instrument could be made usable for any compass.

Degaussing Compensation

740. Degaussing.—As indicated in article 712, a steel vessel has a certain amount of permanent magnetism in its "hard" iron, and induced magnetism in its "soft" iron. Whenever two or more magnetic fields occupy the same space, the total field is the vector sum of the individual fields. Thus, within the effective region of the field of a vessel, the total field is the combined total of the earth's field and that due to the vessel. Consequently, the field due to earth's magnetism alone is altered or distorted due to the field of the vessel. This is indicated by a tendency of the lines of force to crowd into the metal of the vessel (art. 703), as shown in figure 741a.

Certain mines and other explosive devices are designed to be triggered by the magnetic influence of a vessel passing near them. It is therefore desirable to reduce to a practical minimum the magnetic field of a vessel. One method of doing this is to neutralize each component by means of an electromagnetic field produced by direct current of electricity in electric cables installed so as to form coils around the vessel. A unit sometimes used for measuring the strength of a magnetic field is the **gauss.** The reduction of the strength of a magnetic field decreases the number of gauss in that field. Hence, the process is one of **degaussing** the vessel.

When a vessel's degaussing coils are energized, the magnetic field of the vessel is completely altered. This introduces large deviation in the magnetic compasses. This is removed, as nearly as practicable, by introducing at each compass an equal and opposite force of the same type—one caused by direct current in a coil—for each component of the field due to the degaussing currents. This is called **compass compensation.** When there is a possibility of confusion with compass adjustment to neutralize the effects of the natural magnetism of the vessel, the expression **degaussing compensation** is used. Since the neutralization may not be perfect, a small amount of deviation due to degaussing may remain on certain headings. This is the reason for swinging ship twice—once with degaussing off and once with it on—and having two separate columns in the deviation table (fig. 710).

741. A vessel's magnetic signature.—A simplified diagram of the distortion of the earth's magnetic field in the vicinity of a steel vessel is shown in figure 741a. The strength of the field is indicated by the spacing of the lines, being stronger as the lines are closer together. If a vessel passes over a device for detecting and recording the strength of the magnetic field, a certain pattern is traced, as shown in figure 741b. Since the magnetic field of each vessel is different, each has a distinctive trace, known as its **magnetic signature.** The simplified signature shown in figure 741b is one that might result from an uncomplicated field such as that shown in figure 741a.

Several degaussing stations have been established to determine magnetic signatures and recommend the currents needed in the various degaussing coils. Since a vessel's induced magnetism varies with heading and magnetic latitude, the current settings of the coils which neutralize induced magnetism need to be changed to suit the conditions. A "degaussing folder" is provided each vessel to indicate the changes, and to give other pertinent information.

A vessel's permanent magnetism changes somewhat with time and the magnetic history of the vessel. Therefore, the information given in the degaussing folder should be checked from time to time by a return to the magnetic station.

742. Degaussing coils.—For degaussing purposes, the total field of the vessel is divided into three components: (1) vertical, (2) horizontal fore-and-aft, and (3) horizontal athwartships. The positive directions are considered downward, forward, and to port, respectively. These are the normal directions for a vessel headed north or east in north latitude. Each component is opposed by a separate degaussing field just strong enough to neutralize it. Ideally, when this has been done, the earth's field passes through the vessel smoothly and without distortion. The opposing degaussing fields are produced by direct current flowing in coils of wire. Each of the degaussing coils is placed so that the field it produces is directed to oppose one component of the ship's field.

The number of coils installed depends upon the magnetic characteristics of the vessel, and the degree of safety desired. The ship's permanent and induced magnetism may be neutralized separately so that control of induced magnetism can be varied as heading and latitude change, without disturbing the fields opposing the vessel's permanent field. The principal coils employed are the following:

Main (*M*) *coil.* The *M*-coil is placed horizontal, and completely encircles the vessel, usually at or near the waterline. Its function is to oppose the vertical component of the vessel's permanent and induced fields combined. Generally the induced field predominates. Current in the *M*-coil is varied or reversed according to the change of the *induced* component of the vertical field with latitude.

Forecastle (*F*) *and quarterdeck* (*Q*) *coils.* The *F*- and *Q*-coils are placed horizontal just below the forward and after thirds (or quarters), respectively, of the weather deck. The designation "*Q*" for quarterdeck is reminiscent of the days before World War II when the "quarterdeck" of naval vessels was aft along the ship's quarter. These coils, in which current can be individually adjusted, remove much of the fore-and-aft component of the ship's permanent and induced fields. More commonly, the combined *F*- and *Q*-coils consist of two parts; one part the *FP*- and *QP*-coils, to take care of the permanent fore-and-aft field, and the other part, the *FI*- and *QI*-coils, to neutralize the induced fore-and-aft field. Generally, the forward and after coils of each type are connected in series, forming a split-coil installation and designated *FP-PQ* coils and *FI-QI* coils. Current in the *FP-QP* coils is generally constant, but in the *FI-QI* coils is varied according to the heading and magnetic latitude of the vessel. In split-coil installations, the coil designations are often contracted to *P*-coil and *I*-coil.

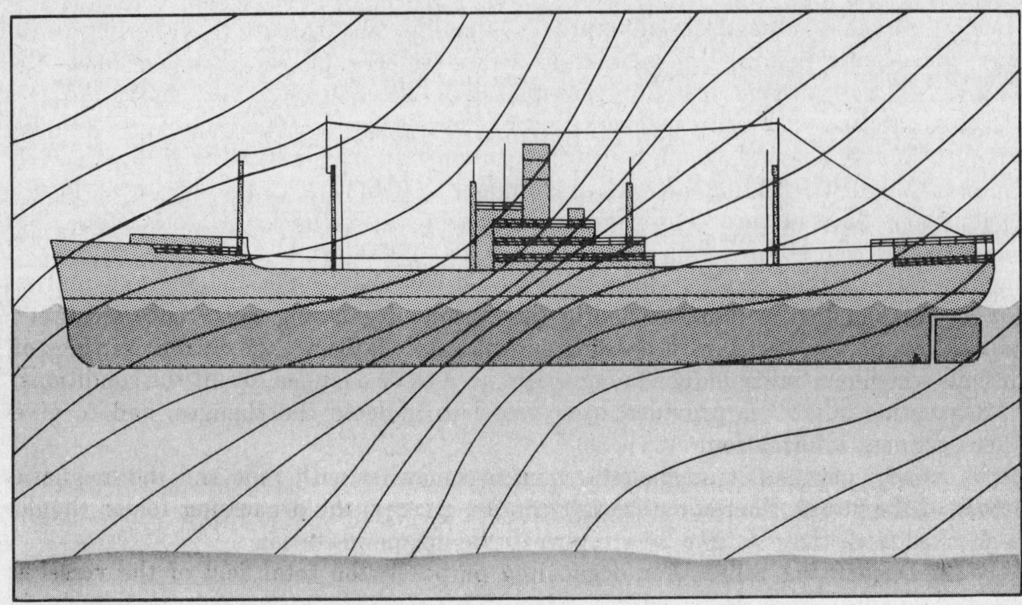

FIGURE 741a.—Simplified diagram of distortion of earth's magnetic field in the vicinity of a steel vessel.

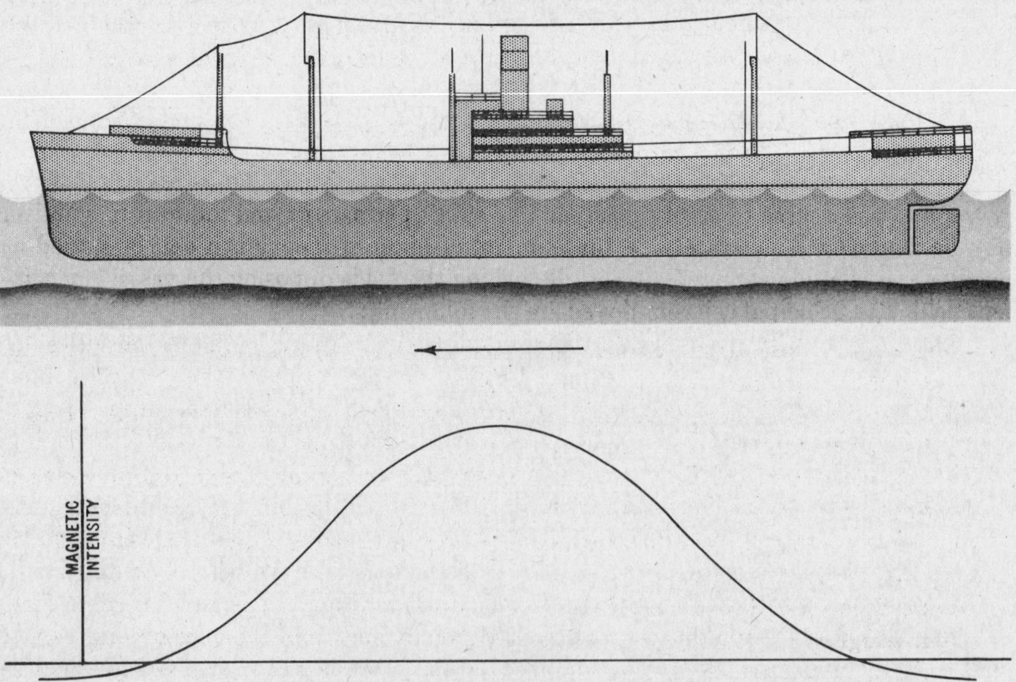

FIGURE 741b.—Simplified signature of vessel of figure 741a.

Longitudinal (*L*) *coil*. Better control of the fore-and-aft components, but at greater installation expense, is provided by placing a series of vertical, athwartships coils along the length of the ship. It is the *field*, not the coils, which is longitudinal. Current in an *L*-coil is varied as with the *FI-QI* coils. It is maximum on north and south headings, and zero on east and west headings.

Athwartship (*A*) *coil.* The *A*-coil is in a vertical fore-and-aft plane, thus producing a horizontal athwartship field which neutralizes the athwartship component of the vessel's field. In most vessels, this component of the permanent field is small and can be ignored. Since the *A*-coil neutralizes the induced field, primarily, the current is changed with magnetic latitude and with heading, being maximum on east or west headings, and zero on north or south headings.

The strength and direction of the current in each coil is indicated and adjusted at a control panel which is normally accessible to the navigator. Current may be controlled directly by rheostats at the control panel or remotely by push buttons which operate rheostats in the engine room.

Since degaussing fields oppose the vessel's fields, the positive directions of the degaussing fields are upward, aft, and to starboard. For positive fields in *M*, *F*, *FI*, *FP*, *Q*, *QI*, and *QP* coils, current flows forward on the starboard side of the vessel; and the north end of a small compass placed *above* any of these coils is deflected outboard. For a positive field in the *L*-coil, current flows upward on the starboard side, and the north end of a compass is deflected aft when placed *below* an upper, athwartship portion of the coil. For a positive field in the *A*-coil, current in the upper, fore-and-aft portion flows aft, and the north end of a compass is deflected to starboard when placed *below* this portion of the coil. The *FI-QI* coils are generally connected so that the field in the *FI*-coil is negative when that in the *QI*-coil is positive.

Appropriate values of the current in each coil are determined at a degaussing station, the various currents being adjusted until the vessel's signature is made as flat as possible. Recommended current values and directions for all headings and magnetic latitudes are set forth in the vessel's degaussing folder. This document is normally retained by the navigator, whose responsibility it is to see that the recommended settings are maintained whenever the degaussing system is energized.

743. Securing the degaussing system.—Unless the degaussing system is properly secured, residual magnetism may remain in the metal of the vessel. During degaussing compensation and at other times, as recommended in the degaussing folder, the "reversal" method is used. The steps in the reversal process are as follows:

1. Start with maximum degaussing current used since the system was last energized.
2. Decrease current to zero and increase it in the opposite direction to the same value as in step 1.
3. Decrease the current to zero and increase it to three-fourths maximum value in the original direction.
4. Decrease the current to zero and increase it to one-half maximum value in the opposite direction.
5. Decrease the current to zero and increase it to one-fourth maximum value in the original direction.
6. Decrease the current to zero and increase it to one-eighth maximum value in the opposite direction.
7. Decrease the current to zero and open switch.

744. Magnetic treatment of vessels.—In some instances, the degaussing can be made more effective by changing the magnetic characteristics of the vessel by a process known as **deperming.** Heavy cables are wound around the vessel in an athwartship direction, forming vertical loops around the longitudinal axis of the vessel. The loops are run beneath the keel, up the sides, and over the top of the weather deck at closely spaced equal intervals along the entire length of the vessel. Predetermined values of direct current are then passed through the coils. When the desired magnetic characteristics have been acquired, the cables are removed.

A vessel which does not have degaussing coils, or which has a degaussing system which is inoperative, can be given some temporary protection by a process known as **flashing.** A horizontal coil is placed around the outside of the vessel and energized with large predetermined values of direct current. When the vessel has acquired a vertical field of permanent magnetism of the correct magnitude and polarity to reduce to a minimum the resultant field below the vessel for the particular magnetic latitude involved, the cable is removed. This type protection is not as satisfactory as that provided by degaussing coils because it is not adjustable for various headings and magnetic latitudes, and also because the vessel's magnetism slowly readjusts itself following treatment.

During magnetic treatment it is a wise precaution to remove all magnetic compasses and Flinders bars from the vessel. Permanent adjusting magnets and quadrantal correctors are not materially affected, and need not be removed. If for any reason it is impractical to remove a compass, the cables used for magnetic treatment should be kept as far as practical from it.

745. Degaussing compensation.—The magnetic fields created by the degaussing coils would render the vessel's magnetic compasses useless unless compensated. This is accomplished by subjecting the compass to compensating fields along three mutually perpendicular axes. These fields are provided by small compensating coils adjacent to the compass. In nearly all installations, one of these coils, the heeling coil, is horizontal and on the same plane as the compass card. Current in the heeling coil is adjusted until the vertical component of the total degaussing field is neutralized. The other compensating coils provide horizontal fields perpendicular to each other. Current is varied in these coils until their resultant field is equal and opposite to the horizontal component of the degaussing field. In early installations, these horizontal fields were directed fore-and-aft and athwartships by placing the coils around the Flinders bar and the quadrantal spheres. Compactness and other advantages are gained by placing the coils on perpendicular axes extending 045°–225° and 315°–135° relative to the heading. A frequently used compensating installation, called the type "K," is shown in figure 745. It consists of a heeling coil extending completely around the top of the binnacle, four "intercardinal" coils, and three control boxes. The intercardinal coils are named for their positions relative to the compass when the vessel is on a heading of north, and also for the compass headings on which the current in the coils is adjusted to the correct amount for compensation. The NE–SW coils operate together as one set, and the NW–SE coils operate as another. One control box is provided for each set, and one for the heeling coil.

The compass compensating coils are connected to the power supply of the degaussing coils, and the currents passing through the compensating coils are adjusted by series resistances so that the compensating field is equal to the degaussing field. Thus, a change in the degaussing currents is accompanied by a proportional change in the compensating currents. Each coil has a separate winding for each degaussing circuit it compensates.

Degaussing compensation is carried out while the vessel is moored at the shipyard where the degaussing coils are installed. This is usually done by personnel of the yard, using the following procedure:

1. The compass is removed from its binnacle and a dip needle is installed in its place. The *M*-coil and heeling coil are then energized, and the current in the heeling coil is adjusted until the dip needle indicates the correct value for the magnetic latitude of the vessel. The system is then secured by the reversing process.

FIGURE 745.—Type "K" degaussing compensation installation.

2. The compass is restored to its usual position in the binnacle. By means of auxiliary magnets, the compass card is deflected until the compass magnets are parallel to one of the compensating coils or set of coils used to produce a horizontal field. The compass magnets are then perpendicular to the field produced by that coil. One of the degaussing circuits producing a horizontal field, and its compensating winding, are then energized, and the current in the compensating winding is adjusted until the compass reading returns to the value it had before the degaussing circuit was energized. The system is then secured by the reversing process. The process is repeated with each additional circuit used to create a horizontal field. The auxiliary magnets are then removed.

3. The auxiliary magnets are placed so that the compass magnets are parallel to the other compensating coils or set of coils used to produce a horizontal field. The procedure of step 2 is then repeated for each circuit producing a horizontal field.

When the vessel gets under way, it proceeds to a suitable maneuvering area. The vessel is then headed so that the compass magnets are parallel first to one compensating coil or set of coils and then the other, and any needed adjustment is made in the compensating circuits to reduce the error to a minimum. The vessel is then swung for residual deviation, first with degaussing off and then with degaussing on, and the correct current settings for each heading at the magnetic latitude of the vessel. From the values thus obtained, the "DG OFF" and "DG ON" columns of the deviation table (fig. 710) are filled in. If the results indicate satisfactory compensation, a record is made of the degaussing coil settings and the resistances, voltages, and currents in the compensating coil circuits. The control boxes are then secured.

Under normal operating conditions, the settings need not be changed unless changes are made in the degaussing system, or unless an alteration is made in the amount of Flinders bar or the setting of the quadrantal correctors. However, it is possible for a ground to occur in the coils or control box if the circuits are not adequately protected from sea water or other moisture. If this occurs, it should be reflected by a change in deviation with degaussing on, or by a decreased installation resistance. Under these conditions, compensation should be carried out again. If the compass is to be needed with degaussing on before the ship can be returned to a shipyard where the compensation can be made by experienced personnel, the compensation should be made at sea on the actual headings needed, rather than by deflection of the compass needles by magnets. More complete information related to this process is given in the degaussing folder.

If a vessel has been given magnetic treatment, its magnetic properties have been changed. This necessitates readjustment of each magnetic compass. This is best delayed for several days to permit stabilization of the magnetic characteristics of the vessel. If this cannot be delayed, the vessel should be swung again for residual deviation after a few days. Degaussing compensation should not be made until after compass adjustment has been completed.

Problems

711a. Fill in the blanks in the following:

	TC °	*V* °	*MC* °	*D* °	*CC* °	*CE* °
(1)	105	15E	—	5W	—	—
(2)	—	—	—	4E	215	14E
(3)	—	12W	—	—	067	7W
(5)	156	—	166	—	160	—
(5)	222	—	216	3W	—	—
(6)	009	—	357	—	—	10E
(7)	—	2W	—	6E	015	—
(8)	—	—	210	—	214	1W

Answers.—(1) MC 090°, CC 095°, CE 10°E; (2) TC 229°, V 10°E, MC 219°; (3) TC 060°, MC 072°, D 5°E; (4) V 10°W, D 6°E, CE 4°W; (5) V 6°E, CC 219°, CE 3°E; (6) V 12°E, D 2°W, CC 359°; (7) TC 019°, MC 021°, CE 4°E; (8) TC 213°, V 3°E, D 4°W.

711b. A vessel is on course 150° by compass in an area where the variation is 19°E. The deviation is as shown in figure 710. Degaussing is on.

Required.—(1) Deviation.

(2) Compass error.

(3) Magnetic heading.

(4) True heading.

Answers.—(1) D 1°E, (2) CE 20°E, (3) MH 151°, (4) TH 170°.

711c. A vessel is on course 055° by gyro and 041° by magnetic compass. The gyro error is 1°W. The variation is 15°E.

Required.—The deviation on this heading.

Answer.—D 2°W.

711d. A vessel is on course 177° by gyro. The gyro error is 0°.5E. A beacon bears 088° by magnetic compass in an area where variation is 11°W. The deviation is as shown in figure 710, degaussing off.

Required.—The true bearing of the beacon.

Answer.—TB 076°.

721a. A magnetic compass is adjusted on the magnetic equator, without any Flinders bar being used. The residual deviation on heading 090° magnetic is 1°E. Some days later, at latitude 37°N, dip 70°, the deviation on heading 090° is 12°W.

Required.—The length and location of Flinders bar required to restore a residual deviation of 1°E (using fig. 721, A) if the magnetic properties of the vessel are unchanged.

Answer.—Fifteen inches of Flinders bar forward of the compass.

721b. The deviation of a magnetic compass of a vessel on heading 270° magnetic is 2°E near Sydney, Australia (south magnetic latitude) and 12°W near Seattle, Wash. (north magnetic latitude). Near Sydney, H=0.258 and Z=0.51. Near Seattle, H=0.188 and Z=0.53. The shielding factor is 0.9.

Required.—The length of Flinders bar to use if (1) no Flinders bar is in place during observations, (2) 12 inches of Flinders bar is in place forward of the compass during observations.

Answers.—(1) 8¼ inches (8.5 inches by computation) of Flinders bar aft of the compass, (2) nine inches (8.8 inches by computation) of Flinders bar forward of the compass.

727. A magnetic compass which has not been adjusted has deviation on cardinal and intercardinal compass headings as follows:

Compass heading °	*Deviation* °	*Compass heading* °	*Deviation* °
000	2.0E	180	6.0E
045	20.5E	225	5.5W
090	18.5E	270	22.0W
135	8.0E	315	23.5W

On heading compass north the deviation is 6°.0W when the vessel heels 7° to starboard.

Required.—(1) The approximate value of each coefficient.

(2) The total deviation to be expected on compass heading 300°, with the vessel on an even keel.

(3) Heeling error on compass heading 060°, with a heel of 10°.

Answers.—(1) *A* (+)0°.5, *B* (+)20°.2, *C* (−)2°.0, *D* (+)7°.6, *E* (+)2°.9, *J* (−)1°.1; (2) d 26°.0W; (3) HE 5°.5.

730a. It is desired to place a vessel on magnetic heading west, using the magnetic steering compass. The deviation table for this compass is shown in figure 710. Degaussing is on.

Required.—Heading per steering compass (p stg c).

Answer.—$H_{p\ stg\ c}$ 272°.

730b. It is desired to place a vessel on magnetic heading south, using the gyrocompass. The variation in this area is 12°E, and the gyro error is 0°.5E.

Required.—Heading per gyrocompass.

Answer.—H_{pgc} 191°.5.

730c. It is desired to place a vessel on magnetic heading southeast in an area where the variation is 6°W. The true bearing for a distant object is 047°.

Required.—(1) The magnetic bearing of the object.

(2) The relative bearing of the object when the vessel is on the desired magnetic heading.

Answers.—(1) MB 053°, (2) RB 278°.

730d. The compass bearings of a distant object are as follows:

CH °	*CB* °	*CH* °	*CB* °
000	358	180	002
045	357	225	006
090	351	270	012
135	353	315	009

Required.—The magnetic bearing of the object, assuming no constant deviation (coefficient *A*).

Answer.—MB 001°.

730e. It is desired to place a vessel on magnetic heading east in an area where the variation is 13°E, and at a time when the computed true azimuth of the sun is 218°.

Required.—(1) The magnetic azimuth of the sun.

(2) The relative azimuth when the vessel is on the desired magnetic heading.

(3) The azimuth by a magnetic compass having deviation as shown in figure 710 (DG on).

(4) The azimuth by a gyrocompass having a gyro error of 1°W.

Answers.—(1) MZn 205°, (2) RZn 115°, (3) CZn 202°, (4) Zn_{pgc} 219°.

732. A vessel is being maneuvered to determine the residual deviation of a magnetic compass. The gyrocompass, which has an error of 1°E, is used for placing the vessel on the magnetic headings indicated below. Variation in the area is 7°.8W. The following readings are obtained:

MH °	*CH* °	*MH* °	*CH* °
000	000.0	180	180.1
045	044.1	225	225.8
090	088.5	270	271.4
135	134.2	315	315.9

Required.—Gyro heading and deviation on each magnetic heading.

Answers.—

MH °	H_{pgc} °	*Dev.* °	*MH* °	H_{pgc} °	*Dev.* °
000	351.2	0.0	180	171.2	0.1W
045	036.2	0.9E	225	216.2	0.8W
090	081.2	1.5E	270	261.2	1.4W
135	126.2	0.8E	315	306.2	0.9W

733. A vessel is being swung for residual deviation during the period and at the place for which the curve of magnetic azimuths of figure 731 has been constructed. The following readings are obtained:

CH °	*Time* h m s	*CZn* °	*CH* °	*Time* h m s	*CZn* °
000	7 56 13	73.7	180	8 16 36	75.2
045	8 01 22	72.9	225	8 22 19	76.8
090	8 04 55	71.9	270	8 27 12	78.7
135	8 11 01	74.0	315	8 33 27	77.2

Required.—Deviation on each compass heading.
Answers.—

CH °	*Deviation* °	*CH* °	*Deviation* °
000	0.1E	180	0.0
045	1.3E	225	1.2W
090	2.6E	270	2.8W
135	0.9E	315	0.8W

734. A vessel being swung for residual deviation crosses a range on various compass headings as indicated below, the compass bearing of the range being observed at each crossing. The true direction of the range is 255°. The variation in the vicinity is 24°.5E.

CH °	*CB* °	*CH* °	*CB* °
000	230.3	180	230.6
045	228.7	225	232.4
090	227.4	270	233.8
135	228.0	315	232.3

Required.—Deviation on each compass heading.
Answers.—

CH °	*Deviation* °	*CH* °	*Deviation* °
000	0.2E	180	0.1W
045	1.8E	225	1.9W
090	3.1E	270	3.3W
135	2.5E	315	1.8W

735. Bearings of a vessel are taken by means of a compass ashore, and simultaneous bearings of the shore position are taken from the vessel, as follows:

CH °	*CB of shore position* °	*MB of vessel* °	*CH* °	*CB of shore position* °	*MB of vessel* °
000	020	198	180	003	184
045	013	189	225	009	194
090	004	174	270	013	204
135	001	172	315	017	205

Required.—(1) Deviation on each heading.
(2) The value of coefficient *A*.
Answers.—
(1)

CH °	*Deviation* °	*CH* °	*Deviation* °
000	2W	180	1E
045	4W	225	5E
090	10W	270	11E
135	9W	315	8E

(2) Coefficient *A* is zero.

CHAPTER VIII

DEAD RECKONING

801. Introduction.—Dead reckoning (**DR**) is the determination of position by advancing a known position for courses and distances. It is reckoning relative to something stationary or "dead" in the water, and hence applies to courses and speeds *through the water*. Because of leeway due to wind, inaccurate allowance for compass error, imperfect steering, or error in measuring speed, the actual motion through the water is seldom determined with complete accuracy. In addition, if the water itself is in motion, the course and speed over the bottom differ from those through the water. It is good practice to use the true course *steered* and the best determination of *measured* speed, which is normally speed *through the water*, for dead reckoning. Hence, geographically, a **dead reckoning position** is an approximate one which is corrected from time to time as the opportunity presents itself. Although of less than the desired accuracy, dead reckoning is the only method by which a position can be determined at *any* time and therefore might be considered *basic* navigation, with all other methods only appendages to provide means for correcting the dead reckoning. The prudent navigator keeps his direction- and speed- or distance-measuring instruments in top condition and accurately calibrated, for his dead reckoning is no more accurate than his measurement of these elements.

If a navigator can accurately assess the disturbing elements introducing geographical errors into his dead reckoning, he can determine a better position than that established by dead reckoning alone. This is properly called an **estimated position** (**EP**). It may be established either by applying an estimated correction to a dead reckoning position, or by estimating the course and speed being made good over the bottom. The expression "dead reckoning" is sometimes applied loosely to such reckoning, but it is better practice to keep this "estimated reckoning" distinct from dead reckoning, if for no other reason than to provide a basis for evaluating the accuracy of one's estimates. When good information regarding current, wind, etc., is available, it should be used, but the practice of applying corrections based upon information of uncertain accuracy is, at best, questionable, and may introduce an error. Estimates should be based upon judgment and experience. Positional information which is incomplete or of uncertain accuracy may be available to assist in making the estimate. However, before adequate experience is gained, one should be cautious in applying corrections, for the estimates of the inexperienced are often quite inaccurate.

Dead reckoning not only provides means for continuously establishing an approximate position, but also is of assistance in determining times of sunrise and sunset, the celestial bodies available for observation, the predicted availability of electronic aids to navigation, the suitability and interpretation of soundings for checking position, the predicted times of making landfalls or sighting lights, estimates of arrival times, and in evaluating the reliability and accuracy of position-determining information. Because of the importance of accurate dead reckoning, a careful log is kept of all courses and speeds, times of all changes, and compass errors. These may be recorded directly in the log or first in a **navigator's notebook** for later recording in the log, but whatever the form, a careful record is important.

Modern navigators almost invariably keep their dead reckoning by plotting directly on the chart or plotting sheet, drawing lines to represent the direction and distance of travel and indicating dead reckoning and estimated positions from time to time. This method is simple and direct. Large errors are often apparent as inconsistencies in an otherwise regular plot. Before the advent of power vessels, when frequent course and speed changes were common, and when charts were sometimes of questionable accuracy, it was common practice to keep the dead reckoning mathematically by one, or a combination, of the "sailings" (chapter IX). Except for great-circle sailing, and occasionally composite and Mercator sailings, these are of little more than historical interest to modern navigators, other than those of small boats.

In determining distance run in a given time, one may find table 7 useful.

802. Plotting position on the chart.—A position is usually expressed in units of latitude and longitude, generally to the nearest 0ʹ.1, but it may be expressed as bearing and distance from a known position, such as a landmark or aid to navigation.

To plot a position on a Mercator chart, or to determine the coordinates of a point on such a chart, proceed as follows:

To plot a position when its latitude and longitude are known: Mark the given latitude on a convenient latitude scale along a meridian, being careful to note the unit of the smallest division on the scale. Place a straightedge at this point and parallel to a parallel of latitude (perpendicular to a meridian). Holding the straightedge in place, set one point of a pair of dividers at the given longitude on the longitude scale at the top or bottom of the chart (or along any parallel) and the other at a convenient printed meridian. Without changing the spread of the dividers, place one point on the same printed meridian at the edge of the straightedge, and the second point at the edge of the straightedge in the direction of the given longitude. This second point is at the given position. *Lightly* prick the chart. Remove first the straightedge and then the dividers, watching the point to be sure of identifying it. Make a dot at the point, enclose it with a small circle or square as appropriate (art. 805), and label it. If the dividers are set to the correct spread for longitude *before* the latitude is marked, one point of the dividers can be used to locate the latitude and place the straightedge, if one is careful not to disturb the setting of the dividers.

To determine the coordinates of a point on the chart: Place a straightedge at the given point and parallel to a parallel of latitude. Read the latitude where the straightedge crosses a latitude scale. Keeping the straightedge in place, set one leg of a pair of dividers at the given point and the other at the intersection of the straightedge and a convenient printed meridian. Without changing the spread of the dividers, place one end on a longitude scale, at the same printed meridian, and the other point on the scale, in the direction of the given point. Read the longitude at this second point.

Several variations of these procedures may suggest themselves. That method which seems most natural and is least likely to result in error should be used.

803. Measuring direction on the chart.—Since the Mercator chart, commonly used by the marine navigator, is *conformal* (art. 302), directions and angles are correctly represented. It is customary to orient the chart with 000° (north) at the top; other directions are in their correct relations to north and each other.

As an aid in measuring direction, **compass roses** are placed at convenient places on the chart or plotting sheet. A desired direction can be measured by placing a straightedge along the line from the center of a compass rose to the circular graduation representing the desired direction. The straightedge is then in the desired direction, which may be transferred to any other part of the chart by parallel motion, as by parallel rulers or two triangles (art. 603). The direction between two points is determined by transferring that direction to a compass rose. If a drafting machine (art. 606) or some form of plotter (art. 605) or protractor (art. 604) is used, measurement can be made directly at the desired point, without using the compass rose.

Measurement of direction, whether or not by compass rose, can be made at any convenient place on a Mercator chart, since meridians are parallel to each other and a line making a desired angle with any one makes the same angle with all others. Such a line is a **rhumb line,** the kind commonly used for course lines, except in polar regions. For direction on a chart having nonparallel meridians, measurement can be made at the meridian involved if the chart is conformal, or by special technique if it is not conformal. The only nonconformal chart commonly used by navigators is the gnomonic, and instructions for measuring direction on this chart are usually given on the chart itself.

Compass roses for both true and magnetic directions may be given. A drafting machine can be oriented to any reference direction—true, magnetic, compass, or grid. When a plotter or protractor is used for measuring an angle with respect to a meridian, the resulting direction is true unless other than true meridians are used. For most purposes of navigation it is good practice to plot true directions only, and to label them in true coordinates.

804. Measuring distance on the chart.—The length of a line on a chart is usually measured in nautical miles, to the nearest 0.1 mile. For this purpose it is customary to use the latitude scale, considering one minute of latitude equal to one nautical mile. The error introduced by this assumption is not great over distances normally measured. It is maximum near the equator or geographical poles. Near the equator a ship traveling 180 miles by measurement on the chart would cover only 179 miles over the earth. Near the poles a run of 220 miles by chart measurement would equal 221 miles over the earth.

Since the latitude scale on a Mercator chart expands with increased latitude, measurement should be made at approximately the mid latitude. For a chart covering a relatively small area, such as a harbor chart, this precaution is not important because of the slight difference in scale over the chart. On such charts a separate mile scale may be given, and it may safely be used over the entire chart. However, habit is strong, and mistakes can probably be avoided by *always* using the mid latitude.

For long distances the line should be broken into a number of parts or *legs*, each one being measured at its mid latitude. The length of a line that should be measured in a single step varies with latitude, decreasing in higher latitudes. No realistic numerical value can be given, since there are too many considerations. With experience a navigator determines this for himself. On the larger scale charts this is not a problem because the usual dividers used for this purpose will not span an excessively long distance.

In measuring distance, the navigator spans with his dividers the length of the line to be measured and then, without altering the setting, transfers this length to the latitude scale, carefully noting the graduations so as to avoid an error in reading. This precaution is needed because of the difference from chart to chart. In measuring a desired length along a line, the navigator spans this length on the latitude scale opposite the line and then transfers his dividers to the line, without changing the setting. For a long line the navigator sets his dividers to some convenient distance and steps off the line, counting the number of steps, multiplying this by the length of the step, and adding any remainder. If the line extends over a sufficient spread of latitude to make scale difference a factor, he resets his dividers to the scale for the approximate mid latitude of each leg. The distance so measured is the length of the rhumb line.

For measuring distance on a nearly-constant-scale chart, such as the Lambert conformal, the mid-latitude precaution is usually unnecessary. Such charts generally have a mile scale independent of the latitude scale. On a gnomonic chart a special procedure is needed, and this is usually explained on the chart.

805. Plotting and labeling the course line and positions.—**Course** is the intended horizontal direction of travel through the water. A **course line** is a line extending in the direction of the course. From a known position of the ship the course line is drawn in the direction indicated by the course. It is good practice to label all lines and points of significance as they are drawn, for an unlabeled line or point can easily be misinterpreted later. Any simple, clear, logical, unambiguous system of labels is suitable. The following is widely used and might well be considered standard.

Label a course line with direction and speed. *Above* the course line place a capital C followed by three figures to indicate the course steered. It is customary to label and steer courses to the nearest whole degree, although they are generally computed to the nearest 0°.1. The course label should indicate *true* direction, starting with 000° at true north and increasing clockwise through 360°. *Below* the course line, and under the direction label, place a capital S followed by figures representing the speed in knots. Since the course is *always* given in degrees true and the speed in knots, it is not necessary to indicate the units or the reference direction (fig. 805).

FIGURE 805.—A course line with labels.

A point to be labeled is enclosed by a small circle in the case of a **fix** (an accurate position determined without reference to any former position), a semicircle in the case of a dead reckoning position, and by a small square in the case of an estimated position. It is labeled with the time, usually to the nearest minute; the nature of the position is indicated by the symbol used. Time is usually expressed in four figures without punctuation, on a 24-hour basis. Zone time is usually used, but Greenwich mean time may be employed. A course line is a succession of an infinite number of dead reckoning positions. Only selected points are labeled.

The times of fixes and estimated positions are placed horizontally; the times of dead reckoning positions are placed at an angle to the course line.

806. Dead reckoning by plot.—As a vessel clears a harbor and proceeds out to sea, the navigator obtains one last good fix while identifiable landmarks are still available. This is called **taking departure,** and the position determined is called the **departure.** Piloting (ch. X) comes to an end and the course is set for the open sea. The course line is drawn and labeled, and some future position is indicated as a DR position. The number of points selected for labeling depends primarily upon the judgment and individual preference of the navigator. It is good practice to label each point where a change of course or speed occurs. If such changes are frequent, no additional points need be labeled. With infrequent changes, it is good practice to label points at some regular interval, as every hour. From departure, the dead reckoning plot continues unbroken until a new well-established position is obtained, when both DR and fix are shown. The fix serves as the start of a new dead reckoning plot. Although estimated positions are shown, it is generally not good practice to begin a new DR at these points.

A typical dead reckoning plot is shown in figure 806, indicating procedures both when there are numerous changes of course and speed and when there is a long continuous course. It is assumed that no fix is obtained after the initial one at 0800 on September 8. Note that course lines are not extended beyond their limits of usefulness, One should keep a neat plot and leave no doubt as to the meaning of each line and

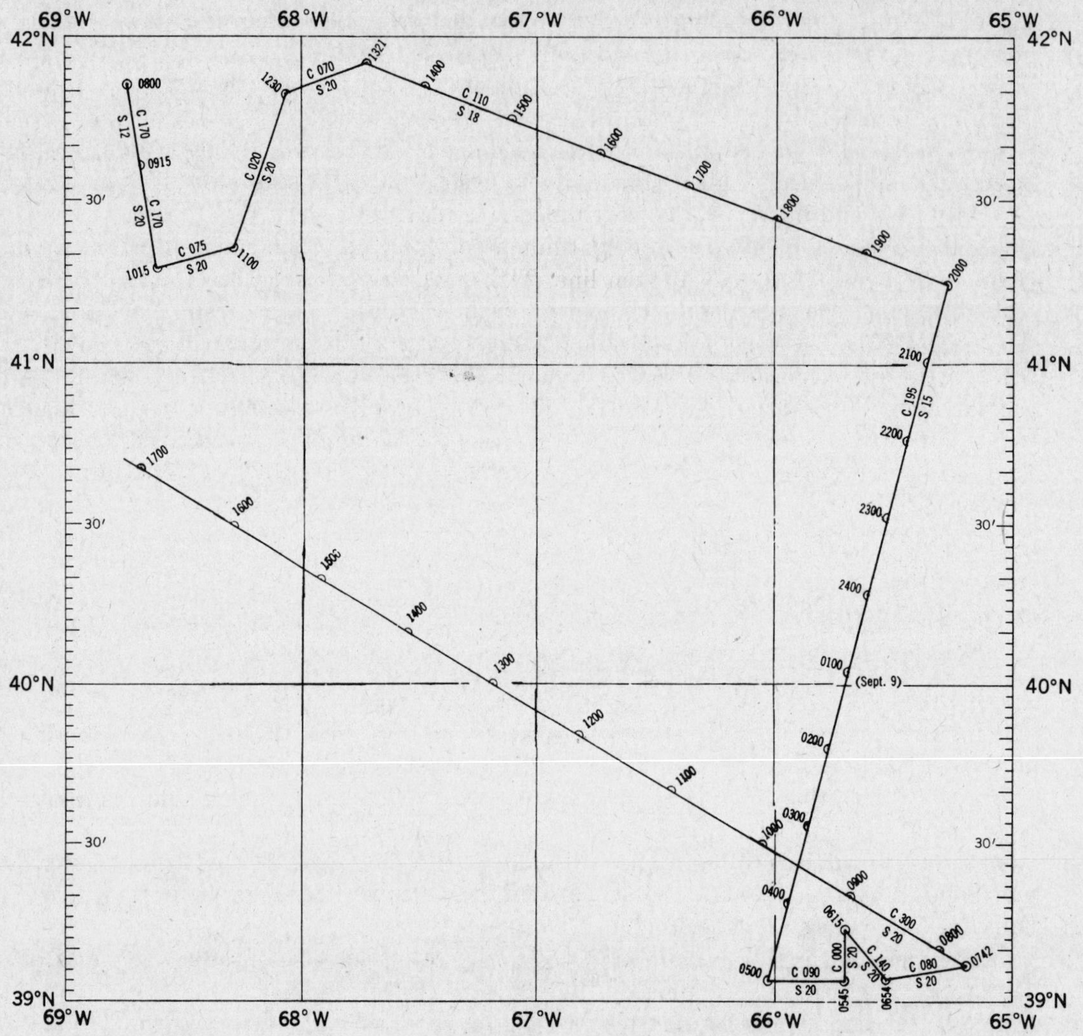

FIGURE 806.—A typical dead reckoning plot.

marked point. *A neat, accurate plot is the mark of a good navigator*. The plot of the **intended track** (art. 207) should be kept extended to some future time. A good navigator is always ahead of his ship. In shoal water or when near the shore, aids to navigation, dangers, etc., it is customary to keep the dead reckoning plot on a chart. A chart overprinted with a lattice of a radionavigation system may be used. But on the open sea, with only dead reckoning and celestial navigation available, it is good practice to use a plotting sheet (art. 323).

807. Current.—Water in essentially horizontal motion over the surface of the earth is called **current.** The direction in which the water is moving is called the **set,** and the speed is called the **drift.** In navigation it is customary to use the term "current" to include all factors introducing geographical error in the dead reckoning, whether their immediate effects are on the vessel or the water. When a fix is obtained, one assumes that the current has set *from* the DR position at the same time *to* the fix, and that the drift is equal to the distance in miles between these positions, divided by the number of hours since the last fix. This is true regardless of the number of changes of course or speed since the last fix.

If set and drift since the last fix are known, or can be estimated, a better position can be obtained by applying a correction to that obtained by dead reckoning. This is conveniently done by drawing a straight line in the direction of the set for a distance equal to the drift multiplied by the number of hours since the last fix, as shown in figure 805. The direction of a straight line from the last fix to the EP is the estimated **course made good,** and the length of this line divided by the time is the estimated **speed made good.** The course and speed actually made good over the ground are called the **course over the ground** (**COG**) and **speed over the ground** (**SOG**)**,** respectively.

As shown in figure 805, the straight line drawn from the 0900 DR in the direction of the set is constructed as a broken line. The capital S above the line represents the set; the capital D below the line represents the drift.

If a current is setting in the same direction as the course, or its reciprocal, the course over the ground is the same as that through the water. The effect on the speed can be found by simple arithmetic. If the course and set are in the same direction, the speeds are added; if in opposite directions, the smaller is subtracted from the larger. This situation is not unusual when a ship encounters a tidal current while entering or leaving port. If a ship is *crossing* a current, solution can be made graphically by vector diagram since velocity over the ground is the vector sum of velocity *through* the water and velocity *of* the water. Although *distances* can be used, it is generally easier to use *speeds*.

Example 1.—A ship on course 080°, speed ten knots, is steaming through a current having an estimated set of 140° and drift of two knots.

Required.—Estimated course and speed made good.

Solution (fig. 807a).—(1) From *A*, any convenient point, draw *AB*, the course and speed of the ship, in direction 080°, for a distance of ten miles.

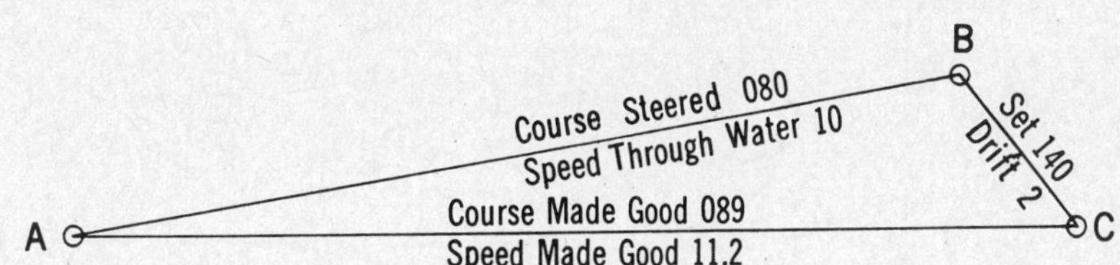

FIGURE 807a.—Finding course and speed made good through a current.

(2) From *B* draw *BC*, the set and drift of the current, in direction 140°, for a distance of two miles.

(3) The direction and length of *AC* are the estimated course and speed made good. Determine these by measurement.

Answers.—Estimated course made good 089°, estimated speed made good 11.2 kn.

If it is required to find the course to steer at a given speed to make good a desired course, plot the current vector from the origin, *A*, instead of from *B*.

Example 2.—The captain desires to make good a course of 095° through a current having a set of 170° and a drift of 2.5 knots, using a speed of 12 knots.

Required.—The course to steer and the speed made good.

Solution (fig. 807b).—(1) From *A*, any convenient point, draw line *AB* extending in the direction of the course to be made good, 095°.

(2) From *A* draw *AC*, the set and drift of the current.

(3) Using C as a center, swing an arc of radius CD, the speed through the water (12 knots), intersecting line AB at D.

(4) Measure the direction of line CD, 083°5. This is the course to steer.

(5) Measure the length AD, 12.4 knots. This is the speed made good.

Answers.—Course to steer 083°5, speed made good 12.4 kn.

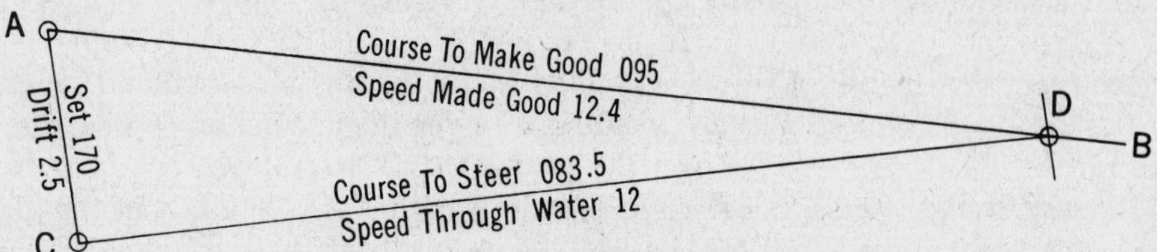

FIGURE 807b.—Finding the course to steer at a given speed to make good a given course through a current.

If it is required to find the course to steer and the speed to use to make good a desired course and speed, proceed as follows:

Example 3.—The captain desires to make good a course of 265° and a speed of 15 knots through a current having a set of 185° and a drift of three knots.

Required.—The course to steer and the speed to use.

Solution (fig. 807c).—(1) From A, any convenient point, draw AB in the direction of the course to be made good, 265°, and for a length equal to the speed to be made good, 15 knots.

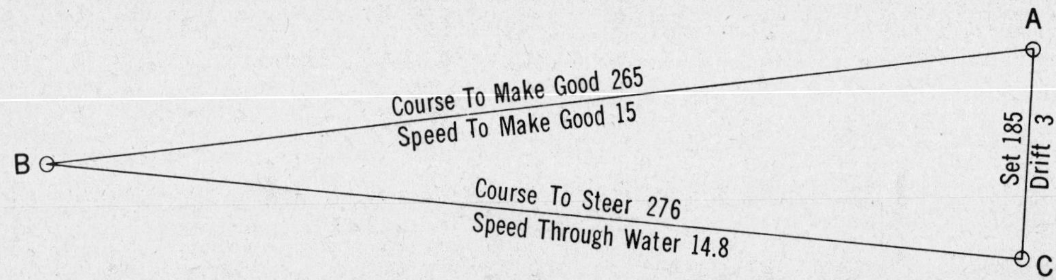

FIGURE 807c.—Finding the course to steer and the speed to use to make good a given course and speed through a current.

(2) From A draw AC, the set and drift of the current.

(3) Draw a straight line from C to B. The direction of this line, 276°, is the required course to steer; and the length, 14.8 knots, is the required speed.

Answers.—Course to steer 276°, speed to use 14.8 kn.

Such vector solutions can be made to any convenient scale and at any convenient place, such as the center of a compass rose, an unused corner of the plotting sheet, a separate sheet, or directly on the plot.

808. Leeway is the leeward motion of a vessel due to wind. It may be expressed as distance, speed, or angular difference between course steered and course through the water. However expressed, its amount varies with the speed and relative direction of the wind, type of vessel, amount of freeboard, trim, speed of the vessel, state of the sea, and depth of water. If information on the amount of leeway to be expected under various conditions is not available for the type vessel involved, it should be determined by observation. When sufficient data have been collected, suitable tables or graphs can be made for quick and convenient estimate. The accuracy of the information should be checked whenever convenient, and corrections made when sufficient evidence indicates the need.

Leeway is most conveniently applied by adding its effect to that of current and other elements introducing geographical error in the dead reckoning. It is customary to consider the combined effect of all such elements as current, and to make allowance for this as explained in article 807. In sailing ship days it was common practice to consider leeway in terms of its effect upon the course only, and to apply it as a correction in the same manner that variation and deviation are applied. While this method has merit even with power vessels, it is generally considered inferior to that of considering leeway as part of current.

809. Automatic dead reckoning.—Several types of devices are in use for performing automatically all or part of the dead reckoning. Perhaps the simplest is the automatic **course recorder,** which provides a graphical record of the various courses steered. In its usual form this device is controlled by the gyrocompass, and so indicates gyro courses.

Dead reckoning equipment receives inputs from the compass, usually the gyrocompass, and a mechanical log or engine revolution counter. It determines *change* in latitude and longitude, the latter by first determining departure and then mechanically multiplying this by the secant of the latitude. The device is provided with counters on which latitude and longitude can be set. As the vessel proceeds, the changes are then mechanically added to or subtracted from these readings to provide a continuous, instantaneous indication of the dead reckoning position. The navigator or an assistant reads these dials at intervals, usually each hour, and records the values in a notebook. Most models of dead reckoning equipment are provided, also, with a tracer for keeping a graphical record of dead reckoning in the form of a plot by moving a pencil or pen across a chart or plotting sheet. This part of the device is called a **dead reckoning tracer.** Whatever the form, dead reckoning equipment is a great convenience, particularly when a ship is maneuvering. However, such mechanical equipment is subject to possible failure. The prudent navigator keeps a hand plot and uses the dead reckoning equipment as a check. In navigation it is never wise to rely upon a single method if a second method is available as a check.

If it were possible to measure, with high accuracy, the direction and distance traveled *with respect to the earth*, an accurate geographical position could be known at all times. The two methods most commonly used are (1) doppler and (2) inertial. By the **doppler** method one or more beams of acoustic energy are directed downward at an angle. The return echo from the bottom is of a slightly different frequency due to the motion of the craft. The amount of the change, or doppler, is proportional to the speed. By proper selection of beams, it is possible to measure speed in a lateral direction as well as in a forward direction. Distance can be determined by mechanical or electronic integration of these measurements, and this can be converted into position. By the **inertial** method, accelerometers measure the acceleration in various directions, and by double integration this is converted to distance, from which position can be determined. Either of these methods can provide considerable accuracy over a period of several hours, but the error increases with time.

Problems

806a. Draw a small area plotting sheet by either method explained in article 324, covering the area between latitude 32°-34°N and longitude 118°-122°W. Plot the following points:

A	L	33°49.′1N	*C*	L	33°38.′0N
	λ	120°52.′0W		λ	118°38.′6W
B	L	32°17.′4N	*D*	L	32°30.′6N
	λ	121°28.′0W		λ	118°36.′2W

Required.—(1) The bearings of *B*, *C*, and *D* from *A*.

(2) The course and distance of *A*, *B*, and *C* from *D*.

Answers.—(1) B_{AB} 198.°5, B_{AC} 095.°5, B_{AD} 124°; (2) C_{DA} 304°, D_{DA} 138.8 mi., C_{DB} 264.°5, D_{DB} 145.7 mi., C_{DC} 358.°5, D_{DC} 67.2 mi.

806b. Use the plot of problem 806a. A ship starts from *A* at 1200, and steams as follows:

Time	*Course*	*Speed*
1200		
	120°	15 kn.
1330		
	240°	15 kn.
1500		
	240°	17 kn.
1800		
	125°	20 kn.
2000		
	090°	20 kn.
2300		
	015°	10 kn.
0500		

Plot and label the dead reckoning course line and DR positions.

Required.—(1) The dead reckoning position of the ship at 0500.

(2) The bearing and distance of *D* from the 2300 DR position.

(3) The course and distance from the 0500 DR position to *C*.

(4) Estimated time of arrival (ETA), to the nearest minute, at *C* if the ship proceeds directly from the 0500 DR position at 20 knots.

Answers.—(1) 0500 DR: L 33°35.′1N, λ 119°35.′8W; (2) B 096°, D 66.0 mi.; (3) C 086°, D 48.1 mi.; (4) ETA 0724.

807a. A ship on course 120°, speed 12 knots, is steaming through a current having a set of 350° and a drift of 1.5 knots.

Required.—Course and speed made good.

Answers.—Course made good 114°, speed made good 11.1 kn.

807b. The captain desires to make good a course of 180° through a current having a set of 090° and a drift of two knots, using a speed of 11 knots.

Required.—The course to steer and the speed made good.

Answers.—Course to steer 190.°5, speed made good 10.8 kn.

807c. The captain desires to make good a course of 325° and a speed of 20 knots through a current having a set of 270° and a drift of one knot.

Required.—The course to steer and the speed to use.

Answers.—Course to steer 327°, speed to use 19.4 kn.

CHAPTER IX

THE SAILINGS

901. Introduction.—Dead reckoning involves the determination of position by means of course and distance from a known position. A closely related problem is that of finding the course and distance from one point to another. Although both of these problems are customarily solved by plotting directly on the chart, it occasionally becomes desirable to solve by computation, frequently by logarithms or traverse table. The various methods of solution are collectively called the **sailings.**

The various kinds of sailings are:

1. **Plane sailing** is a method of solving the various problems involving a single course and distance, difference of latitude, and departure, in which the earth, or that part traversed, is regarded as a plane surface. Hence, the method provides solution for latitude of the point of arrival, but not for longitude of this point, one of the spherical sailings being needed for this problem. Because of the basic assumption that the earth is flat, this method should not be used for distances of more than a few hundred miles.
2. **Traverse sailing** combines the plane sailing solutions when there are two or more courses. This sailing is a method of determining the equivalent course and distance made good by a vessel steaming along a series of rhumb lines.
3. **Parallel sailing** is the interconversion of departure and difference of longitude when a vessel is proceeding due east or due west. This was a common occurrence when the sailings were first employed several hundred years ago, but only an incidental situation now.
4. **Middle-** (or **mid-**) **latitude sailing** involves the use of the mid or mean latitude for converting departure to difference of longitude when the course is not due east or due west and it is assumed such course is steered at the mid latitude.
5. **Mercator sailing** provides a mathematical solution of the plot as made on a Mercator chart. It is similar to plane sailing, but uses meridional difference and difference of longitude in place of difference of latitude and departure, respectively.
6. **Great-circle sailing** involves the solution of courses, distances, and points along a great circle between two points, the earth being regarded as a sphere.
7. **Composite sailing** is a modification of great-circle sailing to limit the maximum latitude.

902. Rhumb lines and great circles.—The principal advantage of a **rhumb line** is that it maintains constant true direction. A ship following the rhumb line between two places does not change true course. A rhumb line makes the same angle with all meridians it crosses and appears as a straight line on a Mercator chart. It is adequate for most purposes of navigation, bearing lines (except long ones, as those obtained by radio) and course lines both being plotted on a Mercator chart as rhumb lines, except in high latitudes. The equator and the meridians are great circles, but may be considered special cases of the rhumb line. For any other case, the difference between the rhumb line and the great circle connecting two points increases (1) as the latitude increases, (2) as the difference of latitude between the two points decreases, and (3) as the difference of longitude increases. It becomes very great for two places widely separated on the same parallel of latitude far from the equator.

A **great circle** is the intersection of the surface of a sphere and a plane through the center of the sphere. It is the largest circle that can be drawn on the surface of the sphere, and is the shortest distance, along the surface, between any two points on the sphere. Any two points are connected by only one great circle unless the points are antipodal (180° apart on the earth), and then an infinite number of great circles passes through them. Thus, two points on the same meridian are not joined by any great circle other than the meridian, unless the two points are antipodal. If they are the poles, *all* meridians pass through them. Every great circle bisects every other great circle. Thus, except for the equator, every great circle lies half in the Northern Hemisphere and half in the Southern Hemisphere. Any two points 180° apart on a great circle have the same latitude numerically, but contrary names, and are 180° apart in longitude. The point of greatest latitude is called the **vertex.** For each great circle there is one of these in each hemisphere, 180° apart. At these points the great circle is tangent to a parallel of latitude, and hence its direction is due east-west. On each side of these vertices the direction changes progressively until the intersection with the equator is reached, 90° away, where the great circle crosses the equator at an angle equal to the latitude of the vertex. As the great circle crosses the equator, its change in direction reverses, again approaching east-west, which it reaches at the next vertex.

On a Mercator chart a great circle appears as a sine curve extending equal distances each side of the equator. The rhumb line connecting any two points of the great circle on the same side of the equator is a chord of the curve, being a straight line nearer the equator than the great circle. Along any intersecting meridian the great circle crosses at a higher latitude than the rhumb line. If the two points are on opposite sides of the equator, the direction of curvature of the great circle relative to the rhumb line changes at the equator. The rhumb line and great circle may intersect each other, and if the points are equal distances on each side of the equator, the intersection takes place at the equator.

903. Great-circle sailing is used when it is desired to take advantage of the shorter distance along the great circle between two points, rather than to follow the longer rhumb line. The arc of the great circle between the points is called the **great-circle track.** If it could be followed exactly, the destination would be dead ahead throughout the voyage (assuming course and heading were the same). The rhumb line *appears* the more direct route on a Mercator chart because of chart distortion. The great circle crosses meridians at higher latitudes, where the distance between them is less.

The decision as to whether or not to use great-circle sailing depends upon the conditions. The saving in distance should be worth the additional effort, and of course the great circle should not cross land, or carry the vessel into dangerous waters or excessively high latitudes. A slight departure from the great circle or a modification called composite sailing (art. 901) may effect a considerable saving over the rhumb line track without leading the vessel into danger. If a fix indicates the vessel is a considerable distance to one side of the great circle, the more desirable practice often is to determine a new great-circle track, rather than to return to the original one.

Since a great circle is continuously changing direction as one proceeds along it, no attempt is customarily made to follow it exactly, except in polar regions. Rather, a number of points are selected along the great circle, and rhumb lines are followed from point to point, taking advantage of the fact that for short distances a great circle and a rhumb line almost coincide.

The number of points to use is a matter of personal preference, a large number of points providing closer approximation to the great circle but requiring more frequent change of course. As a general rule, each 5° of longitude is a convenient length. Legs of equal length are not provided in this way, but this is not objectionable under normal conditions.

If a magnetic compass is used, the variation for the middle of the leg is usually used for the entire leg.

The problems of great-circle sailing can be solved by (1) chart (art. 904), (2) computation, (3) table (art. 905), (4) graphically, or (5) mechanically. Of these, (4) and (5) are but graphical or mechanical solutions of (2). They usually provide solution only for initial course and the distance, and are not in common use.

904. Great-circle sailing by chart.—Problems of great-circle sailing, like those of rhumb line sailing, are most easily solved by plotting directly on a chart. For this purpose the Defense Mapping Agency Hydrographic Center publishes a number of charts on the gnomonic projection (art. 317), covering the principal navigable waters of the world. On this projection any straight line is a great circle, but since the chart is not conformal (art. 302), directions and distances cannot be measured directly, as on a Mercator chart. An indirect method is explained on each chart.

The usual method of using a gnomonic chart is to plot the great circle and, if it provides a satisfactory track, to determine a number of points along the track, using the latitude and longitude scales in the immediate vicinity of each point. These points are then transferred to a Mercator chart or plotting sheet and used as a succession of destinations to be reached by rhumb lines. The course and distance for each leg is determined by measurement on the Mercator chart or plotting sheet. This method is illustrated in figure 904, which shows a great circle plotted as a straight line on a gnomonic chart and a series of points transferred to a Mercator chart. The arrows represent corresponding points on the two charts. The points can be plotted directly

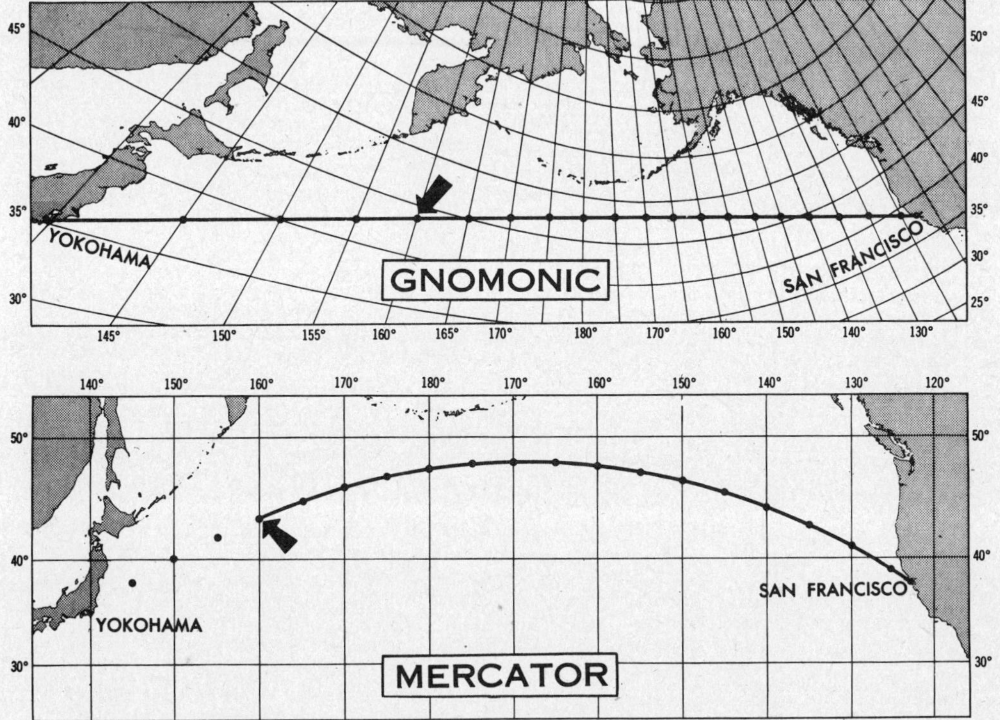

FIGURE 904.—Transferring great-circle points from a gnomonic chart to a Mercator chart.

on plotting sheets without the use of a small-scale chart, but the use of the chart provides a visual check to avoid large errors, and a visual indication of the suitability of the track.

Since gnomonic charts are normally used only because of their great-circle properties, they are often popularly called **great-circle charts.**

A projection on which a straight line is *approximately* a great circle can be used in place of a gnomonic chart with negligible error. If such a projection is conformal, as in the case of the Lambert conformal (art. 314), measurement of course and distance of each leg can be made directly on the chart.

Some great circles are shown on pilot charts and certain other charts, together with the great-circle distances. Where tracks are recommended on charts or in sailing directions, it is good practice to follow such recommendations.

905. Great-circle sailing by table.—Any method of solving the astronomical triangle of celestial navigation can be used for solving great-circle sailing problems. When such an adaptation is made, the point of departure replaces the assumed position of the observer, the destination replaces the geographical position of the body, difference of longitude replaces meridian angle or local hour angle, initial course angle replaces azimuth angle, and great-circle distance replaces zenith distance (90°—altitude), as shown in figure 905. Therefore, any table of azimuths (if the entering values are meridian angle, declination, and latitude) can be used for determining initial great-circle course.

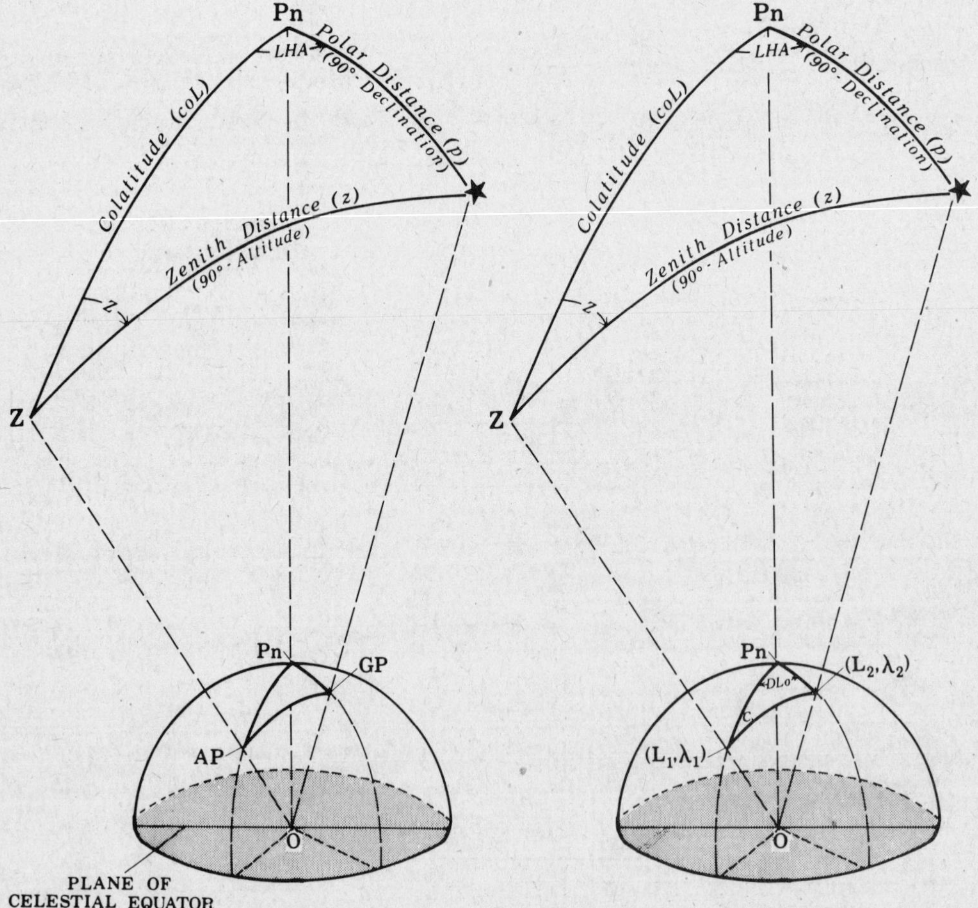

FIGURE 905.—Adapting the astronomical triangle to the navigational triangle of great-circle sailing.

Pubs. Nos. 214, 229, 249, 260, and 261 are examples of tables that can be used for this purpose. Tables which provide solution for altitude, such as Pubs. Nos. 214, 229, and 249, can be used for determining great-circle distance. The required distance is 90° − altitude (90° + negative altitudes).

In inspection tables such as Pubs. Nos. 214, 229, 249, 260, and 261, the given combination of L_1, L_2, and DLo may not be tabulated. In this case reverse the name of L_2 and use 180° − DLo for entering the table. The required course angle is then 180° minus the tabulated azimuth, and distance is 90° plus the altitude. If neither combination can be found, solution cannot be made by that method. By interchanging L_1 and L_2, one can find the supplement of the final course angle.

Solution by table often provides a rapid approximate check, but accurate results usually require triple interpolation. Except for Pub. No. 229, inspection tables do not provide a solution for points along the great circle. Pub. No. 229 provides solutions for these points only if interpolation is not required.

906. Great-circle sailing by Pub. No. 229.—By entering Pub. No. 229 with the latitude of the point of departure as latitude, latitude of destination as declination, and difference of longitude as LHA, the tabular altitude and azimuth angle may be extracted and converted to great-circle distance and course. As in sight reduction, the tables are entered in accordance to whether the name of the latitude of the point of departure is the same as or contrary to the name of the latitude of the destination (declination). If after so entering the tables, the respondent values correspond to those of a celestial body *above* the celestial horizon, 90° minus the arc of the tabular altitude becomes the distance; the tabular azimuth angle becomes the initial great-circle course angle. If the respondents correspond to those of a celestial body *below* the celestial horizon, the arc of the tabular altitude plus 90° becomes the distance; the supplement of the tabular azimuth angle becomes the initial great-circle course angle.

When the C–S Line is crossed in either direction, the altitude becomes negative; the body lies below the celestial horizon. For example: If the tables are entered with the LHA (DLo) at the bottom of a right-hand page and declination (L_2) such that the respondents lie above the C–S Line, the C–S Line has been crossed. Then the distance is 90° plus the tabular altitude; the initial course angle is the supplement of the tabular azimuth angle. Similarly, if the tables are entered with the LHA (DLo) at the top of a right-hand page and the respondents are found below the C–S Line, the distance is 90° plus the tabular altitude; the initial course angle is the supplement of the tabular azimuth angle. If the tables are entered with the LHA (DLo) at the bottom of a right-hand page and the name of L_2 is contrary to L_1, the respondents are found in the column for L_1 on the facing page. In which case, the C–S Line has been crossed; the distance is 90° plus the tabular altitude; the initial course angle is the supplement of the tabular azimuth angle.

The tabular azimuth angle, or its supplement, is prefixed N or S for the latitude of the point of departure and suffixed E or W depending upon the destination being east or west of the point of departure.

If all entering arguments are integral degrees, the distance and course angle are obtained directly from the tables without interpolation. If the latitude of the destination is nonintegral, interpolation for the additional minutes of latitude is done as in correcting altitude for any declination increment; if the latitude of departure or difference of longitude is nonintegral, the additional interpolation is done graphically.

Since the latitude of destination becomes the declination entry, and all declinations appear on every page, the great-circle solution can always be extracted from the volume which covers the latitude of the point of departure.

Example 1.—**By Pub. No. 229 (app. D) find the distance and initial great-circle** course from lat. 32°S, long. 116°E to lat. 30°S, long 31°E.

Solution.—(1) Refer to figure 905. The point of departure (lat. 32°S, long. 116°E) replaces the AP of the observer; the destination (lat. 30°S, long. 31°E) replaces the GP of the celestial body; the difference of longitude (DLo 85°) replaces local hour angle (LHA) of the body.

(2) The solution by Pub. No. 229 is effected by entering volume 3 with lat. 32° (Same Name), LHA 85°, and declination 30°. The respondents as so found correspond to those of a celestial body *above* the celestial horizon. Therefore, 90° minus the tabular altitude (90°−19°12.′4=70°47.′6) becomes the distance; the tabular azimuth angle (S66.°0W) becomes the initial great-circle course angle, prefixed S for the latitude of the point of departure and suffixed W due to the destination being west of the point of departure.

Answers.—(1) D 4248 nautical miles
C S66.°0W
(2) Cn 246.°0.

Example 2.—**By Pub. No. 229 (app. D) find the distance and initial great-circle** course from lat. 38°N, long. 122°W to lat. 24°S, long. 151°E.

Solution.—(1) Refer to figure 905. The point of departure (lat. 38°N, long. 122°W) replaces the AP of the observer; the destination (lat. 24°S, long. 151°E) replaces the GP of the celestial body; the difference of longitude (DLo 87°) replaces local hour angle (LHA) of the body.

(2) The solution by Pub. No. 229 is effected by entering volume 3 with lat. 38° (Contrary Name), LHA 87°, and declination 24°. The respondents as so found correspond to those of a celestial body *below* the celestial horizon. Therefore, the tabular altitude plus 90° (12°17.′0+90°=102°17.′0) becomes the distance; the *supplement* of tabular azimuth angle (180°−69.°0=111.°0) becomes the initial great-circle course angle, prefixed N for the latitude of the point of departure and suffixed W due to the destination being west of the point of departure.

That the tabular data corresponds to a celestial body below the celestial horizon is indicated by the fact that the data is extracted from those tabulations across the C–S Line from the entering argument (LHA 85°).

Answers.—(1) D 6137 nautical miles
C N111.°0W
(2) Cn 249°.

Example 3.—**By Pub. No. 229 (app. D) find the distance and initial great-circle** course from Fremantle (32°03′S, 115°45′E) to Durban (29°52′S, 31°04′E).

Solution.—(1) Refer to figure 905. Since the latitude of the point of departure, the latitude of the destination, and the difference of longitude (DLo) between the point of departure and destination are not integral degrees, the solution is effected from an adjusted point of departure or assumed position of departure chosen as follows: the latitude of the assumed position (AP) is the integral degrees of latitude nearest to the point of departure; the longitude of the AP is chosen to provide integral degrees of DLo. This AP, which should be within 30′ of the longitude of the point of departure, is at latitude 32°S, longitude 116°04′E. The DLo is 85°.

(2) Enter the tables with 32° as the latitude argument (Same Name), 85° as the LHA argument, and 29° as the declination argument.

(3) From the tables extract the tabular altitude, altitude difference, and azimuth angle; interpolate altitude and azimuth angle for declination increment. The Dec. Inc. is the minutes that the latitude of the destination is in excess of the integral degrees used as the declination argument.

	ht (Tab. Hc)	d	Z
LHA 85°, Lat. 32° (Same), Dec. 29°	18°45′.4	(+)27′.0	66°.9
Dec. Inc. 52′, d(+)27′0 Tens	(+)17′.3		
Units	(+) 6′.1		
Interpolated for Dec. Inc.	19°08′.8		C S66°.1W
Initial great-circle course from AP			Cn 246°.1
Great-circle distance from AP(90°–19°08′.8)			4251.2 n.mi.

(4) Using the graphical method for interpolating altitude for latitude and LHA increments, the course line is drawn from the AP in the direction of the initial great-circle course from the AP (246°.1). As shown in figure 906a, a line is drawn from the point of departure perpendicular to the initial great-circle course line or its extension.

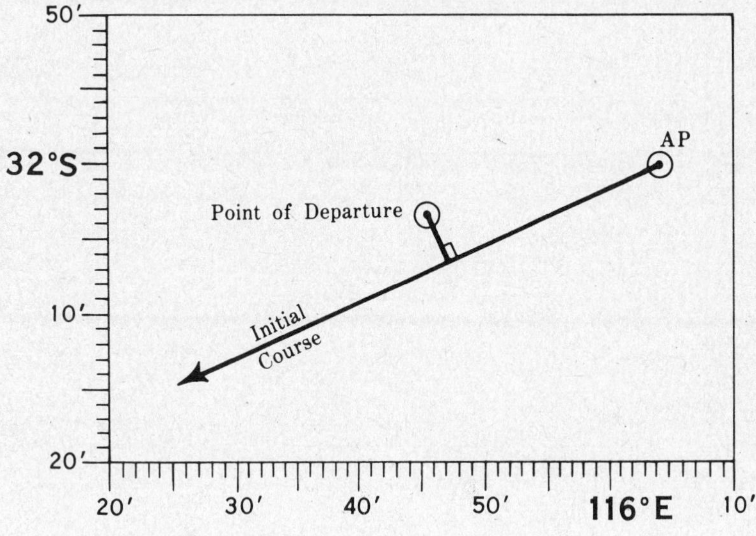

Figure 906a.—Graphical interpolation.

(5) The required correction, in units of minutes of latitude, for the latitude and DLo increments is the length along the course line between the foot of the perpendicular and the AP. The correction as applied to the distance from the AP is −15′.8; the great-circle distance is 4235 nautical miles.

(6) The azimuth angle interpolated for declination, LHA, and latitude increments is S66°.3W; the initial great-circle course from the point of departure is 246°.3.

Example 4.—By Pub. No. 229 (app. D) find the distance and initial great-circle course from San Francisco (37°49′N, 122°25′W) to Gladstone (23°51′S, 151°15′E).

Solution.—(1) Refer to figure 905. Since the latitude of the point of departure, the latitude of the destination, and the difference of longitude (DLo) between the point of departure and destination are not integral degrees, the solution is effected from an adjusted point of departure or assumed position of departure chosen as follows: the latitude of the assumed position (AP) is the integral degrees of latitude nearest to the point of departure; the longitude of the AP is chosen to provide integral degrees of

DLo. This AP, which should be within 30′ of the longitude of the point of departure, is at latitude 38°N, longitude 122°45′W. The DLo is 86°.

(2) Enter the tables with 38° as the latitude argument (Contrary Name), 86° as the LHA argument, and 23° as the declination argument.

(3) From the tables extract the tabular altitude, altitude difference, and azimuth angle; interpolate altitude for Dec. Inc. as if the altitude were positive, adhering strictly to the sign given d. After interpolation regard the results as negative. Subtract tabular azimuth angle from 180°; interpolate for Dec. Inc.

	ht(Tab. Hc)	d	Z
LHA 86°, Lat. 38° (Contrary), Dec. 23°	10°57′.0	(+)35′.9	69°.3
Dec. Inc. 51′, d(+)35′.9	Tens (+)25′.5		180°−Z=110°.7
	Units (+)5′.1		
Interpolated for Dec. Inc.	(−)11°27′.6		C N111°.4W
Initial great-circle course from AP			Cn 248°.6
Great-circle distance from AP (90°+11°27′.6)			6087.6 n.mi.

(4) Using the graphical method for interpolating altitude for latitude and LHA increments, the course line is drawn from the AP in the direction of the initial great-circle course from the AP (248°.6). As shown in figure 906b, a line is drawn from the point of departure perpendicular to the course line or its extension.

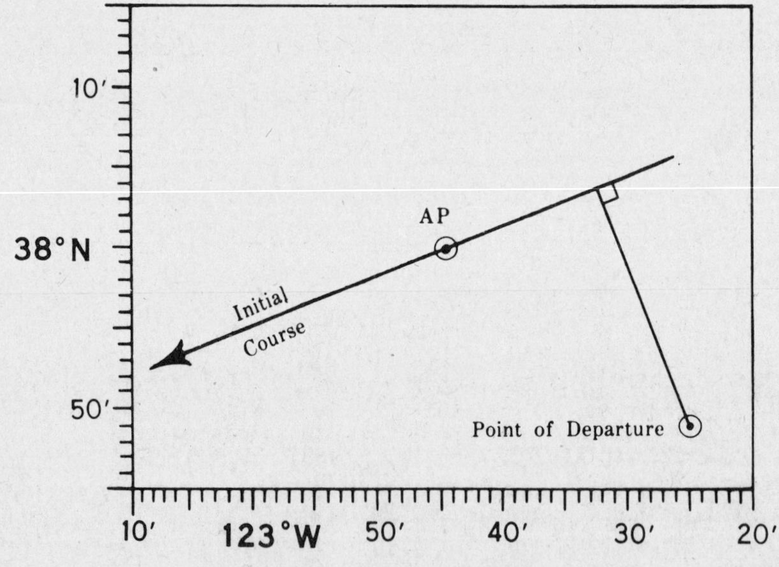

FIGURE 906b.—Graphical interpolation.

(5) The required additional correction, in units of minutes of latitude, for the latitude and DLo increments is the length along the course line between the foot of the perpendicular and the AP. The correction as applied to the distance from the AP is +10′.7; the great-circle distance is 6098 nautical miles.

(6) The azimuth angle interpolated for declination, LHA, and latitude increments is 111°.2; the initial great-circle course from the point of departure is 248°.8.

Example 5.—By Pub. No. 229 (app. D) find the distance and initial great-circle course from Cabo Pilar (52°43′S, 74°41′W) to Wake Island (19°17′N, 166°39′E).

Solution.—(1) Refer to figure 905. Since the latitude of the point of departure, the latitude of the destination, and the difference of longitude (DLo) between the point of departure and destination are not integral degrees, the solution is effected from an adjusted point of departure or assumed position of departure chosen as follows: the latitude of the assumed position (AP) is the integral degrees of latitude nearest to the point of departure; the longitude of the AP is chosen to provide integral degrees of DLo. This AP, which should be within 30′ of the longitude of the point of departure, is at latitude 53°S, longitude 74°21′W; the DLo is 119°.

(2) Enter the tables with 53° as the latitude argument (Contrary Name), 119° as the LHA argument, and 19° as the declination argument. Since the tables are entered with the LHA (DLo) at the bottom of a right-hand page and the name of L_2 is contrary to the name L_1, the respondents are found in the column for L_1 on the facing page. In which case the C–S Line has been crossed, and the respondents correspond to those of a celestial body below the celestial horizon.

(3) From the table, extract the tabular latitude, altitude difference, and azimuth angle; interpolate altitude for Dec. Inc. as if the altitude were positive, adhering strictly to the sign given d. After interpolation regard the results as negative. Subtract tabular azimuth angle from 180°; interpolate for Dec. Inc.

		ht (Tab. Hc)	d	Z
LHA 119°, Lat. 53° (Contrary), Dec. 19°		32°24′.2	(+)46′.8	101°.6
Dec. Inc. 17′, d(+)47′.1	Tens	(+)11′.3		180°−Z=S78°.6W
	Units	(+) 2′.0		
Interpolated for Dec. Inc.		(−)32°37′.5		C S78°.6W
Initial great-circle course from AP				Cn 258°.6
Great-circle distance from AP (90°+32°37′.5)				7357.5 n.mi.

(4) Using the graphical method for interpolating altitude for latitude and LHA increments, the course line is drawn from the AP in the direction of the initial great-circle course from the AP (258°.6). As shown in figure 906c a line is drawn from the point of departure perpendicular to the course line or its extension.

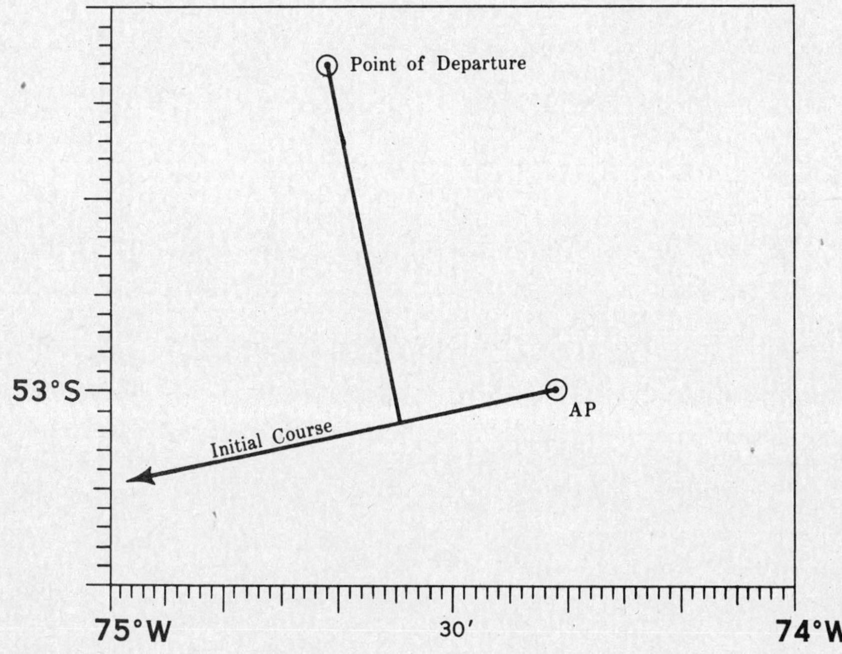

FIGURE 906c.—Graphical interpolation.

(5) The required additional correction, in units of minutes of latitude, for the latitude and DLo increments is the length along the course line between the foot of the perpendicular and the AP. The correction as applied to the distance from the AP is −8.'5; the great-circle distance is 7349 nautical miles.

(6) The azimuth angle interpolated for declination, LHA, and latitude increments is 79.°1; the initial great-circle course from the point of departure is 259.°1.

Points Along Great Circle

If, as in examples 1 and 2, the latitude of the point of departure and the initial great-circle course angle are integral degrees, points along the great circle are found by entering the tables with the latitude of departure as the latitude argument (always Same Name), the initial great-circle course angle as the LHA argument, and 90° minus distance to a point on the great circle as the declination argument. The latitude of the point on the great circle and the difference of longitude between that point and the point of departure are the tabular altitude and azimuth angle respondents, respectively. If, however, the respondents are extracted from across the C–S Line, the tabular altitude corresponds to a latitude on the side of the equator opposite from that of the point of departure; the tabular azimuth angle is the supplement of the difference of longitude.

Example 6.—Find a number of points along the great-circle from latitude 38°N, longitude 125°W when the initial great-circle course angle is N111°W.

Solution.—(1) Entering the tables with latitude 38° (Same Name), LHA 111°, and with successive declinations of 85°, 80°, 75° . . . the latitudes and differences in longitude, from 125°W, are found as tabular altitudes and azimuth angles respectively:

Distance n.mi. (arc)	*300(5°)*	*600(10°)*	*900(15°)*	*3600(60°)*	*4800(80°)*
Latitude	36.°1N	33.°9N	31.°4N	3.°6N	3.°1S
DLo	5.°8	11.°3	16.°5	54.°1	61.°5
Longitude	130.°8W	136.°3W	141.°5W	179.°1W	173.°5E

Example 7.—Find a number of points along the great-circle from latitude 38°N, long. 125°W when the initial great-circle course angle is N69°W.

Solution.—Entering the tables with latitude 38° (Same Name), LHA 69°, and with successive declinations of 85°, 80°, 75° . . . the latitudes and differences of longitude, from 125°W, are found as tabular altitudes and azimuth angles, respectively:

Distance n.mi.(arc)	*300(5°)*	*600(10°)*	*900(15°)*	*6600(110°)*	*7200(120°)*
Latitude	39.°6N	40.°9N	41.°9N	3.°1N	3.°6S
DLo	6.°1	12.°4	18.°9	118.°5	125.°9
Longitude	131.°1W	137.°4W	143.°9W	116.°5E	109.°1E

The latitude and difference of longitude of the point 6600 miles from the point of departure are found among the data for the latitude of departure continued on the facing page. Since the respondents for the point 7200 miles from the point of departure are found across the C–S Line on the facing page, the tabular altitude corresponds to a latitude on the side of the equator opposite from that of the point of departure; the tabular azimuth angle is the supplement of the difference of longitude.

Finding The Vertex

The use of Pub. No. 229 to find the approximate position of the vertex of a great-circle track provides a rapid check on the solution by computation. This approximate solution is also useful for voyage planning purposes.

Using the procedures for finding points along the great circle, the column of data for the latitude of the point of departure is inspected to find the maximum value of tabular altitude. This maximum tabular altitude and the tabular azimuth angle correspond to the latitude of the vertex and the difference of longitude of the vertex and the point of departure.

Example 7.—Find the vertex of the great-circle track from lat. 38°N, long. 125°W when the initial great-circle course angle is N69°W.

Solution.—(1) Enter Pub. No. 229 with lat. 38° (Same Name), LHA 69°, and inspect the column for lat. 38° to find the maximum tabular altitude.

(2) The maximum tabular altitude is found to be 42°38′.1 at a distance of 1500 nautical miles (90°−65°=25°) from the point of departure. The corresponding tabular azimuth angle is 32°.4. Therefore, the difference of longitude of vertex and point of departure is 32°.4.

Answers.—(1) Latitude of vertex 42°38′.1N.
(2) Longitude of vertex 157°.4W.

907. Altering a great-circle track to avoid obstructions.—Great-circle sailing cannot be used unless the great-circle track is free from obstructions. It does not start until one clears the harbor and takes his departure (art. 806), and often ends near the entrance to the destination. However, islands, points of land, or other obstructions may prevent the use of great-circle sailing over the entire distance. One of the principal advantages of solution by great-circle chart is that the presence of any obstructions is immediately apparent.

Often a relatively short run by rhumb line is sufficient to reach a point from which the great-circle track can be followed. Where a choice is possible, the rhumb line selected should conform as nearly as practicable to the direct great circle.

If the great circle crosses a small island, one or more legs may be altered slightly, or perhaps the drift of the vessel will be sufficient to make any planned alteration unnecessary. The possible use of the island in obtaining an en route fix should not be overlooked. If a larger obstruction is encountered, as in the case of the Aleutian Islands on a great circle from Seattle to Yokohama, some judgment may be needed in selecting the track. It may be satisfactory to follow a great circle to the vicinity of the obstruction, one or more rhumb lines along the edge of the obstruction, and another great circle to the destination. Another possible solution is the use of composite sailing (art. 908), and still another the use of two great circles, one from the point of departure to a point near the maximum latitude of unobstructed water, and the second from this point to the destination.

It is sometimes desirable to alter a great-circle track to avoid unfavorable winds or currents. The shortest route is not always the quickest.

Whatever the problem, a great-circle chart can be helpful in its solution.

908. Composite sailing.—When the great circle would carry a vessel to a higher latitude than desired, a modification of great-circle sailing, called **composite sailing,** may be used to good advantage. The composite track consists of a great circle from the point of departure and tangent to the limiting parallel, a course line along the parallel, and a great circle tangent to the limiting parallel and through the destination.

Solution of composite sailing problems is most easily made by means of a great-circle chart. Lines from the point of departure and the destination are drawn tangent to the limiting parallel. The coordinates of various selected points along the composite track are then measured and transferred to a Mercator chart, as in great-circle sailing (art. 904).

Composite sailing problems can also be solved by computation (art. 1011, vol. II).

CHAPTER X

PILOTING

General

1001. Introduction.—On the high seas, where there is no immediate danger of grounding, navigation is a comparatively leisurely process. Courses and speeds are maintained over relatively long periods, and fixes are obtained at convenient intervals. Under favorable conditions a vessel might continue for several days with no positions other than those obtained by dead reckoning, or by estimate, and with no anxiety on the part of the captain or navigator. Errors in position can usually be detected and corrected before danger threatens.

In the vicinity of shoal water the situation is different. Frequent or continuous positional information is usually essential to the safety of the vessel. An error, which on the high seas may be considered small, may in what are called **pilot waters** be intolerably large. Frequent changes of course and speed are common. The proximity of other vessels increases the possibility of collisions and restricts movements.

In some waters the services of a specially qualified navigator having local knowledge may be necessary to insure safe navigation. **Local knowledge** extends beyond that publicly available in charts and publications, being more detailed, intimate, and current. The pilot's knowledge of his waters is gained not only through his own experience and familiarity, but by his availing himself of all local information resources, public and private, recent and longstanding, particularly concerning underwater hazards and obstructions, uncharted above-water landmarks and topographical configurations, local tides and currents, recent shoaling, temporary changes or deficiencies in aids to navigation, and similar matters of local concern. This local knowledge should enable a pilot to traverse his waters safely without reliance on man-made aids to navigation and to detect any unusual conditions or departure from a safe course. This service does not substitute for the ship's own safe navigation, but complements it. Prudence may also dictate the use of this specially qualified navigator to better insure safe navigation in situations where local knowledge is not essential. This navigator specially qualified for specific waters is called a **pilot**; his services are referred to as **pilotage** or **piloting.**

In its more general sense, the term **piloting** is used to mean the art of safely conducting a vessel on waters the hazards of which make necessary frequent or continuous positioning with respect to *charted* features and close attention to the vessel's draft with respect to the depth of water. Except for special circumstances, such as proceeding along a **range** (art. 1004), this positioning normally must be effected by constructing a plot on the chart based upon accurate navigational observations of charted features.

No other form of navigation requires the continuous alertness needed in piloting. At no other time is navigational experience and judgment so valuable. The ability to work rapidly and to correctly interpret all available information, always keeping "ahead of the vessel," may mean the difference between safety and disaster.

1002. Preparation for piloting.—Because the time element is often of vital importance in piloting, adequate preparation is important. Long-range preparation includes the organization and training of those who will assist in any way. This includes the steersman, who will be granted less tolerance in straying from the prescribed course than when farther offshore.

The more immediate preparation includes a study of the charts and publications of the area to familiarize oneself with the channels, shoals, tides, currents, aids to navigation, etc. One seldom has time to seek such information once he is proceeding in pilot waters. This preparation also includes the development of a definite plan for transiting the hazardous waters. Since the services provided by pilots having local knowledge are usually *advisory*, prudence dictates that the regularly assigned navigational personnel be advised of the pilot's plan. Otherwise, their ability to counteract any imprudent action on the part of the pilot may be severely limited. Also, knowledge of the pilot's plan enables the regularly assigned navigational personnel to act more effectively in verifying that the pilot is making a safe passage.

Position

1003. Lines of position.—As in celestial and radionavigation, piloting makes extensive use of **lines or position.** Such a line is one on some point of which the vessel may be presumed to be located, as a result of observation or measurement. It may be highly reliable, or of questionable accuracy. Lines of position are of great value, but one should always keep in mind that *they can be in error* because of imperfections in instruments used for obtaining them and human limitations in those who use the instruments and utilize the results. The extent to which one can have confidence in various lines of position is a matter of judgment acquired from experience.

A line of position might be a straight line (actually a part of a great circle), an arc of a circle, or part of some other curve such as a hyperbola. An appropriate label should be placed on the plot of a line of position *at the time it is drawn*, to avoid possible error or confusion. A label should include all information essential for identification, but no extraneous information. *The labels shown in this volume are recommended.*

1004. Bearings.—A **bearing** is the horizontal direction of one terrestrial point from another. It is usually expressed as the angular difference between a reference direction and the given direction. In navigation, north is generally used as the reference direction, and angles are measured clockwise through 360°. It is customary to express all bearings in three digits, using preliminary zeros where needed. Thus, north is 000° or 360°, a direction 7° to the right of north is 007°, east is 090°, southwest is 225°, etc.

For plotting, *true* north is used as the reference direction. A bearing measured from this reference is called a **true bearing.** A **magnetic, compass,** or **grid bearing** results from using magnetic, compass, or grid north, respectively, as the reference direction. This is similar to the designation of courses. In the case of bearings, however, one additional reference direction is often convenient. This is the heading of the ship. A bearing expressed as angular distance from the heading is called a **relative bearing.** It is usually measured clockwise through 360°. A relative bearing may be expressed in still another way, as indicated in figure 1004. Except for dead ahead and points at 45° intervals from it, this method is used principally for indicating directions obtained visually, without precise measurement. An even more general indication of relative bearing may be given by such directions as "ahead," "on the starboard bow," "on the port quarter," "astern." The term *abeam* may be used as the equivalent of either the general "on the beam" or, sometimes, the more precise "broad on the beam." Degrees are sometimes used instead of points to express relative bearings by the system illustrated in figure 1004. However, if degrees are used, a better practice is to use the 360°

system. Thus, a relative bearing of "20° forward of the port beam" is better expressed as "290°."

True, magnetic, and compass bearings are interconverted by the use of variation and deviation, or compass error, in the same manner as courses. Interconversion of relative and other bearings is accomplished by means of the heading. If true heading is added to relative bearing, true bearing results. If magnetic, compass, or grid heading is added to relative bearing, the corresponding magnetic, compass, or grid bearing is obtained.

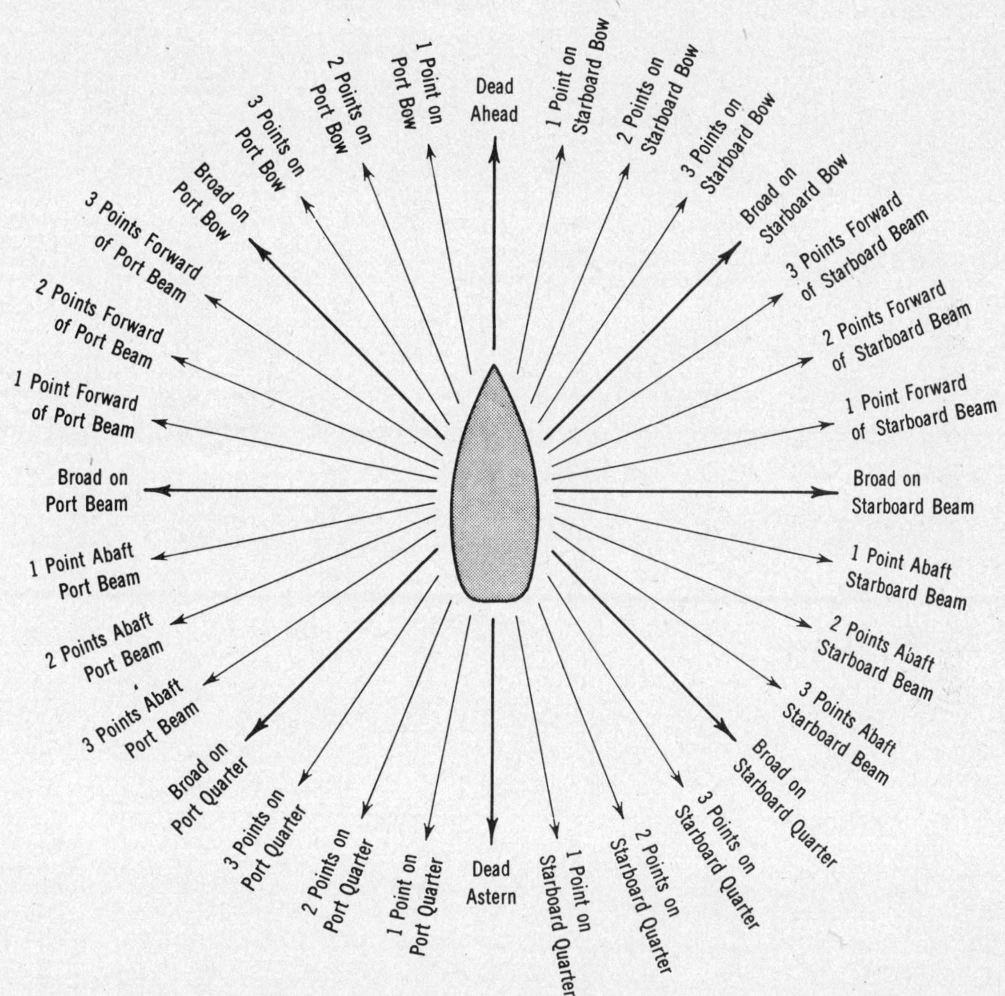

FIGURE 1004.—One method of expressing relative bearings.

A bearing line extending in the direction of an observed bearing of a charted object is one of the most widely used lines of position. If one knows that an identified landmark has a certain bearing from his vessel, the vessel can only be on the line at which such a bearing might be observed, for at any other point the bearing would be different. This line extends outward from the landmark, along the *reciprocal* of the observed bearing. Thus, if a lighthouse is *east* of a ship, that ship is *west* of the lighthouse. If a beacon bears 156°, the observer must be on a line extending 156°+180°=336° from the beacon. Since observed bearing lines are great circles, this relationship is not strictly accurate, but the error is significant only where the great circle departs materially from the rhumb line, as in high latitudes.

Bearings are obtained by compass, gyro repeater, pelorus, alidade, radar, etc. One type of bearing can be obtained by eye without measurement. When two objects appear directly in line, one behind the other, they are said to be "in range," and together they constitute a **range**. For accurately charted objects, a range may provide the most accurate line of position obtainable, and one of the easiest to observe. Tanks, steeples, towers, cupolas, etc., sometimes form **natural ranges.** A navigator should be familiar with prominent ranges in his operating area, particularly those which can be used to mark turning points, indicate limits of shoals, or define an approach heading or let-go point of the anchorage of a naval vessel. So useful is the range in marking a course that artificial ranges, usually in the form of two lighted beacons, have been installed in line with channels in many ports. A vessel proceeding along the channel has only to keep the beacons in range to remain in the center of the channel. If the *farther* beacon (customarily the higher one) appears to "open out" (move) to the right of the forward (lower) beacon, one knows that he is to the right of his desired track. Similarly, if it opens out to the left, the vessel is off track to the left.

The line defined by the range is called a **range line** or **leading line**. Range daybeacons (art. 412) and other charted objects forming a range are often called **leading marks**. Range lights (art. 402) are often called **leading lights**.

It is good practice to plot only a short part of a line of position in the vicinity of the vessel, to avoid unnecessary confusion and to reduce the chart wear by erasure. Particularly, one should avoid the drawing of lines through the chart symbol indicating the landmark used. In the case of a range, a straightedge is placed along the two objects, and the desired portion of the line is plotted. One need not know the numerical value of the bearing represented by the line. However, if there is any doubt as to the identification of the objects observed, the measurement of the bearing should prove useful.

A single bearing line is labeled with the time above the line.

1005. Distance.—If a vessel is known to be a certain distance from an identified point on the chart, it must be somewhere on a circle with that point as the center and the distance as the radius. A single distance (range) arc is labeled with the time above the line.

Distances are obtained by radar, range finder, stadimeter, synchronized sound and radio signals, synchronized air and water sounds, vertical sextant angles (table 5), etc. If vertical sextant angles are used, measurement should be made from the top of the object to the visible sea horizon, if it is available. If measurement is made to a water line not vertically below the top of the object, a problem may be encountered because distance from table 5 is to the point vertically below the top of the object, while the distance used for entering table 8 to determine dip short of the horizon is to the water line. Generally, any differences in these two distances can be determined from the chart. This problem may, in some cases, be avoided by decreasing the height of eye sufficiently to bring the horizon between the observer and the object.

1006. The fix.—A line of position, however obtained, represents a series of possible positions, but not a single position. However, if *two simultaneous, nonparallel* lines of position are available, the only position that satisfies the requirements of being on both lines at the same time is the intersection of the two lines. This point is one form of **fix.** Examples of several types of fix are given in the illustrations. In figure 1006a a fix is obtained from two bearing lines. The fix of figure 1006b is obtained by two distance circles. Figure 1006c illustrates a fix from a range and a distance. In figure 1006d a bearing and distance of a single object are used. A small circle is used to indicate the fix at the intersection of the lines of position. The time of the fix is the time at which the lines of position were established.

Some consideration should be given to the selection of objects to provide a fix. It is essential, for instance, that the objects be identified. The angle between lines of position is important. The ideal is 90°. If the angle is small, a slight error in measuring or plotting either line results in a relatively large error in the indicated position. In the case of a bearing line, nearby objects are preferable to those at a considerable distance, because the linear (distance) error resulting from an angular error increases with distance.

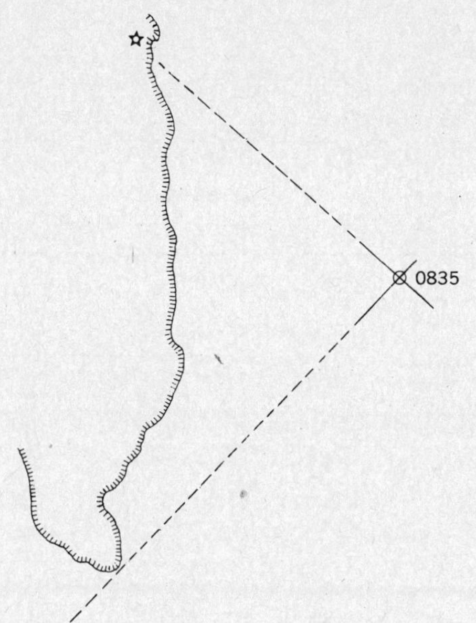

FIGURE 1006a.—A fix by two bearing lines.

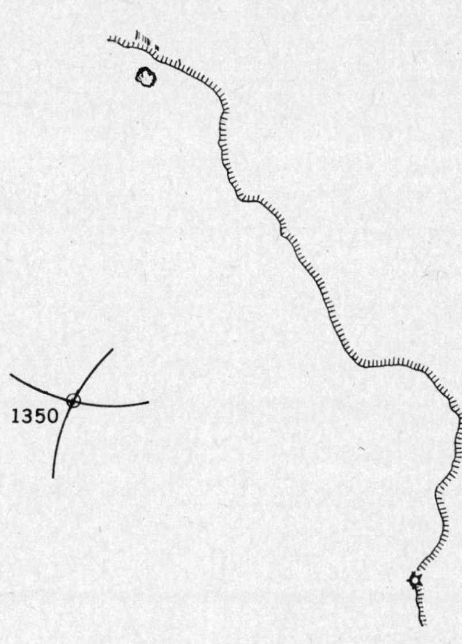

FIGURE 1006b.—A fix by two distances.

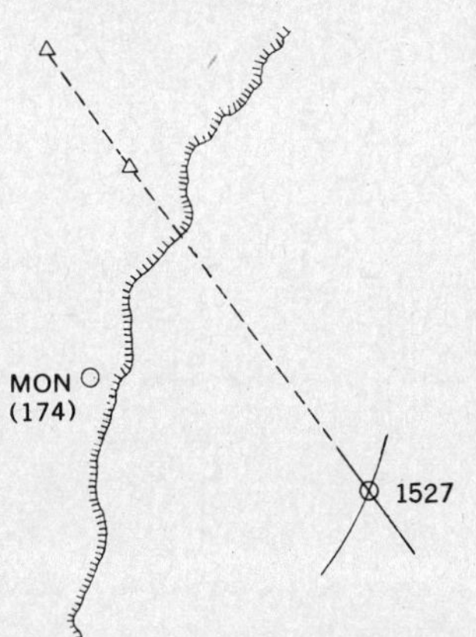

FIGURE 1006c.—A fix by a range and distance.

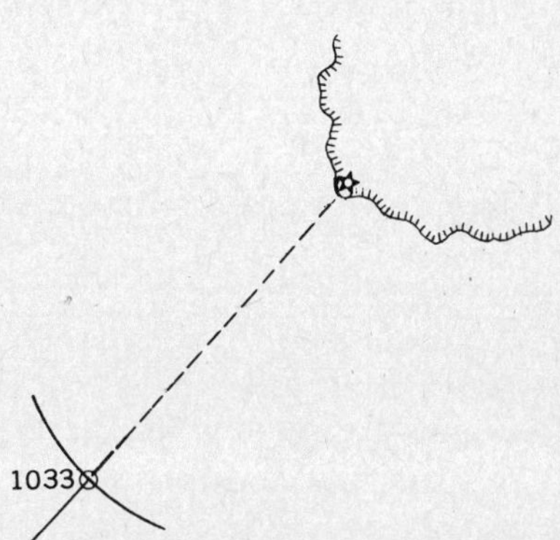

FIGURE 1006d.—A fix by distance and bearing of single object.

Another consideration is the type of object. Lighthouses, spires, flagpoles, etc., are good objects because the point of observation is well defined. A large building, most nearby mountains, a point of land, etc., may leave some reasonable doubt as to the exact point used for observation. If a tangent is used (fig. 1006a), there is a possibility that a low spit may extend seaward from the part observed. A number of towers, chimneys, etc., close together require careful identification. A buoy or a lightship may drag anchor and be out of position. Most buoys are secured by a single anchor and so have a certain radius of swing as the tide, current, and wind change.

Although two accurate nonparallel lines of position completely define a position, if they are taken at the same time, an element of doubt always exists as to the accuracy of the lines. Additional lines of position can serve as a check on those already obtained, and, usually, to reduce any existing error. If three lines of position cross at a common point, or form a small triangle, it is usually a reasonable assumption that the position is reliable, and defined by the center of the figure. However, this is not *necessarily* so, and one should be aware of the possibility of an erroneously indicated position.

A single bearing line of an accurately charted object will be offset from the observer's actual position by an amount dependent upon the net angular error of the observation and plot, and the distance of the charted object from the observer. The amount of offset is expressed approximately in the **Rule of Sixty,** which may be stated as follows: *The offset of the plotted bearing line from the observer's actual position is 1/60th of the distance to the object observed for each degree of error.* In the derivation of the Rule of Sixty, the assumption is made that the angular error is small, i.e., not more than the small errors normally associated with compass observations and plotting. Using this assumption, the sine function of the angular error is taken as equal to the same number of radians as the error. As shown in figure 1006e, the offset is equal to 1/60th of the distance to the charted object observed times the sine of the angular error of the bearing line as plotted. Thus, an error of 1° represents an error of about 100 feet if the object is 1 mile distant, 1,000 feet if the object is 10 miles away, and 1 mile if the object is 60 miles from the observer.

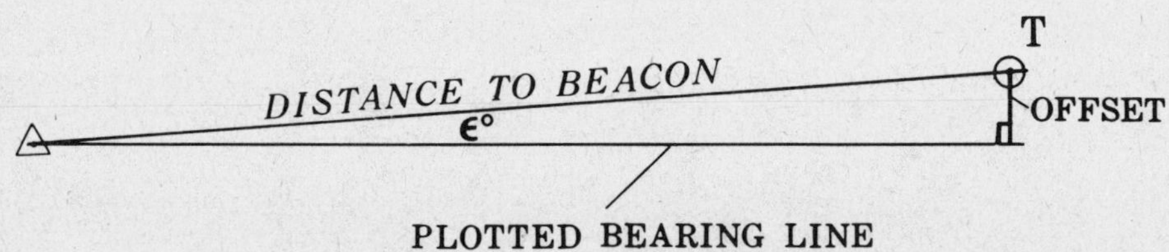

FIGURE 1006e.—Basis of the Rule of Sixty.

1007. Two-bearing plot.—If as shown in figure 1007a, the observer is located at point T and the bearings of a beacon and cupola are observed and plotted without error, the intersection of the bearing lines lies on the circumference of a circle passing through the beacon, cupola, and the observer. With *constant error*, i.e., an error of fixed magnitude and sign (or direction) for a given set of observations, the angular difference of the bearings of the beacon and the cupola is not affected. Thus, the angle formed at point F by the bearing lines plotted with constant error is equal to the angle formed at point T by the bearing lines plotted without error. From geometry it is known that angles having their apexes on the circumference of a circle and that are subtended by the same chord are equal. Since the angles at points T and F are equal and the angles are subtended by the same chord, the intersection at point F lies on the circumference of a circle passing through the beacon, cupola, and the observer.

Assuming only constant error in the plot, the direction of displacement of the two-bearing fix from the position of the observer is in accordance with the sign (or direction) of the constant error. However, a third bearing is required to determine the direction of the constant error.

Assuming only constant error in the plot, the two-bearing fix lies on the circumference of the circle passing through the two charted objects observed and the observer. The fix error, i.e., the length of the chord FT in figure 1007b, is dependent upon the magnitude of the constant error ϵ, the distance between the charted objects, and the cosecant of the angle of cut, angle θ. In figure 1007b,

$$\text{fix error} = FT = \frac{\epsilon\, BC \csc \theta}{2} \qquad \text{(where } \epsilon \text{ is a small angle).}$$

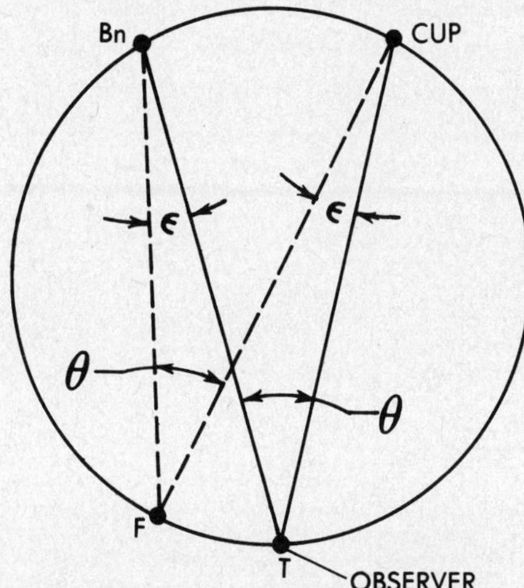

FIGURE 1007a.—Two-bearing plot.

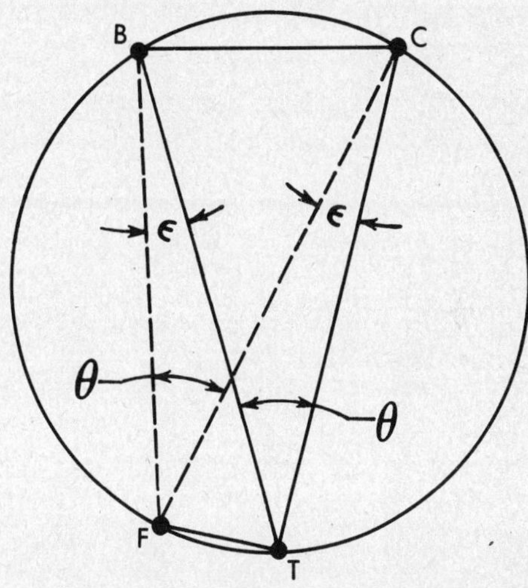

FIGURE 1007b.—Two-bearing plot with constant error.

Thus, the fix error is least when the angle of cut is 90°. As illustrated in figure 1007c, the error increases in accordance with the cosecant function as the angle of cut decreases. The increase in the error becomes quite rapid after the angle of cut has decreased to below about 30°. With an angle of cut of 30°, the fix error is about twice that at 90°.

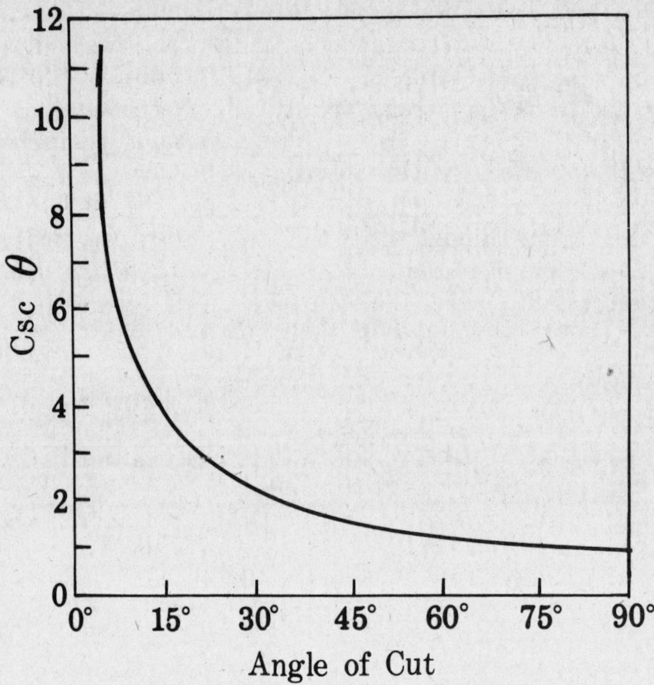

FIGURE 1007c.—Error of two-bearing plot.

1008. Three-bearing plot.—Assuming only constant error in the plot, the plot of three bearing lines forms a **triangle of error,** sometimes called **cocked hat.** As shown in figure 1008a, each apex of the triangle lies on the circumference of a circle passing through the two respective beacons and the observer at point *T*.

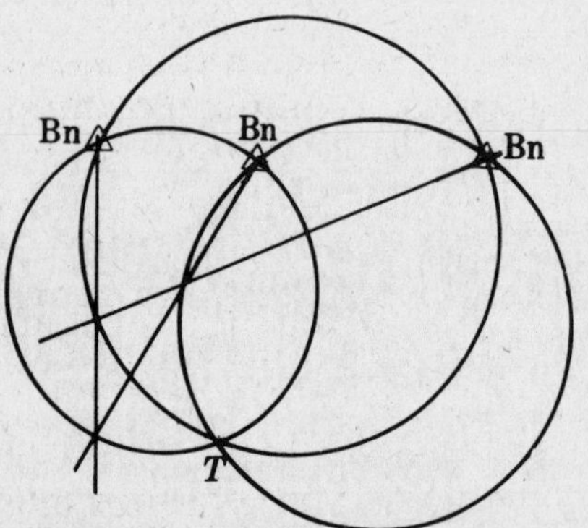

FIGURE 1008a.—Triangle of error.

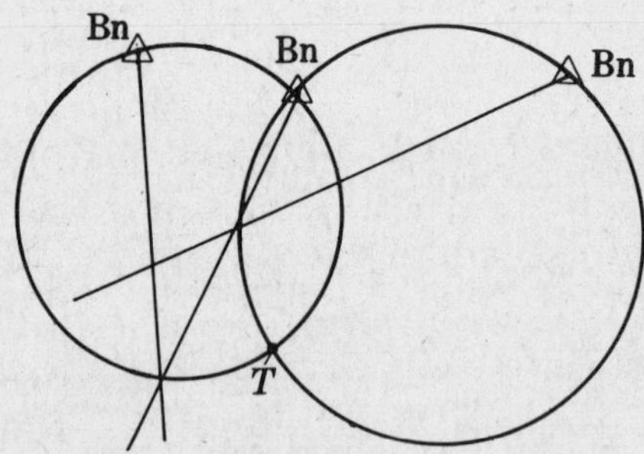

FIGURE 1008b.—Three-bearing plot.

The same situation is shown in figure 1008b, but only two of the circles are drawn through their respective beacons. For the set of angular differences established by the differences of the bearing observations, the observer can be located only at the intersection of the two circles at point *T*. Note that point *T* is not inside the triangle in this instance. If all error is due to constant error and the bearing spread, i.e., the angular difference between the extreme left and right beacons, is less than 180°, point *T* is *always* outside the triangle. If all error is due to constant error, and the bearing spread is greater than 180°, point *T* is always inside the triangle as shown in figure 1008c.

With a bearing spread greater than 180°, and assuming only constant error, the fix position in a three-bearing plot forming a triangle of error is the geometric center of the triangle as shown in figure 1008c. The geometric center is located at the intersection of the bisectors of the three interior angles as illustrated in figure 1008d.

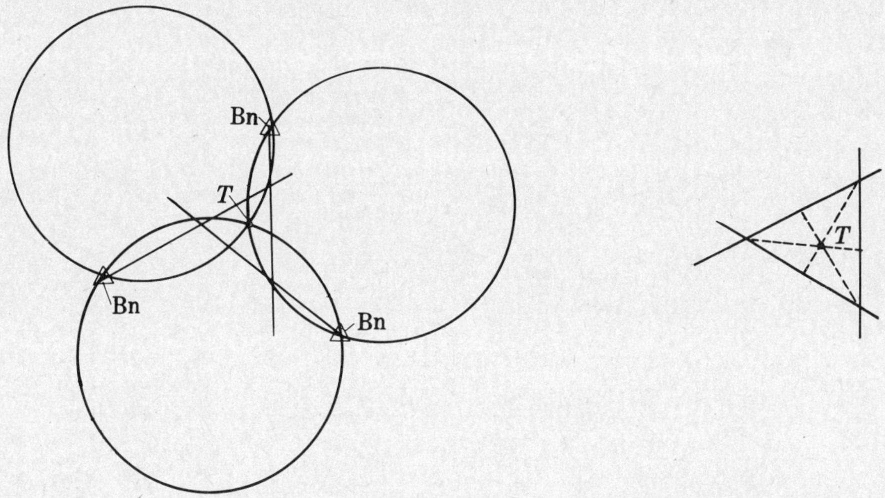

FIGURE 1008c.—Three-bearing plot.

FIGURE 1008d.—Bisecting the interior angles of a triangle of error.

With a bearing spread less than 180°, and assuming only constant error, the fix position in a three-bearing plot forming a triangle of error lies outside the triangle at the point of common intersection obtained by rotating each bearing line an equal amount in the same direction. This common intersection lies at the intersection of the bisectors of the appropriate two adjacent exterior angles and the opposite interior angle. Examination of figure 1008e, and similar constructions for bearing spreads of less than 180°, reveals that the common intersection cannot lie within the area bounded by the bearing lines extending from the triangle toward their respective objects. Further examination reveals that of the two remaining sets of adjacent exterior angles being investigated to determine that set which, with its opposite interior angle, should be bisected to determine the common intersection, only one set is immediately adjacent to the area bounded by the bearing lines extending from the triangle toward their respective objects. The set adjacent to the latter area is the set to be bisected.

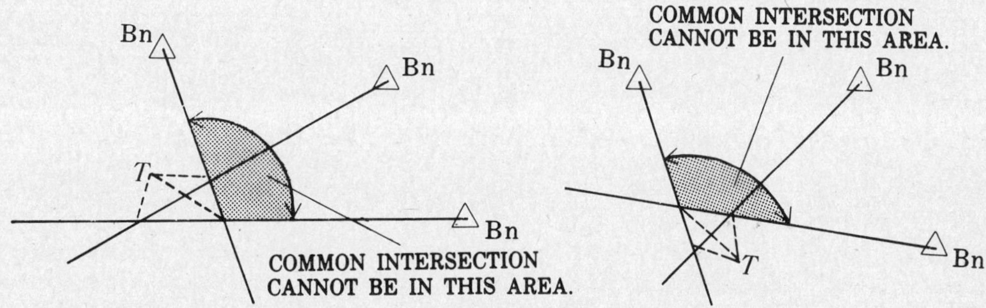

FIGURE 1008e.—Bisecting the exterior angles of a triangle of error.

1009. Adjusting a fix for constant error.—If several fixes obtained by bearings on three objects produce triangles of error of about the same size, one might reasonably suspect a constant error in the observation of the bearings, particularly if the same instrument is used for all observations, or in the plotting of the lines. If the application of a constant error to all bearings results in a point, or near-point fix, the navigator is usually justified in applying such a correction. This situation is illustrated in figure 1009a, where the solid lines indicate the original plot, and the broken lines indicate each line of position moved 3° in a clockwise direction. If different instruments are used for observation, one of them might be consistently in error. This might be detected by altering all bearings observed by that instrument by a fixed amount and producing good fixes.

When there is indication of constant error in a cross-bearing plot, the **Franklin Piloting Technique** can be used for rapid determination of the direction and magnitude of the error. The use of the technique avoids the delays associated with the trial and error method (fig. 1009a). Being a rapid method for determining with sufficient accuracy the normally small errors of the compass, the technique provides a means for maintaining the cross-bearing plot even when the compass error is variable from one round of bearings to the next. To apply the technique when there is indication of constant error in the plot, the navigator selects three objects for his next round of bearings in accordance with the following rules:

1. Two of the three objects should be nearby so that the displacements of their plotted bearings lines from the observer's actual position, as a result of a small constant error, will be small.

2. The third object should be at least two and one-half times the distance of the farther of the two nearby objects so that the displacement of its plotted bearing line from the observer's actual position, as a result of a small constant error, will be relatively large.

3. Preferably, the third object should lie in a direction from the observer approximately parallel to a line between the two nearby objects.

With selection as in (3) above, the line drawn from the third object to the intersection of the bearing lines of the two nearby objects is nearly tangent to the circle through these nearby objects and the observer's actual position (fig. 1009b). Being nearly tangent to this circle, the line drawn from the most distant object passes close to the observer's actual position, which is close to the point of tangency for small constant errors.

As shown in figure 1009b, the bearing lines through nearby objects A and B intersect at F on the circle through A, B, and the observer's actual position at point T. The acute angle between the plotted bearing line through distant object C and a line from C to T is exactly equal to the error, assuming that all error is due to a constant compass error. It follows that the acute angle between the plotted bearing line through distant object C and the line from C to F is approximately equal to the error.

Because the objects observed in figure 1009b lie within a bearing spread of 180°, the most probable position of the fix is outside the triangle of error. The fix is determined from the set of adjacent exterior angles (and opposite interior angle) which are immediately adjacent to the area formed by the three lines extending from the triangle of error toward the observed objects.

From geometry, the fix cannot lie within the shaded area (fig. 1009c); the fix cannot lie within the triangle of error; the fix is determined by the set of adjacent exterior angles of the triangle of error which are immediately adjacent to the shaded area. The adjacent set establishes the fix at T.

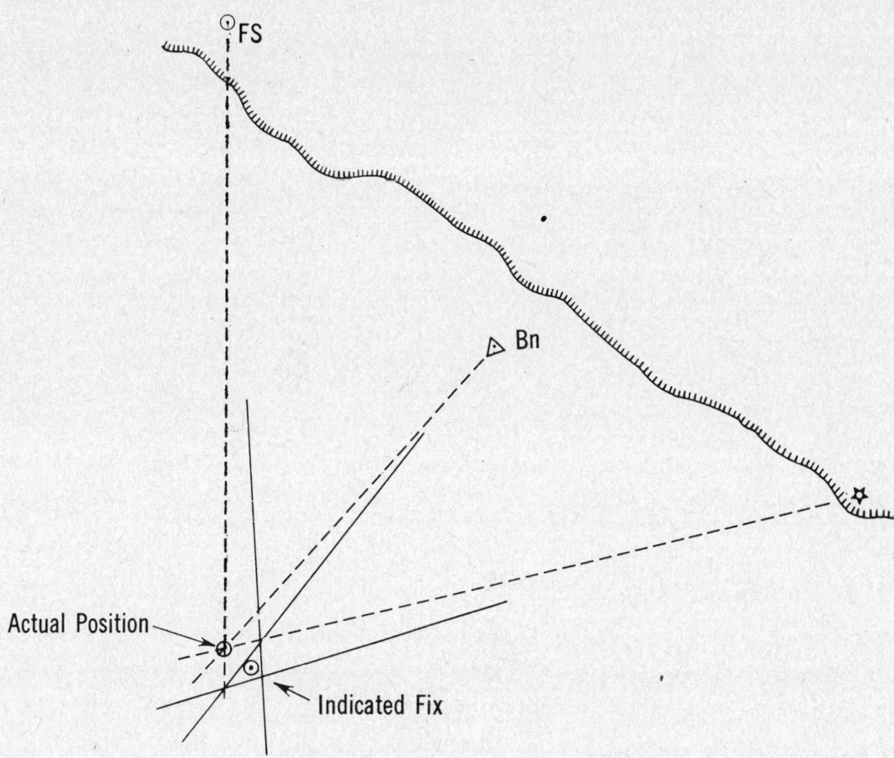

FIGURE 1009a.—Adjusting a fix for constant error.

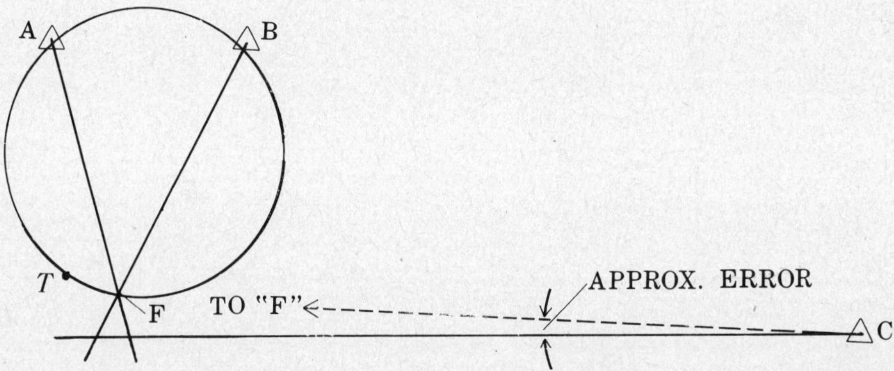

FIGURE 1009b.—Selection of charted objects for observation.

Although the foregoing use of the geometry of the cross-bearing plot could be used to find the direction of the constant error, the Franklin technique provides a simpler means. However, a reference direction must first be established. This reference direction is used to determine whether the plotted bearing line of one of the three objects lies to the left or right of the intersection of the bearing lines of the other two. For example, in the left-hand plot of figure 1009d the intersection at *F* is taken as being to the right of the plotted bearing line of object *C*.

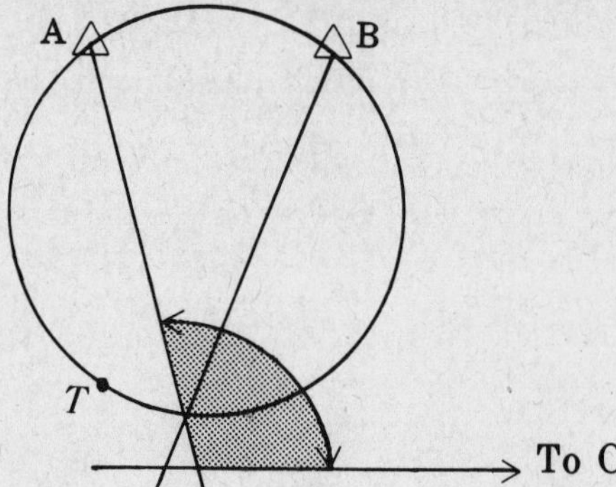

FIGURE 1009c.—Determining the most probable position of the fix.

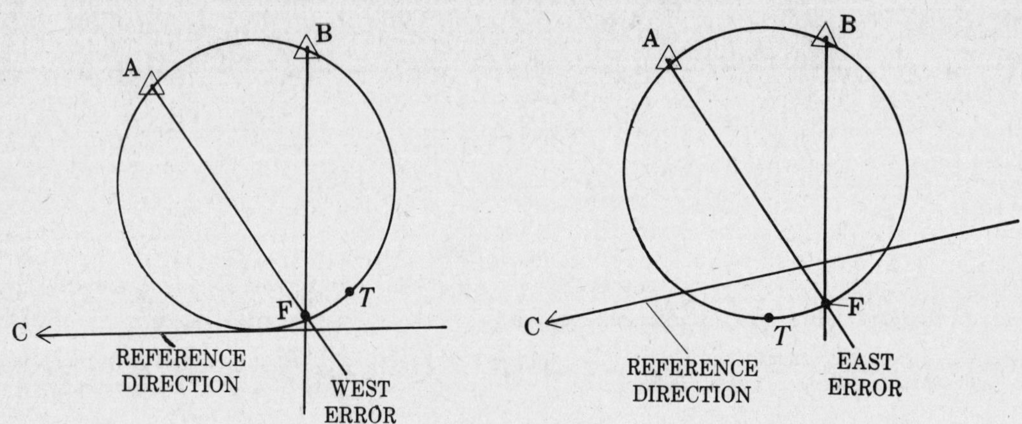

FIGURE 1009d.—Determining constant error when bearing spread is less than 180°.

When the bearing spread is less than 180°, the direction of either the extreme left-hand or right-hand object from the observer's approximate position is used as the reference direction. When the bearing spread is greater than 180°, the direction of any one of the three objects from the observer's position can be used as the reference direction.

If the bearing spread is less than 180° and the plotted bearing line extended through the extreme left-hand or right-hand object lies to the right of the intersection of the other two plotted bearing lines (fig. 1009d), the error is east; otherwise the error is west.

If the bearing spread is greater than 180° and the plotted bearing line through one object lies to the right of the intersection of the other two plotted bearing lines, the error is east; otherwise the error is west.

1010. Nonsimultaneous observations.—For fully accurate results, observations made to fix the position of a moving vessel should be made simultaneously, or nearly so. On a slow-moving vessel, relatively little error is introduced by making several observations in quick succession. A wise precaution is to observe the objects more nearly ahead or astern first, since these are least affected by the motion of the observer. However, when it is desired to obtain a good estimate of the speed being made good, it may be desirable to observe the most rapidly changing bearing first, assuming that such observation can be better coordinated with the time "mark."

Sometimes it is not possible or desirable to make simultaneous or nearly simultaneous observations. Such a situation may arise, for instance, when a single object is available for observation, or when all available objects are on nearly the same or reciprocal bearings, and there is no means of determining distance. Under such conditions, a period of several minutes or more may be permitted to elapse between observations to provide lines of position crossing at suitable angles. When this occurs, the lines can be adjusted to a common time to obtain a **running fix.** Refer to figure 1010a. A ship is proceeding along a coast on course 020°, speed 15 knots. At 1505 lighthouse *L* bears 310°. If the line of position is accurate, the ship is somewhere on it at the time of observation. Ten minutes later the ship will have traveled 2.5 miles in direction 020°. If the ship was at *A* at 1505, it will be at *A*′ at 1515. However, if the position at 1505 was *B*, the position at 1515 will be *B*′. A similar relationship exists between *C* and *C*′, *D* and *D*′, *E* and *E*′, etc. Thus, if *any* point on the original line of position is moved a distance equal to the distance run, and in the direction of the motion, a line through this point, parallel to the original line of position, represents all possible positions of the ship at the later time. This process is called **advancing** a line of position. The moving of a line *back* to an *earlier* time is called **retiring** a line of position.

The accuracy of an adjusted line of position depends not only upon the accuracy of the original line, but also upon the reliability of the information used in moving the line. A small error in the course made good has little effect upon the accuracy of a bearing line of an object near the beam, but maximum effect upon the bearing line of an object nearly ahead or astern. Conversely, the effect of an error in speed is maximum upon the bearing line of an object abeam. The opposite is true of circles of position. The best estimate of course and speed made good should be used in advancing or retiring a line of position.

If there are any changes of course or speed, these should be considered, for the motion of the line of position should reflect as accurately as possible the motion of the observer between the time of observation and the time to which the line is adjusted.

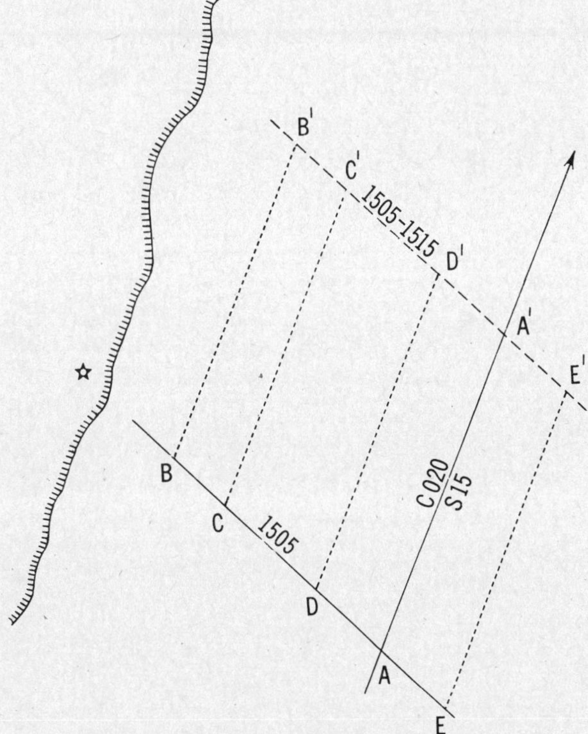

Figure 1010a.—Advancing a line of position.

Perhaps the easiest way to do this is to measure the direction and distance between dead reckoning or estimated positions at the two times, and use these to adjust some point on the line of position. This method is shown in figure 1010b. In this illustration

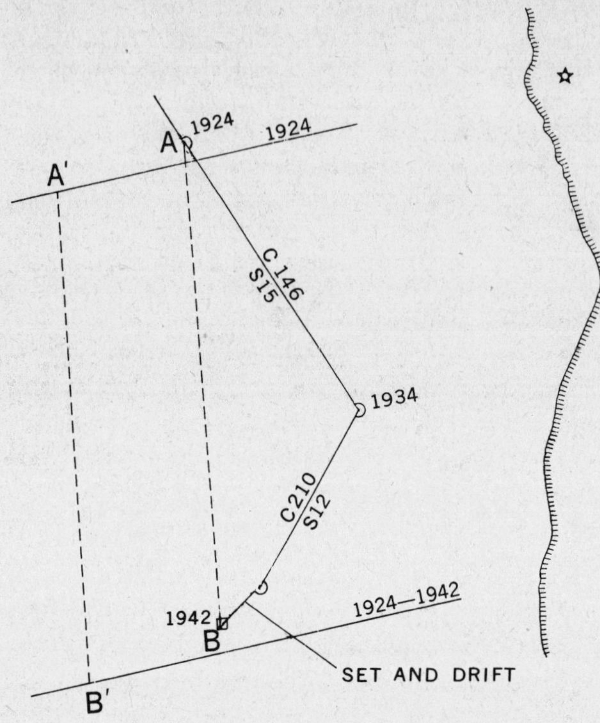

FIGURE 1010b.—Advancing a line of position with a change in course and speed, and allowing for current.

allowance is made for the estimated combined effect of wind and current, this effect being plotted as an additional course and distance. If courses and speeds made good over the ground are used, the separate plotting of the wind and current effect is not used. In the illustration, point *A* is the DR position at the time of observation, and point *B* is the estimated position (the DR position adjusted for wind and current) at the time to which the line of position is adjusted. Line *A′B′* is of the same length and in the same direction as line *AB*.

Other techniques may be used. The position of the object observed may be advanced or retired, and the line of position drawn in relation to the adjusted position. This is the most satisfactory method for a circle of position, as shown in figure 1010c. When the position of the landmark is adjusted, the advanced line of position can be laid down without plotting the original line, which need be shown only if it serves a useful purpose. This not only eliminates part of the work, but reduces the number of lines on the chart, and thereby decreases the possibility of error. Another method is to draw any line, such as a perpendicular, from the dead reckoning position at the time of observation to the line of position. A line of the same length and in the same direction, drawn from the DR position or EP at the time to which the line is adjusted, locates a point on the adjusted line, as shown in figure 1010d. If a single course and speed is involved, common practice is to measure from the intersection of the line of position and the course line. If the dividers are set to the distance run between bearings and placed on the chart so that one point is on the first bearing line and the other point

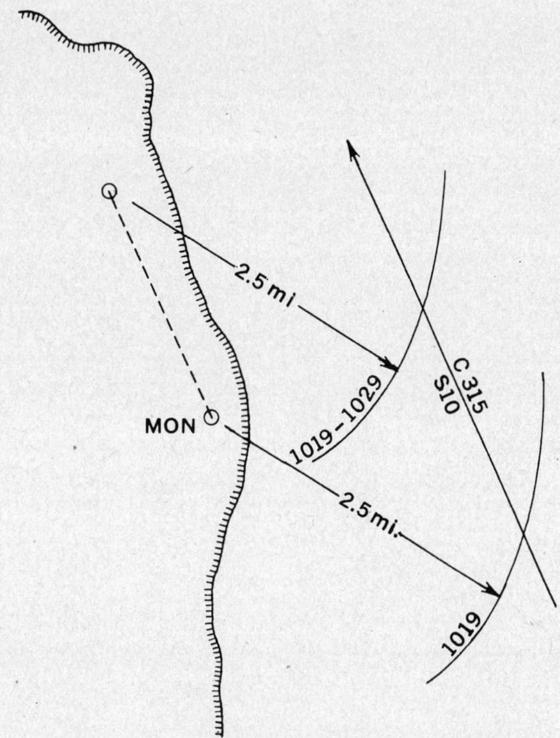

FIGURE 1010c.—Advancing a circle of position.

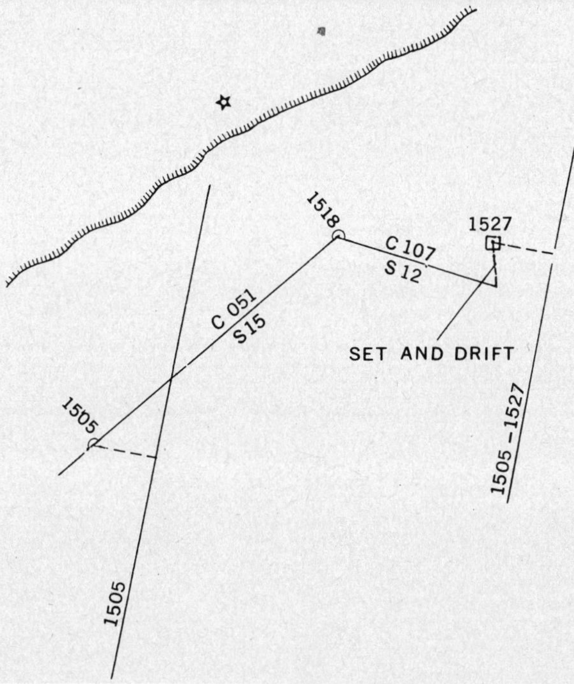

FIGURE 1010d.—Advancing a line of position by its relation to the dead reckoning.

is on the second bearing line, and the line connecting the points is parallel to the course line, the points will indicate the positions of the vessel at the times of the bearings.

An adjusted line of position is labeled the same as an unadjusted one, except that both the time of observation and the time to which the line is adjusted are shown, as in the illustrations of this article and article 1011. Because of additional sources of error in adjusted lines of position, they are not used when satisfactory simultaneous lines can be obtained.

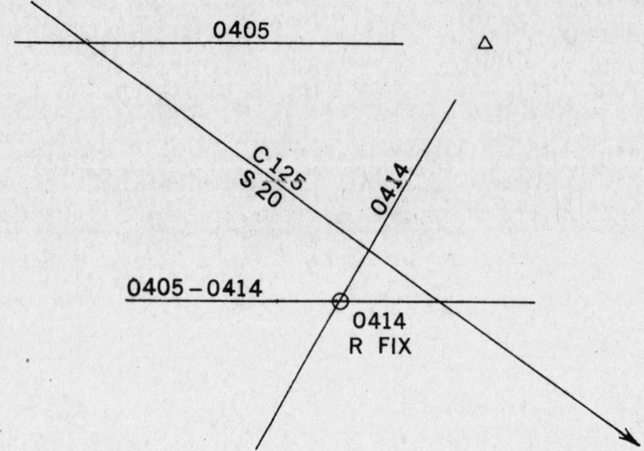

FIGURE 1011a.—A running fix by two bearings on the same object.

1011. The running fix.—As stated in article 1010, a fix obtained by means of lines of position taken at different times and adjusted to a common time is called a **running fix.** In piloting, common practice is to *advance* earlier lines to the time of the last observation. Figure 1011a illustrates a running fix obtained from two bearings of the same object. In figure 1011b the ship changes course and speed between observations of two objects. A running fix by two circles of position is shown in figure 1011c.

When simultaneous observations are not available, a running fix may provide the most reliable position obtainable. The time between observations should be no longer than about 30 minutes, for the uncertainty of course and distance made good increases with time.

The errors applicable to a running fix are those resulting from errors of the individual lines of position. However, a given error may have quite a different effect upon the fix than upon the line of position. Consider, for example, the situation of an unknown head current. In figure 1011d a ship is proceeding along a coast, on course 250°, speed 12 knots. At 0920 light *A* bears 190°, and at 0930 it bears 143°. If the earlier bearing line is advanced a distance of two miles (ten minutes at 12 knots) in the direction of the course, the running fix is as shown by the solid lines. However, if there is a head current of two knots, the ship is making good a speed of only ten knots, and in ten minutes will travel a distance of only 1⅔ miles. If the first bearing line is advanced this distance, as shown by the broken line, the actual position of the ship is at *B*. *This is nearer the beach than the running fix,* and therefore a dangerous situation. A following current gives an indication of position too far from the object. Therefore, if a current *parallel* to the course (either head or following) is suspected, a *minimum* estimate of speed made good will result in a possible margin of safety. If the second bearing is of a different object, a *maximum* estimate of speed should be made if the second object is on the same side and farther forward, or on the opposite side and farther aft, than the first object was when observed. All of these situations assume that danger

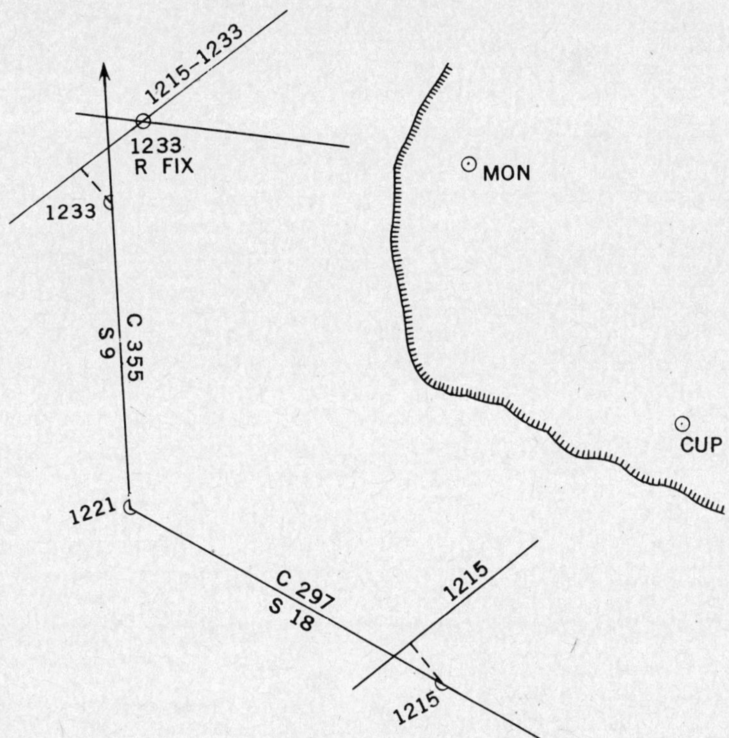

FIGURE 1011b.—A running fix with a change of course and speed between observations on separate landmarks.

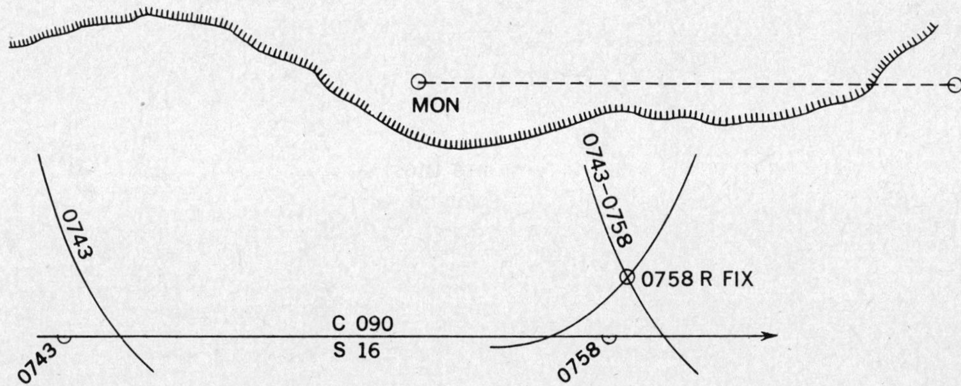

FIGURE 1011c.—A running fix by two circles of position.

is on the same side as the object observed first. If there is either a head or following current, a series of running fixes based upon a number of bearings of the same object will plot in a straight line parallel to the course line, as shown in figure 1011e. The plotted line will be too close to the object observed if there is a following current, and too far out if there is a head current. The existence of the current will not be apparent unless the actual speed over the ground is known. The position of the plotted line relative to the dead reckoning course line is not a reliable guide.

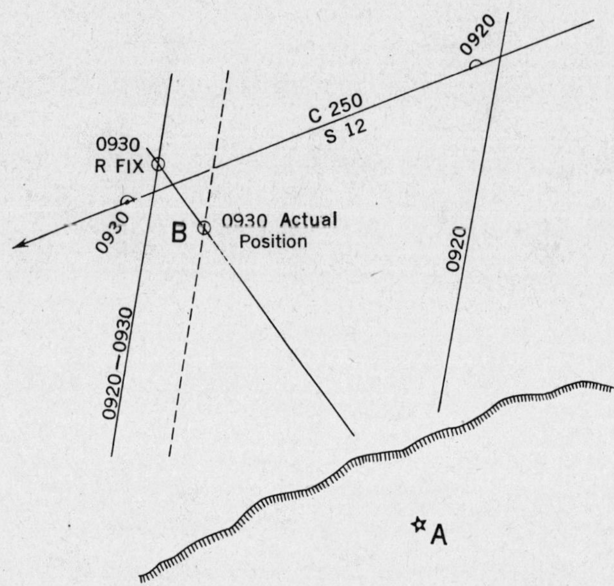

FIGURE 1011d.—Effect of a head current on a running fix.

A current oblique to the course will result in an incorrect position, but the direction of the error is indeterminate. In general, the effect of a current with a strong head or following component is similar to that of a head or following current, respectively. The existence of an oblique current, but not its amount, can be detected by observing and plotting several bearings of the same object. The running fix obtained by advancing one bearing line to the time of the next one will not agree with the running fix obtained by advancing an earlier line. Thus, if bearings *A*, *B*, and *C* are observed at five-minute intervals, the running fix obtained by advancing *B* to the time of *C* will not be the same as that obtained by advancing *A* to the time of *C*, as shown in figure 1011f.

Whatever the current, the *direction* of the course made good (assuming constant current and constant course and speed) can be determined. Three bearings of a charted object *O* are observed and plotted (fig. 1011g). Through *O* draw *XY* in any direction. Using a convenient scale, determine points *A* and *B* so that *OA* and *OB* are proportional to the time intervals between the first and second bearings and the second and third bearings, respectively. From *A* and *B* draw lines parallel to the second bearing line, intersecting the first and third bearing lines at *C* and *D*, respectively. The direction of the line from *C* and *D* is the course being made good.

The principle of the method shown in figure 1011g is based on the property of similar triangles. A frequently desirable variation of the method is to use the first bearing line as the side of the triangle that is divided in proportion to the time intervals between bearings (fig. 1011h). This method of solution of the **three-bearing problem** is presented in *The Complete Coastal Navigator* by Charles H. Cotter.

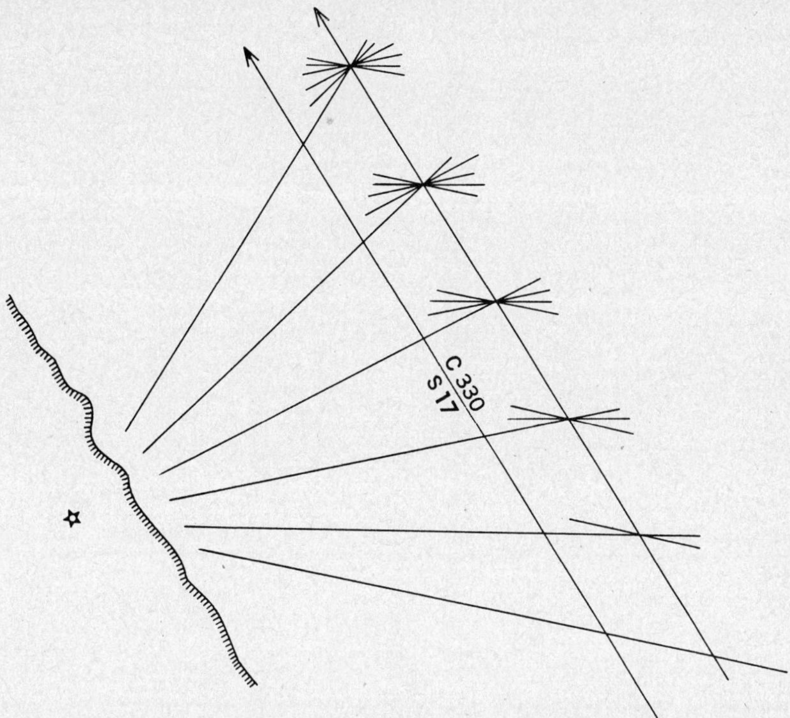

FIGURE 1011e.—A number of running fixes with a following current.

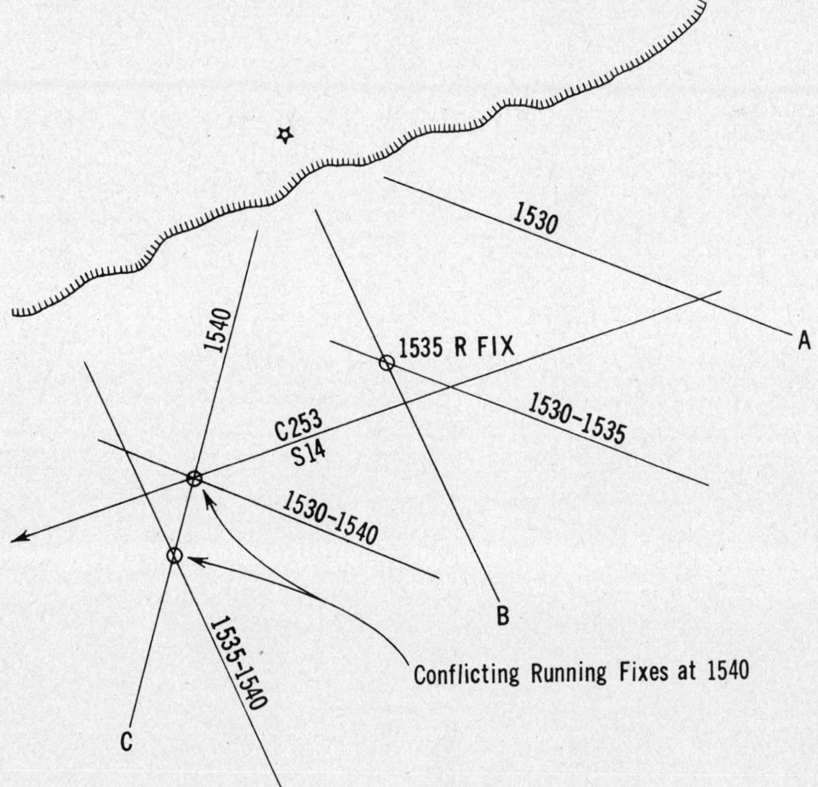

FIGURE 1011f.—Detecting the existence of an oblique current, by a series of running fixes.

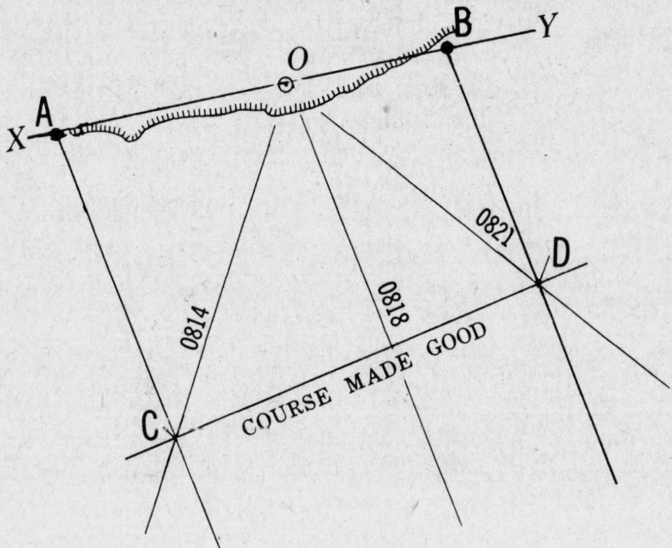

FIGURE 1011g.—Determining the course made good.

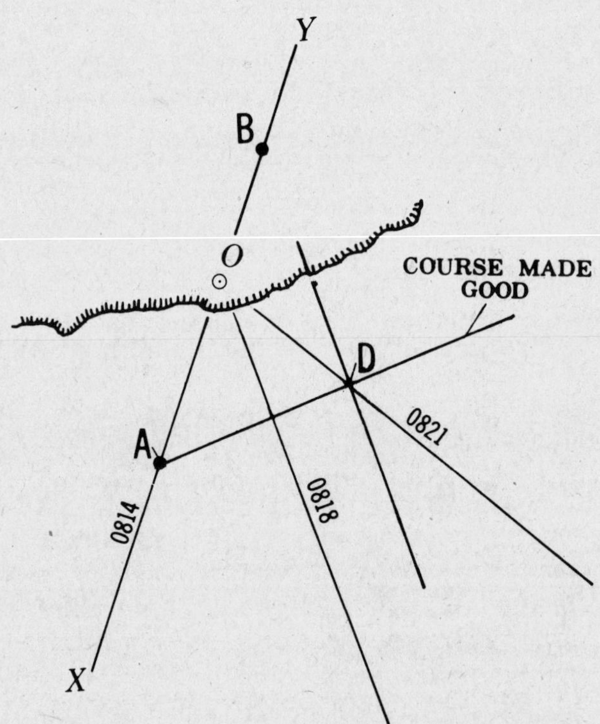

FIGURE 1011h.—Determining the course made good.

The distance of the line *CD* in figure 1011g from the track is in error by an amount proportional to the ratio of the speed being made good to the speed assumed for the solution. If a good fix (not a running fix) is obtained at some time before the first bearing for the running fix, and the current has not changed, the track can be determined by drawing a line from the fix, in the direction of the course made good. The intersection of the track with any of the bearing lines is an actual position.

The current can be determined whenever a dead reckoning position and fix are available for the same time. The direction *from* the dead reckoning position *to* the fix is the set of the current. The distance between these two positions, divided by the time (expressed in hours and tenths) since the last fix, is the drift of the current in knots. For accurate results, the dead reckoning position must be run up from the previous fix without any allowance for current. Any error in either the dead reckoning position (such as poor steering, unknown compass error, inaccurate log, wind, etc.) or the fix will be reflected in the determination of current. *When the dead reckoning position and fix are close together, a relatively small error in either may introduce a large error in the apparent set of the current.*

1012. Distance of an object by two bearings.—A running fix can be obtained by utilizing the mathematical relationships involved. A ship steams past landmark *D* (fig. 1012). At any point *A* a bearing of *D* is observed and expressed as degrees right or left of the course (*a relative bearing if the ship is on course*). At some later time, at *B*, a second bearing of *D* is observed and expressed as before. At *C* the landmark is broad on the beam. The angles at *A*, *B*, and *C* are known, and also the distance run between points. The various triangles could be solved by trigonometry to find the distance from *D* at any bearing. Distance and bearing provide a fix. Table 3 provides a quick and easy solution.

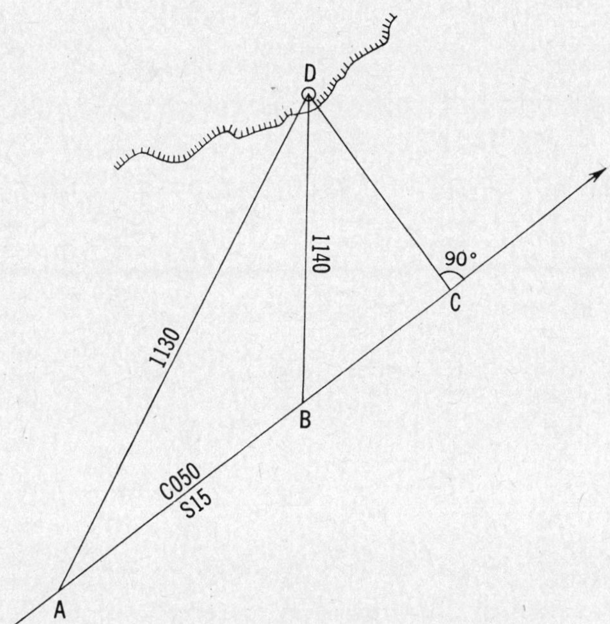

FIGURE 1012.—Triangles involved in a running fix.

Solution by table 3 or one of the special cases is accurate only *if a steady course has been steered,* the *vessel is unaffected by current, and the speed used is the speed over ground.*

There are certain *special cases* arising under the method of obtaining a running fix from two bearings and the intervening run which do not require the use of tables. Two of these cases arise when the multiplier is equal to unity, and the distance run is therefore equal to the distance from the object.

If the second difference (angle *CBD* of figure 1012) is double the first difference (angle *BAD*), triangle *BAD* is isoceles with equal angles at *A* and *D*. Therefore, side *AB* (the run) is equal to side *BD* (the distance off at the time of the second bearing). This is called **doubling the angle on the bow.** If the first angle is 45° and the second 90°, the distance run equals the distance when broad on the beam. These are called **bow and beam bearings.**

1013. Safe piloting without a fix.—A fix or running fix is not always necessary to insure safety of the vessel. If a ship is proceeding up a dredged channel, for instance, the only knowledge needed to prevent grounding is that the ship is within the limits of the dredged area. This information might be provided by a range in line with the channel. A fix is not needed except to mark the point at which the range can no longer be followed with safety.

Under favorable conditions a **danger bearing** might be used to insure safe passage past a shoal or other danger. Refer to figure 1013. A vessel is proceeding along a coast, on intended track *AB*. A shoal is to be avoided. A line *HX* is drawn from light-

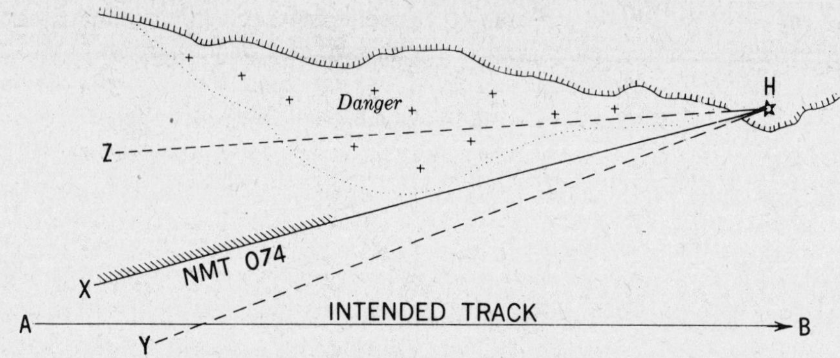

FIGURE 1013.—A danger bearing.

house *H*, tangent to the outer edge of the danger. As long as the bearing of light *H* is *less* than *XH*, the danger bearing, the vessel is in safe water. An example is *YH*, no part of the bearing line passing through the danger area. Any bearing *greater* than *XH*, such as *ZH*, indicates a *possible* dangerous situation. If the object is passed on the port side, the safe bearing is *less* than the danger bearing, as shown in figure 1013. If the object is passed on the starboard side, the danger bearing represents the minimum bearing, safe ones being *greater*. To be effective, a danger bearing should not differ greatly from the course, and the object of which bearings are to be taken should be easily identifiable and visible over the entire area of usefulness of the danger bearing. A margin of safety might be provided by drawing line *HX* through a point a short distance off the danger. In figure 1013, the danger bearing is labeled NMT 074 to indicate that the bearing of the light should not be more than 074°. The hazardous side of the bearing line is hatched. If a natural or artifical range is available as a danger bearing, it should be used.

A vessel proceeding along a coast may be in safe water as long as it remains a minimum distance off the beach. This information may be provided by any means available. One method useful in avoiding particular dangers is the use of a **danger angle** (art. 1109).

A vessel may sometimes be kept in safe water by means of a **danger sounding.** The value selected depends upon the draft of the vessel and the slope of the bottom. It should be sufficiently deep to provide adequate maneuvering room for the vessel to reach deeper water before grounding, once the minimum depth is obtained. In an area where the shoaling is gradual, a smaller margin of depth can be considered than in an area of rapid shoaling. Where the shoaling is very abrupt, as off Point Conception, California, no danger sounding is practical. It is good practice to prominently mark the danger sounding line on the chart. A colored pencil is useful for this purpose.

If it is desired to round a point marked by a prominent landmark, without approaching closer than a given minimum distance, this can be done by steaming until the minimum distance is reached and then immediately changing course so as to bring the landmark broad on the beam. Frequent small changes of course are then used to keep the landmark near, *but not forward of*, the beam. This method is not reliable if the vessel is being moved laterally by wind or current.

An approximation of the distance off can be found by noting the rate at which the bearing changes. If the landmark is kept abeam, the change is indicated by a change of heading. During a change of 57°5, the distance off is about the same as the distance run. For a change of 28°5, the distance is about twice the run; for 19° it is about three times the run; for 14°5 it is about four times the run; and for 11°5 it is about five times the run. Another variation is to measure the number of seconds required for a change of 16°. The distance off is equal to this interval multiplied by the speed in knots and divided by 1,000. That is, $D=\frac{St}{1,000}$, where D is the distance in nautical miles, S is the speed in knots, and t is the time interval in seconds. This method can also be used for straight courses (with bearings 8° forward and abaft the beam), but with somewhat reduced accuracy.

1014. Soundings.—The most important use of soundings is to determine whether the depth is sufficient to provide a reasonable margin of safety for the vessel. For this reason, soundings should be taken continuously in pilot waters. A study of the chart and the establishment of a danger sounding (art. 1013) should indicate the degree of safety of the vessel at any time.

Under favorable conditions, soundings can be a valuable aid in establishing the position of the vessel. Their value in this regard depends upon the configuration of the bottom, the amount and accuracy of information given on the chart, the type and accuracy of the sounding equipment available aboard ship, and the knowledge and skill of the navigator. In an area having a flat bottom devoid of distinctive features, or in an area where detailed information is not given on the chart, little positional information can be gained from soundings. However, in an area where depth curves run roughly parallel to the shore, a sounding might indicate distance from the beach. In any area where a given depth curve is sharply defined and relatively straight, it serves as a line of position which can be used with other lines, such as those obtained by bearings of landmarks, to obtain a fix. The 100-fathom curve at the outer edge of the continental shelf might be crossed with a line of position from celestial observation or Loran. The crossing of a sharply defined trench, ridge, shoal, or flat-topped seamount (a **guyot**) might provide valuable positional information.

In any such use, identification of the feature observed is important. In an area of rugged underwater terrain, identification might be difficult unless an almost continuous determination of position is maintained, for it is not unusual for a number of features within a normal radius of uncertainty to be similar. If the echo sounder produces a continuous recording of the depth, called a **bottom profile,** this can be matched to the chart in the vicinity of the course line. If no profile is available, a rough approximation of one can be constructed as follows: Record a series of soundings at short intervals, the length being dictated by the scale of the chart and the existing situation. For most purposes the interval might be each minute, or perhaps each half-mile or mile, Draw a straight line on transparent material and, at the scale of the chart, place marks along the line at the distance intervals at which soundings were made. For this purpose the line might be superimposed over the latitude scale or a distance scale of the chart. At each mark record the corresponding sounding. Then place the transparency over the chart and, by trial and error, match the recorded soundings to those indicated on the chart. Keep the line on the transparency parallel or nearly parallel to the course line plotted on the chart. A current may cause some difference between the plotted course line and the course made good. Also, speed over the bottom might be somewhat different from that used for the plot. This should be reflected in the match. This method should be used with caution, because it may be possible to fit the **line of soundings** to several places on the chart.

Exact agreement with the charted bottom should not be expected at all times. Inaccuracies in the soundings, tide, or incomplete data on the chart may affect the match, but general agreement should be sought. Any marked discrepancy should be investigated, particularly if it indicates less depth than anticipated. If such a discrepancy cannot be reconciled, the wisest decision might well be to haul off into deeper water or anchor and wait for more favorable conditions or additional information.

1015. Most probable position (MPP).—Since information sufficient to establish an *exact* position is seldom available, the navigator is frequently faced with the problem of establishing the most probable position of the vessel. If three reliable bearing lines cross at a point, there is usually little doubt as to the position, and little or no judgment is needed. But when conflicting information or information of questionable reliability is received, a decision is required to establish the MPP. At such a time the experience of the navigator can be of great value. Judgment can be improved if the navigator will continually try to account for all apparent discrepancies, even under favorable conditions. If a navigator habitually analyzes the situation whenever positional information is received, he will develop judgment as to the reliability of various types of information, and will learn something of the conditions under which certain types should be treated with caution.

When complete positional information is lacking, or when the available information is considered of questionable reliability, the most probable position might well be considered an **estimated position (EP)**. Such a position might be determined from a single line of position, from a line of soundings, from lines of position which are somewhat inconsistent, from a dead reckoning position with a correction for current or wind, etc.

Whether the most probable position is a fix, running fix, estimated position, or dead reckoning position, it should be kept continually in mind, together with some estimate of its reliability. The practice of continuing a dead reckoning plot from one good fix to another is advisable, whether or not information is available to indicate a most probable position differing from the dead reckoning position, for the DR plot provides an indication of current and leeway. A series of estimated positions may not be consistent because of the continual revision of the estimate as additional information is received. However, it is good practice to plot all MPP's, and sometimes to maintain a separate EP plot based upon the best estimate of course and speed being made good over the ground, for this should furnish valuable information to indicate whether the present course is a safe one.

1016. Allowing for turning characteristics of vessel.—When precise piloting is necessary (as in an area where maneuvering space is limited, when a specified anchorage is approached, or when steaming in formation with other ships), the turning characteristics of the vessel should be considered. That is, a ship does not complete a turn instantaneously, but follows a curve the characteristics of which depend upon the vessel's length, beam, underwater contour, draft, trim, rudder angle, speed, effects of wind and sea, etc. At the moment the rudder is put over, the vessel begins to follow a

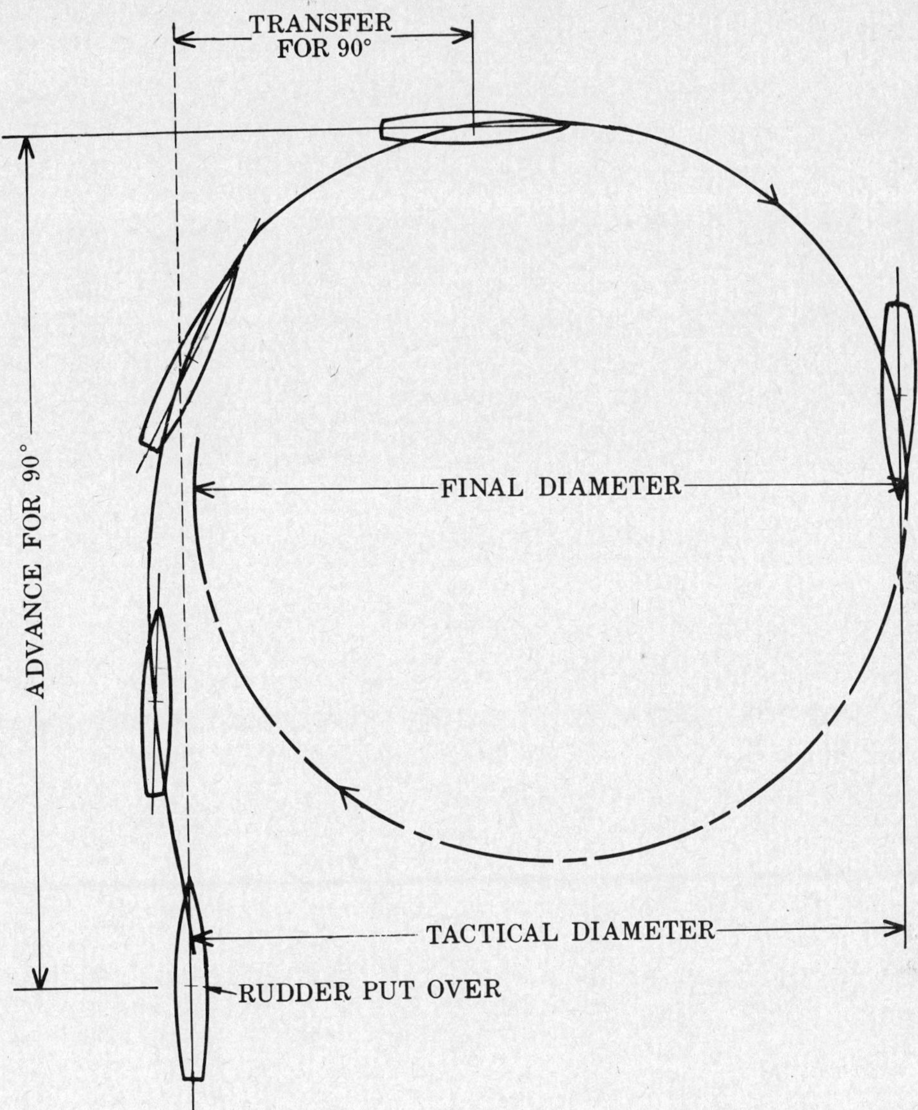

FIGURE 1016a.—Turning circle.

spiral path (fig. 1016a). This path becomes circular when the vessel has turned about 90°. The distance the vessel moves in the direction of the original course until the new course is reached is called **advance.** The distance the vessel moves perpendicular to the original course during the turn is called **transfer.** The **tactical diameter** is the distance gained to the right or left of the original course after a turn of 180° with a constant rudder angle. The **final diameter** is the diameter of a circle traversed by a vessel after turning through 360° and maintaining the same speed and rudder angle. This diameter is always less than the tactical diameter. It is measured perpendicular to the original course and between the tangents at the points where 180° and 360° of the turn have been completed. The vessel turns with its bow inside and its stern outside the tangent to the path of its center of gravity. The angle between the tangent to this path, the **turning circle,** and the centerline of the vessel is the **drift angle.** After the vessel has assumed its drift angle in a turn, the point on the centerline between the bow and the center of gravity at which the resultant of the velocities of rotation and translation is directed along the centerline is the **pivot point.** To an observer on board, the vessel appears to rotate about this point, which is normally at one-third to one-sixth of the distance from the bow to the center of gravity.

The amount of advance and transfer for a given vessel depends primarily upon the amount of rudder used and the angle through which the ship is to be turned. The speed of the vessel has little effect. Figure 1016b is a simplified illustration of advance and transfer for a turn of less than 90°. This figure does not include the initial drift away from the center of turning due to a lateral force caused by rudder action.

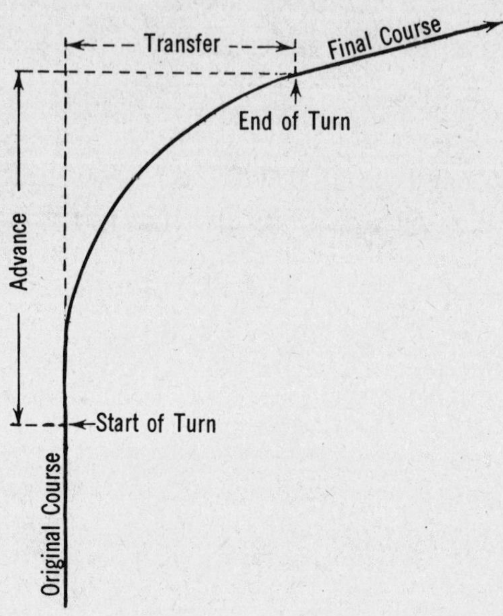

FIGURE 1016b.—Advance and transfer.

Allowance for advance and transfer is illustrated in the following example.

Example (fig. 1016c).—A ship proceeding on course 100° is to turn 60° to the left to come on a range which will guide it up a channel. For a 60° turn and the amount of rudder used, the advance is 920 yards and the transfer is 350 yards.

Required.—The bearing of flagpole "FP." when the rudder is put over.

Solution.—(1) Extend the original course line, *AB*.

(2) At a perpendicular distance of 350 yards, the transfer, draw a line *A'B'* parallel to the original course line *AB*. The point of intersection, *C*, of *A'B'* with the new course line (located by the range) is the place at which the turn is to be completed.

(3) From *C* draw a perpendicular, *CD*, to the original course line, intersecting it at *D*.

(4) From *D* measure the advance, 920 yards, *back* along the original course line. This locates *E*, the point at which the turn should be started.

(5) The direction of "FP." from *E*, 058°, is the bearing when the turn should be started.

Answer.—B 058°.

A frequently useful alternative procedure is the **distance to new course method.** From the vessel's tactical characteristics, a table is constructed to indicate, for various course alterations, speeds, and rudder angles, the distance from the point where the rudder is put over to the intersection (fig. 1016d) of the original course line and the extension of the intended new course line.

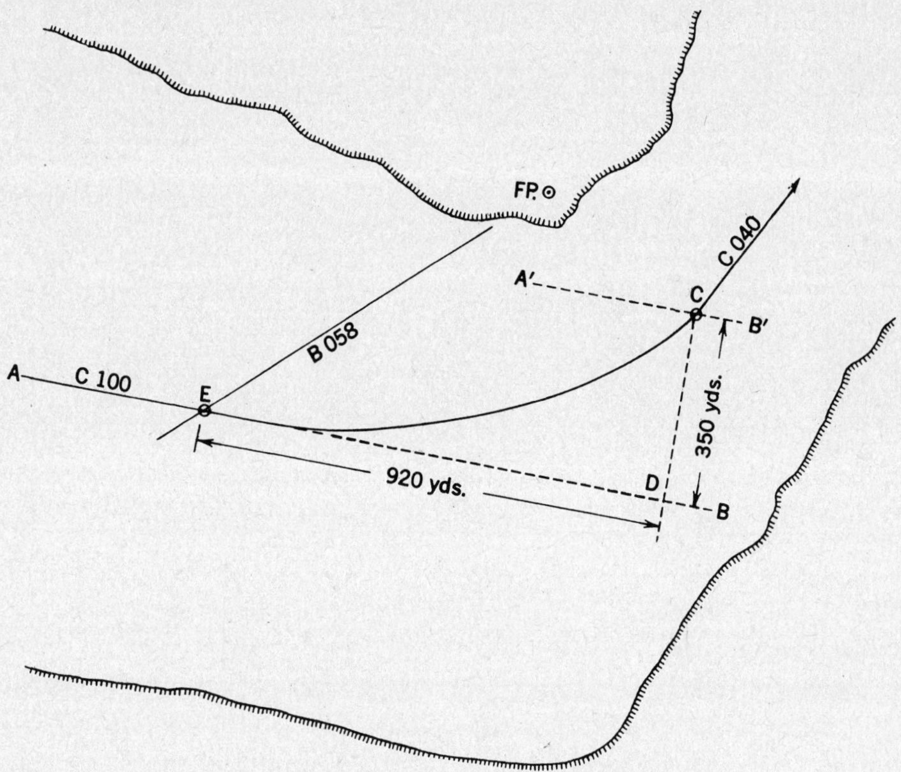

FIGURE 1016c.—Allowing for advance and transfer.

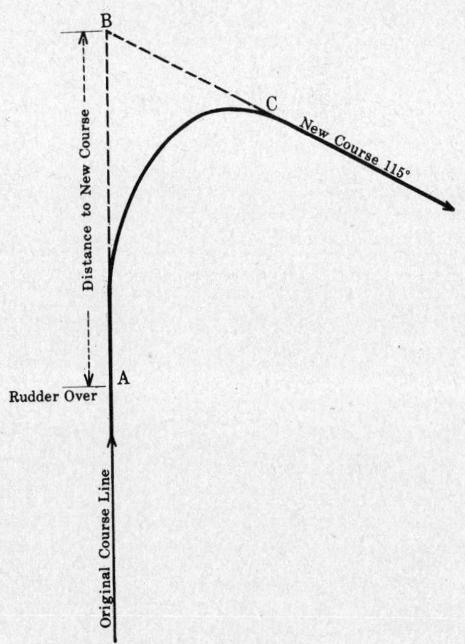

FIGURE 1016d.—Distance to new course method.

In application, the extension of the intended new course line is drawn to intersect the original course line. The table is referred to to determine the distance from this intersection to the point where the rudder should be put over. When the vessel reaches this point the rudder is put over.

Although the distance to new course method does not indicate where the vessel will be first on the new course line, it is simpler and faster to use than advance and transfer. However, practical considerations limit its use with course alterations greater than about 120°.

1017. Turning bearing.—The turning bearing is the predetermined bearing to a charted object from that point on the original track at which the rudder must be put over in order to effect the desired turn.

If the turning bearing is such that it is not nearly parallel to the predetermined course to which the vessel is turning, a large error may occur if the vessel is not on the intended track before the turn as shown in figure 1017.

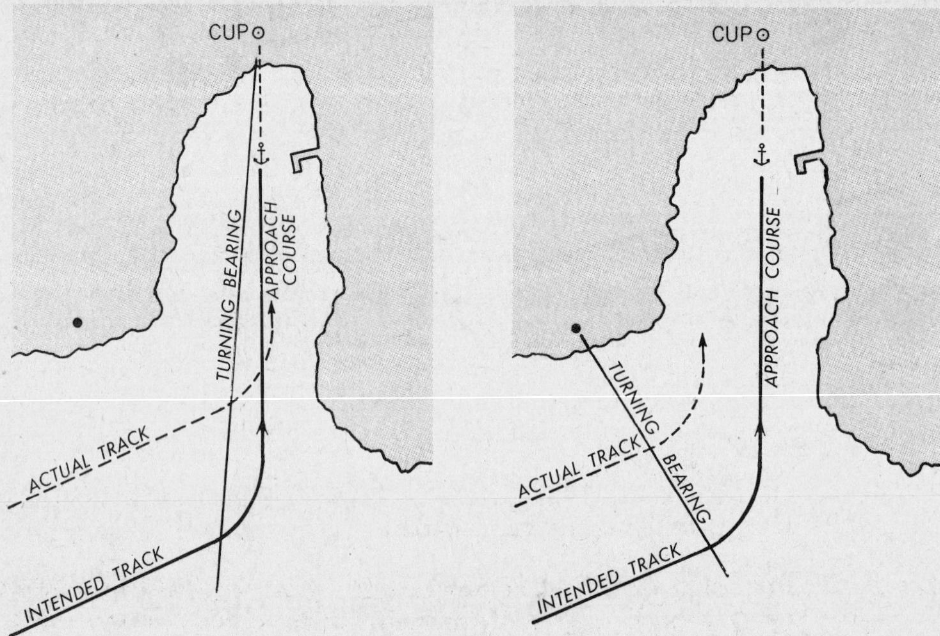

FIGURE 1017.—Selection of turning bearing to avoid large error when turning to predetermined course.

1018. Anchoring.—If a vessel is to anchor at a predetermined point, as in an assigned berth, an established procedure should be followed to insure accuracy of placing the anchor. Several procedures have been devised. The following is representative (fig. 1018). The use of a turning bearing not nearly parallel to the predetermined course, as in figure 1018, may result in a large error (art. 1017).

The position selected for anchoring is located on the chart. The direction of approach is then determined, considering limitations of land, shoals, other vessels, etc. Where conditions permit, the approach should be made heading into the current or, if the wind has a greater effect upon the vessel, into the wind. It is desirable to approach from such direction that a prominent object, or preferably a range, is available dead ahead to serve as a steering guide. It is also desirable to have a range or prominent object near the beam at the point of letting go the anchor. If practicable a straight

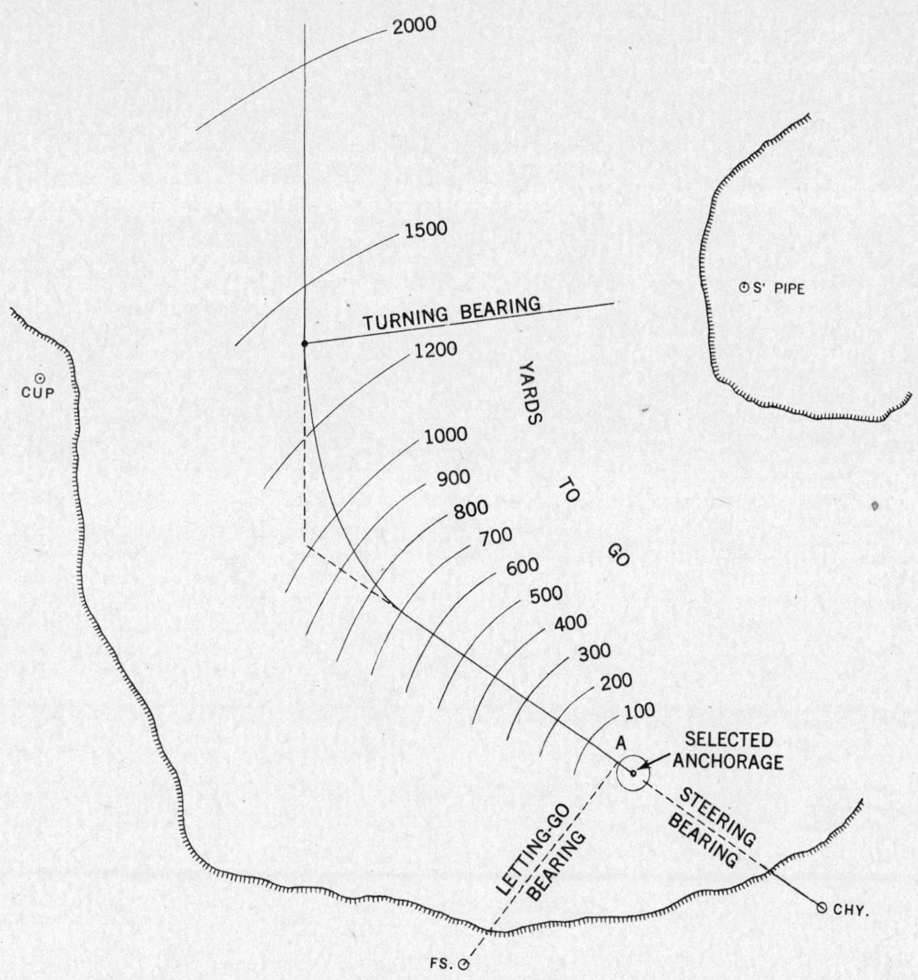

FIGURE 1018.—Anchoring.

approach of at least 500 yards should be provided to permit the vessel to steady on the required course. The track is then drawn in, allowing for advance and transfer during any turns.

Next, a circle is drawn with the selected position of the anchor as the center, and with a radius equal to the distance between the hawsepipe and pelorus, alidade, etc., used for measuring bearings. The intersection of this circle and the approach track, point *A*, is the position of the vessel (bearing-measuring instrument) at the moment of letting go. A number of arcs of circles are then drawn and labeled as shown in figure 1018. The desired position of the anchor is the common center of these arcs. The selected radii may be chosen at will. Those shown in figure 1018 have been found to be generally suitable. In each case the distance indicated is from the small circle. Turning bearings may also be indicated.

During the approach to the anchorage, fixes are plotted at frequent intervals, the measurement and plotting of bearings going on continuously, usually to the nearest half or quarter degree. The navigator advises the captain of any tendency of the vessel to drift from the desired track, so that adjustments can be made. The navigator also keeps the captain informed of the distance to go, to permit adjustment of the speed so that the vessel will be nearly dead in the water when the anchor is let go.

At the moment of letting go, the position of the vessel should be determined as accurately as possible, preferably by two simultaneous horizontal sextant angles, or by simultaneous or nearly simultaneous bearings of a number of prominent landmarks.

The exact procedure to use depends upon local conditions, number and training of available personnel, equipment, and personal preference of individuals concerned. Whatever the procedure, it should be carefully planned, and any needed advance preparations should be made early enough to avoid haste and the attendant danger of making a mistake. Teamwork is important. Each person involved should understand precisely what is expected of him.

1019. Piloting and electronics.—Many of the familiar electronic aids to navigation are used primarily in piloting. The radio direction finder provides bearings through fog and at greater distance from the aids. The sonic depth finder provides frequent or continuous soundings. Radar provides bearings, distances, and information on the location and identity of various targets. Some of the longer range systems such as Loran, Omega, and Decca extend piloting techniques far to sea, where nearness of shoals and similar dangers is not a problem.

1020. Practical piloting.—In pilot waters navigation is primarily an art. It is essential that the principles explained in this chapter be mastered and applied intelligently. From every experience the wise navigator acquires additional knowledge and improves his judgment. The mechanical following of a set procedure should not be expected to produce satisfactory results always.

While piloting, the successful navigator is somewhat of an opportunist, fitting his technique to the situation at hand. If a vessel is steaming in a large area having relatively weak currents and moderate traffic, like Chesapeake Bay, fixes may be obtained at relatively long intervals, with a dead reckoning plot between. In a narrow channel with swift currents and heavy traffic, an almost continuous fix is needed. In such an area the navigator may draw the desired track on the chart and obtain fixes every few minutes, or less, directing the vessel back on the track as it begins to drift to one side.

If the navigator is to traverse unfamiliar waters, he studies the chart, sailing directions or coast pilot, tide and tidal current tables, and light lists to familiarize himself with local conditions. The experienced navigator learns to interpret the signs around him. The ripple of water around buoys and other obstructions, the direction and angle of tilt of buoys, the direction at which vessels ride at anchor, provide meaningful information regarding currents. The wise navigator learns to interpret such signs when the position of his vessel is not in doubt. When visibility is poor, or available information is inconsistent, the ability developed at favorable times can be of great value.

With experience, a navigator learns when a danger angle or danger bearing is useful, and what ranges are reliable and how they should be used. However familiar one is with an area, he should not permit himself to become careless in the matter of timing lights for identification, plotting his progress on a chart, or keeping a good recent position. Fog sometimes creeps in unnoticed, obscuring landmarks before one realizes its presence. A series of frequent fixes obtained while various aids are visible provides valuable information on position and current.

Practical piloting requires a thorough familiarity with principles involved and local conditions, constant alertness, and judgment. A study of avoidable groundings reveals that in most cases the problem is not lack of knowledge, but failure to use or interpret available information. Among the more common errors are:

1. Failure to obtain or evaluate soundings.
2. Failure to identify aids to navigation.
3. Failure to use available navigational aids effectively.
4. Failure to correct charts.

5. Failure to adjust a magnetic compass or maintain an accurate table of corrections.
6. Failure to apply deviation, or error in its application.
7. Failure to apply variation, or to allow for change in variation.
8. Failure to check gyro and magnetic compass readings at frequent and regular intervals.
9. Failure to keep a dead reckoning plot.
10. Failure to plot information received.
11. Failure to properly evaluate information received.
12. Poor judgment.
13. Failure to do own navigating (following another vessel).
14. Failure to obtain and use information available on charts and in various publications.
15. Poor ship organization.
16. Failure to "keep ahead of the vessel."

Further discussion on practical piloting is given in chapter XXIII.

CHAPTER XI

USE OF SEXTANT IN PILOTING

1101. Introduction.—The marine sextant provides the most accurate means generally available to the mariner for fixing his position in confined waters. But following the widespread use of the highly reliable gyrocompass, the mariner's use of the sextant for piloting has declined to such an extent that it is seldom if ever used by many. This is unfortunate because the sextant can be used to advantage in situations where other methods or tools, including the gyrocompass, are inadequate.

The applications of the sextant during daylight in coastal waters, harbor approaches, and more confined waters may be summarized as follows:

1. fixing to make a safe transit of hazardous waters;
2. fixing to take a specific geographic position;
3. fixing to establish accurately the position of the anchor on anchoring;
4. fixing to determine whether or not the ship is dragging anchor;
5. using horizontal and vertical danger angles;
6. using vertical angles to determine distance off;
7. fixing to determine the positions of uncharted objects, or to verify the positions of charted features;
8. using the sextant to evaluate the accuracy of navigation by other means.

Because the use of the sextant has declined, many navigators, unfortunately, do not have the proficiency necessary to use it to advantage in those situations where other methods are inadequate. Proficiency in the use of the sextant can be invaluable in situations where even a small error in either observing or plotting cross bearings can result in a grounding.

1102. Three-point problem.—Normally, three charted objects are selected for measuring horizontal sextant angles to determine the observer's position, one of the objects being common to each angular measurement. With simultaneous or nearly simultaneous measurements of the horizontal angles between each pair of charted

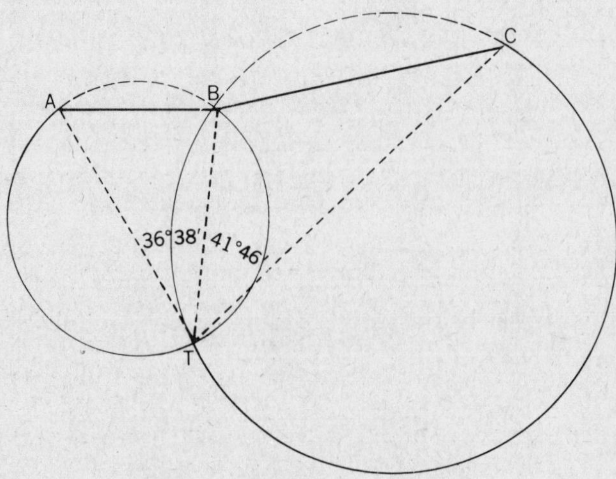

FIGURE 1102a.—Solving the three-point problem.

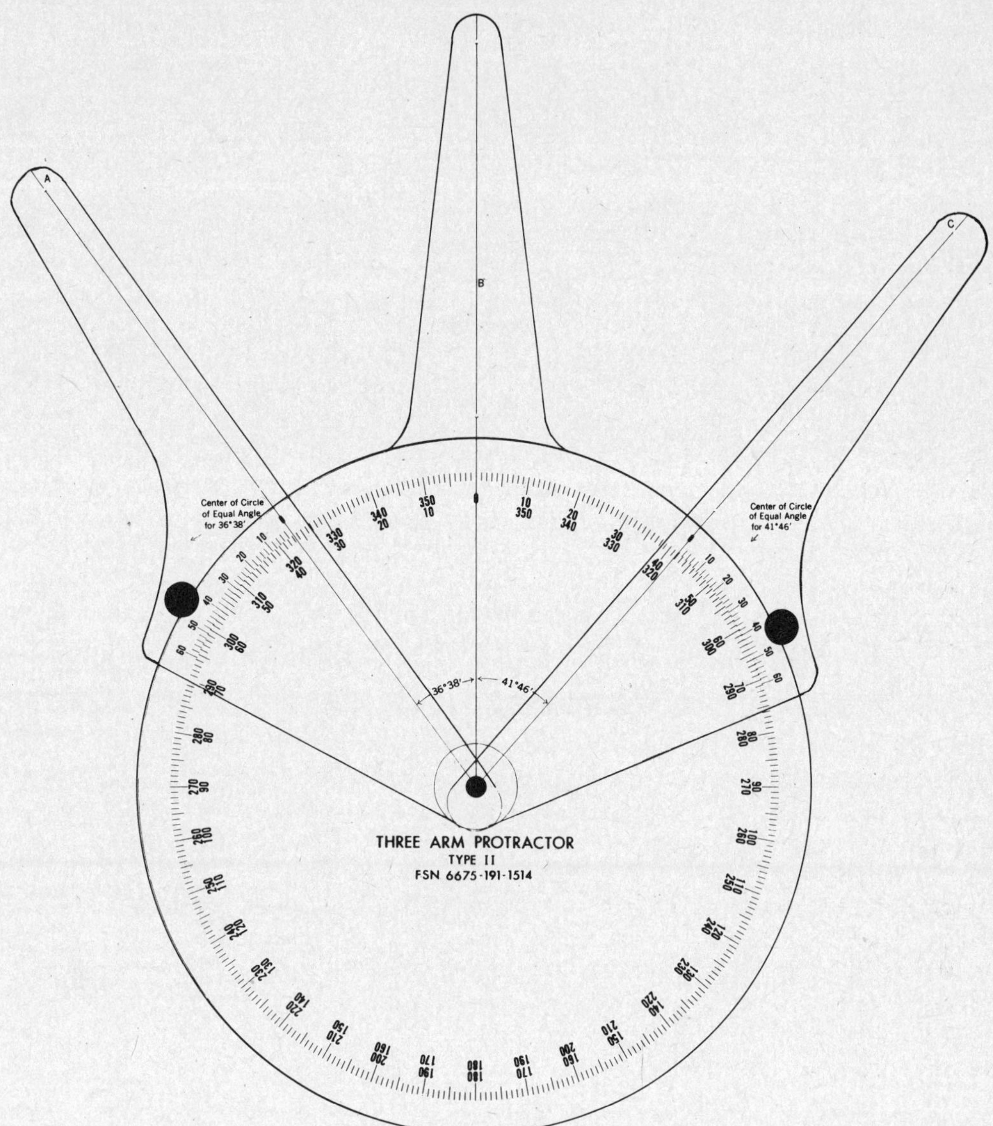

FIGURE 1102b.—Use of three-arm protractor.

objects, the observer establishes two circles of position. For each pair of objects, there is only one circle which passes through the two objects and the observer's position. Thus, there are two circles, intersecting at two points as shown in figure 1102a, which pass through the observer's position at *T*.

Since the observer knows that he is not at the intersection at *B*, he must be at *T*.

The solution of what is known as the **three-point problem** is effected by placing the hairlines of the arms of a plastic three-arm protractor over the three observed objects on the chart as shown in figure 1102b. With the arms so placed, the center of the protractor disk is over the observer's position on the chart at the time of the measurements.

1103. Solution without three-arm protractor.—Although the conventional solution of the three-point problem is obtained by placing the arms of a three-arm protractor over the three observed objects on the chart, the use of the protractor is not necessary. The use of the protractor may not be practicable because of limited room and facilities for plotting, as in a small open boat. Where a common charted object cannot be used in the horizontal angle observations, a means other than the three-arm protractor must be employed to determine the position of the observer. Also, point fixes as obtained from the three-arm protractor can be misleading if the navigator has limited skill in evaluating the strengths of the three-point solutions.

In plotting the three-point fix without a three-arm protractor, the procedure is to find the center of each circle of position, sometimes called **circle of equal angle** (fig. 1103a), and then, about such center, to strike an arc of radius equal to the distance on the chart from the circle center to one of the two objects through which the circle passes. The same procedure is applied to the other pair of objects to establish the fix at the intersection of the two arcs.

Some of the methods for finding the center of a circle of equal angle are described in the following text.

The center of the circle of equal angle lies on the perpendicular bisector of the baseline of the pair of objects. With the bisector properly graduated (fig. 1103b), one need only to place one point of the compasses at the appropriate graduation, the other point at one of the observed objects, and then to strike the circle of equal angle or an arc of it in the vicinity of the DR.

The bisector can be graduated through calculation or by means of either the simple protractor or the three-arm protractor.

As shown in figure 1103a when the observed angle is 90°, the center of the circle of equal angle lies at the center of the baseline or at the foot of the perpendicular bisector of the baseline. When the observed angle is less than 90°, for example 40°, the center of the circle lies on the perpendicular bisector on the same side of the baseline as the observer. When the observed angle is 26°34′, the center of the circle lies on the bisector at a distance from its foot equal to the distance between the two objects. When the observed angle is greater than 90°, the center of the circle lies on the perpendicular

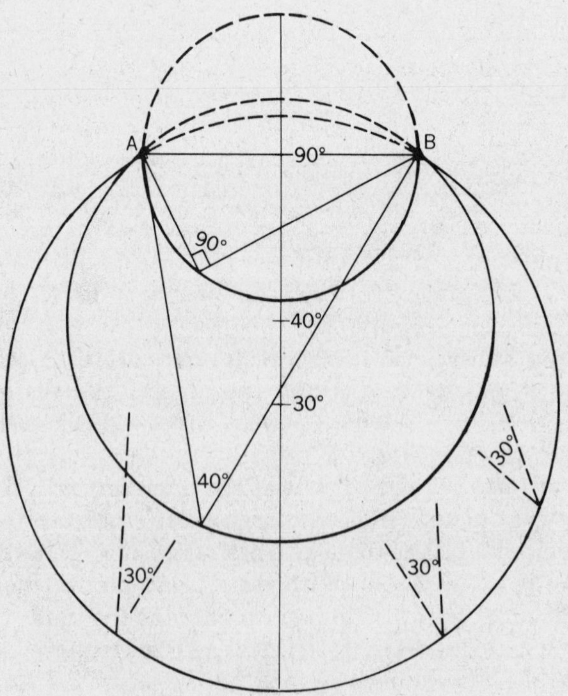

Figure 1103a.—Circles of equal angle.

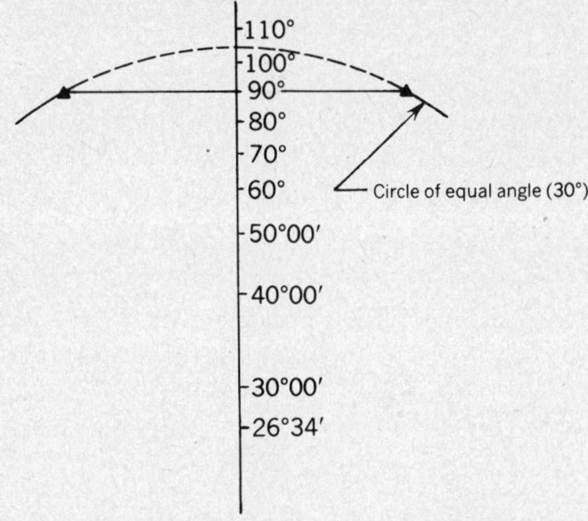

FIGURE 1103b.—Graduated perpendicular bisector.

bisector on the side of the baseline opposite from the observer. The center for 100° is the same distance from the baseline as the center for 80°; the center for 110° is the same distance as the center for 70°, etc. These facts can be used to construct a nomogram for finding the distances of circles of equal angle from the foot of the perpendicular for various angles.

From geometry the central angle subtended by a chord is twice the angle with its vertex on the circle and subtended by the same chord. Therefore, when the observed horizontal angle is 30°, the central angle subtended by the baseline is 60°. Or, the angle at the center of the circle between the perpendicular bisector and the line in the direction of one of the observed objects is equal to the observed angle, or 30° as shown in figure 1103c. The angle at the object between the baseline and the center of the circle on the bisector is 90° minus observed angle, or 60°.

The 30° graduation can be located quickly using a suitable protractor as shown in figure 1103d. The placement of the protractor as shown in the upper part of the figure requires moving its center along the bisector until the straightedge passes through the object. The method shown in the lower part enables more rapid location of the 30° graduation because there is no need to slide the protractor after its center is placed over the object and the angle is set.

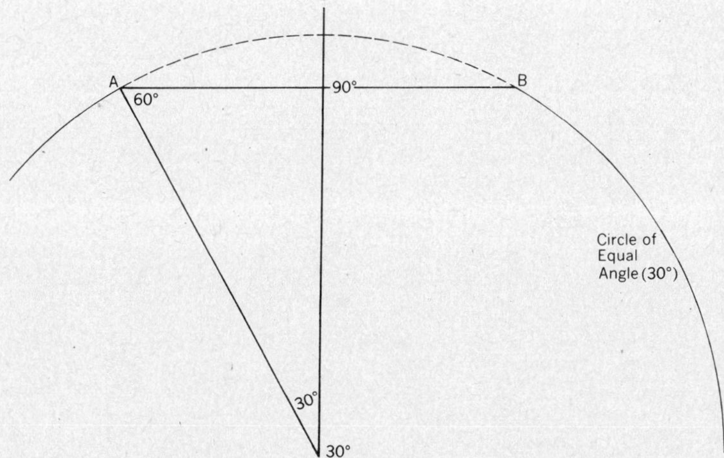

FIGURE 1103c.—Circle of equal angle (30°).

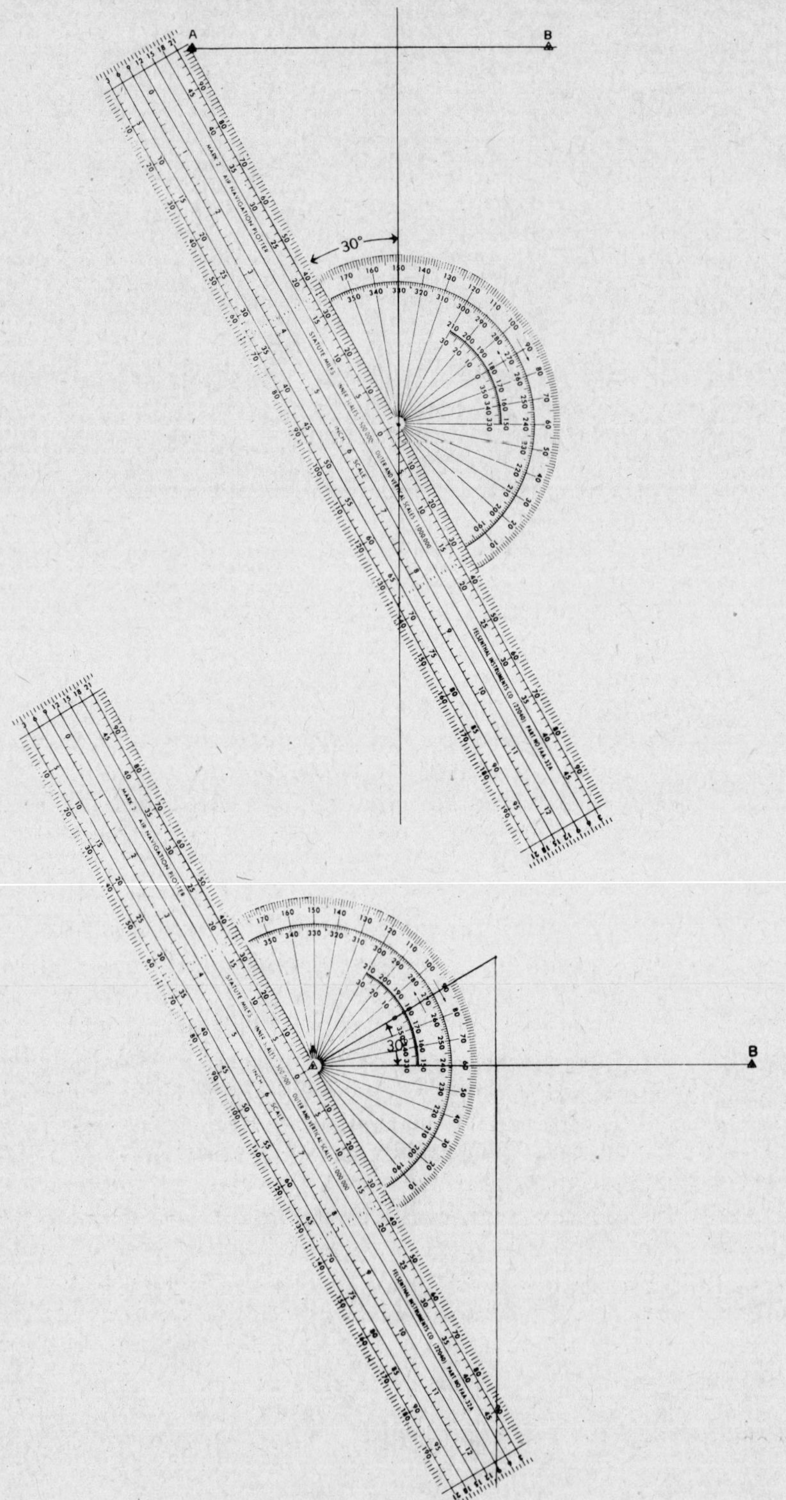

FIGURE 1103d.—Graduating perpendicular bisector.

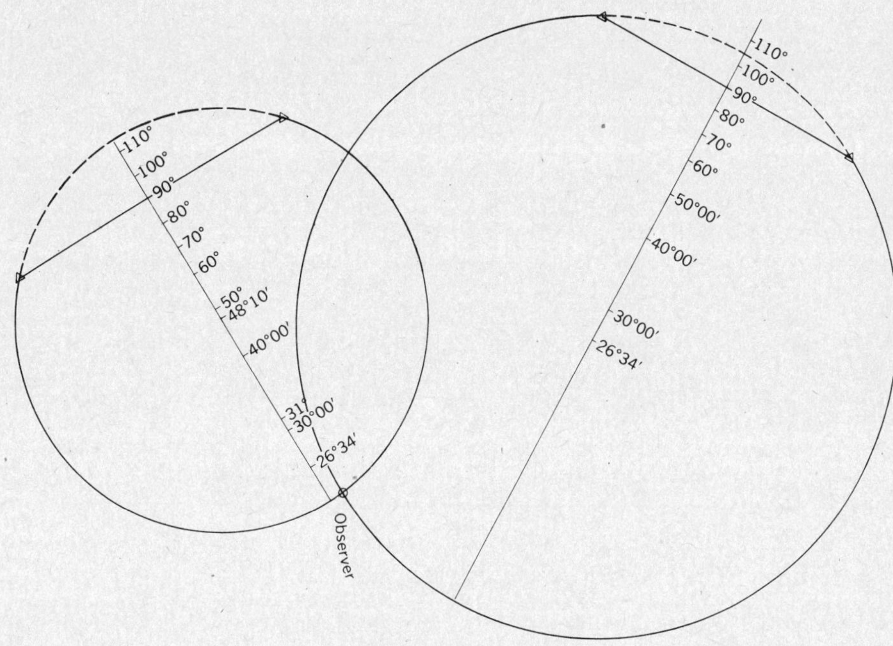

FIGURE 1104.—Split fix.

1104. Split fix.—Occasions when a common charted object cannot be used in horizontal angle observations are not infrequent. On these occasions the mariner must obtain what is called a **split fix** through observation of two pairs of charted objects, with no object being common. As with the three-point fix, the mariner will obtain two circles of equal angle, intersecting at two points. As shown in figure 1104, one of these two intersections will fix the observer's position.

1105. Conning aid.—Preconstructed circles of equal angle can be helpful in conning the vessel to a specific geographic position when fixing by horizontal angles. In one application, the vessel is conned to keep one angle constant, or nearly constant, in order to follow the circumference of the associated circle of equal angle to the desired position; the other angle is changing rapidly and is approaching the value for the second circle of equal angle passing through the desired position.

1106. Strength of three-point fix.—Although an experienced hydrographer can readily estimate the strength of a three-point fix, and is able to select the objects providing the strongest fix available quickly, others often have difficulty in visualizing the problem and may select a weak fix when strong ones are available. The following generally useful but not infallible rules apply to selection of charted objects to be observed:

1. The strongest fix is obtained when the observer is inside the triangle formed by the three objects. And in such case the fix is strongest where the three objects form an equilateral triangle (fig. 1106, view A), the observer is at the center, and the objects are close to the observer.

2. The fix is strong when the sum of the two angles is equal to or greater than 180° and neither angle is less than 30°. The nearer the angles are equal to each other, the stronger is the fix (view B).

3. The fix is strong when the three objects lie in a straight line and the center object is nearest the observer (view C).

4. The fix is strong when the center object lies between the observer and a line joining the other two, and the center object is nearest the observer (view D).

5. The fix is strong when two objects a considerable distance apart are in range and the angle to the third object is not less than 45° (view E).

6. Small angles should be avoided as they result in weak fixes in most cases and are difficult to plot. However, a strong fix is obtained when two objects are nearly in range and the nearest one is used as the common object. The small angle must be measured very accurately, and the position of the two objects in range must be very accurately plotted. Otherwise, large errors in position will result. Such fixes are strong only when the common object is nearest the observer. The fix will become very weak when the observer moves to a position where the distant object is the common object (view F).

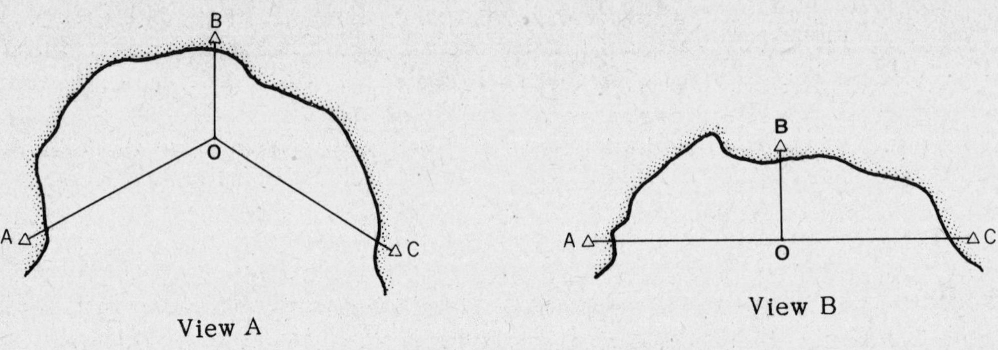

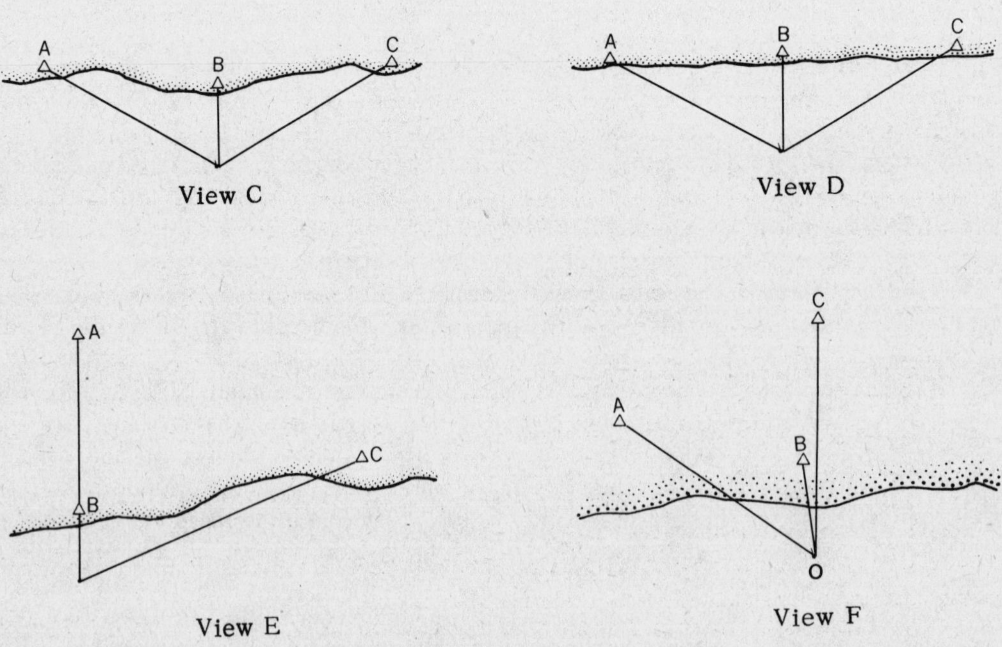

Figure 1106.—Strengths of three-point fixes.

7. A fix is strong when at least one of the angles changes rapidly as the vessel moves from one location to another.

8. The sum of the two angles should not be less than 50°; better results are obtained when neither angle is less than 30°.

9. Do not observe an angle between objects of considerably different elevation. Indefinite objects such as tangents, hill-tops, and other poorly defined or located points should not be used. Take care to select prominent objects such as major lights, church spires, towers or buildings which are charted and are readily distinguished from surrounding objects.

Beginners should demonstrate the validity of the above rules by plotting examples of each and their opposites. It should be noted that a fix is strong if, in plotting, a slight movement of the center of the protractor moves the arms away from one or more of the stations, and is weak if such movement does not appreciably change the relation of the arms to the three points. An appreciation of the accuracy required in measuring angles can be obtained by changing one angle about five minutes in arc in each example and noting the resulting shift in the plotted positions.

The **error of the three-point fix** will be due to:

1. error in measurement of the horizontal angles;
2. error resulting from observer and observed objects not lying in a horizontal plane;
3. instrument error; and
4. plotting error.

The magnitude of the error varies directly as the error in measurement, the distance of the common object from the observer, (D) and inversely as the sine function of the angle of cut (θ). The magnitude of the error also depends upon the following ratios:

1. The distance to the object to the left of the observer divided by the distance from this object to the center object (r_1).

2. The distance to the object to the right of the observer divided by the distance from this object to the center object (r_2).

Assuming that each horizontal angle has the same error (α), the magnitude of the error (E) is expressed in the formula

$$E=\frac{\alpha D}{\sin\theta}\sqrt{r^2_1+r^2_2+2r_1r_2\cos\theta},$$

where error in measurement (α) is expressed in radians.

The magnitude of the error (E) is expressed in the formula

$$E=\frac{.00029\alpha D}{\sin\theta}\sqrt{r^2_1+r^2_2+2r_1r_2\cos\theta},$$

where error in measurement (α) is expressed in minutes of arc.

To avoid mistakes in the identification of charted objects observed, either a check bearing or a check angle should be used to insure that the objects used in observation and plotting are the same.

1107. Avoiding the swinger.—Avoid a selection of objects which will result in a "**revolver**" or "**swinger**"; that is, when the three objects observed on shore and the ship are all on, or near, the circumference of a circle (fig. 1107). In such a case the ship's position is indeterminate by three-point fix.

If *bearings* as plotted are affected by unknown and uncorrected compass error, the bearing lines may intersect at a point when the objects observed ashore and the ship are all on, or near, the circumference of a circle.

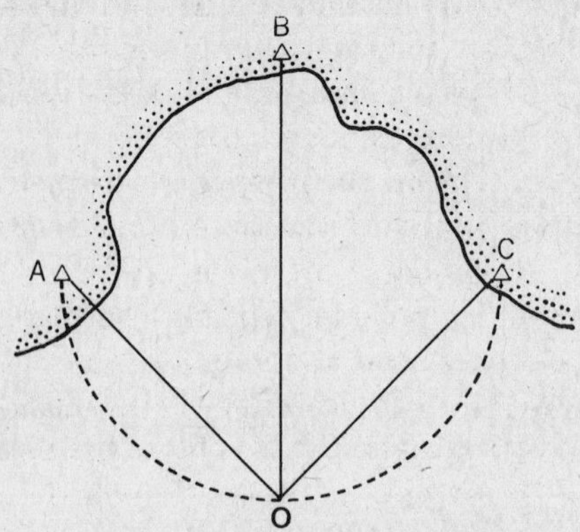

FIGURE 1107.—Revolver or swinger.

1108. Cutting in uncharted objects.—To cut in or locate on the chart uncharted objects, such as newly discovered offshore wrecks or objects ashore which may be useful for future observations, proceed as follows:

1. Fix successive positions of the ship or ship's boat by three-point fixes, i.e., by horizontal sextant angles. At each fix, simultaneously measure the sextant angle between one of the objects used in the fix and the object to be charted (fig. 1108a). For more accurate results, the craft from which the observations are made should be either lying to or proceeding slowly.

2. For best results, the angles should be measured simultaneously. If verification is undertaken, the angles observed should be interchanged among observers.

3. The fix positions should be selected carefully to give strong fixes, and so that the cuts to the object will provide a good intersection at the next station taken for observations. A minimum of three cuts should be taken.

An alternative procedure is to select observing positions so that the object to be charted will be in range with one of the charted objects used to obtain the three-point fix (fig. 1108b). The charted objects should be selected to provide the best possible intersections at the position of the uncharted object.

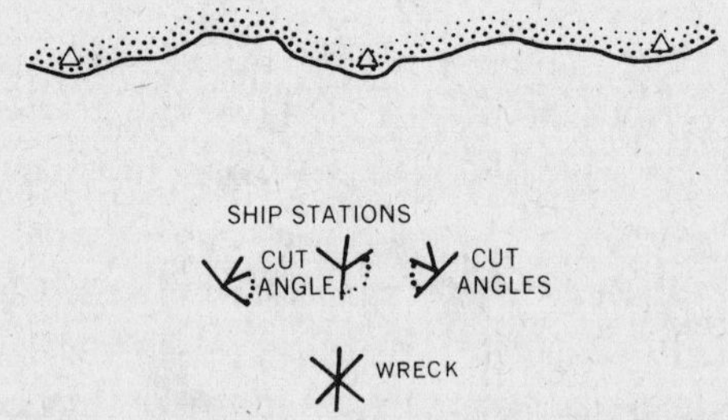

FIGURE 1108a.—Cutting in uncharted objects.

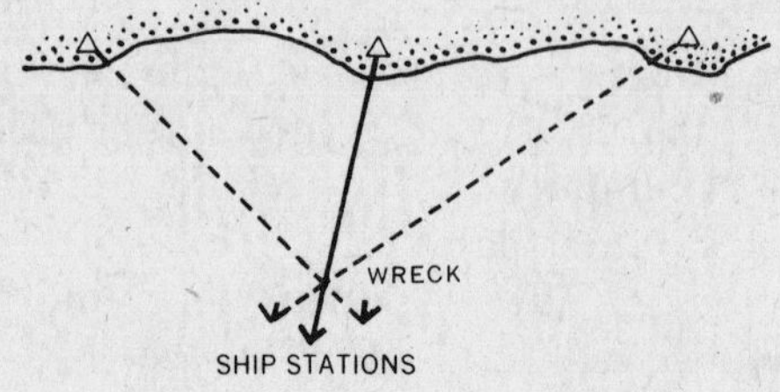

FIGURE 1108b.—On range method.

1109. Horizontal and vertical danger angles.—A vessel proceeding along a coast may be in safe water as long as it remains a minimum distance off the beach. This information may be provided by any means available. One method useful in avoiding particular dangers is the use of a **danger angle.** Refer to figure 1109. A ship is proceeding along a coast on course line *AB*, and the captain wishes to remain outside a danger *D*. Prominent landmarks are located at *M* and *N*. A circle is drawn through *M* and *N* and tangent to the outer edge of the danger. If *X* is a point on this circle, angle *MXN* is the same as at any other point on the circle (except that part between *M* and *N*). Anywhere within the circle the angle is *larger* and anywhere outside the circle it is *smaller*. Therefore, any angle smaller than *MXN* indicates a safe position and any angle larger than *MXN* indicates possible danger. Angle *MXN* is therefore a maximum **horizontal danger angle.** A minimum horizontal danger angle is used when a vessel is to pass *inside* an offlying danger, as at *D′* in figure 1109. In this case the circle is drawn through *M* and *N* and tangent to the *inner* edge of the danger area. The angle is kept larger than *MYN*. If a vessel is to pass *between* two danger areas, as in figure 1109, the horizontal angle should be kept smaller than *MXN* but larger than *MYN*. The minimum danger angle is effective only while the vessel is inside the larger circle through *M* and *N*. Bearings on either landmark might be used to indicate the entering and leaving of the larger circle. A margin of safety can be provided by drawing the circles through points a short distance off the dangers. Any method of measuring the angles, or difference of bearing of *M* and *N*, can be used. Perhaps the most accurate is by horizontal sextant angle. If a single landmark of known height is available, similar procedure can be used with a **vertical danger angle** between top and bottom of the object. In this case the charted position of the object is used as the center of the circles.

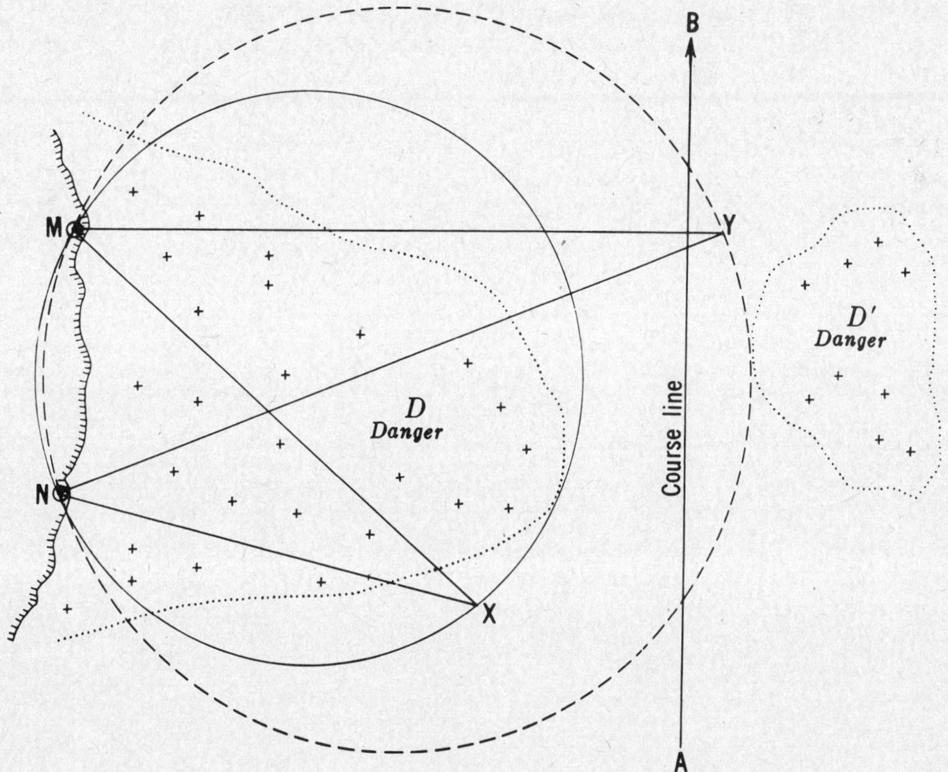

FIGURE 1109.—Horizontal danger angles.

1110. Distance by vertical angle.—Table 5 provides means for determining the distance of an object of known height above sea level. The vertical angle between the top of the object and the visible (sea) horizon (the sextant altitude) is measured and corrected for index error and dip only. If the visible horizon is not available as a reference, the angle should be measured to the bottom of the object, and dip short of the horizon (tab. 8) used in place of the usual dip correction. This may require several approximations of distance by alternate entries of tables 5 and 8 until the same value is obtained twice. The table is entered with the difference in the height of the object and the height of eye of the observer, in feet, and the corrected vertical angle; and the distance in nautical miles is taken directly from the table. An error may be introduced if refraction differs from the standard value used in the computation of the table.

1111. Evaluation.—As time and conditions permit, it behooves the navigator to use the sextant to evaluate the accuracy of navigation by other means in pilot waters. Such accuracy comparisons tend to provide navigators with better appreciation of the limitations of fixing by various methods in a given piloting situation.

CHAPTER XII

TIDE AND CURRENT PREDICTIONS

1201. Tidal effects.—The daily rise and fall of the **tide,** with its attendant flood and ebb of **tidal current,** is familiar to every mariner. He is aware, also, that at **high water** and **low water** the depth of water is momentarily constant, a condition called **stand.** Similarly, there is a moment of **slack water** as a tidal current reverses direction. As a general rule, the *change* in height or the current speed is at first very slow, increasing to a maximum about midway between the two extremes, and then decreasing again. If plotted against time, the height of tide or speed of a tidal current takes the general form of a sine curve. The present chapter is concerned primarily with the application of tides and currents to piloting, and predicting the tidal conditions that might be encountered at any given time.

Although tides and tidal currents are caused by the same phenomena, the time relationship between them varies considerably from place to place. For instance, if an estuary has a wide entrance and does not extend far inland, the time of maximum speed of current occurs at about the mid time between high water and low water. However, if an extensive tidal basin is connected to the sea by a small opening, the maximum current may occur at about the time of high water or low water outside the basin, when the difference in height is maximum.

The *height of tide* should not be confused with *depth of water.* For reckoning tides a reference level is selected. Soundings shown on the largest scale charts are the vertical distances from this level to the bottom. At any time the actual depth is this charted depth *plus* the height of tide. In most places the reference level is some form of low water. But all low waters at a place are not the same height, and the selected reference level is seldom the *lowest* tide that occurs at the place. When lower tides occur, these are indicated by a negative sign. Thus, at a spot where the charted depth is 15 feet, the actual depth is 15 feet plus height of tide. When the tide is three feet, the depth is $15+3=18$ feet. When it is (−) 1 foot, the depth is $15-1=14$ feet. It is well to remember that *the actual depth can be less than the charted depth.* In an area where there is a considerable **range of tide** (the difference between high water and low water), the height of tide might be an important consideration in using soundings to assist in determining position, or whether the vessel is in safe water.

One should remember that heights given in the tide tables are *predictions*, and that when conditions vary considerably from those used in making the predictions, the heights shown may be considerably in error. Heights lower than predicted are particularly to be anticipated when the atmospheric pressure is higher than normal, or when there is a persistent strong offshore wind. Along coasts where there is a large inequality between the two high or two low tides during a tidal day the height predictions are less reliable than elsewhere.

The current encountered in pilot waters is due primarily to tidal action, but other causes are sometimes present. The tidal current tables give the best prediction of total current, regardless of cause. The predictions for a river may be considerably in error following heavy rains or a drought. The effect of current is to alter the course and speed made good over the bottom. Due to the configuration of land (or shoal areas) and water, the set and drift may vary considerably over different parts of a harbor. Since this is generally an area in which small errors in position of a vessel are of considerable importance to its safety, a knowledge of predicted currents can be critical, particularly if the visibility is reduced by fog, snow, etc. If the vessel is proceeding at reduced speed, the effect of current with respect to distance traveled is greater than normal. Strong currents are particularly to be anticipated in narrow passages connecting larger bodies of water. Currents of more than five knots are encountered from time to time in the Golden Gate at San Francisco. Currents of more than 13 knots sometimes occur at Seymour Narrows, British Columbia.

In straight portions of rivers and channels the strongest currents usually occur in the middle, but in curved portions the swiftest currents (and deepest water) usually occur near the outer edge of the curve. Countercurrents and eddies may occur on either side of the main current of a river or narrow passage, especially near obstructions and in bights.

In general, the range of tide and the speed of tidal current are at a minimum upon the open ocean or along straight coasts. The greatest tidal effects are usually encountered in rivers, bays, harbors, inlets, bights, etc. A vessel proceeding along a coast can be expected to encounter stronger sets toward or away from the shore while passing an indentation than when the coast is straight.

1202. Predictions of tides and currents to be expected at various places are published annually by the National Ocean Survey. These are supplemented by eleven sets of tidal current charts (art. 1211), each set consisting of charts for each hour of the tidal cycle. On these charts the set of the current at various places in the area is shown by arrows, and the drift by numbers. Since these are *average* conditions, they indicate in a general way the tidal conditions on any day and during *any* year. They are designed to be used with tidal current diagrams (art. 1211) or the tidal current tables (except those for New York Harbor, and Narragansett Bay, which are used with the tide tables). These charts are available for Boston Harbor, Narragansett Bay to Nantucket Sound, Narragansett Bay, Long Island Sound and Block Island Sound, New York Harbor, Delaware Bay and River, upper Chesapeake Bay, Charleston Harbor, San Francisco Bay, Puget Sound (northern part), and Puget Sound (southern part). Current arrows are sometimes shown on nautical charts. These represent average conditions and should not be considered reliable predictions of the conditions to be encountered at any given time. When a strong current sets over an irregular bottom, or meets an opposing current, ripples may occur on the surface. These are called **tide rips.** Areas where they occur frequently are shown on charts.

Usually, the mariner obtains tidal information from tide and tidal current tables. However, if these are not available, or if they do not include information at a desired place, the mariner may be able to obtain locally the **mean high water lunitidal interval** or the **high water full and change.** The approximate *time* of high water can be found by adding either interval to the time of transit (either upper or lower) of the moon. Low water occurs approximately ¼ tidal day (about $6^h 12^m$) before and after the time of high water. The actual interval varies somewhat from day to day, but approximate results can be obtained in this manner. Similar information for tidal currents **(lunicurrent interval)** is seldom available.

1203. Tide tables for various parts of the world are published in four volumes by the National Ocean Survey. Each volume is arranged as follows:

Table 1 contains a complete list of the predicted times and heights of the tide for each day of the year at a number of places designated as **reference stations.**

Table 2 gives differences and ratios which can be used to modify the tidal information for the reference stations to make it applicable to a relatively large number of **subordinate stations.**

Table 3 provides information for use in finding the approximate height of the tide at any time between high water and low water.

Table 4 is a sunrise-sunset table at five-day intervals for various latitudes from 76°N to 60°S (40°S in one volume).

Table 5 provides an adjustment to convert the local mean time of table 4 to zone or standard time.

Table 6 (two volumes only) gives the zone time of moonrise and moonset for each day of the year at certain selected places.

Certain astonomical data are contained on the inside back cover of each volume.

Extracts from tables 1, 2, and 3 for the East Coast of North and South America are given in appendix B.

1204. Tide predictions for reference stations.—The first page of appendix B is the table 1 daily predictions for New York (The Battery) for the first quarter of 1975. As indicated at the bottom of the page, times are for Eastern Standard Time (+5 zone, time meridian 75°W). Daylight saving time is not used. Times are given on the 24-hour basis. The tidal reference level for this station is mean low water.

For each day, the date and day of week are given, and the time and height of each high and low water are given in chronological order. Although high and low waters are not labeled as such, they can be distinguished by the relative heights given immediately to the right of the times. Since *two* high tides and *two* low tides occur each tidal day, the type of tide at this place is *semidiurnal*. The *tidal* day being longer than the *civil* day (because of the revolution of the moon eastward around the earth), any given tide occurs *later* from day to day. Thus, on Saturday, March 29, 1975, the first tide that occurs is the lower low water (−1.2 feet at 0334). The following high water (lower high water) is 4.9 feet above the reference level (a 6.1 foot rise from the preceding low water), and occurs at 0942. This is followed by the higher low water (−0.9 feet) at 1547, and then the higher high water of 5.5 feet at 2206. The cycle is repeated on the following day with variations in height, and later times.

Because of later times of corresponding tides from day to day, certain days have only one high water or only one low water. Thus, on January 17 high tides occur at 1120 and 2357. The next following high tides are at 1154 on January 18 and 0029 on January 19. Thus, only one high tide occurs on January 18, the previous one being shortly before midnight on the seventeenth, and the next one occurring early in the morning of the nineteenth, as shown.

1205. Tide predictions for subordinate stations.—The second page of appendix B is a page of table 2 of the tide tables. For each subordinate station listed, the following information is given:

Number. The stations are listed in geographical order and given consecutive numbers. At the end of each volume an alphabetical listing is given, and for each entry the consecutive number is shown, to assist in finding the entry in table 2.

Place. The list of places includes both subordinate and reference stations, the latter being given in bold type.

Position. The approximate latitude and longitude are given to assist in locating the station. The latitude is north or south, and the longitude east or west, depending upon the letters (N, S, E, W) next *above* the entry. These may not be the same as those at the *top* of the column.

Differences. The differences are to be applied to the predictions for the reference station shown in bold capitals next *above* the entry on the page. Time and height differences are given separately for high and low waters. Where differences are omitted, they are either unreliable or unknown.

The time difference is the number of hours and minutes to be applied to the time at the reference station to find the time of the corresponding tide at the subordinate station. This interval is added if preceded by a plus sign (+), and subtracted if preceded by a minus sign (−). The results obtained by the application of the time differences will be in the zone time of the time meridian shown directly above the difference for the subordinate station. Special conditions occurring at a few stations are indicated by footnotes on the applicable pages. In some instances, the corresponding tide falls on a different date at reference and subordinate stations.

Height differences are shown in a variety of ways. For most entries separate height differences in feet are given for high water and low water. These are applied to the height given for the reference station. In many cases a *ratio* is given for either high water or low water, or both. The height at the reference station is multiplied by this ratio to find the height at the subordinate station. For a few stations, *both* a ratio and difference are given. In this case the height at the reference station is first multiplied by the ratio, and the difference is then applied. An example is given in each volume of tide tables. Special conditions are indicated in the table or by footnote. Thus, a footnote on the second page of appendix B indicates that "Values for the Hudson River above George Washington Bridge are based upon averages for the six months May to October, when the fresh-water discharge is a minimum."

Ranges. Various ranges are given, as indicated in the tables. In each case this is the difference in height between high water and low water for the tides indicated.

Example.—List chronologically the times and heights of all tides at Yonkers. (No. 1531) on January 2, 1975.

Solution.—

Date	January 2, 1975
Subordinate station	Yonkers
Reference station	New York
High water time difference	(+) 1^h09^m
Low water time difference	(+) 1^h10^m
High water height difference	(−) 0.8 ft.
Low water height difference	0.0 ft.

	New York		*Yonkers*	
HW	2321 (1st)	4.6 ft.	0030	3.8 ft.
LW	0516	(−) 0.6 ft.	0626	(−) 0.6 ft.
HW	1138	4.9 ft.	1247	4.1 ft.
LW	1749	(−) 0.9 ft.	1859	(−) 0.9 ft.

1206. Finding height of tide at any time.—Table 3 of the tide tables provides means for determining the approximate height of tide at any time. It is based upon the assumption that a plot of height versus time is a sine curve. Instructions for use of the table are given in a footnote below the table, which is reproduced in appendix B.

Example 1.—Find the height of tide at Yonkers (No. 1531) at 1000 on January 2, 1975.

Solution.—The given time is between the low water at 0626 and the high water at 1247 (example of art. 1205). Therefore, the tide is rising. The duration of rise is $1247-0626=6^h21^m$. The range of tide is $4.1-(-0.6)=4.7$ feet. The given time is 2^h47^m *before* high water, the nearest tide. Enter the upper part of the table with duration of rise 6^h20^m (the nearest tabulated value to 6^h21^m), and follow the line horizontally to 2^h45^m (the nearest tabulated value to 2^h47^m). Follow this column vertically downward to the entry 1.8 feet in the line for a range of tide of 4.5 feet (the nearest tabulated value to 4.7 feet). This is the correction to be applied to the nearest tide. Since the nearest tide is high water, subtract 1.8 from 4.1 feet. The answer, 2.3 feet, is the height of tide at the given time.

Answer.—Ht. of tide at 1000, 2.3 ft. A suitable form (fig. 1206a) is used to facilitate the solution.

Interpolation in this table is not considered justified.

TIDE AND CURRENT TABLES
SRNC-USNA-NC&M-3161/31(1-71)

NAVIGATION DEPARTMENT — DIVISION OF NAVAL COMMAND AND MANAGEMENT

COMPLETE TIDE TABLE

Date: Jan. 2, 1975

Substation: Yonkers

Reference Station: New York

HW Time Difference: (+) $1^h\ 09^m$

LW Time Difference: (+) $1^h\ 10^m$

Difference in height of HW: (−) 0.8ft.

Difference in height of LW: 0.0ft.

	Reference Station		Substation	
HW	2231	4.6ft.	0030	3.8ft.
LW	0516	(−) 0.6ft.	0626	(−) 0.6ft.
HW	1138	4.9ft.	1247	4.1ft.
LW	1749	(−) 0.9ft.	1859	(−) 0.9ft.
HW				
LW				

HEIGHT OF TIDE AT ANY TIME

Locality: Yonkers Time: 1000 Date: Jan. 2, 1975

Duration of Rise or Fall: $6^h\ 21^m$

Time from Nearest Tide: $2^h\ 47^m$

Range of Tide: 4.7ft.

Height of Nearest Tide: 4.1ft.

Corr. from Table 3: 1.8ft.

Height of Tide at: 1000 2.3ft.

FIGURE 1206a.—U.S. Naval Academy tide form.

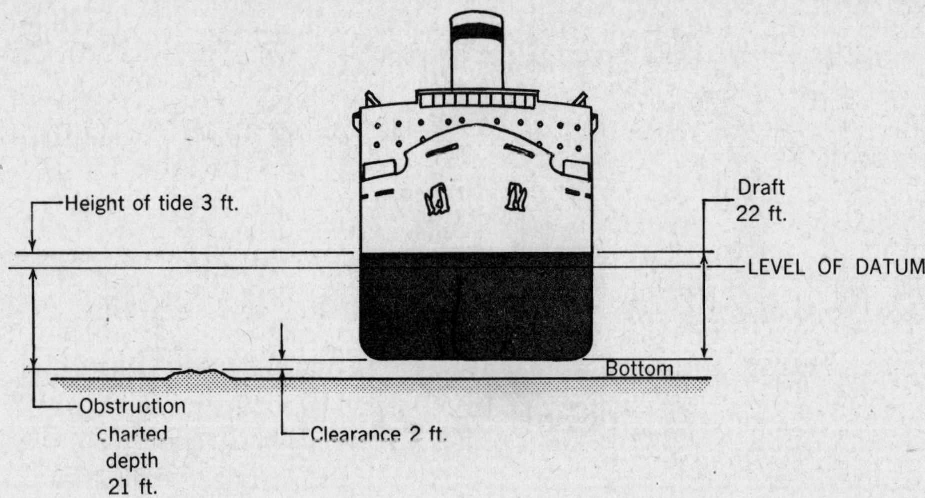

FIGURE 1206b.—Height of tide required to pass clear of charted obstruction.

It may be desired to know at what time a given depth of water will occur. In this case, the problem is solved in reverse.

Example 2.—The captain of a vessel drawing 22 feet wishes to pass over a temporary obstruction near Days Point, Weehawken (No. 1521), having a charted depth of 21 feet, passage to be made during the morning of January 31, 1975. Refer to figure 1206b.

Required.—The earliest time after 0800 that this passage can be made, allowing a safety margin of two feet.

Solution.—The least acceptable depth of water is 24 feet, which is three feet more than the charted depth. Therefore, the height of tide must be three feet or more. At the New York reference station a low tide of (−)0.9 foot occurs at 0459, followed by a high tide of 4.9 feet at 1120. At Days Point the corresponding low tide is (−)0.9 foot at 0522, and the high tide is 4.6 feet at 1144. The duration of rise is 6^h22^m, and the range of tide is 5.5 feet. The least acceptable tide is 3.0 feet, or 1.6 feet less than high tide. Enter the *lower* part of table 3 with range 5.5 feet and follow the horizontal line until 1.6 feet is reached. Follow this column vertically *upward* until the value of 2^h19^m is reached on the line for a duration of 6^h20^m (the nearest tabulated value to 6^h22^m). The minimum depth will occur about 2^h19^m *before* high water or at about 0925.

Answer.—A depth of 24 feet occurs at 0925.

If the range of tide is more than 20 feet, *half* the range (*one third* if the range is greater than 40 feet) is used to enter table 3, and the correction to height is *doubled* (*trebled* if one third is used).

A diagram for a graphical solution is given in figure 1206c. Eye interpolation can be used if desired. The steps in this solution are as follows:

1. Enter the upper graph with the duration of rise or fall. This is represented by a horizontal line.
2. Find the intersection of this line and the curve representing the interval from the nearest *low* water (point *A*).
3. From *A*, follow a vertical line to the sine curve of the lower diagram (point *B*).
4. From *B*, follow horizontally to the vertical line representing the range of tide (point *C*).
5. Using *C*, read the correction from the series of curves.
6. Add (algebraically) the correction of step 5 to the *low* water height, to find the height at the given time.

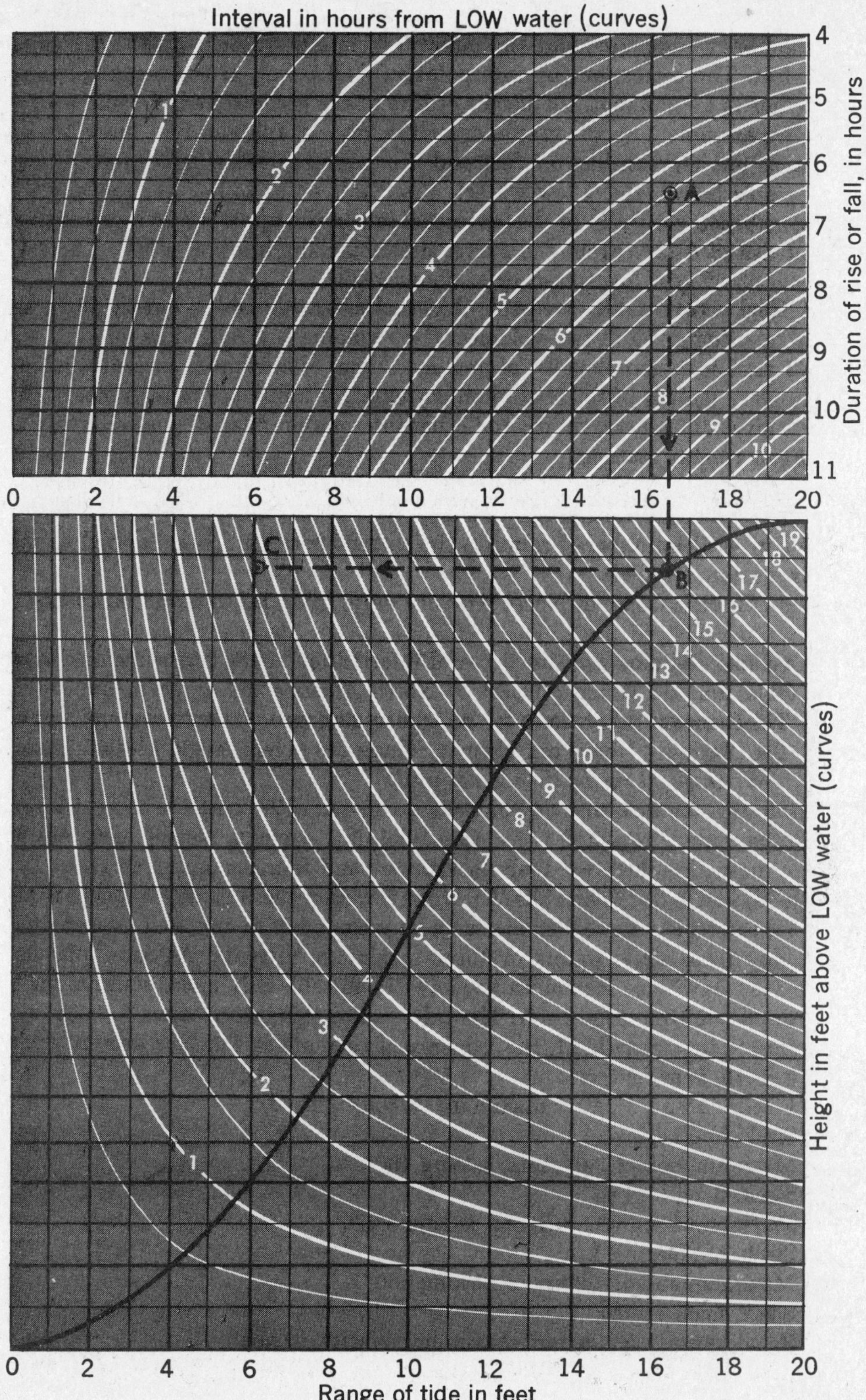

FIGURE 1206c.—Graphical solution for height of tide at any time.

The problem illustrated in figure 1206c is similar to that of example 1 given above. The duration of rise is 6^h25^m, and the interval from *low* water is 5^h23^m. The range of tide is 6.1 feet. The correction (by interpolation) is 5.7 feet. If the height of the preceding low tide is (−)0.2 foot, the height of tide at the given time is (−)0.2+5.7=5.5 feet. To solve example 2 by the graph, enter the lower graph and find the intersection of the vertical line representing 5.5 feet and the curve representing 3.9 feet (the minimum acceptable height above low water). From this point follow horizontally to the sine curve, and then vertically to the horizontal line in the upper figure representing the duration of rise of 6^h22^m. From the curve, determine the interval 4^h00^m. The earliest time is about 4^h00^m *after* low water, or at about 0922.

1207. Tidal current tables are somewhat similar to tide tables, but the coverage is less extensive, being given in two volumes. Each volume is arranged as follows:

Table 1 contains a complete list of predicted times of maximum currents and slack, with the velocity (speed) of the maximum currents, for a number of reference stations.

Table 2 gives differences, ratios, and other information related to a relatively large number of subordinate stations.

Table 3 provides information for use in finding the speed of the current at any time between tabulated entries in tables 1 and 2.

Table 4 gives the number of minutes the current does not exceed stated amounts, for various maximum speeds.

Table 5 (Atlantic Coast of North America only) gives information on rotary tidal currents.

Each volume contains additional useful information related to currents. Extracts from the tables for the Atlantic Coast of North America are given in appendix C.

1208. Tidal current predictions for reference stations.—The extracts of appendix M are for The Narrows, New York Harbor. Times are given on the 24-hour basis, for meridian 75°W. *Daylight saving time is not used.*

For each day, the date and day of week are given, with complete current information. Since the cycle is repeated twice each tidal day, currents at this place are semidiurnal. On most days there are four slack waters and four maximum currents, two of them floods (F) and two of them ebbs (E). However, since the tidal day is longer than the civil day, the corresponding condition occurs later from day to day, and on certain days there are only three slack waters or three maximum currents. At some places, the current on some days runs maximum flood twice, but ebb only once, a minimum flood occurring in place of the second ebb. The tables show this information.

As indicated by appendix C, the sequence of currents at The Narrows on Monday, February 3, 1975, is as follows:

0000 Flood current, 5^m after maximum velocity (speed).
0305 Slack, ebb begins.
0621 Maximum ebb of 2.0 knots, setting 160°.
1005 Slack, flood begins.
1222 Maximum flood of 1.5 knots, setting 340°.
1516 Slack, ebb begins.
1839 Maximum ebb of 1.9 knots, setting 160°.
2216 Slack, flood begins.
2400 Flood current, 56^m before maximum velocity (speed).

Only one maximum flood occurs on this day, the previous one having occurred 5 minutes before the day began, and the following one predicted for 56 minutes after the day ends.

1209. Tidal current predictions for subordinate stations.—For each subordinate station listed in table 2 of the tidal current tables, the following information is given:

Number. The stations are listed in geographical order and given consecutive numbers, as in the tide tables (art. 1205). At the end of each volume an alphabetical listing is given, and for each entry the consecutive number is shown, to assist in finding the entry in table 2.

Place. The list of places includes both subordinate and reference stations, the latter being given in bold type.

Position. The approximate latitude and longitude are given to assist in locating the station. The latitude is north or south and the longitude east or west as indicated by the letters (N, S, E, W) next *above* the entry. The current given is for the center of the channel unless another location is indicated by the station name.

Time difference. Two time differences are tabulated. One is the number of hours and minutes to be applied to the tabulated times of slack water at the reference station to find the times of slack waters at the subordinate station. The other time difference is applied to the times of maximum current at the reference station to find the times of the corresponding maximum current at the subordinate station. The intervals, which are added or subtracted in accordance with their signs, include any difference in time between the two stations, so that the answer is correct for the standard time of the subordinate station. Limited application and special conditions are indicated by footnotes.

Velocity (speed) ratios. Speed of the current at the subordinate station is found by multiplying the speed at the reference station by the tabulated ratio. Separate ratios may be given for flood and ebb currents. Special conditions are indicated by footnotes.

As indicated in appendix C, the currents at The Battery (No. 2375) can be found by *adding* 1^h30^m for slack water and 1^h35^m for maximum current to the times for The Narrows, and multiplying flood currents by 0.9 and ebb currents by 1.2. Applying these to the values for Monday, February 3, 1975, the sequence is as follows:

0000 Flood current, 1^h30^m before maximum velocity (speed).
0130 Maximum flood of 1.8 knots, setting 015°.
0435 Slack, ebb begins.
0756 Maximum ebb of 2.4 knots, setting 195°.
1135 Slack, flood begins.
1357 Maximum flood of 1.4 knots, setting 015°.
1646 Slack, ebb begins.
2014 Maximum ebb of 2.3 knots setting 195°.
2346 Slack, flood begins.
2400 Flood current, 14^m after slack.

1210. Finding speed of tidal current at any time.—Table 3 of the tidal current table provides means for determining the approximate velocity (speed) at any time. Instructions for its use are given below the table, which is reproduced in appendix C.

Example 1.—Find the speed of the current at The Battery at 1500 on February 3, 1975.

Solution.—The given time is between the maximum flood of 1.4 knots at 1357 and the slack at 1646 (art. 1209). The interval between slack and maximum current (1646 −1357) is 2^h49^m. The interval between slack and the desired time (1646−1500) is 1^h46^m. Enter the table (A) with 2^h40^m at the top, and 1^h40^m at the left side (the nearest tabulated values to 2^h49^m and 1^h46^m, respectively), and find the factor 0.8 in the body of the table. The approximate speed at 1500 is $0.8\times1.4=1.1$ knots, and it is flooding.

Answer.—Speed 1.1 kn. A suitable form (fig. 1210) is used to facilitate the solution.

It may be desired to determine the period during which the current is less (or greater) than a given amount. Table 4 of the tidal current tables can be used to determine the period during which the speed does not exceed 0.5 knot. For greater

NAVIGATION DEPARTMENT DIVISION OF NAVAL COMMAND AND MANAGEMENT

COMPLETE CURRENT TABLE

Locality: The Battery Date: Feb. 3, 1975

Reference Station: The Narrows

Time Difference: Slack Water: (+) $1^h 30^m$
Maximum Current: (+) $1^h 35^m$

Velocity Ratio: Maximum Flood: 0.9
Maximum Ebb: 1.2

Flood Direction: 015°
Ebb Direction: 195°

Reference Station: The Narrows		Locality: The Battery	
		0000	F
2355	2.0F	0130	1.8F
0305	0	0435	0
0621	2.0E	0756	2.4E
1005	0	1135	0
1222	1.5F	1357	1.4F
1516	0	1646	0
1839	1.9E	2014	2.3E
2216	0	2346	0
2400	F	2400	F

VELOCITY OF CURRENT AT ANY TIME

Int. between slack and desired time:	$1^h 46^m$	
Int. between slack and maximum current:	$2^h 49^m$	(Ebb) (Flood) [circled]
Maximum current:	1.4kn	
Factor, Table 3	0.8	
Velocity:	1.1kn	
Direction:	015°	

DURATION OF SLACK

Times of maximum current:	0756	1357
Maximum current:	2.4kn	1.4kn
Desired maximum:	0.3	0.3
Period – Table 4:	35^m	46^m
Sum of periods:		81^m
Average period:		40^m
Time of slack:		1135

Duration of slack: From: 1115 To: 1155

FIGURE 1210.—U.S. Naval Academy tidal current form.

speeds, and for more accurate results under some conditions, table 3 of the tidal current tables can be used, solving by reversing the process used in example 1.

Example 2.—During what period on the evening of February 3, 1975, does the ebb current equal or exceed 1.0 knot at The Battery?

Solution.—The maximum ebb of 2.3 knots occurs at 2014. This is preceded by a slack at 1646, and followed by the next slack at 2346. The interval between the earlier slack and the maximum ebb is 3^h28^m, and the interval between the ebb and following slack is 3^h32^m. The desired factor is $\frac{1.0}{2.3}=0.4$. Enter table A with 3^h20^m (the nearest tabulated value to 3^h28^m) at the top, and follow down the column to 0.4 (midway between 0.3 and 0.5). At the left margin the interval between slack and the desired time is found to be 0^h50^m (midway between 0^h40^m and 1^h00^m). Therefore, the current becomes 1.0 knot at $1646+0^h50^m=1736$. Next, enter table A with 3^h40^m (the nearest tabulated value to 3^h32^m) at the top, and follow down the column to 0.4. Follow this line to the left margin, where the interval between slack and desired time is found to be 1^h00^m. Therefore, the current is 1.0 knot or greater until $2346-1^h00^m=2246$. If the two intervals between maximum current and slack were nearest the same 20^m interval, table A would have to be entered only once.

Answer.—The speed equals or exceeds 1.0 knot between 1736 and 2246.

The predicted times of slack water given in the tidal current tables indicate the instant of zero velocity. There is a period each side of slack water, however, during which the current is so weak that for practical purposes it may be considered as negligible. Table 4 of the tidal current tables gives, for various maximum currents, the approximate period of time during which weak currents not exceeding 0.1 to 0.5 knot will be encountered. This duration includes the last of the flood or ebb and the beginning of the following flood or ebb, that is, half of the duration will be before and half after the time of slack water.

When there is a difference between the velocities of the maximum flood and ebb preceding and following the slack for which the duration is desired, it will be sufficiently accurate for practical purposes to find a separate duration for each maximum velocity and take the average of the two as the duration of the weak current.

Of the two subtables of table 4, table A should be used for all places *except* those listed for table B; table B should be used for all places listed, and all stations in table 2 which are referred to them.

Example 3.—Find the period from just before until just after the slack at The Battery at 1135 on February 3, 1975, that the current does not exceed 0.3 kn.

Solution.—Refer to table 4. Table A of table 4 of the tidal current tables is entered with the maximum current before the slack to find the period during which the current does not exceed 0.3 kn. Since there is a difference between the velocities of the maximum ebb and flood preceding and following the slack for which the duration is desired, table A is re-entered with the maximum current after the slack to find the period during which the current does not exceed 0.3 kn. The average of the two values so found is taken as the duration of the weak current. The form shown in figure 1210 is used to facilitate the solution.

Answer.—Duration 40 min. (from 1115 to 1155).

1211. Tidal current charts present a comprehensive view of the hourly speed and direction of the current in 11 bodies of water (art. 1202). They also provide a means for determining the speed and direction of the current at various localities throughout these bodies of water. The arrows show the direction of the current; the figures give the speed in knots at the time of spring tides, that is, during the time of new or full moon when the currents are stronger than average. When the current is given as weak, the speed is less than 0.1 knot. The decimal point locates the position of the station.

The charts depict the flow of the tidal current under normal weather conditions. Strong winds and freshets, however, bring about nontidal currents which may modify considerably the speed and direction shown on the charts.

The speed of the tidal current varies from day to day principally in accordance with the phase, distance, and declination of the moon. Therefore, to obtain the speed for any particular day and hour, the *spring speeds* shown on the charts must be modified by correction factors. A correction table given in the charts can be used for this purpose.

The **tidal current diagrams** are a series of 12 monthly diagrams to be used with the tidal current charts. There is one diagram for each month of the year. A new set of diagrams must be used each year. The diagrams are computer constructed lines that locate each chart throughout all hours of every month. The diagrams indicate directly the chart and the speed correction factor to use at any desired time.

1212. Current diagrams.—A current diagram is a graph showing the speed of the current along a channel at different stages of the tidal current cycle. The current tables include such diagrams for Vineyard and Nantucket Sounds (one diagram); East River, New York; New York Harbor; Delaware Bay and River (one diagram); and Chesapeake Bay. The diagram for New York Harbor is reproduced in appendix C.

On this diagram each vertical line represents a given instant identified in terms of the number of hours before or after slack at The Narrows. Each horizontal line represents a distance from Ambrose Channel Entrance, measured along the usually traveled route. The names along the left margin are placed at the correct distances from Ambrose Channel Entrance. The current is for the center of the channel opposite these points. The intersection of any vertical line with any horizontal line represents a given moment in the current cycle at a given place in the channel. If this intersection is in a shaded area, the current is flooding; if in an unshaded area, it is ebbing. The speed in knots can be found by interpolation (if necessary) between the numbers given in the body of the diagram. The given values are *averages*. To find the value at any given time, multiply the speed found from the diagram by the ratio of *maximum speed of the current involved* to the *maximum shown on the diagram*, both values being taken for The Narrows. If the diurnal inequality is large, the accuracy can be improved by altering the width of the shaded area to fit conditions. The diagram covers 1½ current cycles, so that the right-hand third is a duplication of the left-hand third.

If the current for a single station is desired, table 1 or 2 should be used. The current diagrams are intended for use in either of two ways: First, to determine a favorable time for passage through the channel. Second, to find the average current to be expected during any passage through the channel. For both of these uses a number of "speed lines" are provided. When the appropriate line is transferred to the correct part of the diagram, the current to be encountered during passage is indicated along the line.

Example.—During the morning of January 3, 1975, a ship is to leave Pier 83 at W. 42nd St., and proceed down the bay at ten knots.

Required.—(1) Time to get underway to take maximum advantage of a favorable current, allowing 15 minutes to reach mid channel.

(2) Average speed over the bottom during passage down the bay.

Solution.—(1) Transfer the line (slope) for ten knots southbound to the diagram, locating it so that it is centered on the unshaded ebb current section between W. 42nd St. and Ambrose Channel Entrance. This line crosses a horizontal line through W. 42nd St. about one-half of the distance between the vertical lines representing three and two hours, respectively, after ebb begins at The Narrows. The setting is not critical. Any time within about half an hour of the correct time will result in about the same current. Between the points involved, the entire speed line is in the ebb current area.

(2) Table 1 indicates that on the morning of January 3 ebb begins at The Narrows at 0132. Two hours twenty-eight minutes after ebb begins, the time is 0400. Therefore, the ship should reach mid channel at 0400. It should get underway 15 minutes earlier, at 0345.

(3) To find the average current, determine the current at intervals (as every two miles), add, and divide by the number of entries.

Distance	*Current*
18	1.2
16	1.4
14	1.9
12	1.5
10	2.0
8	1.9
6	1.3
4	1.2
2	1.4
0	1.2
sum	15.0

The sum of 15.0 is for ten entries. The average is therefore 15.0÷10=1.5 knots.

(4) This value of current is correct only if the ebb current is an average one. From table 1 the maximum ebb involved is 2.2 knots. From the diagram the maximum value at The Narrows is 2.0 knots. Therefore, the average current found in step (3) should be increased by the ratio 2.2÷2.0=1.1. The average for the run is therefore 1.5×1.1=1.6 knots. Speed over the botton is 10+1.6=11.6 knots.

Answers.—(1) T 0345, (2) S 11.6 kn.

In the example, an ebb current is carried throughout the run. If the transferred speed line had been partly in a flood current area, all ebb currents (those increasing the ship's speed) should be given a positive sign (+), and all flood currents a negative sign (−). A separate ratio should be determined for each current (flood or ebb), and applied to the entries for that current. In Chesapeake Bay it is not unusual for an outbound vessel to encounter three or even four separate currents during passage down the bay. Under the latter condition, it is good practice to multiply *each* current taken from the diagram by the ratio for the current involved.

If the time of starting the passage is fixed, and the current during passage is desired, the starting time is identified in terms of the reference tidal cycle. The speed line is then drawn through the intersection of this vertical time line and the horizontal line through the place. The average current is then determined in the same manner as when the speed line is located as described above.

Problems

1202. The mean high water lunitidal interval at a certain port is 2^h17^m.

Required.—The approximate times of each high and low water on a day when the moon transits the local meridian at 1146.

Answers.—HW at 0139 and 1403, LW at 0751 and 2015.

1204. List chronologically the times and heights of all tides at New York (The Battery) on February 11, 1975.

Answer.—

Time	*Tide*	*Height*
0222	LW	(−) 0.4 ft.
0829	HW	4.6 ft.
1449	LW	(−) 0.6 ft.
2053	HW	4.2 ft.

1205. List chronologically the times and heights of all tides at Castle Point, Hoboken, N.J. (No. 1519) on March 18, 1975.

Answer.—

Time	*Tide*	*Height*
0533	LW	0.2 ft.
1141	HW	3.5 ft.
1724	LW	0.3 ft.
0003	HW	4.1 ft.

1206a. Find the height of tide at Union Stock Yards, New York (No. 1523) at 0600 on February 6, 1975.

Answer.—Ht. of tide at 0600, 3.8 ft.

1206b. The captain of a vessel drawing 24 feet wishes to pass over a temporary obstruction near Bayonne, N.J. (No. 1505) having a charted depth of 23 feet, passage to be made during the afternoon of March 5, 1975.

Required.—The earliest and latest times that the passage can be made, allowing a safety margin of two feet.

Answers.—Earliest time 1316, latest time 1531.

1208. Determine the sequence of currents at The Narrows on January 15, 1975.

Answer.—

0000 Ebb current, 42^m after slack.
0231 Maximum ebb of 1.9 knots.
0557 Slack, flood begins.
0822 Maximum flood of 1.7 knots.
1137 Slack, ebb begins.
1455 Maximum ebb of 2.1 knots.
1836 Slack, flood begins.
2051 Maximum flood of 1.5 knots.
2400 Flood current, 2^m before slack.

1209. Determine the sequence of currents at Ambrose Channel Entrance (No. 2310) on January 12, 1975.

Answer.—

0000 Ebb current, 42^m after maximum velocity (speed).
0241 Slack, flood begins.
0533 Maximum flood of 2.0 knots, setting 310°.
0828 Slack, ebb begins.
1155 Maximum ebb of 2.5 knots.
1527 Slack, flood begins.
1801 Maximum flood of 1.5 knots, setting 310°.
2040 Slack, ebb begins.
2400 Ebb current, 3^m before maximum velocity (speed).

1210a. Find the speed of the current at Bear Mountain Bridge (No. 2445) at 0900 on February 19, 1975.

Answer.—Speed 0.8 kn.

1210b. At about what time during the afternoon of February 3, 1975, does the flood current northwest of The Battery (No. 2375) reach a speed of 1.0 knot?

Answer.—T 1245.

1212. A vessel arrives at Ambrose Channel Entrance two hours after flood begins at The Narrows on the morning of February 16, 1975.

Required.—(1) The speed through the water required to take fullest advantage of the flood tide in steaming to Chelsea Docks.

(2) The average current to be expected.

(3) Estimated time of arrival off Chelsea Docks.

Answers.—(1) S 9 kn., (2) S 1.4 kn., (3) ETA 1035.

CHAPTER XIII

SAILING DIRECTIONS AND LIGHT LISTS

1301. Introduction.—Sailing directions (pilots) and light lists provide the information that cannot be shown graphically on the nautical chart and that is not readily available elsewhere. In pilot waters, the prudent navigator makes effective use of all three tools: the nautical chart, sailing directions, and light lists. He does not use one to the exclusion of the others.

Sailing Directions

1302. Format.—The format of the 70 volumes of the sailing directions produced by the Defense Mapping Agency Hydrographic Center prior to 1971 was such that each volume, as it related to specific foreign areas, provided detailed descriptions of coasts, channels, dangers, aids, winds, currents, tides, port facilities, signal systems, pilotage, instructions for approaching and entering harbors, as well as a variety of other material required by mariners. This format differed little from sailing directions of centuries past. There were the same geographic divisions and lengthy descriptions of approaches or harbors even though improved charts had obviated the necessity for such detail.

In the earlier format the limited geographic coverage of a given volume precluded inclusion of important information pertaining to transoceanic passages.

Using a new format, the Defense Mapping Agency Hydrographic Center is replacing the previous 70 volumes with 43 volumes: 35 *Sailing Directions* (*Enroute*) and 8 *Sailing Directions* (*Planning Guide*). Port facilities data is contained in Pub. No. 150, *World Port Index.*

The old sailing directions described and located features by bearing and distance from previously described landmarks and formed a maze of descriptive hydrography covering the coasts of the world. Sometimes, the description amounted to a mass of verbosity, especially when it pertained to an archipelago. The new Index-Gazetteer, listing each feature by its coordinates, eliminates the need for lengthy, unwieldy descriptive text. Another innovation is the fact that the features described are referred to in the text by page numbers rather than by the chapter-paragraph method used in the old sailing directions.

1303. *Sailing Directions* (*Planning Guide*).—Each of the 8 *Sailing Directions* (*Planning Guide*) contains five chapters, the titles of which are shown in figure 1303a.

The Planning Guides are relatively permanent because of the nature of the material they contain. The *Sailing Directions* (*Enroute*) must be updated by relatively frequent changes, and so must the *World Port Index.*

The new sailing directions are designed to assist the navigator in planning a voyage of any extent, particularly if it involves an ocean passage. Each of the *Sailing Directions* (*Planning Guide*) covers one of the world's great land-sea areas based on an arbitrary division of the world's seaways into eight "ocean basins" as shown in figure 1303b.

Chapter 1 of the Planning Guide, COUNTRIES, contains useful information about all of the countries adjacent to the particular ocean basin being covered by one of the eight publications. This is the chapter concerned with pratique, pilotage, signals, and

CHAPTER	
1. COUNTRIES	Governments Regulations Search & Rescue Communications Signals
2. OCEAN BASIN ENVIRONMENT	Oceanography Magnetic Disturbances Climatology
3. WARNING AREAS	Operating Areas, Firing Areas Reference Guide to Warnings and Cautions
4. OCEAN ROUTES	Route Chart & Text Traffic Separation Schemes
5. NAVAID SYSTEMS	Electronic Navigation Systems Systems of Lights & Buoyage

FIGURE 1303a.—Table of contents of *Sailing Directions* (*Planning Guide*).

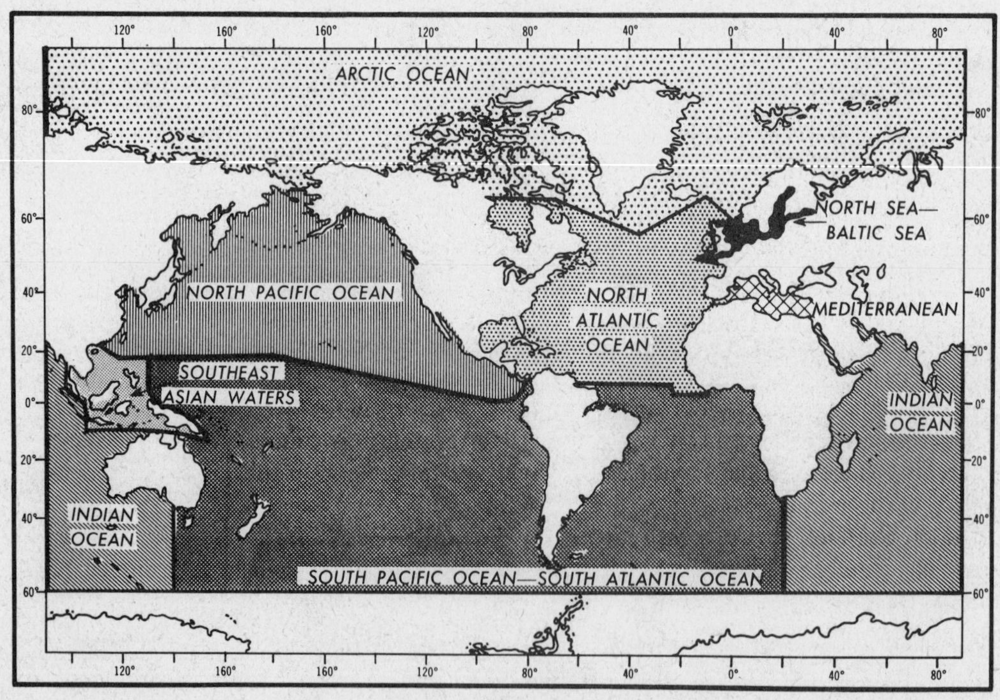

FIGURE 1303b.—Division of world's great land-sea areas into eight ocean basins.

pertinent regulations for shipping. A treatment of Search and Rescue includes graphics showing all lifesaving stations and radio stations open to public correspondence.

Chapter 2 of the Planning Guide, OCEAN BASIN ENVIRONMENT, contains important information relative to the physical environment of an ocean basin. It consists of Ocean

Summaries and local coastal phenomena not found in referenced atlases, and provides the mariner with general, concise information concerning the physical forces he must consider in planning a route.

Chapter 3 of the Planning Guide, WARNING AREAS, includes firing danger areas published in foreign sailing directions and not already shown on nautical charts or in other Defense Mapping Agency Hydrographic Center publications. A graphic key identifies Submarine Operating Areas. References are made to publications and periodicals which list danger areas, for example *Notice to Mariners No. 1* which gives an annual listing of Atlantic and Pacific danger areas. General cautions pertinent to navigation are given.

In Chapter 4 of the Planning Guide, ROUTES, the recommended steamship routes are described and shown graphically. To facilitate planning, the new publication shows entire routes as they originate from all major U. S. ports and naval bases and terminate at foreign ports in the Planning Guide area. The new concept is in sharp contrast to the localized method used in the old sailing directions. Chapter 4 also includes all applicable Traffic Separation Schemes.

The Planning Guide concludes with Chapter 5, NAVAID SYSTEMS. In keeping with the principles of the new concept, all radionavigation systems pertaining to the ocean area are described. The national and international systems of lights, beaconage, and buoyage are also described and illustrated.

1304. *Sailing Directions* (*Enroute*).—Each volume of the 35 *Sailing Directions* (*Enroute*) is divided into numbered sectors. Figure 1304a shows a portion of the sectors covered by one of the two *Sailing Directions* (*Enroute*) covering the English Channel. Figure 1304b illustrates a typical table of contents for a sector.

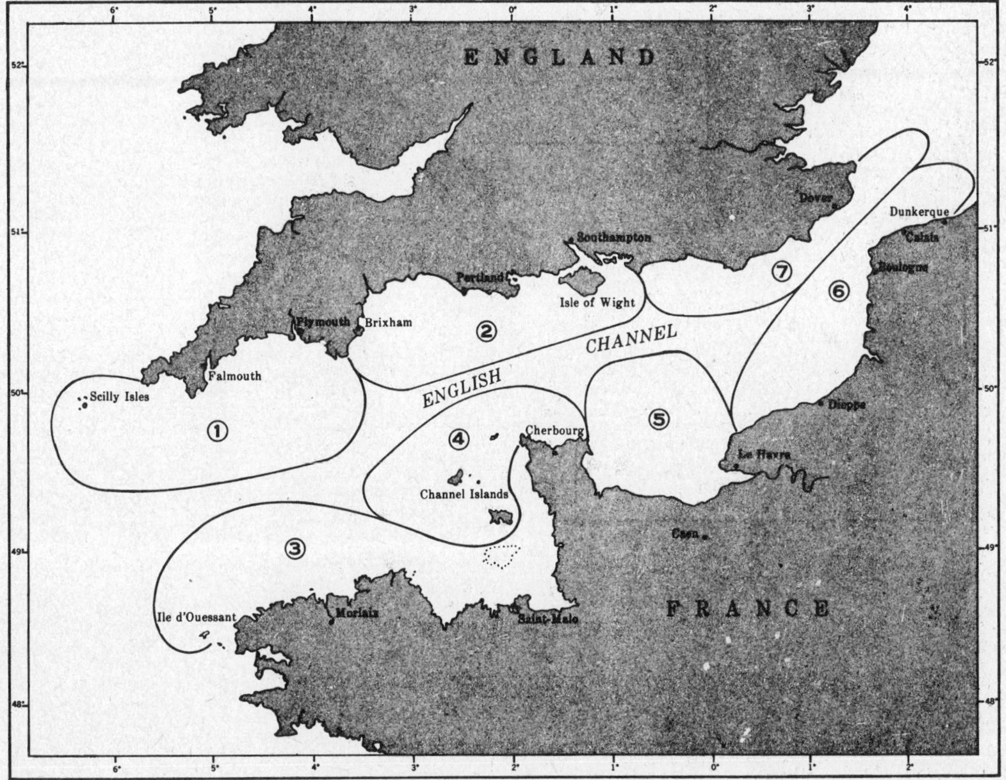

FIGURE 1304a.—Typical diagram of sector limits.

SECTOR 1

CHART INFORMATION GRAPHIC
COASTAL WINDS & CURRENTS GRAPHIC
OUTER DANGERS
COASTAL FEATURES
ANCHORAGES (COASTAL)
MAJOR PORTS

—Directions; Landmarks; Navaids; Depths;
Limitations; Restrictions; Pilotage; Regulations;
Winds; Tides; Currents; Anchorages

FIGURE 1304b.—Typical table of contents of *Sailing Directions* (*Enroute*).

Chart Information, the first subtitle in the sample table of contents, refers to a graphic key to charts pertaining to a sector. Figure 1304c is an actual sample of the graphic key for Sector 1, "English Channel—Scilly Isles to Start Point." The graduation of the border scale of the chartlet in five-minute increments enables navigators to quickly identify the largest scale chart for a location and to find a feature listed in the publications Index-Gazetteer.

The Index-Gazetteer is simply an alphabetical listing, including both described features and charted features. Each feature is listed with its geographic coordinates and sector number for use with the graphic key. Only features mentioned in the text are given a page number.

Coastal Winds and Currents, the second subtitle in the table of contents, refers to a graphic depicting coastal winds, weather, tides, and currents. Figure 1304d is a

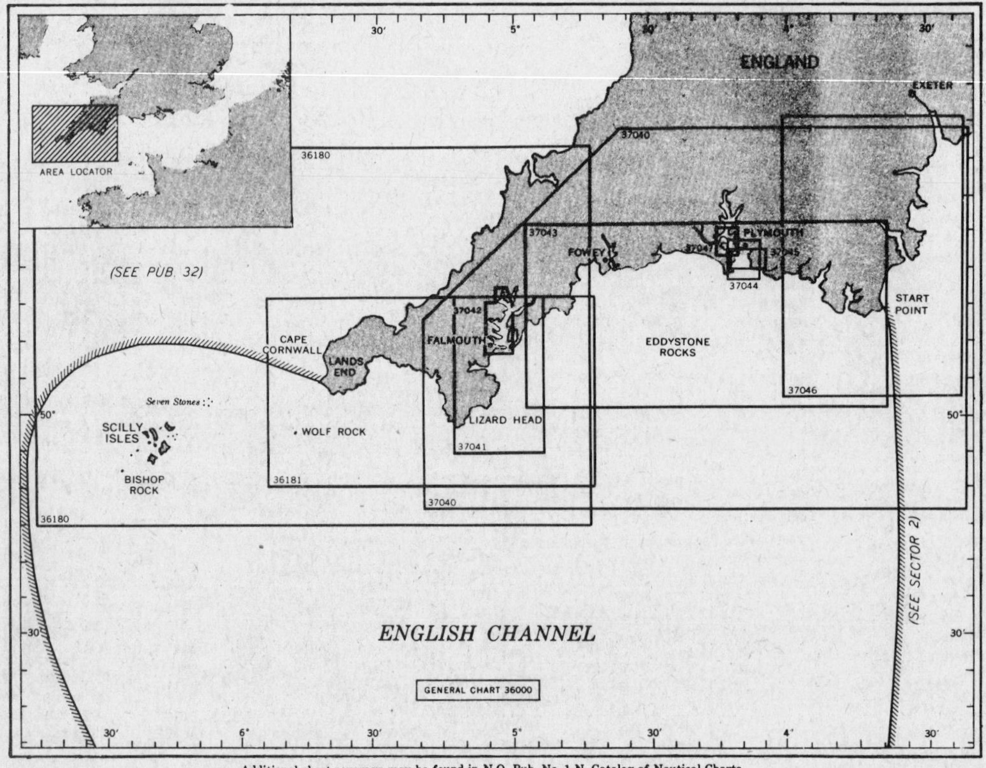

FIGURE 1304c.—Graphic key to charts within a sector.

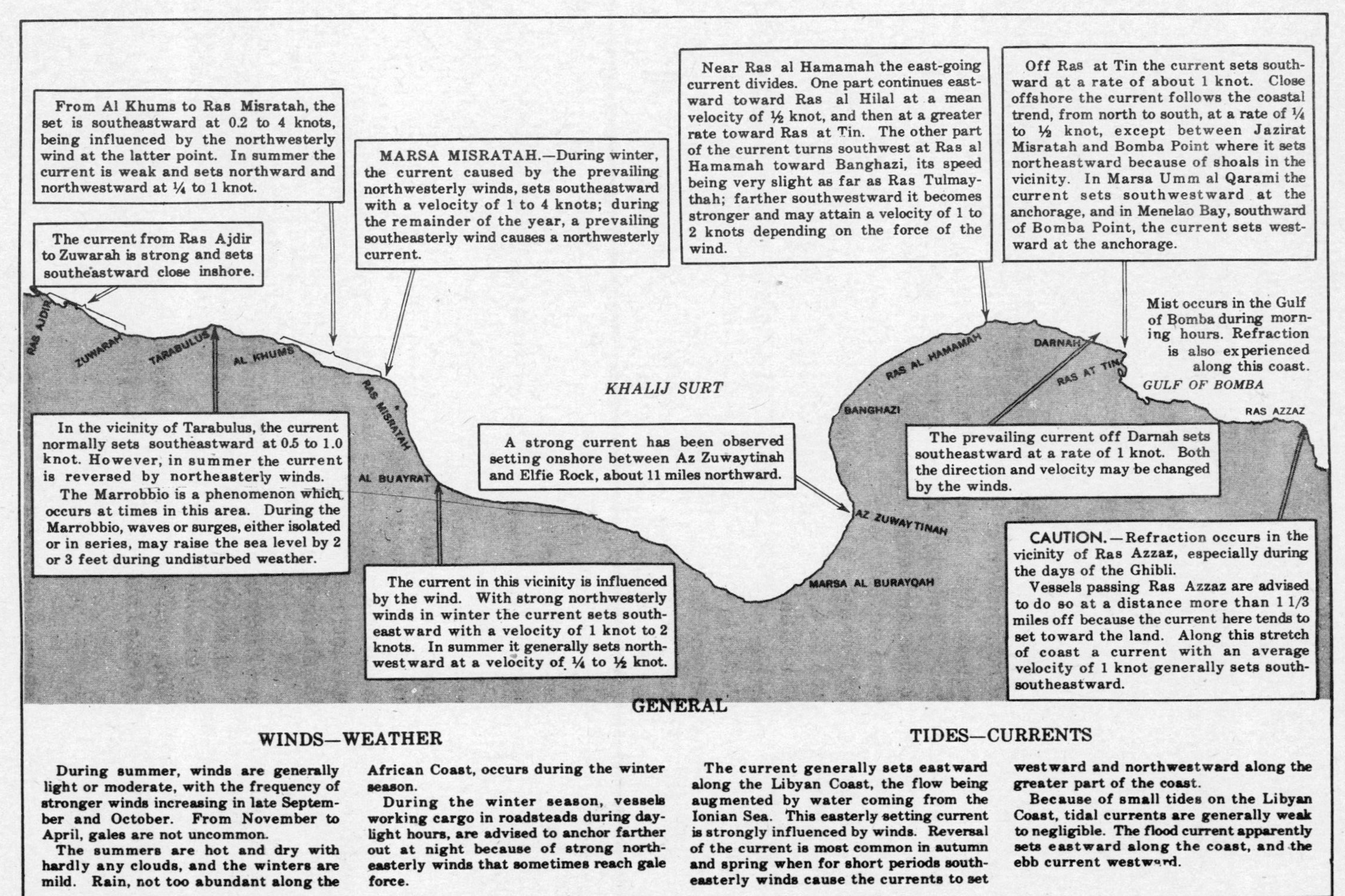

From Al Khums to Ras Misratah, the set is southeastward at 0.2 to 4 knots, being influenced by the northwesterly wind at the latter point. In summer the current is weak and sets northward and northwestward at ¼ to 1 knot.
The current from Ras Ajdir to Zuwarah is strong and sets southeastward close inshore.
MARSA MISRATAH.—During winter, the current caused by the prevailing northwesterly winds, sets southeastward with a velocity of 1 to 4 knots; during the remainder of the year, a prevailing southeasterly wind causes a northwesterly current.
Near Ras al Hamamah the east-going current divides. One part continues eastward toward Ras al Hilal at a mean velocity of ½ knot, and then at a greater rate toward Ras at Tin. The other part of the current turns southwest at Ras al Hamamah toward Banghazi, its speed being very slight as far as Ras Tulmaythah; farther southwestward it becomes stronger and may attain a velocity of 1 to 2 knots depending on the force of the wind.
Off Ras at Tin the current sets southward at a rate of about 1 knot. Close offshore the current follows the coastal trend, from north to south, at a rate of ¼ to ½ knot, except between Jazirat Misratah and Bomba Point where it sets northeastward because of shoals in the vicinity. In Marsa Umm al Qarami the current sets southwestward at the anchorage, and in Menelao Bay, southward of Bomba Point, the current sets westward at the anchorage.
Mist occurs in the Gulf of Bomba during morning hours. Refraction is also experienced along this coast.
RAS AJDIR
ZUWARAH
TARABULUS
AL KHUMS
RAS MISRATAH
KHALIJ SURT
RAS AL HAMAMAH
DARNAH
RAS AT TIN
GULF OF BOMBA
BANGHAZI
RAS AZZAZ
In the vicinity of Tarabulus, the current normally sets southeastward at 0.5 to 1.0 knot. However, in summer the current is reversed by northeasterly winds.
The Marrobbio is a phenomenon which occurs at times in this area. During the Marrobbio, waves or surges, either isolated or in series, may raise the sea level by 2 or 3 feet during undisturbed weather.
AL BUAYRAT
A strong current has been observed setting onshore between Az Zuwaytinah and Elfie Rock, about 11 miles northward.
The prevailing current off Darnah sets southeastward at a rate of 1 knot. Both the direction and velocity may be changed by the winds.
AZ ZUWAYTINAH
CAUTION.—Refraction occurs in the vicinity of Ras Azzaz, especially during the days of the Ghibli.
Vessels passing Ras Azzaz are advised to do so at a distance more than 1 1/3 miles off because the current here tends to set toward the land. Along this stretch of coast a current with an average velocity of 1 knot generally sets south-southeastward.
The current in this vicinity is influenced by the wind. With strong northwesterly winds in winter the current sets southeastward with a velocity of 1 knot to 2 knots. In summer it generally sets northwestward at a velocity of ¼ to ½ knot.
MARSA AL BURAYQAH
GENERAL
WINDS—WEATHER
During summer, winds are generally light or moderate, with the frequency of stronger winds increasing in late September and October. From November to April, gales are not uncommon.
The summers are hot and dry with hardly any clouds, and the winters are mild. Rain, not too abundant along the African Coast, occurs during the winter season.
During the winter season, vessels working cargo in roadsteads during daylight hours, are advised to anchor farther out at night because of strong northeasterly winds that sometimes reach gale force.
TIDES—CURRENTS
The current generally sets eastward along the Libyan Coast, the flow being augmented by water coming from the Ionian Sea. This easterly setting current is strongly influenced by winds. Reversal of the current is most common in autumn and spring when for short periods southeasterly winds cause the currents to set westward and northwestward along the greater part of the coast.
Because of small tides on the Libyan Coast, tidal currents are generally weak to negligible. The flood current apparently sets eastward along the coast, and the ebb current westward.

FIGURE 1304d.—Graphic depicting coastal winds, weather, tides and currents.

reproduction of the graphic for a sector covering the coast of Libya and which appears in one of the new *Sailing Directions* (*Enroute*). In the new format all of the information previously scattered throughout a chapter of the old sailing directions is given on a single graphic to facilitate use by navigators.

Outer Dangers, the third subtitle in the table of contents, refers to that part of Sector 1 which describes dangers to navigation in the outer portion of a harbor, bay, river, etc. In the old format all dangers, both inner and outer, were described at length. In the new format the outer dangers are fully described, but inner dangers which are well-charted are for the most part omitted. The greatest offshore distance of the 20-meter (10-fathom) curve, or other appropriate curve, is stated. Numerous offshore dangers, grouped together, are mentioned only in general terms. Dangers adjacent to a coastal passage or fairway are described along with supplementary information to ensure safe passage.

Coastal Features, the fourth subtitle in the table of contents, consists of both text and graphics and includes information in geographical sequence that supplements the charted landmarks, aids to navigation, salient points, fringing reefs, shoals, river mouths, coastal islets, inlets, and bays. In compiling this section it is assumed that the majority of ships have radar and, hence, annotated radarscope photographs have been included whenever possible. Aerial and surface views of harbors and approaches are included to aid mariners in identifying features. Where no photographs or sketches are available, features are described in the text.

Anchorages, the fifth subtitle in the table of contents, describes in geographical sequence all coastal anchoring information pertaining to a sector. A tabulated listing of these anchorages is included in an appendix at the back of the book.

Major Ports, the sixth and final subtitle in the table of contents, gives specific information for the major seaports within a sector. In keeping with the precepts of the new format every effort is made to limit such information to essential facts, thus permitting a significant reduction in the textual material presented. An example is the use of graphic directions for entering a particular port. These graphic directions consist of an annotated chartlet with line drawings of aids to navigation and prominent landmarks. Orientation photos may be included. Port facilities are given in the *World Port Index*.

1305. *United States Coast Pilots* published by the National Ocean Survey supplement the navigational information shown on nautical charts. These *sailing directions* for United States coastal and intracoastal waters provide information that cannot be shown graphically on nautical charts and that is not readily available elsewhere. *Coast Pilot* subjects include navigation regulations, outstanding landmarks, channel and anchorage peculiarities, dangers, weather, ice, freshets, routes, pilotage, and port facilities.

Each of the eight *Coast Pilots* is corrected through the dates of *Notice to Mariners* shown on the title page, and should not be used without reference to the *Notices to Mariners* issued subsequent to those dates.

The ***Great Lakes Pilot,*** also published by the National Ocean Survey, provides similar information for the Great Lakes. Distances given in this publication are expressed in statute miles.

Light Lists

1306. Light lists furnish more complete information concerning aides to navigation than can be conveniently shown on charts. They are not intended to be used for navigation in place of charts and sailing directions (pilots), and should not be so used. The charts should be consulted for the location of all aids to navigation. It may be dangerous to use aids to navigation without reference to charts. Likewise, the charts should not be used without reference to the more detailed information given in the light list, even during daylight. For example: Only the light list may reveal that certain channel buoys are actually located some 50 yards beyond the charted channel limits. Or, only the light list may reveal that a certain charted lighted buoy with a radar reflector is replaced by a nun buoy when endangered by ice. Since this replacement is indicated in the light list, it would not normally be included in *Notice to Mariners*.

Light lists give detailed information regarding navigational lights and sound signals. The U. S. Coast Guard *Light List* for the United States and its possessions, including the Intracoastal Waterway, the Great Lakes (both United States and certain aids on Canadian shores), and the Mississippi River and its navigable tributaries also gives information on unlighted buoys, radiobeacons, radio direction finder calibration stations, daybeacons, racons, and Loran stations. The *Light List* does not include aeronautical lights.

In addition to information on lighted aids to navigation and sound signals, the Defense Mapping Agency Hydrographic Center *List of Lights* for coasts other than the United States and its possessions provides information on storm signals, signal stations, racons, radiobeacons, and radio direction finder calibration stations located at or near lights. However, for detailed information on radio aids the navigator should refer to Pubs. Nos. 117A and 117B, *Radio Navigational Aids*. The *List of Lights* does not include information on lighted buoys in harbors. Those aeronautical lights situated near the coast are listed in the *List of Lights* in order that the marine navigator may be able to obtain more complete information concerning their description. However, it should be borne in mind that these lights are not designed or maintained for marine navigation, and they are subject to changes of which the marine navigator may not receive prompt notification.

Within each volume of the *Light List* aids to navigation are listed in geographic order from north to south along the Atlantic coast, from east to west along the gulf coast, and from south to north along the Pacific coast. Seacoast aids are listed first, followed by entrance and harbor aids listed from seaward to the head of navigation. In volumes I and II, Intracoastal Waterway aids are listed last and in geographic order from north to south along the Atlantic coast and south to north and east to west along the gulf coast.

The introductions to the light lists contain useful information pertaining to the contents which should be carefully studied by the user. In addition to the notes in the remarks columns of the lists, *the user should be sure to refer to all other notes, such as those which may be given near the head of the location column.*

The U. S. Coast Guard *Light List* is published in five volumes; the Defense Mapping Agency Hydrographic Center *List of Lights* is published in seven volumes. The data in both lists are corrected through the *Notice to Mariners* specified in the preface of each volume. For example, the 1975 *Light List, Volume* I, *Atlantic Coast,* is corrected through *Local Notice to Mariners* issued by the 1st, 3rd, and 5th U. S. Coast Guard District Commanders through October 5, 1974, and *Notice to Mariners* No. 45 of November 9, 1974, published by the Defense Mapping Agency Hydrographic Center. Corrections which have accumulated since the latter date are included in section IV weekly. All of these corrections should be applied in the appropriate places and their insertion noted in the "Record of Corrections."

1307. Visual range of lights.—Usually a navigator wants to know not only the identity of a light, but also the area in which he might reasonably expect to observe it. His track is planned to take him within range of lights which can prove useful during periods of darkness. If lights are not sighted within a reasonable time after prediction, a dangerous situation may exist, requiring resolution or action to insure safety of the vessel.

The area in which a light can be observed is normally a circle with the light as the center, and the visual range as the radius. However, on some bearings the range may be reduced by obstructions. In this case the obstructed arc might differ with height of eye and distance. Also, lights of different colors may be seen at different distances. This fact should be considered not only in predicting the distance at which a light can be seen, but also in identifying it. The condition of the atmosphere has a considerable effect upon the distance at which lights can be seen. Sometimes lights are obscured by fog, haze, dust, smoke, or precipitation which may be present at the light, or between it and the observer, but not at the observer, and possibly unknown to him. There is always the possibility of a light being extinguished. In the case of unwatched lights, this condition might not be detected and corrected at once. During periods of armed conflict, certain lights might be deliberately extinguished if they are considered of greater value to the enemy than to one's own vessels.

On a dark, clear night the visual range is limited primarily by one of two ways: (1) luminous intensity and (2) curvature of the earth. A weak light cannot normally be expected to be seen beyond a certain range, regardless of the height of eye. This distance is called luminous range. Light travels in almost straight lines, so that an observer below the visible horizon of the light should not expect to see the light, although the loom extending upward from the light can sometimes be seen at greater distances. Table 8 gives the distance to the horizon at various heights. A condensed version of table 8 is given in the light lists. The tabulated distances assume normal refraction. Abnormal conditions might extend this range somewhat (or in some cases reduce it). Hence, the geographic range, as the luminous range, is not subject to exact prediction at any given time.

The **luminous range** is the maximum distance at which a light can be seen under existing visibility conditions. This luminous range takes no account of the elevation of the light, the observer's height of eye, the curvature of the earth, or interference from background lighting. The luminous range is determined from the known nominal luminous range, called the nominal range, and the existing visibility conditions. The **nominal range** is the maximum distance at which a light can be seen in clear weather as defined by the International Visibility Code (meteorological visibility of 10 nautical miles). The **geographic range** is the maximum distance at which the curvature of the earth permits a light to be seen from a particular height of eye *without* regard to the luminous intensity of the light. The geographic range *sometimes* printed on charts or tabulated in light lists is the maximum distance at which the curvature of the earth permits a light to be seen from a height of eye of 15 feet above the water when the elevation of the light is taken above the height datum of the largest scale chart of the locality.

The geographic range depends upon the height of both the light and the observer, as shown in figure 1307a. In this illustration a light 150 feet above the water is shown. At this height, the distance to the horizon, by table 4, is 14.0 miles. Within this range the light, *if powerful enough and atmospheric conditions permit,* is visible regardless of the height of eye of the observer (if there is no obstruction). Beyond this range, the visual range depends on the height of the eye. Thus, by table 4 an observer with height of eye of five feet can see the light on his horizon if he is 2.6 miles beyond the horizon of the light, or a total of 16.6 miles. For a height of 30 feet the distance is $14.0+6.3=20.3$ miles. If the height of eye is 70 feet, the geographic range is $14.0+9.6=23.6$ miles.

Except for range and some directional lights, the nominal range is listed in the U. S. Coast Guard *Light List.* The **Luminous Range Diagram** shown in the *Light List* and figure 1307b is used to convert the nominal range to the luminous range. When using this diagram, it must be remembered that the ranges obtained are approximate, the transmissivity of the atmosphere may vary between the observer and the light, and *glare from background lighting will reduce considerably the range at which lights are sighted.* After estimating the meteorological visibility with the aid of the Meteorological Optical Range Table shown in table 1307, the Luminous Range Diagram is entered with the nominal range on the horizontal nominal range scale; a vertical line is followed until it intersects the curve or reaches the region on the diagram representing the meteorological visibility; from this point or region a horizontal line is followed until it intersects the vertical luminous range scale.

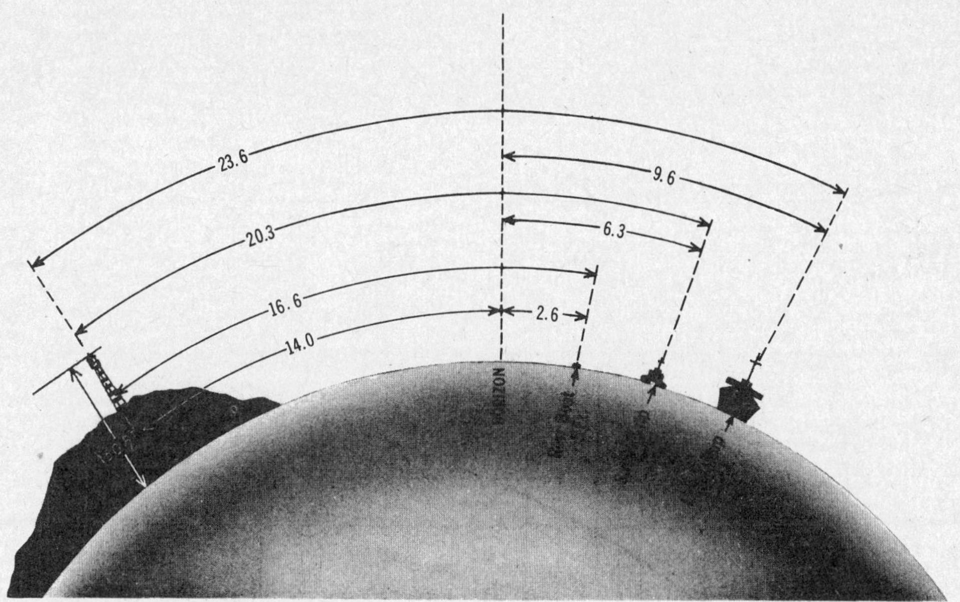

FIGURE 1307a.—Geographic range of a light.

Example 1.—The nominal range of a light as extracted from the *Light List* is 15 nautical miles.

Required.—The luminous range when the meteorological visibility is (1) 11 nautical miles and (2) 1 nautical mile.

Solution.—To find the luminous range when the meteorological visibility is 11 nautical miles, the Luminous Range Diagram is entered with nominal range 15 nautical miles on the horizontal nominal range scale; a vertical line is followed until it intersects the curve on the diagram representing a meteorological visibility of 11 nautical miles; from this point a horizontal line is followed until it intersects the vertical luminous range scale at 16 nautical miles. A similar procedure is followed to find the luminous range when the meteorological visibility is 1 nautical mile.

Answers.—(1) 16 nautical miles; (2) 3 nautical miles.

In predicting the range at which a light can be seen, one should first determine the geographic range to compare this range with the luminous range, if known. If the geographic range is less than the luminous range, the geographic range must be taken as the limiting range. If the luminous range is less than the geographic range, the luminous range must be taken as the limiting range.

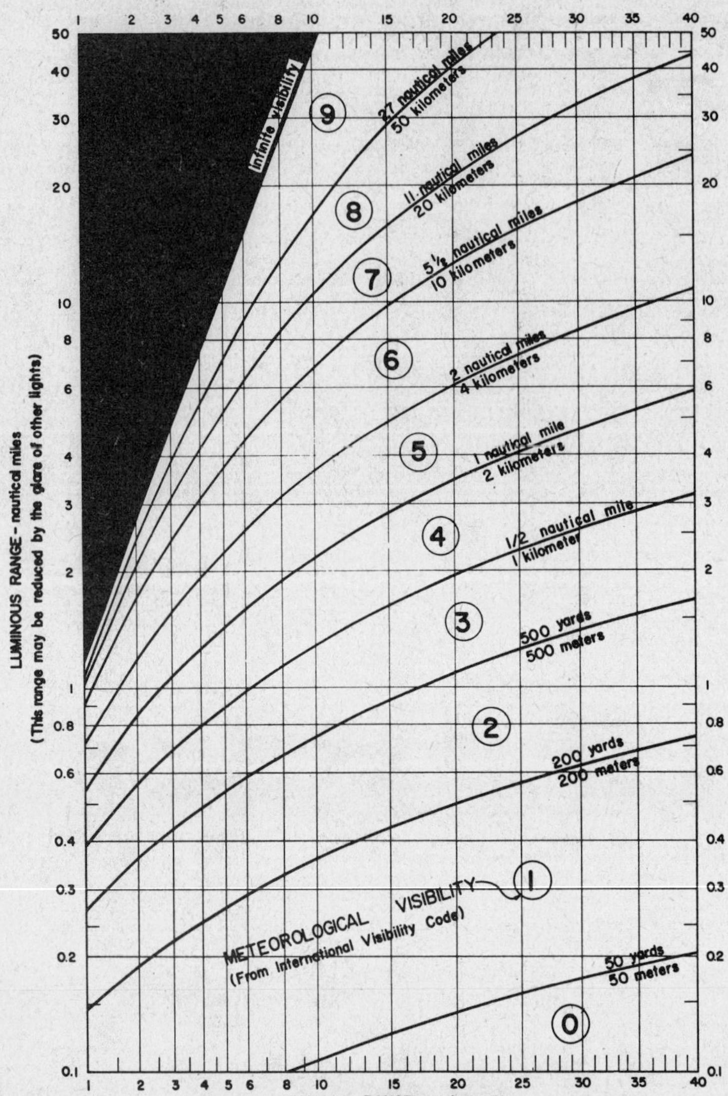

FIGURE 1307b.—Luminous Range Diagram.

These predictions are simple when using the U. S. Coast Guard *Light List* because only nominal ranges are tabulated. Also the current practice of the National Ocean Survey is to follow the *Light List* when printing the range of a light on a chart.

Example 2.—The nominal range of a navigational light 120 feet above the chart datum is 20 nautical miles. The meteorological visibility is 27 nautical miles.

Required.—The distance at which an observer at a height of eye of 60 feet can expect to see the light.

Solution.—The maximum range at which the light may be seen is the lesser of the luminous and geographic ranges.

At 120 feet the distance to the horizon, by table 4, is 12.5 miles. Adding 8.9 miles, the distance to the horizon at a height of eye of 60 feet, the geographic range (12.5 mi.+8.9 mi.=21.4 mi.) is found to be less than the luminous range, which is 40 nautical miles.

Answer.—21 nautical miles. Because of various uncertainties, the range is given only to the nearest whole mile.

If the range of a light as printed on a chart, particularly a foreign chart or a reproduction of a foreign chart, or tabulated in a light list other than the U. S. Coast Guard *Light List*, approximates the geographic range for a 15-foot height of eye of the observer, one is generally safe in assuming that this range is the geographic range. With lesser certainty, one may also assume that the lesser of the geographic and nominal ranges is printed on the chart or tabulated in the light list. Using these assumptions, the predicted range is then found by adding the distance to the horizon for both the light and the observer, or approximately, by the *difference* between 4.4 miles (the distance to the horizon at a height of 15 feet) and the distance for the height of eye of the observer (a constant for any given height) and *adding* this value to the tabulated or charted geographic range (subtracting if the height of eye is less than 15 feet). In making a prediction, one should keep in mind the possibility of the luminous range being *between* the tabulated or charted geographic range and the predicted range. The intensity of the light, if known, should be of assistance in identifying this condition.

Code No.	Weather	Yards
0	Dense fog	Less than 50
1	Thick fog....................	50–200
2	Moderate fog.................	200–500
3	Light fog....................	500–1000
		Nautical Miles
4	Thin fog....................	½–1
5	Haze	1–2
6	Light haze.................	2–5½
7	Clear......................	5½–11
8	Very clear.................	11.0–27.0
9	Exceptionally clear.........	Over 27.0

From the International Visibility Code

TABLE 1307.—Meteorological Optical Range Table.

Example 3.—The range of a light as printed on a foreign chart is 17 miles. The light is 120 feet above chart datum. The meteorological visibility is 10 nautical miles.

Required.—The distance at which an observer at a height of eye of 60 feet can expect to see the light.

Solution.—At 120 feet the distance to the horizon, by table 4, is 12.5 miles. Adding 4.4 miles (the distance to the horizon at a height of 15 feet), the geographic range is found to approximate the range printed on the chart. Then assuming that the latter range is the geographic range for a 15-foot height of eye of the observer and that the nominal range is the greater value, the predicted range is found by adding the distance to the horizon for both the light and the observer (predicted range = 12.5 mi. + 8.9 mi. = 21.4 mi.). The additional distance, i.e., the distance in excess of the assumed charted geographic range, is dependent upon the luminous intensity of the light and the meteorological visibility.

If one is approaching a light, and wishes to predict the *time* at which it should be sighted, he first predicts the range. It is then good practice to draw an arc indicating the visual range. The point at which the course line crosses the arc of visual range is the predicted position of the vessel at the time of sighting the light. The predicted time of arrival at this point is the predicted time of sighting the light. The direction of the light from this point is the predicted bearing at which the light should be sighted. Conversion of the true bearing to a relative bearing is usually helpful in sighting the light. The accuracy of the predictions depends upon the accuracy of the predicted range, and the accuracy of the predicted time and place of crossing the visual range arc. If the course line crosses the visual range arc at a small angle, a small lateral error in track may result in a large error of prediction, both of bearing and time. This is particularly apparent if the vessel is *farther* from the light than predicted, in which case the light might be passed without being sighted. Thus, if a light is not sighted at the predicted time, the error *may* be on the side of safety. However, such an interpretation should not be given unless confirmed by other information, for there is always the possibility of reduced meteorological visibility, or of the light being extinguished.

When a light is first sighted, one might determine whether it is on the horizon by immediately reducing the height of eye by several feet, as by squatting or changing position to a lower height. If the light disappears, and reappears when the original height is resumed, it is on the horizon. This process is called **bobbing a light.** If a vessel has considerable vertical motion due to the condition of the sea, a light sighted on the horizon may alternately appear and disappear. This may lead the unwary to assign faulty characteristics and hence to err in its identification. The true characteristics should be observed after the distance has decreased, or by increasing the height of eye of the observer.

CHAPTER XIV

RADIO DIRECTION FINDING

1401. Introduction.—Medium frequency radio direction finders on board ships enable measurement of the bearings of radio transmissions from other ships, aircraft, shore stations, marine radiobeacons, aeronautical radiobeacons, and the coastal stations of the radio communications network.

Depending upon the design of the **radio direction finder (RDF),** the bearings of the radio transmissions are measured as relative bearings or as both relative and true bearings. In one design, the true bearing dial is manually set with respect to the relative bearing dial in accordance with the ship's heading. In another design, the true bearing dial is rotated electrically in accordance with a course input from the gyrocompass. In some of the earlier designs, the RDF is mounted over the ship's compass so as to permit the bearings to be read directly from the compass card.

Whatever means is used to read the bearings, corrections for errors of radio bearings (art. 1404) must be applied. In some designs two distinct means are employed for automatic error compensation. An electrical compensating system provides for automatic compensation of errors which are symmetrically distributed, fore-and-aft or athwartship. A mechanical compensating system provides for automatic compensation of residual errors up to a limiting value. The mechanical compensator may consist of a stationary cam which is cut for each calibration (art. 1407), a movable roller, and associated linkage for causing the goniometer (art. 1403) pointer to lead or lag the actual goniometer setting.

When plotting radio bearings on a Mercator chart, conversion angle must be applied to convert the radio bearing (great-circle direction) to the equivalent rhumb line bearing. Conversion angles are given in table 1.

1402. Radiobeacons established to be of primary usefulness to mariners are known as **marine radiobeacons;** beacons established to be of primary usefulness to airmen are known as **aeronautical radiobeacons;** other beacons established for both classes of user are sometimes known as **aeromarine radiobeacons.** The most common type of marine radiobeacon transmits radio waves of approximately uniform strength in all directions. These *omnidirectional* beacons are known as **circular radiobeacons.**

Directional radiobeacons transmit radio waves within a narrow sector. Compared with the circular radiobeacon, the transmissions from the directional radiobeacons have relatively short range. The rotating loop radiobeacon is discussed in article 1411.

Most United States and Canadian radiobeacons are grouped together on the same operating frequency and are assigned a specific sequence of transmission within this group. This reduces station interference and undesirable retuning. Normally the stations operate in groups of six, each station in a group of **sequenced radiobeacons** using the same frequency and transmitting for 1 minute in its proper sequence. A few radiobeacons transmit for 1 minute with 2 minutes of silence, and some radiobeacons transmit continuously without interruption.

Except for **calibration radiobeacons,** radiobeacons operate during all periods either sequenced or continuously, regardless of weather conditions.

Simple combinations of dots and dashes are used for station identification. These combinations and the duration of the dots, dashes, and spaces are chosen for ease of identification. Where applicable, the Morse equivalent character or characters are shown in conjunction with the station characteristic. All radiobeacons superimpose the characteristic on a carrier which is on continuously during the period of transmission. This extends the usefulness of marine radiobeacons to an airborne or marine user of an **automatic radio direction finder (ADF)**. Users of the "aural null" type radio direction finder will notice no change in quality of service. A 10-second dash is incorporated in the characteristic signal to enable the user of the aural null type of radio direction finder to refine his bearing.

Aeronautical radiobeacons are sometimes used by marine navigators for determining lines of position when marine radiobeacons are not available. Since it is not possible to predict the extent to which land effect (art. 1404) may render mariners' observations of the bearings of these beacons unreliable, their inclusion in Pubs. Nos. 117A and 117B, *Radio Navigational Aids*, does not imply that the beacons have been found reliable for marine use. Those aeronautical radiobeacons included in Pubs. Nos. 117A and 117B may be useful to the marine navigator who recognizes their limitations. These aeronautical aids become less trustworthy, so far as marine applications are concerned, as they are situated farther inland or when high land intervenes between them and the coast.

Pubs. Nos. 117A and 117B, *Radio Navigational Aids*, include in the details of many radiobeacons located at or near light stations a statement of the distance and bearing of the radiobeacon transmitting antenna from the light tower. Use should be made of this information when calibrating (art. 1407) the radio direction finder.

1403. Direction measurement at the receiving site is accomplished by means of a directional antenna. Nearly all antennas have some directional properties, but in the usual antenna used for radio communication, these properties are not sufficiently critical for navigational use.

A widely used directional antenna is in the form of a loop. Suppose a transmitted radio signal encounters such a loop oriented in the direction of travel of the radio signal, as shown in figure 1403a. If the diameter of the loop is half the wavelength, the crest of one wave arrives at one side of the loop at the same time that the trough arrives at the opposite side, as shown. Thus, the currents induced in the two sides reinforce each other, causing maximum output from the antenna. A short time later, as the wave continues to move past the antenna, the crest reaches the other side of the loop, and a new trough reaches the approach side. A maximum current now flows in the opposite direction. Therefore, with the antenna in this orientation, an alternating current flows in the loop. If the loop diameter is less than half a wavelength, the current is less than maximum.

If the antenna is rotated 90°, the alternate crests and troughs arrive at both sides at the same time, tending to cause currents to flow in opposite directions around the loop. Under these conditions the two parts cancel each other, resulting in zero antenna output. This condition is called a **null.**

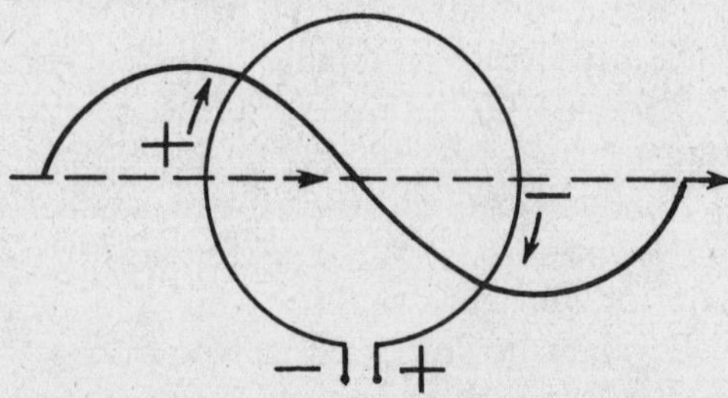

FIGURE 1403a.—Principle of the loop antenna.

As the antenna is rotated, its output varies with the angle relative to the direction of motion of the radio signal. This condition is illustrated in figure 1403b. The length of a line from the center to the outer edge of the shaded area represents the strength of the antenna output at that bearing, relative to the direction of motion of the radio wave. Thus, when it is in line, *with either side of the loop toward the approaching signal,* the output is maximum, and at 90° it is minimum. Since the change with bearing is most rapid near the region of minimum signal, this is the portion used for determination of direction.

Because of the characteristics of the simple loop antenna, a 180° **ambiguity** exists. That is, a signal approaching from either of two directions 180° apart would cause the same antenna output. This ambiguity can be resolved by using a vertical **sense antenna** in connection with a loop. The output from this wire, if the direction of motion of the signal is horizontal, is the same in all directions. Therefore, the polar diagram of its output is a circle, with the same polarity in all directions. If this output is exactly equal to the maximum of the loop, it will cancel the output from one side and double that from the other, since the polarity in the two sides is opposite. The resulting diagram of antenna output is shown in figure 1403c. With this arrangement, a single minimum exists, permitting the determination of which of the two reciprocal bearings is correct, thereby removing the ambiguity. The loop antenna is then used for making the reading. This is the type of equipment commonly used with a radio direction finder.

Two variations of the loop antenna are also used in radio direction finders. In one of these, the **crossed loop** type, two loops are rigidly mounted in such manner that one is rotated 90° with respect to the other. The *relative* output of the two antennas is related to the orientation of each with respect to the direction of travel of the radio wave, and is measured by a device called a **goniometer.** This is the type antenna used in an automatic direction finder. In the other variation, the **rotating loop** type, a single loop is

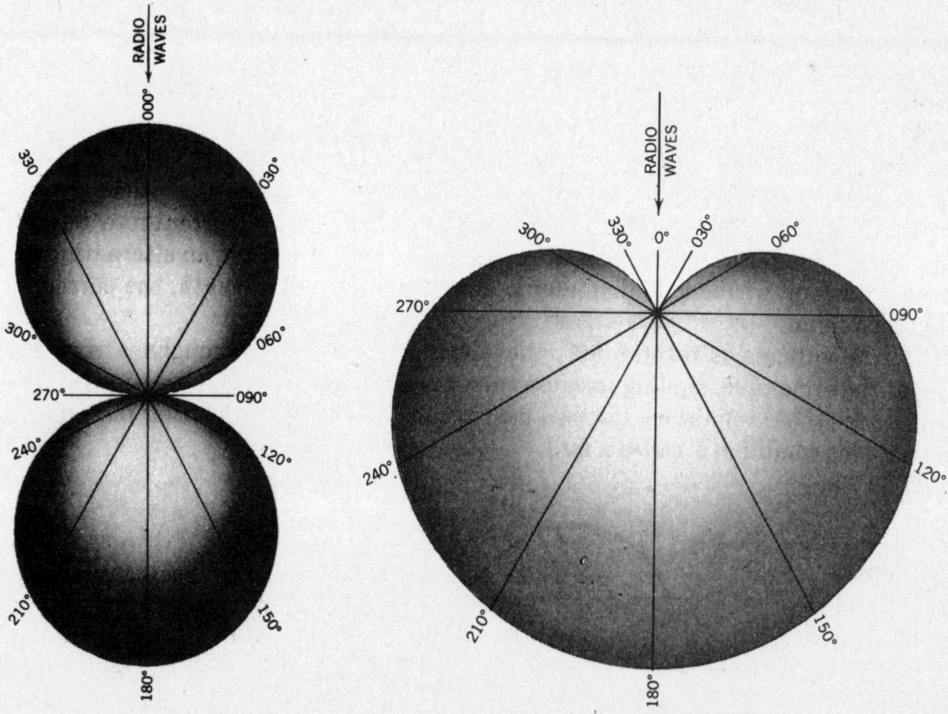

FIGURE 1403b.—Polar diagram of output of loop antenna.

FIGURE 1403c.—Polar diagram of output of loop antenna with vertical sense antenna.

kept in rapid rotation by means of a motor. The antenna output is shown on a cathode-ray tube, and the resulting display shows the direction of the signal.

1404. Errors of radio bearings.—Bearings obtained by radio direction finder are subject to certain errors, as follows:

Quadrantal error. When radio waves arrive at a receiver, they are influenced somewhat by the environment. An erroneous radio direction finder bearing results from currents induced in the direction finder antenna by re-radiation from the structural features of the vessel's superstructure and distortion of the radio wave front due to the physical dimensions and contour of the vessel's hull. This quadrantal error is a function of the *relative* bearing, normally being maximum for bearings broad on the bow and broad on the quarter. Its value for various bearings can be determined, and a **calibration table** made (art. 1407).

Coastal refraction. A radio wave crossing a coastline at an oblique angle undergoes a change of direction due to difference in conducting and reflecting properties of land and water. This is sometimes called **land effect.** It is avoided by not using, or regarding as of doubtful accuracy, bearings of waves which cross a shoreline at an oblique angle. Bearings within 15° to 20° of being parallel to a shoreline should not be trusted. If the transmitter is near the coast, negligible error is introduced because of the short distance the waves travel before undergoing refraction.

Polarization error. The direction of travel of radio waves may undergo an alteration during the confused period near sunrise or sunset, when great changes are taking place in the ionosphere. This error is sometimes called **night effect.** The error can be minimized by averaging several readings, but any radio bearings taken during this period should be considered of doubtful accuracy.

Reciprocal bearings. Unless a radio direction finder has a vertical sensing wire (art. 1403), there is a possible 180° ambiguity in the reading. If such an error is discovered, one should take the reciprocal of the *uncorrected* reading, and apply the correction for the new direction. If there is doubt as to which of the two possible directions is the correct one, one should wait long enough for the bearing to change appreciably and take another reading. The transmitter should draw *aft* between readings. If the reciprocal is used, the station will appear to have drawn *forward.* A reciprocal bearing furnished by a direction finder station should not be used because the quadrantal error is not known, either on the given bearing or its reciprocal.

1405. Accuracy of radio bearings.—In general, good radio bearings should not be in error by more than 2° for distances under 150 nautical miles. However, conditions vary considerably, and skill is an important factor. By observing the technical instructions for the equipment and practicing frequently when results can be checked by visual observation or by other means, one can develop skill and learn to what extent radio bearings can be relied upon under various conditions.

Other factors affecting accuracy include the errors discussed in article 1404, range, the condition of the equipment, and the accuracy of the calibration (art. 1407). Errors in bearing can result if the selectivity (art. 1406) of a radio direction finder is poor.

1406. Factors affecting maximum range.—The service range of a radiobeacon is determined by the strength of the radiated signal. Field strength requirements for a given service range vary with latitude, being higher in the southern latitudes. The actual useful range may vary considerably from the service range with different types of radio direction finders and during varying atmospheric conditions.

Sensitivity is a measure of the ability of a receiver to detect transmissions. All direction finder receivers do not have the same sensitivity. Some will detect a radiobeacon signal at its rated range whereas others will not detect the same signal until such time that the distance to the beacon has decreased. For example, radio direction finders having a sensitivity of 75 microvolts per meter on the radiobeacon band should be capable of detecting a signal whose intensity is 75 microvolts per meter or more. A radio direction finder having a sensitivity of 120 microvolts per meter will be unable to receive a radiobeacon signal rated at 75 microvolts per meter at 100 miles until 56 miles from the radiobeacon. At 56 miles the signal strength of the transmitted signal is 120 microvolts per meter, which is equal to the sensitivity of the receiver. It follows that the sensitivity of a radio direction finder determines the degree to which the full range capability of the radiobeacon system can be utilized.

Selectivity is a measure of the ability of a receiver to choose one frequency and reject all others. The selectivity varies with the type of receiver and its condition. The transmitted radiobeacon signal is comprised of a band of frequencies, 286.000 kHz to 287.020 kHz for example. A radio direction finder capable of accepting only this narrow band of frequencies would be ideal. If a radio direction finder accepts a wide band of frequencies (280 to 292 kHz) when tuned to 286 kHz, it will admit more noise and signals than desired. This additional interference may reduce the usefulness of the desired signal, and effectively decrease the maximum range of reception of the radiobeacon.

1407. Calibration.—The reliability of a radio direction finder is largely dependent upon the accuracy of the calibration. A good initial calibration not only increases the reliability of operation but also reduces the need for repeated recalibration, provided the superstructure and rigging of the vessel are not altered. Correct radio direction finder calibration compensates for errors caused by induced currents and vessel configuration, i.e., quadrantal error (art. 1404), also known as **direction finder error.**

Proper preliminary procedures for this calibration include accurately aligning the vessel's pelorus fore-and-aft, providing adequate communications between the pelorus and the radio direction finder, developing a plan for coordination between the calibrator and conning officer, determining that the equipment is in proper operating condition, and determining that metal booms, cranes, antennas, etc., are in their normal positions.

While the vessel is enroute to the calibration site, it may be advisable to take a number of bearings on the station to be used for calibration and on one or more other charted stations whose relative bearings can be ascertained. If it is feasible to take an RDF bearing on such a station when it bears broad on the bow or quarter, the magnitude of the quadrantal error can be estimated. Then the electrical error compensator, if installed, should be set to correct the error. It is also desirable to take RDF bearings while the vessel is enroute to the calibration site on a station at 135°, 225°, and 315° from the vessel's heading. These additional readings serve to check the setting of the electrical error compensator and to indicate whether additional adjustment of the compensator is required. Generally, if the magnitudes of the bearing errors on 135°, 225°, and 315° are less than the initial error used to adjust the compensator, the setting should be left unaltered.

The source of the radio signals used in calibration may be a radiobeacon operating on schedule or on request.

Sequenced radiobeacons cannot broadcast at any time other than on their assigned operating minute for the purpose of enabling vessels to calibrate their radio direction finders without causing interference. Special radio direction finder calibration transmitters of short range are operated at certain localities to provide calibration service during specified periods or on request. These stations with information as to position, frequency, characteristic, times of service, requests for use, etc., are listed in Pubs. Nos. 117A and 117B, *Radio Navigational Aids* and the *Light List.*

The position given for the antenna is the point from which the radiobeacon signal is emitted.

The calibration must be made on approximately the same frequency or frequencies as will be used to take RDF bearings because the direction finder error for several frequencies is not likely to be the same. It is believed that one calibration curve or table is satisfactory for the normal radiobeacon frequency (285 to 325 kHz); but the instructions issued by the manufacturer of the particular radio direction finder to be calibrated should be studied in this respect.

The usual method of calibration is to obtain a series of simultaneous radio and visual bearings on a transmitter. This can be done while a vessel swings at anchor or more quickly by steaming in a circle at the greatest distance compatible with clear visual observation of the transmitter, preferably over 1 mile. The simultaneous bearings should be observed and recorded at least every 10°, preferably every 5°.

The difference between a radio bearing and a simultaneously observed visual bearing, using the same reference, is the direction finder error. The error is positive if the visual bearing is greater than the radio bearing; otherwise, the error is negative.

The quadrantal error being maximum, generally, when the station is broad on the bow or quarter, setting of the electrical error compensator for a correction equal to the error measured when the visual bearing is 45° or 315° should provide marked reduction in errors corresponding to visual bearings of 45°, 135°, 225°, and 315°. If the vessel is swung again and another set of visual and RDF bearings are observed, the errors computed from this swing should comprise primarily the residual nonsymmetrical error components. This residual error can be corrected by cutting a cam for the mechanical error compensator.

The radio direction finder should be recalibrated after any changes have been made in the set or its surroundings, whenever there is reason to believe that the previous calibration has become inaccurate, and also at periodic intervals.

While RDF bearings are being taken, other radio antennas on board must be in the same condition as they were when the calibration was made; movable parts of the ship's superstructure such as booms, davits, wire rigging, etc., must be secured in the positions which they occupied when the radio direction finder was calibrated. Unusual cargoes such as large quantities of metals and extraordinary conditions of loading may cause errors.

1408. Using radio bearings.—A bearing obtained by radio, like one determined in any other manner, provides means for establishing a line of position. By heading in the direction from which the signal is coming, one can proceed toward, or **home** on, the transmitter. In thick weather one should avoid heading directly toward the source of radiation unless he has reliable information to indicate that he is some distance away. In 1934 the Nantucket Lightship was rammed and sunk by a ship homing on its radiobeacon.

Due to the many factors which enter into the transmission and reception of radio signals, a mariner cannot practically estimate his distance from a radiobeacon either by the strength of the signals received or by the time at which the signals were first heard. Mariners should give this fact careful consideration in approaching radiobeacons. When approaching a lightship, large navigational buoy, ocean station vessel, or a station on a submarine site, on radio bearings, the risk of collision will be avoided by insuring that the radio bearing does not remain constant.

It should be borne in mind that most lightships and large buoys are anchored to a very long scope of chain and, as a result, the radius of their swinging circle is considerable. The charted position is the location of the anchor. Furthermore, under certain conditions of wind and current, they are subject to sudden and unexpected sheers which are certain to hazard a vessel attempting to pass close aboard.

Radio waves, like light, travel along great circles. Except in high latitudes, visual bearings can usually be plotted as straight lines on a Mercator chart, without significant error. Radio bearings, however, are often observed at such positions with respect to the transmitter that the use of a rhumb line is not satisfactory. Under these conditions it is customary to apply the **conversion angle** as a correction to the observed angle, to find the equivalent rhumb line. Such a correction is not needed when a bearing is plotted on a gnomonic chart or one on which a straight line is a good approximation of a great circle. In other situations, a correction may be necessary.

If the transmitter and receiver are on the same meridian, or are both on the equator, no correction is needed because rhumb lines and great circles coincide under these conditions. The size of the correction increases with degree of departure from these conditions, and with greater distance between transmitter and receiver.

Conversion angles are given in table 1. This table is used to convert great circle to rhumb line directions. If the difference of longitude is not more than 4°5, and the mid-latitude between transmitter and receiver is not more than 85°, the first part of the table should be used. The simplifying assumptions used in the computation of this part of the table do not introduce a significant error within the limits of the table.

The sign of the correction can be determined by referring to the rules given at the bottom of each page of table 1. These follow from the fact that the great circle is nearer the pole than the rhumb line.

Before taking bearings on a commercial broadcasting station, the mariner should consider the following:

1. The operating frequency of the commercial station may differ widely from the frequency for which the radio direction finder is calibrated.
2. The broadcast antenna may be remote from the broadcast station.
3. The commercial stations are usually inland.

Accordingly, the use of commercial broadcasting stations to obtain a direction finder bearing is not recommended. If these stations are used, the mariner should recognize the limitations of the bearings obtained.

1409. Radio direction finder stations.—Radio direction finder stations are stations equipped with special apparatus for determining the direction of radio signals transmitted by ships and other stations. The bearings taken by radio direction finder stations, and reported to ships, are corrected for all determinable errors except conversion angle.

The bearings are normally accurate within 2° for distances under 150 nautical miles. The best bearings are obtained on ships whose signals are steady, clear, and strong. Therefore, the ship's transmitter should be finely tuned to the frequency of the transmitter. If the ship's transmitter is not finely tuned, it is difficult for the station to obtain bearings sufficiently accurate for navigational purposes.

Where bearing lines intersect an intervening coastline at an oblique angle or cross high intervening land, errors of from 4° to 5° may be expected due to refraction (art. 1404). However, the sectors in which such refraction may be expected is normally known by station personnel. Such sectors may not be included in the published sectors of calibration or are indicated as **sectors of uncertain calibration.**

The **sector of calibration** of a radio direction finder station is the sector about the receiving coil of the station in which the deviation of radio bearings is known. In Pubs. Nos. 117A and 117B, *Radio Navigational Aids*, the sectors are measured clockwise from 0° (true north) to 360° and are given looking from the station to seaward. Bearings which do not lie within the sector of calibration of a station should be considered unreliable.

1410. Distance finding stations.—At some locations a radio signal is synchronized with a sound signal which may be transmitted through either air or water or both. The travel time of the radio signal is negligible compared to that of the sound signal. Consequently, the difference in time between reception of the two signals is proportional to the distance from the station. The distance in nautical miles is equal to the number of seconds of time interval divided by 5½ if the sound travels through air, or by 1¼ if through water (or multiplied by 0.18 or 0.8, respectively). The distance so found is from the origin of the *sound* signal, which might differ somewhat from that of the radio signal. Table 1410 can be used for finding the distance in nautical miles from a sound signal source.

Interval in seconds	Distance in nautical miles from sound signal source	
	Air	Submarine
1	0.18	0.8
2	.36	1.6
3	.54	2.4
4	.72	3.2
5	.90	4.0
6	1.08	4.8
7	1.26	5.6
8	1.44	6.4
9	1.62	7.2
10	1.80	8.0
20	3.60	16.0
30	5.40	24.0
40	7.20	
50	9.00	
60	10.80	

TABLE 1410.—Table for finding distance from a sound source.

The speed of sound travel is influenced by a number of conditions making it impracticable to state a factor that will give exact results under all conditions. The results obtained by the methods described may be accepted as being accurate to within 10 percent of the distance.

Ordinarily, the sound signals do not operate during the transmission period of the radio signal in clear weather. The methods in use employ, as a rule, distinctive signals to indicate the point of synchronization. Methods of synchronizing the signals vary and are described or illustrated in official announcements regarding them. It is essential to note carefully the point of synchronization used so that no error will be made through taking time on the wrong signal or the wrong part of it.

An example of the synchronized signals is shown in figure 1410. In this example, the beginning of the 10-second radio dash and the beginning of the 5-second fog signal blast are synchronized. The observer may use as the time interval the interval from the time of hearing the beginning of the long radio dash to the instant of hearing the beginning of the long blast of the fog signal.

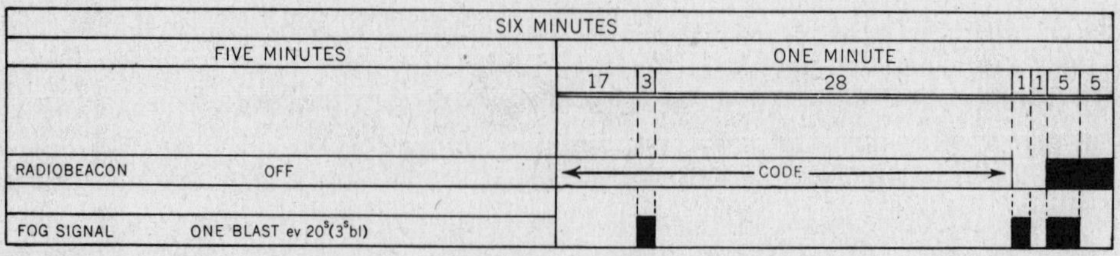

SIX MINUTES
FIVE MINUTES
ONE MINUTE
17 3 28 1 1 5 5
RADIOBEACON OFF
CODE
FOG SIGNAL ONE BLAST ev 20s(3s bl)

FIGURE 1410.—Synchronized radio and fog signals.

In observing air signals it is usually sufficient to use a watch with second hand, although a stopwatch is helpful. For submarine signals where the interval is shorter and a time error correspondingly more important, it is essential that a stopwatch or other timing device be used. Where the radiobeacon and submarine signals are not received at the same point on the vessel, means of instant communication between two observers should be available or synchronized stopwatches provided for each.

In the case of some sound signals a series of short radio dashes is transmitted at intervals following the synchronizing point, so that by counting the number of such short dashes heard after the distinctive radio signal and before hearing the corresponding distinctive sound signal, the observer obtains his distance, in miles equal to the number of dashes counted, from the sound signal apparatus unless stated otherwise.

Ships not equipped with an RDF receiver can take advantage of the distance finding feature of a radiobeacon station, if equipped with a radio receiver capable of receiving the transmission. In the case of obtaining distance from a radiobeacon station which is synchronized with a submarine sound signal, the ship must also be equipped with a device for picking up submarine sound signals.

1411. Rotating loop radiobeacon.—The rotating loop radiobeacon *used in Japanese waters* consists of a rotating loop transmitter having directional properties by which an observer in a ship can obtain his bearing from the beacon without the use of a radio direction finder. Any radio receiving set capable of being tuned to the radiobeacon frequency can be used. The only other equipment required is a reliable stopwatch with a sweep second hand. Stopwatches and clocks with dials graduated in degrees can be used, from which bearings can be read off directly without any mathematical calculation.

During each revolution of the beacon, the signals received by the observer will rise and fall in intensity, passing through a maximum and a minimum twice each minute. The positions of minimum intensity, which occur at intervals of 30 seconds from one another, are very sharp and can be accurately observed. These are, therefore, used for navigation purposes.

The beacon may be regarded as having a line or beam of minimum intensity which rotates at a uniform speed of 360° in 1 minute (i.e. 6° in 1 second) based on the true meridian as starting point. Therefore, if the observer can (1) identify the beacon and (2) measure the number of seconds which this minimum beam takes to reach his position starting from the true meridian, this number multiplied by six will give his true bearing from the beacon or its reciprocal.

Each transmission (fig. 1411) from the beacon lasts for 4 minutes, and automatically starts again at the end of the silent period. Each transmission consists of two parts: (1) the identification signal of the station set at a slow speed for the first minute, commencing when the minimum beam is true east and west and followed by a long dash of about 12 seconds duration and (2) the signal group commencing when the minimum beam is approaching the true meridian and consisting of (i) the north starting signal, which is Morse V followed by two dots (. . . — . .); (ii) a long dash of about 12 seconds duration; (iii) the east starting signal, which is Morse B followed by two dots (— . . . . .); and (iv) a long dash for about 42 seconds.

The navigation signals are repeated during the remainder of the transmission and signals cease when the minimum beam is in the east-west position.

1412. Using the rotating loop radiobeacon.—Procedures for using the rotating loop radiobeacon are as follows:

1. Set stopwatch to zero.
2. Listen for identification signal.

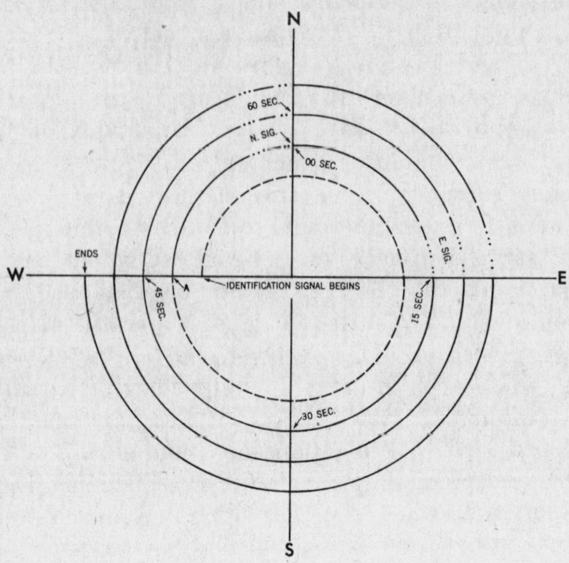

FIGURE 1411.—Transmissions from rotating loop radiobeacon.

3. When the first long dash begins (at *A* of figure 1411) stand by for the north starting signal (Morse V followed by two dots); start stopwatch exactly at beginning of long dash (00^s of figure 1411), counting "one"-"two" with the two preceding dots and "three" for the start of the stopwatch.

4. Listen for minimum and record its exact time by stopwatch.

5. Multiply the number of seconds by 6° for bearing.

6. Determine whether bearing is reciprocal or direct.

7. If the north signal is faint, use the east signal but add 90° to the bearing.

The true bearing established is *from* the beacon. Therefore, if conversion angle is to be used it should be applied to the true bearing of the observer *from* the beacon, as in correcting bearings obtained by shore direction finder stations for conversion angle.
for conversion angle.

The following precautions should be observed:

1. Stopwatch should be started exactly at the beginning of the long dash.

2. The time of the minimum should be observed to the nearest fifth of a second, if possible.

3. Be sure to determine whether the bearing is the direct bearing to the beacon or its reciprocal.

4. If the east signal is used, be sure to add 90°.

5. The stopwatch should be checked before use. This can be done by checking the time by stopwatch of the complete revolution of the beacon transmission. A comparatively large bearing error can result from inaccurate timing.

TABLES AND APPENDICES

APPENDIX A

ABBREVIATIONS

Abbreviations used on nautical charts are given in appendix Z.

A, amplitude; augmentation; away (altitude intercept).

***a*,** altitude intercept (Ho∼Hc); altitude factor (change of altitude in 1 minute of time from meridian transit); assumed.

a_0, first Polaris correction.

a_1, second Polaris correction.

a_2, third Polaris correction.

AC, alternating current.

add'l, additional.

ADF, automatic radio direction finder.

AF, audio frequency.

***a*L,** assumed latitude.

AM, amplitude modulation.

AM, ante meridian (before noon).

AMVER, Automated Mutual-assistance Vessel Rescue System.

antilog, antilogarithm.

AP, assumed position.

approx., approximate, approximately.

ASF, Additional Secondary Phase Factor.

AT, Atomic Time.

AU, astronomical unit.

AUSREP, Australian Ships Reporting System.

***a*λ,** assumed longitude.

B, atmospheric pressure correction (altitude); bearing, bearing angle.

B_A, difference between heading and apparent wind direction.

BIH, Bureau Internationale de l'Heure.

Brg., bearing (as distinguished from bearing angle).

B_{pgc}, bearing per gyrocompass.

B_T, difference between heading and true wind direction.

C, Celsius (centigrade); chronometer time; compass (direction); correction; course, course angle.

CB, compass bearing.

CC, compass course; chronometer correction.

CCIR, International Radio Consultative Committee.

CCZ, Coastal Confluence Zone.

CE, chronometer error; compass error.

cec, centicycle.

cel, centilane.

CEP, circular probable error.

CFR, Code of Federal Regulations.

CH, compass heading.

cm, centimeter, centimeters.

CMG, course made good.

Cn, course (as distinguished from course angle).

co-, the complement of (90° minus).

COA, course of advance.

COG, course over ground.

coL, colatitude.

colog, cologarithm.

corr., correction.

cos, cosine.

cot, cotangent.

cov, coversine.

CPE, circular probable error.

cps, cycles per second.

C_{pgc}, course per gyrocompass.

C_{psc}, course per standard compass.

$C_{p\ stg\ c}$, course per steering compass.

CRT, cathode-ray tube.

csc, cosecant.

CW, continuous wave.

CZn, compass azimuth.

D, deviation; dip (of horizon); distance.

d, declination (astronomical); altitude difference.

***d*,** declination change in 1 hour.

DC, direct current.

D. Lat., difference of latitude.

Dec., declination.

Dec. Inc., declination increment.

Dep., departure.

Dev., deviation.

DG, degaussing.

diff., difference.
Dist., distance.
DLo, difference of longitude (arc units).
DMAHC, Defense Mapping Agency Hydrographic Center.
DR, dead reckoning, dead reckoning position.
DRE, dead reckoning equipment.
DRT, dead reckoning tracer.
D_s, dip short of horizon.
DSD, double second difference.
dur., duration.
dλ, difference of longitude (time units).
E, east.
e, base of Naperian logarithms.
e, eccentricity.
EDD, estimated date of departure.
EHF, extremely high frequency.
EM, electromagnetic (underwater log).
EP, estimated position.
Eq.T, equation of time.
ET, Ephemeris Time.
ETA, estimated time of arrival.
ETD, estimated time of departure.
F, Fahrenheit; fast; longitude factor; phase correction (altitude).
f, latitude factor.
f, flattening or ellipticity.
FM, frequency modulation.
ft., foot, feet.
G, Greenwich, Greenwich meridian (upper branch); grid (direction).
g, acceleration due to gravity; Greenwich meridian (lower branch).
GAT, Greenwich apparent time.
GB, grid bearing.
GC, grid course.
GE, gyro error.
GH, grid heading.
GHA, Greenwich hour angle.
GMT, Greenwich mean time.
GP, geographical position.
Gr., Greenwich.
GRI, group repetition interval.
GST, Greenwich sidereal time.
GV, grid variation.
GZn, grid azimuth.
h, altitude (astronomical); height above sea level.
ha, apparent altitude.
hav, haversine.
Hc, computed altitude.
Hdg., heading.
HE, heeling error; height of eye.
HF, high frequency.
h_f, height above sea level in feet.
HHW, higher high water.
HLW, higher low water.
hm, height above sea level in meters.
Ho, observed altitude.
HP, horizontal parallax.
Hp, precomputed altitude.
H_{pgc}, heading per gyrocompass.
H_{psc}, heading per standard compass.
$H_{p\ stg\ c}$, heading per steering compass.
hr, rectified (apparent) altitude.
hr., hour.
hrs., hours.
hs, sextant altitude.
ht, tabulated altitude.
HW, high water.
HWF & C, high water full and change.
I, instrument correction.
IALA, International Association of Lighthouse Authorities.
IAU, International Astronomical Union.
IC, index correction.
ICW, Intracoastal Waterway.
IHB, International Hydrographic Bureau.
IHO, International Hydrographic Organization.
IMCO, Inter-Governmental Maritime Consultative Organization.
in., inch, inches.
INM, International Nautical Mile.
INS, inertial navigation system.
int., interval.
ISLW, Indian spring low water.
ITU, International Telecommunications Union.
IUGG, International Union of Geodesy and Geophysics.
J, irradiation correction (altitude).
K, Kelvin (temperature).
kHz, kilohertz.
km, kilometer, kilometers.
kn, knot, knots.
L, latitude; lower limb correction for moon (from *Nautical Almanac*).
l, difference of latitude; logarithm, logarithmic.
LAN, local apparent noon.

LAT, local apparent time.
lat., latitude.
LF, low frequency.
LHA, local hour angle.
LHW, lower high water.
LL, lower limb.
LLW, lower low water.
Lm, middle latitude; mean latitude.
LMT, local mean time.
log, logarithm, logarithmic.
$\log_e$, natural logarithm (to the base e).
$\log_{10}$, common logarithm (to the base 10).
long., longitude.
LOP, line of position.
LST, local sidereal time.
LW, low water.
M, celestial body; meridian (upper branch); magnetic (direction); meridional parts; nautical mile, miles.
m, meridian (lower branch); meridional difference ($M_1 \sim M_2$); meter, meters; statute mile, miles.
mag., magnetic; magnitude.
MB, magnetic bearing.
mb, millibar, millibars.
MC, magnetic course.
mc, megacycle, megacycles; megacycles per second.
Mer. Pass., meridian passage.
MF, medium frequency.
MH, magnetic heading.
MHHW, mean higher high water.
MHW, mean high water.
MHWN, mean high water neaps.
MHWS, mean high water springs.
MHz, megahertz.
mi., mile, miles.
mid, middle.
min., minute, minutes.
MLLW, mean lower low water.
MLW, mean low water.
MLWN, mean low water neaps.
MLWS, mean low water springs.
mm, millimeter.
mo., month.
mos., months.
mph, miles (statute) per hour.
MPP, most probable position.
ms, millisecond, milliseconds.
MSL, mean sea level.
MZn, magnetic azimuth.
N, north.
***n*,** natural (trigonometric function).
Na, nadir.
NASA, National Aeronautics and Space Administration.
NAVSAT, Navy Navigation Satellite System.
NBS, National Bureau of Standards.
NLT, not less than (used with danger bearing).
NM, nautical mile, miles.
n. mi., nautical mile, miles.
NMT, not more than (used with danger bearing).
NNSS, Navy Navigation Satellite System.
NOAA, National Oceanic and Atmospheric Administration.
NOS, National Ocean Survey.
OTSR, Optimum Track Ship Routing.
P, atmospheric pressure; parallax; planet; pole.
p, departure, polar distance.
PC, personal correction.
PCA, polar cap absorption.
PCD, polar cap disturbance.
pgc, per gyrocompass.
P in A, parallax in altitude.
PM, pulse modulation.
PM, post meridian (after noon).
Pn, north pole; north celestial pole.
PPC, predicted propagation correction.
PPI, plan position indicator.
PRR, pulse repetition rate.
Ps, south pole; south celestial pole.
psc, per standard compass.
p stg c, per steering compass.
Pub., publication.
PV, prime vertical.
***Q*,** Polaris correction (*Air Almanac*).
QQ′, celestial equator.
R, Rankine (temperature); refraction.
RA, right ascension.
rad, radian, radians.
RB, relative bearing.
R Bn, radiobeacon.
RDF, radio direction finder.
rev., reversed.
RF, radio frequency.
R Fix, running fix.
RMS, root mean square.
RSS, root sum square.

RZn, relative azimuth.

S, sea-air temperature difference correction (altitude); slow; south; set; speed.

S_A, speed of apparent wind in units of ship's speed.

SAM, system area monitor.

SAR, Search and Rescue.

SD, semidiameter.

sec, secant.

sec., second, seconds.

semidur., semiduration.

SF, Secondary Phase Factor.

SH, ship's head (heading).

SHA, sidereal hour angle.

SHF, super high frequency.

SI, International System of Units.

SID, sudden ionospheric disturbance.

sin, sine.

SINS, Ships Inertial Navigation System.

SMG, speed made good.

SOA, speed of advance.

SOG, speed over ground.

SPA, sudden phase anomoly.

S_T, speed of true wind in units of ship's speed.

St M, statute mile, miles.

T, air temperature correction (altitude); table; temperature; time; toward (altitude intercept); true (direction).

t, dry-bulb temperature; elapsed time; meridian angle.

t′, wet-bulb temperature.

tab., table.

TAI, International Atomic Time scale.

tan, tangent.

TB, true bearing; turning bearing; air temperature-atmos pheric pressure correction (altitude).

TC, true course.

TcHHW, tropic higher high water.

TcHLW, tropic higher low water.

TcLHW, tropic lower high water.

TcLLW, tropic lower low water.

TD, time difference (Loran-C).

T_G, time difference of groundwaves from master and secondary (slave) stations (Loran).

T_{GS}, time difference of groundwave from master and skywave from secondary (slave) station (Loran).

TH, true heading.

TMG, track made good.

TOD, time of day (clock).

TR, track.

Tr., transit.

T_S, time difference of skywaves from master and secondary (slave) stations (Loran).

T_{SG}, time difference of skywave from master and groundwave from secondary (slave) station (Loran).

TZn, true azimuth.

U, upper limb correction for moon (from *Nautical Almanac*).

UHF, ultra high frequency.

UL, upper limb.

UPS, Universal Polar Stereographic.

USWMS, Uniform State Waterway Marking System.

UT, Universal Time.

UTC, Coordinated Universal Time.

UT0, Universal Time 0.

UT1, Universal Time 1.

UT2, Universal Time 2.

UTM, Universal Transverse Mercator.

V, variation; vertex.

***v*,** excess of GHA change from adopted value for 1 hour.

Var., variation.

ver, versine.

VHF, very high frequency.

VLF, very low frequency.

W, west.

WARC, World Administrative Radio Council.

WE, watch error.

WGS, World Geodetic System.

WMO, World Meteorological Organization.

WT, watch time.

X, parallactic angle.

yd., yard.

yds., yards.

yr., year.

yrs., years.

Z, azimuth angle; zenith.

z, zenith distance.

ZD, zone description.

Z Diff., azimuth angle difference.

Zn, azimuth (as distinguished fom azimuth angle).

Zn_{pgc}, azimuth per gyrocompass.

ZT, zone time.

Δ, a small increment, or the change in one quantity corresponding to unit change in another.

λ, longitude; wavelength (radiant energy).

σ, standard deviation.

μ, index of refraction.

μS, microsecond.

π, ratio of circumference of circle to diameter=3.14159+.

APPENDIX B

EXTRACTS FROM TIDE TABLES

NEW YORK (THE BATTERY), N.Y., 1975

TIMES AND HEIGHTS OF HIGH AND LOW WATERS

JANUARY

DAY	TIME H.M.	HT. FT.	DAY	TIME H.M.	HT. FT.
1	0422	-0.8	16	0431	0.0
W	1043	5.1	TH	1045	4.1
	1659	-1.1		1656	-0.2
	2321	4.6		2319	3.8
2	0516	-0.6	17	0501	0.2
TH	1138	4.9	F	1120	3.9
	1749	-0.9		1722	0.0
				2357	3.7
3	0017	4.6	18	0533	0.4
F	0615	-0.4	SA	1154	3.7
	1234	4.6		1746	0.2
	1847	-0.6			
4	0111	4.6	19	0029	3.7
SA	0724	-0.1	SU	0613	0.6
	1329	4.3		1228	3.5
	1951	-0.4		1818	0.3
5	0207	4.6	20	0108	3.8
SU	0835	0.0	M	0727	0.7
	1428	4.0		1311	3.4
	2053	-0.3		1917	0.4
6	0307	4.5	21	0156	3.9
M	0939	-0.1	TU	0856	0.7
	1530	3.7		1404	3.3
	2153	-0.3		2050	0.4
7	0407	4.5	22	0255	4.0
TU	1038	-0.2	W	1001	0.4
	1635	3.6		1515	3.2
	2247	-0.3		2157	0.2
8	0508	4.6	23	0404	4.2
W	1131	-0.3	TH	1057	0.1
	1735	3.7		1637	3.4
	2339	-0.3		2256	0.0
9	0603	4.7	24	0510	4.5
TH	1222	-0.4	F	1150	-0.2
	1828	3.8		1742	3.7
				2352	-0.3
10	0028	-0.4	25	0609	4.9
F	0649	4.8	SA	1242	-0.6
	1310	-0.5		1838	4.0
	1915	3.9			
11	0117	-0.4	26	0048	-0.6
SA	0733	4.8	SU	0701	5.2
	1354	-0.6		1330	-1.0
	1959	3.9		1929	4.4
12	0202	-0.4	27	0140	-0.9
SU	0814	4.8	M	0749	5.4
	1436	-0.6		1419	-1.3
	2040	3.9		2019	4.7
13	0242	-0.4	28	0231	-1.1
M	0854	4.7	TU	0840	5.5
	1516	-0.6		1505	-1.4
	2122	3.9		2110	4.9
14	0321	-0.3	29	0321	-1.2
TU	0931	4.5	W	0931	5.4
	1552	-0.5		1550	-1.5
	2202	3.9		2203	5.0
15	0358	-0.1	30	0410	-1.2
W	1011	4.3	TH	1024	5.2
	1625	-0.4		1635	-1.3
	2242	3.8		2258	5.0
			31	0459	-0.9
			F	1120	4.9
				1725	-1.0
				2354	4.9

FEBRUARY

DAY	TIME H.M.	HT. FT.	DAY	TIME H.M.	HT. FT.
1	0554	-0.6	16	0503	0.2
SA	1213	4.5	SU	1111	3.8
	1818	-0.7		1704	0.1
				2338	4.0
2	0047	4.8	17	0535	0.3
SU	0659	-0.2	M	1149	3.6
	1309	4.1		1733	0.2
	1919	-0.3			
3	0142	4.6	18	0020	4.0
M	0808	0.0	TU	0621	0.5
	1405	3.8		1231	3.5
	2024	-0.1		1818	0.4
4	0240	4.4	19	0108	4.1
TU	0915	0.1	W	0759	0.6
	1508	3.6		1329	3.4
	2129	0.0		1932	0.5
5	0341	4.3	20	0211	4.1
W	1015	0.0	TH	0926	0.5
	1612	3.5		1439	3.3
	2225	0.0		2125	0.4
6	0444	4.3	21	0327	4.2
TH	1110	-0.1	F	1026	0.2
	1715	3.5		1607	3.5
	2320	0.0		2233	0.1
7	0542	4.4	22	0444	4.5
F	1200	-0.2	SA	1123	-0.2
	1811	3.7		1718	3.9
				2334	-0.3
8	0009	-0.1	23	0545	4.8
SA	0629	4.5	SU	1214	-0.6
	1246	-0.3		1816	4.4
	1856	3.9			
9	0057	-0.2	24	0030	-0.7
SU	0713	4.6	M	0640	5.2
	1329	-0.5		1306	-1.0
	1937	4.0		1909	4.8
10	0141	-0.3	25	0123	-1.0
M	0752	4.6	TU	0731	5.4
	1410	-0.5		1354	-1.2
	2015	4.1		1959	5.2
11	0222	-0.4	26	0215	-1.3
TU	0829	4.6	W	0820	5.4
	1449	-0.6		1441	-1.4
	2053	4.2		2048	5.4
12	0300	-0.4	27	0305	-1.4
W	0906	4.5	TH	0912	5.3
	1523	-0.5		1526	-1.4
	2129	4.2		2139	5.4
13	0335	-0.3	28	0352	-1.3
TH	0941	4.3	F	1003	5.1
	1555	-0.4		1612	-1.2
	2203	4.1		2232	5.3
14	0407	-0.2			
F	1011	4.1			
	1622	-0.2			
	2235	4.1			
15	0435	0.0			
SA	1043	3.9			
	1643	-0.1			
	2307	4.0			

MARCH

DAY	TIME H.M.	HT. FT.	DAY	TIME H.M.	HT. FT.
1	0442	-1.0	16	0416	-0.1
SA	1058	4.8	SU	1013	4.0
	1658	-0.9		1613	0.0
	2325	5.1		2223	4.4
2	0533	-0.6	17	0443	0.0
SU	1152	4.4	M	1043	3.8
	1749	-0.5		1637	0.2
				2259	4.4
3	0021	4.9	18	0517	0.2
M	0631	-0.2	TU	1124	3.7
	1247	4.1		1708	0.3
	1847	0.0		2346	4.3
4	0115	4.6	19	0602	0.4
TU	0739	0.1	W	1218	3.6
	1344	3.8		1752	0.5
	1956	0.3			
5	0212	4.3	20	0042	4.3
W	0848	0.3	TH	0724	0.5
	1443	3.6		1318	3.6
	2103	0.4		1906	0.6
6	0312	4.1	21	0146	4.3
TH	0949	0.3	F	0853	0.4
	1545	3.5		1429	3.6
	2204	0.4		2106	0.5
7	0415	4.1	22	0300	4.3
F	1041	0.2	SA	0959	0.2
	1649	3.6		1548	3.9
	2258	0.3		2217	0.2
8	0513	4.2	23	0417	4.5
SA	1131	0.0	SU	1056	-0.2
	1744	3.8		1658	4.3
	2347	0.1		2315	-0.2
9	0603	4.3	24	0524	4.8
SU	1216	-0.1	M	1147	-0.5
	1830	4.1		1755	4.8
10	0033	0.0	25	0011	-0.6
M	0645	4.4	TU	0620	5.0
	1259	-0.3		1238	-0.8
	1909	4.3		1848	5.2
11	0117	-0.2	26	0107	-1.0
TU	0726	4.5	W	0712	5.2
	1341	-0.4		1328	-1.1
	1946	4.4		1938	5.6
12	0158	-0.3	27	0157	-1.2
W	0803	4.5	TH	0802	5.3
	1418	-0.4		1416	-1.2
	2022	4.5		2025	5.7
13	0237	-0.4	28	0247	-1.3
TH	0837	4.5	F	0852	5.2
	1453	-0.4		1502	-1.1
	2054	4.5		2114	5.7
14	0313	-0.4	29	0334	-1.2
F	0912	4.3	SA	0942	4.9
	1525	-0.3		1547	-0.9
	2126	4.5		2206	5.5
15	0346	-0.3	30	0422	-0.9
SA	0941	4.2	SU	1037	4.7
	1551	-0.1		1632	-0.6
	2152	4.5		2259	5.3
			31	0512	-0.6
			M	1132	4.3
				1721	-0.2
				2352	4.9

TIME MERIDIAN 75° W. 0000 IS MIDNIGHT. 1200 IS NOON.
HEIGHTS ARE RECKONED FROM THE DATUM OF SOUNDINGS ON CHARTS OF THE LOCALITY WHICH IS MEAN LOW WATER.

TABLE 2.—TIDAL DIFFERENCES AND OTHER CONSTANTS

No.	PLACE	POSITION		DIFFERENCES				RANGES		Mean Tide Level
		Lat.	Long.	Time		Height		Mean	Spring	
				High water	Low water	High water	Low water			
		° ′	° ′	*h. m.*	*h. m.*	*feet*	*feet*	*feet*	*feet*	*feet*
	NEW YORK and NEW JERSEY — Continued									
	Hudson River‡	N.	W.	**on NEW YORK, p.56**						
	Time meridian, 75°W.									
1513	Jersey City, Pa. RR. Ferry, N. J----	40 43	74 02	+0 07	+0 07	−0.1	0.0	4.4	5.3	2.2
1515	New York, Desbrosses Street---------	40 43	74 01	+0 10	+0 10	−0.1	0.0	4.4	5.3	2.2
1517	New York, Chelsea Docks------------	40 45	74 01	+0 17	+0 16	−0.2	0.0	4.3	5.2	2.1
1519	Hoboken, Castle Point, N. J---------	40 45	74 01	+0 17	+0 16	−0.2	0.0	4.3	5.2	2.1
1521	Weehawken, Days Point, N. J---------	40 46	74 01	+0 24	+0 23	−0.3	0.0	4.2	5.0	2.1
1523	New York, Union Stock Yards---------	40 47	74 00	+0 27	+0 26	−0.3	0.0	4.2	5.0	2.1
1525	New York, 130th Street-------------	40 49	73 58	+0 37	+0 35	−0.5	0.0	4.0	4.8	2.0
1527	George Washington Bridge------------	40 51	73 57	+0 46	+0 43	−0.6	0.0	3.9	4.6	1.9
1529	Spuyten Duyvil, West of RR. bridge--	40 53	73 56	+0 58	+0 53	−0.7	0.0	3.8	4.5	1.9
1531	Yonkers----------------------------	40 56	73 54	+1 09	+1 10	−0.8	0.0	3.7	4.4	1.8
1533	Dobbs Ferry------------------------	41 01	73 53	+1 29	+1 40	−1.1	0.0	3.4	4.0	1.7
1535	Tarrytown--------------------------	41 05	73 52	+1 45	+1 54	−1.3	0.0	3.2	3.7	1.6
1537	Ossining---------------------------	41 10	73 52	+1 53	+2 14	−1.4	0.0	3.1	3.6	1.5
1539	Haverstraw-------------------------	41 12	73 58	+1 59	+2 25	−1.6	0.0	2.9	3.4	1.4
1541	Peekskill--------------------------	41 17	73 56	+2 24	+3 00	−1.3	+0.3	2.9	3.4	1.7
1543	West Point-------------------------	41 24	73 57	+3 16	+3 37	−1.5	+0.3	2.7	3.1	1.6
1545	Newburgh---------------------------	41 30	74 00	+3 42	+4 00	−1.5	+0.2	2.8	3.2	1.6
1547	New Hamburg------------------------	41 35	73 57	+4 00	+4 25	−1.5	+0.1	2.9	3.3	1.5
1549	Poughkeepsie-----------------------	41 42	73 57	+4 30	+4 43	−1.3	+0.1	3.1	3.5	1.6
1551	Hyde Park--------------------------	41 47	73 57	+4 56	+5 09	−1.3	0.0	3.2	3.6	1.6
1553	Kingston Point---------------------	41 56	73 58	+5 16	+5 31	−0.9	−0.1	3.7	4.2	1.7
1555	Tivoli-----------------------------	42 04	73 56	+5 46	+6 01	−0.8	−0.2	3.9	4.4	1.7
1557	Catskill---------------------------	42 13	73 51	+6 37	+6 55	−0.7	−0.3	4.1	4.6	1.7
1559	Hudson-----------------------------	42 15	73 48	+6 54	+7 09	−0.9	−0.4	4.0	4.4	1.6
				on ALBANY, p.60						
1561	Coxsackie--------------------------	42 21	73 48	−1 01	−1 38	−0.5	+0.2	3.9	4.3	2.1
1563	New Baltimore----------------------	42 27	73 47	−0 34	−0 56	−0.1	+0.4	4.1	4.5	2.4
1565	Castleton-on-Hudson----------------	42 32	73 46	−0 17	−0 29	−0.2	+0.1	4.3	4.7	2.2
1567	ALBANY-----------------------------	42 39	73 45	Daily predictions				4.6	5.0	2.5
1569	Troy-------------------------------	42 44	73 42	+0 08	+0 10	+0.1	0.0	4.7	5.1	2.3
	The Kills and Newark Bay			**on NEW YORK, p.56**						
	Kill Van Kull									
1571	Constable Hook---------------------	40 39	74 05	−0 34	−0 21	0.0	0.0	4.5	5.4	2.2
1573	New Brighton-----------------------	40 39	74 05	−0 12	−0 18	0.0	0.0	4.5	5.4	2.2
1575	Port Richmond----------------------	40 38	74 08	−0 03	+0 05	0.0	0.0	4.5	5.4	2.2
1577	Bergen Point-----------------------	40 39	74 08	+0 03	+0 03	+0.1	0.0	4.6	5.5	2.3
1579	Shooters Island--------------------	40 39	74 10	+0 06	+0 18	+0.1	0.0	4.6	5.5	2.3
1581	Port Newark Terminal---------------	40 41	74 08	−0 01	+0 18	+0.6	0.0	5.1	6.1	2.5
1583	Newark, Passaic River--------------	40 44	74 10	+0 22	+0 52	+0.6	0.0	5.1	6.1	2.5
1585	Passaic, Gregory Ave. bridge-------	40 51	74 07	+0 49	+1 57	+0.6	0.0	5.1	6.1	2.5
	Hackensack River									
1586	Kearny Point-----------------------	40 44	74 06	+0 09	+0 33	+0.5	0.0	5.0	6.0	2.5
1587	Secaucus---------------------------	40 48	74 04	+1 13	+1 09	+0.6	0.0	5.1	6.1	2.6
1588	Little Ferry-----------------------	40 51	74 02	+1 22	+1 14	+0.8	0.0	5.3	6.4	2.7
1589	Hackensack-------------------------	40 53	74 02	+1 33	+1 58	+0.8	0.0	5.3	6.4	2.6
				on SANDY HOOK, p.64						
	Arthur Kill									
1591	Elizabethport----------------------	40 39	74 11	+0 25	+0 39	+0.3	0.0	4.9	5.9	2.4
1593	Chelsea----------------------------	40 36	74 12	+0 24	+0 35	+0.4	0.0	5.0	6.0	2.5
1595	Carteret---------------------------	40 35	74 13	+0 23	+0 31	+0.5	0.0	5.1	6.2	2.6
1597	Rossville--------------------------	40 33	74 13	+0 17	+0 25	+0.7	0.0	5.3	6.4	2.6
1599	Tottenville------------------------	40 31	74 15	+0 03	+0 13	+0.7	0.0	5.3	6.4	2.6
1601	Perth Amboy------------------------	40 30	74 16	+0 13	+0 19	+0.6	0.0	5.2	6.3	2.6

‡Values for the Hudson River above the George Washington Bridge are based upon averages for the six months May to October, when the fresh-water discharge is a minimum.

TABLE 3.—HEIGHT OF TIDE AT ANY TIME

Duration of rise or fall, see footnote	Time from the nearest high water or low water														
h. m.	*h. m.*	*h. m.*	*h. m.*	*h. m.*	*h. m.*	*h. m.*	*h. m.*	*h. m.*	*h. m.*	*h. m.*	*h. m.*	*h. m.*	*h. m.*	*h. m.*	*h. m.*
4 00	0 08	0 16	0 24	0 32	0 40	0 48	0 56	1 04	1 12	1 20	1 28	1 36	1 44	1 52	2 00
4 20	0 09	0 17	0 26	0 35	0 43	0 52	1 01	1 09	1 18	1 27	1 35	1 44	1 53	2 01	2 10
4 40	0 09	0 19	0 28	0 37	0 47	0 56	1 05	1 15	1 24	1 33	1 43	1 52	2 01	2 11	2 20
5 00	0 10	0 20	0 30	0 40	0 50	1 00	1 10	1 20	1 30	1 40	1 50	2 00	2 10	2 20	2 30
5 20	0 11	0 21	0 32	0 43	0 53	1 04	1 15	1 25	1 36	1 47	1 57	2 08	2 19	2 29	2 40
5 40	0 11	0 23	0 34	0 45	0 57	1 08	1 19	1 31	1 42	1 53	2 05	2 16	2 27	2 39	2 50
6 00	0 12	0 24	0 36	0 48	1 00	1 12	1 24	1 36	1 48	2 00	2 12	2 24	2 36	2.48	3 00
6 20	0 13	0 25	0 38	0 51	1 03	1 16	1 29	1 41	1 54	2 07	2 19	2 32	2 45	2 57	3 10
6 40	0 13	0 27	0 40	0 53	1 07	1 20	1 33	1 47	2 00	2 13	2 27	2 40	2 53	3 07	3 20
7 00	0 14	0 28	0 42	0 56	1 10	1 24	1 38	1 52	2 06	2 20	2 34	2 48	3 02	3 16	3 30
7 20	0 15	0 29	0 44	0 59	1 13	1 28	1 43	1 57	2 12	2 27	2 41	2 56	3 11	3 25	3 40
7 40	0 15	0 31	0 46	1 01	1 17	1 32	1 47	2 03	2 18	2 33	2 49	3 04	3 19	3 35	3 50
8 00	0 16	0 32	0 48	1 04	1 20	1 36	1 52	2 08	2 24	2 40	2 56	3 12	3 28	3 44	4 00
8 20	0 17	0 33	0 50	1 07	1 23	1 40	1 57	2 13	2 30	2 47	3 03	3 20	3 37	3 53	4 10
8 40	0 17	0 35	0 52	1 09	1 27	1 44	2 01	2 19	2 36	2 53	3 11	3 28	3 45	4 03	4 20
9 00	0 18	0 36	0 54	1 12	1 30	1 48	2 06	2 24	2 42	3 00	3 18	3 36	3 54	4 12	4 30
9 20	0 19	0 37	0 56	1 15	1 33	1 52	2 11	2 29	2 48	3 07	3 25	3 44	4 03	4 21	4 40
9 40	0 19	0 39	0 58	1 17	1 37	1 56	2 15	2 35	2 54	3 13	3 33	3 52	4 11	4 31	4 50
10 00	0 20	0 40	1 00	1 20	1 40	2 00	2 20	2 40	3 00	3 20	3 40	4 00	4 20	4 40	5 00
10 20	0 21	0 41	1 02	1 23	1 43	2 04	2 25	2 45	3 00	3 27	3 47	4 08	4 29	4 49	5 10
10 40	0 21	0 43	1 04	1 25	1 47	2 08	2 29	2 51	3 12	3 33	3 55	4 16	4 37	4 59	5 20

Range of tide, see footnote	Correction to height														
Ft.	*Ft.*	*Ft.*	*Ft.*	*Ft.*	*Ft.*	*Ft.*	*Ft.*	*Ft.*	*Ft.*	*Ft.*	*Ft.*	*Ft.*	*Ft.*	*Ft.*	*Ft.*
0.5	0.0	0.0	0.0	0.0	0.0	0.0	0.1	0.1	0.1	0.1	0.1	0.2	0.2	0.2	0.2
1.0	0.0	0.0	0.0	0.0	0.1	0.1	0.1	0.2	0.2	0.2	0.3	0.3	0.4	0.4	0.5
1.5	0.0	0.0	0.0	0.1	0.1	0.1	0.2	0.2	0.3	0.4	0.4	0.5	0.0	0.7	0.8
2.0	0.0	0.0	0.0	0.1	0.1	0.2	0.3	0.3	0.4	0.5	0.6	0.7	0.8	0.9	1.0
2.5	0.0	0.0	0.1	0.1	0.2	0.2	0.3	0.4	0.5	0.6	0.7	0.9	1.0	1.1	1.2
3.0	0.0	0.0	0.1	0.1	0.2	0.3	0.4	0.5	0.6	0.8	0.9	1.0	1.2	1.3	1.5
3.5	0.0	0.0	0.1	0.2	0.2	0.3	0.4	0.6	0.7	0.9	1.0	1.2	1.4	1.6	1.8
4.0	0.0	0.0	0.1	0.2	0.3	0.4	0.5	0.7	0.8	1.0	1.2	1.4	1.6	1.8	2.0
4.5	0.0	0.0	0.1	0.2	0.3	0.4	0.6	0.7	0.9	1.1	1.3	1.6	1.8	2.0	2.2
5.0	0.0	0.1	0.1	0.2	0.3	0.5	0.6	0.8	1.0	1.2	1.5	1.7	2.0	2.2	2.5
5.5	0.0	0.1	0.1	0.2	0.4	0.5	0.7	0.9	1.1	1.4	1.6	1.9	2.2	2.5	2.8
6.0	0.0	0.1	0.1	0.3	0.4	0.6	0.8	1.0	1.2	1.5	1.8	2.1	2.4	2.7	3.0
6.5	0.0	0.1	0.2	0.3	0.4	0.6	0.8	1.1	1.3	1.6	1.9	2.2	2.6	2.9	3.2
7.0	0.0	0.1	0.2	0.3	0.5	0.7	0.9	1.2	1.4	1.8	2.1	2.4	2.8	3.1	3.5
7.5	0.0	0.1	0.2	0.3	0.5	0.7	1.0	1.2	1.5	1.9	2.2	2.6	3.0	3.4	3.8
8.0	0.0	0.1	0.2	0.3	0.5	0.8	1.0	1.3	1.6	2.0	2.4	2.8	3.2	3.6	4.0
8.5	0.0	0.1	0.2	0.4	0.6	0.8	1.1	1.4	1.8	2.1	2.5	2.9	3.4	3.8	4.2
9.0	0.0	0.1	0.2	0.4	0.6	0.9	1.2	1.5	1.9	2.2	2.7	3.1	6.6	4.0	4.5
9.5	0.0	0.1	0.2	0.4	0.6	0.9	1.2	1.6	2.0	2.4	2.8	3.3	3.8	4.3	4.8
10.0	0.0	0.1	0.2	0.4	0.7	1.0	1.3	1.7	2.1	2.5	3.0	3.5	4.0	4.5	5.0
10.5	0.0	0.1	0.3	0.5	0.7	1.0	1.3	1.7	2.2	2.6	3.1	3.6	4.2	4.7	5.2
11.0	0.0	0.1	0.3	0.5	0.7	1.1	1.4	1.8	2.3	2.8	3.3	3.8	4.4	4.9	5.5
11.5	0.0	0.1	0.3	0.5	0.8	1.1	1.5	1.9	2.4	2.9	3.4	4.0	4.6	5.1	5.8
12.0	0.0	0.1	0.3	0.5	0.8	1.1	1.5	2.0	2.5	3.0	3.6	4.1	4.8	5.4	6.0
12.5	0.0	0.1	0.3	0.5	0.8	1.2	1.6	2.1	2.6	3.1	3.7	4.3	5.0	5.6	6.2
13.0	0.0	0.1	0.3	0.6	0.9	1.2	1.7	2.2	2.7	3.2	3.9	4.5	5.1	5.8	6.5
13.5	0.0	0.1	0.3	0.6	0.9	1.3	1.7	2.2	2.8	3.4	4.0	4.7	5.3	6.0	6.8
14.0	0.0	0.2	0.3	0.6	0.9	1.3	1.8	2.3	2.9	3.5	4.2	4.8	5.5	6.3	7.0
14.5	0.0	0.2	0.4	0.6	1.0	1.4	1.9	2.4	3.0	3.6	4.3	5.0	5.7	6.5	7.2
15.0	0.0	0.2	0.4	0.6	1.0	1.4	1.9	2.5	3.1	3.8	4.4	5.2	5.9	6.7	7.5
15.5	0.0	0.2	0.4	0.7	1.0	1.5	2.0	2.6	3.2	3.9	4.6	5.4	6.1	6.9	7.8
16.0	0.0	0.2	0.4	0.7	1.1	1.5	2.1	2.6	3.3	4.0	4.7	5.5	6.3	7.2	8.0
16.5	0.0	0.2	0.4	0.7	1.1	1.6	2.1	2.7	3.4	4.1	4.9	5.7	6.5	7.4	8.2
17.0	0.0	0.2	0.4	0.7	1.1	1.6	2.2	2.8	3.5	4.2	5.0	5.9	6.7	7.6	8.5
17.5	0.0	0.2	0.4	0.8	1.2	1.7	2.2	2.9	3.6	4.4	5.2	6.0	6.9	7.8	8.8
18.0	0.0	0.2	0.4	0.8	1.2	1.7	2.3	3.0	3.7	4.5	5.3	6.2	7.1	8.1	9.0
18.5	0.1	0.2	0.5	0.8	1.2	1.8	2.4	3.1	3.8	4.6	5.5	6.4	7.3	8.3	9.2
19.0	0.1	0.2	0.5	0.8	1.3	1.8	2.4	3.1	3.9	4.8	5.6	6.6	7.5	8.5	9.5
19.5	0.1	0.2	0.5	0.8	1.3	1.9	2.5	3.2	4.0	4.9	5.8	6.7	7.7	8.7	9.8
20.0	0.1	0.2	0.5	0.9	1.3	1.9	2.6	3.3	4.1	5.0	5.9	6.9	7.9	9.0	10.0

Obtain from the predictions the high water and low water, one of which is before and the other after the time for which the height is required. The difference between the times of occurrence of these tides is the duration of rise or fall, and the difference between their heights is the range of tide for the above table. Find the difference between the nearest high or low water and the time for which the height is required.

Enter the table with the duration of rise or fall, printed in heavy-faced type, which most nearly agrees with the actual value, and on that horizontal line find the time from the nearest high or low water which agrees most nearly with the corresponding actual difference. The correction sought is in the column directly below, on the line with the range of tide.

When the nearest tide is high water, subtract the correction.

When the nearest tide is low water, add the correction.

APPENDIX C

EXTRACTS FROM TIDAL CURRENT TABLES

THE NARROWS, NEW YORK HARBOR, N.Y., 1975

F-FLOOD, DIR. 340° TRUE E-EBB, DIR. 160° TRUE

JANUARY

DAY	SLACK WATER TIME H.M.	MAXIMUM CURRENT TIME H.M.	VEL. KNOTS
1		0254	2.4E
W	0617	0857	2.2F
	1211	1526	2.5E
	1901	2132	2.0F
2	0037	0345	2.3E
TH	0716	0952	2.1F
	1301	1614	2.4E
	1954	2227	2.0F
3	0132	0440	2.2E
F	0819	1049	1.9F
	1352	1708	2.3E
	2050	2321	2.0F
4	0230	0542	2.1E
SA	0924	1147	1.7F
	1445	1807	2.1E
	2146		
5		0018	1.9F
SU	0331	0648	2.0E
	1027	1244	1.5F
	1543	1909	2.0E
	2242		
6		0119	1.9F
M	0434	0751	2.0E
	1129	1352	1.4F
	1643	2007	2.0E
	2337		
7		0232	1.9F
TU	0537	0850	2.0E
	1230	1515	1.3F
	1744	2102	2.0E
8	0033	0343	1.9F
W	0635	0946	2.0E
	1328	1623	1.4F
	1841	2154	1.9E
9	0127	0442	2.0F
TH	0727	1037	2.1E
	1423	1714	1.4F
	1932	2242	1.9E
10	0219	0527	2.0F
F	0814	1126	2.1E
	1511	1757	1.5F
	2020	2336	1.9E
11	0307	0609	2.0F
SA	0857	1215	2.1E
	1556	1836	1.5F
	2106		
12		0023	1.9E
SU	0351	0638	2.0F
	0938	1300	2.1E
	1637	1906	1.5F
	2150		
13		0108	1.9E
M	0434	0709	1.9F
	1018	1340	2.2E
	1717	1937	1.5F
	2235		
14		0151	1.9E
TU	0515	0743	1.8F
	1058	1418	2.1E
	1756	2010	1.5F
	2318		
15		0231	1.9E
W	0557	0822	1.7F
	1137	1455	2.1E
	1836	2051	1.5F

DAY	SLACK WATER TIME H.M.	MAXIMUM CURRENT TIME H.M.	VEL. KNOTS
16	0002	0310	1.8E
TH	0641	0907	1.6F
	1217	1532	2.0E
	1917	2139	1.5F
17	0046	0351	1.7E
F	0730	0954	1.5F
	1257	1611	1.9E
	2000	2224	1.5F
18	0131	0437	1.6E
SA	0823	1043	1.4F
	1339	1654	1.8E
	2045	2309	1.5F
19	0218	0530	1.6E
SU	0920	1130	1.3F
	1424	1745	1.7E
	2132	2358	1.5F
20	0310	0631	1.5E
M	1017	1220	1.2F
	1514	1842	1.6E
	2220		
21		0047	1.6F
TU	0407	0728	1.6E
	1114	1313	1.1F
	1610	1940	1.6E
	2310		
22		0140	1.6F
W	0505	0823	1.7E
	1211	1410	1.1F
	1710	2033	1.7E
23	0001	0237	1.7F
TH	0602	0917	1.9E
	1305	1509	1.2F
	1808	2124	1.8E
24	0055	0337	1.9F
F	0655	1007	2.0E
	1357	1612	1.4F
	1903	2215	2.0E
25	0148	0434	2.1F
SA	0745	1059	2.2E
	1445	1703	1.6F
	1955	2309	2.1E
26	0240	0523	2.3F
SU	0834	1150	2.4E
	1531	1751	1.8F
	2046		
27		0003	2.3E
M	0330	0611	2.4F
	0922	1241	2.5E
	1615	1838	2.0F
	2138		
28		0057	2.4E
TU	0420	0658	2.5F
	1011	1329	2.6E
	1659	1925	2.2F
	2231		
29		0148	2.5E
W	0510	0745	2.4F
	1100	1416	2.7E
	1745	2015	2.2F
	2324		
30		0237	2.6E
TH	0602	0838	2.3F
	1149	1503	2.6E
	1833	2106	2.2F
31	0017	0327	2.5E
F	0659	0932	2.1F
	1238	1551	2.5E
	1925	2201	2.1F

FEBRUARY

DAY	SLACK WATER TIME H.M.	MAXIMUM CURRENT TIME H.M.	VEL. KNOTS
1	0111	0420	2.3E
SA	0759	1027	1.9F
	1328	1643	2.3E
	2021	2258	2.1F
2	0207	0517	2.1E
SU	0902	1124	1.7F
	1420	1738	2.1E
	2118	2355	2.0F
3	0305	0621	2.0E
M	1005	1222	1.5F
	1516	1839	1.9E
	2216		
4		0056	1.8F
TU	0408	0727	1.9E
	1107	1331	1.3F
	1617	1943	1.8E
	2314		
5		0207	1.7F
W	0511	0830	1.9E
	1208	1455	1.2F
	1720	2039	1.8E
6	0011	0322	1.7F
TH	0611	0925	1.9E
	1306	1602	1.3F
	1820	2133	1.8E
7	0107	0422	1.8F
F	0704	1016	1.9E
	1359	1655	1.4F
	1913	2226	1.8E
8	0200	0511	1.8F
SA	0751	1104	2.0E
	1447	1741	1.5F
	2001	2313	1.8E
9	0248	0552	1.9F
SU	0833	1149	2.0E
	1530	1818	1.5F
	2045		
10		0000	1.9E
M	0333	0625	1.9F
	0912	1232	2.1E
	1609	1845	1.6F
	2128		
11		0044	1.9E
TU	0414	0650	1.8F
	0951	1312	2.1E
	1647	1911	1.6F
	2209		
12		0127	2.0E
W	0455	0718	1.8F
	1029	1350	2.1E
	1723	1942	1.7F
	2251		
13		0207	2.0E
TH	0534	0757	1.7F
	1108	1426	2.1E
	1800	2019	1.7F
	2332		
14		0245	1.9E
F	0616	0838	1.6F
	1147	1501	2.0E
	1836	2102	1.7F
15	0015	0323	1.9E
SA	0700	0923	1.5F
	1226	1536	1.9E
	1915	2149	1.6F

DAY	SLACK WATER TIME H.M.	MAXIMUM CURRENT TIME H.M.	VEL. KNOTS
16	0058	0404	1.8E
SU	0751	1011	1.4F
	1307	1615	1.8E
	1958	2236	1.6F
17	0144	0451	1.7E
M	0846	1100	1.3F
	1350	1656	1.7E
	2046	2325	1.6F
18	0233	0547	1.6E
TU	0944	1151	1.2F
	1439	1800	1.6E
	2138		
19		0015	1.6F
W	0329	0650	1.6E
	1041	1242	1.1F
	1535	1903	1.6E
	2234		
20		0108	1.6F
TH	0429	0752	1.7E
	1138	1337	1.1F
	1638	2004	1.7E
	2331		
21		0205	1.7F
F	0529	0848	1.9E
	1233	1439	1.2F
	1741	2100	1.9E
22	0030	0308	1.8F
SA	0627	0941	2.1E
	1325	1544	1.5F
	1840	2154	2.1E
23	0127	0408	2.0F
SU	0720	1032	2.2E
	1415	1639	1.7F
	1935	2248	2.2E
24	0222	0504	2.2F
M	0810	1123	2.4E
	1502	1730	2.0F
	2027	2343	2.4E
25	0315	0552	2.4F
TU	0859	1214	2.5E
	1547	1818	2.2F
	2119		
26		0037	2.6E
W	0405	0641	2.4F
	0947	1304	2.6E
	1632	1903	2.4F
	2211		
27		0129	2.7E
TH	0455	0726	2.4F
	1036	1353	2.7E
	1718	1952	2.4F
	2303		
28		0218	2.7E
F	0547	0816	2.2F
	1125	1439	2.6E
	1805	2041	2.3F
	2356		

TIME MERIDIAN 75° W. 0000 IS MIDNIGHT. 1200 IS NOON.

TABLE 2.—CURRENT DIFFERENCES AND OTHER CONSTANTS

No.	PLACE	POSITION		TIME DIFFERENCES		VELOCITY RATIOS		MAXIMUM CURRENTS			
								Flood		Ebb	
		Lat.	Long.	Slack water	Maximum current	Maximum flood	Maximum ebb	Direction (true)	Average velocity	Direction (true)	Average velocity
		° ′	° ′	h. m.	h. m.			deg.	knots	deg.	knots
	LONG ISLAND, South Coast—Continued	**N.**	**W.**	**on THE NARROWS, p.52** *Time meridian, 75°W.*							
2250	Shinnecock Inlet	40 51	72 29	-0 20	-0 40	1.5	1.2	350	2.5	170	2.3
2255	Fire I. Inlet, 0.5 mi. S. of Oak Beach	40 38	73 18	+0 15	0 00	1.4	1.2	80	2.4	245	2.4
2260	Jones Inlet	40 35	73 34	-1 00	-0 55	1.8	1.3	35	3.1	215	2.6
2265	Long Beach, inside, between bridges	40 36	73 40	-0 10	+0 10	0.3	0.3	75	0.5	275	0.6
2270	East Rockaway Inlet	40 35	73 45	-1 25	-1 35	1.3	1.2	40	2.2	225	2.3
2275	Ambrose Light	40 27	73 49	See table 5.							
2280	Sandy Hook App. Lighted Horn Buoy 2A	40 27	73 55	See table 5.							
	JAMAICA BAY										
2285	Rockaway Inlet	40 34	73 56	-1 45	-2 15	1.1	1.3	85	1.8	245	2.7
2290	Barren Island, east of	40 35	73 53	-2 00	-2 25	0.7	0.9	5	1.2	190	1.7
2295	Canarsie (midchannel, off Pier)	40 38	73 53	-1 35	-1 50	0.3	0.3	45	0.5	220	0.7
2300	Beach Channel (bridge)	40 35	73 49	-1 20	-1 20	1.1	1.0	60	1.9	225	2.0
2305	Grass Hassock Channel	40 37	73 47	-1 10	-1 00	0.6	0.5	50	1.0	230	1.0
	NEW YORK HARBOR ENTRANCE										
2310	Ambrose Channel entrance	40 30	73 58	-1 10	-1 05	1.0	1.2	310	1.7	110	2.3
2315	Ambrose Channel, SE. of West Bank Lt	40 32	74 01	(1)	-0 25	0.8	0.9	310	1.3	170	1.8
2320	Coney Island Lt., 1.6 miles SSW. of	40 33	74 01	-0 10	(2)	0.5	0.8	330	0.8	145	1.5
2325	Ambrose Channel, north end	40 34	74 02	+0 05	+0 15	0.8	0.9	330	1.3	175	1.9
2330	Coney Island, 0.2 mile west of	40 35	74 01	-0 55	-0 55	0.9	1.0	330	1.5	170	2.0
2335	Ft. Lafayette, channel east of	40 36	74 02	(3)	(3)	0.6	0.5	345	1.1	195	0.9
2340	THE NARROWS, midchannel	40 37	74 03	Daily predictions				340	1.7	160	2.0
	NEW YORK HARBOR, Upper Bay										
2345	Tompkinsville	40 38	74 04	-0 10	+0 20	0.9	1.0	5	1.6	170	2.0
2350	Bay Ridge Channel	40 39	74 02	-0 35	-0 45	0.6	0.6	40	1.0	220	1.1
2355	Red Hook Channel	40 40	74 01	-0 35	-0 35	0.6	0.4	355	1.0	170	0.7
2360	Robbins Reef Light, east of	40 39	74 03	+0 10	+0 20	0.8	0.8	15	1.3	205	1.6
2365	Red Hook, 1 mile west of	40 41	74 02	+0 45	+1 00	0.8	1.2	25	1.3	205	2.3
2370	Statue of Liberty, east of	40 42	74 02	+0 55	+1 00	0.8	1.0	30	1.4	205	1.9
	HUDSON RIVER, Midchannel[4]										
2375	The Battery, northwest of	40 43	74 02	+1 30	+1 35	0.9	1.2	15	1.5	195	2.3
2380	Desbrosses Street	40 43	74 01	+1 35	+1 40	0.9	1.2	10	1.5	----	2.3
2385	Chelsea Docks	40 45	74 01	+1 30	+1 40	1.0	1.0	20	1.7	185	2.0
2390	Forty-second Street	40 46	74 00	+1 35	+1 45	1.0	1.2	30	1.7	----	2.3
2395	Ninety-sixth Street	40 48	73 59	+1 40	+1 50	1.0	1.2	30	1.7	----	2.3
2400	Grants Tomb, 123d Street	40 49	73 58	+1 45	+1 55	0.9	1.2	25	1.6	----	2.3
2405	George Washington Bridge	40 51	73 57	+1 45	+2 00	0.9	1.1	20	1.6	200	2.2
2410	Spuyten Duyvil	40 53	73 56	+2 00	+2 10	0.9	1.1	20	1.6	----	2.1
2415	Riverdale	40 54	73 55	+2 05	+2 20	0.8	1.0	15	1.4	200	2.0
2420	Dobbs Ferry	41 01	73 53	+2 25	+2 40	0.8	0.9	10	1.3	----	1.7
2425	Tarrytown	41 05	73 53	+2 40	+2 55	0.6	0.8	0	1.1	----	1.5
2430	Ossining	41 10	73 54	+2 55	+3 10	0.5	0.7	320	0.9	----	1.3
2435	Haverstraw	41 12	73 57	+3 05	+3 15	0.5	0.7	335	0.8	----	1.3
2440	Peekskill	41 17	73 57	+3 20	+3 35	0.5	0.6	0	0.8	----	1.2
2445	Bear Mountain Bridge	41 19	73 59	+3 25	+3 40	0.5	0.6	0	0.8	----	1.1
2450	Highland Falls	41 22	73 58	+3 35	+3 50	0.6	0.6	5	1.0	185	1.2
2455	West Point, off Duck Island	41 24	73 57	+3 40	+3 55	0.5	0.6	10	1.0	----	1.1

[1] Current is rotary, turning clockwise. Minimum current of 0.9 knot sets SW. about time of "Slack, flood begins" at The Narrows. Minimum current of 0.5 knot sets NE. about 1 hour before "Slack, ebb begins" at The Narrows.

[2] Maximum flood, $-0^h\ 50^m$; maximum ebb, $+0^h\ 55^m$.

[3] Flood begins, $-2^h\ 15^m$; maximum flood, $-0^h\ 05^m$; ebb begins, $+0^h\ 05^m$; maximum ebb, $-1^h\ 50^m$.

[4] The values for the Hudson River are for the summer months, when the fresh-water discharge is a minimum.

TABLE 3.—VELOCITY OF CURRENT AT ANY TIME

TABLE A

Interval between slack and desired time	Interval between slack and maximum current													
	h. m. 1 20	*h. m.* 1 40	*h. m.* 2 00	*h. m.* 2 20	*h. m.* 2 40	*h. m.* 3 00	*h. m.* 3 20	*h. m.* 3 40	*h. m.* 4 00	*h. m.* 4 20	*h. m.* 4 40	*h. m.* 5 00	*h. m.* 5 20	*h. m.* 5 40
h. m.	*f.*	*f.*	*f.*	*f.*	*f.*	*f.*	*f.*	*f.*	*f.*	*f.*	*f.*	*f.*	*f.*	*f.*
0 20	0.4	0.3	0.3	0.2	0.2	0.2	0.2	0.1	0.1	0.1	0.1	0.1	0.1	0.1
0 40	0.7	0.6	0.5	0.4	0.4	0.3	0.3	0.3	0.3	0.2	0.2	0.2	0.2	0.2
1 00	0.9	0.8	0.7	0.6	0.6	0.5	0.5	0.4	0.4	0.4	0.3	0.3	0.3	0.3
1 20	1.0	1.0	0.9	0.8	0.7	0.6	0.6	0.5	0.5	0.5	0.4	0.4	0.4	0.4
1 40	------	1.0	1.0	0.9	0.8	0.8	0.7	0.7	0.6	0.6	0.5	0.5	0.5	0.4
2 00	------	------	1.0	1.0	0.9	0.9	0.8	0.8	0.7	0.7	0.6	0.6	0.6	0.5
2 20	------	------	------	1.0	1.0	0.9	0.9	0.8	0.8	0.7	0.7	0.7	0.6	0.6
2 40	------	------	------	------	1.0	1.0	1.0	0.9	0.9	0.8	0.8	0.7	0.7	0.7
3 00	------	------	------	------	------	1.0	1.0	1.0	0.9	0.9	0.8	0.8	0.8	0.7
3 20	------	------	------	------	------	------	1.0	1.0	1.0	0.9	0.9	0.9	0.8	0.8
3 40	------	------	------	------	------	------	------	1.0	1.0	1.0	0.9	0.9	0.9	0.9
4 00	------	------	------	------	------	------	------	------	1.0	1.0	1.0	1.0	0.9	0.9
4 20	------	------	------	------	------	------	------	------	------	1.0	1.0	1.0	1.0	0.9
4 40	------	------	------	------	------	------	------	------	------	------	1.0	1.0	1.0	1.0
5 00	------	------	------	------	------	------	------	------	------	------	------	1.0	1.0	1.0
5 20	------	------	------	------	------	------	------	------	------	------	------	------	1.0	1.0
5 40	------	------	------	------	------	------	------	------	------	------	------	------	------	1.0

TABLE B

Interval between slack and desired time	Interval between slack and maximum current													
	h. m. 1 20	*h. m.* 1 40	*h. m.* 2 00	*h. m.* 2 20	*h. m.* 2 40	*h. m.* 3 00	*h. m.* 3 20	*h. m.* 3 40	*h. m.* 4 00	*h. m.* 4 20	*h. m.* 4 40	*h. m.* 5 00	*h. m.* 5 20	*h. m.* 5 40
h. m.	*f.*	*f.*	*f.*	*f.*	*f.*	*f.*	*f.*	*f.*	*f.*	*f.*	*f.*	*f.*	*f.*	*f.*
0 20	0.5	0.4	0.4	0.3	0.3	0.3	0.3	0.3	0.2	0.2	0.2	0.2	0.2	0.2
0 40	0.8	0.7	0.6	0.5	0.5	0.5	0.4	0.4	0.4	0.4	0.3	0.3	0.3	0.3
1 00	0.9	0.8	0.8	0.7	0.7	0.6	0.6	0.5	0.5	0.5	0.4	0.4	0.4	0.4
1 20	1.0	1.0	0.9	0.8	0.8	0.7	0.7	0.6	0.6	0.6	0.5	0.5	0.5	0.5
1 40	------	1.0	1.0	0.9	0.9	0.8	0.8	0.7	0.7	0.7	0.6	0.6	0.6	0.6
2 00	------	------	1.0	1.0	0.9	0.9	0.9	0.8	0.8	0.7	0.7	0.7	0.7	0.6
2 20	------	------	------	1.0	1.0	1.0	0.9	0.9	0.8	0.8	0.8	0.7	0.7	0.7
2 40	------	------	------	------	1.0	1.0	1.0	0.9	0.9	0.9	0.8	0.8	0.8	0.7
3 00	------	------	------	------	------	1.0	1.0	1.0	0.9	0.9	0.9	0.9	0.8	0.8
3 20	------	------	------	------	------	------	1.0	1.0	1.0	1.0	0.9	0.9	0.9	0.8
3 40	------	------	------	------	------	------	------	1.0	1.0	1.0	1.0	0.9	0.9	0.9
4 00	------	------	------	------	------	------	------	------	1.0	1.0	1.0	1.0	0.9	0.9
4 20	------	------	------	------	------	------	------	------	------	1.0	1.0	1.0	1.0	0.9
4 40	------	------	------	------	------	------	------	------	------	------	1.0	1.0	1.0	1.0
5 00	------	------	------	------	------	------	------	------	------	------	------	1.0	1.0	1.0
5 20	------	------	------	------	------	------	------	------	------	------	------	------	1.0	1.0
5 40	------	------	------	------	------	------	------	------	------	------	------	------	------	1.0

Use Table A for all places except those listed below for Table B.
Use Table B for Cape Cod Canal, Hell Gate, Chesapeake and Delaware Canal and all stations in Table 2 which are referred to them.

1. From predictions find the time of slack water and the time and velocity of maximum current (flood or ebb), one of which is immediately before and the other after the time for which the velocity is desired.
2. Find the interval of time between the above slack and maximum current, and enter the top of Table A or B with the interval which most nearly agrees with this value.
3. Find the interval of time between the above slack and the time desired, and enter the side of Table A or B with the interval which most nearly agrees with this value.
4. Find, in the table, the factor corresponding to the above two intervals and multiply the maximum velocity by this factor. The result will be the approximate velocity at the time desired.

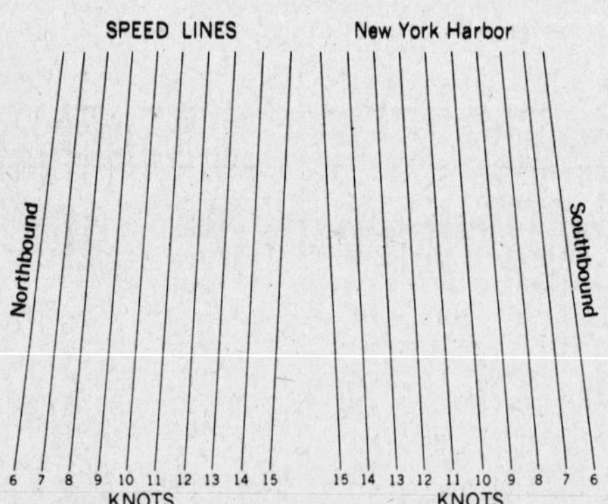
SPEED LINES
New York Harbor
Northbound
Southbound
6 7 8 9 10 11 12 13 14 15
15 14 13 12 11 10 9 8 7 6
KNOTS
KNOTS

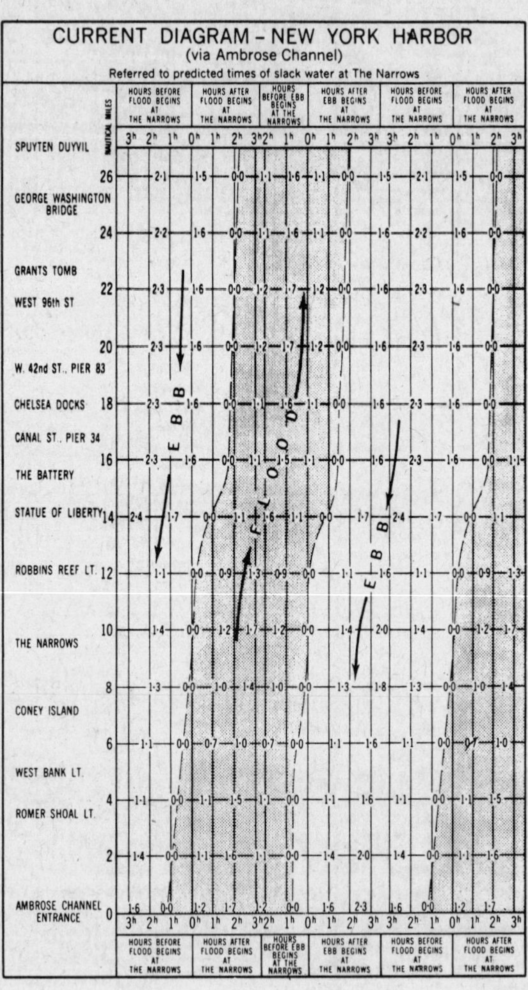
CURRENT DIAGRAM – NEW YORK HARBOR
(via Ambrose Channel)
Referred to predicted times of slack water at The Narrows
HOURS BEFORE FLOOD BEGINS AT THE NARROWS
HOURS AFTER FLOOD BEGINS AT THE NARROWS
HOURS BEFORE EBB BEGINS AT THE NARROWS
HOURS AFTER EBB BEGINS AT THE NARROWS
NAUTICAL MILES
SPUYTEN DUYVIL
GEORGE WASHINGTON BRIDGE
GRANTS TOMB
WEST 96th ST
W. 42nd ST., PIER 83
CHELSEA DOCKS
CANAL ST., PIER 34
THE BATTERY
STATUE OF LIBERTY
ROBBINS REEF LT.
THE NARROWS
CONEY ISLAND
WEST BANK LT.
ROMER SHOAL LT.
AMBROSE CHANNEL ENTRANCE
EBB
FLOOD
EBB

APPENDIX D

EXTRACTS FROM PUB. NO. 229

INTERPOLATION TABLE

Dec. Inc.	Altitude Difference (d) Tens 10'	20'	30'	40'	50'	Decimals ↓	Units 0'	1'	2'	3'	4'	5'	6'	7'	8'	9'	Double Second Diff. and Corr.
0.0	0.0	0.0	0.0	0.0	0.0	.0	0.0	0.0	0.0	0.0	0.0	0.0	0.0	0.1	0.1	0.1	
0.1	0.0	0.0	0.0	0.0	0.1	.1	0.0	0.0	0.0	0.0	0.0	0.0	0.1	0.1	0.1	0.1	0.0 (0.0)
0.2	0.0	0.0	0.1	0.1	0.1	.2	0.0	0.0	0.0	0.0	0.0	0.0	0.1	0.1	0.1	0.1	48.2
0.3	0.0	0.1	0.1	0.2	0.2	.3	0.0	0.0	0.0	0.0	0.0	0.0	0.1	0.1	0.1	0.1	
0.4	0.1	0.1	0.2	0.3	0.3	.4	0.0	0.0	0.0	0.0	0.0	0.0	0.1	0.1	0.1	0.1	
0.5	0.1	0.2	0.3	0.3	0.4	.5	0.0	0.0	0.0	0.0	0.0	0.0	0.1	0.1	0.1	0.1	
0.6	0.1	0.2	0.3	0.4	0.5	.6	0.0	0.0	0.0	0.0	0.0	0.0	0.1	0.1	0.1	0.1	16.2 (0.1)
0.7	0.1	0.3	0.4	0.5	0.6	.7	0.0	0.0	0.0	0.0	0.0	0.0	0.1	0.1	0.1	0.1	48.6
0.8	0.2	0.3	0.4	0.6	0.7	.8	0.0	0.0	0.0	0.0	0.0	0.0	0.1	0.1	0.1	0.1	
0.9	0.2	0.3	0.5	0.6	0.8	.9	0.0	0.0	0.0	0.0	0.0	0.0	0.1	0.1	0.1	0.1	
1.0	0.1	0.3	0.5	0.6	0.8	.0	0.0	0.0	0.0	0.1	0.1	0.1	0.1	0.2	0.2	0.2	
1.1	0.2	0.3	0.5	0.7	0.9	.1	0.0	0.0	0.1	0.1	0.1	0.1	0.2	0.2	0.2	0.2	
1.2	0.2	0.4	0.6	0.8	1.0	.2	0.0	0.0	0.1	0.1	0.1	0.1	0.2	0.2	0.2	0.2	
1.3	0.2	0.4	0.6	0.9	1.1	.3	0.0	0.0	0.1	0.1	0.1	0.1	0.2	0.2	0.2	0.2	
1.4	0.2	0.5	0.7	0.9	1.2	.4	0.0	0.0	0.1	0.1	0.1	0.1	0.2	0.2	0.2	0.2	8.2 (0.1) 24.6 (0.2)
1.5	0.3	0.5	0.8	1.0	1.3	.5	0.0	0.0	0.1	0.1	0.1	0.1	0.2	0.2	0.2	0.2	41.0
1.6	0.3	0.5	0.8	1.1	1.3	.6	0.0	0.0	0.1	0.1	0.1	0.1	0.2	0.2	0.2	0.2	
1.7	0.3	0.6	0.9	1.2	1.4	.7	0.0	0.0	0.1	0.1	0.1	0.1	0.2	0.2	0.2	0.2	
1.8	0.3	0.6	0.9	1.2	1.5	.8	0.0	0.0	0.1	0.1	0.1	0.1	0.2	0.2	0.2	0.2	
1.9	0.4	0.7	1.0	1.3	1.6	.9	0.0	0.0	0.1	0.1	0.1	0.1	0.2	0.2	0.2	0.2	
2.0	0.3	0.6	1.0	1.3	1.6	.0	0.0	0.0	0.1	0.1	0.2	0.2	0.2	0.3	0.3	0.4	
2.1	0.3	0.7	1.0	1.4	1.7	.1	0.0	0.0	0.1	0.1	0.2	0.2	0.3	0.3	0.3	0.4	
2.2	0.3	0.7	1.1	1.4	1.8	.2	0.0	0.0	0.1	0.1	0.2	0.2	0.3	0.3	0.3	0.4	
2.3	0.4	0.8	1.1	1.5	1.9	.3	0.0	0.1	0.1	0.1	0.2	0.2	0.3	0.3	0.3	0.4	5.0 (0.1)
2.4	0.4	0.8	1.2	1.6	2.0	.4	0.0	0.1	0.1	0.1	0.2	0.2	0.3	0.3	0.3	0.4	15.0 (0.2)
2.5	0.4	0.8	1.3	1.7	2.1	.5	0.0	0.1	0.1	0.1	0.2	0.2	0.3	0.3	0.4	0.4	25.0 (0.3)
2.6	0.4	0.9	1.3	1.7	2.2	.6	0.0	0.1	0.1	0.1	0.2	0.2	0.3	0.3	0.4	0.4	35.1
2.7	0.5	0.9	1.4	1.8	2.3	.7	0.0	0.1	0.1	0.2	0.2	0.2	0.3	0.3	0.4	0.4	
2.8	0.5	1.0	1.4	1.9	2.4	.8	0.0	0.1	0.1	0.2	0.2	0.2	0.3	0.3	0.4	0.4	
2.9	0.5	1.0	1.5	2.0	2.5	.9	0.0	0.1	0.1	0.2	0.2	0.2	0.3	0.3	0.4	0.4	
3.0	0.5	1.0	1.5	2.0	2.5	.0	0.0	0.1	0.1	0.2	0.2	0.3	0.3	0.4	0.5	0.5	
3.1	0.5	1.0	1.5	2.0	2.6	.1	0.0	0.1	0.1	0.2	0.2	0.3	0.4	0.4	0.5	0.5	
3.2	0.5	1.0	1.6	2.1	2.6	.2	0.0	0.1	0.1	0.2	0.2	0.3	0.4	0.4	0.5	0.5	3.6 (0.1)
3.3	0.5	1.1	1.6	2.2	2.7	.3	0.0	0.1	0.1	0.2	0.3	0.3	0.4	0.4	0.5	0.5	10.9 (0.2)
3.4	0.6	1.1	1.7	2.3	2.8	.4	0.0	0.1	0.1	0.2	0.3	0.3	0.4	0.4	0.5	0.5	18.2 (0.3)
3.5	0.6	1.2	1.8	2.3	2.9	.5	0.0	0.1	0.1	0.2	0.3	0.3	0.4	0.4	0.5	0.6	25.5 (0.4)
3.6	0.6	1.2	1.8	2.4	3.0	.6	0.0	0.1	0.2	0.2	0.3	0.3	0.4	0.4	0.5	0.6	32.8 (0.5)
3.7	0.6	1.3	1.9	2.5	3.1	.7	0.0	0.1	0.2	0.2	0.3	0.3	0.4	0.4	0.5	0.6	40.1
3.8	0.7	1.3	1.9	2.6	3.2	.8	0.0	0.1	0.2	0.2	0.3	0.3	0.4	0.5	0.5	0.6	
3.9	0.7	1.3	2.0	2.6	3.3	.9	0.1	0.1	0.2	0.2	0.3	0.3	0.4	0.5	0.5	0.6	
4.0	0.6	1.3	2.0	2.6	3.3	.0	0.0	0.1	0.1	0.2	0.3	0.4	0.4	0.5	0.6	0.7	
4.1	0.7	1.3	2.0	2.7	3.4	.1	0.0	0.1	0.2	0.2	0.3	0.4	0.5	0.5	0.6	0.7	
4.2	0.7	1.4	2.1	2.8	3.5	.2	0.0	0.1	0.2	0.2	0.3	0.4	0.5	0.5	0.6	0.7	2.9 (0.1)
4.3	0.7	1.4	2.1	2.9	3.6	.3	0.0	0.1	0.2	0.2	0.3	0.4	0.5	0.5	0.6	0.7	8.6 (0.2)
4.4	0.7	1.5	2.2	2.9	3.7	.4	0.0	0.1	0.2	0.3	0.3	0.4	0.5	0.6	0.6	0.7	14.4 (0.3) 20.2 (0.4)
4.5	0.8	1.5	2.3	3.0	3.8	.5	0.0	0.1	0.2	0.3	0.3	0.4	0.5	0.6	0.6	0.7	25.9 (0.5)
4.6	0.8	1.5	2.3	3.1	3.8	.6	0.0	0.1	0.2	0.3	0.3	0.4	0.5	0.6	0.6	0.7	31.7 (0.6)
4.7	0.8	1.6	2.4	3.2	3.9	.7	0.1	0.1	0.2	0.3	0.4	0.4	0.5	0.6	0.7	0.7	37.5
4.8	0.8	1.6	2.4	3.2	4.0	.8	0.1	0.1	0.2	0.3	0.4	0.4	0.5	0.6	0.7	0.7	
4.9	0.9	1.7	2.5	3.3	4.1	.9	0.1	0.1	0.2	0.3	0.4	0.4	0.5	0.6	0.7	0.7	
5.0	0.8	1.6	2.5	3.3	4.1	.0	0.0	0.1	0.2	0.3	0.4	0.5	0.5	0.6	0.7	0.8	
5.1	0.8	1.7	2.5	3.4	4.2	.1	0.0	0.1	0.2	0.3	0.4	0.5	0.6	0.7	0.7	0.8	2.4 (0.1)
5.2	0.8	1.7	2.6	3.4	4.3	.2	0.0	0.1	0.2	0.3	0.4	0.5	0.6	0.7	0.8	0.8	7.2 (0.2)
5.3	0.9	1.8	2.6	3.5	4.4	.3	0.0	0.1	0.2	0.3	0.4	0.5	0.6	0.7	0.8	0.9	12.0 (0.3)
5.4	0.9	1.8	2.7	3.6	4.5	.4	0.0	0.1	0.2	0.3	0.4	0.5	0.6	0.7	0.8	0.9	16.8 (0.4)
5.5	0.9	1.8	2.8	3.7	4.6	.5	0.0	0.1	0.2	0.3	0.4	0.5	0.6	0.7	0.8	0.9	21.6 (0.5)
5.6	0.9	1.9	2.8	3.7	4.7	.6	0.1	0.1	0.2	0.3	0.4	0.5	0.6	0.7	0.8	0.9	26.4 (0.6)
5.7	1.0	1.9	2.9	3.8	4.8	.7	0.1	0.2	0.2	0.3	0.4	0.5	0.6	0.7	0.8	0.9	31.2 (0.7)
5.8	1.0	2.0	2.9	3.9	4.9	.8	0.1	0.2	0.3	0.3	0.4	0.5	0.6	0.7	0.8	0.9	36.0
5.9	1.0	2.0	3.0	4.0	5.0	.9	0.1	0.2	0.3	0.4	0.4	0.5	0.6	0.7	0.8	0.9	
6.0	1.0	2.0	3.0	4.0	5.0	.0	0.0	0.1	0.2	0.3	0.4	0.5	0.6	0.8	0.9	1.0	
6.1	1.0	2.0	3.0	4.0	5.1	.1	0.0	0.1	0.2	0.3	0.4	0.6	0.7	0.8	0.9	1.0	2.1 (0.1)
6.2	1.0	2.0	3.1	4.1	5.1	.2	0.0	0.1	0.2	0.3	0.5	0.6	0.7	0.8	0.9	1.0	6.2 (0.2)
6.3	1.0	2.1	3.1	4.2	5.2	.3	0.0	0.1	0.2	0.4	0.5	0.6	0.7	0.8	0.9	1.0	10.4 (0.3)
6.4	1.1	2.1	3.2	4.3	5.3	.4	0.0	0.2	0.3	0.4	0.5	0.6	0.7	0.8	0.9	1.0	14.5 (0.4) 18.6 (0.5)
6.5	1.1	2.2	3.3	4.3	5.4	.5	0.1	0.2	0.3	0.4	0.5	0.6	0.7	0.8	0.9	1.0	22.8 (0.6)
6.6	1.1	2.2	3.3	4.4	5.5	.6	0.1	0.2	0.3	0.4	0.5	0.6	0.7	0.8	0.9	1.0	26.9 (0.7)
6.7	1.1	2.3	3.4	4.5	5.6	.7	0.1	0.2	0.3	0.4	0.5	0.6	0.7	0.8	0.9	1.1	31.1 (0.8)
6.8	1.2	2.3	3.4	4.6	5.7	.8	0.1	0.2	0.3	0.4	0.5	0.6	0.7	0.8	1.0	1.1	35.2
6.9	1.2	2.3	3.5	4.6	5.8	.9	0.1	0.2	0.3	0.4	0.5	0.6	0.7	0.9	1.0	1.1	
7.0	1.1	2.3	3.5	4.6	5.8	.0	0.0	0.1	0.2	0.4	0.5	0.6	0.7	0.9	1.0	1.1	1.8 (0.1)
7.1	1.2	2.3	3.5	4.7	5.9	.1	0.0	0.1	0.3	0.4	0.5	0.6	0.8	0.9	1.0	1.1	5.5 (0.2)
7.2	1.2	2.4	3.6	4.8	6.0	.2	0.0	0.1	0.3	0.4	0.5	0.6	0.8	0.9	1.0	1.1	9.1 (0.3)
7.3	1.2	2.4	3.6	4.9	6.1	.3	0.0	0.2	0.3	0.4	0.5	0.7	0.8	0.9	1.0	1.2	12.8 (0.4)
7.4	1.2	2.5	3.7	4.9	6.2	.4	0.0	0.2	0.3	0.4	0.5	0.7	0.8	0.9	1.0	1.2	16.5 (0.5)
7.5	1.3	2.5	3.8	5.0	6.3	.5	0.1	0.2	0.3	0.4	0.6	0.7	0.8	0.9	1.1	1.2	20.1 (0.6)
7.6	1.3	2.5	3.8	5.1	6.3	.6	0.1	0.2	0.3	0.4	0.6	0.7	0.8	0.9	1.1	1.2	23.8 (0.7)
7.7	1.3	2.6	3.9	5.2	6.4	.7	0.1	0.2	0.3	0.5	0.6	0.7	0.8	1.0	1.1	1.2	27.4 (0.8)
7.8	1.3	2.6	3.9	5.2	6.5	.8	0.1	0.2	0.3	0.5	0.6	0.7	0.8	1.0	1.1	1.2	31.1 (0.9)
7.9	1.4	2.7	4.0	5.3	6.6	.9	0.1	0.2	0.4	0.5	0.6	0.7	0.9	1.0	1.1	1.2	34.7
	10'	20'	30'	40'	50'		0'	1'	2'	3'	4'	5'	6'	7'	8'	9'	

Dec. Inc.	Altitude Difference (d) Tens 10'	20'	30'	40'	50'	Decimals ↓	Units 0'	1'	2'	3'	4'	5'	6'	7'	8'	9'	Double Second Diff. and Corr.
8.0	1.3	2.6	4.0	5.3	6.6	.0	0.0	0.1	0.3	0.4	0.6	0.7	0.8	1.0	1.1	1.3	
8.1	1.3	2.7	4.0	5.4	6.7	.1	0.0	0.2	0.3	0.4	0.6	0.7	0.9	1.0	1.1	1.3	
8.2	1.3	2.7	4.1	5.4	6.8	.2	0.0	0.2	0.3	0.5	0.6	0.7	0.9	1.0	1.2	1.3	1.6 (0.1)
8.3	1.4	2.8	4.1	5.5	6.9	.3	0.0	0.2	0.3	0.5	0.6	0.8	0.9	1.0	1.2	1.3	4.8 (0.2)
8.4	1.4	2.8	4.2	5.6	7.0	.4	0.1	0.2	0.3	0.5	0.6	0.8	0.9	1.0	1.2	1.3	8.0 (0.3)
8.5	1.4	2.8	4.3	5.7	7.1	.5	0.1	0.2	0.4	0.5	0.6	0.8	0.9	1.1	1.2	1.3	11.2 (0.4)
8.6	1.4	2.9	4.3	5.7	7.2	.6	0.1	0.2	0.4	0.5	0.7	0.8	0.9	1.1	1.2	1.4	14.5 (0.5)
8.7	1.5	2.9	4.4	5.8	7.3	.7	0.1	0.2	0.4	0.5	0.7	0.8	0.9	1.1	1.2	1.4	17.7 (0.6)
8.8	1.5	3.0	4.4	5.9	7.4	.8	0.1	0.3	0.4	0.5	0.7	0.8	1.0	1.1	1.2	1.4	20.9 (0.7)
8.9	1.5	3.0	4.5	6.0	7.5	.9	0.1	0.3	0.4	0.6	0.7	0.8	1.0	1.1	1.3	1.4	24.1 (0.8) 27.3 (0.9)
9.0	1.5	3.0	4.5	6.0	7.5	.0	0.0	0.2	0.3	0.5	0.6	0.8	0.9	1.1	1.3	1.4	30.5 (1.0)
9.1	1.5	3.0	4.5	6.0	7.6	.1	0.0	0.2	0.3	0.5	0.6	0.8	1.0	1.1	1.3	1.4	33.7 (1.1)
9.2	1.5	3.0	4.6	6.1	7.6	.2	0.0	0.2	0.3	0.5	0.7	0.8	1.0	1.1	1.3	1.5	36.9
9.3	1.5	3.1	4.6	6.2	7.7	.3	0.0	0.2	0.4	0.5	0.7	0.8	1.0	1.2	1.3	1.5	
9.4	1.6	3.1	4.7	6.3	7.8	.4	0.1	0.2	0.4	0.5	0.7	0.9	1.0	1.2	1.3	1.5	
9.5	1.6	3.2	4.8	6.3	7.9	.5	0.1	0.2	0.4	0.6	0.7	0.9	1.0	1.2	1.3	1.5	
9.6	1.6	3.2	4.8	6.4	8.0	.6	0.1	0.3	0.4	0.6	0.7	0.9	1.0	1.2	1.4	1.5	
9.7	1.6	3.3	4.9	6.5	8.1	.7	0.1	0.3	0.4	0.6	0.7	0.9	1.1	1.2	1.4	1.5	1.4 (0.1)
9.8	1.7	3.3	4.9	6.6	8.2	.8	0.1	0.3	0.4	0.6	0.8	0.9	1.1	1.2	1.4	1.6	4.2 (0.2)
9.9	1.7	3.3	5.0	6.6	8.3	.9	0.1	0.3	0.5	0.6	0.8	0.9	1.1	1.3	1.4	1.6	7.1 (0.3) 9.9 (0.4)
10.0	1.6	3.3	5.0	6.6	8.3	.0	0.0	0.2	0.3	0.5	0.7	0.9	1.0	1.2	1.4	1.6	12.7 (0.5)
10.1	1.7	3.3	5.0	6.7	8.4	.1	0.0	0.2	0.4	0.5	0.7	0.9	1.1	1.2	1.4	1.6	15.5 (0.6)
10.2	1.7	3.4	5.1	6.8	8.5	.2	0.0	0.2	0.4	0.6	0.7	0.9	1.1	1.3	1.4	1.6	18.4 (0.7)
10.3	1.7	3.4	5.1	6.9	8.6	.3	0.1	0.2	0.4	0.6	0.8	0.9	1.1	1.3	1.5	1.6	21.2 (0.8)
10.4	1.7	3.5	5.2	6.9	8.7	.4	0.1	0.2	0.4	0.6	0.8	0.9	1.1	1.3	1.5	1.6	24.0 (0.9) 26.8 (1.0)
10.5	1.8	3.5	5.3	7.0	8.8	.5	0.1	0.3	0.4	0.6	0.8	1.0	1.1	1.3	1.5	1.7	29.7 (1.1)
10.6	1.8	3.5	5.3	7.1	8.8	.6	0.1	0.3	0.5	0.6	0.8	1.0	1.2	1.3	1.5	1.7	32.5 (1.2)
10.7	1.8	3.6	5.4	7.2	8.9	.7	0.1	0.3	0.5	0.6	0.8	1.0	1.2	1.3	1.5	1.7	35.3
10.8	1.8	3.6	5.4	7.2	9.0	.8	0.1	0.3	0.5	0.7	0.8	1.0	1.2	1.4	1.5	1.7	
10.9	1.9	3.7	5.5	7.3	9.1	.9	0.2	0.3	0.5	0.7	0.9	1.0	1.2	1.4	1.6	1.7	
11.0	1.8	3.6	5.5	7.3	9.1	.0	0.0	0.2	0.4	0.6	0.8	1.0	1.1	1.3	1.5	1.7	
11.1	1.8	3.7	5.5	7.4	9.2	.1	0.0	0.2	0.4	0.6	0.8	1.0	1.2	1.4	1.6	1.7	1.3 (0.1)
11.2	1.8	3.7	5.6	7.4	9.3	.2	0.0	0.2	0.4	0.6	0.8	1.0	1.2	1.4	1.6	1.8	3.8 (0.2)
11.3	1.9	3.8	5.6	7.5	9.4	.3	0.1	0.2	0.4	0.6	0.8	1.0	1.2	1.4	1.6	1.8	6.3 (0.3)
11.4	1.9	3.8	5.7	7.6	9.5	.4	0.1	0.3	0.5	0.7	0.8	1.0	1.2	1.4	1.6	1.8	8.9 (0.4)
11.5	1.9	3.8	5.8	7.7	9.6	.5	0.1	0.3	0.5	0.7	0.9	1.1	1.2	1.4	1.6	1.8	11.4 (0.5)
11.6	1.9	3.9	5.8	7.7	9.7	.6	0.1	0.3	0.5	0.7	0.9	1.1	1.3	1.5	1.6	1.8	14.0 (0.6)
11.7	2.0	3.9	5.9	7.8	9.8	.7	0.1	0.3	0.5	0.7	0.9	1.1	1.3	1.5	1.7	1.9	16.5 (0.7)
11.8	2.0	4.0	5.9	7.9	9.9	.8	0.2	0.3	0.5	0.7	0.9	1.1	1.3	1.5	1.7	1.9	19.0 (0.8)
11.9	2.0	4.0	6.0	8.0	10.0	.9	0.2	0.4	0.6	0.7	0.9	1.1	1.3	1.5	1.7	1.9	21.6 (0.9) 24.1 (1.0)
12.0	2.0	4.0	6.0	8.0	10.0	.0	0.0	0.2	0.4	0.6	0.8	1.0	1.2	1.5	1.7	1.9	26.7 (1.1)
12.1	2.0	4.0	6.0	8.0	10.1	.1	0.0	0.2	0.4	0.6	0.9	1.1	1.3	1.5	1.7	1.9	29.2 (1.2)
12.2	2.0	4.0	6.1	8.1	10.1	.2	0.0	0.2	0.5	0.7	0.9	1.1	1.3	1.5	1.7	1.9	31.7 (1.3)
12.3	2.0	4.1	6.1	8.2	10.2	.3	0.1	0.3	0.5	0.7	0.9	1.1	1.3	1.5	1.7	1.9	34.3
12.4	2.1	4.1	6.2	8.3	10.3	.4	0.1	0.3	0.5	0.7	0.9	1.1	1.3	1.5	1.7	2.0	
12.5	2.1	4.2	6.3	8.3	10.4	.5	0.1	0.3	0.5	0.7	0.9	1.1	1.4	1.6	1.8	2.0	1.2 (0.1)
12.6	2.1	4.2	6.3	8.4	10.5	.6	0.1	0.3	0.5	0.7	1.0	1.2	1.4	1.6	1.8	2.0	3.5 (0.2)
12.7	2.1	4.3	6.4	8.5	10.6	.7	0.1	0.4	0.6	0.8	1.0	1.2	1.4	1.6	1.8	2.0	5.8 (0.3)
12.8	2.2	4.3	6.4	8.6	10.7	.8	0.2	0.4	0.6	0.8	1.0	1.2	1.4	1.6	1.8	2.0	8.1 (0.4)
12.9	2.2	4.3	6.5	8.6	10.8	.9	0.2	0.4	0.6	0.8	1.0	1.2	1.4	1.6	1.9	2.1	10.5 (0.5) 12.8 (0.6)
13.0	2.1	4.3	6.5	8.6	10.8	.0	0.0	0.2	0.4	0.7	0.9	1.1	1.3	1.6	1.8	2.0	15.1 (0.7)
13.1	2.2	4.3	6.5	8.7	10.9	.1	0.0	0.2	0.5	0.7	0.9	1.1	1.4	1.6	1.8	2.0	17.4 (0.8)
13.2	2.2	4.4	6.6	8.8	11.0	.2	0.0	0.3	0.5	0.7	0.9	1.2	1.4	1.6	1.8	2.1	19.8 (0.9)
13.3	2.2	4.4	6.6	8.9	11.1	.3	0.1	0.3	0.5	0.7	1.0	1.2	1.4	1.6	1.9	2.1	22.1 (1.0)
13.4	2.2	4.5	6.7	8.9	11.2	.4	0.1	0.3	0.5	0.8	1.0	1.2	1.4	1.7	1.9	2.1	24.4 (1.1)
13.5	2.3	4.5	6.8	9.0	11.3	.5	0.1	0.3	0.6	0.8	1.0	1.2	1.5	1.7	1.9	2.1	26.7 (1.2)
13.6	2.3	4.5	6.8	9.1	11.3	.6	0.1	0.4	0.6	0.8	1.0	1.3	1.5	1.7	1.9	2.2	29.1 (1.3)
13.7	2.3	4.6	6.9	9.2	11.4	.7	0.2	0.4	0.6	0.8	1.1	1.3	1.5	1.7	2.0	2.2	31.4 (1.4)
13.8	2.3	4.6	6.9	9.2	11.5	.8	0.2	0.4	0.6	0.9	1.1	1.3	1.5	1.8	2.0	2.2	33.7 (1.5)
13.9	2.4	4.7	7.0	9.3	11.6	.9	0.2	0.4	0.7	0.9	1.1	1.3	1.6	1.8	2.0	2.2	36.0
14.0	2.3	4.6	7.0	9.3	11.6	.0	0.0	0.2	0.5	0.7	1.0	1.2	1.4	1.7	1.9	2.2	
14.1	2.3	4.7	7.0	9.4	11.7	.1	0.0	0.3	0.5	0.7	1.0	1.2	1.5	1.7	2.0	2.2	
14.2	2.3	4.7	7.1	9.4	11.8	.2	0.0	0.3	0.5	0.8	1.0	1.3	1.5	1.7	2.0	2.2	
14.3	2.4	4.8	7.1	9.5	11.9	.3	0.1	0.3	0.6	0.8	1.0	1.3	1.5	1.8	2.0	2.2	1.1 (0.1)
14.4	2.4	4.8	7.2	9.6	12.0	.4	0.1	0.3	0.6	0.8	1.1	1.3	1.5	1.8	2.0	2.3	3.2 (0.2) 5.3 (0.3)
14.5	2.4	4.8	7.3	9.7	12.1	.5	0.1	0.4	0.6	0.8	1.1	1.3	1.6	1.8	2.1	2.3	7.5 (0.4)
14.6	2.4	4.9	7.3	9.7	12.2	.6	0.1	0.4	0.6	0.9	1.1	1.4	1.6	1.8	2.1	2.3	9.6 (0.5)
14.7	2.5	4.9	7.4	9.8	12.3	.7	0.2	0.4	0.7	0.9	1.1	1.4	1.6	1.9	2.1	2.3	11.7 (0.6)
14.8	2.5	5.0	7.4	9.9	12.4	.8	0.2	0.4	0.7	0.9	1.2	1.4	1.6	1.9	2.1	2.4	13.9 (0.7)
14.9	2.5	5.0	7.5	10.0	12.5	.9	0.2	0.5	0.7	0.9	1.2	1.4	1.7	1.9	2.2	2.4	16.0 (0.8) 18.1 (0.9)
15.0	2.5	5.0	7.5	10.0	12.5	.0	0.0	0.3	0.5	0.8	1.0	1.3	1.5	1.8	2.1	2.3	20.3 (1.0)
15.1	2.5	5.0	7.5	10.0	12.6	.1	0.0	0.3	0.5	0.8	1.1	1.3	1.6	1.8	2.1	2.4	22.4 (1.1)
15.2	2.5	5.0	7.6	10.1	12.6	.2	0.1	0.3	0.6	0.8	1.1	1.3	1.6	1.9	2.1	2.4	24.5 (1.2)
15.3	2.5	5.1	7.6	10.2	12.7	.3	0.1	0.3	0.6	0.9	1.1	1.4	1.6	1.9	2.1	2.4	26.7 (1.3)
15.4	2.6	5.1	7.7	10.3	12.8	.4	0.1	0.4	0.6	0.9	1.1	1.4	1.7	1.9	2.2	2.4	28.8 (1.4) 30.9 (1.5)
15.5	2.6	5.2	7.8	10.3	12.9	.5	0.1	0.4	0.6	0.9	1.2	1.4	1.7	1.9	2.2	2.5	33.1 (1.6)
15.6	2.6	5.2	7.8	10.4	13.0	.6	0.2	0.4	0.7	0.9	1.2	1.4	1.7	2.0	2.2	2.5	35.2
15.7	2.6	5.3	7.9	10.5	13.1	.7	0.2	0.4	0.7	1.0	1.2	1.5	1.7	2.0	2.2	2.5	
15.8	2.7	5.3	7.9	10.6	13.2	.8	0.2	0.5	0.7	1.0	1.2	1.5	1.8	2.0	2.3	2.5	
15.9	2.7	5.3	8.0	10.6	13.3	.9	0.2	0.5	0.7	1.0	1.3	1.5	1.8	2.0	2.3	2.6	
	10'	20'	30'	40'	50'		0'	1'	2'	3'	4'	5'	6'	7'	8'	9'	

The Double-Second-Difference correction (Corr.) is always to be added to the tabulated altitude.

INTERPOLATION TABLE

Dec. Inc.	Tens 10'	20'	30'	40'	50'	Decimals	Units 0'	1'	2'	3'	4'	5'	6'	7'	8'	9'	Double Second Diff.	and Corr.
16.0	2.6	5.3	8.0	10.6	13.3	.0	0.0	0.3	0.5	0.8	1.1	1.4	1.6	1.9	2.2	2.5		
16.1	2.7	5.3	8.0	10.7	13.4	.1	0.0	0.3	0.6	0.9	1.1	1.4	1.7	2.0	2.2	2.5		
16.2	2.7	5.4	8.1	10.8	13.5	.2	0.1	0.3	0.6	0.9	1.2	1.4	1.7	2.0	2.3	2.5	1.0	0.1
16.3	2.7	5.4	8.1	10.9	13.6	.3	0.1	0.4	0.6	0.9	1.2	1.5	1.7	2.0	2.3	2.6	3.0	0.2
16.4	2.7	5.5	8.2	10.9	13.7	.4	0.1	0.4	0.7	0.9	1.2	1.5	1.8	2.0	2.3	2.6	4.9	0.3
16.5	2.8	5.5	8.3	11.0	13.8	.5	0.1	0.4	0.7	1.0	1.2	1.5	1.8	2.1	2.3	2.6	6.9	0.4
16.6	2.8	5.5	8.3	11.1	13.8	.6	0.2	0.4	0.7	1.0	1.3	1.5	1.8	2.1	2.4	2.6	8.9	0.5
16.7	2.8	5.6	8.4	11.2	13.9	.7	0.2	0.5	0.7	1.0	1.3	1.6	1.8	2.1	2.4	2.7	10.8	0.6
16.8	2.8	5.6	8.4	11.2	14.0	.8	0.2	0.5	0.8	1.0	1.3	1.6	1.9	2.1	2.4	2.7	12.8	0.7
16.9	2.9	5.7	8.5	11.3	14.1	.9	0.2	0.5	0.8	1.1	1.3	1.6	1.9	2.2	2.4	2.7	14.8	0.8
																	16.7	0.9
17.0	2.8	5.6	8.5	11.3	14.1	.0	0.0	0.3	0.6	0.9	1.2	1.5	1.7	2.0	2.3	2.6	18.7	1.0
17.1	2.8	5.7	8.5	11.4	14.2	.1	0.0	0.3	0.6	0.9	1.2	1.5	1.8	2.1	2.4	2.7	20.7	1.1
17.2	2.8	5.7	8.6	11.4	14.3	.2	0.1	0.3	0.6	0.9	1.2	1.5	1.8	2.1	2.4	2.7	22.7	1.2
17.3	2.9	5.8	8.6	11.5	14.4	.3	0.1	0.4	0.7	1.0	1.3	1.5	1.8	2.1	2.4	2.7	24.6	1.3
17.4	2.9	5.8	8.7	11.6	14.5	.4	0.1	0.4	0.7	1.0	1.3	1.6	1.9	2.2	2.4	2.7	26.6	1.4
17.5	2.9	5.8	8.8	11.7	14.6	.5	0.1	0.4	0.7	1.0	1.3	1.6	1.9	2.2	2.5	2.8	28.6	1.5
17.6	2.9	5.9	8.8	11.7	14.7	.6	0.2	0.5	0.8	1.0	1.3	1.6	1.9	2.2	2.5	2.8	30.5	1.6
17.7	3.0	5.9	8.9	11.8	14.8	.7	0.2	0.5	0.8	1.1	1.4	1.7	2.0	2.2	2.5	2.8	32.5	1.7
17.8	3.0	6.0	8.9	11.9	14.9	.8	0.2	0.5	0.8	1.1	1.4	1.7	2.0	2.3	2.6	2.9	34.5	
17.9	3.0	6.0	9.0	12.0	15.0	.9	0.3	0.6	0.8	1.1	1.4	1.7	2.0	2.3	2.6	2.9		
18.0	3.0	6.0	9.0	12.0	15.0	.0	0.0	0.3	0.6	0.9	1.2	1.5	1.8	2.2	2.5	2.8		
18.1	3.0	6.0	9.0	12.0	15.1	.1	0.0	0.3	0.6	1.0	1.3	1.6	1.9	2.2	2.5	2.8	0.9	0.1
18.2	3.0	6.0	9.1	12.1	15.1	.2	0.1	0.4	0.7	1.0	1.3	1.6	1.9	2.2	2.5	2.8	2.8	0.2
18.3	3.0	6.1	9.1	12.2	15.2	.3	0.1	0.4	0.7	1.0	1.3	1.6	1.9	2.3	2.6	2.9	4.6	0.3
18.4	3.1	6.1	9.2	12.3	15.3	.4	0.1	0.4	0.7	1.0	1.4	1.7	2.0	2.3	2.6	2.9	6.5	0.4
18.5	3.1	6.2	9.3	12.3	15.4	.5	0.2	0.5	0.8	1.1	1.4	1.7	2.0	2.3	2.6	2.9	8.3	0.5
18.6	3.1	6.2	9.3	12.4	15.5	.6	0.2	0.5	0.8	1.1	1.4	1.7	2.0	2.3	2.7	3.0	10.2	0.6
18.7	3.1	6.3	9.4	12.5	15.6	.7	0.2	0.5	0.8	1.1	1.4	1.8	2.1	2.4	2.7	3.0	12.0	0.7
18.8	3.2	6.3	9.4	12.6	15.7	.8	0.2	0.6	0.9	1.2	1.5	1.8	2.1	2.4	2.7	3.0	13.9	0.8
18.9	3.2	6.3	9.5	12.6	15.8	.9	0.3	0.6	0.9	1.2	1.5	1.8	2.1	2.4	2.7	3.1	15.7	0.9
																	17.6	1.0
19.0	3.1	6.3	9.5	12.6	15.8	.0	0.0	0.3	0.6	1.0	1.3	1.6	1.9	2.3	2.6	2.9	19.4	1.1
19.1	3.2	6.3	9.5	12.7	15.9	.1	0.0	0.4	0.7	1.0	1.3	1.7	2.0	2.3	2.6	3.0	21.3	1.2
19.2	3.2	6.4	9.6	12.8	16.0	.2	0.1	0.4	0.7	1.0	1.4	1.7	2.0	2.3	2.7	3.0	23.1	1.3
19.3	3.2	6.4	9.6	12.9	16.1	.3	0.1	0.4	0.7	1.1	1.4	1.7	2.0	2.4	2.7	3.0	25.0	1.4
19.4	3.2	6.5	9.7	12.9	16.2	.4	0.1	0.5	0.8	1.1	1.4	1.8	2.1	2.4	2.7	3.1	26.8	1.5
19.5	3.3	6.5	9.8	13.0	16.3	.5	0.2	0.5	0.8	1.1	1.5	1.8	2.1	2.4	2.8	3.1	28.7	1.6
19.6	3.3	6.5	9.8	13.1	16.3	.6	0.2	0.5	0.8	1.2	1.5	1.8	2.1	2.5	2.8	3.1	30.5	1.7
19.7	3.3	6.6	9.9	13.2	16.4	.7	0.2	0.6	0.9	1.2	1.5	1.9	2.2	2.5	2.8	3.2	32.3	1.8
19.8	3.3	6.6	9.9	13.2	16.5	.8	0.3	0.6	0.9	1.2	1.6	1.9	2.2	2.5	2.9	3.2	34.2	
19.9	3.4	6.7	10.0	13.3	16.6	.9	0.3	0.6	0.9	1.3	1.6	1.9	2.2	2.6	2.9	3.2		
20.0	3.3	6.6	10.0	13.3	16.6	.0	0.0	0.3	0.7	1.0	1.4	1.7	2.0	2.4	2.7	3.1		
20.1	3.3	6.7	10.0	13.4	16.7	.1	0.0	0.4	0.7	1.1	1.4	1.7	2.1	2.4	2.8	3.1	0.9	0.1
20.2	3.3	6.7	10.1	13.4	16.8	.2	0.1	0.4	0.8	1.1	1.4	1.8	2.1	2.5	2.8	3.1	2.6	0.2
20.3	3.4	6.8	10.1	13.5	16.9	.3	0.1	0.4	0.8	1.1	1.5	1.8	2.2	2.5	2.8	3.2	4.4	0.3
20.4	3.4	6.8	10.2	13.6	17.0	.4	0.1	0.5	0.8	1.2	1.5	1.8	2.2	2.5	2.9	3.2	6.2	0.4
20.5	3.4	6.8	10.3	13.7	17.1	.5	0.2	0.5	0.9	1.2	1.5	1.9	2.2	2.6	2.9	3.2	7.9	0.5
20.6	3.4	6.9	10.3	13.7	17.2	.6	0.2	0.5	0.9	1.2	1.6	1.9	2.3	2.6	2.9	3.3	9.7	0.6
20.7	3.5	6.9	10.4	13.8	17.3	.7	0.2	0.6	0.9	1.3	1.6	1.9	2.3	2.6	3.0	3.3	11.4	0.7
20.8	3.5	7.0	10.4	13.9	17.4	.8	0.3	0.6	1.0	1.3	1.6	2.0	2.3	2.7	3.0	3.3	13.2	0.8
20.9	3.5	7.0	10.5	14.0	17.5	.9	0.3	0.6	1.0	1.3	1.7	2.0	2.4	2.7	3.0	3.4	14.9	0.9
																	16.7	1.0
21.0	3.5	7.0	10.5	14.0	17.5	.0	0.0	0.4	0.7	1.1	1.4	1.8	2.1	2.5	2.9	3.2	18.5	1.1
21.1	3.5	7.0	10.5	14.0	17.6	.1	0.0	0.4	0.8	1.1	1.5	1.8	2.2	2.5	2.9	3.3	20.2	1.2
21.2	3.5	7.0	10.6	14.1	17.6	.2	0.1	0.4	0.8	1.1	1.5	1.9	2.2	2.6	2.9	3.3	22.0	1.3
21.3	3.5	7.1	10.6	14.2	17.7	.3	0.1	0.5	0.8	1.2	1.5	1.9	2.3	2.6	3.0	3.3	23.7	1.4
21.4	3.6	7.1	10.7	14.3	17.8	.4	0.1	0.5	0.9	1.2	1.6	1.9	2.3	2.7	3.0	3.4	25.5	1.5
21.5	3.6	7.2	10.8	14.3	17.9	.5	0.2	0.5	0.9	1.3	1.6	2.0	2.3	2.7	3.0	3.4	27.3	1.6
21.6	3.6	7.2	10.8	14.4	18.0	.6	0.2	0.6	0.9	1.3	1.6	2.0	2.4	2.7	3.1	3.4	29.0	1.7
21.7	3.6	7.3	10.9	14.5	18.1	.7	0.3	0.6	1.0	1.3	1.7	2.0	2.4	2.8	3.1	3.5	30.8	1.8
21.8	3.7	7.3	10.9	14.6	18.2	.8	0.3	0.6	1.0	1.4	1.7	2.1	2.4	2.8	3.2	3.5	32.5	1.9
21.9	3.7	7.3	11.0	14.6	18.3	.9	0.3	0.7	1.0	1.4	1.8	2.1	2.5	2.8	3.2	3.5	34.3	
22.0	3.6	7.3	11.0	14.6	18.3	.0	0.0	0.4	0.7	1.1	1.5	1.9	2.2	2.6	3.0	3.4	0.8	0.1
22.1	3.7	7.3	11.0	14.7	18.4	.1	0.0	0.4	0.8	1.2	1.5	1.9	2.3	2.7	3.0	3.4	2.5	0.2
22.2	3.7	7.4	11.1	14.8	18.5	.2	0.1	0.4	0.8	1.2	1.6	1.9	2.3	2.7	3.1	3.4	4.2	0.3
22.3	3.7	7.4	11.1	14.9	18.6	.3	0.1	0.5	0.9	1.2	1.6	2.0	2.4	2.7	3.1	3.5	5.9	0.4
22.4	3.7	7.5	11.2	14.9	18.7	.4	0.1	0.5	0.9	1.3	1.6	2.0	2.4	2.8	3.1	3.5	7.6	0.5
22.5	3.8	7.5	11.3	15.0	18.8	.5	0.2	0.6	0.9	1.3	1.7	2.1	2.4	2.8	3.2	3.6	9.3	0.6
22.6	3.8	7.5	11.3	15.1	18.8	.6	0.2	0.6	1.0	1.3	1.7	2.1	2.5	2.8	3.2	3.6	11.0	0.7
22.7	3.8	7.6	11.4	15.2	18.9	.7	0.3	0.6	1.0	1.4	1.8	2.1	2.5	2.9	3.3	3.6	12.7	0.8
22.8	3.8	7.6	11.4	15.2	19.0	.8	0.3	0.7	1.0	1.4	1.8	2.2	2.5	2.9	3.3	3.7	14.4	0.9
22.9	3.9	7.7	11.5	15.3	19.1	.9	0.3	0.7	1.1	1.5	1.8	2.2	2.6	3.0	3.3	3.7	16.1	1.0
																	17.8	1.1
23.0	3.8	7.6	11.5	15.3	19.1	.0	0.0	0.4	0.8	1.2	1.6	2.0	2.3	2.7	3.1	3.5	19.5	1.2
23.1	3.8	7.7	11.5	15.4	19.2	.1	0.0	0.4	0.8	1.2	1.6	2.0	2.4	2.8	3.2	3.6	21.2	1.3
23.2	3.8	7.7	11.6	15.4	19.3	.2	0.1	0.5	0.9	1.3	1.6	2.0	2.4	2.8	3.2	3.6	22.8	1.4
23.3	3.9	7.8	11.6	15.5	19.4	.3	0.1	0.5	0.9	1.3	1.7	2.1	2.5	2.9	3.3	3.6	24.5	1.5
23.4	3.9	7.8	11.7	15.6	19.5	.4	0.2	0.5	0.9	1.3	1.7	2.1	2.5	2.9	3.3	3.7	26.2	1.6
23.5	3.9	7.8	11.8	15.7	19.6	.5	0.2	0.6	1.0	1.4	1.8	2.2	2.5	2.9	3.3	3.7	27.9	1.7
23.6	3.9	7.9	11.8	15.7	19.7	.6	0.2	0.6	1.0	1.4	1.8	2.2	2.6	3.0	3.4	3.8	29.6	1.8
23.7	4.0	7.9	11.9	15.8	19.8	.7	0.3	0.7	1.1	1.4	1.8	2.2	2.6	3.0	3.4	3.8	31.3	1.9
23.8	4.0	8.0	11.9	15.9	19.9	.8	0.3	0.7	1.1	1.5	1.9	2.3	2.7	3.1	3.4	3.8	33.0	2.0
23.9	4.0	8.0	12.0	16.0	20.0	.9	0.4	0.7	1.1	1.5	1.9	2.3	2.7	3.1	3.5	3.9	34.7	
	10'	20'	30'	40'	50'		0'	1'	2'	3'	4'	5'	6'	7'	8'	9'		

Dec. Inc.	Tens 10'	20'	30'	40'	50'	Decimals	Units 0'	1'	2'	3'	4'	5'	6'	7'	8'	9'	Double Second Diff.	and Corr.
24.0	4.0	8.0	12.0	16.0	20.0	.0	0.0	0.4	0.8	1.2	1.6	2.0	2.4	2.9	3.3	3.7	0.8	0.1
24.1	4.0	8.0	12.0	16.0	20.1	.1	0.0	0.4	0.9	1.3	1.7	2.1	2.5	2.9	3.3	3.7	2.5	0.2
24.2	4.0	8.0	12.1	16.1	20.1	.2	0.1	0.5	0.9	1.3	1.7	2.1	2.5	2.9	3.3	3.8	4.1	0.3
24.3	4.0	8.1	12.1	16.2	20.2	.3	0.1	0.5	0.9	1.3	1.8	2.2	2.6	3.0	3.4	3.8	5.8	0.4
24.4	4.1	8.1	12.2	16.3	20.3	.4	0.2	0.6	1.0	1.4	1.8	2.2	2.6	3.0	3.4	3.8	7.4	0.5
																	9.1	0.6
24.5	4.1	8.2	12.3	16.3	20.4	.5	0.2	0.6	1.0	1.4	1.8	2.2	2.7	3.1	3.5	3.9	10.7	0.7
24.6	4.1	8.2	12.3	16.4	20.5	.6	0.2	0.7	1.1	1.5	1.9	2.3	2.7	3.1	3.5	3.9	12.3	0.8
24.7	4.1	8.3	12.4	16.5	20.6	.7	0.3	0.7	1.1	1.5	1.9	2.3	2.7	3.1	3.6	4.0	14.0	0.9
24.8	4.2	8.3	12.4	16.6	20.7	.8	0.3	0.7	1.1	1.6	2.0	2.4	2.8	3.2	3.6	4.0	15.6	1.0
24.9	4.2	8.3	12.5	16.6	20.8	.9	0.4	0.8	1.2	1.6	2.0	2.4	2.8	3.2	3.6	4.0	17.3	1.1
																	18.9	1.2
25.0	4.1	8.3	12.5	16.6	20.8	.0	0.0	0.4	0.8	1.3	1.7	2.1	2.5	3.0	3.4	3.8	20.6	1.3
25.1	4.2	8.3	12.5	16.7	20.9	.1	0.0	0.5	0.9	1.3	1.7	2.2	2.6	3.0	3.4	3.9	22.2	1.4
25.2	4.2	8.4	12.6	16.8	21.0	.2	0.1	0.5	0.9	1.4	1.8	2.2	2.6	3.1	3.5	3.9	23.9	1.5
25.3	4.2	8.4	12.6	16.9	21.1	.3	0.1	0.6	1.0	1.4	1.8	2.3	2.7	3.1	3.5	4.0	25.5	1.6
25.4	4.2	8.5	12.7	16.9	21.2	.4	0.2	0.6	1.0	1.4	1.9	2.3	2.7	3.1	3.6	4.0	27.2	1.7
25.5	4.3	8.5	12.8	17.0	21.3	.5	0.2	0.6	1.1	1.5	1.9	2.3	2.8	3.2	3.6	4.0	28.8	1.8
25.6	4.3	8.5	12.8	17.1	21.3	.6	0.3	0.7	1.1	1.5	2.0	2.4	2.8	3.2	3.7	4.1	30.4	1.9
25.7	4.3	8.6	12.9	17.2	21.4	.7	0.3	0.7	1.1	1.6	2.0	2.4	2.8	3.3	3.7	4.1	32.1	2.0
25.8	4.3	8.6	12.9	17.2	21.5	.8	0.3	0.8	1.2	1.6	2.0	2.5	2.9	3.3	3.7	4.2	33.7	2.1
25.9	4.4	8.7	13.0	17.3	21.6	.9	0.4	0.8	1.2	1.7	2.1	2.5	2.9	3.4	3.8	4.2	35.4	
26.0	4.3	8.6	13.0	17.3	21.6	.0	0.0	0.4	0.9	1.3	1.8	2.2	2.6	3.1	3.5	4.0	0.8	0.1
26.1	4.3	8.7	13.0	17.4	21.7	.1	0.0	0.5	0.9	1.4	1.8	2.3	2.7	3.1	3.6	4.0	2.4	0.2
26.2	4.3	8.7	13.1	17.4	21.8	.2	0.1	0.5	1.0	1.4	1.9	2.3	2.7	3.2	3.6	4.1	4.0	0.3
26.3	4.4	8.8	13.1	17.5	21.9	.3	0.1	0.6	1.0	1.5	1.9	2.3	2.8	3.2	3.7	4.1	5.7	0.4
26.4	4.4	8.8	13.2	17.6	22.0	.4	0.2	0.6	1.1	1.5	1.9	2.4	2.8	3.3	3.7	4.2	7.3	0.5
																	8.9	0.6
26.5	4.4	8.8	13.3	17.7	22.1	.5	0.2	0.7	1.1	1.5	2.0	2.4	2.9	3.3	3.8	4.2	10.5	0.7
26.6	4.4	8.9	13.3	17.7	22.2	.6	0.3	0.7	1.1	1.6	2.0	2.5	2.9	3.4	3.8	4.2	12.1	0.8
26.7	4.5	8.9	13.4	17.8	22.3	.7	0.3	0.8	1.2	1.6	2.1	2.5	3.0	3.4	3.8	4.3	13.7	0.9
26.8	4.5	9.0	13.4	17.9	22.4	.8	0.4	0.8	1.2	1.7	2.1	2.6	3.0	3.4	3.9	4.3	15.4	1.0
26.9	4.5	9.0	13.5	18.0	22.5	.9	0.4	0.8	1.3	1.7	2.2	2.6	3.0	3.5	3.9	4.4	17.0	1.1
																	18.6	1.2
27.0	4.5	9.0	13.5	18.0	22.5	.0	0.0	0.5	0.9	1.4	1.8	2.3	2.7	3.2	3.7	4.1	20.2	1.3
27.1	4.5	9.0	13.5	18.0	22.6	.1	0.0	0.5	1.0	1.4	1.9	2.3	2.8	3.3	3.7	4.2	21.8	1.4
27.2	4.5	9.0	13.6	18.1	22.6	.2	0.1	0.5	1.0	1.5	1.9	2.4	2.8	3.3	3.8	4.2	23.4	1.5
27.3	4.5	9.1	13.6	18.2	22.7	.3	0.1	0.6	1.1	1.5	2.0	2.4	2.9	3.3	3.8	4.3	25.1	1.6
27.4	4.6	9.1	13.7	18.3	22.8	.4	0.2	0.6	1.1	1.6	2.0	2.5	2.9	3.4	3.8	4.3	26.7	1.7
27.5	4.6	9.2	13.8	18.3	22.9	.5	0.2	0.7	1.1	1.6	2.1	2.5	3.0	3.4	3.9	4.4	28.3	1.8
27.6	4.6	9.2	13.8	18.4	23.0	.6	0.3	0.7	1.2	1.6	2.1	2.6	3.0	3.5	3.9	4.4	29.9	1.9
27.7	4.6	9.3	13.9	18.5	23.1	.7	0.3	0.8	1.2	1.7	2.2	2.6	3.1	3.5	4.0	4.4	31.5	2.0
27.8	4.7	9.3	13.9	18.6	23.2	.8	0.4	0.8	1.3	1.7	2.2	2.7	3.1	3.6	4.0	4.5	33.1	2.1
27.9	4.7	9.3	14.0	18.6	23.3	.9	0.4	0.9	1.3	1.8	2.2	2.7	3.2	3.6	4.1	4.5	34.7	
28.0	4.6	9.3	14.0	18.6	23.3	.0	0.0	0.5	0.9	1.4	1.9	2.4	2.8	3.3	3.8	4.3	0.8	0.1
28.1	4.7	9.3	14.0	18.7	23.4	.1	0.0	0.5	1.0	1.5	1.9	2.4	2.9	3.4	3.8	4.3	2.4	0.2
28.2	4.7	9.4	14.1	18.8	23.5	.2	0.1	0.6	1.0	1.5	2.0	2.5	2.9	3.4	3.9	4.4	4.0	0.3
28.3	4.7	9.4	14.1	18.9	23.6	.3	0.1	0.6	1.1	1.6	2.0	2.5	3.0	3.5	3.9	4.4	5.6	0.4
28.4	4.7	9.5	14.2	18.9	23.7	.4	0.2	0.7	1.1	1.6	2.1	2.6	3.0	3.5	4.0	4.5	7.2	0.5
																	8.8	0.6
28.5	4.8	9.5	14.3	19.0	23.8	.5	0.2	0.7	1.2	1.7	2.1	2.6	3.1	3.6	4.0	4.5	10.4	0.7
28.6	4.8	9.5	14.3	19.1	23.8	.6	0.3	0.8	1.2	1.7	2.2	2.7	3.1	3.6	4.1	4.6	12.0	0.8
28.7	4.8	9.6	14.4	19.2	23.9	.7	0.3	0.8	1.3	1.8	2.2	2.7	3.2	3.7	4.1	4.6	13.6	0.9
28.8	4.8	9.6	14.4	19.2	24.0	.8	0.4	0.9	1.3	1.8	2.3	2.8	3.2	3.7	4.2	4.7	15.2	1.0
28.9	4.9	9.7	14.5	19.3	24.1	.9	0.4	0.9	1.4	1.9	2.3	2.8	3.3	3.8	4.2	4.7	16.8	1.1
																	18.4	1.2
29.0	4.8	9.6	14.5	19.3	24.1	.0	0.0	0.5	1.0	1.5	2.0	2.5	2.9	3.4	3.9	4.4	20.0	1.3
29.1	4.8	9.7	14.5	19.4	24.2	.1	0.0	0.5	1.0	1.5	2.0	2.5	3.0	3.5	4.0	4.5	21.6	1.4
29.2	4.8	9.7	14.6	19.4	24.3	.2	0.1	0.6	1.1	1.6	2.1	2.6	3.0	3.5	4.0	4.5	23.2	1.5
29.3	4.9	9.8	14.6	19.5	24.4	.3	0.1	0.6	1.1	1.6	2.1	2.6	3.1	3.6	4.1	4.6	24.8	1.6
29.4	4.9	9.8	14.7	19.6	24.5	.4	0.2	0.7	1.2	1.7	2.2	2.7	3.1	3.6	4.1	4.6	26.4	1.7
29.5	4.9	9.8	14.8	19.7	24.6	.5	0.2	0.7	1.2	1.7	2.2	2.7	3.2	3.7	4.2	4.7	28.0	1.8
29.6	4.9	9.9	14.8	19.7	24.7	.6	0.3	0.8	1.3	1.8	2.3	2.8	3.2	3.7	4.2	4.7	29.6	1.9
29.7	5.0	9.9	14.9	19.8	24.8	.7	0.3	0.8	1.3	1.8	2.3	2.8	3.3	3.8	4.3	4.8	31.2	2.0
29.8	5.0	10.0	14.9	19.9	24.9	.8	0.4	0.9	1.4	1.9	2.4	2.9	3.3	3.8	4.3	4.8	32.8	2.1
29.9	5.0	10.0	15.0	20.0	25.0	.9	0.4	0.9	1.4	1.9	2.4	2.9	3.4	3.9	4.4	4.9	34.4	
30.0	5.0	10.0	15.0	20.0	25.0	.0	0.0	0.5	1.0	1.5	2.0	2.5	3.0	3.6	4.1	4.6	0.8	0.1
30.1	5.0	10.0	15.0	20.0	25.1	.1	0.1	0.6	1.1	1.6	2.1	2.6	3.1	3.6	4.1	4.6	2.4	0.2
30.2	5.0	10.0	15.1	20.1	25.1	.2	0.1	0.6	1.1	1.6	2.1	2.6	3.2	3.7	4.2	4.7	4.0	0.3
30.3	5.0	10.1	15.1	20.2	25.2	.3	0.2	0.7	1.2	1.7	2.2	2.7	3.2	3.7	4.2	4.7	5.6	0.4
30.4	5.1	10.1	15.2	20.3	25.3	.4	0.2	0.7	1.2	1.7	2.2	2.7	3.3	3.8	4.3	4.8	7.2	0.5
																	8.8	0.6
30.5	5.1	10.2	15.3	20.3	25.4	.5	0.3	0.8	1.3	1.8	2.3	2.8	3.3	3.8	4.3	4.8	10.4	0.7
30.6	5.1	10.2	15.3	20.4	25.5	.6	0.3	0.8	1.3	1.8	2.3	2.8	3.4	3.9	4.4	4.9	12.0	0.8
30.7	5.1	10.3	15.4	20.5	25.6	.7	0.4	0.9	1.4	1.9	2.4	2.9	3.4	3.9	4.4	4.9	13.6	0.9
30.8	5.2	10.3	15.4	20.6	25.7	.8	0.4	0.9	1.4	1.9	2.4	2.9	3.5	4.0	4.5	5.0	15.2	1.0
30.9	5.2	10.3	15.5	20.6	25.8	.9	0.5	1.0	1.5	2.0	2.5	3.0	3.5	4.0	4.5	5.0	16.8	1.1
																	18.4	[illegible]
31.0	5.1	10.3	15.5	20.6	25.8	.0	0.0	0.5	1.0	1.6	2.1	2.6	3.1	3.7	4.2	4.7	20.0	[illegible]
31.1	5.2	10.3	15.5	20.7	25.9	.1	0.1	0.6	1.1	1.6	2.2	2.7	3.2	3.7	4.3	4.8	21.6	[illegible]
31.2	5.2	10.4	15.6	20.8	26.0	.2	0.1	0.6	1.2	1.7	2.2	2.7	3.3	3.8	4.3	4.8	23.2	[illegible]
31.3	5.2	10.4	15.6	20.9	26.1	.3	0.2	0.7	1.2	1.7	2.3	2.8	3.3	3.8	4.4	4.9	24.8	[illegible]
31.4	5.2	10.5	15.7	20.9	26.2	.4	0.2	0.7	1.3	1.8	2.3	2.8	3.4	3.9	4.4	4.9	26.4	[illegible]
31.5	5.3	10.5	15.8	21.0	26.3	.5	0.3	0.8	1.3	1.8	2.4	2.9	3.4	3.9	4.5	5.0	28.0	[illegible]
31.6	5.3	10.5	15.8	21.1	26.3	.6	0.3	0.8	1.4	1.9	2.4	2.9	3.5	4.0	4.5	5.0	29.6	[illegible]
31.7	5.3	10.6	15.9	21.2	26.4	.7	0.4	0.9	1.4	1.9	2.5	3.0	3.5	4.0	4.6	5.1	31.2	[illegible]
31.8	5.3	10.6	15.9	21.2	26.5	.8	0.4	0.9	1.5	2.0	2.5	3.0	3.6	4.1	4.6	5.1	32.8	[illegible]
31.9	5.4	10.7	16.0	21.3	26.6	.9	0.5	1.0	1.5	2.0	2.6	3.1	3.6	4.1	4.7	5.2	34.4	
	10'	20'	30'	40'	50'		0'	1'	2	3'	4'	5'	6'	7'	8'	9'		

The Double-Second-Difference correction (Corr.) is always to be added to the tabulated altitude.

60°, 300° L.H.A. LATITUDE SAME NAME AS DECLINATION

N. Lat. { L.H.A. greater than 180°......Zn=Z ; L.H.A. less than 180°............Zn=360°−Z }

Dec.	38° Hc	d	Z	39° Hc	d	Z	40° Hc	d	Z	41° Hc	d	Z
°	° ′	′	°	° ′	′	°	° ′	′	°	° ′	′	°
0	23 12.2	+40.1	109.6	22 51.9	+40.9	110.0	22 31.3	+41.6	110.4	22 10.2	+42.4	110.7
1	23 52.3	39.8	108.8	23 32.8	40.6	109.2	23 12.9	41.4	109.6	22 52.6	42.2	110.0
2	24 32.1	39.5	107.9	24 13.4	40.4	108.4	23 54.3	41.2	108.8	23 34.8	41.9	109.2
3	25 11.6	39.3	107.1	24 53.8	40.1	107.6	24 35.5	40.9	108.0	24 16.7	41.7	108.4
4	25 50.9	39.0	106.3	25 33.9	39.8	106.7	25 16.4	40.6	107.2	24 58.4	41.5	107.6
5	26 29.9	+38.6	105.4	26 13.7	+39.5	105.9	25 57.0	+40.4	106.4	25 39.9	+41.1	106.8
6	27 08.5	38.4	104.6	26 53.2	39.2	105.1	26 37.4	40.0	105.5	26 21.0	40.9	106.0
7	27 46.9	38.0	103.7	27 32.4	38.9	104.2	27 17.4	39.8	104.7	27 01.9	40.7	105.2
8	28 24.9	37.7	102.8	28 11.3	38.6	103.3	27 57.2	39.5	103.9	27 42.6	40.3	104.4
9	29 02.6	37.3	101.9	28 49.9	38.2	102.5	28 36.7	39.1	103.0	28 22.9	40.0	103.5
10	29 39.9	+37.0	101.0	29 28.1	+37.9	101.6	29 15.8	+38.8	102.1	29 02.9	+39.7	102.7
11	30 16.9	36.5	100.1	30 06.0	37.5	100.7	29 54.6	38.4	101.3	29 42.6	39.3	101.8
12	30 53.4	36.2	99.2	30 43.5	37.2	99.8	30 33.0	38.1	100.4	30 21.9	39.0	101.0
13	31 29.6	35.8	98.3	31 20.7	36.7	98.9	31 11.1	37.7	99.5	31 00.9	38.6	100.1
14	32 05.4	35.3	97.3	31 57.4	36.3	97.9	31 48.8	37.3	98.6	31 39.5	38.3	99.2
15	32 40.7	+34.9	96.4	32 33.7	+35.9	97.0	32 26.1	+36.9	97.6	32 17.8	+37.8	98.3
16	33 15.6	34.5	95.4	33 09.6	35.5	96.1	33 03.0	36.4	96.7	32 55.6	37.5	97.3
17	33 50.1	33.9	94.4	33 45.1	35.0	95.1	33 39.4	36.0	95.7	33 33.1	37.0	96.4
18	34 24.0	33.5	93.4	34 20.1	34.5	94.1	34 15.4	35.6	94.8	34 10.1	36.5	95.5
19	34 57.5	33.0	92.4	34 54.6	34.0	93.1	34 51.0	35.1	93.8	34 46.6	36.1	94.5
20	35 30.5	+32.4	91.4	35 28.6	+33.6	92.1	35 26.1	+34.5	92.8	35 22.7	+35.7	93.5
21	36 02.9	31.9	90.4	36 02.2	32.9	91.1	36 00.6	34.1	91.8	35 58.4	35.1	92.5
22	36 34.8	31.3	89.3	36 35.1	32.5	90.0	36 34.7	33.6	90.8	36 33.5	34.6	91.5
23	37 06.1	30.8	88.2	37 07.6	31.9	89.0	37 08.3	32.9	89.8	37 08.1	34.1	90.5
24	37 36.9	30.2	87.2	37 39.5	31.3	87.9	37 41.2	32.5	88.7	37 42.2	33.5	89.5
25	38 07.1	+29.5	86.1	38 10.8	+30.7	86.8	38 13.7	+31.8	87.6	38 15.7	+33.0	88.4
26	38 36.6	28.9	85.0	38 41.5	30.0	85.7	38 45.5	31.2	86.5	38 48.7	32.4	87.4
27	39 05.5	28.3	83.8	39 11.5	29.5	84.6	39 16.7	30.6	85.4	39 21.1	31.7	86.3
28	39 33.8	27.5	82.7	39 41.0	28.7	83.5	39 47.3	30.0	84.3	39 52.8	31.1	85.2
29	40 01.3	26.9	81.5	40 09.7	28.1	82.4	40 17.3	29.2	83.2	40 23.9	30.5	84.0
30	40 28.2	+26.1	80.4	40 37.8	+27.4	81.2	40 46.5	+28.6	82.1	40 54.4	+29.8	82.9
31	40 54.3	25.5	79.2	41 05.2	26.6	80.0	41 15.1	27.9	80.9	41 24.2	29.1	81.8
32	41 19.8	24.6	78.0	41 31.8	25.9	78.8	41 43.0	27.1	79.7	41 53.3	28.3	80.6
33	41 44.4	23.9	76.8	41 57.7	25.1	77.6	42 10.1	26.4	78.5	42 21.6	27.6	79.4
34	42 08.3	23.0	75.5	42 22.8	24.4	76.4	42 36.5	25.6	77.3	42 49.2	26.9	78.2
35	42 31.3	+22.3	74.3	42 47.2	+23.5	75.2	43 02.1	+24.8	76.1	43 16.1	+26.0	77.0
36	42 53.6	21.4	73.0	43 10.7	22.7	73.9	43 26.9	23.9	74.8	43 42.1	25.3	75.7
37	43 15.0	20.5	71.7	43 33.4	21.8	72.6	43 50.8	23.1	73.5	44 07.4	24.3	74.5
38	43 35.5	19.7	70.4	43 55.2	20.9	71.3	44 13.9	22.2	72.3	44 31.7	23.6	73.2
39	43 55.2	18.7	69.1	44 16.1	20.0	70.0	44 36.1	21.4	71.0	44 55.3	22.6	71.9
40	44 13.9	+17.8	67.8	44 36.1	+19.2	68.7	44 57.5	+20.4	69.6	45 17.9	+21.7	70.6
41	44 31.7	16.9	66.5	44 55.3	18.1	67.4	45 17.9	19.5	68.3	45 39.6	20.8	69.3
42	44 48.6	15.9	65.1	45 13.4	17.2	66.0	45 37.4	18.5	67.0	46 00.4	19.8	67.9
43	45 04.5	15.0	63.8	45 30.6	16.3	64.7	45 55.9	17.5	65.6	46 20.2	18.8	66.5
44	45 19.5	13.9	62.4	45 46.9	15.2	63.3	46 13.4	16.5	64.2	46 39.0	17.9	65.2
45	45 33.4	+12.9	61.0	46 02.1	+14.2	61.9	46 29.9	+15.5	62.8	46 56.9	+16.8	63.8
46	45 46.3	11.9	59.6	46 16.3	13.1	60.5	46 45.4	14.5	61.4	47 13.7	15.7	62.4
47	45 58.2	10.9	58.2	46 29.4	12.1	59.1	46 59.9	13.3	60.0	47 29.4	14.7	60.9
48	46 09.1	9.7	56.8	46 41.5	11.1	57.7	47 13.2	12.4	58.6	47 44.1	13.6	59.5
49	46 18.8	8.8	55.3	46 52.6	9.9	56.2	47 25.6	11.2	57.1	47 57.7	12.5	58.0
50	46 27.6	+7.6	53.9	47 02.5	+8.9	54.8	47 36.8	+10.1	55.7	48 10.2	+11.4	56.6
51	46 35.2	6.5	52.5	47 11.4	7.7	53.3	47 46.9	8.9	54.2	48 21.6	10.2	55.1
52	46 41.7	5.5	51.0	47 19.1	6.7	51.9	47 55.8	7.9	52.7	48 31.8	9.1	53.6
53	46 47.2	4.3	49.6	47 25.8	5.5	50.4	48 03.7	6.7	51.2	48 40.9	7.9	52.1
54	46 51.5	3.3	48.1	47 31.3	4.3	48.9	48 10.4	5.5	49.8	48 48.8	6.7	50.6
55	46 54.8	+2.1	46.6	47 35.6	+3.3	47.4	48 15.9	+4.4	48.3	48 55.5	+5.6	49.1
56	46 56.9	+1.0	45.2	47 38.9	2.0	46.0	48 20.3	3.2	46.8	49 01.1	4.3	47.6
57	46 57.9	-0.2	43.7	47 40.9	+1.0	44.5	48 23.5	2.0	45.3	49 05.4	3.1	46.1
58	46 57.7	1.2	42.3	47 41.9	-0.2	43.0	48 25.5	+0.8	43.8	49 08.5	2.0	44.5
59	46 56.5	2.4	40.8	47 41.7	1.4	41.5	48 26.3	-0.3	42.2	49 10.5	+0.7	43.0
60	46 54.1	-3.5	39.3	47 40.3	-2.5	40.0	48 26.0	-1.5	40.7	49 11.2	-0.5	41.5
61	46 50.6	4.6	37.9	47 37.8	3.7	38.5	48 24.5	2.7	39.2	49 10.7	1.7	40.0
62	46 46.0	5.7	36.4	47 34.1	4.8	37.1	48 21.8	3.9	37.7	49 09.0	2.9	38.4
63	46 40.3	6.8	35.0	47 29.3	6.0	35.6	48 17.9	5.1	36.2	49 06.1	4.1	36.9
64	46 33.5	7.9	33.5	47 23.3	7.0	34.1	48 12.8	6.2	34.7	49 02.0	5.4	35.4
65	46 25.6	-9.0	32.1	47 16.3	-8.2	32.6	48 06.6	-7.3	33.2	48 56.6	-6.5	33.9
66	46 16.6	10.0	30.6	47 08.1	9.3	31.2	47 59.3	8.5	31.8	48 50.1	7.7	32.4
67	46 06.6	11.1	29.2	46 58.8	10.4	29.7	47 50.8	9.6	30.3	48 42.4	8.8	30.8
68	45 55.5	12.1	27.8	46 48.4	11.4	28.3	47 41.2	10.8	28.8	48 33.6	10.0	29.4
69	45 43.4	13.2	26.4	46 37.0	12.5	26.9	47 30.4	11.8	27.4	48 23.6	11.2	27.9
70	45 30.2	-14.2	25.0	46 24.5	-13.6	25.4	47 18.6	-13.0	25.9	48 12.4	-12.3	26.4
71	45 16.0	15.1	23.6	46 10.9	14.6	24.0	47 05.6	14.0	24.5	48 00.1	13.4	24.9
72	45 00.9	16.2	22.2	45 56.3	15.6	22.6	46 51.6	15.0	23.0	47 46.7	14.4	23.5
73	44 44.7	17.1	20.9	45 40.7	16.6	21.2	46 36.6	16.1	21.6	47 32.3	15.6	22.0
74	44 27.6	18.0	19.5	45 24.1	17.6	19.9	46 20.5	17.1	20.2	47 16.7	16.6	20.6
75	44 09.6	-19.0	18.2	45 06.5	-18.5	18.5	46 03.4	-18.1	18.8	47 00.1	-17.7	19.2
76	43 50.6	19.8	16.9	44 48.0	19.5	17.2	45 45.3	19.1	17.5	46 42.4	18.6	17.8
77	43 30.8	20.8	15.6	44 28.5	20.4	15.8	45 26.2	20.0	16.1	46 23.8	19.6	16.4
78	43 10.0	21.6	14.3	44 08.1	21.3	14.5	45 06.2	21.0	14.8	46 04.2	20.6	15.0
79	42 48.4	22.4	13.0	43 46.8	22.1	13.2	44 45.2	21.8	13.5	45 43.6	21.6	13.7
80	42 26.0	-23.3	11.8	43 24.7	-23.0	11.9	44 23.4	-22.8	12.1	45 22.0	-22.5	12.4
81	42 02.7	24.0	10.5	43 01.7	23.8	10.7	44 00.6	23.6	10.9	44 59.5	23.3	11.0
82	41 38.7	24.9	9.3	42 37.9	24.7	9.4	43 37.0	24.4	9.6	44 36.2	24.2	9.7
83	41 13.8	25.6	8.1	42 13.2	25.4	8.2	43 12.6	25.2	8.3	44 12.0	25.1	8.5
84	40 48.2	26.3	6.9	41 47.8	26.2	7.0	42 47.4	26.1	7.1	43 46.9	25.9	7.2
85	40 21.9	-27.0	5.7	41 21.6	-26.9	5.8	42 21.3	-26.8	5.9	43 21.0	-26.7	6.0
86	39 54.9	27.7	4.5	40 54.7	27.7	4.6	41 54.5	27.6	4.7	42 54.3	27.5	4.7
87	39 27.2	28.5	3.4	40 27.0	28.3	3.4	41 26.9	28.2	3.5	42 26.8	28.2	3.5
88	38 58.7	29.0	2.2	39 58.7	29.0	2.3	40 58.7	29.0	2.3	41 58.6	28.9	2.3
89	38 29.7	29.7	1.1	39 29.7	29.7	1.1	40 29.7	29.7	1.1	41 29.7	29.7	1.2
90	38 00.0	-30.3	0.0	39 00.0	-30.3	0.0	40 00.0	-30.3	0.0	41 00.0	-30.3	0.0
	38°			39°			40°			41°		

42° Hc	d	Z	43° Hc	d	Z	44° Hc	d	Z	45° Hc	d	Z	Dec.
° ′	′	°	° ′	′	°	° ′	′	°	° ′	′	°	°
21 48.8	+43.1	111.1	21 27.0	+43.8	111.5	21 04.8	+44.6	111.9	20 42.3	+45.3	112.2	0
22 31.9	42.9	110.4	22 10.8	43.7	110.8	21 49.4	44.4	111.1	21 27.6	45.0	111.5	1
23 14.8	42.7	109.6	22 54.5	43.4	110.0	22 33.8	44.2	110.4	22 12.6	45.0	110.8	2
23 57.5	42.5	108.8	23 37.9	43.3	109.3	23 18.0	43.9	109.7	22 57.6	44.7	110.1	3
24 40.0	42.3	108.1	24 21.2	43.0	108.5	24 01.9	43.8	108.9	23 42.3	44.5	109.3	4
25 22.3	+41.9	107.3	25 04.2	+42.8	107.7	24 45.7	+43.5	108.2	24 26.8	+44.3	108.6	5
26 04.2	41.8	106.5	25 47.0	42.5	107.0	25 29.2	43.3	107.4	25 11.1	44.0	107.9	6
26 46.0	41.4	105.7	26 29.5	42.3	106.2	26 12.5	43.1	106.7	25 55.1	43.8	107.1	7
27 27.4	41.2	104.9	27 11.8	41.9	105.4	26 55.6	42.8	105.9	26 38.9	43.6	106.4	8
28 08.6	40.8	104.1	27 53.7	41.7	104.6	27 38.4	42.5	105.1	27 22.5	43.3	105.6	9
28 49.4	+40.6	103.2	28 35.4	+41.4	103.8	28 20.9	+42.2	104.3	28 05.8	+43.1	104.8	10
29 30.0	40.2	102.4	29 16.8	41.1	102.9	29 03.1	42.0	103.5	28 48.9	42.8	104.0	11
30 10.2	39.9	101.5	29 57.9	40.8	102.1	29 45.1	41.6	102.7	29 31.7	42.4	103.2	12
30 50.1	39.6	100.7	30 38.7	40.5	101.2	30 26.7	41.3	101.8	30 14.1	42.2	102.4	13
31 29.7	39.1	99.8	31 19.2	40.0	100.4	31 08.0	41.0	101.0	30 56.3	41.9	101.6	14
32 08.8	+38.8	98.9	31 59.2	+39.8	99.5	31 49.0	+40.6	100.1	31 38.2	+41.5	100.7	15
32 47.6	38.4	98.0	32 39.0	39.3	98.6	32 29.6	40.3	99.3	32 19.7	41.1	99.9	16
33 26.0	38.0	97.1	33 18.3	38.9	97.7	33 09.9	39.9	98.4	33 00.8	40.8	99.0	17
34 04.0	37.6	96.1	33 57.2	38.6	96.8	33 49.8	39.5	97.5	33 41.6	40.5	98.1	18
34 41.6	37.1	95.2	34 35.8	38.1	95.9	34 29.3	39.1	96.6	34 22.1	40.0	97.2	19
35 18.7	+36.6	94.2	35 13.9	+37.7	94.9	35 08.4	+38.6	95.6	35 02.1	+39.6	96.3	20
35 55.3	36.2	93.3	35 51.6	37.2	94.0	35 47.0	38.2	94.7	35 41.7	39.2	95.4	21
36 31.5	35.7	92.3	36 28.8	36.7	93.0	36 25.2	37.8	93.7	36 20.9	38.8	94.5	22
37 07.2	35.2	91.3	37 05.5	36.2	92.0	37 03.0	37.2	92.8	36 59.7	38.2	93.5	23
37 42.4	34.6	90.2	37 41.7	35.7	91.0	37 40.2	36.8	91.8	37 37.9	37.8	92.6	24
38 17.0	+34.0	89.2	38 17.4	+35.2	90.0	38 17.0	+36.2	90.8	38 15.7	+37.3	91.6	25
38 51.0	33.5	88.2	38 52.6	34.6	89.0	38 53.2	35.7	89.8	38 53.0	36.8	90.6	26
39 24.5	32.9	87.1	39 27.2	34.0	87.9	39 28.9	35.2	88.7	39 29.8	36.3	89.6	27
39 57.4	32.3	86.0	40 01.2	33.4	86.8	40 04.1	34.5	87.7	40 06.1	35.6	88.5	28
40 29.7	31.7	84.9	40 34.6	32.8	85.7	40 38.6	34.0	86.6	40 41.7	35.1	87.5	29
41 01.4	+30.9	83.8	41 07.4	+32.2	84.6	41 12.6	+33.3	85.5	41 16.8	+34.5	86.4	30
41 32.3	30.3	82.6	41 39.6	31.4	83.5	41 45.9	32.6	84.4	41 51.3	33.8	85.3	31
42 02.6	29.6	81.5	42 11.0	30.8	82.4	42 18.5	32.0	83.3	42 25.1	33.2	84.2	32
42 32.2	28.8	80.3	42 41.8	30.1	81.2	42 50.5	31.3	82.1	42 58.3	32.5	83.0	33
43 01.0	28.1	79.1	43 11.9	29.3	80.0	43 21.8	30.6	81.0	43 30.8	31.8	81.9	34
43 29.1	+27.3	77.9	43 41.2	+28.6	78.8	43 52.4	+29.8	79.8	44 02.6	+31.0	80.7	35
43 56.4	26.5	76.7	44 09.8	27.8	77.6	44 22.2	29.0	78.6	44 33.6	30.3	79.5	36
44 22.9	25.7	75.4	44 37.6	26.9	76.4	44 51.2	28.3	77.3	45 03.9	29.5	78.3	37
44 48.6	24.8	74.1	45 04.5	26.1	75.1	45 19.5	27.4	76.1	45 33.4	28.7	77.1	38
45 13.4	24.0	72.9	45 30.6	25.3	73.8	45 46.9	26.5	74.8	46 02.1	27.8	75.8	39
45 37.4	+23.0	71.5	45 55.9	+24.3	72.5	46 13.4	+25.6	73.5	46 29.9	+27.0	74.5	40
46 00.4	22.1	70.2	46 20.2	23.4	71.2	46 39.0	24.8	72.2	46 56.9	26.0	73.2	41
46 22.5	21.1	68.9	46 43.6	22.5	69.9	47 03.8	23.8	70.9	47 22.9	25.2	71.9	42
46 43.6	20.2	67.5	47 06.1	21.5	68.5	47 27.6	22.8	69.5	47 48.1	24.1	70.5	43
47 03.8	19.1	66.1	47 27.6	20.5	67.1	47 50.4	21.8	68.1	48 12.2	23.2	69.2	44
47 22.9	+18.2	64.7	47 48.1	+19.4	65.7	48 12.2	+20.8	66.8	48 35.4	+22.2	67.8	45
47 41.1	17.0	63.3	48 07.5	18.4	64.3	48 33.0	19.8	65.3	48 57.6	21.1	66.4	46
47 58.1	16.0	61.9	48 25.9	17.4	62.9	48 52.8	18.7	63.9	49 18.7	20.0	65.0	47
48 14.1	15.0	60.5	48 43.3	16.2	61.4	49 11.5	17.6	62.5	49 38.7	19.0	63.5	48
48 29.1	13.7	59.0	48 59.5	15.1	60.0	49 29.1	16.4	61.0	49 57.7	17.8	62.0	49
48 42.8	+12.7	57.5	49 14.6	+14.0	58.5	49 45.5	+15.3	59.5	50 15.5	+16.7	60.5	50
48 55.5	11.5	56.0	49 28.6	12.8	57.0	50 00.8	14.2	58.0	50 32.2	15.4	59.0	51
49 07.0	10.3	54.5	49 41.4	11.6	55.5	50 15.0	12.9	56.5	50 47.6	14.3	57.5	52
49 17.3	9.2	53.0	49 53.0	10.4	54.0	50 27.9	11.7	55.0	51 01.9	13.0	56.0	53
49 26.5	7.9	51.5	50 03.4	9.2	52.5	50 39.6	10.5	53.4	51 14.9	11.8	54.4	54
49 34.4	+6.8	50.0	50 12.6	+8.0	50.9	50 50.1	+9.2	51.9	51 26.7	+10.6	52.8	55
49 41.2	5.5	48.5	50 20.6	6.7	49.4	50 59.3	8.0	50.3	51 37.3	9.2	51.3	56
49 46.7	4.3	46.9	50 27.3	5.5	47.8	51 07.3	6.7	48.7	51 46.5	7.9	49.7	57
49 51.0	3.1	45.4	50 32.8	4.2	46.2	51 14.0	5.4	47.1	51 54.4	6.7	48.1	58
49 54.1	1.8	43.8	50 37.0	3.0	44.7	51 19.4	4.1	45.5	52 01.1	5.3	46.4	59
49 55.9	+0.5	42.3	50 40.0	+1.6	43.1	51 23.5	+2.8	43.9	52 06.4	+3.9	44.8	60
49 56.4	-0.6	40.7	50 41.6	+0.4	41.5	51 26.3	1.5	42.3	52 10.3	2.6	43.2	61
49 55.8	2.0	39.2	50 42.0	-0.9	39.9	51 27.8	+0.1	40.7	52 12.9	+1.3	41.6	62
49 53.8	3.1	37.6	50 41.1	2.1	38.4	51 27.9	-1.1	39.1	52 14.2	-0.1	39.9	63
49 50.7	4.4	36.1	50 39.0	3.5	36.8	51 26.8	2.5	37.5	52 14.1	1.4	38.3	64
49 46.3	-5.7	34.5	50 35.5	-4.7	35.2	51 24.3	-3.8	35.9	52 12.7	-2.8	36.7	65
49 40.6	6.8	33.0	50 30.8	6.0	33.6	51 20.5	5.0	34.3	52 09.9	4.1	35.0	66
49 33.8	8.1	31.4	50 24.8	7.2	32.1	51 15.5	6.4	32.7	52 05.8	5.5	33.4	67
49 25.7	9.2	29.9	50 17.6	8.5	30.5	51 09.1	7.6	31.1	52 00.3	6.8	31.8	68
49 16.5	10.5	28.4	50 09.1	9.7	29.0	51 01.5	9.0	29.6	51 53.5	8.1	30.2	69
49 06.0	-11.6	26.9	49 59.4	10.9	27.4	50 52.5	-10.1	28.0	51 45.4	-9.4	28.6	70
48 54.4	12.7	25.4	49 48.5	12.1	25.9	50 42.4	11.4	26.4	51 36.0	10.7	27.0	71
48 41.7	13.9	23.9	49 36.4	13.2	24.4	50 31.0	12.7	24.9	51 25.3	12.0	25.4	72
48 27.8	15.0	22.4	49 23.2	14.5	22.9	50 18.3	13.8	23.4	51 13.3	13.2	23.8	73
48 12.8	16.1	21.0	49 08.7	15.5	21.4	50 04.5	15.0	21.8	51 00.1	14.4	22.3	74
47 56.7	-17.2	19.5	48 53.2	16.7	19.9	49 49.5	-16.2	20.3	50 45.7	-15.6	20.8	75
47 39.5	18.2	18.1	48 36.5	17.8	18.5	49 33.3	17.3	18.8	50 30.1	16.9	19.2	76
47 21.3	19.2	16.7	48 18.7	18.8	17.0	49 16.0	18.4	17.4	50 13.2	17.9	17.7	77
47 02.1	20.3	15.3	47 59.9	19.9	15.6	48 57.6	19.5	15.9	49 55.3	19.1	16.2	78
46 41.8	21.2	13.9	47 40.0	20.9	14.2	48 38.1	20.5	14.5	49 36.2	20.2	14.8	79
46 20.6	-22.2	12.6	47 19.1	-21.9	12.8	48 17.6	-21.6	13.1	49 16.0	-21.2	13.3	80
45 58.4	23.1	11.2	46 57.2	22.8	11.4	47 56.0	22.6	11.7	48 54.8	22.3	11.9	81
45 35.3	24.0	9.9	46 34.4	23.8	10.1	47 33.4	23.5	10.3	48 32.5	23.3	10.5	82
45 11.3	24.9	8.6	46 10.6	24.7	8.8	47 09.9	24.5	8.9	48 09.2	24.3	9.1	83
44 46.4	25.7	7.3	45 45.9	25.6	7.5	46 45.4	25.4	7.6	47 44.9	25.3	7.7	84
44 20.7	-26.6	6.1	45 20.3	-26.4	6.2	46 20.0	-26.3	6.3	47 19.6	-26.2	6.4	85
43 54.1	27.4	4.8	44 53.9	27.3	4.9	45 53.7	27.2	5.0	46 53.4	27.1	5.1	86
43 26.7	28.1	3.6	44 26.6	28.1	3.6	45 26.5	28.1	3.7	46 26.3	27.9	3.8	87
42 58.6	29.0	2.4	43 58.5	28.9	2.4	44 58.4	28.8	2.4	45 58.4	28.8	2.5	88
42 29.6	29.6	1.2	43 29.6	29.6	1.2	44 29.6	29.6	1.2	45 29.6	29.6	1.2	89
42 00.0	-30.3	0.0	43 00.0	-30.4	0.0	44 00.0	-30.4	0.0	45 00.0	-30.4	0.0	90
42°			43°			44°			45°			

60°, 300° L.H.A. LATITUDE SAME NAME AS DECLINATION

LATITUDE CONTRARY NAME TO DECLINATION   L.H.A. 60°, 300°

Dec.	38°			39°			40°			41°			42°			43°			44°			45°			Dec.
	Hc	d	Z	Hc	d	Z	Hc	d	Z	Hc	d	Z	Hc	d	Z	Hc	d	Z	Hc	d	Z	Hc	d	Z	
°	° ′	′	°	° ′	′	°	° ′	′	°	° ′	′	°	° ′	′	°	° ′	′	°	° ′	′	°	° ′	′	°	°
0	23 12.2	−40.3	109.6	22 51.9	−41.1	110.0	22 31.3	−41.9	110.4	22 10.2	−42.6	110.7	21 48.8	−43.4	111.1	21 27.0	−44.1	111.5	21 04.8	−44.8	111.9	20 42.3	−45.5	112.2	0
1	22 31.9	40.5	110.4	22 10.8	41.3	110.8	21 49.4	42.1	111.1	21 27.6	42.8	111.5	21 05.4	43.5	111.9	20 42.9	44.2	112.2	20 20.0	44.9	112.6	19 56.8	45.6	112.9	1
2	21 51.4	40.8	111.2	21 29.5	41.5	111.5	21 07.3	42.3	111.9	20 44.8	43.0	112.3	20 21.9	43.7	112.6	19 58.7	44.5	112.9	19 35.1	45.1	113.3	19 11.2	45.7	113.6	2
3	21 10.6	41.0	112.0	20 48.0	41.8	112.3	20 25.0	42.4	112.7	20 01.8	43.2	113.0	19 38.2	43.9	113.3	19 14.2	44.5	113.7	18 50.0	45.2	114.0	18 25.5	45.9	114.3	3
4	20 29.6	41.2	112.7	20 06.2	41.9	113.1	19 42.6	42.7	113.4	19 18.6	43.4	113.7	18 54.3	44.1	114.1	18 29.7	44.8	114.4	18 04.8	45.4	114.7	17 39.6	46.0	115.0	4
5	19 48.4	−41.4	113.5	19 24.3	−42.1	113.8	18 59.9	−42.8	114.2	18 35.2	−43.5	114.5	18 10.2	−44.2	114.8	17 44.9	−44.9	115.1	17 19.4	−45.6	115.3	16 53.6	−46.2	115.6	5
6	19 07.0	41.6	114.3	18 42.2	42.3	114.6	18 17.1	43.0	114.9	17 51.7	43.7	115.2	17 26.0	44.4	115.5	17 00.0	45.0	115.8	16 33.8	45.6	116.0	16 07.4	46.3	116.3	6
7	18 25.4	41.8	115.0	17 59.9	42.5	115.3	17 34.1	43.2	115.6	17 08.0	43.9	115.9	16 41.6	44.5	116.2	16 15.0	45.1	116.4	15 48.2	45.8	116.7	15 21.1	46.4	117.0	7
8	17 43.6	41.9	115.8	17 17.4	42.6	116.1	16 50.9	43.3	116.4	16 24.1	44.0	116.6	15 57.1	44.6	116.9	15 29.9	45.3	117.1	15 02.4	45.9	117.4	14 34.7	46.5	117.6	8
9	17 01.7	42.1	116.5	16 34.8	42.8	116.8	16 07.6	43.5	117.1	15 40.1	44.1	117.3	15 12.5	44.8	117.6	14 44.6	45.4	117.8	14 16.5	46.0	118.0	13 48.2	46.6	118.3	9
10	16 19.6	−42.3	117.3	15 52.0	−43.0	117.5	15 24.1	−43.6	117.8	14 56.0	−44.2	118.0	14 27.7	−44.9	118.3	13 59.2	−45.5	118.5	13 30.5	−46.1	118.7	13 01.6	−46.7	118.9	10
11	15 37.3	42.4	118.0	15 09.0	43.1	118.3	14 40.5	43.7	118.5	14 11.8	44.4	118.7	13 42.8	45.0	118.9	13 13.7	45.6	119.2	12 44.4	46.3	119.4	12 14.9	46.9	119.6	11
12	14 54.9	42.5	118.8	14 25.9	43.2	119.0	13 56.8	43.9	119.2	13 27.4	44.5	119.4	12 57.8	45.1	119.6	12 28.1	45.7	119.8	11 58.1	46.3	120.0	11 28.0	46.8	120.2	12
13	14 12.4	42.7	119.5	13 42.7	43.3	119.7	13 12.9	44.0	119.9	12 42.9	44.6	120.1	12 12.7	45.2	120.3	11 42.4	45.8	120.5	11 11.8	46.4	120.7	10 41.2	47.0	120.8	13
14	13 29.7	42.8	120.2	12 59.4	43.4	120.4	12 28.9	44.0	120.6	11 58.3	44.7	120.8	11 27.5	45.3	121.0	10 56.6	45.9	121.1	10 25.4	46.4	121.3	9 54.2	47.0	121.5	14
15	12 46.9	−42.9	120.9	12 16.0	−43.6	121.1	11 44.9	−44.2	121.3	11 13.6	−44.8	121.5	10 42.2	−45.4	121.6	10 10.7	−46.0	121.8	9 39.0	−46.6	121.9	9 07.2	−47.1	122.1	15
16	12 04.0	43.1	121.6	11 32.4	43.6	121.8	11 00.7	44.3	122.0	10 28.8	44.8	122.2	9 56.8	45.4	122.3	9 24.7	46.0	122.5	8 52.4	46.6	122.6	8 20.1	47.2	122.7	16
17	11 20.9	43.1	122.4	10 48.8	43.8	122.5	10 16.4	44.3	122.7	9 44.0	45.0	122.8	9 11.4	45.6	123.0	8 38.7	46.1	123.1	8 05.8	46.6	123.2	7 32.9	47.2	123.3	17
18	10 37.8	43.2	123.1	10 05.0	43.8	123.2	9 32.1	44.5	123.4	8 59.0	45.0	123.5	8 25.8	45.6	123.6	7 52.6	46.2	123.7	7 19.2	46.7	123.9	6 45.7	47.3	124.0	18
19	9 54.6	43.3	123.8	9 21.2	43.9	123.9	8 47.6	44.5	124.0	8 14.0	45.1	124.2	7 40.2	45.6	124.3	7 06.4	46.2	124.4	6 32.5	46.8	124.5	5 58.4	47.2	124.6	19
20	9 11.3	−43.4	124.5	8 37.3	−44.0	124.6	8 03.1	−44.5	124.7	7 28.9	−45.1	124.8	6 54.6	−45.7	124.9	6 20.2	−46.3	125.0	5 45.7	−46.8	125.1	5 11.2	−47.4	125.2	20
21	8 27.9	43.5	125.2	7 53.3	44.1	125.3	7 18.6	44.7	125.4	6 43.8	45.2	125.5	6 08.9	45.8	125.6	5 23.9	46.3	125.7	4 58.9	46.8	125.8	4 23.8	47.3	125.8	21
22	7 44.4	43.5	125.9	7 09.2	44.1	126.0	6 33.9	44.7	126.1	5 58.6	45.3	126.2	5 23.1	45.8	126.2	4 47.6	46.3	126.3	4 12.1	46.9	126.4	3 36.5	47.4	126.4	22
23	7 00.9	43.6	126.6	6 25.1	44.2	126.7	5 49.2	44.7	126.7	5 13.3	45.3	126.8	4 37.3	45.8	126.9	4 01.3	46.4	127.0	3 25.2	46.9	127.0	2 49.1	47.4	127.0	23
24	6 17.3	43.7	127.3	5 40.9	44.2	127.3	5 04.5	44.8	127.4	4 28.0	45.3	127.5	3 51.5	45.9	127.5	3 14.9	46.4	127.6	2 38.3	46.9	127.6	2 01.7	47.5	127.7	24
25	5 33.6	−43.7	127.9	4 56.7	−44.2	128.0	4 19.7	−44.8	128.1	3 42.7	−45.3	128.1	3 05.6	−45.9	128.2	2 28.5	−46.4	128.2	1 51.4	−46.9	128.3	1 14.2	−47.4	128.3	25
26	4 49.9	43.7	128.6	4 12.5	44.3	128.7	3 34.9	44.8	128.7	2 57.4	45.4	128.8	2 19.7	45.9	128.8	1 42.1	46.4	128.9	1 04.5	47.0	128.9	0 26.8	−47.4	128.9	26
27	4 06.2	43.8	129.3	3 28.2	44.4	129.4	2 50.1	44.9	129.4	2 12.0	45.4	129.4	1 33.8	45.9	129.5	0 55.7	46.4	129.5	0 17.5	−46.9	129.5	0 20.6	+47.5	50.5	27
28	3 22.4	43.8	130.0	2 43.8	44.3	130.0	2 05.2	44.9	130.1	1 26.6	45.4	130.1	0 47.9	45.9	130.1	0 09.3	−46.5	130.1	0 29.4	+46.9	49.9	1 08.1	47.4	49.9	28
29	2 38.6	43.8	130.7	1 59.5	44.4	130.7	1 20.3	44.8	130.7	0 41.2	−45.4	130.8	0 02.0	−45.9	130.8	0 37.2	+46.4	49.2	1 16.3	47.0	49.3	1 55.5	47.4	49.3	29
30	1 54.8	−43.8	131.4	1 15.1	−44.3	131.4	0 35.5	−44.9	131.4	0 04.2	+45.4	48.6	0 43.9	+45.9	48.6	1 23.6	+46.4	48.6	2 03.3	+46.9	48.6	2 42.9	+47.4	48.7	30
31	1 11.0	43.9	132.1	0 30.8	−44.4	132.1	0 09.4	+44.9	47.9	0 49.6	45.4	47.9	1 29.8	45.9	48.0	2 10.0	46.4	48.0	2 50.2	46.9	48.0	3 30.3	47.4	48.0	31
32	0 27.1	−43.9	132.7	0 13.6	+44.4	47.3	0 54.3	44.9	47.3	1 35.0	45.4	47.3	2 15.7	45.9	47.3	2 56.4	46.4	47.3	3 37.1	46.8	47.4	4 17.7	47.3	47.4	32
33	0 16.8	+43.8	46.6	0 58.0	44.4	46.6	1 39.2	44.9	46.6	2 20.4	45.4	46.6	3 01.6	45.9	46.7	3 42.8	46.3	46.7	4 23.9	46.8	46.8	5 05.0	47.3	46.8	33
34	1 00.6	43.8	45.9	1 42.4	44.3	45.9	2 24.1	44.8	45.9	3 05.8	45.4	46.0	3 47.5	45.8	46.0	4 29.1	46.4	46.1	5 10.7	46.8	46.1	5 52.3	47.3	46.2	34
35	1 44.4	+43.9	45.2	2 26.7	+44.3	45.2	3 08.9	+44.9	45.3	3 51.2	+45.3	45.3	4 33.3	+45.8	45.4	5 15.5	+46.2	45.4	5 57.5	+46.8	45.5	6 39.6	+47.2	45.6	35
36	2 28.3	43.8	44.5	3 11.0	44.3	44.6	3 53.8	44.8	44.6	4 36.5	45.3	44.7	5 19.1	45.8	44.7	6 01.7	46.3	44.8	6 44.3	46.7	44.9	7 26.8	47.1	45.0	36
37	3 12.1	43.8	43.8	3 55.3	44.3	43.9	4 38.6	44.7	43.9	5 21.8	45.2	44.0	6 04.9	45.7	44.1	6 48.0	46.1	44.1	7 31.0	46.6	44.2	8 13.9	47.1	44.3	37
38	3 55.9	43.7	43.2	4 39.6	44.3	43.2	5 23.3	44.7	43.3	6 07.0	45.2	43.3	6 50.6	45.7	43.4	7 34.1	46.2	43.5	8 17.6	46.6	43.6	9 01.0	47.1	43.7	38
39	4 39.6	43.7	42.5	5 23.9	44.1	42.5	6 08.0	44.7	42.6	6 52.2	45.1	42.7	7 36.3	45.6	42.8	8 20.3	46.0	42.9	9 04.2	46.5	43.0	9 48.1	47.0	43.1	39
40	5 23.3	+43.7	41.8	6 08.0	+44.2	41.9	6 52.7	+44.6	41.9	7 37.3	+45.1	42.0	8 21.9	+45.5	42.1	9 06.3	+46.0	42.2	9 50.7	+46.5	42.3	10 35.1	+46.9	42.4	40
41	6 07.0	43.6	41.1	6 52.2	44.1	41.2	7 37.3	44.6	41.3	8 22.4	45.0	41.3	9 07.4	45.5	41.5	9 52.3	46.0	41.6	10 37.2	46.4	41.7	11 22.0	46.8	41.8	41
42	6 50.6	43.5	40.4	7 36.3	44.0	40.5	8 21.9	44.4	40.6	9 07.4	44.9	40.7	9 52.9	45.4	40.8	10 38.3	45.8	40.9	11 23.6	46.2	41.0	12 08.8	46.7	41.2	42
43	7 34.1	43.5	39.7	8 20.3	43.9	39.8	9 06.3	44.4	39.9	9 52.3	44.9	40.0	10 38.3	45.3	40.1	11 24.1	45.7	40.2	12 09.8	46.2	40.4	12 55.5	46.6	40.5	43
44	8 17.6	43.4	39.0	9 04.2	43.9	39.1	9 50.7	44.4	39.2	10 37.2	44.8	39.3	11 23.6	45.2	39.5	12 09.8	45.7	39.6	12 56.0	46.1	39.7	13 42.1	46.6	39.9	44
45	9 01.0	+43.4	38.3	9 48.1	+43.8	38.4	10 35.1	+44.2	38.5	11 22.0	+44.6	38.7	12 08.8	+45.1	38.8	12 55.5	+45.5	38.9	13 42.1	+46.0	39.1	14 28.7	+46.4	39.2	45
46	9 44.4	43.2	37.6	10 31.9	43.7	37.7	11 19.3	44.1	37.8	12 06.6	44.6	38.0	12 53.9	45.0	38.1	13 41.0	45.5	38.3	14 28.1	45.9	38.4	15 15.1	46.3	38.6	46
47	10 27.6	43.2	36.9	11 15.6	43.6	37.0	12 03.4	44.0	37.2	12 51.2	44.5	37.3	13 38.9	44.9	37.4	14 26.5	45.3	37.6	15 14.0	45.7	37.7	16 01.4	46.2	37.9	47
48	11 10.8	43.0	36.2	11 59.2	43.4	36.3	12 47.4	44.0	36.5	13 35.7	44.3	36.6	14 23.8	44.8	36.7	15 11.8	45.2	36.9	15 59.7	45.7	37.1	16 47.6	46.0	37.3	48
49	11 53.8	43.0	35.5	12 42.6	43.4	35.6	13 31.4	43.8	35.8	14 20.0	44.2	35.9	15 08.6	44.6	36.1	15 57.0	45.1	36.2	16 45.4	45.5	36.4	17 33.6	45.9	36.6	49
50	12 36.8	+42.8	34.8	13 26.0	+43.3	34.9	14 15.2	+43.7	35.1	15 04.2	+44.1	35.2	15 53.2	+44.5	35.4	16 42.1	+44.9	35.5	17 30.9	+45.3	35.7	18 19.5	+45.8	35.9	50
51	13 19.6	42.7	34.1	14 09.3	43.1	34.2	14 58.9	43.5	34.3	15 48.3	44.0	34.5	16 37.7	44.4	34.7	17 27.0	44.8	34.8	18 16.2	45.2	35.0	19 05.3	45.6	35.2	51
52	14 02.3	42.6	33.3	14 52.4	43.0	33.5	15 42.4	43.4	33.6	16 32.3	43.8	33.8	17 22.1	44.3	34.0	18 11.8	44.7	34.1	19 01.4	45.1	34.3	19 50.9	45.5	34.5	52
53	14 44.9	42.4	32.6	15 35.4	42.8	32.8	16 25.8	43.3	32.9	17 16.1	43.7	33.1	18 06.4	44.0	33.3	18 56.5	44.5	33.4	19 46.5	44.9	33.6	20 36.4	45.3	33.8	53
54	15 27.3	42.3	31.9	16 18.2	42.7	32.0	17 09.1	43.1	32.2	17 59.8	43.5	32.4	18 50.4	43.9	32.5	19 41.0	44.3	32.7	20 31.4	44.7	32.9	21 21.7	45.1	33.1	54
55	16 09.6	+42.2	31.1	17 00.9	+42.6	31.3	17 52.2	+42.9	31.5	18 43.3	+43.3	31.6	19 34.3	+43.8	31.8	20 25.3	+44.1	32.0	21 16.1	+44.5	32.2	22 06.8	+44.9	32.4	55
56	16 51.8	42.0	30.4	17 43.5	42.4	30.6	18 35.1	42.8	30.7	19 26.6	43.2	30.9	20 18.1	43.5	31.1	21 09.4	43.9	31.3	22 00.6	44.4	31.5	22 51.7	44.8	31.7	56
57	17 33.8	41.8	29.7	18 25.9	42.2	29.8	19 17.9	42.6	30.0	20 09.8	43.0	30.2	21 01.6	43.4	30.4	21 53.3	43.8	30.6	22 45.0	44.1	30.8	23 36.5	44.5	31.0	57
58	18 15.6	41.6	28.9	19 08.1	42.0	29.1	20 00.5	42.3	29.2	20 52.8	42.7	29.4	21 45.0	43.1	29.6	22 37.1	43.5	29.8	23 29.1	43.9	30.0	24 21.0	44.3	30.2	58
59	18 57.2	41.4	28.1	19 50.1	41.8	28.3	20 42.8	42.2	28.5	21 35.5	42.6	28.7	22 28.1	43.0	28.9	23 20.6	43.4	29.1	24 13.0	43.7	29.3	25 05.3	44.1	29.5	59
60	19 38.6	+41.3	27.4	20 31.9	+41.6	27.5	21 25.0	+42.0	27.7	22 18.1	+42.4	27.9	23 11.1	+42.7	28.1	24 04.0	+43.1	28.3	24 56.7	+43.5	28.5	25 49.4	+43.8	28.8	60
61	20 19.9	41.0	26.6	21 13.5	41.4	26.8	22 07.0	41.8	26.9	23 00.5	42.1	27.1	23 53.8	42.5	27.3	24 47.1	42.8	27.5	25 40.2	43.3	27.8	26 33.2	43.7	28.0	61
62	21 00.9	40.9	25.8	21 54.9	41.2	26.0	22 48.8	41.5	26.2	23 42.6	41.9	26.4	24 36.3	42.3	26.6	25 29.9	42.7	26.8	26 23.5	42.9	27.0	27 16.9	43.3	27.2	62
63	21 41.8	40.6	25.0	22 36.1	40.9	25.2	23 30.3	41.3	25.4	24 24.5	41.7	25.6	25 18.6	42.0	25.8	26 12.6	42.3	26.0	27 06.4	42.8	26.2	28 00.2	43.1	26.4	63
64	22 22.4	40.3	24.2	23 17.0	40.8	24.4	24 11.6	41.1	24.6	25 06.2	41.4	24.8	26 00.6	41.7	25.0	26 54.9	42.1	25.2	27 49.2	42.4	25.4	28 43.3	42.8	25.7	64
65	23 02.7	+40.2	23.4	23 57.8	+40.4	23.6	24 52.7	+40.8	23.8	25 47.6	+41.1	24.0	26 42.3	+41.5	24.2	27 37.0	+41.8	24.4	28 31.6	+42.2	24.6	29 26.1	+42.5	24.9	65
66	23 42.9	39.8	22.6	24 38.2	40.2	22.8	25 33.5	40.5	23.0	26 28.7	40.8	23.2	27 23.8	41.2	23.4	28 18.8	41.6	23.6	29 13.8	41.8	23.8	30 08.6	42.2	24.0	66
67	24 22.7	39.6	21.8	25 18.4	39.9	22.0	26 14.0	40.3	22.2	27 09.5	40.6	22.4	28 05.0	40.9	22.6	29 00.4	41.2	22.8	29 55.6	41.6	23.0	30 50.8	41.9	23.2	67
68	25 02.3	39.4	21.0	25 58.3	39.7	21.2	26 54.3	39.9	21.3	27 50.1	40.3	21.5	28 45.9	40.6	21.7	29 41.6	40.9	21.9	30 37.2	41.2	22.1	31 32.7	41.6	22.4	68
69	25 41.7	39.0	20.1	26 38.0	39.3	20.3	27 34.2	39.6	20.5	28 30.4	39.9	20.7	29 26.5	40.2	20.9	30 22.5	40.6	21.1	31 18.4	40.9	21.3	32 14.3	41.2	21.5	69
70	26 20.7	+38.7	19.3	27 17.3	+39.0	19.5	28 13.8	+39.4	19.6	29 10.3	+39.6	19.8	30 06.7	+39.9	20.0	31 03.1	+40.2	20.2	31 59.3	+40.6	20.4	32 55.5	+40.9	20.7	70
71	26 59.4	38.5	18.4	27 56.3	38.7	18.6	28 53.2	38.9	18.8	29 49.9	39.3	19.0	30 46.6	39.6	19.2	31 43.3	39.9	19.4	32 39.9	40.1	19.6	33 36.4	40.4	19.8	71
72	27 37.9	38.1	17.6	28 35.0	38.4	17.7	29 32.1	38.7	17.9	30 29.2	38.9	18.1	31 26.2	39.2	18.3	32 23.2	39.4	18.5	33 20.0	39.8	18.7	34 16.8	40.1	18.9	72
73	28 16.0	37.7	16.7	29 13.4	38.0	16.9	30 10.8	38.3	17.0	31 08.1	38.6	17.2	32 05.4	38.8	17.4	33 02.6	39.2	17.6	33 59.8	39.4	17.8	34 56.9	39.7	18.0	73
74	28 53.7	37.4	15.8	29 51.4	37.7	16.0	30 49.1	37.9	16.1	31 46.7	38.2	16.3	32 44.2	38.5	16.5	33 41.8	38.7	16.7	34 39.2	39.0	16.9	35 36.6	39.2	17.1	74
75	29 31.1	+37.1	14.9	30 29.1	+37.3	15.1	31 27.0	+37.5	15.2	32 24.9	+37.7	15.4	33 22.7	+38.0	15.6	34 20.5	+38.2	15.8	35 18.2	+38.5	15.9	36 15.8	+38.8	16.1	75
76	30 08.2	36.6	14.0	31 06.4	36.9	14.2	32 04.5	37.1	14.3	33 02.6	37.4	14.5	34 00.7	37.6	14.6	34 58.7	37.9	14.8	35 56.7	38.1	15.0	36 54.6	38.4	15.2	76
77	30 44.8	36.3	13.1	31 43.3	36.4	13.2	32 41.6	36.7	13.4	33 40.0	36.9	13.5	34 38.3	37.2	13.7	35 36.6	37.4	13.9	36 34.8	37.6	14.0	37 33.0	37.9	14.2	77
78	31 21.1	35.9	12.2	32 19.7	36.1	12.3	33 18.3	36.3	12.4	34 16.9	36.5	12.6	35 15.5	36.7	12.7	36 14.0	36.9	12.9	37 12.4	37.2	13.1	38 10.9	37.3	13.2	78
79	31 57.0	35.4	11.2	32 55.8	35.6	11.4	33 54.6	35.8	11.5	34 53.4	36.0	11.6	35 52.2	36.2	11.8	36 50.9	36.4	11.9	37 49.6	36.6	12.1	38 48.2	36.9	12.2	79
80	32 32.4	+35.0	10.3	33 31.4	+35.2	10.4	34 30.4	+35.4	10.5	35 29.4	+35.6	10.6	36 28.4	+35.7	10.8	37 27.3	+35.9	10.9	38 26.2	+36.1	11.1	39 25.1	+36.3	11.2	80
81	33 07.4	34.6	9.3	34 06.6	34.7	9.4	35 05.8	34.9	9.5	36 05.0	35.0	9.7	37 04.1	35.2	9.8	38 03.2	35.4	9.9	39 02.3	35.6	10.0	40 01.4	35.7	10.2	81
82	33 42.0	34.0	8.3	34 41.3	34.2	8.4	35 40.7	34.3	8.5	36 40.0	34.5	8.6	37 39.3	34.7	8.8	38 38.6	34.8	8.9	39 37.9	35.0	9.0	40 37.1	35.2	9.1	82
83	34 16.0	33.6	7.3	35 15.5	33.8	7.4	36 15.0	33.9	7.5	37 14.5	34.0	7.6	38 14.0	34.1	7.7	39 13.4	34.3	7.8	40 12.9	34.4	7.9	41 12.3	34.5	8.1	83
84	34 49.6	33.1	6.3	35 49.3	33.2	6.4	36 48.9	33.3	6.5	37 48.5	33.4	6.6	38 48.1	33.5	6.7	39 47.7	33.6	6.8	40 47.3	33.7	6.9	41 46.8	33.9	7.0	84
85	35 22.7	+32.6	5.3	36 22.5	+32.6	5.4	37 22.2	+32.8	5.4	38 21.9	+32.9	5.5	39 21.6	+33.0	5.6	40 21.3	+33.1	5.7	41 21.0	+33.2	5.8	42 20.7	+33.3	5.9	85
86	35 55.3	32.0	4.3	36 55.1	32.1	4.3	37 55.0	32.1	4.4	38 54.8	32.2	4.5	39 54.6	32.3	4.5	40 54.4	32.4	4.6	41 54.2	32.5	4.7	42 54.0	32.6	4.7	86
87	36 27.3	31.5	3.2	37 27.2	31.6	3.3	38 27.1	31.6	3.3	39 27.0	31.7	3.4	40 26.9	31.7	3.4	41 26.8	31.8	3.5	42 26.7	31.8	3.5	43 26.6	31.9	3.6	87
88	36 58.8	30.9	2.2	37 58.8	30.9	2.2	38 58.7	31.0	2.2	39 58.7	31.0	2.3	40 58.6	31.1	2.3	41 58.6	31.0	2.3	42 58.5	31.1	2.4	43 58.5	31.1	2.4	88
89	37 29.7	30.3	1.1	38 29.7	30.3	1.1	39 29.7	30.3	1.1	40 29.7	30.3	1.1	41 29.7	30.3	1.2	42 29.6	30.4	1.2	43 29.6	30.4	1.2	44 29.6	30.4	1.2	89
90	38 00.0	+29.7	0.0	39 00.0	+29.7	0.0	40 00.0	+29.7	0.0	41 00.0	+29.7	0.0	42 00.0	+29.6	0.0	43 00.0	+29.6	0.0	44 00.0	+29.6	0.0	45 00.0	+29.6	0.0	90
	38°			39°			40°			41°			42°			43°			44°			45°			

S. Lat. { L.H.A. greater than 180°......Zn=180°−Z
L.H.A. less than 180°............Zn=180°+Z

LATITUDE SAME NAME AS DECLINATION   L.H.A. 120°, 240°

INTERPOLATION TABLE

Dec. Inc.	Tens 10′	20′	30′	40′	50′	Decimals	Units 0′	1′	2′	3′	4′	5′	6′	7′	8′	9′	Double Second Diff. and Corr.
28.0	4.6	9.3	14.0	18.6	23.3	.0	0.0	0.5	0.9	1.4	1.9	2.4	2.8	3.3	3.8	4.3	0.8 (0.1) 2.4 (0.2) 4.0 (0.3) 5.6 (0.4) 7.2 (0.5) 8.8 (0.6) 10.4 (0.7) 12.0 (0.8) 13.6 (0.9) 15.2 (1.0) 16.8 (1.1) 18.4 (1.2) 20.0 (1.3) 21.6 (1.4) 23.2 (1.5) 24.8 (1.6) 26.4 (1.7) 28.0 (1.8) 29.6 (1.9) 31.2 (2.0) 32.8 (2.1) 34.4
28.1	4.7	9.3	14.0	18.7	23.4	.1	0.0	0.5	1.0	1.5	1.9	2.4	2.9	3.4	3.8	4.3	
28.2	4.7	9.4	14.1	18.8	23.5	.2	0.1	0.6	1.0	1.5	2.0	2.5	2.9	3.4	3.9	4.4	
28.3	4.7	9.4	14.1	18.9	23.6	.3	0.1	0.6	1.1	1.6	2.0	2.5	3.0	3.5	3.9	4.4	
28.4	4.7	9.5	14.2	18.9	23.7	.4	0.2	0.7	1.1	1.6	2.1	2.6	3.0	3.5	4.0	4.5	
28.5	4.8	9.5	14.3	19.0	23.8	.5	0.2	0.7	1.2	1.7	2.1	2.6	3.1	3.6	4.0	4.5	
28.6	4.8	9.5	14.3	19.1	23.8	.6	0.3	0.8	1.2	1.7	2.2	2.7	3.1	3.6	4.1	4.6	
28.7	4.8	9.6	14.4	19.2	23.9	.7	0.3	0.8	1.3	1.8	2.2	2.7	3.2	3.7	4.1	4.6	
28.8	4.8	9.6	14.4	19.2	24.0	.8	0.4	0.9	1.3	1.8	2.3	2.8	3.2	3.7	4.2	4.7	
28.9	4.9	9.7	14.5	19.3	24.1	.9	0.4	0.9	1.4	1.9	2.3	2.8	3.3	3.8	4.2	4.7	
29.0	4.8	9.6	14.5	19.3	24.1	.0	0.0	0.5	1.0	1.5	2.0	2.5	2.9	3.4	3.9	4.4	
29.1	4.8	9.7	14.5	19.4	24.2	.1	0.0	0.5	1.0	1.5	2.0	2.5	3.0	3.5	4.0	4.5	
29.2	4.8	9.7	14.6	19.4	24.3	.2	0.1	0.6	1.1	1.6	2.1	2.6	3.0	3.5	4.0	4.5	
29.3	4.9	9.8	14.6	19.5	24.4	.3	0.1	0.6	1.1	1.6	2.1	2.6	3.1	3.6	4.1	4.6	
29.4	4.9	9.8	14.7	19.6	24.5	.4	0.2	0.7	1.2	1.7	2.2	2.7	3.1	3.6	4.1	4.6	
29.5	4.9	9.8	14.8	19.7	24.6	.5	0.2	0.7	1.2	1.7	2.2	2.7	3.2	3.7	4.2	4.7	
29.6	4.9	9.9	14.8	19.7	24.7	.6	0.3	0.8	1.3	1.8	2.3	2.8	3.2	3.7	4.2	4.7	
29.7	5.0	9.9	14.9	19.8	24.8	.7	0.3	0.8	1.3	1.8	2.3	2.8	3.3	3.8	4.3	4.8	
29.8	5.0	10.0	14.9	19.9	24.9	.8	0.4	0.9	1.4	1.9	2.4	2.9	3.3	3.8	4.3	4.8	
29.9	5.0	10.0	15.0	20.0	25.0	.9	0.4	0.9	1.4	1.9	2.4	2.9	3.4	3.9	4.4	4.9	
30.0	5.0	10.0	15.0	20.0	25.0	.0	0.0	0.5	1.0	1.5	2.0	2.5	3.0	3.6	4.1	4.6	0.8 (0.1) 2.4 (0.2) 4.0 (0.3) 5.6 (0.4) 7.2 (0.5) 8.8 (0.6) 10.4 (0.7) 12.0 (0.8) 13.6 (0.9) 15.2 (1.0) 16.8 (1.1) 18.4 (1.2) 20.0 (1.3) 21.6 (1.4) 23.2 (1.5) 24.8 (1.6) 26.4 (1.7) 28.0 (1.8) 29.6 (1.9) 31.2 (2.0) 32.8 (2.1) 34.4
30.1	5.0	10.0	15.0	20.0	25.1	.1	0.1	0.6	1.1	1.6	2.1	2.6	3.1	3.6	4.1	4.6	
30.2	5.0	10.0	15.1	20.1	25.1	.2	0.1	0.6	1.1	1.6	2.1	2.6	3.2	3.7	4.2	4.7	
30.3	5.0	10.1	15.1	20.2	25.2	.3	0.2	0.7	1.2	1.7	2.2	2.7	3.2	3.7	4.2	4.7	
30.4	5.1	10.1	15.2	20.3	25.3	.4	0.2	0.7	1.2	1.7	2.2	2.7	3.3	3.8	4.3	4.8	
30.5	5.1	10.2	15.3	20.3	25.4	.5	0.3	0.8	1.3	1.8	2.3	2.8	3.3	3.8	4.3	4.8	
30.6	5.1	10.2	15.3	20.4	25.5	.6	0.3	0.8	1.3	1.8	2.3	2.8	3.4	3.9	4.4	4.9	
30.7	5.1	10.3	15.4	20.5	25.6	.7	0.4	0.9	1.4	1.9	2.4	2.9	3.4	3.9	4.4	4.9	
30.8	5.2	10.3	15.4	20.6	25.7	.8	0.4	0.9	1.4	1.9	2.4	2.9	3.5	4.0	4.5	5.0	
30.9	5.2	10.3	15.5	20.6	25.8	.9	0.5	1.0	1.5	2.0	2.5	3.0	3.5	4.0	4.5	5.0	
31.0	5.1	10.3	15.5	20.6	25.8	.0	0.0	0.5	1.0	1.6	2.1	2.6	3.1	3.7	4.2	4.7	
31.1	5.2	10.3	15.5	20.7	25.9	.1	0.1	0.6	1.1	1.6	2.2	2.7	3.2	3.7	4.3	4.8	
31.2	5.2	10.4	15.6	20.8	26.0	.2	0.1	0.6	1.2	1.7	2.2	2.7	3.3	3.8	4.3	4.8	
31.3	5.2	10.4	15.6	20.9	26.1	.3	0.2	0.7	1.2	1.7	2.3	2.8	3.3	3.8	4.4	4.9	
31.4	5.2	10.5	15.7	20.9	26.2	.4	0.2	0.7	1.3	1.8	2.3	2.8	3.4	3.9	4.4	4.9	
31.5	5.3	10.5	15.8	21.0	26.3	.5	0.3	0.8	1.3	1.8	2.4	2.9	3.4	3.9	4.5	5.0	
31.6	5.3	10.5	15.8	21.1	26.3	.6	0.3	0.8	1.4	1.9	2.4	2.9	3.5	4.0	4.5	5.0	
31.7	5.3	10.6	15.9	21.2	26.4	.7	0.4	0.9	1.4	1.9	2.5	3.0	3.5	4.0	4.6	5.1	
31.8	5.3	10.6	15.9	21.2	26.5	.8	0.4	0.9	1.5	2.0	2.5	3.0	3.6	4.1	4.6	5.1	
31.9	5.4	10.7	16.0	21.3	26.6	.9	0.5	1.0	1.5	2.0	2.6	3.1	3.6	4.1	4.7	5.2	
32.0	5.3	10.6	16.0	21.3	26.6	.0	0.0	0.5	1.1	1.6	2.2	2.7	3.2	3.8	4.3	4.9	0.8 (0.1) 2.4 (0.2) 4.0 (0.3) 5.7 (0.4) 7.3 (0.5) 8.9 (0.6) 10.5 (0.7) 12.1 (0.8) 13.7 (0.9) 15.4 (1.0) 17.0 (1.1) 18.6 (1.2) 20.2 (1.3) 21.8 (1.4) 23.4 (1.5) 25.1 (1.6) 26.7 (1.7) 28.3 (1.8) 29.9 (1.9) 31.5 (2.0) 33.1 (2.1) 34.7
32.1	5.3	10.7	16.0	21.4	26.7	.1	0.1	0.6	1.1	1.7	2.2	2.8	3.3	3.8	4.4	4.9	
32.2	5.3	10.7	16.1	21.4	26.8	.2	0.1	0.6	1.2	1.7	2.3	2.8	3.4	3.9	4.4	5.0	
32.3	5.4	10.8	16.1	21.5	26.9	.3	0.2	0.7	1.2	1.8	2.3	2.9	3.4	4.0	4.5	5.0	
32.4	5.4	10.8	16.2	21.6	27.0	.4	0.2	0.8	1.3	1.8	2.4	2.9	3.5	4.0	4.5	5.1	
32.5	5.4	10.8	16.3	21.7	27.1	.5	0.3	0.8	1.4	1.9	2.4	3.0	3.5	4.1	4.6	5.1	
32.6	5.4	10.9	16.3	21.7	27.2	.6	0.3	0.9	1.4	1.9	2.5	3.0	3.6	4.1	4.7	5.2	
32.7	5.5	10.9	16.4	21.8	27.3	.7	0.4	0.9	1.5	2.0	2.5	3.1	3.6	4.2	4.7	5.3	
32.8	5.5	11.0	16.4	21.9	27.4	.8	0.4	1.0	1.5	2.1	2.6	3.1	3.7	4.2	4.8	5.3	
32.9	5.5	11.0	16.5	22.0	27.5	.9	0.5	1.0	1.6	2.1	2.7	3.2	3.7	4.3	4.8	5.4	
33.0	5.5	11.0	16.5	22.0	27.5	.0	0.0	0.6	1.1	1.7	2.2	2.8	3.3	3.9	4.5	5.0	
33.1	5.5	11.0	16.5	22.0	27.6	.1	0.1	0.6	1.2	1.7	2.3	2.8	3.4	4.0	4.5	5.1	
33.2	5.5	11.0	16.6	22.1	27.6	.2	0.1	0.7	1.2	1.8	2.3	2.9	3.5	4.0	4.6	5.1	
33.3	5.5	11.1	16.6	22.2	27.7	.3	0.2	0.7	1.3	1.8	2.4	3.0	3.5	4.1	4.6	5.2	
33.4	5.6	11.1	16.7	22.3	27.8	.4	0.2	0.8	1.3	1.9	2.5	3.0	3.6	4.1	4.7	5.2	
33.5	5.6	11.2	16.8	22.3	27.9	.5	0.3	0.8	1.4	2.0	2.5	3.1	3.6	4.2	4.7	5.3	
33.6	5.6	11.2	16.8	22.4	28.0	.6	0.3	0.9	1.5	2.0	2.6	3.1	3.7	4.2	4.8	5.4	
33.7	5.6	11.3	16.9	22.5	28.1	.7	0.4	0.9	1.5	2.1	2.6	3.2	3.7	4.3	4.9	5.4	
33.8	5.7	11.3	16.9	22.6	28.2	.8	0.4	1.0	1.6	2.1	2.7	3.2	3.8	4.4	4.9	5.5	
33.9	5.7	11.3	17.0	22.6	28.3	.9	0.5	1.1	1.6	2.2	2.7	3.3	3.9	4.4	5.0	5.5	
34.0	5.6	11.3	17.0	22.6	28.3	.0	0.0	0.6	1.1	1.7	2.3	2.9	3.4	4.0	4.6	5.2	0.8 (0.1) 2.5 (0.2) 4.1 (0.3) 5.8 (0.4) 7.4 (0.5) 9.1 (0.6) 10.7 (0.7) 12.3 (0.8) 14.0 (0.9) 15.6 (1.0) 17.3 (1.1) 18.9 (1.2) 20.6 (1.3) 22.2 (1.4) 23.9 (1.5) 25.5 (1.6) 27.2 (1.7) 28.8 (1.8) 30.4 (1.9) 32.1 (2.0) 33.7 (2.1) 35.4
34.1	5.7	11.3	17.0	22.7	28.4	.1	0.1	0.6	1.2	1.8	2.4	2.9	3.5	4.1	4.7	5.2	
34.2	5.7	11.4	17.1	22.8	28.5	.2	0.1	0.7	1.3	1.8	2.4	3.0	3.6	4.1	4.7	5.3	
34.3	5.7	11.4	17.1	22.9	28.6	.3	0.2	0.7	1.3	1.9	2.5	3.0	3.6	4.2	4.8	5.3	
34.4	5.7	11.5	17.2	22.9	28.7	.4	0.2	0.8	1.4	2.0	2.5	3.1	3.7	4.3	4.8	5.4	
34.5	5.8	11.5	17.3	23.0	28.8	.5	0.3	0.9	1.4	2.0	2.6	3.2	3.7	4.3	4.9	5.5	
34.6	5.8	11.5	17.3	23.1	28.8	.6	0.3	0.9	1.5	2.1	2.6	3.2	3.8	4.4	4.9	5.5	
34.7	5.8	11.6	17.4	23.2	28.9	.7	0.4	1.0	1.6	2.1	2.7	3.3	3.9	4.4	5.0	5.6	
34.8	5.8	11.6	17.4	23.2	29.0	.8	0.5	1.0	1.6	2.2	2.8	3.3	3.9	4.5	5.1	5.6	
34.9	5.9	11.7	17.5	23.3	29.1	.9	0.5	1.1	1.7	2.2	2.8	3.4	4.0	4.5	5.1	5.7	
35.0	5.8	11.6	17.5	23.3	29.1	.0	0.0	0.6	1.2	1.8	2.4	3.0	3.5	4.1	4.7	5.3	
35.1	5.8	11.7	17.5	23.4	29.2	.1	0.1	0.7	1.2	1.8	2.4	3.0	3.6	4.2	4.8	5.4	
35.2	5.8	11.7	17.6	23.4	29.3	.2	0.1	0.7	1.3	1.9	2.5	3.1	3.7	4.3	4.9	5.4	
35.3	5.9	11.8	17.6	23.5	29.4	.3	0.2	0.8	1.4	2.0	2.5	3.1	3.7	4.3	4.9	5.5	
35.4	5.9	11.8	17.7	23.6	29.5	.4	0.2	0.8	1.4	2.0	2.6	3.2	3.8	4.4	5.0	5.6	
35.5	5.9	11.8	17.8	23.7	29.6	.5	0.3	0.9	1.5	2.1	2.7	3.3	3.8	4.4	5.0	5.6	
35.6	5.9	11.9	17.8	23.7	29.7	.6	0.4	0.9	1.5	2.1	2.7	3.3	3.9	4.5	5.1	5.7	
35.7	6.0	11.9	17.9	23.8	29.8	.7	0.4	1.0	1.6	2.2	2.8	3.4	4.0	4.6	5.1	5.7	
35.8	6.0	12.0	17.9	23.9	29.9	.8	0.5	1.1	1.7	2.2	2.8	3.4	4.0	4.6	5.2	5.8	
35.9	6.0	12.0	18.0	24.0	30.0	.9	0.5	1.1	1.7	2.3	2.9	3.5	4.1	4.7	5.3	5.9	
	10′	20′	30′	40′	50′		0′	1′	2′	3′	4′	5′	6′	7′	8′	9′	

Dec. Inc.	Tens 10′	20′	30′	40′	50′	Decimals	Units 0′	1′	2′	3′	4′	5′	6′	7′	8′	9′	Double Second Diff. and Corr.
36.0	6.0	12.0	18.0	24.0	30.0	.0	0.0	0.6	1.2	1.8	2.4	3.0	3.6	4.3	4.9	5.5	0.8 (0.1) 2.5 (0.2) 4.2 (0.3) 5.9 (0.4) 7.6 (0.5) 9.3 (0.6) 11.0 (0.7) 12.7 (0.8) 14.4 (0.9) 16.1 (1.0) 17.8 (1.1) 19.5 (1.2) 21.2 (1.3) 22.8 (1.4) 24.5 (1.5) 26.2 (1.6) 27.9 (1.7) 29.6 (1.8) 31.3 (1.9) 33.0 (2.0) 34.7
36.1	6.0	12.0	18.0	24.0	30.1	.1	0.1	0.7	1.3	1.9	2.5	3.1	3.7	4.3	4.9	5.5	
36.2	6.0	12.0	18.1	24.1	30.1	.2	0.1	0.7	1.3	1.9	2.6	3.2	3.8	4.4	5.0	5.6	
36.3	6.0	12.1	18.1	24.2	30.2	.3	0.2	0.8	1.4	2.0	2.6	3.2	3.8	4.4	5.0	5.7	
36.4	6.1	12.1	18.2	24.3	30.3	.4	0.2	0.9	1.5	2.1	2.7	3.3	3.9	4.5	5.1	5.7	
36.5	6.1	12.2	18.3	24.3	30.4	.5	0.3	0.9	1.5	2.1	2.7	3.3	4.0	4.6	5.2	5.8	
36.6	6.1	12.2	18.3	24.4	30.5	.6	0.4	1.0	1.6	2.2	2.8	3.4	4.0	4.6	5.2	5.8	
36.7	6.1	12.3	18.4	24.5	30.6	.7	0.4	1.0	1.6	2.3	2.9	3.5	4.1	4.7	5.3	5.9	
36.8	6.2	12.3	18.4	24.6	30.7	.8	0.5	1.1	1.7	2.3	2.9	3.5	4.1	4.7	5.4	6.0	
36.9	6.2	12.3	18.5	24.6	30.8	.9	0.5	1.2	1.8	2.4	3.0	3.6	4.2	4.8	5.4	6.0	
37.0	6.1	12.3	18.5	24.6	30.8	.0	0.0	0.6	1.2	1.9	2.5	3.1	3.7	4.4	5.0	5.6	
37.1	6.2	12.3	18.5	24.7	30.9	.1	0.1	0.7	1.3	1.9	2.6	3.2	3.8	4.4	5.1	5.7	
37.2	6.2	12.4	18.6	24.8	31.0	.2	0.1	0.7	1.4	2.0	2.6	3.2	3.9	4.5	5.1	5.7	
37.3	6.2	12.4	18.6	24.9	31.1	.3	0.2	0.8	1.4	2.1	2.7	3.3	3.9	4.6	5.2	5.8	
37.4	6.2	12.5	18.7	24.9	31.2	.4	0.2	0.9	1.5	2.1	2.7	3.4	4.0	4.6	5.2	5.9	
37.5	6.3	12.5	18.8	25.0	31.3	.5	0.3	0.9	1.6	2.2	2.8	3.4	4.1	4.7	5.3	5.9	
37.6	6.3	12.5	18.8	25.1	31.3	.6	0.4	1.0	1.6	2.2	2.9	3.5	4.1	4.7	5.4	6.0	
37.7	6.3	12.6	18.9	25.2	31.4	.7	0.4	1.1	1.7	2.3	2.9	3.6	4.2	4.8	5.4	6.1	
37.8	6.3	12.6	18.9	25.2	31.5	.8	0.5	1.1	1.7	2.4	3.0	3.6	4.2	4.9	5.5	6.1	
37.9	6.4	12.7	19.0	25.3	31.6	.9	0.6	1.2	1.8	2.4	3.1	3.7	4.3	4.9	5.6	6.2	
38.0	6.3	12.6	19.0	25.3	31.6	.0	0.0	0.6	1.3	1.9	2.6	3.2	3.8	4.5	5.1	5.8	0.9 (0.1) 2.6 (0.2) 4.4 (0.3) 6.2 (0.4) 7.9 (0.5) 9.7 (0.6) 11.4 (0.7) 13.2 (0.8) 14.9 (0.9) 16.7 (1.0) 18.5 (1.1) 20.2 (1.2) 22.0 (1.3) 23.7 (1.4) 25.5 (1.5) 27.3 (1.6) 29.0 (1.7) 30.8 (1.8) 32.5 (1.9) 34.3
38.1	6.3	12.7	19.0	25.4	31.7	.1	0.1	0.7	1.3	2.0	2.6	3.3	3.9	4.6	5.2	5.8	
38.2	6.3	12.7	19.1	25.4	31.8	.2	0.1	0.8	1.4	2.1	2.7	3.3	4.0	4.6	5.3	5.9	
38.3	6.4	12.8	19.1	25.5	31.9	.3	0.2	0.8	1.5	2.1	2.8	3.4	4.0	4.7	5.3	6.0	
38.4	6.4	12.8	19.2	25.6	32.0	.4	0.3	0.9	1.5	2.2	2.8	3.5	4.1	4.7	5.4	6.0	
38.5	6.4	12.8	19.3	25.7	32.1	.5	0.3	1.0	1.6	2.2	2.9	3.5	4.2	4.8	5.5	6.1	
38.6	6.4	12.9	19.3	25.7	32.2	.6	0.4	1.0	1.7	2.3	3.0	3.6	4.2	4.9	5.5	6.2	
38.7	6.5	12.9	19.4	25.8	32.3	.7	0.4	1.1	1.7	2.4	3.0	3.7	4.3	4.9	5.6	6.2	
38.8	6.5	13.0	19.4	25.9	32.4	.8	0.5	1.2	1.8	2.4	3.1	3.7	4.4	5.0	5.6	6.3	
38.9	6.5	13.0	19.5	26.0	32.5	.9	0.6	1.2	1.9	2.5	3.1	3.8	4.4	5.1	5.7	6.4	
39.0	6.5	13.0	19.5	26.0	32.5	.0	0.0	0.7	1.3	2.0	2.6	3.3	3.9	4.6	5.3	5.9	
39.1	6.5	13.0	19.5	26.0	32.6	.1	0.1	0.7	1.4	2.0	2.7	3.4	4.0	4.7	5.3	6.0	
39.2	6.5	13.0	19.6	26.1	32.6	.2	0.1	0.8	1.4	2.1	2.8	3.4	4.1	4.7	5.4	6.1	
39.3	6.5	13.1	19.6	26.2	32.7	.3	0.2	0.9	1.5	2.2	2.8	3.5	4.1	4.8	5.5	6.1	
39.4	6.6	13.1	19.7	26.3	32.8	.4	0.3	0.9	1.6	2.2	2.9	3.6	4.2	4.9	5.5	6.2	
39.5	6.6	13.2	19.8	26.3	32.9	.5	0.3	1.0	1.6	2.3	3.0	3.6	4.3	4.9	5.6	6.3	
39.6	6.6	13.2	19.8	26.4	33.0	.6	0.4	1.1	1.7	2.4	3.0	3.7	4.3	5.0	5.7	6.3	
39.7	6.6	13.3	19.9	26.5	33.1	.7	0.5	1.1	1.8	2.4	3.1	3.8	4.4	5.1	5.7	6.4	
39.8	6.7	13.3	19.9	26.6	33.2	.8	0.5	1.2	1.8	2.5	3.2	3.8	4.5	5.1	5.8	6.5	
39.9	6.7	13.3	20.0	26.6	33.3	.9	0.6	1.3	1.9	2.6	3.2	3.9	4.5	5.2	5.9	6.5	
40.0	6.6	13.3	20.0	26.6	33.3	.0	0.0	0.7	1.3	2.0	2.7	3.4	4.0	4.7	5.4	6.1	0.9 (0.1) 2.8 (0.2) 4.6 (0.3) 6.5 (0.4) 8.3 (0.5) 10.2 (0.6) 12.0 (0.7) 13.9 (0.8) 15.7 (0.9) 17.6 (1.0) 19.4 (1.1) 21.3 (1.2) 23.1 (1.3) 25.0 (1.4) 26.8 (1.5) 28.7 (1.6) 30.5 (1.7) 32.3 (1.8) 34.2
40.1	6.7	13.3	20.0	26.7	33.4	.1	0.1	0.7	1.4	2.1	2.8	3.4	4.1	4.8	5.5	6.1	
40.2	6.7	13.4	20.1	26.8	33.5	.2	0.1	0.8	1.5	2.2	2.8	3.5	4.2	4.9	5.5	6.2	
40.3	6.7	13.4	20.1	26.9	33.6	.3	0.2	0.9	1.6	2.2	2.9	3.6	4.3	4.9	5.6	6.3	
40.4	6.7	13.5	20.2	26.9	33.7	.4	0.3	0.9	1.6	2.3	3.0	3.6	4.3	5.0	5.7	6.3	
40.5	6.8	13.5	20.3	27.0	33.8	.5	0.3	1.0	1.7	2.4	3.0	3.7	4.4	5.1	5.7	6.4	
40.6	6.8	13.5	20.3	27.1	33.8	.6	0.4	1.1	1.8	2.4	3.1	3.8	4.5	5.1	5.8	6.5	
40.7	6.8	13.6	20.4	27.2	33.9	.7	0.5	1.1	1.8	2.5	3.2	3.8	4.5	5.2	5.9	6.5	
40.8	6.8	13.6	20.4	27.2	34.0	.8	0.5	1.2	1.9	2.6	3.2	3.9	4.6	5.3	5.9	6.6	
40.9	6.9	13.7	20.5	27.3	34.1	.9	0.6	1.3	2.0	2.6	3.3	4.0	4.7	5.3	6.0	6.7	
41.0	6.8	13.6	20.5	27.3	34.1	.0	0.0	0.7	1.4	2.1	2.8	3.5	4.1	4.8	5.5	6.2	
41.1	6.8	13.7	20.5	27.4	34.2	.1	0.1	0.8	1.5	2.1	2.8	3.5	4.2	4.9	5.6	6.3	
41.2	6.8	13.7	20.6	27.4	34.3	.2	0.1	0.8	1.5	2.2	2.9	3.6	4.3	5.0	5.7	6.4	
41.3	6.9	13.8	20.6	27.5	34.4	.3	0.2	0.9	1.6	2.3	3.0	3.7	4.4	5.0	5.7	6.4	
41.4	6.9	13.8	20.7	27.6	34.5	.4	0.3	1.0	1.7	2.4	3.0	3.7	4.4	5.1	5.8	6.5	
41.5	6.9	13.8	20.8	27.7	34.6	.5	0.3	1.0	1.7	2.4	3.1	3.8	4.5	5.2	5.9	6.6	
41.6	6.9	13.9	20.8	27.7	34.7	.6	0.4	1.1	1.8	2.5	3.2	3.9	4.6	5.3	5.9	6.6	
41.7	7.0	13.9	20.9	27.8	34.8	.7	0.5	1.2	1.9	2.6	3.3	3.9	4.6	5.3	6.0	6.7	
41.8	7.0	14.0	20.9	27.9	34.9	.8	0.6	1.2	1.9	2.6	3.3	4.0	4.7	5.4	6.1	6.8	
41.9	7.0	14.0	21.0	28.0	35.0	.9	0.6	1.3	2.0	2.7	3.4	4.1	4.8	5.5	6.2	6.8	
42.0	7.0	14.0	21.0	28.0	35.0	.0	0.0	0.7	1.4	2.1	2.8	3.5	4.2	5.0	5.7	6.4	1.0 (0.1) 3.0 (0.2) 4.9 (0.3) 6.9 (0.4) 8.9 (0.5) 10.8 (0.6) 12.8 (0.7) 14.8 (0.8) 16.7 (0.9) 18.7 (1.0) 20.7 (1.1) 22.7 (1.2) 24.6 (1.3) 26.6 (1.4) 28.6 (1.5) 30.5 (1.6) 32.5 (1.7) 34.5
42.1	7.0	14.0	21.0	28.0	35.1	.1	0.1	0.8	1.5	2.2	2.9	3.6	4.3	5.0	5.7	6.4	
42.2	7.0	14.0	21.1	28.1	35.1	.2	0.1	0.8	1.6	2.3	3.0	3.7	4.4	5.1	5.8	6.5	
42.3	7.0	14.1	21.1	28.2	35.2	.3	0.2	0.9	1.6	2.3	3.0	3.8	4.5	5.2	5.9	6.6	
42.4	7.1	14.1	21.2	28.3	35.3	.4	0.3	1.0	1.7	2.4	3.1	3.8	4.5	5.2	5.9	6.7	
42.5	7.1	14.2	21.3	28.3	35.4	.5	0.4	1.1	1.8	2.5	3.2	3.9	4.6	5.3	6.0	6.7	
42.6	7.1	14.2	21.3	28.4	35.5	.6	0.4	1.1	1.8	2.5	3.3	4.0	4.7	5.4	6.1	6.8	
42.7	7.1	14.3	21.4	28.5	35.6	.7	0.5	1.2	1.9	2.6	3.3	4.0	4.7	5.5	6.2	6.9	
42.8	7.2	14.3	21.4	28.6	35.7	.8	0.6	1.3	2.0	2.7	3.4	4.1	4.8	5.5	6.2	6.9	
42.9	7.2	14.3	21.5	28.6	35.8	.9	0.6	1.3	2.1	2.8	3.5	4.2	4.9	5.6	6.3	7.0	
43.0	7.1	14.3	21.5	28.6	35.8	.0	0.0	0.7	1.4	2.2	2.9	3.6	4.3	5.1	5.8	6.5	
43.1	7.2	14.3	21.5	28.7	35.9	.1	0.1	0.8	1.5	2.2	3.0	3.7	4.4	5.1	5.9	6.6	
43.2	7.2	14.4	21.6	28.8	36.0	.2	0.1	0.9	1.6	2.3	3.0	3.8	4.5	5.2	5.9	6.7	
43.3	7.2	14.4	21.6	28.9	36.1	.3	0.2	0.9	1.7	2.4	3.1	3.8	4.6	5.3	6.0	6.7	
43.4	7.2	14.5	21.7	28.9	36.2	.4	0.3	1.0	1.7	2.5	3.2	3.9	4.6	5.4	6.1	6.8	
43.5	7.3	14.5	21.8	29.0	36.3	.5	0.4	1.1	1.8	2.5	3.3	4.0	4.7	5.4	6.2	6.9	
43.6	7.3	14.5	21.8	29.1	36.3	.6	0.4	1.2	1.9	2.6	3.3	4.1	4.8	5.5	6.2	7.0	
43.7	7.3	14.6	21.9	29.2	36.4	.7	0.5	1.2	2.0	2.7	3.4	4.1	4.9	5.6	6.3	7.0	
43.8	7.3	14.6	21.9	29.2	36.5	.8	0.6	1.3	2.0	2.8	3.5	4.2	4.9	5.7	6.4	7.1	
43.9	7.4	14.7	22.0	29.3	36.6	.9	0.7	1.4	2.1	2.8	3.6	4.3	5.0	5.7	6.5	7.2	
	10′	20′	30′	40′	50′		0′	1′	2′	3′	4′	5′	6′	7′	8′	9′	

The Double-Second-Difference correction (Corr.) is always to be added to the tabulated altitude.

INTERPOLATION TABLE

Dec. Inc.	Tens 10′	20′	30′	40′	50′	Decimals	Units 0′	1′	2′	3′	4′	5′	6′	7′	8′	9′	Double Second Diff. and Corr.
°	′	′	′	′	′	′	′	′	′	′	′	′	′	′	′	′	′ ′
44.0	7.3	14.6	22.0	29.3	36.6	.0	0.0	0.7	1.5	2.2	3.0	3.7	4.4	5.2	5.9	6.7	1.1 0.1 3.2 0.2 5.3 0.3 7.5 0.4 9.6 0.5 11.7 0.6 13.9 0.7 16.0 0.8 18.1 0.9 20.3 1.0 22.4 1.1 24.5 1.2 26.7 1.3 28.8 1.4 30.9 1.5 33.1 1.6 35.2
44.1	7.3	14.7	22.0	29.4	36.7	.1	0.1	0.8	1.6	2.3	3.0	3.8	4.5	5.3	6.0	6.7	
44.2	7.3	14.7	22.1	29.4	36.8	.2	0.1	0.9	1.6	2.4	3.1	3.9	4.6	5.3	6.1	6.8	
44.3	7.4	14.8	22.1	29.5	36.9	.3	0.2	1.0	1.7	2.4	3.2	3.9	4.7	5.4	6.2	6.9	
44.4	7.4	14.8	22.2	29.6	37.0	.4	0.3	1.0	1.8	2.5	3.3	4.0	4.7	5.5	6.2	7.0	
44.5	7.4	14.8	22.3	29.7	37.1	.5	0.4	1.1	1.9	2.6	3.3	4.1	4.8	5.6	6.3	7.0	
44.6	7.4	14.9	22.3	29.7	37.2	.6	0.4	1.2	1.9	2.7	3.4	4.2	4.9	5.6	6.4	7.1	
44.7	7.5	14.9	22.4	29.8	37.3	.7	0.5	1.3	2.0	2.7	3.5	4.2	5.0	5.7	6.5	7.2	
44.8	7.5	15.0	22.4	29.9	37.4	.8	0.6	1.3	2.1	2.8	3.6	4.3	5.0	5.8	6.5	7.3	
44.9	7.5	15.0	22.5	30.0	37.5	.9	0.7	1.4	2.2	2.9	3.6	4.4	5.1	5.9	6.6	7.3	
45.0	7.5	15.0	22.5	30.0	37.5	.0	0.0	0.8	1.5	2.3	3.0	3.8	4.5	5.3	6.1	6.8	
45.1	7.5	15.0	22.5	30.0	37.6	.1	0.1	0.8	1.6	2.4	3.1	3.9	4.6	5.4	6.1	6.9	
45.2	7.5	15.0	22.6	30.1	37.6	.2	0.2	0.9	1.7	2.4	3.2	3.9	4.7	5.5	6.2	7.0	
45.3	7.5	15.1	22.6	30.2	37.7	.3	0.2	1.0	1.7	2.5	3.3	4.0	4.8	5.5	6.3	7.1	
45.4	7.6	15.1	22.7	30.3	37.8	.4	0.3	1.1	1.8	2.6	3.3	4.1	4.9	5.6	6.4	7.1	
45.5	7.6	15.2	22.8	30.3	37.9	.5	0.4	1.1	1.9	2.7	3.4	4.2	4.9	5.7	6.4	7.2	
45.6	7.6	15.2	22.8	30.4	38.0	.6	0.5	1.2	2.0	2.7	3.5	4.2	5.0	5.8	6.5	7.3	
45.7	7.6	15.3	22.9	30.5	38.1	.7	0.5	1.3	2.0	2.8	3.6	4.3	5.1	5.8	6.6	7.4	
45.8	7.7	15.3	22.9	30.6	38.2	.8	0.6	1.4	2.1	2.9	3.6	4.4	5.2	5.9	6.7	7.4	
45.9	7.7	15.3	23.0	30.6	38.3	.9	0.7	1.4	2.2	3.0	3.7	4.5	5.2	6.0	6.7	7.5	
46.0	7.6	15.3	23.0	30.6	38.3	.0	0.0	0.8	1.5	2.3	3.1	3.9	4.6	5.4	6.2	7.0	1.2 0.1 3.5 0.2 5.8 0.3 8.1 0.4 10.5 0.5 12.8 0.6 15.1 0.7 17.4 0.8 19.8 0.9 22.1 1.0 24.4 1.1 26.7 1.2 29.1 1.3 31.4 1.4 33.7 1.5 36.0
46.1	7.7	15.3	23.0	30.7	38.4	.1	0.1	0.9	1.6	2.4	3.2	4.0	4.7	5.5	6.3	7.1	
46.2	7.7	15.4	23.1	30.8	38.5	.2	0.2	0.9	1.7	2.5	3.3	4.0	4.8	5.6	6.4	7.1	
46.3	7.7	15.4	23.1	30.9	38.6	.3	0.2	1.0	1.8	2.6	3.3	4.1	4.9	5.7	6.4	7.2	
46.4	7.7	15.5	23.2	30.9	38.7	.4	0.3	1.1	1.9	2.6	3.4	4.2	5.0	5.7	6.5	7.3	
46.5	7.8	15.5	23.3	31.0	38.8	.5	0.4	1.2	1.9	2.7	3.5	4.3	5.0	5.8	6.6	7.4	
46.6	7.8	15.5	23.3	31.1	38.8	.6	0.5	1.2	2.0	2.8	3.6	4.3	5.1	5.9	6.7	7.4	
46.7	7.8	15.6	23.4	31.2	38.9	.7	0.5	1.3	2.1	2.9	3.6	4.4	5.2	6.0	6.7	7.5	
46.8	7.8	15.6	23.4	31.2	39.0	.8	0.6	1.4	2.2	2.9	3.7	4.5	5.3	6.0	6.8	7.6	
46.9	7.9	15.7	23.5	31.3	39.1	.9	0.7	1.5	2.2	3.0	3.8	4.6	5.3	6.1	6.9	7.7	
47.0	7.8	15.6	23.5	31.3	39.1	.0	0.0	0.8	1.6	2.4	3.2	4.0	4.7	5.5	6.3	7.1	
47.1	7.8	15.7	23.5	31.4	39.2	.1	0.1	0.9	1.7	2.5	3.2	4.0	4.8	5.6	6.4	7.2	
47.2	7.8	15.7	23.6	31.4	39.3	.2	0.2	0.9	1.7	2.5	3.3	4.1	4.9	5.7	6.5	7.3	
47.3	7.9	15.8	23.6	31.5	39.4	.3	0.2	1.0	1.8	2.6	3.4	4.2	5.0	5.8	6.6	7.4	
47.4	7.9	15.8	23.7	31.6	39.5	.4	0.3	1.1	1.9	2.7	3.5	4.3	5.1	5.9	6.6	7.4	
47.5	7.9	15.8	23.8	31.7	39.6	.5	0.4	1.2	2.0	2.8	3.6	4.4	5.1	5.9	6.7	7.5	1.3 0.1 3.8 0.2 6.3 0.3 8.9 0.4 11.4 0.5 14.0 0.6 16.5 0.7 19.0 0.8 21.6 0.9 24.1 1.0 26.7 1.1 29.2 1.2 31.7 1.3 34.3
47.6	7.9	15.9	23.8	31.7	39.7	.6	0.5	1.3	2.1	2.8	3.6	4.4	5.2	6.0	6.8	7.6	
47.7	8.0	15.9	23.9	31.8	39.8	.7	0.6	1.3	2.1	2.9	3.7	4.5	5.3	6.1	6.9	7.7	
47.8	8.0	16.0	23.9	31.9	39.9	.8	0.6	1.4	2.2	3.0	3.8	4.6	5.4	6.2	7.0	7.8	
47.9	8.0	16.0	24.0	32.0	40.0	.9	0.7	1.5	2.3	3.1	3.9	4.7	5.5	6.3	7.0	7.8	
48.0	8.0	16.0	24.0	32.0	40.0	.0	0.0	0.8	1.6	2.4	3.2	4.0	4.8	5.7	6.5	7.3	
48.1	8.0	16.0	24.0	32.0	40.1	.1	0.1	0.9	1.7	2.5	3.3	4.1	4.9	5.7	6.5	7.4	
48.2	8.0	16.0	24.1	32.1	40.1	.2	0.2	1.0	1.8	2.6	3.4	4.2	5.0	5.8	6.6	7.4	
48.3	8.0	16.1	24.1	32.2	40.2	.3	0.2	1.1	1.9	2.7	3.5	4.3	5.1	5.9	6.7	7.5	
48.4	8.1	16.1	24.2	32.3	40.3	.4	0.3	1.1	1.9	2.7	3.6	4.4	5.2	6.0	6.8	7.6	
48.5	8.1	16.2	24.3	32.3	40.4	.5	0.4	1.2	2.0	2.8	3.6	4.4	5.3	6.1	6.9	7.7	
48.6	8.1	16.2	24.3	32.4	40.5	.6	0.5	1.3	2.1	2.9	3.7	4.5	5.3	6.1	7.0	7.8	
48.7	8.1	16.3	24.4	32.5	40.6	.7	0.6	1.4	2.2	3.0	3.8	4.6	5.4	6.2	7.0	7.8	
48.8	8.2	16.3	24.4	32.6	40.7	.8	0.6	1.5	2.3	3.1	3.9	4.7	5.5	6.3	7.1	7.9	
48.9	8.2	16.3	24.5	32.6	40.8	.9	0.7	1.5	2.3	3.2	4.0	4.8	5.6	6.4	7.2	8.0	
49.0	8.1	16.3	24.5	32.6	40.8	.0	0.0	0.8	1.6	2.5	3.3	4.1	4.9	5.8	6.6	7.4	1.4 0.1 4.2 0.2 7.1 0.3 9.9 0.4 12.7 0.5 15.5 0.6 18.4 0.7 21.2 0.8 24.0 0.9 26.8 1.0 29.7 1.1 32.5 1.2 35.3
49.1	8.2	16.3	24.5	32.7	40.9	.1	0.1	0.9	1.7	2.6	3.4	4.2	5.0	5.9	6.7	7.5	
49.2	8.2	16.4	24.6	32.8	41.0	.2	0.2	1.0	1.8	2.6	3.5	4.3	5.1	5.9	6.8	7.6	
49.3	8.2	16.4	24.6	32.9	41.1	.3	0.2	1.1	1.9	2.7	3.5	4.4	5.2	6.0	6.8	7.7	
49.4	8.2	16.5	24.7	32.9	41.2	.4	0.3	1.2	2.0	2.8	3.6	4.5	5.3	6.1	6.9	7.8	
49.5	8.3	16.5	24.8	33.0	41.3	.5	0.4	1.2	2.1	2.9	3.7	4.5	5.4	6.2	7.0	7.8	
49.6	8.3	16.5	24.8	33.1	41.3	.6	0.5	1.3	2.1	3.0	3.8	4.6	5.4	6.3	7.1	7.9	
49.7	8.3	16.6	24.9	33.2	41.4	.7	0.6	1.4	2.2	3.1	3.9	4.7	5.5	6.4	7.2	8.0	
49.8	8.3	16.6	24.9	33.2	41.5	.8	0.7	1.5	2.3	3.1	4.0	4.8	5.6	6.4	7.3	8.1	
49.9	8.4	16.7	25.0	33.3	41.6	.9	0.7	1.6	2.4	3.2	4.0	4.9	5.7	6.5	7.3	8.2	
50.0	8.3	16.6	25.0	33.3	41.6	.0	0.0	0.8	1.7	2.5	3.4	4.2	5.0	5.9	6.7	7.6	
50.1	8.3	16.7	25.0	33.4	41.7	.1	0.1	0.9	1.8	2.6	3.5	4.3	5.1	6.0	6.8	7.7	
50.2	8.3	16.7	25.1	33.4	41.8	.2	0.2	1.0	1.9	2.7	3.5	4.4	5.2	6.1	6.9	7.7	
50.3	8.4	16.8	25.1	33.5	41.9	.3	0.3	1.1	1.9	2.8	3.6	4.5	5.3	6.1	7.0	7.8	
50.4	8.4	16.8	25.2	33.6	42.0	.4	0.3	1.2	2.0	2.9	3.7	4.5	5.4	6.2	7.1	7.9	
50.5	8.4	16.8	25.3	33.7	42.1	.5	0.4	1.3	2.1	2.9	3.8	4.6	5.5	6.3	7.2	8.0	1.6 0.1 4.8 0.2 8.0 0.3 11.2 0.4 14.5 0.5 17.7 0.6 20.9 0.7 24.1 0.8 27.3 0.9 30.5 1.0 33.7 1.1 36.9
50.6	8.4	16.9	25.3	33.7	42.2	.6	0.5	1.3	2.2	3.0	3.9	4.7	5.6	6.4	7.2	8.1	
50.7	8.5	16.9	25.4	33.8	42.3	.7	0.6	1.4	2.3	3.1	4.0	4.8	5.6	6.5	7.3	8.2	
50.8	8.5	17.0	25.4	33.9	42.4	.8	0.7	1.5	2.4	3.2	4.0	4.9	5.7	6.6	7.4	8.2	
50.9	8.5	17.0	25.5	34.0	42.5	.9	0.8	1.6	2.4	3.3	4.1	5.0	5.8	6.6	7.5	8.3	
51.0	8.5	17.0	25.5	34.0	42.5	.0	0.0	0.9	1.7	2.6	3.4	4.3	5.1	6.0	6.9	7.7	
51.1	8.5	17.0	25.5	34.0	42.6	.1	0.1	0.9	1.8	2.7	3.5	4.4	5.2	6.1	7.0	7.8	
51.2	8.5	17.0	25.6	34.1	42.6	.2	0.2	1.0	1.9	2.7	3.6	4.5	5.3	6.2	7.0	7.9	
51.3	8.5	17.1	25.6	34.2	42.7	.3	0.3	1.1	2.0	2.8	3.7	4.5	5.4	6.3	7.1	8.0	
51.4	8.6	17.1	25.7	34.3	42.8	.4	0.3	1.2	2.1	2.9	3.8	4.6	5.5	6.4	7.2	8.1	
51.5	8.6	17.2	25.8	34.3	42.9	.5	0.4	1.3	2.1	3.0	3.9	4.7	5.6	6.4	7.3	8.2	
51.6	8.6	17.2	25.8	34.4	43.0	.6	0.5	1.4	2.2	3.1	3.9	4.8	5.7	6.5	7.4	8.2	
51.7	8.6	17.3	25.9	34.5	43.1	.7	0.6	1.5	2.3	3.2	4.0	4.9	5.8	6.6	7.5	8.3	
51.8	8.7	17.3	25.9	34.6	43.2	.8	0.7	1.5	2.4	3.3	4.1	5.0	5.8	6.7	7.6	8.4	
51.9	8.7	17.3	26.0	34.6	43.3	.9	0.8	1.6	2.5	3.3	4.2	5.1	5.9	6.8	7.6	8.5	
	10′	20′	30′	40′	50′		0′	1′	2′	3′	4′	5′	6′	7′	8′	9′	

Dec. Inc.	Tens 10′	20′	30′	40′	50′	Decimals	Units 0′	1′	2′	3′	4′	5′	6′	7′	8′	9′	Double Second Diff. and Corr.
°	′	′	′	′	′	′	′	′	′	′	′	′	′	′	′	′	′ ′
52.0	8.6	17.3	26.0	34.6	43.3	.0	0.0	0.9	1.7	2.6	3.5	4.4	5.2	6.1	7.0	7.9	1.8 0.1 5.5 0.2 9.1 0.3 12.8 0.4 16.5 0.5 20.1 0.6 23.8 0.7 27.4 0.8 31.1 0.9 34.7
52.1	8.7	17.3	26.0	34.7	43.4	.1	0.1	1.0	1.8	2.7	3.6	4.5	5.3	6.2	7.1	8.0	
52.2	8.7	17.4	26.1	34.8	43.5	.2	0.2	1.0	1.9	2.8	3.7	4.5	5.4	6.3	7.2	8.0	
52.3	8.7	17.4	26.1	34.9	43.6	.3	0.3	1.1	2.0	2.9	3.8	4.6	5.5	6.4	7.3	8.1	
52.4	8.7	17.5	26.2	34.9	43.7	.4	0.3	1.2	2.1	3.0	3.8	4.7	5.6	6.5	7.3	8.2	
52.5	8.8	17.5	26.3	35.0	43.8	.5	0.4	1.3	2.2	3.1	3.9	4.8	5.7	6.6	7.4	8.3	
52.6	8.8	17.5	26.3	35.1	43.8	.6	0.5	1.4	2.3	3.1	4.0	4.9	5.8	6.6	7.5	8.4	
52.7	8.8	17.6	26.4	35.2	43.9	.7	0.6	1.5	2.4	3.2	4.1	5.0	5.9	6.7	7.6	8.5	
52.8	8.8	17.6	26.4	35.2	44.0	.8	0.7	1.6	2.4	3.3	4.2	5.1	5.9	6.8	7.7	8.6	
52.9	8.9	17.7	26.5	35.3	44.1	.9	0.8	1.7	2.5	3.4	4.3	5.2	6.0	6.9	7.8	8.7	
53.0	8.8	17.6	26.5	35.3	44.1	.0	0.0	0.9	1.8	2.7	3.6	4.5	5.3	6.2	7.1	8.0	2.1 0.1 6.2 0.2 10.4 0.3 14.5 0.4 18.6 0.5 22.8 0.6 26.9 0.7 31.1 0.8 35.2
53.1	8.8	17.7	26.5	35.4	44.2	.1	0.1	1.0	1.9	2.8	3.7	4.5	5.4	6.3	7.2	8.1	
53.2	8.8	17.7	26.6	35.4	44.3	.2	0.2	1.1	2.0	2.9	3.7	4.6	5.5	6.4	7.3	8.2	
53.3	8.9	17.8	26.6	35.5	44.4	.3	0.3	1.2	2.1	2.9	3.8	4.7	5.6	6.5	7.4	8.3	
53.4	8.9	17.8	26.7	35.6	44.5	.4	0.4	1.2	2.1	3.0	3.9	4.8	5.7	6.6	7.5	8.4	
53.5	8.9	17.8	26.8	35.7	44.6	.5	0.4	1.3	2.2	3.1	4.0	4.9	5.8	6.7	7.6	8.5	
53.6	8.9	17.9	26.8	35.7	44.7	.6	0.5	1.4	2.3	3.2	4.1	5.0	5.9	6.8	7.7	8.6	
53.7	9.0	17.9	26.9	35.8	44.8	.7	0.6	1.5	2.4	3.3	4.2	5.1	6.0	6.9	7.8	8.6	
53.8	9.0	18.0	26.9	35.9	44.9	.8	0.7	1.6	2.5	3.4	4.3	5.2	6.1	7.0	7.8	8.7	
53.9	9.0	18.0	27.0	36.0	45.0	.9	0.8	1.7	2.6	3.5	4.4	5.3	6.2	7.0	7.9	8.8	
54.0	9.0	18.0	27.0	36.0	45.0	.0	0.0	0.9	1.8	2.7	3.6	4.5	5.4	6.4	7.3	8.2	2.4 0.1 7.2 0.2 12.0 0.3 16.8 0.4 21.6 0.5 26.4 0.6 31.2 0.7 36.0
54.1	9.0	18.0	27.0	36.0	45.1	.1	0.1	1.0	1.9	2.8	3.7	4.6	5.5	6.4	7.4	8.3	
54.2	9.0	18.0	27.1	36.1	45.1	.2	0.2	1.1	2.0	2.9	3.8	4.7	5.6	6.5	7.4	8.4	
54.3	9.0	18.1	27.1	36.2	45.2	.3	0.3	1.2	2.1	3.0	3.9	4.8	5.7	6.6	7.5	8.4	
54.4	9.1	18.1	27.2	36.3	45.3	.4	0.4	1.3	2.2	3.1	4.0	4.9	5.8	6.7	7.6	8.5	
54.5	9.1	18.2	27.3	36.3	45.4	.5	0.5	1.4	2.3	3.2	4.1	5.0	5.9	6.8	7.7	8.6	
54.6	9.1	18.2	27.3	36.4	45.5	.6	0.5	1.5	2.4	3.3	4.2	5.1	6.0	6.9	7.8	8.7	
54.7	9.1	18.3	27.4	36.5	45.6	.7	0.6	1.5	2.5	3.4	4.3	5.2	6.1	7.0	7.9	8.8	
54.8	9.2	18.3	27.4	36.6	45.7	.8	0.7	1.6	2.5	3.5	4.4	5.3	6.2	7.1	8.0	8.9	
54.9	9.2	18.3	27.5	36.6	45.8	.9	0.8	1.7	2.6	3.5	4.5	5.4	6.3	7.2	8.1	9.0	
55.0	9.1	18.3	27.5	36.6	45.8	.0	0.0	0.9	1.8	2.8	3.7	4.6	5.5	6.5	7.4	8.3	2.9 0.1 8.6 0.2 14.4 0.3 20.2 0.4 25.9 0.5 31.7 0.6 37.5
55.1	9.2	18.3	27.5	36.7	45.9	.1	0.1	1.0	1.9	2.9	3.8	4.7	5.6	6.6	7.5	8.4	
55.2	9.2	18.4	27.6	36.8	46.0	.2	0.2	1.1	2.0	3.0	3.9	4.8	5.7	6.7	7.6	8.5	
55.3	9.2	18.4	27.6	36.9	46.1	.3	0.3	1.2	2.1	3.1	4.0	4.9	5.8	6.8	7.7	8.6	
55.4	9.2	18.5	27.7	36.9	46.2	.4	0.4	1.3	2.2	3.1	4.1	5.0	5.9	6.8	7.8	8.7	
55.5	9.3	18.5	27.8	37.0	46.3	.5	0.5	1.4	2.3	3.2	4.2	5.1	6.0	6.9	7.9	8.8	
55.6	9.3	18.5	27.8	37.1	46.3	.6	0.6	1.5	2.4	3.3	4.3	5.2	6.1	7.0	8.0	8.9	
55.7	9.3	18.6	27.9	37.2	46.4	.7	0.6	1.6	2.5	3.4	4.3	5.3	6.2	7.1	8.0	9.0	
55.8	9.3	18.6	27.9	37.2	46.5	.8	0.7	1.7	2.6	3.5	4.4	5.4	6.3	7.2	8.1	9.1	
55.9	9.4	18.7	28.0	37.3	46.6	.9	0.8	1.8	2.7	3.6	4.5	5.5	6.4	7.3	8.2	9.2	
56.0	9.3	18.6	28.0	37.3	46.6	.0	0.0	0.9	1.9	2.8	3.8	4.7	5.6	6.6	7.5	8.5	3.6 0.1 10.9 0.2 18.2 0.3 25.5 0.4 32.8 0.5 40.1
56.1	9.3	18.7	28.0	37.4	46.7	.1	0.1	1.0	2.0	2.9	3.9	4.8	5.7	6.7	7.6	8.6	
56.2	9.3	18.7	28.1	37.4	46.8	.2	0.2	1.1	2.1	3.0	4.0	4.9	5.8	6.8	7.7	8.7	
56.3	9.4	18.8	28.1	37.5	46.9	.3	0.3	1.2	2.2	3.1	4.0	5.0	5.9	6.9	7.8	8.8	
56.4	9.4	18.8	28.2	37.6	47.0	.4	0.4	1.3	2.3	3.2	4.1	5.1	6.0	7.0	7.9	8.9	
56.5	9.4	18.8	28.3	37.7	47.1	.5	0.5	1.4	2.4	3.3	4.2	5.2	6.1	7.1	8.0	8.9	
56.6	9.4	18.9	28.3	37.7	47.2	.6	0.6	1.5	2.4	3.4	4.3	5.3	6.2	7.2	8.1	9.0	
56.7	9.5	18.9	28.4	37.8	47.3	.7	0.7	1.6	2.5	3.5	4.4	5.4	6.3	7.3	8.2	9.1	
56.8	9.5	19.0	28.4	37.9	47.4	.8	0.8	1.7	2.6	3.6	4.5	5.5	6.4	7.3	8.3	9.2	
56.9	9.5	19.0	28.5	38.0	47.5	.9	0.8	1.8	2.7	3.7	4.6	5.6	6.5	7.4	8.4	9.3	
57.0	9.5	19.0	28.5	38.0	47.5	.0	0.0	1.0	1.9	2.9	3.8	4.8	5.7	6.7	7.7	8.6	5.0 0.1 15.0 0.2 25.0 0.3 35.1
57.1	9.5	19.0	28.5	38.0	47.6	.1	0.1	1.1	2.0	3.0	3.9	4.9	5.8	6.8	7.8	8.7	
57.2	9.5	19.0	28.6	38.1	47.6	.2	0.2	1.1	2.1	3.1	4.0	5.0	5.9	6.9	7.9	8.8	
57.3	9.5	19.1	28.6	38.2	47.7	.3	0.3	1.2	2.2	3.2	4.1	5.1	6.0	7.0	8.0	8.9	
57.4	9.6	19.1	28.7	38.3	47.8	.4	0.4	1.3	2.3	3.3	4.2	5.2	6.1	7.1	8.0	9.0	
57.5	9.6	19.2	28.8	38.3	47.9	.5	0.5	1.4	2.4	3.4	4.3	5.3	6.2	7.2	8.1	9.1	
57.6	9.6	19.2	28.8	38.4	48.0	.6	0.6	1.5	2.5	3.4	4.4	5.4	6.3	7.3	8.2	9.2	
57.7	9.6	19.3	28.9	38.5	48.1	.7	0.7	1.6	2.6	3.5	4.5	5.5	6.4	7.4	8.3	9.3	
57.8	9.7	19.3	28.9	38.6	48.2	.8	0.8	1.7	2.7	3.6	4.6	5.6	6.5	7.5	8.4	9.4	
57.9	9.7	19.3	29.0	38.6	48.3	.9	0.9	1.8	2.8	3.7	4.7	5.7	6.6	7.6	8.5	9.5	
58.0	9.6	19.3	29.0	38.6	48.3	.0	0.0	1.0	1.9	2.9	3.9	4.9	5.8	6.8	7.8	8.8	8.2 0.1 24.6 0.2 41.0
58.1	9.7	19.3	29.0	38.7	48.4	.1	0.1	1.1	2.0	3.0	4.0	5.0	5.9	6.9	7.9	8.9	
58.2	9.7	19.4	29.1	38.8	48.5	.2	0.2	1.2	2.1	3.1	4.1	5.1	6.0	7.0	8.0	9.0	
58.3	9.7	19.4	29.1	38.9	48.6	.3	0.3	1.3	2.2	3.2	4.2	5.2	6.1	7.1	8.1	9.1	
58.4	9.7	19.5	29.2	38.9	48.7	.4	0.4	1.4	2.3	3.3	4.3	5.3	6.2	7.2	8.2	9.2	
58.5	9.8	19.5	29.3	39.0	48.8	.5	0.5	1.5	2.4	3.4	4.4	5.4	6.3	7.3	8.3	9.3	
58.6	9.8	19.5	29.3	39.1	48.8	.6	0.6	1.6	2.5	3.5	4.5	5.5	6.4	7.4	8.4	9.4	
58.7	9.8	19.6	29.4	39.2	48.9	.7	0.7	1.7	2.6	3.6	4.6	5.6	6.5	7.5	8.5	9.5	
58.8	9.8	19.6	29.4	39.2	49.0	.8	0.8	1.8	2.7	3.7	4.7	5.7	6.6	7.6	8.6	9.6	
58.9	9.9	19.7	29.5	39.3	49.1	.9	0.9	1.9	2.8	3.8	4.8	5.8	6.7	7.7	8.7	9.7	
59.0	9.8	19.6	29.5	39.3	49.1	.0	0.0	1.0	2.0	3.0	4.0	5.0	5.9	6.9	7.9	8.9	16.2 0.1 48.6
59.1	9.8	19.7	29.5	39.4	49.2	.1	0.1	1.1	2.1	3.1	4.1	5.1	6.0	7.0	8.0	9.0	
59.2	9.8	19.7	29.6	39.4	49.3	.2	0.2	1.2	2.2	3.2	4.2	5.2	6.1	7.1	8.1	9.1	
59.3	9.9	19.8	29.6	39.5	49.4	.3	0.3	1.3	2.3	3.3	4.3	5.3	6.2	7.2	8.2	9.2	
59.4	9.9	19.8	29.7	39.6	49.5	.4	0.4	1.4	2.4	3.4	4.4	5.4	6.3	7.3	8.3	9.3	
59.5	9.9	19.8	29.8	39.7	49.6	.5	0.5	1.5	2.5	3.5	4.5	5.5	6.4	7.4	8.4	9.4	0.0 0.0 48.2
59.6	9.9	19.9	29.8	39.7	49.7	.6	0.6	1.6	2.6	3.6	4.6	5.6	6.5	7.5	8.5	9.5	
59.7	10.0	19.9	29.9	39.8	49.8	.7	0.7	1.7	2.7	3.7	4.7	5.7	6.6	7.6	8.6	9.6	
59.8	10.0	20.0	29.9	39.9	49.9	.8	0.8	1.8	2.8	3.8	4.8	5.8	6.7	7.7	8.7	9.7	
59.9	10.0	20.0	30.0	40.0	50.0	.9	0.9	1.9	2.9	3.9	4.9	5.9	6.8	7.8	8.8	9.8	
	10′	20′	30′	40′	50′		0′	1′	2′	3′	4′	5′	6′	7′	8′	9′	

The Double-Second-Difference correction (Corr.) is always to be added to the tabulated altitude.

TABLE 1

Conversion Angle

Mid lat.	Difference of longitude										Mid lat.
	0°	0°5	1°	1°5	2°	2°5	3°	3°5	4°	4°5	
°	°	°	°	°	°	°	°	°	°	°	°
0	0.0	0.0	0.0	0.0	0.0	0.0	0.0	0.0	0.0	0.0	0
2	0.0	0.0	0.0	0.0	0.0	0.0	0.1	0.1	0.1	0.1	2
4	0.0	0.0	0.0	0.0	0.0	0.1	0.1	0.1	0.1	0.2	4
6	0.0	0.0	0.1	0.1	0.1	0.1	0.2	0.2	0.2	0.2	6
8	0.0	0.0	0.1	0.1	0.1	0.2	0.2	0.2	0.3	0.3	8
10	0.0	0.0	0.1	0.1	0.1	0.2	0.2	0.3	0.4	0.4	10
11	0.0	0.0	0.1	0.1	0.2	0.2	0.3	0.3	0.4	0.4	11
12	0.0	0.1	0.1	0.1	0.2	0.3	0.3	0.4	0.4	0.5	12
13	0.0	0.1	0.1	0.2	0.2	0.3	0.3	0.4	0.4	0.5	13
14	0.0	0.1	0.1	0.2	0.2	0.3	0.4	0.4	0.5	0.6	14
15	0.0	0.1	0.1	0.2	0.3	0.3	0.4	0.4	0.5	0.6	15
16	0.0	0.1	0.1	0.2	0.3	0.4	0.4	0.5	0.6	0.6	16
17	0.0	0.1	0.2	0.2	0.3	0.4	0.4	0.5	0.6	0.6	17
18	0.0	0.1	0.2	0.2	0.3	0.4	0.5	0.5	0.6	0.7	18
19	0.0	0.1	0.2	0.2	0.3	0.4	0.5	0.6	0.6	0.7	19
20	0.0	0.1	0.2	0.2	0.3	0.4	0.5	0.6	0.7	0.8	20
21	0.0	0.1	0.2	0.3	0.4	0.5	0.5	0.6	0.7	0.8	21
22	0.0	0.1	0.2	0.3	0.4	0.5	0.6	0.6	0.8	0.8	22
23	0.0	0.1	0.2	0.3	0.4	0.5	0.6	0.7	0.8	0.9	23
24	0.0	0.1	0.2	0.3	0.4	0.5	0.6	0.7	0.8	0.9	24
25	0.0	0.1	0.2	0.3	0.4	0.5	0.6	0.7	0.8	1.0	25
26	0.0	0.1	0.2	0.3	0.4	0.6	0.6	0.8	0.9	1.0	26
27	0.0	0.1	0.2	0.3	0.4	0.6	0.7	0.8	0.9	1.0	27
28	0.0	0.1	0.2	0.4	0.5	0.6	0.7	0.8	0.9	1.1	28
29	0.0	0.1	0.2	0.4	0.5	0.6	0.7	0.8	1.0	1.1	29
30	0.0	0.1	0.2	0.4	0.5	0.6	0.8	0.9	1.0	1.1	30
31	0.0	0.1	0.2	0.4	0.5	0.6	0.8	0.9	1.0	1.2	31
32	0.0	0.1	0.3	0.4	0.5	0.7	0.8	0.9	1.1	1.2	32
33	0.0	0.1	0.3	0.4	0.6	0.7	0.8	1.0	1.1	1.2	33
34	0.0	0.1	0.3	0.4	0.6	0.7	0.8	1.0	1.1	1.2	34
35	0.0	0.1	0.3	0.4	0.6	0.7	0.9	1.0	1.2	1.3	35
36	0.0	0.1	0.3	0.4	0.6	0.7	0.9	1.0	1.2	1.3	36
37	0.0	0.2	0.3	0.4	0.6	0.8	0.9	1.1	1.2	1.4	37
38	0.0	0.2	0.3	0.5	0.6	0.8	0.9	1.1	1.2	1.4	38
39	0.0	0.2	0.3	0.5	0.6	0.8	1.0	1.1	1.2	1.4	39
40	0.0	0.2	0.3	0.5	0.6	0.8	1.0	1.1	1.3	1.4	40
41	0.0	0.2	0.3	0.5	0.6	0.8	1.0	1.2	1.3	1.5	41
42	0.0	0.2	0.3	0.5	0.7	0.8	1.0	1.2	1.3	1.5	42
43	0.0	0.2	0.3	0.5	0.7	0.8	1.0	1.2	1.4	1.5	43
44	0.0	0.2	0.4	0.5	0.7	0.9	1.1	1.2	1.4	1.6	44
45	0.0	0.2	0.4	0.5	0.7	0.9	1.1	1.2	1.4	1.6	45
46	0.0	0.2	0.4	0.5	0.7	0.9	1.1	1.3	1.4	1.6	46
47	0.0	0.2	0.4	0.6	0.7	0.9	1.1	1.3	1.5	1.7	47
48	0.0	0.2	0.4	0.6	0.8	0.9	1.1	1.3	1.5	1.7	48
49	0.0	0.2	0.4	0.6	0.8	1.0	1.1	1.3	1.5	1.7	49
50	0.0	0.2	0.4	0.6	0.8	1.0	1.1	1.3	1.5	1.7	50
51	0.0	0.2	0.4	0.6	0.8	1.0	1.2	1.4	1.6	1.8	51
52	0.0	0.2	0.4	0.6	0.8	1.0	1.2	1.4	1.6	1.8	52
53	0.0	0.2	0.4	0.6	0.8	1.0	1.2	1.4	1.6	1.8	53
54	0.0	0.2	0.4	0.6	0.8	1.0	1.2	1.4	1.6	1.8	54
55	0.0	0.2	0.4	0.6	0.8	1.0	1.2	1.4	1.6	1.8	55
56	0.0	0.2	0.4	0.6	0.8	1.0	1.2	1.4	1.7	1.9	56
57	0.0	0.2	0.4	0.6	0.8	1.1	1.2	1.5	1.7	1.9	57
58	0.0	0.2	0.4	0.6	0.8	1.1	1.3	1.5	1.7	1.9	58
59	0.0	0.2	0.4	0.6	0.8	1.1	1.3	1.5	1.7	1.9	59
60	0.0	0.2	0.4	0.7	0.9	1.1	1.3	1.5	1.7	2.0	60

Receiver (latitude)	Transmitter (direction from receiver)	Correction Sign	Receiver (latitude)	Transmitter (direction from receiver)	Correction Sign
North	Eastward	+	South	Eastward	−
North	Westward	−	South	Westward	+

TABLE 1

Conversion Angle

Mid lat.	Difference of longitude										Mid lat.
	0°	0°.5	1°	1°.5	2°	2°.5	3°	3°.5	4°	4°.5	
°	°	°	°	°	°	°	°	°	°	°	°
61	0.0	0.2	0.4	0.7	0.9	1.1	1.3	1.5	1.7	2.0	61
62	0.0	0.2	0.4	0.7	0.9	1.1	1.3	1.5	1.8	2.0	62
63	0.0	0.2	0.4	0.7	0.9	1.1	1.3	1.6	1.8	2.0	63
64	0.0	0.2	0.4	0.7	0.9	1 1	1.3	1.6	1.8	2.0	64
65	0.0	0.2	0.5	0.7	0.9	1.1	1.4	1.6	1.8	2.0	65
66	0.0	0.2	0.5	0.7	0.9	1.1	1.4	1.6	1.8	2.1	66
67	0.0	0.2	0.5	0.7	0.9	1.2	1.4	1.6	1.8	2.1	67
68	0.0	0.2	0.5	0.7	0.9	1.2	1.4	1.6	1.9	2.1	68
69	0.0	0.2	0.5	0.7	0.9	1.2	1.4	1.6	1.9	2.1	69
70	0.0	0.2	0.5	0.7	0.9	1.2	1.4	1.6	1.9	2.1	70
71	0.0	0.2	0.5	0.7	0.9	1.2	1.4	1.7	1.9	2.1	71
72	0.0	0.2	0.5	0.7	1.0	1.2	1.4	1.7	1.9	2.1	72
73	0.0	0.2	0.5	0.7	1.0	1.2	1.4	1.7	1.9	2.2	73
74	0.0	0.2	0.5	0.7	1.0	1.2	1.4	1.7	1.9	2.2	74
75	0.0	0.2	0.5	0.7	1.0	1.2	1.4	1.7	1.9	2.2	75
76	0.0	0.2	0.5	0.7	1.0	1.2	1.5	1.7	1.9	2.2	76
77	0.0	0.2	0.5	0.7	1.0	1.2	1.5	1.7	1.9	2.2	77
78	0.0	0.2	0.5	0.7	1.0	1.2	1.5	1.7	2.0	2.2	78
79	0.0	0.2	0.5	0.7	1.0	1.2	1.5	1.7	2.0	2.2	79
80	0.0	0.2	0.5	0.7	1.0	1.2	1.5	1.7	2.0	2.2	80
81	0.0	0.2	0.5	0.7	1.0	1.2	1.5	1.7	2.0	2.2	81
82	0.0	0.2	0.5	0.7	1.0	1.2	1.5	1.7	2.0	2.2	82
83	0.0	0.2	0.5	0.7	1.0	1.2	1.5	1.7	2.0	2.2	83
84	0.0	0.2	0.5	0.7	1.0	1.2	1.5	1.7	2.0	2.2	84
85	0.0	0.2	0.5	0.7	1.0	1.2	1.5	1.7	2.0	2.2	85

DLo	0° Latitude of Receiver					5° Latitude of Receiver					DLo
	Latitude of Transmitter					Latitude of Transmitter					
	10°	5°	0°	5°	10°	5°	0°	5°	10°	15°	
°	°	°	°	°	°	°	°	°	°	°	°
0	0.0	0.0	0.0	0.0	0.0	0.0	0.0	0.0	0.0	0.0	0
5	0.3	0.3	0.0	0.3	0.3	0.1	0.0	0.3	0.5	0.5	5
10	0.5	0.3	0.0	0.3	0.5	0.0	0.1	0.4	0.7	0.9	10
15	0.6	0.3	0.0	0.3	0.6	0.0	0.3	0.7	1.0	1.3	15

DLo	10° Latitude of Receiver					15° Latitude of Receiver					DLo
	Latitude of Transmitter					Latitude of Transmitter					
	0°	5°	10°	15°	20°	5°	10°	15°	20°	25°	
°	°	°	°	°	°	°	°	°	°	°	°
0	0.0	0.0	0.0	0.0	0.0	0.0	0.0	0.0	0.0	0.0	0
5	0.1	0.2	0.5	0.7	0.7	0.4	0.4	0.7	0.9	0.9	5
10	0.4	0.6	0.9	1.2	1.3	0.8	1.0	1.3	1.6	1.7	10
15	0.7	1.0	1.3	1.6	1.9	1.4	1.6	2.0	2.3	2.5	15

Receiver (latitude)	Transmitter (direction from receiver)	Correction Sign	Receiver (latitude)	Transmitter (direction from receiver)	Correction Sign
North	Eastward	+	South	Eastward	–
North	Westward	–	South	Westward	+

TABLE 1

Conversion Angle

DLo	20° Latitude of Receiver					25° Latitude of Receiver					DLo
	Latitude of Transmitter					Latitude of Transmitter					
	10°	15°	20°	25°	30°	15°	20°	25°	30°	35°	
°	°	°	°	°	°	°	°	°	°	°	°
0	0.0	0.0	0.0	0.0	0.0	0.0	0.0	0.0	0.0	0.0	0
5	0.6	0.6	0.9	1.1	1.1	0.8	0.8	1.1	1.3	1.3	5
10	1.3	1.4	1.7	2.0	2.1	1.7	1.9	2.1	2.4	2.5	10
15	2.0	2.3	2.6	2.9	3.1	2.7	2.9	3.2	3.5	3.7	15

DLo	30° Latitude of Receiver					35° Latitude of Receiver					DLo
	Latitude of Transmitter					Latitude of Transmitter					
	20°	25°	30°	35°	40°	25°	30°	35°	40°	45°	
°	°	°	°	°	°	°	°	°	°	°	°
0	0.0	0.0	0.0	0.0	0.0	0.0	0.0	0.0	0.0	0.0	0
5	1.0	1.0	1.3	1.4	1.4	1.2	1.3	1.5	1.6	1.6	5
10	2.1	2.3	2.5	2.7	2.8	2.5	2.7	2.9	3.1	3.2	10
15	3.3	3.5	3.8	4.0	4.2	3.9	4.1	4.3	4.5	4.7	15

DLo	40° Latitude of Receiver					45° Latitude of Receiver					DLo
	Latitude of Transmitter					Latitude of Transmitter					
	30°	35°	40°	45°	50°	35°	40°	45°	50°	55°	
°	°	°	°	°	°	°	°	°	°	°	°
0	0.0	0.0	0.0	0.0	0.0	0.0	0.0	0.0	0.0	0.0	0
5	1.4	1.5	1.6	1.7	1.7	1.6	1.6	1.8	1.9	1.9	5
10	2.9	3.0	3.2	3.4	3.4	3.3	3.4	3.6	3.7	3.7	10
15	4.5	4.6	4.8	5.0	5.1	5.0	5.2	5.3	5.5	5.5	15
20	6.0	6.3	6.5	6.7	6.8	6.8	6.9	7.1	7.3	7.4	20
25	7.6	7.9	8.1	8.3	8.5	8.5	8.7	8.9	9.1	9.2	25
30	9.2	9.5	9.8	10.0	10.2	10.3	10.5	10.7	10.9	11.0	30

DLo	50° Latitude of Receiver					55° Latitude of Receiver					DLo
	Latitude of Transmitter					Latitude of Transmitter					
	40°	45°	50°	55°	60°	45°	50°	55°	60°	65°	
°	°	°	°	°	°	°	°	°	°	°	°
0	0.0	0.0	0.0	0.0	0.0	0.0	0.0	0.0	0.0	0.0	0
5	1.8	1.8	1.9	2.0	2.0	2.0	2.0	2.1	2.1	2.1	5
10	3.7	3.7	3.8	3.9	3.9	4.0	4.0	4.1	4.2	4.1	10
15	5.6	5.6	5.8	5.9	5.9	6.0	6.1	6.2	6.2	6.1	15
20	7.5	7.6	7.7	7.8	7.8	8.1	8.2	8.2	8.2	8.2	20
25	9.4	9.5	9.6	9.7	9.8	10.2	10.2	10.3	10.3	10.2	25
30	11.3	11.5	11.6	11.7	11.7	12.3	12.3	12.4	12.4	12.3	30

Receiver (latitude)	Transmitter (direction from receiver)	Correction Sign	Receiver (latitude)	Transmitter (direction from receiver)	Correction Sign
North	Eastward	+	South	Eastward	−
North	Westward	−	South	Westward	+

TABLE 1

Conversion Angle

DLo	60° Latitude of Receiver					65° Latitude of Receiver					DLo
	Latitude of Transmitter					Latitude of Transmitter					
	50°	55°	60°	65°	70°	55°	60°	65°	70°	75°	
°	°	°	°	°	°	°	°	°	°	°	°
0	0.0	0.0	0.0	0.0	0.0	0.0	0.0	0.0	0.0	0.0	0
5	2.2	2.1	2.2	2.2	2.1	2.3	2.3	2.3	2.2	2.2	5
10	4.3	4.3	4.3	4.3	4.2	4.6	4.6	4.5	4.5	4.3	10
15	6.5	6.5	6.5	6.5	6.3	6.9	6.9	6.8	6.7	6.5	15
20	8.7	8.7	8.7	8.6	8.5	9.3	9.2	9.1	8.9	8.6	20
25	10.9	10.9	10.9	10.8	10.6	11.6	11.5	11.4	11.1	10.8	25
30	13.1	13.1	13.1	12.9	12.7	14.0	13.8	13.7	13.4	12.9	30
35	15.4	15.4	15.3	15.1	14.8	16.3	16.2	16.0	15.6	15.1	35
40	17.7	17.6	17.5	17.3	17.0	18.7	18.5	18.3	17.9	17.2	40
45	19.9	19.9	19.7	19.5	19.1	21.1	20.9	20.6	20.1	19.4	45

DLo	70° Latitude of Receiver					75° Latitude of Receiver					DLo
	Latitude of Transmitter					Latitude of Transmitter					
	60°	65°	70°	75°	80°	65°	70°	75°	80°	85°	
°	°	°	°	°	°	°	°	°	°	°	°
0	0.0	0.0	0.0	0.0	0.0	0.0	0.0	0.0	0.0	0.0	0
5	2.4	2.4	2.4	2.3	2.1	2.6	2.5	2.4	2.3	2.0	5
10	4.9	4.8	4.7	4.5	4.3	5.1	5.0	4.8	4.6	4.0	10
15	7.3	7.2	7.1	6.8	6.4	7.7	7.5	7.3	6.8	6.1	15
20	9.8	9.6	9.4	9.1	8.6	10.3	10.0	9.7	9.1	8.1	20
25	12.2	12.0	11.8	11.4	10.7	12.9	12.6	12.1	11.4	10.1	25
30	14.7	14.5	14.1	13.6	12.8	15.5	15.1	14.5	13.7	12.1	30
35	17.2	16.9	16.5	15.9	15.0	18.1	17.6	16.9	15.9	14.1	35
40	19.7	19.4	18.9	18.2	17.1	20.7	20.1	19.4	18.2	16.2	40
45	22.2	21.8	21.3	20.5	19.3	23.3	22.7	21.8	20.5	18.2	45

DLo	80° Latitude of Receiver					80° Latitude of Receiver					DLo
	Latitude of Transmitter					Latitude of Transmitter					
	70°	75°	80°	85°	90°	70°	75°	80°	85°	90°	
°	°	°	°	°	°	°	°	°	°	°	°
0	0.0	0.0	0.0	0.0	0.0	49.6	47.5	44.6	39.4	0.0	90
5	2.7	2.6	2.6	2.2	0.0	52.4	50.2	47.1	41.6	0.0	95
10	5.4	5.2	4.9	4.4	0.0	55.2	52.9	49.6	43.7	0.0	100
15	8.1	7.8	7.4	6.6	0.0	58.1	55.7	52.1	45.9	0.0	105
20	10.9	10.5	9.9	8.8	0.0	61.0	58.4	54.6	48.1	0.0	110
25	13.6	13.1	12.3	11.0	0.0	63.8	61.1	57.1	50.2	0.0	115
30	16.3	15.7	14.8	13.2	0.0	66.7	63.8	59.6	52.4	0.0	120
35	19.0	18.3	17.3	15.4	0.0	69.6	66.6	62.1	54.5	0.0	125
40	21.8	20.9	19.7	17.5	0.0	72.6	69.3	64.7	56.7	0.0	130
45	24.5	23.6	22.2	19.7	0.0	75.5	72.1	67.2	58.8	0.0	135
50	27.3	26.2	24.7	21.9	0.0	78.5	74.9	69.7	60.9	0.0	140
55	30.0	28.9	27.2	24.1	0.0	81.4	77.7	72.2	63.0	0.0	145
60	32.8	31.5	29.6	26.3	0.0	84.4	80.5	74.8	65.1	0.0	150
65	35.6	34.2	32.1	28.5	0.0	87.4	83.2	77.3	67.2	0.0	155

Receiver (latitude)	Transmitter (direction from receiver)	Correction Sign	Receiver (latitude)	Transmitter (direction from receiver)	Correction Sign
North	Eastward	+	South	Eastward	−
North	Westward	−	South	Westward	+

TABLE 1

Conversion Angle

DLo	80° Latitude of Receiver					80° Latitude of Receiver					DLo
	Latitude of Transmitter					Latitude of Transmitter					
	70°	75°	80°	85°	90°	70°	75°	80°	85°	90°	
°	°	°	°	°	°	°	°	°	°	°	°
70	38. 3	36. 8	34. 6	30. 7	0. 0	90. 4	86. 0	79. 8	69. 3	0. 0	160
75	41. 1	39. 5	37. 1	32. 9	0. 0	93. 5	88. 9	82. 4	71. 4	0. 0	165
80	43. 9	42. 2	39. 6	35. 0	0. 0	96. 5	91. 7	84. 9	73. 4	0. 0	170
85	46. 7	44. 8	42. 1	37. 2	0. 0	99. 6	94. 6	87. 5	75. 5	0. 0	175
90	49. 6	47. 5	44. 6	39. 4	0. 0	102. 6	97. 4	90. 0	77. 5	0. 0	180

DLo	85° Latitude of Receiver				85° Latitude of Receiver				DLo
	Latitude of Transmitter				Latitude of Transmitter				
	75°	80°	85°	90°	75°	80°	85°	80°	
°	°	°	°	°	°	°	°	°	°
0	0. 0	0. 0	0. 0	0. 0	53. 1	50. 2	44. 9	0. 0	90
5	2. 9	2. 8	2. 6	0. 0	56. 1	53. 0	47. 4	0. 0	95
10	5. 9	5. 5	5. 0	0. 0	59. 2	55. 9	49. 9	0. 0	100
15	8. 8	8. 3	7. 5	0. 0	62. 2	58. 7	52. 4	0. 0	105
20	11. 7	11. 1	10. 0	0. 0	65. 2	61. 5	54. 9	0. 0	110
25	14. 6	13. 8	12. 5	0. 0	68. 3	64. 4	57. 4	0. 0	115
30	17. 6	16. 6	14. 9	0. 0	71. 4	67. 3	59. 9	0. 0	120
35	20. 5	19. 4	17. 4	0. 0	74. 4	70. 1	62. 4	0. 0	125
40	23. 4	22. 2	19. 9	0. 0	77. 5	73. 0	64. 9	0. 0	130
45	26. 4	25. 0	22. 4	0. 0	80. 6	75. 9	67. 4	0. 0	135
50	29. 3	27. 7	24. 9	0. 0	83. 7	78. 8	69. 9	0. 0	140
55	32. 3	30. 5	27. 4	0. 0	86. 9	81. 8	72. 4	0. 0	145
60	35. 2	33. 3	29. 9	0. 0	90. 1	84. 7	74. 9	0. 0	150
65	38. 2	36. 1	32. 4	0. 0	93. 2	87. 6	77. 5	0. 0	155
70	41. 1	38. 9	34. 9	0. 0	96. 4	90. 6	80. 0	0. 0	160
75	44. 1	41. 7	37. 4	0. 0	99. 6	93. 6	82. 5	0. 0	165
80	47. 1	44. 5	39. 9	0. 0	102. 8	96. 5	85. 0	0. 0	170
85	50. 1	47. 4	42. 4	0. 0	106. 1	99. 5	87. 5	0. 0	175
90	53. 1	50. 2	44. 9	0. 0	109. 4	102. 5	90. 0	0. 0	180

Receiver (latitude)	Transmitter (direction from receiver)	Correction Sign	Receiver (latitude)	Transmitter (direction from receiver)	Correction Sign
North	Eastward	+	South	Eastward	–
North	Westward	–	South	Westward	+

TABLE 2

Conversion of Compass Points to Degrees

	Points	Angular measure		Points	Angular measure
NORTH TO EAST		° ′ ″	SOUTH TO WEST		° ′ ″
North	0	0 00 00	South	16	180 00 00
N¼E	¼	2 48 45	S¼W	16¼	182 48 45
N½E	½	5 37 30	S½W	16½	185 37 30
N¾E	¾	8 26 15	S¾W	16¾	188 26 15
N by E	1	11 15 00	S by W	17	191 15 00
N by E¼E	1¼	14 03 45	S by W¼W	17¼	194 03 45
N by E½E	1½	16 52 30	S by W½W	17½	196 52 30
N by E¾E	1¾	19 41 15	S by W¾W	17¾	199 41 15
NNE	2	22 30 00	SSW	18	202 30 00
NNE¼E	2¼	25 18 45	SSW¼W	18¼	205 18 45
NNE½E	2½	28 07 30	SSW½W	18½	208 07 30
NNE¾E	2¾	30 56 15	SSW¾W	18¾	210 56 15
NE by N	3	33 45 00	SW by S	19	213 45 00
NE¾N	3¼	36 33 45	SW¾S	19¼	216 33 45
NE½N	3½	39 22 30	SW½S	19½	219 22 30
NE¼N	3¾	42 11 15	SW¼S	19¾	222 11 15
NE	4	45 00 00	SW	20	225 00 00
NE¼E	4¼	47 48 45	SW¼W	20¼	227 48 45
NE½E	4½	50 37 30	SW½W	20½	230 37 30
NE¾E	4¾	53 26 15	SW¾W	20¾	233 26 15
NE by E	5	56 15 00	SW by W	21	236 15 00
NE by E¼E	5¼	59 03 45	SW by W¼W	21¼	239 03 45
NE by E½E	5½	61 52 30	SW by W½W	21½	241 52 30
NE by E¾E	5¾	64 41 15	SW by W¾W	21¾	244 41 15
ENE	6	67 30 00	WSW	22	247 30 00
ENE¼E	6¼	70 18 45	WSW¼W	22¼	250 18 45
ENE½E	6½	73 07 30	WSW½W	22½	253 07 30
ENE¾E	6¾	75 56 15	WSW¾W	22¾	255 56 15
E by N	7	78 45 00	W by S	23	258 45 00
E¾N	7¼	81 33 45	W¾S	23¼	261 33 45
E½N	7½	84 22 30	W½S	23½	264 22 30
E¼N	7¾	87 11 15	W¼S	23¾	267 11 15
EAST TO SOUTH			WEST TO NORTH		
East	8	90 00 00	West	24	270 00 00
E¼S	8¼	92 48 45	W¼N	24¼	272 48 45
E½S	8½	95 37 30	W½N	24½	275 37 30
E¾S	8¾	98 26 15	W¾N	24¾	278 26 15
E by S	9	101 15 00	W by N	25	281 15 00
ESE¾E	9¼	104 03 45	WNW¾W	25¼	284 03 45
ESE½E	9½	106 52 30	WNW½W	25½	286 52 30
ESE¼E	9¾	109 41 15	WNW¼W	25¾	289 41 15
ESE	10	112 30 00	WNW	26	292 30 00
SE by E¾E	10¼	115 18 45	NW by W¾W	26¼	295 18 45
SE by E½E	10½	118 07 30	NW by W½W	26½	298 07 30
SE by E¼E	10¾	120 56 15	NW by W¼W	26¾	300 56 15
SE by E	11	123 45 00	NW by W	27	303 45 00
SE¾E	11¼	126 33 45	NW¾W	27¼	306 33 45
SE½E	11½	129 22 30	NW½W	27½	309 22 30
SE¼E	11¾	132 11 15	NW¼W	27¾	312 11 15
SE	12	135 00 00	NW	28	315 00 00
SE¼S	12¼	137 48 45	NW¼N	28¼	317 48 45
SE½S	12½	140 37 30	NW½N	28½	320 37 30
SE¾S	12¾	143 26 15	NW¾N	28¾	323 26 15
SE by S	13	146 15 00	NW by N	29	326 15 00
SSE¾E	13¼	149 03 45	NNW¾W	29¼	329 03 45
SSE½E	13½	151 52 30	NNW½W	29½	331 52 30
SSE¼E	13¾	154 41 15	NNW¼W	29¾	334 41 15
SSE	14	157 30 00	NNW	30	337 30 00
S by E¾E	14¼	160 18 45	N by W¾W	30¼	340 18 45
S by E½E	14½	163 07 30	N by W½W	30½	343 07 30
S by E¼E	14¾	165 56 15	N by W¼W	30¾	345 56 15
S by E	15	168 45 00	N by W	31	348 45 00
S¾E	15¼	171 33 45	N¾W	31¼	351 33 45
S½E	15½	174 22 30	N½W	31½	354 22 30
S¼E	15¾	177 11 15	N¼W	31¾	357 11 15
South	16	180 00 00	North	32	360 00 00

TABLE 3

Distance of an Object by Two Bearings

Difference between the course and second bearing	Difference between the course and first bearing													
	20°		22°		24°		26°		28°		30°		32°	
°														
30	1.97	0.98												
32	1.64	0.87	2.16	1.14										
34	1.41	0.79	1.80	1.01	2.34	1.31								
36	1.24	0.73	1.55	0.91	1.96	1.15	2.52	1.48						
38	1.11	0.68	1.36	0.84	1.68	1.04	2.11	1.30	2.70	1.66				
40	1.00	0.64	1.21	0.78	1.48	0.95	1.81	1.16	2.26	1.45	2.88	1.85		
42	0.91	0.61	1.10	0.73	1.32	0.88	1.59	1.06	1.94	1.30	2.40	1.61	3.05	2.04
44	0.84	0.58	1.00	0.69	1.19	0.83	1.42	0.98	1.70	1.18	2.07	1.44	2.55	1.77
46	0.78	0.56	0.92	0.66	1.09	0.78	1.28	0.92	1.52	1.09	1.81	1.30	2.19	1.58
48	0.73	0.54	0.85	0.64	1.00	0.74	1.17	0.87	1.37	1.02	1.62	1.20	1.92	1.43
50	0.68	0.52	0.80	0.61	0.93	0.71	1.08	0.83	1.25	0.96	1.46	1.12	1.71	1.31
52	0.65	0.51	0.75	0.59	0.87	0.68	1.00	0.79	1.15	0.91	1.33	1.05	1.55	1.22
54	0.61	0.49	0.71	0.57	0.81	0.66	0.93	0.76	1.07	0.87	1.23	0.99	1.41	1.14
56	0.58	0.48	0.67	0.56	0.77	0.64	0.88	0.73	1.00	0.83	1.14	0.95	1.30	1.08
58	0.56	0.47	0.64	0.54	0.73	0.62	0.83	0.70	0.94	0.80	1.07	0.90	1.21	1.03
60	0.53	0.46	0.61	0.53	0.69	0.60	0.78	0.68	0.89	0.77	1.00	0.87	1.13	0.98
62	0.51	0.45	0.58	0.51	0.66	0.58	0.75	0.66	0.84	0.74	0.94	0.83	1.06	0.94
64	0.49	0.44	0.56	0.50	0.63	0.57	0.71	0.64	0.80	0.72	0.89	0.80	1.00	0.90
66	0.48	0.43	0.54	0.49	0.61	0.56	0.68	0.62	0.76	0.70	0.85	0.78	0.95	0.87
68	0.46	0.43	0.52	0.48	0.59	0.54	0.66	0.61	0.73	0.68	0.81	0.75	0.90	0.84
70	0.45	0.42	0.50	0.47	0.57	0.53	0.63	0.59	0.70	0.66	0.78	0.73	0.86	0.81
72	0.43	0.41	0.49	0.47	0.55	0.52	0.61	0.58	0.68	0.64	0.75	0.71	0.82	0.78
74	0.42	0.41	0.48	0.46	0.53	0.51	0.59	0.57	0.65	0.63	0.72	0.69	0.79	0.76
76	0.41	0.40	0.46	0.45	0.52	0.50	0.57	0.56	0.63	0.61	0.70	0.67	0.76	0.74
78	0.40	0.39	0.45	0.44	0.50	0.49	0.56	0.54	0.61	0.60	0.67	0.66	0.74	0.72
80	0.39	0.39	0.44	0.44	0.49	0.48	0.54	0.53	0.60	0.59	0.65	0.64	0.71	0.70
82	0.39	0.38	0.43	0.43	0.48	0.47	0.53	0.52	0.58	0.57	0.63	0.63	0.69	0.69
84	0.38	0.38	0.42	0.42	0.47	0.47	0.52	0.51	0.57	0.56	0.62	0.61	0.67	0.67
86	0.37	0.37	0.42	0.42	0.46	0.46	0.51	0.51	0.55	0.55	0.60	0.60	0.66	0.65
88	0.37	0.37	0.41	0.41	0.45	0.45	0.50	0.50	0.54	0.54	0.59	0.59	0.64	0.64
90	0.36	0.36	0.40	0.40	0.45	0.45	0.49	0.49	0.53	0.53	0.58	0.58	0.62	0.62
92	0.36	0.36	0.40	0.40	0.44	0.44	0.48	0.48	0.52	0.52	0.57	0.57	0.61	0.61
94	0.36	0.35	0.39	0.39	0.43	0.43	0.47	0.47	0.51	0.51	0.56	0.55	0.60	0.60
96	0.35	0.35	0.39	0.39	0.43	0.43	0.47	0.46	0.51	0.50	0.55	0.54	0.59	0.59
98	0.35	0.35	0.39	0.38	0.42	0.42	0.46	0.46	0.50	0.50	0.54	0.53	0.58	0.57
100	0.35	0.34	0.38	0.38	0.42	0.41	0.46	0.45	0.49	0.49	0.53	0.52	0.57	0.56
102	0.35	0.34	0.38	0.37	0.42	0.41	0.45	0.44	0.49	0.48	0.53	0.51	0.56	0.55
104	0.34	0.33	0.38	0.37	0.41	0.40	0.45	0.43	0.48	0.47	0.52	0.50	0.56	0.54
106	0.34	0.33	0.38	0.36	0.41	0.39	0.45	0.43	0.48	0.46	0.52	0.50	0.55	0.53
108	0.34	0.32	0.38	0.36	0.41	0.39	0.44	0.42	0.48	0.45	0.51	0.49	0.55	0.52
110	0.34	0.32	0.37	0.35	0.41	0.38	0.44	0.41	0.47	0.44	0.51	0.48	0.54	0.51
112	0.34	0.32	0.37	0.35	0.41	0.38	0.44	0.41	0.47	0.44	0.50	0.47	0.54	0.50
114	0.34	0.31	0.37	0.34	0.41	0.37	0.44	0.40	0.47	0.43	0.50	0.46	0.54	0.49
116	0.34	0.31	0.38	0.34	0.41	0.37	0.44	0.39	0.47	0.42	0.50	0.45	0.53	0.48
118	0.35	0.31	0.38	0.33	0.41	0.36	0.44	0.39	0.47	0.41	0.50	0.44	0.53	0.47
120	0.35	0.30	0.38	0.33	0.41	0.36	0.44	0.38	0.47	0.41	0.50	0.43	0.53	0.46
122	0.35	0.30	0.38	0.32	0.41	0.35	0.44	0.37	0.47	0.40	0.50	0.42	0.53	0.45
124	0.35	0.29	0.38	0.32	0.41	0.34	0.44	0.37	0.47	0.39	0.50	0.42	0.53	0.44
126	0.36	0.29	0.39	0.31	0.42	0.34	0.45	0.36	0.47	0.38	0.50	0.41	0.53	0.43
128	0.36	0.28	0.39	0.31	0.42	0.33	0.45	0.35	0.48	0.38	0.50	0.40	0.53	0.42
130	0.36	0.28	0.39	0.30	0.42	0.32	0.45	0.35	0.48	0.37	0.51	0.39	0.54	0.41
132	0.37	0.27	0.40	0.30	0.43	0.32	0.46	0.34	0.48	0.36	0.51	0.38	0.54	0.40
134	0.37	0.27	0.40	0.29	0.43	0.31	0.46	0.33	0.49	0.35	0.52	0.37	0.54	0.39
136	0.38	0.26	0.41	0.28	0.44	0.30	0.47	0.32	0.49	0.34	0.52	0.36	0.55	0.38
138	0.39	0.26	0.42	0.28	0.45	0.30	0.47	0.32	0.50	0.33	0.53	0.35	0.55	0.37
140	0.39	0.25	0.42	0.27	0.45	0.29	0.48	0.31	0.51	0.33	0.53	0.34	0.56	0.36
142	0.40	0.25	0.43	0.27	0.46	0.28	0.49	0.30	0.51	0.32	0.54	0.33	0.56	0.35
144	0.41	0.24	0.44	0.26	0.47	0.28	0.50	0.29	0.52	0.31	0.55	0.32	0.57	0.34
146	0.42	0.24	0.45	0.25	0.48	0.27	0.51	0.28	0.53	0.30	0.56	0.31	0.58	0.32
148	0.43	0.23	0.46	0.25	0.49	0.26	0.52	0.27	0.54	0.29	0.57	0.30	0.59	0.31
150	0.45	0.22	0.48	0.24	0.50	0.25	0.53	0.26	0.55	0.28	0.58	0.29	0.60	0.30
152	0.46	0.22	0.49	0.23	0.52	0.24	0.54	0.25	0.57	0.27	0.59	0.28	0.61	0.29
154	0.48	0.21	0.50	0.22	0.53	0.23	0.56	0.24	0.58	0.25	0.60	0.26	0.62	0.27
156	0.49	0.20	0.52	0.21	0.55	0.22	0.57	0.23	0.60	0.24	0.62	0.25	0.64	0.26
158	0.51	0.19	0.54	0.20	0.57	0.21	0.59	0.22	0.61	0.23	0.63	0.24	0.66	0.25
160	0.53	0.18	0.56	0.19	0.59	0.20	0.61	0.21	0.63	0.22	0.65	0.22	0.67	0.23

TABLE 3

Distance of an Object by Two Bearings

Difference between the course and second bearing	Difference between the course and first bearing													
	34°		36°		38°		40°		42°		44°		46°	
°														
44	3.22	2.24												
46	2.69	1.93	3.39	2.43										
48	2.31	1.72	2.83	2.10	3.55	2.63								
50	2.03	1.55	2.43	1.86	2.96	2.27	3.70	2.84						
52	1.81	1.43	2.13	1.68	2.54	2.01	3.09	2.44	3.85	3.04				
54	1.63	1.32	1.90	1.54	2.23	1.81	2.66	2.15	3.22	2.60	4.00	3.24		
56	1.49	1.24	1.72	1.42	1.99	1.65	2.33	1.93	2.77	2.29	3.34	2.77	4.14	3.43
58	1.37	1.17	1.57	1.33	1.80	1.53	2.08	1.76	2.43	2.06	2.87	2.44	3.46	2.93
60	1.28	1.10	1.45	1.25	1.64	1.42	1.88	1.63	2.17	1.88	2.52	2.18	2.97	2.57
62	1.19	1.05	1.34	1.18	1.51	1.34	1.72	1.52	1.96	1.73	2.25	1.98	2.61	2.30
64	1.12	1.01	1.25	1.13	1.40	1.26	1.58	1.42	1.79	1.61	2.03	1.83	2.33	2.09
66	1.06	0.96	1.18	1.07	1.31	1.20	1.47	1.34	1.65	1.51	1.85	1.69	2.10	1.92
68	1.00	0.93	1.11	1.03	1.23	1.14	1.37	1.27	1.53	1.42	1.71	1.58	1.92	1.78
70	0.95	0.89	1.05	0.99	1.16	1.09	1.29	1.21	1.43	1.34	1.58	1.49	1.77	1.66
72	0.91	0.86	1.00	0.95	1.10	1.05	1.21	1.15	1.34	1.27	1.48	1.41	1.64	1.56
74	0.87	0.84	0.95	0.92	1.05	1.01	1.15	1.10	1.26	1.21	1.39	1.34	1.53	1.47
76	0.84	0.81	0.91	0.89	1.00	0.97	1.09	1.06	1.20	1.16	1.31	1.27	1.44	1.40
78	0.80	0.79	0.88	0.86	0.96	0.94	1.04	1.02	1.14	1.11	1.24	1.22	1.36	1.33
80	0.78	0.77	0.85	0.83	0.92	0.91	1.00	0.98	1.09	1.07	1.18	1.16	1.28	1.27
82	0.75	0.75	0.82	0.81	0.89	0.88	0.96	0.95	1.04	1.03	1.13	1.12	1.22	1.21
84	0.73	0.73	0.79	0.79	0.86	0.85	0.93	0.92	1.00	0.99	1.08	1.07	1.17	1.16
86	0.71	0.71	0.77	0.77	0.83	0.83	0.89	0.89	0.96	0.96	1.04	1.04	1.12	1.12
88	0.69	0.69	0.75	0.75	0.80	0.80	0.86	0.86	0.93	0.93	1.00	1.00	1.08	1.07
90	0.67	0.67	0.73	0.73	0.78	0.78	0.84	0.84	0.90	0.90	0.97	0.97	1.04	1.04
92	0.66	0.66	0.71	0.71	0.76	0.76	0.82	0.82	0.87	0.87	0.93	0.93	1.00	1.00
94	0.65	0.64	0.69	0.69	0.74	0.74	0.79	0.79	0.85	0.85	0.91	0.90	0.97	0.97
96	0.63	0.63	0.68	0.67	0.73	0.72	0.78	0.77	0.83	0.82	0.88	0.88	0.94	0.93
98	0.62	0.62	0.67	0.66	0.71	0.70	0.76	0.75	0.81	0.80	0.86	0.85	0.91	0.90
100	0.61	0.60	0.65	0.64	0.70	0.69	0.74	0.73	0.79	0.78	0.84	0.83	0.89	0.88
102	0.60	0.59	0.64	0.63	0.68	0.67	0.73	0.71	0.77	0.76	0.82	0.80	0.87	0.85
104	0.60	0.58	0.63	0.61	0.67	0.65	0.72	0.69	0.76	0.74	0.80	0.78	0.85	0.82
106	0.59	0.57	0.63	0.60	0.66	0.64	0.70	0.68	0.74	0.72	0.79	0.76	0.83	0.80
108	0.58	0.55	0.62	0.59	0.66	0.62	0.69	0.66	0.73	0.70	0.77	0.74	0.81	0.77
110	0.58	0.54	0.61	0.57	0.65	0.61	0.68	0.64	0.72	0.68	0.76	0.71	0.80	0.75
112	0.57	0.53	0.61	0.56	0.64	0.59	0.68	0.63	0.71	0.66	0.75	0.69	0.79	0.73
114	0.57	0.52	0.60	0.55	0.63	0.58	0.67	0.61	0.70	0.64	0.74	0.68	0.78	0.71
116	0.56	0.51	0.60	0.54	0.63	0.57	0.66	0.60	0.70	0.63	0.73	0.66	0.77	0.69
118	0.56	0.50	0.59	0.52	0.63	0.55	0.66	0.58	0.69	0.61	0.72	0.64	0.76	0.67
120	0.56	0.49	0.59	0.51	0.62	0.54	0.65	0.57	0.68	0.59	0.72	0.62	0.75	0.65
122	0.56	0.47	0.59	0.50	0.62	0.53	0.65	0.55	0.68	0.58	0.71	0.60	0.74	0.63
124	0.56	0.46	0.59	0.49	0.62	0.51	0.65	0.54	0.68	0.56	0.71	0.58	0.74	0.61
126	0.56	0.45	0.59	0.48	0.62	0.50	0.64	0.52	0.67	0.54	0.70	0.57	0.73	0.59
128	0.56	0.44	0.59	0.46	0.62	0.49	0.64	0.51	0.67	0.53	0.70	0.55	0.73	0.57
130	0.56	0.43	0.59	0.45	0.62	0.47	0.64	0.49	0.67	0.51	0.70	0.53	0.72	0.55
132	0.56	0.42	0.59	0.44	0.62	0.46	0.64	0.48	0.67	0.50	0.70	0.52	0.72	0.54
134	0.57	0.41	0.59	0.43	0.62	0.45	0.64	0.46	0.67	0.48	0.69	0.50	0.72	0.52
136	0.57	0.40	0.60	0.41	0.62	0.43	0.65	0.45	0.67	0.47	0.70	0.48	0.72	0.50
138	0.58	0.39	0.60	0.40	0.63	0.42	0.65	0.43	0.67	0.45	0.70	0.47	0.72	0.48
140	0.58	0.37	0.61	0.39	0.63	0.40	0.65	0.42	0.68	0.43	0.70	0.45	0.72	0.46
142	0.59	0.36	0.61	0.38	0.63	0.39	0.66	0.41	0.68	0.42	0.70	0.43	0.72	0.45
144	0.60	0.35	0.62	0.36	0.64	0.38	0.66	0.39	0.68	0.40	0.71	0.41	0.73	0.43
146	0.60	0.34	0.63	0.35	0.65	0.36	0.67	0.37	0.69	0.39	0.71	0.40	0.73	0.41
148	0.61	0.32	0.63	0.34	0.66	0.35	0.68	0.36	0.70	0.37	0.72	0.38	0.74	0.39
150	0.62	0.31	0.64	0.32	0.66	0.33	0.68	0.34	0.70	0.35	0.72	0.36	0.74	0.37
152	0.63	0.30	0.65	0.31	0.67	0.32	0.69	0.33	0.71	0.33	0.73	0.34	0.75	0.35
154	0.65	0.28	0.67	0.29	0.68	0.30	0.70	0.31	0.72	0.32	0.74	0.32	0.76	0.33
156	0.66	0.27	0.68	0.28	0.70	0.28	0.72	0.29	0.73	0.30	0.75	0.30	0.77	0.31
158	0.67	0.25	0.69	0.26	0.71	0.27	0.73	0.27	0.74	0.28	0.76	0.28	0.78	0.29
160	0.69	0.24	0.71	0.24	0.73	0.25	0.74	0.25	0.76	0.26	0.77	0.26	0.79	0.27

TABLE 3

Distance of an Object by Two Bearings

Difference between the course and second bearing	Difference between the course and first bearing													
	48°		50°		52°		54°		56°		58°		60°	
°														
58	4. 28	3. 63												
60	3. 57	3. 10	4. 41	3. 82										
62	3. 07	2. 71	3. 68	3. 25	4. 54	4. 01								
64	2. 70	2. 42	3. 17	2. 85	3. 79	3. 41	4. 66	4. 19						
66	2. 40	2. 20	2. 78	2. 54	3. 26	2. 98	3. 89	3. 55	4. 77	4. 36				
68	2. 17	2. 01	2. 48	2. 30	2. 86	2. 65	3. 34	3. 10	3. 99	3. 71	4. 88	4. 53		
70	1. 98	1. 86	2. 24	2. 10	2. 55	2. 39	2. 94	2. 76	3. 43	3. 22	4. 08	3. 83	4. 99	4. 69
72	1. 83	1. 74	2. 04	1. 94	2. 30	2. 19	2. 62	2. 49	3. 01	2. 86	3. 51	3. 33	4. 17	3. 96
74	1. 70	1. 63	1. 88	1. 81	2. 10	2. 02	2. 37	2. 27	2. 68	2. 58	3. 08	2. 96	3. 58	3. 44
76	1. 58	1. 54	1. 75	1. 70	1. 94	1. 88	2. 16	2. 10	2. 42	2. 35	2. 74	2. 66	3. 14	3. 05
78	1. 49	1. 45	1. 63	1. 60	1. 80	1. 76	1. 99	1. 95	2. 21	2. 16	2. 48	2. 43	2. 80	2. 74
80	1. 40	1. 38	1. 53	1. 51	1. 68	1. 65	1. 85	1. 82	2. 04	2. 01	2. 26	2. 23	2. 53	2. 49
82	1. 33	1. 32	1. 45	1. 43	1. 58	1. 56	1. 72	1. 71	1. 89	1. 87	2. 08	2. 06	2. 31	2. 29
84	1. 26	1. 26	1. 37	1. 36	1. 49	1. 48	1. 62	1. 61	1. 77	1. 76	1. 93	1. 92	2. 13	2. 12
86	1. 21	1. 20	1. 30	1. 30	1. 41	1. 41	1. 53	1. 52	1. 66	1. 65	1. 81	1. 80	1. 98	1. 97
88	1. 16	1. 16	1. 24	1. 24	1. 34	1. 34	1. 45	1. 45	1. 56	1. 56	1. 70	1. 70	1. 84	1. 84
90	1. 11	1. 11	1. 19	1. 19	1. 28	1. 28	1. 38	1. 38	1. 48	1. 48	1. 60	1. 60	1. 73	1. 73
92	1. 07	1. 07	1. 14	1. 14	1. 23	1. 23	1. 31	1. 31	1. 41	1. 41	1. 52	1. 52	1. 63	1. 63
94	1. 03	1. 03	1. 10	1. 10	1. 18	1. 17	1. 26	1. 26	1. 35	1. 34	1. 44	1. 44	1. 55	1. 54
96	1. 00	0. 99	1. 06	1. 06	1. 13	1. 13	1. 21	1. 20	1. 29	1. 28	1. 38	1. 37	1. 47	1. 47
98	0. 97	0. 96	1. 03	1. 02	1. 10	1. 08	1. 16	1. 15	1. 24	1. 23	1. 32	1. 31	1. 41	1. 39
100	0. 94	0. 93	1. 00	0. 98	1. 06	1. 04	1. 12	1. 11	1. 19	1. 18	1. 27	1. 25	1. 35	1. 33
102	0. 92	0. 90	0. 97	0. 95	1. 03	1. 01	1. 09	1. 06	1. 15	1. 13	1. 22	1. 19	1. 29	1. 27
104	0. 90	0. 87	0. 95	0. 92	1. 00	0. 97	1. 06	1. 02	1. 12	1. 08	1. 18	1. 14	1. 25	1. 21
106	0. 88	0. 84	0. 92	0. 89	0. 97	0. 94	1. 03	0. 99	1. 09	1. 04	1. 14	1. 10	1. 20	1. 16
108	0. 86	0. 82	0. 90	0. 86	0. 95	0. 90	1. 00	0. 95	1. 05	1. 00	1. 11	1. 05	1. 17	1. 11
110	0. 84	0. 79	0. 88	0. 83	0. 93	0. 87	0. 98	0. 92	1. 02	0. 96	1. 08	1. 01	1. 13	1. 06
112	0. 83	0. 77	0. 87	0. 80	0. 91	0. 84	0. 95	0. 88	1. 00	0. 93	1. 05	0. 97	1. 10	1. 02
114	0. 81	0. 74	0. 85	0. 78	0. 89	0. 82	0. 93	0. 85	0. 98	0. 89	1. 02	0. 93	1. 07	0. 98
116	0. 80	0. 72	0. 84	0. 75	0. 88	0. 79	0. 92	0. 82	0. 96	0. 85	1. 00	0. 90	1. 04	0. 94
118	0. 79	0. 70	0. 83	0. 73	0. 86	0. 76	0. 90	0. 79	0. 94	0. 83	0. 98	0. 86	1. 02	0. 90
120	0. 78	0. 68	0. 82	0. 71	0. 85	0. 74	0. 89	0. 77	0. 91	0. 80	0. 96	0. 83	1. 00	0. 87
122	0. 77	0. 66	0. 81	0. 68	0. 84	0. 71	0. 87	0. 74	0. 90	0. 77	0. 95	0. 80	0. 98	0. 83
124	0. 77	0. 63	0. 80	0. 66	0. 83	0. 69	0. 86	0. 71	0. 90	0. 74	0. 93	0. 77	0. 96	0. 80
126	0. 76	0. 61	0. 79	0. 64	0. 82	0. 66	0. 85	0. 69	0. 88	0. 71	0. 91	0. 74	0. 95	0. 77
128	0. 75	0. 59	0. 78	0. 62	0. 81	0. 64	0. 84	0. 66	0. 87	0. 69	0. 90	0. 71	0. 93	0. 74
130	0. 75	0. 57	0. 78	0. 60	0. 81	0. 62	0. 83	0. 64	0. 86	0. 66	0. 89	0. 68	0. 92	0. 71
132	0. 75	0. 56	0. 77	0. 57	0. 80	0. 59	0. 83	0. 61	0. 85	0. 64	0. 88	0. 66	0. 91	0. 68
134	0. 74	0. 54	0. 77	0. 55	0. 80	0. 57	0. 82	0. 59	0. 85	0. 61	0. 87	0. 63	0. 90	0. 65
136	0. 74	0. 52	0. 77	0. 53	0. 80	0. 55	0. 82	0. 57	0. 84	0. 58	0. 87	0. 60	0. 89	0. 62
138	0. 74	0. 50	0. 77	0. 51	0. 79	0. 53	0. 81	0. 54	0. 84	0. 56	0. 86	0. 58	0. 89	0. 59
140	0. 74	0. 48	0. 77	0. 49	0. 79	0. 51	0. 81	0. 52	0. 83	0. 54	0. 86	0. 55	0. 88	0. 57
142	0. 74	0. 46	0. 77	0. 47	0. 79	0. 49	0. 81	0. 50	0. 83	0. 51	0. 85	0. 52	0. 87	0. 54
144	0. 75	0. 44	0. 77	0. 45	0. 79	0. 46	0. 81	0. 48	0. 83	0. 49	0. 85	0. 50	0. 87	0. 51
146	0. 75	0. 42	0. 77	0. 43	0. 79	0. 44	0. 81	0. 45	0. 83	0. 46	0. 85	0. 47	0. 87	0. 49
148	0. 76	0. 40	0. 77	0. 41	0. 79	0. 42	0. 81	0. 43	0. 83	0. 44	0. 85	0. 45	0. 87	0. 46
150	0. 76	0. 38	0. 78	0. 39	0. 80	0. 40	0. 81	0. 41	0. 83	0. 42	0. 85	0. 42	0. 87	0. 43
152	0. 77	0. 36	0. 78	0. 37	0. 80	0. 38	0. 82	0. 38	0. 83	0. 39	0. 85	0. 40	0. 87	0. 41
154	0. 77	0. 34	0. 79	0. 35	0. 81	0. 35	0. 82	0. 36	0. 84	0. 37	0. 85	0. 37	0. 87	0. 38
156	0. 78	0. 32	0. 80	0. 32	0. 81	0. 33	0. 83	0. 34	0. 84	0. 34	0. 86	0. 35	0. 87	0. 35
158	0. 79	0. 30	0. 81	0. 30	0. 82	0. 31	0. 83	0. 31	0. 85	0. 32	0. 86	0. 32	0. 87	0. 33
160	0. 80	0. 27	0. 82	0. 28	0. 83	0. 28	0. 84	0. 29	0. 85	0. 29	0. 86	0. 30	0. 88	0. 30

TABLE 3

Distance of an Object by Two Bearings

Difference between the course and second bearing	Difference between the course and first bearing															
	62°		64°		66°		68°		70°		72°		74°		76°	
°																
72	5. 08	4. 84														
74	4. 25	4. 08	5. 18	4. 98												
76	3. 65	3. 54	4. 32	4. 19	5. 26	5. 10										
78	3. 20	3. 13	3. 72	3. 63	4. 39	4. 30	5. 34	5. 22								
80	2. 86	2. 81	3. 26	3. 21	3. 78	3. 72	4. 46	4. 39	5. 41	5. 33						
82	2. 58	2. 56	2. 91	2. 88	3. 31	3. 28	3. 83	3. 80	4. 52	4. 48	5. 48	5. 42				
84	2. 36	2. 34	2. 63	2. 61	2. 96	2. 94	3. 36	3. 35	3. 88	3. 86	4. 57	4. 55	5. 54	5. 51		
86	2. 17	2. 17	2. 40	2. 39	2. 67	2. 66	3. 00	2. 99	3. 41	3. 40	3. 93	3. 92	4. 62	4. 61	5. 59	5. 57
88	2. 01	2. 01	2. 21	2. 21	2. 44	2. 44	2. 71	2. 71	3. 04	3. 04	3. 45	3. 45	3. 97	3. 97	4. 67	4. 66
90	1. 88	1. 88	2. 05	2. 05	2. 25	2. 25	2. 48	2. 48	2. 75	2. 75	3. 08	3. 08	3. 49	3. 49	4. 01	4. 01
92	1. 77	1. 76	1. 91	1. 91	2. 08	2. 08	2. 28	2. 28	2. 51	2. 51	2. 78	2. 78	3. 11	3. 11	3. 52	3. 52
94	1. 67	1. 66	1. 80	1. 79	1. 95	1. 94	2. 12	2. 11	2. 31	2. 30	2. 54	2. 53	2. 81	2. 80	3. 14	3. 13
96	1. 58	1. 57	1. 70	1. 69	1. 83	1. 82	1. 97	1. 96	2. 14	2. 13	2. 34	2. 33	2. 57	2. 55	2. 84	2. 82
98	1. 50	1. 49	1. 61	1. 59	1. 72	1. 71	1. 85	1. 84	2. 00	1. 98	2. 17	2. 15	2. 36	2. 34	2. 59	2. 56
100	1. 43	1. 41	1. 53	1. 51	1. 63	1. 61	1. 75	1. 72	1. 88	1. 85	2. 03	2. 00	2. 19	2. 16	2. 39	2. 35
102	1. 37	1. 34	1. 46	1. 43	1. 55	1. 52	1. 66	1. 62	1. 77	1. 73	1. 90	1. 86	2. 05	2. 00	2. 21	2. 16
104	1. 32	1. 28	1. 40	1. 36	1. 48	1. 44	1. 58	1. 53	1. 68	1. 63	1. 79	1. 74	1. 92	1. 87	2. 07	2. 01
106	1. 27	1. 22	1. 34	1. 29	1. 42	1. 37	1. 51	1. 45	1. 60	1. 54	1. 70	1. 63	1. 81	1. 74	1. 94	1. 87
108	1. 23	1. 17	1. 29	1. 23	1. 37	1. 30	1. 44	1. 37	1. 53	1. 45	1. 62	1. 54	1. 72	1. 63	1. 83	1. 74
110	1. 19	1. 12	1. 25	1. 17	1. 32	1. 24	1. 39	1. 30	1. 46	1. 37	1. 54	1. 45	1. 64	1. 54	1. 74	1. 63
112	1. 15	1. 07	1. 21	1. 12	1. 27	1. 18	1. 33	1. 24	1. 40	1. 30	1. 48	1. 37	1. 56	1. 45	1. 65	1. 53
114	1. 12	1. 02	1. 17	1. 07	1. 23	1. 12	1. 29	1. 18	1. 35	1. 24	1. 42	1. 30	1. 50	1. 37	1. 58	1. 44
116	1. 09	0. 98	1. 14	1. 03	1. 19	1. 07	1. 25	1. 12	1. 31	1. 17	1. 37	1. 23	1. 44	1. 29	1. 51	1. 36
118	1. 07	0. 94	1. 11	0. 98	1. 16	1. 02	1. 21	1. 07	1. 26	1. 12	1. 32	1. 17	1. 38	1. 22	1. 45	1. 28
120	1. 04	0. 90	1. 08	0. 94	1. 13	0. 98	1. 18	1. 02	1. 23	1. 06	1. 28	1. 11	1. 34	1. 16	1. 40	1. 21
122	1. 02	0. 86	1. 06	0. 90	1. 10	0. 93	1. 15	0. 97	1. 19	1. 01	1. 24	1. 05	1. 29	1. 10	1. 35	1. 14
124	1. 00	0. 83	1. 04	0. 86	1. 08	0. 89	1. 12	0. 93	1. 16	0. 96	1. 21	1. 00	1. 25	1. 04	1. 31	1. 08
126	0. 98	0. 79	1. 02	0. 82	1. 05	0. 85	1. 09	0. 88	1. 13	0. 92	1. 18	0. 95	1. 22	0. 99	1. 27	1. 02
128	0. 97	0. 76	1. 00	0. 79	1. 03	0. 82	1. 07	0. 84	1. 11	0. 87	1. 15	0. 90	1. 19	0. 94	1. 23	0. 97
130	0. 95	0. 73	0. 98	0. 75	1. 02	0. 78	1. 05	0. 80	1. 09	0. 83	1. 12	0. 86	1. 16	0. 89	1. 20	0. 92
132	0. 94	0. 70	0. 97	0. 72	1. 00	0. 74	1. 03	0. 77	1. 06	0. 79	1. 10	0. 82	1. 13	0. 84	1. 17	0. 87
134	0. 93	0. 67	0. 96	0. 69	0. 99	0. 71	1. 01	0. 73	1. 04	0. 75	1. 08	0. 77	1. 11	0. 80	1. 14	0. 82
136	0. 92	0. 64	0. 95	0. 66	0. 97	0. 68	1. 00	0. 69	1. 03	0. 71	1. 06	0. 74	1. 09	0. 76	1. 12	0. 78
138	0. 91	0. 61	0. 94	0. 63	0. 96	0. 64	0. 99	0. 66	1. 01	0. 68	1. 04	0. 70	1. 07	0. 72	1. 10	0. 74
140	0. 90	0. 58	0. 93	0. 60	0. 95	0. 61	0. 97	0. 63	1. 00	0. 64	1. 03	0. 66	1. 05	0. 68	1. 08	0. 70
142	0. 90	0. 55	0. 92	0. 57	0. 94	0. 58	0. 96	0. 59	0. 99	0. 61	1. 01	0. 62	1. 04	0. 64	1. 06	0. 65
144	0. 89	0. 52	0. 91	0. 54	0. 93	0. 55	0. 96	0. 56	0. 98	0. 57	1. 00	0. 59	1. 02	0. 60	1. 05	0. 62
146	0. 89	0. 50	0. 91	0. 51	0. 93	0. 52	0. 95	0. 53	0. 97	0. 54	0. 99	0. 55	1. 01	0. 57	1. 03	0. 58
148	0. 89	0. 47	0. 90	0. 48	0. 92	0. 49	0. 94	0. 50	0. 96	0. 51	0. 98	0. 52	1. 00	0. 53	1. 02	0. 54
150	0. 88	0. 44	0. 90	0. 45	0. 92	0. 46	0. 94	0. 47	0. 95	0. 48	0. 97	0. 49	0. 99	0. 50	1. 01	0. 50
152	0. 88	0. 41	0. 90	0. 42	0. 92	0. 43	0. 93	0. 44	0. 95	0. 45	0. 97	0. 45	0. 98	0. 46	1. 00	0. 47
154	0. 88	0. 39	0. 90	0. 39	0. 91	0. 40	0. 93	0. 41	0. 94	0. 41	0. 96	0. 42	0. 98	0. 43	0. 99	0. 43
156	0. 89	0. 36	0. 90	0. 37	0. 91	0. 37	0. 93	0. 38	0. 94	0. 38	0. 96	0. 39	0. 97	0. 39	0. 99	0. 40
158	0. 89	0. 33	0. 90	0. 34	0. 91	0. 34	0. 93	0. 35	0. 94	0. 35	0. 95	0. 36	0. 97	0. 36	0. 98	0. 37
160	0. 89	0. 30	0. 90	0. 31	0. 91	0. 31	0. 93	0. 32	0. 94	0. 32	0. 95	0. 33	0. 96	0. 33	0. 98	0. 33

TABLE 3

Distance of an Object by Two Bearings

Difference between the course and second bearing.	Difference between the course and first bearing. 110°		112°		114°		116°		118°		120°		122°	
°														
120	5.41	4.69												
122	4.52	3.83	5.34	4.53										
124	3.88	3.22	4.46	3.70	5.26	4.36								
126	3.41	2.76	3.83	3.10	4.39	3.55	5.18	4.19						
128	3.04	2.40	3.36	2.65	3.78	2.98	4.32	3.41	5.08	4.01				
130	2.75	2.10	3.00	2.30	3.31	2.54	3.72	2.85	4.25	3.25	4.99	3.82		
132	2.51	1.86	2.71	2.01	2.96	2.20	3.26	2.42	3.65	2.71	4.17	3.10	4.88	3.63
134	2.31	1.66	2.48	1.78	2.67	1.92	2.91	2.09	3.20	2.30	3.58	2.57	4.08	2.93
136	2,14	1.49	2.28	1.58	2.44	1.69	2.63	1.83	2.86	1.98	3.14	2.18	3.51	2.44
138	2.00	1.34	2.12	1.42	2.25	1.50	2.40	1.61	2.58	1.73	2.80	1.88	3.08	2.06
140	1.88	1.21	1.97	1.27	2.08	1.34	2.21	1.42	2.36	1.52	2.53	1.63	2.74	1.76
142	1.77	1.09	1.85	1.14	1.95	1.20	2.05	1.26	2.17	1.34	2.31	1.42	2.48	1.53
144	1.68	0.99	1.75	1.03	1.83	1.07	1.91	1.13	2.01	1.18	2.13	1.25	2.26	1.33
146	1.60	0.89	1.66	0.93	1.72	0.96	1.80	1.01	1.88	1.05	1.98	1.10	2.08	1.17
148	1.53	0.81	1.58	0.84	1.63	0.87	1.70	0.90	1.77	0.94	1.84	0.98	1.93	1.03
150	1.46	0.73	1.51	0.75	1.55	0.78	1.61	0.80	1.67	0.83	1.73	0.87	1.81	0.90
152	1.40	0.66	1.44	0.68	1.48	0.70	1.53	0.72	1.58	0.74	1.63	0.77	1.70	0.80
154	1.35	0.59	1.39	0.61	1.42	0.62	1.46	0.64	1.50	0.66	1.55	0.68	1.60	0.70
156	1.31	0.53	1.33	0.54	1.37	0.56	1.40	0.57	1.43	0.58	1.47	0.60	1.52	0.62
158	1.26	0.47	1.29	0.48	1.32	0.49	1.34	0.50	1.37	0.51	1.41	0.53	1.44	0.54
160	1.23	0.42	1.25	0.43	1.27	0.43	1.29	0.44	1.32	0.45	1.35	0.46	1.38	0.47

	124°		126°		128°		130°		132°		134°		136°	
134	4.77	3.43												
136	3.99	2.77	4.66	3.23										
138	3.43	2.29	3.89	2.60	4.54	3.04								
140	3.01	1.93	3.34	2.15	3.79	2.44	4.41	2.84						
142	2.68	1.65	2.94	1.81	3.26	2.01	3.68	2.27	4.28	2.63				
144	2.42	1.42	2.62	1.54	2.86	1.68	3.17	1.86	3.57	2.10	4.14	2.43		
146	2.21	1.24	2.37	1.32	2.55	1.43	2.78	1.55	3.07	1.72	3.46	1.93	4.00	2.24
148	2.04	1.08	2.16	1.14	2.30	1.22	2.48	1.31	2.70	1.43	2.97	1.58	3.34	1.77
150	1.89	0.95	1.99	0.99	2.10	1.05	2.24	1.12	2.40	1.20	2.61	1.30	2.87	1.44
152	1.77	0.83	1.85	0.87	1.94	0.91	2.04	0.96	2.17	1.02	2.33	1.09	2.52	1.18
154	1.66	0.73	1.72	0.76	1.80	0.79	1.88	0.83	1.98	0.87	2.10	0.92	2.25	0.99
156	1.56	0.64	1.62	0.66	1.68	0.68	1.75	0.71	1.83	0.74	1.92	0.78	2.03	0.83
158	1.48	0.56	1.53	0.57	1.58	0.59	1.63	0.61	1.70	0.64	1.77	0.66	1.85	0.69
160	1.41	0.48	1.45	0.49	1.49	0.51	1.53	0.52	1.58	0.54	1.64	0.56	1.71	0.58

	138°		140°		142°		144°		146°		148°		150°	
148	3.85	2.04												
150	3.22	1.61	3.70	1.85										
152	2.77	1.30	3.09	1.45	3.55	1.66								
154	2.43	1.06	2.66	1.16	2.96	1.30	3.38	1.48						
156	2.17	0.88	2.33	0.95	2.54	1.04	2.83	1.15	3.22	1.31				
158	1.96	0.73	2.08	0.78	2.23	0.84	2.43	0.91	2.69	1.01	3.05	1.14		
160	1.79	0.61	1.88	0.64	1.99	0.68	2.13	0.73	2.31	0.79	2.55	0.87	2.88	0.98

TABLE 3

Distance of an Object by Two Bearings

Difference between the course and second bearing	Difference between the course and first bearing															
	78°		80°		82°		84°		86°		88°		90°		92°	
°																
88	5. 63	5. 63														
90	4. 70	4. 70	5. 67	5. 67												
92	4. 04	4. 04	4. 74	4. 73	5. 70	5. 70										
94	3. 55	3. 54	4. 07	4. 06	4. 76	4. 75	5. 73	5. 71								
96	3. 17	3. 15	3. 57	3. 55	4. 09	4. 07	4. 78	4. 76	5. 74	5. 71						
98	2. 86	2. 83	3. 19	3. 16	3. 59	3. 56	4. 11	4. 07	4. 80	4. 75	5. 76	5. 70				
100	2. 61	2. 57	2. 88	2. 84	3. 20	3. 16	3. 61	3. 55	4. 12	4. 06	4. 81	4. 73	5. 76	5. 67		
102	2. 40	2. 35	2. 63	2. 57	2. 90	2. 83	3. 22	3. 15	3. 62	3. 54	4. 13	4. 04	4. 81	4. 70	5. 76	5. 63
104	2. 23	2. 16	2. 42	2. 35	2. 64	2. 56	2. 91	2. 82	3. 23	3. 13	3. 63	3. 52	4. 13	4. 01	4. 81	4. 66
106	2. 08	2. 00	2. 25	2. 16	2. 43	2. 34	2. 65	2. 55	2. 92	2. 80	3. 23	3. 11	3. 63	3. 49	4. 13	3. 97
108	1. 96	1. 86	2. 10	2. 00	2. 26	2. 15	2. 45	2. 33	2. 66	2. 53	2. 92	2. 78	3. 24	3. 08	3. 63	3. 45
110	1. 85	1. 73	1. 97	1. 85	2. 11	1. 98	2. 27	2. 13	2. 45	2. 31	2. 67	2. 51	2. 92	2. 75	3. 23	3. 04
112	1. 75	1. 62	1. 86	1. 72	1. 98	1. 83	2. 12	1. 96	2. 28	2. 11	2. 46	2. 28	2. 67	2. 48	2. 92	2. 71
114	1. 66	1. 52	1. 76	1. 61	1. 87	1. 71	1. 99	1. 82	2. 12	1. 94	2. 28	2. 08	2. 46	2. 25	2. 67	2. 44
116	1. 59	1. 43	1. 68	1. 51	1. 77	1. 59	1. 88	1. 69	2. 00	1. 79	2. 13	1. 91	2. 28	2. 05	2. 46	2. 21
118	1. 52	1. 34	1. 60	1. 41	1. 68	1. 49	1. 78	1. 57	1. 88	1. 66	2. 00	1. 76	2. 13	1. 88	2. 28	2. 01
120	1. 46	1. 27	1. 53	1. 33	1. 61	1. 39	1. 69	1. 47	1. 78	1. 54	1. 89	1. 63	2. 00	1. 73	2. 13	1. 84
122	1. 41	1. 19	1. 47	1. 25	1. 54	1. 31	1. 62	1. 37	1. 70	1. 44	1. 79	1. 52	1. 89	1. 60	2. 00	1. 70
124	1. 36	1. 13	1. 42	1. 18	1. 48	1. 23	1. 55	1. 28	1. 62	1. 34	1. 70	1. 41	1. 79	1. 48	1. 89	1. 56
126	1. 32	1. 06	1. 37	1. 11	1. 43	1. 15	1. 48	1. 20	1. 55	1. 26	1. 62	1. 31	1. 70	1. 38	1. 79	1. 45
128	1. 28	1. 01	1. 33	1. 04	1. 38	1. 08	1. 43	1. 13	1. 49	1. 17	1. 55	1. 23	1. 62	1. 28	1. 70	1. 34
130	1. 24	0. 95	1. 29	0. 98	1. 33	1. 02	1. 38	1. 06	1. 44	1. 10	1. 49	1. 14	1. 56	1. 19	1. 62	1. 24
132	1. 21	0. 90	1. 25	0. 93	1. 29	0. 96	1. 34	0. 99	1. 39	1. 03	1. 44	1. 07	1. 49	1. 11	1. 55	1. 16
134	1. 18	0. 85	1. 22	0. 88	1. 26	0. 90	1. 30	0. 93	1. 34	0. 97	1. 39	1. 00	1. 44	1. 04	1. 49	1. 07
136	1. 15	0. 80	1. 19	0. 83	1. 22	0. 85	1. 26	0. 88	1. 30	0. 90	1. 34	0. 93	1. 39	0. 97	1. 44	1. 00
138	1. 13	0. 76	1. 16	0. 78	1. 19	0. 80	1. 23	0. 82	1. 27	0. 85	1. 30	0. 87	1. 35	0. 90	1. 39	0. 93
140	1. 11	0. 71	1. 14	0. 73	1. 17	0. 75	1. 20	0. 77	1. 23	0. 79	1. 27	0. 82	1. 31	0. 84	1. 34	0. 86
142	1. 09	0. 67	1. 12	0. 69	1. 14	0. 70	1. 17	0. 72	1. 20	0. 74	1. 24	0. 76	1. 27	0. 78	1. 30	0. 80
144	1. 07	0. 63	1. 10	0. 64	1. 12	0. 66	1. 15	0. 67	1. 18	0. 69	1. 21	0. 71	1. 24	0. 73	1. 27	0. 75
146	1. 05	0. 59	1. 08	0. 60	1. 10	0. 62	1. 13	0. 63	1. 15	0. 64	1. 18	0. 66	1. 21	0. 67	1. 24	0. 69
148	1. 04	0. 55	1. 06	0. 56	1. 08	0. 57	1. 11	0. 59	1. 13	0. 60	1. 15	0. 61	1. 18	0. 62	1. 21	0. 64
150	1. 03	0. 51	1. 05	0. 52	1. 07	0. 53	1. 09	0. 54	1. 11	0. 55	1. 13	0. 57	1. 15	0. 58	1. 18	0. 59
152	1. 02	0. 48	1. 04	0. 49	1. 05	0. 49	1. 07	0. 50	1. 09	0. 51	1. 11	0. 52	1. 13	0. 53	1. 15	0. 54
154	1. 01	0. 44	1. 02	0. 45	1. 04	0. 46	1. 06	0. 46	1. 08	0. 47	1. 09	0. 48	1. 11	0. 49	1. 13	0. 50
156	1. 00	0. 41	1. 01	0. 41	1. 03	0. 42	1. 05	0. 43	1. 06	0. 43	1. 08	0. 44	1. 09	0. 45	1. 11	0. 45
158	0. 99	0. 37	1. 01	0. 38	1. 02	0. 38	1. 03	0. 39	1. 05	0. 39	1. 06	0. 40	1. 08	0. 40	1. 09	0. 41
160	0. 99	0. 34	1. 00	0. 34	1. 01	0. 35	1. 02	0. 35	1. 04	0. 35	1. 05	0. 36	1. 06	0. 36	1. 08	0. 37
	94°		96°		98°		100°		102°		104°		106°		108°	
°																
104	5. 74	5. 57														
106	4. 80	4. 61	5. 73	5. 51												
108	4. 12	3. 92	4. 78	4. 55	5. 70	5. 42										
110	3. 62	3. 40	4. 11	3. 86	4. 76	4. 48	5. 67	5. 33								
112	3. 23	2. 99	3. 61	3. 35	4. 09	3. 80	4. 74	4. 40	5. 63	5. 22						
114	2. 92	2. 66	3. 22	2. 94	3. 59	3. 28	4. 07	3. 72	4. 70	4. 30	5. 59	5. 10				
116	2. 66	2. 39	2. 91	2. 61	3. 20	2. 88	3. 57	3. 21	4. 04	3. 63	4. 67	4. 19	5. 54	4. 98		
118	2. 45	2. 17	2. 65	2. 34	2. 90	2. 56	3. 19	2. 81	3. 55	3. 13	4. 01	3. 54	4. 62	4. 08	5. 48	4. 84
120	2. 28	1. 97	2. 45	2. 12	2. 64	2. 29	2. 88	2. 49	3. 17	2. 74	3. 52	3. 05	3. 97	3. 44	4. 57	3. 96
122	2. 12	1. 80	2. 27	1. 92	2. 43	2. 06	2. 63	2. 23	2. 86	2. 43	3. 14	2. 66	3. 49	2. 96	3. 93	3. 33
124	2. 00	1. 65	2. 12	1. 76	2. 26	1. 87	2. 42	2. 01	2. 61	2. 16	2. 84	2. 35	3. 11	2. 58	3. 45	2. 86
126	1. 88	1. 52	1. 99	1. 61	2. 11	1. 71	2. 25	1. 82	2. 40	1. 95	2. 59	2. 10	2. 81	2. 27	3. 08	2. 49
128	1. 78	1. 41	1. 88	1. 48	1. 98	1. 56	2. 10	1. 65	2. 23	1. 76	2. 39	1. 88	2. 57	2. 02	2. 78	2. 19
130	1. 70	1. 30	1. 78	1. 36	1. 87	1. 43	1. 97	1. 51	2. 08	1. 60	2. 21	1. 70	2. 36	1. 81	2. 54	1. 94
132	1. 62	1. 20	1. 69	1. 26	1. 77	1. 32	1. 86	1. 38	1. 96	1. 45	2. 07	1. 54	2. 19	1. 63	2. 34	1. 74
134	1. 55	1. 12	1. 62	1. 16	1. 68	1. 21	1. 76	1. 27	1. 85	1. 33	1. 94	1. 40	2. 05	1. 47	2. 17	1. 56
136	1. 49	1. 04	1. 55	1. 07	1. 61	1. 12	1. 68	1. 16	1. 75	1. 22	1. 83	1. 27	1. 92	1. 34	2. 03	1. 41
138	1. 44	0. 96	1. 49	0. 99	1. 54	1. 03	1. 60	1. 07	1. 66	1. 11	1. 74	1. 16	1. 81	1. 21	1. 90	1. 27
140	1. 39	0. 89	1. 43	0. 92	1. 48	0. 95	1. 53	0. 98	1. 59	1. 02	1. 65	1. 06	1. 72	1. 10	1. 79	1. 15
142	1. 34	0. 83	1. 38	0. 85	1. 43	0. 88	1. 47	0. 91	1. 52	0. 94	1. 58	0. 97	1. 64	1. 01	1. 70	1. 05
144	1. 30	0. 77	1. 34	0. 79	1. 38	0. 81	1. 42	0. 83	1. 46	0. 86	1. 51	0. 89	1. 56	0. 92	1. 62	0. 95
146	1. 27	0. 71	1. 30	0. 73	1. 33	0. 75	1. 37	0. 77	1. 41	0. 79	1. 45	0. 81	1. 50	0. 84	1. 54	0. 86
148	1. 23	0. 65	1. 26	0. 67	1. 29	0. 69	1. 33	0. 70	1. 36	0. 72	1. 40	0. 74	1. 44	0. 76	1. 48	0. 78
150	1. 20	0. 60	1. 23	0. 61	1. 26	0. 63	1. 29	0. 64	1. 32	0. 66	1. 35	0. 67	1. 38	0. 69	1. 42	0. 71
152	1. 18	0. 55	1. 20	0. 56	1. 22	0. 57	1. 25	0. 59	1. 28	0. 60	1. 31	0. 61	1. 34	0. 63	1. 37	0. 64
154	1. 15	0. 50	1. 17	0. 51	1. 19	0. 52	1. 22	0. 53	1. 24	0. 54	1. 27	0. 56	1. 29	0. 57	1. 32	0. 58
156	1. 13	0. 46	1. 15	0. 47	1. 17	0. 47	1. 19	0. 48	1. 21	0. 49	1. 23	0. 50	1. 25	0. 51	1. 28	0. 52
158	1. 11	0. 42	1. 13	0. 42	1. 14	0. 43	1. 16	0. 44	1. 18	0. 44	1. 20	0. 45	1. 22	0. 46	1. 24	0. 47
160	1. 09	0. 37	1. 11	0. 38	1. 12	0. 38	1. 14	0. 39	1. 15	0. 39	1. 17	0. 40	1. 19	0. 41	1. 21	0. 41

TABLE 4

Distance of the Horizon

Height feet	Nautical miles	Statute miles	Height feet	Nautical miles	Statute miles	Height feet	Nautical miles	Statute miles
1	1. 1	1. 3	120	12. 5	14. 4	940	35. 1	40. 4
2	1. 6	1. 9	125	12. 8	14. 7	960	35. 4	40. 8
3	2. 0	2. 3	130	13. 0	15. 0	980	35. 8	41. 2
4	2. 3	2. 6	135	13. 3	15. 3	1, 000	36. 2	41. 6
5	2. 6	2. 9	140	13. 5	15. 6	1, 100	37. 9	43. 7
6	2. 8	3. 2	145	13. 8	15. 9	1, 200	39. 6	45. 6
7	3. 0	3. 5	150	14. 0	16. 1	1, 300	41. 2	47. 5
8	3. 2	3. 7	160	14. 5	16. 7	1, 400	42. 8	49. 3
9	3. 4	4. 0	170	14. 9	17. 2	1, 500	44. 3	51. 0
10	3. 6	4. 2	180	15. 3	17. 7	1, 600	45. 8	52. 7
11	3. 8	4. 4	190	15. 8	18. 2	1, 700	47. 2	54. 3
12	4. 0	4. 6	200	16. 2	18. 6	1, 800	48. 5	55. 9
13	4. 1	4. 7	210	16. 6	19. 1	1, 900	49. 9	57. 4
14	4. 3	4. 9	220	17. 0	19. 5	2, 000	51. 2	58. 9
15	4. 4	5. 1	230	17. 3	20. 0	2, 100	52. 4	60. 4
16	4. 6	5. 3	240	17. 7	20. 4	2, 200	53. 7	61. 8
17	4. 7	5. 4	250	18. 1	20. 8	2, 300	54. 9	63. 2
18	4. 9	5. 6	260	18. 4	21. 2	2, 400	56. 0	64. 5
19	5. 0	5. 7	270	18. 8	21. 6	2, 500	57. 2	65. 8
20	5. 1	5. 9	280	19. 1	22. 0	2, 600	58. 3	67. 2
21	5. 2	6. 0	290	19. 5	22. 4	2, 700	59. 4	68. 4
22	5. 4	6. 2	300	19. 8	22. 8	2, 800	60. 5	69. 7
23	5. 5	6. 3	310	20. 1	23. 2	2, 900	61. 6	70. 9
24	5. 6	6. 5	320	20. 5	23. 6	3, 000	62. 7	72. 1
25	5. 7	6. 6	330	20. 8	23. 9	3, 100	63. 7	73. 3
26	5. 8	6. 7	340	21. 1	24. 3	3, 200	64. 7	74. 5
27	5. 9	6. 8	350	21. 4	24. 6	3, 300	65. 7	75. 7
28	6. 1	7. 0	360	21. 7	25. 0	3, 400	66. 7	76. 8
29	6. 2	7. 1	370	22. 0	25. 3	3, 500	67. 7	77. 9
30	6. 3	7. 2	380	22. 3	25. 7	3, 600	68. 6	79. 0
31	6. 4	7. 3	390	22. 6	26. 0	3, 700	69. 6	80. 1
32	6. 5	7. 5	400	22. 9	26. 3	3, 800	70. 5	81. 2
33	6. 6	7. 6	410	23. 2	26. 7	3, 900	71. 4	82. 2
34	6. 7	7. 7	420	23. 4	27. 0	4, 000	72. 4	83. 3
35	6. 8	7. 8	430	23. 7	27. 3	4, 100	73. 3	84. 3
36	6. 9	7. 9	440	24. 0	27. 6	4, 200	74. 1	85. 4
37	7. 0	8. 0	450	24. 3	27. 9	4, 300	75. 0	86. 4
38	7. 1	8. 1	460	24. 5	28. 2	4, 400	75. 9	87. 4
39	7. 1	8. 2	470	24. 8	28. 6	4, 500	76. 7	88. 3
40	7. 2	8. 3	480	25. 1	28. 9	4, 600	77. 6	89. 3
41	7. 3	8. 4	490	25. 3	29. 2	4, 700	78. 4	90. 3
42	7. 4	8. 5	500	25. 6	29. 4	4, 800	79. 3	91. 2
43	7. 5	8. 6	520	26. 1	30. 0	4, 900	80. 1	92. 2
44	7. 6	8. 7	540	26. 6	30. 6	5, 000	80. 9	93. 1
45	7. 7	8. 8	560	27. 1	31. 2	6, 000	88. 6	102. 0
46	7. 8	8. 9	580	27. 6	31. 7	7, 000	95. 7	110. 2
47	7. 8	9. 0	600	28. 0	32. 3	8, 000	102. 3	117. 8
48	7. 9	9. 1	620	28. 5	32. 8	9, 000	108. 5	124. 9
49	8. 0	9. 2	640	28. 9	33. 3	10, 000	114. 4	131. 7
50	8. 1	9. 3	660	29. 4	33. 8	15, 000	140. 1	161. 3
55	8. 5	9. 8	680	29. 8	34. 3	20, 000	161. 8	186. 3
60	8. 9	10. 2	700	30. 3	34. 8	25, 000	180. 9	208. 2
65	9. 2	10. 6	720	30. 7	35. 3	30, 000	198. 1	228. 1
70	9. 6	11. 0	740	31. 1	35. 8	35, 000	214. 0	246. 4
75	9. 9	11. 4	760	31. 5	36. 3	40, 000	228. 8	263. 4
80	10. 2	11. 8	780	31. 9	36. 8	45, 000	242. 7	279. 4
85	10. 5	12. 1	800	32. 4	37. 3	50, 000	255. 8	294. 5
90	10. 9	12. 5	820	32. 8	37. 7	60, 000	280. 2	322. 6
95	11. 2	12. 8	840	33. 2	38. 2	70, 000	302. 7	348. 4
100	11. 4	13. 2	860	33. 5	38. 6	80, 000	323. 6	372. 5
105	11. 7	13. 5	880	33. 9	39. 1	90, 000	343. 2	395. 1
110	12. 0	13. 8	900	34. 3	39. 5	100, 000	361. 8	416. 5
115	12. 3	14. 1	920	34. 7	39. 9	200, 000	511. 6	589. 0

TABLE 5

Distance by Vertical Angle

Angle	Difference in feet between height of object and height of eye of observer										Angle
	25	30	35	40	45	50	60	70	80	90	
° ′	*Miles*	*Miles*	*Miles*	*Miles*	*Miles*	*Miles*	*Miles*	*Miles*	*Miles*	*Miles*	° ′
−0 04	12.3	12.7	13.1	13.5	13.9	14.2	14.9	15.6	16.2	16.8	−0 04
−0 03	10.4	10.9	11.3	11.7	12.1	12.5	13.2	13.9	14.6	15.2	−0 03
−0 02	8.7	9.2	9.7	10.1	10.5	10.9	11.7	12.4	13.0	13.7	−0 02
−0 01	7.1	7.7	8.2	8.6	9.1	9.5	10.3	11.0	11.6	12.3	−0 01
0 00	5.8	6.4	6.9	7.3	7.8	8.2	9.0	9.7	10.4	11.0	0 00
0 01	4.7	5.3	5.8	6.3	6.7	7.1	7.9	8.6	9.3	9.9	0 01
0 02	3.9	4.4	4.9	5.3	5.8	6.2	6.9	7.6	8.3	8.9	0 02
0 03	3.2	3.7	4.2	4.6	5.0	5.4	6.1	6.8	7.4	8.0	0 03
0 04	2.6	3.2	3.6	4.0	4.4	4.7	5.4	6.1	6.7	7.2	0 04
0 05	2.4	2.8	3.1	3.5	3.9	4.2	4.8	5.4	6.0	6.6	0 05
0 06	2.1	2.4	2.8	3.1	3.4	3.7	4.3	4.9	5.5	6.0	0 06
0 07	1.8	2.1	2.5	2.8	3.1	3.4	3.9	4.5	5.0	5.5	0 07
0 08	1.6	1.9	2.2	2.5	2.8	3.0	3.6	4.1	4.6	5.0	0 08
0 09	1.5	1.7	2.0	2.3	2.5	2.8	3.3	3.7	4.2	4.6	0 09
0 10	1.3	1.6	1.8	2.1	2.3	2.6	3.0	3.5	3.9	4.3	0 10
0 15	.9	1.1	1.3	1.5	1.6	1.8	2.1	2.5	2.8	3.1	0 15
0 20	.7	.8	1.0	1.1	1.2	1.4	1.6	1.9	2.2	2.4	0 20
0 25	.6	.7	.8	.9	1.0	1.1	1.3	1.5	1.8	2.0	0 25
0 30	.5	.6	.7	.7	.8	.9	1.1	1.3	1.5	1.7	0 30
0 35		.5	.6	.6	.7	.8	1.0	1.1	1.3	1.4	0 35
0 40			.5	.6	.6	.7	.8	1.0	1.1	1.3	0 40
0 45				.5	.6	.6	.7	.9	1.0	1.1	0 45
0 50				.5	.5	.6	.7	.8	.9	1.0	0 50
0 55					.5	.5	.6	.7	.8	.9	0 55
1 00						.5	.6	.7	.8	.8	1 00
1 10							.5	.6	.6	.7	1 10
1 20								.5	.6	.6	1 20
1 30									.5	.6	1 30
1 40									.5	.5	1 40
1 50										.5	1 50

TABLE 6

Speed Table for Measured Mile

Sec.	Minutes												Sec.
	1	2	3	4	5	6	7	8	9	10	11	12	
	Knots	*Knots*	*Knots*	*Knots*	*Knots*	*Knots*	*Knots*	*Knots*	*Knots*	*Knots*	*Knots*	*Knots*	
0	60. 000	30. 000	20. 000	15. 000	12. 000	10. 000	8. 571	7. 500	6. 667	6. 000	5. 455	5. 000	0
1	59. 016	29. 752	19. 890	14. 938	11. 960	9. 972	8. 551	7. 484	6. 654	5. 990	5. 446	4. 993	1
2	58. 065	29. 508	19. 780	14. 876	11. 921	9. 945	8. 531	7. 469	6. 642	5. 980	5. 438	4. 986	2
3	57. 143	29. 268	19. 672	14. 815	11. 881	9. 917	8. 511	7. 453	6. 630	5. 970	5. 430	4. 979	3
4	56. 250	29. 032	19. 565	14. 754	11. 842	9. 890	8. 491	7. 438	6. 618	5. 960	5. 422	4. 972	4
5	55. 385	28. 800	19. 459	14. 694	11. 803	9. 863	8. 471	7. 423	6. 606	5. 950	5. 414	4. 966	5
6	54. 545	28. 571	19. 355	14. 634	11. 765	9. 836	8. 451	7. 407	6. 593	5. 941	5. 405	4. 959	6
7	53. 731	28. 346	19. 251	14. 575	11. 726	9. 809	8. 431	7. 392	6. 581	5. 931	5. 397	4. 952	7
8	52. 941	28. 125	19. 149	14. 516	11. 688	9. 783	8. 411	7. 377	6. 569	5. 921	5. 389	4. 945	8
9	52. 174	27. 907	19. 048	14. 458	11. 650	9. 756	8. 392	7. 362	6. 557	5. 911	5. 381	4. 938	9
10	51. 429	27. 692	18. 947	14. 400	11. 613	9. 730	8. 372	7. 347	6. 545	5. 902	5. 373	4. 932	10
11	50. 704	27. 481	18. 848	14. 343	11. 576	9. 704	8. 353	7. 332	6. 534	5. 892	5. 365	4. 925	11
12	50. 000	27. 273	18. 750	14. 286	11. 538	9. 677	8. 333	7. 317	6. 522	5. 882	5. 357	4. 918	12
13	49. 315	27. 068	18. 653	14. 229	11. 502	9. 651	8. 314	7. 302	6. 510	5. 873	5. 349	4. 911	13
14	48. 649	26. 866	18. 557	14. 173	11. 465	9. 626	8. 295	7. 287	6. 498	5. 863	5. 341	4. 905	14
15	48. 000	26. 667	18. 462	14. 118	11. 429	9. 600	8. 276	7. 273	6. 486	5. 854	5. 333	4. 898	15
16	47. 368	26. 471	18. 367	14. 062	11. 392	9. 574	8. 257	7. 258	6. 475	5. 844	5. 325	4. 891	16
17	46. 753	26. 277	18. 274	14. 008	11. 356	9. 549	8. 238	7. 243	6. 463	5. 835	5. 318	4. 885	17
18	46. 154	26. 087	18. 182	13. 953	11. 321	9. 524	8. 219	7. 229	6. 452	5. 825	5. 310	4. 878	18
19	45. 570	25. 899	18. 090	13. 900	11. 285	9. 499	8. 200	7. 214	6. 440	5. 816	5. 302	4. 871	19
20	45. 000	25. 714	18. 000	13. 846	11. 250	9. 474	8. 182	7. 200	6. 429	5. 806	5. 294	4. 865	20
21	44. 444	25. 532	17. 910	13. 793	11. 215	9. 449	8. 163	7. 186	6. 417	5. 797	5. 286	4. 858	21
22	43. 902	25. 352	17. 822	13. 740	11. 180	9. 424	8. 145	7. 171	6. 406	5. 788	5. 279	4. 852	22
23	43. 373	25. 175	17. 734	13. 688	11. 146	9. 399	8. 126	7. 157	6. 394	5. 778	5. 271	4. 845	23
24	42. 857	25. 000	17. 647	13. 636	11. 111	9. 375	8. 108	7. 143	6. 383	5. 769	5. 263	4. 839	24
25	42. 353	24. 828	17. 561	13. 585	11. 077	9. 351	8. 090	7. 129	6. 372	5. 760	5. 255	4. 832	25
26	41. 860	24. 658	17. 476	13. 534	11. 043	9. 326	8. 072	7. 115	6. 360	5. 751	5. 248	4. 826	26
27	41. 379	24. 490	17. 391	13. 483	11. 009	9. 302	8. 054	7. 101	6. 349	5. 742	5. 240	4. 819	27
28	40. 909	24. 324	17. 308	13. 433	10. 976	9. 278	8. 036	7. 087	6. 338	5. 732	5. 233	4. 813	28
29	40. 449	24. 161	17. 225	13. 383	10. 942	9. 254	8. 018	7. 073	6. 327	5. 723	5. 225	4. 806	29
30	40. 000	24. 000	17. 143	13. 333	10. 909	9. 231	8. 000	7. 059	6. 316	5. 714	5. 217	4. 800	30
31	39. 560	23. 841	17. 062	13. 284	10. 876	9. 207	7. 982	7. 045	6. 305	5. 705	5. 210	4. 794	31
32	39. 130	23. 684	16. 981	13. 235	10. 843	9. 184	7. 965	7. 031	6. 294	5. 696	5. 202	4. 787	32
33	38. 710	23. 529	16. 901	13. 187	10. 811	9. 160	7. 947	7. 018	6. 283	5. 687	5. 195	4. 781	33
34	38. 298	23. 377	16. 822	13. 139	10. 778	9. 137	7. 930	7. 004	6. 272	5. 678	5. 187	4. 775	34
35	37. 895	23. 226	16. 744	13. 091	10. 746	9. 114	7. 912	6. 990	6. 261	5. 669	5. 180	4. 768	35
36	37. 500	23. 077	16. 667	13. 043	10. 714	9. 091	7. 895	6. 977	6. 250	5. 660	5. 172	4. 762	36
37	37. 113	22. 930	16. 590	12. 996	10. 682	9. 068	7. 877	6. 963	6. 239	5. 651	5. 165	4. 756	37
38	36. 735	22. 785	16. 514	12. 950	10. 651	9. 045	7. 860	6. 950	6. 228	5. 643	5. 158	4. 749	38
39	36. 364	22. 642	16. 438	12. 903	10. 619	9. 023	7. 843	6. 936	6. 218	5. 634	5. 150	4. 743	39
40	36. 000	22. 500	16. 364	12. 857	10. 588	9. 000	7. 826	6. 923	6. 207	5. 625	5. 143	4. 737	40
41	35. 644	22. 360	16. 290	12. 811	10. 557	8. 978	7. 809	6. 910	6. 196	5. 616	5. 136	4. 731	41
42	35. 294	22. 222	16. 216	12. 766	10. 526	8. 955	7. 792	6. 897	6. 186	5. 607	5. 128	4. 724	42
43	34. 951	22. 086	16. 143	12. 721	10. 496	8. 933	7. 775	6. 883	6. 175	5. 599	5. 121	4. 718	43
44	34. 615	21. 951	16. 071	12. 676	10. 465	8. 911	7. 759	6. 870	6. 164	5. 590	5. 114	4. 712	44
45	34. 286	21. 818	16. 000	12. 632	10. 435	8. 889	7. 742	6. 857	6. 154	5. 581	5. 106	4. 706	45
46	33. 962	21. 687	15. 929	12. 587	10. 405	8. 867	7. 725	6. 844	6. 143	5. 573	5. 099	4. 700	46
47	33. 645	21. 557	15. 859	12. 544	10. 375	8. 845	7. 709	6. 831	6. 133	5. 564	5. 092	4. 694	47
48	33. 333	21. 429	15. 789	12. 500	10. 345	8. 824	7. 692	6. 818	6. 122	5. 556	5. 085	4. 688	48
49	33. 028	21. 302	15. 721	12. 457	10. 315	8. 802	7. 676	6. 805	6. 112	5. 547	5. 078	4. 681	49
50	32. 727	21. 176	15. 652	12. 414	10. 286	8. 780	7. 660	6. 792	6. 102	5. 538	5. 070	4. 675	50
51	32. 432	21. 053	15. 584	12. 371	10. 256	8. 759	7. 643	6. 780	6. 091	5. 530	5. 063	4. 669	51
52	32. 143	20. 930	15. 517	12. 329	10. 227	8. 738	7. 627	6. 767	6. 081	5. 521	5. 056	4. 663	52
53	31. 858	20. 809	15. 451	12. 287	10. 198	8. 717	7. 611	6. 754	6. 071	5. 513	5. 049	4. 657	53
54	31. 579	20. 690	15. 385	12. 245	10. 169	8. 696	7. 595	6. 742	6. 061	5. 505	5. 042	4. 651	54
55	31. 304	20. 571	15. 319	12. 203	10. 141	8. 675	7. 579	6. 729	6. 050	5. 496	5. 035	4. 645	55
56	31. 034	20. 455	15. 254	12. 162	10. 112	8. 654	7. 563	6. 716	6. 040	5. 488	5. 028	4. 639	56
57	30. 769	20. 339	15. 190	12. 121	10. 084	8. 633	7. 547	6. 704	6. 030	5. 479	5. 021	4. 633	57
58	30. 508	20. 225	15. 126	12. 081	10. 056	8. 612	7. 531	6. 691	6. 020	5. 471	5. 014	4. 627	58
59	30. 252	20. 112	15. 063	12. 040	10. 028	8. 592	7. 516	6. 679	6. 010	5. 463	5. 007	4. 621	59
60	30. 000	20. 000	15. 000	12. 000	10. 000	8. 571	7. 500	6. 667	6. 000	5. 455	5. 000	4. 615	60
Sec.	1	2	3	4	5	6	7	8	9	10	11	12	Sec.

TABLE 7

Speed, Time, and Distance

Minutes	Speed in knots																Minutes
	0.5	1.0	1.5	2.0	2.5	3.0	3.5	4.0	4.5	5.0	5.5	6.0	6.5	7.0	7.5	8.0	
	Miles	*Miles*	*Miles*	*Miles*	*Miles*	*Miles*	*Miles*	*Miles*	*Miles*	*Miles*	*Miles*	*Miles*	*Miles*	*Miles*	*Miles*	*Miles*	
1	0.0	0.0	0.0	0.0	0.0	0.0	0.1	0.1	0.1	0.1	0.1	0.1	0.1	0.1	0.1	0.1	1
2	0.0	0.0	0.0	0.1	0.1	0.1	0.1	0.1	0.2	0.2	0.2	0.2	0.2	0.2	0.2	0.3	2
3	0.0	0.0	0.1	0.1	0.1	0.2	0.2	0.2	0.2	0.2	0.3	0.3	0.3	0.4	0.4	0.4	3
4	0.0	0.1	0.1	0.1	0.2	0.2	0.2	0.3	0.3	0.3	0.4	0.4	0.4	0.5	0.5	0.5	4
5	0.0	0.1	0.1	0.2	0.2	0.2	0.3	0.3	0.4	0.4	0.5	0.5	0.5	0.6	0.6	0.7	5
6	0.0	0.1	0.2	0.2	0.2	0.3	0.4	0.4	0.4	0.5	0.6	0.6	0.6	0.7	0.8	0.8	6
7	0.1	0.1	0.2	0.2	0.3	0.4	0.4	0.5	0.5	0.6	0.6	0.7	0.8	0.8	0.9	0.9	7
8	0.1	0.1	0.2	0.3	0.3	0.4	0.5	0.5	0.6	0.7	0.7	0.8	0.9	0.9	1.0	1.1	8
9	0.1	0.2	0.2	0.3	0.4	0.4	0.5	0.6	0.7	0.8	0.8	0.9	1.0	1.0	1.1	1.2	9
10	0.1	0.2	0.2	0.3	0.4	0.5	0.6	0.7	0.8	0.8	0.9	1.0	1.1	1.2	1.2	1.3	10
11	0.1	0.2	0.3	0.4	0.5	0.6	0.6	0.7	0.8	0.9	1.0	1.1	1.2	1.3	1.4	1.5	11
12	0.1	0.2	0.3	0.4	0.5	0.6	0.7	0.8	0.9	1.0	1.1	1.2	1.3	1.4	1.5	1.6	12
13	0.1	0.2	0.3	0.4	0.5	0.6	0.8	0.9	1.0	1.1	1.2	1.3	1.4	1.5	1.6	1.7	13
14	0.1	0.2	0.4	0.5	0.6	0.7	0.8	0.9	1.0	1.2	1.3	1.4	1.5	1.6	1.8	1.9	14
15	0.1	0.2	0.4	0.5	0.6	0.8	0.9	1.0	1.1	1.2	1.4	1.5	1.6	1.8	1.9	2.0	15
16	0.1	0.3	0.4	0.5	0.7	0.8	0.9	1.1	1.2	1.3	1.5	1.6	1.7	1.9	2.0	2.1	16
17	0.1	0.3	0.4	0.6	0.7	0.8	1.0	1.1	1.3	1.4	1.6	1.7	1.8	2.0	2.1	2.3	17
18	0.2	0.3	0.4	0.6	0.8	0.9	1.0	1.2	1.4	1.5	1.6	1.8	2.0	2.1	2.2	2.4	18
19	0.2	0.3	0.5	0.6	0.8	1.0	1.1	1.3	1.4	1.6	1.7	1.9	2.1	2.2	2.4	2.5	19
20	0.2	0.3	0.5	0.7	0.8	1.0	1.2	1.3	1.5	1.7	1.8	2.0	2.2	2.3	2.5	2.7	20
21	0.2	0.4	0.5	0.7	0.9	1.0	1.2	1.4	1.6	1.8	1.9	2.1	2.3	2.4	2.6	2.8	21
22	0.2	0.4	0.6	0.7	0.9	1.1	1.3	1.5	1.6	1.8	2.0	2.2	2.4	2.6	2.8	2.9	22
23	0.2	0.4	0.6	0.8	1.0	1.2	1.3	1.5	1.7	1.9	2.1	2.3	2.5	2.7	2.9	3.1	23
24	0.2	0.4	0.6	0.8	1.0	1.2	1.4	1.6	1.8	2.0	2.2	2.4	2.6	2.8	3.0	3.2	24
25	0.2	0.4	0.6	0.8	1.0	1.2	1.5	1.7	1.9	2.1	2.3	2.5	2.7	2.9	3.1	3.3	25
26	0.2	0.4	0.6	0.9	1.1	1.3	1.5	1.7	2.0	2.2	2.4	2.6	2.8	3.0	3.2	3.5	26
27	0.2	0.4	0.7	0.9	1.1	1.4	1.6	1.8	2.0	2.2	2.5	2.7	2.9	3.2	3.4	3.6	27
28	0.2	0.5	0.7	0.9	1.2	1.4	1.6	1.9	2.1	2.3	2.6	2.8	3.0	3.3	3.5	3.7	28
29	0.2	0.5	0.7	1.0	1.2	1.4	1.7	1.9	2.2	2.4	2.7	2.9	3.1	3.4	3.6	3.9	29
30	0.2	0.5	0.8	1.0	1.2	1.5	1.8	2.0	2.2	2.5	2.8	3.0	3.2	3.5	3.8	4.0	30
31	0.3	0.5	0.8	1.0	1.3	1.6	1.8	2.1	2.3	2.6	2.8	3.1	3.4	3.6	3.9	4.1	31
32	0.3	0.5	0.8	1.1	1.3	1.6	1.9	2.1	2.4	2.7	2.9	3.2	3.5	3.7	4.0	4.3	32
33	0.3	0.6	0.8	1.1	1.4	1.6	1.9	2.2	2.5	2.8	3.0	3.3	3.6	3.8	4.1	4.4	33
34	0.3	0.6	0.8	1.1	1.4	1.7	2.0	2.3	2.6	2.8	3.1	3.4	3.7	4.0	4.2	4.5	34
35	0.3	0.6	0.9	1.2	1.5	1.8	2.0	2.3	2.6	2.9	3.2	3.5	3.8	4.1	4.4	4.7	35
36	0.3	0.6	0.9	1.2	1.5	1.8	2.1	2.4	2.7	3.0	3.3	3.6	3.9	4.2	4.5	4.8	36
37	0.3	0.6	0.9	1.2	1.5	1.8	2.2	2.5	2.8	3.1	3.4	3.7	4.0	4.3	4.6	4.9	37
38	0.3	0.6	1.0	1.3	1.6	1.9	2.2	2.5	2.8	3.2	3.5	3.8	4.1	4.4	4.8	5.1	38
39	0.3	0.6	1.0	1.3	1.6	2.0	2.3	2.6	2.9	3.2	3.6	3.9	4.2	4.6	4.9	5.2	39
40	0.3	0.7	1.0	1.3	1.7	2.0	2.3	2.7	3.0	3.3	3.7	4.0	4.3	4.7	5.0	5.3	40
41	0.3	0.7	1.0	1.4	1.7	2.0	2.4	2.7	3.1	3.4	3.8	4.1	4.4	4.8	5.1	5.5	41
42	0.4	0.7	1.0	1.4	1.8	2.1	2.4	2.8	3.2	3.5	3.8	4.2	4.6	4.9	5.2	5.6	42
43	0.4	0.7	1.1	1.4	1.8	2.2	2.5	2.9	3.2	3.6	3.9	4.3	4.7	5.0	5.4	5.7	43
44	0.4	0.7	1.1	1.5	1.8	2.2	2.6	2.9	3.3	3.7	4.0	4.4	4.8	5.1	5.5	5.9	44
45	0.4	0.8	1.1	1.5	1.9	2.2	2.6	3.0	3.4	3.8	4.1	4.5	4.9	5.2	5.6	6.0	45
46	0.4	0.8	1.2	1.5	1.9	2.3	2.7	3.1	3.4	3.8	4.2	4.6	5.0	5.4	5.8	6.1	46
47	0.4	0.8	1.2	1.6	2.0	2.4	2.7	3.1	3.5	3.9	4.3	4.7	5.1	5.5	5.9	6.3	47
48	0.4	0.8	1.2	1.6	2.0	2.4	2.8	3.2	3.6	4.0	4.4	4.8	5.2	5.6	6.0	6.4	48
49	0.4	0.8	1.2	1.6	2.0	2.4	2.9	3.3	3.7	4.1	4.5	4.9	5.3	5.7	6.1	6.5	49
50	0.4	0.8	1.2	1.7	2.1	2.5	2.9	3.3	3.8	4.2	4.6	5.0	5.4	5.8	6.2	6.7	50
51	0.4	0.8	1.3	1.7	2.1	2.6	3.0	3.4	3.8	4.2	4.7	5.1	5.5	6.0	6.4	6.8	51
52	0.4	0.9	1.3	1.7	2.2	2.6	3.0	3.5	3.9	4.3	4.8	5.2	5.6	6.1	6.5	6.9	52
53	0.4	0.9	1.3	1.8	2.2	2.6	3.1	3.5	4.0	4.4	4.9	5.3	5.7	6.2	6.6	7.1	53
54	0.4	0.9	1.4	1.8	2.2	2.7	3.2	3.6	4.0	4.5	5.0	5.4	5.8	6.3	6.8	7.2	54
55	0.5	0.9	1.4	1.8	2.3	2.8	3.2	3.7	4.1	4.6	5.0	5.5	6.0	6.4	6.9	7.3	55
56	0.5	0.9	1.4	1.9	2.3	2.8	3.3	3.7	4.2	4.7	5.1	5.6	6.1	6.5	7.0	7.5	56
57	0.5	1.0	1.4	1.9	2.4	2.8	3.3	3.8	4.3	4.8	5.2	5.7	6.2	6.6	7.1	7.6	57
58	0.5	1.0	1.4	1.9	2.4	2.9	3.4	3.9	4.4	4.8	5.3	5.8	6.3	6.8	7.2	7.7	58
59	0.5	1.0	1.5	2.0	2.5	3.0	3.4	3.9	4.4	4.9	5.4	5.9	6.4	6.9	7.4	7.9	59
60	0.5	1.0	1.5	2.0	2.5	3.0	3.5	4.0	4.5	5.0	5.5	6.0	6.5	7.0	7.5	8.0	60

TABLE 7

Speed, Time, and Distance

Minutes	Speed in knots																Minutes
	8.5	9.0	9.5	10.0	10.5	11.0	11.5	12.0	12.5	13.0	13.5	14.0	14.5	15.0	15.5	16.0	
	Miles	*Miles*	*Miles*	*Miles*	*Miles*	*Miles*	*Miles*	*Miles*	*Miles*	*Miles*	*Miles*	*Miles*	*Miles*	*Miles*	*Miles*	*Miles*	
1	0.1	0.2	0.2	0.2	0.2	0.2	0.2	0.2	0.2	0.2	0.2	0.2	0.2	0.2	0.3	0.3	1
2	0.3	0.3	0.3	0.3	0.4	0.4	0.4	0.4	0.4	0.4	0.4	0.5	0.5	0.5	0.5	0.5	2
3	0.4	0.4	0.5	0.5	0.5	0.6	0.6	0.6	0.6	0.6	0.7	0.7	0.7	0.8	0.8	0.8	3
4	0.6	0.6	0.6	0.7	0.7	0.7	0.8	0.8	0.8	0.9	0.9	0.9	1.0	1.0	1.0	1.1	4
5	0.7	0.8	0.8	0.8	0.9	0.9	1.0	1.0	1.0	1.1	1.1	1.2	1.2	1.2	1.3	1.3	5
6	0.8	0.9	1.0	1.0	1.0	1.1	1.2	1.2	1.2	1.3	1.4	1.4	1.4	1.5	1.6	1.6	6
7	1.0	1.0	1.1	1.2	1.2	1.3	1.3	1.4	1.5	1.5	1.6	1.6	1.7	1.8	1.8	1.9	7
8	1.1	1.2	1.3	1.3	1.4	1.5	1.5	1.6	1.7	1.7	1.8	1.9	1.9	2.0	2.1	2.1	8
9	1.3	1.4	1.4	1.5	1.6	1.6	1.7	1.8	1.9	2.0	2.0	2.1	2.2	2.2	2.3	2.4	9
10	1.4	1.5	1.6	1.7	1.8	1.8	1.9	2.0	2.1	2.2	2.2	2.3	2.4	2.5	2.6	2.7	10
11	1.6	1.6	1.7	1.8	1.9	2.0	2.1	2.2	2.3	2.4	2.5	2.6	2.7	2.8	2.8	2.9	11
12	1.7	1.8	1.9	2.0	2.1	2.2	2.3	2.4	2.5	2.6	2.7	2.8	2.9	3.0	3.1	3.2	12
13	1.8	2.0	2.1	2.2	2.3	2.4	2.5	2.6	2.7	2.8	2.9	3.0	3.1	3.2	3.4	3.5	13
14	2.0	2.1	2.2	2.3	2.4	2.6	2.7	2.8	2.9	3.0	3.2	3.3	3.4	3.5	3.6	3.7	14
15	2.1	2.2	2.4	2.5	2.6	2.8	2.9	3.0	3.1	3.2	3.4	3.5	3.6	3.8	3.9	4.0	15
16	2.3	2.4	2.5	2.7	2.8	2.9	3.1	3.2	3.3	3.5	3.6	3.7	3.9	4.0	4.1	4.3	16
17	2.4	2.6	2.7	2.8	3.0	3.1	3.3	3.4	3.5	3.7	3.8	4.0	4.1	4.2	4.4	4.5	17
18	2.6	2.7	2.8	3.0	3.2	3.3	3.4	3.6	3.8	3.9	4.0	4.2	4.4	4.5	4.6	4.8	18
19	2.7	2.8	3.0	3.2	3.3	3.5	3.6	3.8	4.0	4.1	4.3	4.4	4.6	4.8	4.9	5.1	19
20	2.8	3.0	3.2	3.3	3.5	3.7	3.8	4.0	4.2	4.3	4.5	4.7	4.8	5.0	5.2	5.3	20
21	3.0	3.2	3.3	3.5	3.7	3.8	4.0	4.2	4.4	4.6	4.7	4.9	5.1	5.2	5.4	5.6	21
22	3.1	3.3	3.5	3.7	3.8	4.0	4.2	4.4	4.6	4.8	5.0	5.1	5.3	5.5	5.7	5.9	22
23	3.3	3.4	3.6	3.8	4.0	4.2	4.4	4.6	4.8	5.0	5.2	5.4	5.6	5.8	5.9	6.1	23
24	3.4	3.6	3.8	4.0	4.2	4.4	4.6	4.8	5.0	5.2	5.4	5.6	5.8	6.0	6.2	6.4	24
25	3.5	3.8	4.0	4.2	4.4	4.6	4.8	5.0	5.2	5.4	5.6	5.8	6.0	6.2	6.5	6.7	25
26	3.7	3.9	4.1	4.3	4.6	4.8	5.0	5.2	5.4	5.6	5.8	6.1	6.3	6.5	6.7	6.9	26
27	3.8	4.0	4.3	4.5	4.7	5.0	5.2	5.4	5.6	5.8	6.1	6.3	6.5	6.8	7.0	7.2	27
28	4.0	4.2	4.4	4.7	4.9	5.1	5.4	5.6	5.8	6.1	6.3	6.5	6.8	7.0	7.2	7.5	28
29	4.1	4.4	4.6	4.8	5.1	5.3	5.6	5.8	6.0	6.3	6.5	6.8	7.0	7.2	7.5	7.7	29
30	4.2	4.5	4.8	5.0	5.2	5.5	5.8	6.0	6.2	6.5	6.8	7.0	7.2	7.5	7.8	8.0	30
31	4.4	4.6	4.9	5.2	5.4	5.7	5.9	6.2	6.5	6.7	7.0	7.2	7.5	7.8	8.0	8.3	31
32	4.5	4.8	5.1	5.3	5.6	5.9	6.1	6.4	6.7	6.9	7.2	7.5	7.7	8.0	8.3	8.5	32
33	4.7	5.0	5.2	5.5	5.8	6.0	6.3	6.6	6.9	7.2	7.4	7.7	8.0	8.2	8.5	8.8	33
34	4.8	5.1	5.4	5.7	6.0	6.2	6.5	6.8	7.1	7.4	7.6	7.9	8.2	8.5	8.8	9.1	34
35	5.0	5.2	5.5	5.8	6.1	6.4	6.7	7.0	7.3	7.6	7.9	8.2	8.5	8.8	9.0	9.3	35
36	5.1	5.4	5.7	6.0	6.3	6.6	6.9	7.2	7.5	7.8	8.1	8.4	8.7	9.0	9.3	9.6	36
37	5.2	5.6	5.9	6.2	6.5	6.8	7.1	7.4	7.7	8.0	8.3	8.6	8.9	9.2	9.6	9.9	37
38	5.4	5.7	6.0	6.3	6.6	7.0	7.3	7.6	7.9	8.2	8.6	8.9	9.2	9.5	9.8	10.1	38
39	5.5	5.8	6.2	6.5	6.8	7.2	7.5	7.8	8.1	8.4	8.8	9.1	9.4	9.8	10.1	10.4	39
40	5.7	6.0	6.3	6.7	7.0	7.3	7.7	8.0	8.3	8.7	9.0	9.3	9.7	10.0	10.3	10.7	40
41	5.8	6.2	6.5	6.8	7.2	7.5	7.9	8.2	8.5	8.9	9.2	9.6	9.9	10.2	10.6	10.9	41
42	6.0	6.3	6.6	7.0	7.4	7.7	8.0	8.4	8.8	9.1	9.4	9.8	10.2	10.5	10.8	11.2	42
43	6.1	6.4	6.8	7.2	7.5	7.9	8.2	8.6	9.0	9.3	9.7	10.0	10.4	10.8	11.1	11.5	43
44	6.2	6.6	7.0	7.3	7.7	8.1	8.4	8.8	9.2	9.5	9.9	10.3	10.6	11.0	11.4	11.7	44
45	6.4	6.8	7.1	7.5	7.9	8.2	8.6	9.0	9.4	9.8	10.1	10.5	10.9	11.2	11.6	12.0	45
46	6.5	6.9	7.3	7.7	8.0	8.4	8.8	9.2	9.6	10.0	10.4	10.7	11.1	11.5	11.9	12.3	46
47	6.7	7.0	7.4	7.8	8.2	8.6	9.0	9.4	9.8	10.2	10.6	11.0	11.4	11.8	12.1	12.5	47
48	6.8	7.2	7.6	8.0	8.4	8.8	9.2	9.6	10.0	10.4	10.8	11.2	11.6	12.0	12.4	12.8	48
49	6.9	7.4	7.8	8.2	8.6	9.0	9.4	9.8	10.2	10.6	11.0	11.4	11.8	12.2	12.7	13.1	49
50	7.1	7.5	7.9	8.3	8.8	9.2	9.6	10.0	10.4	10.8	11.2	11.7	12.1	12.5	12.9	13.3	50
51	7.2	7.6	8.1	8.5	8.9	9.4	9.8	10.2	10.6	11.0	11.5	11.9	12.3	12.8	13.2	13.6	51
52	7.4	7.8	8.2	8.7	9.1	9.5	10.0	10.4	10.8	11.3	11.7	12.1	12.6	13.0	13.4	13.9	52
53	7.5	8.0	8.4	8.8	9.3	9.7	10.2	10.6	11.0	11.5	11.9	12.4	12.8	13.2	13.7	14.1	53
54	7.6	8.1	8.6	9.0	9.4	9.9	10.4	10.8	11.2	11.7	12.2	12.6	13.0	13.5	14.0	14.4	54
55	7.8	8.2	8.7	9.2	9.6	10.1	10.5	11.0	11.5	11.9	12.4	12.8	13.3	13.8	14.2	14.7	55
56	7.9	8.4	8.9	9.3	9.8	10.3	10.7	11.2	11.7	12.1	12.6	13.1	13.5	14.0	14.5	14.9	56
57	8.1	8.6	9.0	9.5	10.0	10.4	10.9	11.4	11.9	12.4	12.8	13.3	13.8	14.2	14.7	15.2	57
58	8.2	8.7	9.2	9.7	10.2	10.6	11.1	11.6	12.1	12.6	13.0	13.5	14.0	14.5	15.0	15.5	58
59	8.4	8.8	9.3	9.8	10.3	10.8	11.3	11.8	12.3	12.8	13.3	13.8	14.3	14.8	15.2	15.7	59
60	8.5	9.0	9.5	10.0	10.5	11.0	11.5	12.0	12.5	13.0	13.5	14.0	14.5	15.0	15.5	16.0	60

TABLE 7

Speed, Time, and Distance

Minutes	Speed in knots																Minutes
	16.5	17.0	17.5	18.0	18.5	19.0	19.5	20.0	20.5	21.0	21.5	22.0	22.5	23.0	23.5	24.0	
	Miles	*Miles*	*Miles*	*Miles*	*Miles*	*Miles*	*Miles*	*Miles*	*Miles*	*Miles*	*Miles*	*Miles*	*Miles*	*Miles*	*Miles*	*Miles*	
1	0.3	0.3	0.3	0.3	0.3	0.3	0.3	0.3	0.3	0.4	0.4	0.4	0.4	0.4	0.4	0.4	1
2	0.6	0.6	0.6	0.6	0.6	0.6	0.6	0.7	0.7	0.7	0.7	0.7	0.8	0.8	0.8	0.8	2
3	0.8	0.8	0.9	0.9	0.9	1.0	1.0	1.0	1.0	1.0	1.1	1.1	1.1	1.2	1.2	1.2	3
4	1.1	1.1	1.2	1.2	1.2	1.3	1.3	1.3	1.4	1.4	1.4	1.5	1.5	1.5	1.6	1.6	4
5	1.4	1.4	1.5	1.5	1.5	1.6	1.6	1.7	1.7	1.8	1.8	1.8	1.9	1.9	2.0	2.0	5
6	1.6	1.7	1.8	1.8	1.8	1.9	2.0	2.0	2.0	2.1	2.2	2.2	2.2	2.3	2.4	2.4	6
7	1.9	2.0	2.0	2.1	2.2	2.2	2.3	2.3	2.4	2.4	2.5	2.6	2.6	2.7	2.7	2.8	7
8	2.2	2.3	2.3	2.4	2.5	2.5	2.6	2.7	2.7	2.8	2.9	2.9	3.0	3.1	3.1	3.2	8
9	2.5	2.6	2.6	2.7	2.8	2.8	2.9	3.0	3.1	3.2	3.2	3.3	3.4	3.4	3.5	3.6	9
10	2.8	2.8	2.9	3.0	3.1	3.2	3.2	3.3	3.4	3.5	3.6	3.7	3.8	3.8	3.9	4.0	10
11	3.0	3.1	3.2	3.3	3.4	3.5	3.6	3.7	3.8	3.8	3.9	4.0	4.1	4.2	4.3	4.4	11
12	3.3	3.4	3.5	3.6	3.7	3.8	3.9	4.0	4.1	4.2	4.3	4.4	4.5	4.6	4.7	4.8	12
13	3.6	3.7	3.8	3.9	4.0	4.1	4.2	4.3	4.4	4.6	4.7	4.8	4.9	5.0	5.1	5.2	13
14	3.8	4.0	4.1	4.2	4.3	4.4	4.6	4.7	4.8	4.9	5.0	5.1	5.2	5.4	5.5	5.6	14
15	4.1	4.2	4.4	4.5	4.6	4.8	4.9	5.0	5.1	5.2	5.4	5.5	5.6	5.8	5.9	6.0	15
16	4.4	4.5	4.7	4.8	4.9	5.1	5.2	5.3	5.5	5.6	5.7	5.9	6.0	6.1	6.3	6.4	16
17	4.7	4.8	5.0	5.1	5.2	5.4	5.5	5.7	5.8	6.0	6.1	6.2	6.4	6.5	6.7	6.8	17
18	5.0	5.1	5.2	5.4	5.6	5.7	5.8	6.0	6.2	6.3	6.4	6.6	6.8	6.9	7.0	7.2	18
19	5.2	5.4	5.5	5.7	5.9	6.0	6.2	6.3	6.5	6.6	6.8	7.0	7.1	7.3	7.4	7.6	19
20	5.5	5.7	5.8	6.0	6.2	6.3	6.5	6.7	6.8	7.0	7.2	7.3	7.5	7.7	7.8	8.0	20
21	5.8	6.0	6.1	6.3	6.5	6.6	6.8	7.0	7.2	7.4	7.5	7.7	7.9	8.0	8.2	8.4	21
22	6.0	6.2	6.4	6.6	6.8	7.0	7.2	7.3	7.5	7.7	7.9	8.1	8.2	8.4	8.6	8.8	22
23	6.3	6.5	6.7	6.9	7.1	7.3	7.5	7.7	7.9	8.0	8.2	8.4	8.6	8.8	9.0	9.2	23
24	6.6	6.8	7.0	7.2	7.4	7.6	7.8	8.0	8.2	8.4	8.6	8.8	9.0	9.2	9.4	9.6	24
25	6.9	7.1	7.3	7.5	7.7	7.9	8.1	8.3	8.5	8.8	9.0	9.2	9.4	9.6	9.8	10.0	25
26	7.2	7.4	7.6	7.8	8.0	8.2	8.4	8.7	8.9	9.1	9.3	9.5	9.8	10.0	10.2	10.4	26
27	7.4	7.6	7.9	8.1	8.3	8.6	8.8	9.0	9.2	9.4	9.7	9.9	10.1	10.4	10.6	10.8	27
28	7.7	7.9	8.2	8.4	8.6	8.9	9.1	9.3	9.6	9.8	10.0	10.3	10.5	10.7	11.0	11.2	28
29	8.0	8.2	8.5	8.7	8.9	9.2	9.4	9.7	9.9	10.2	10.4	10.6	10.9	11.1	11.4	11.6	29
30	8.2	8.5	8.8	9.0	9.2	9.5	9.8	10.0	10.2	10.5	10.8	11.0	11.2	11.5	11.8	12.0	30
31	8.5	8.8	9.0	9.3	9.6	9.8	10.1	10.3	10.6	10.8	11.1	11.4	11.6	11.9	12.1	12.4	31
32	8.8	9.1	9.3	9.6	9.9	10.1	10.4	10.7	10.9	11.2	11.5	11.7	12.0	12.3	12.5	12.8	32
33	9.1	9.4	9.6	9.9	10.2	10.4	10.7	11.0	11.3	11.6	11.8	12.1	12.4	12.6	12.9	13.2	33
34	9.4	9.6	9.9	10.2	10.5	10.8	11.0	11.3	11.6	11.9	12.2	12.5	12.8	13.0	13.3	13.6	34
35	9.6	9.9	10.2	10.5	10.8	11.1	11.4	11.7	12.0	12.2	12.5	12.8	13.1	13.4	13.7	14.0	35
36	9.9	10.2	10.5	10.8	11.1	11.4	11.7	12.0	12.3	12.6	12.9	13.2	13.5	13.8	14.1	14.4	36
37	10.2	10.5	10.8	11.1	11.4	11.7	12.0	12.3	12.6	13.0	13.3	13.6	13.9	14.2	14.5	14.8	37
38	10.4	10.8	11.1	11.4	11.7	12.0	12.4	12.7	13.0	13.3	13.6	13.9	14.2	14.6	14.9	15.2	38
39	10.7	11.0	11.4	11.7	12.0	12.4	12.7	13.0	13.3	13.6	14.0	14.3	14.6	15.0	15.3	15.6	39
40	11.0	11.3	11.7	12.0	12.3	12.7	13.0	13.3	13.7	14.0	14.3	14.7	15.0	15.3	15.7	16.0	40
41	11.3	11.6	12.0	12.3	12.6	13.0	13.3	13.7	14.0	14.4	14.7	15.0	15.4	15.7	16.1	16.4	41
42	11.6	11.9	12.2	12.6	13.0	13.3	13.6	14.0	14.4	14.7	15.0	15.4	15.8	16.1	16.4	16.8	42
43	11.8	12.2	12.5	12.9	13.3	13.6	14.0	14.3	14.7	15.0	15.4	15.8	16.1	16.5	16.8	17.2	43
44	12.1	12.5	12.8	13.2	13.6	13.9	14.3	14.7	15.0	15.4	15.8	16.1	16.5	16.9	17.2	17.6	44
45	12.4	12.8	13.1	13.5	13.9	14.2	14.6	15.0	15.4	15.8	16.1	16.5	16.9	17.2	17.6	18.0	45
46	12.6	13.0	13.4	13.8	14.2	14.6	15.0	15.3	15.7	16.1	16.5	16.9	17.2	17.6	18.0	18.4	46
47	12.9	13.3	13.7	14.1	14.5	14.9	15.3	15.7	16.1	16.4	16.8	17.2	17.6	18.0	18.4	18.8	47
48	13.2	13.6	14.0	14.4	14.8	15.2	15.6	16.0	16.4	16.8	17.2	17.6	18.0	18.4	18.8	19.2	48
49	13.5	13.9	14.3	14.7	15.1	15.5	15.9	16.3	16.7	17.2	17.6	18.0	18.4	18.8	19.2	19.6	49
50	13.8	14.2	14.6	15.0	15.4	15.8	16.2	16.7	17.1	17.5	17.9	18.3	18.8	19.2	19.6	20.0	50
51	14.0	14.4	14.9	15.3	15.7	16.2	16.6	17.0	17.4	17.8	18.3	18.7	19.1	19.6	20.0	20.4	51
52	14.3	14.7	15.2	15.6	16.0	16.5	16.9	17.3	17.8	18.2	18.6	19.1	19.5	19.9	20.4	20.8	52
53	14.6	15.0	15.5	15.9	16.3	16.8	17.2	17.7	18.1	18.6	19.0	19.4	19.9	20.3	20.8	21.2	53
54	14.8	15.3	15.8	16.2	16.6	17.1	17.6	18.0	18.4	18.9	19.4	19.8	20.2	20.7	21.2	21.6	54
55	15.1	15.6	16.0	16.5	17.0	17.4	17.9	18.3	18.8	19.2	19.7	20.2	20.6	21.1	21.5	22.0	55
56	15.4	15.9	16.3	16.8	17.3	17.7	18.2	18.7	19.1	19.6	20.1	20.5	21.0	21.5	21.9	22.4	56
57	15.7	16.2	16.6	17.1	17.6	18.0	18.5	19.0	19.5	20.0	20.4	20.9	21.4	21.8	22.3	22.8	57
58	16.0	16.4	16.9	17.4	17.9	18.4	18.8	19.3	19.8	20.3	20.8	21.3	21.8	22.2	22.7	23.2	58
59	16.2	16.7	17.2	17.7	18.2	18.7	19.2	19.7	20.2	20.6	21.1	21.6	22.1	22.6	23.1	23.6	59
60	16.5	17.0	17.5	18.0	18.5	19.0	19.5	20.0	20.5	21.0	21.5	22.0	22.5	23.0	23.5	24.0	60

TABLE 7

Speed, Time, and Distance

Minutes	24.5	25.0	25.5	26.0	26.5	27.0	27.5	28.0	28.5	29.0	29.5	30.0	30.5	31.0	31.5	32.0	Minutes
	Speed in knots																
	Miles	*Miles*	*Miles*	*Miles*	*Miles*	*Miles*	*Miles*	*Miles*	*Miles*	*Miles*	*Miles*	*Miles*	*Miles*	*Miles*	*Miles*	*Miles*	
1	0.4	0.4	0.4	0.4	0.4	0.4	0.5	0.5	0.5	0.5	0.5	0.5	0.5	0.5	0.5	0.5	1
2	0.8	0.8	0.8	0.9	0.9	0.9	0.9	0.9	1.0	1.0	1.0	1.0	1.0	1.0	1.0	1.1	2
3	1.2	1.2	1.3	1.3	1.3	1.4	1.4	1.4	1.4	1.4	1.5	1.5	1.5	1.6	1.6	1.6	3
4	1.6	1.7	1.7	1.7	1.8	1.8	1.8	1.9	1.9	1.9	2.0	2.0	2.0	2.1	2.1	2.1	4
5	2.0	2.1	2.1	2.2	2.2	2.2	2.3	2.3	2.4	2.4	2.5	2.5	2.5	2.6	2.6	2.7	5
6	2.4	2.5	2.6	2.6	2.6	2.7	2.8	2.8	2.8	2.9	3.0	3.0	3.0	3.1	3.2	3.2	6
7	2.9	2.9	3.0	3.0	3.1	3.2	3.2	3.3	3.3	3.4	3.4	3.5	3.6	3.6	3.7	3.7	7
8	3.3	3.3	3.4	3.5	3.5	3.6	3.7	3.7	3.8	3.9	3.9	4.0	4.1	4.1	4.2	4.3	8
9	3.7	3.8	3.8	3.9	4.0	4.0	4.1	4.2	4.3	4.4	4.4	4.5	4.6	4.6	4.7	4.8	9
10	4.1	4.2	4.2	4.3	4.4	4.5	4.6	4.7	4.8	4.8	4.9	5.0	5.1	5.2	5.2	5.3	10
11	4.5	4.6	4.7	4.8	4.9	5.0	5.0	5.1	5.2	5.3	5.4	5.5	5.6	5.7	5.8	5.9	11
12	4.9	5.0	5.1	5.2	5.3	5.4	5.5	5.6	5.7	5.8	5.9	6.0	6.1	6.2	6.3	6.4	12
13	5.3	5.4	5.5	5.6	5.7	5.8	6.0	6.1	6.2	6.3	6.4	6.5	6.6	6.7	6.8	6.9	13
14	5.7	5.8	6.0	6.1	6.2	6.3	6.4	6.5	6.6	6.8	6.9	7.0	7.1	7.2	7.4	7.5	14
15	6.1	6.2	6.4	6.5	6.6	6.8	6.9	7.0	7.1	7.2	7.4	7.5	7.6	7.8	7.9	8.0	15
16	6.5	6.7	6.8	6.9	7.1	7.2	7.3	7.5	7.6	7.7	7.9	8.0	8.1	8.3	8.4	8.5	16
17	6.9	7.1	7.2	7.4	7.5	7.6	7.8	7.9	8.1	8.2	8.4	8.5	8.6	8.8	8.9	9.1	17
18	7.4	7.5	7.6	7.8	8.0	8.1	8.2	8.4	8.6	8.7	8.8	9.0	9.2	9.3	9.4	9.6	18
19	7.8	7.9	8.1	8.2	8.4	8.6	8.7	8.9	9.0	9.2	9.3	9.5	9.7	9.8	10.0	10.1	19
20	8.2	8.3	8.5	8.7	8.8	9.0	9.2	9.3	9.5	9.7	9.8	10.0	10.2	10.3	10.5	10.7	20
21	8.6	8.8	8.9	9.1	9.3	9.4	9.6	9.8	10.0	10.2	10.3	10.5	10.7	10.8	11.0	11.2	21
22	9.0	9.2	9.4	9.5	9.7	9.9	10.1	10.3	10.4	10.6	10.8	11.0	11.2	11.4	11.6	11.7	22
23	9.4	9.6	9.8	10.0	10.2	10.4	10.5	10.7	10.9	11.1	11.3	11.5	11.7	11.9	12.1	12.3	23
24	9.8	10.0	10.2	10.4	10.6	10.8	11.0	11.2	11.4	11.6	11.8	12.0	12.2	12.4	12.6	12.8	24
25	10.2	10.4	10.6	10.8	11.0	11.2	11.5	11.7	11.9	12.1	12.3	12.5	12.7	12.9	13.1	13.3	25
26	10.6	10.8	11.0	11.3	11.5	11.7	11.9	12.1	12.4	12.6	12.8	13.0	13.2	13.4	13.6	13.9	26
27	11.0	11.2	11.5	11.7	11.9	12.2	12.4	12.6	12.8	13.0	13.3	13.5	13.7	14.0	14.2	14.4	27
28	11.4	11.7	11.9	12.1	12.4	12.6	12.8	13.1	13.3	13.5	13.8	14.0	14.2	14.5	14.7	14.9	28
29	11.8	12.1	12.3	12.6	12.8	13.0	13.3	13.5	13.8	14.0	14.3	14.5	14.7	15.0	15.2	15.5	29
30	12.2	12.5	12.8	13.0	13.2	13.5	13.8	14.0	14.2	14.5	14.8	15.0	15.2	15.5	15.8	16.0	30
31	12.7	12.9	13.2	13.4	13.7	14.0	14.2	14.5	14.7	15.0	15.2	15.5	15.8	16.0	16.3	16.5	31
32	13.1	13.3	13.6	13.9	14.1	14.4	14.7	14.9	15.2	15.5	15.7	16.0	16.3	16.5	16.8	17.1	32
33	13.5	13.8	14.0	14.3	14.6	14.8	15.1	15.4	15.7	16.0	16.2	16.5	16.8	17.0	17.3	17.6	33
34	13.9	14.2	14.4	14.7	15.0	15.3	15.6	15.9	16.2	16.4	16.7	17.0	17.3	17.6	17.8	18.1	34
35	14.3	14.6	14.9	15.2	15.5	15.8	16.0	16.3	16.6	16.9	17.2	17.5	17.8	18.1	18.4	18.7	35
36	14.7	15.0	15.3	15.6	15.9	16.2	16.5	16.8	17.1	17.4	17.7	18.0	18.3	18.6	18.9	19.2	36
37	15.1	15.4	15.7	16.0	16.3	16.6	17.0	17.3	17.6	17.9	18.2	18.5	18.8	19.1	19.4	19.7	37
38	15.5	15.8	16.2	16.5	16.8	17.1	17.4	17.7	18.0	18.4	18.7	19.0	19.3	19.6	20.0	20.3	38
39	15.9	16.2	16.6	16.9	17.2	17.6	17.9	18.2	18.5	18.8	19.2	19.5	19.8	20.2	20.5	20.8	39
40	16.3	16.7	17.0	17.3	17.7	18.0	18.3	18.7	19.0	19.3	19.7	20.0	20.3	20.7	21.0	21.3	40
41	16.7	17.1	17.4	17.8	18.1	18.4	18.8	19.1	19.5	19.8	20.2	20.5	20.8	21.2	21.5	21.9	41
42	17.2	17.5	17.8	18.2	18.6	18.9	19.2	19.6	20.0	20.3	20.6	21.0	21.4	21.7	22.0	22.4	42
43	17.6	17.9	18.3	18.6	19.0	19.4	19.7	20.1	20.4	20.8	21.1	21.5	21.9	22.2	22.6	22.9	43
44	18.0	18.3	18.7	19.1	19.4	19.8	20.2	20.5	20.9	21.3	21.6	22.0	22.4	22.7	23.1	23.5	44
45	18.4	18.8	19.1	19.5	19.9	20.2	20.6	21.0	21.4	21.8	22.1	22.5	22.9	23.2	23.6	24.0	45
46	18.8	19.2	19.6	19.9	20.3	20.7	21.1	21.5	21.8	22.2	22.6	23.0	23.4	23.8	24.2	24.5	46
47	19.2	19.6	20.0	20.4	20.8	21.2	21.5	21.9	22.3	22.7	23.1	23.5	23.9	24.3	24.7	25.1	47
48	19.6	20.0	20.4	20.8	21.2	21.6	22.0	22.4	22.8	23.2	23.6	24.0	24.4	24.8	25.2	25.6	48
49	20.0	20.4	20.8	21.2	21.6	22.0	22.5	22.9	23.3	23.7	24.1	24.5	24.9	25.3	25.7	26.1	49
50	20.4	20.8	21.2	21.7	22.1	22.5	22.9	23.3	23.8	24.2	24.6	25.0	25.4	25.8	26.2	26.7	50
51	20.8	21.2	21.7	22.1	22.5	23.0	23.4	23.8	24.2	24.6	25.1	25.5	25.9	26.4	26.8	27.2	51
52	21.2	21.7	22.1	22.5	23.0	23.4	23.8	24.3	24.7	25.1	25.6	26.0	26.4	26.9	27.3	27.7	52
53	21.6	22.1	22.5	23.0	23.4	23.8	24.3	24.7	25.2	25.6	26.1	26.5	26.9	27.4	27.8	28.3	53
54	22.0	22.5	23.0	23.4	23.8	24.3	24.8	25.2	25.6	26.1	26.6	27.0	27.4	27.9	28.4	28.8	54
55	22.5	22.9	23.4	23.8	24.3	24.8	25.2	25.7	26.1	26.6	27.0	27.5	28.0	28.4	28.9	29.3	55
56	22.9	23.3	23.8	24.3	24.7	25.2	25.7	26.1	26.6	27.1	27.5	28.0	28.5	28.9	29.4	29.9	56
57	23.3	23.8	24.2	24.7	25.2	25.6	26.1	26.6	27.1	27.6	28.0	28.5	29.0	29.4	29.9	30.4	57
58	23.7	24.2	24.6	25.1	25.6	26.1	26.6	27.1	27.6	28.0	28.5	29.0	29.5	30.0	30.4	30.9	58
59	24.1	24.6	25.1	25.6	26.1	26.6	27.0	27.5	28.0	28.5	29.0	29.5	30.0	30.5	31.0	31.5	59
60	24.5	25.0	25.5	26.0	26.5	27.0	27.5	28.0	28.5	29.0	29.5	30.0	30.5	31.0	31.5	32.0	60

TABLE 7

Speed, Time, and Distance

Minutes	Speed in knots																Minutes
	32.5	33.0	33.5	34.0	34.5	35.0	35.5	36.0	36.5	37.0	37.5	38.0	38.5	39.0	39.5	40.0	
	Miles	*Miles*	*Miles*	*Miles*	*Miles*	*Miles*	*Miles*	*Miles*	*Miles*	*Miles*	*Miles*	*Miles*	*Miles*	*Miles*	*Miles*	*Miles*	
1	0.5	0.6	0.6	0.6	0.6	0.6	0.6	0.6	0.6	0.6	0.6	0.6	0.6	0.6	0.7	0.7	1
2	1.1	1.1	1.1	1.1	1.2	1.2	1.2	1.2	1.2	1.2	1.2	1.3	1.3	1.3	1.3	1.3	2
3	1.6	1.6	1.7	1.7	1.7	1.8	1.8	1.8	1.8	1.8	1.9	1.9	1.9	2.0	2.0	2.0	3
4	2.2	2.2	2.2	2.3	2.3	2.3	2.4	2.4	2.4	2.5	2.5	2.5	2.6	2.6	2.6	2.7	4
5	2.7	2.8	2.8	2.8	2.9	2.9	3.0	3.0	3.0	3.1	3.1	3.2	3.2	3.2	3.3	3.3	5
6	3.2	3.3	3.4	3.4	3.4	3.5	3.6	3.6	3.6	3.7	3.8	3.8	3.8	3.9	4.0	4.0	6
7	3.8	3.8	3.9	4.0	4.0	4.1	4.1	4.2	4.3	4.3	4.4	4.4	4.5	4.6	4.6	4.7	7
8	4.3	4.4	4.5	4.5	4.6	4.7	4.7	4.8	4.9	4.9	5.0	5.1	5.1	5.2	5.3	5.3	8
9	4.9	5.0	5.0	5.1	5.2	5.2	5.3	5.4	5.5	5.6	5.6	5.7	5.8	5.8	5.9	6.0	9
10	5.4	5.5	5.6	5.7	5.8	5.8	5.9	6.0	6.1	6.2	6.2	6.3	6.4	6.5	6.6	6.7	10
11	6.0	6.0	6.1	6.2	6.3	6.4	6.5	6.6	6.7	6.8	6.9	7.0	7.1	7.2	7.2	7.3	11
12	6.5	6.6	6.7	6.8	6.9	7.0	7.1	7.2	7.3	7.4	7.5	7.6	7.7	7.8	7.9	8.0	12
13	7.0	7.2	7.3	7.4	7.5	7.6	7.7	7.8	7.9	8.0	8.1	8.2	8.3	8.4	8.6	8.7	13
14	7.6	7.7	7.8	7.9	8.0	8.2	8.3	8.4	8.5	8.6	8.8	8.9	9.0	9.1	9.2	9.3	14
15	8.1	8.2	8.4	8.5	8.6	8.8	8.9	9.0	9.1	9.2	9.4	9.5	9.6	9.8	9.9	10.0	15
16	8.7	8.8	8.9	9.1	9.2	9.3	9.5	9.6	9.7	9.9	10.0	10.1	10.3	10.4	10.5	10.7	16
17	9.2	9.4	9.5	9.6	9.8	9.9	10.1	10.2	10.3	10.5	10.6	10.8	10.9	11.0	11.2	11.3	17
18	9.8	9.9	10.0	10.2	10.4	10.5	10.6	10.8	11.0	11.1	11.2	11.4	11.6	11.7	11.8	12.0	18
19	10.3	10.4	10.6	10.8	10.9	11.1	11.2	11.4	11.6	11.7	11.9	12.0	12.2	12.4	12.5	12.7	19
20	10.8	11.0	11.2	11.3	11.5	11.7	11.8	12.0	12.2	12.3	12.5	12.7	12.8	13.0	13.2	13.3	20
21	11.4	11.6	11.7	11.9	12.1	12.2	12.4	12.6	12.8	13.0	13.1	13.3	13.5	13.6	13.8	14.0	21
22	11.9	12.1	12.3	12.5	12.6	12.8	13.0	13.2	13.4	13.6	13.8	13.9	14.1	14.3	14.5	14.7	22
23	12.5	12.6	12.8	13.0	13.2	13.4	13.6	13.8	14.0	14.2	14.4	14.6	14.8	15.0	15.1	15.3	23
24	13.0	13.2	13.4	13.6	13.8	14.0	14.2	14.4	14.6	14.8	15.0	15.2	15.4	15.6	15.8	16.0	24
25	13.5	13.8	14.0	14.2	14.4	14.6	14.8	15.0	15.2	15.4	15.6	15.8	16.0	16.2	16.5	16.7	25
26	14.1	14.3	14.5	14.7	15.0	15.2	15.4	15.6	15.8	16.0	16.2	16.5	16.7	16.9	17.1	17.3	26
27	14.6	14.8	15.1	15.3	15.5	15.8	16.0	16.2	16.4	16.6	16.9	17.1	17.3	17.6	17.8	18.0	27
28	15.2	15.4	15.6	15.9	16.1	16.3	16.6	16.8	17.0	17.3	17.5	17.7	18.0	18.2	18.4	18.7	28
29	15.7	16.0	16.2	16.4	16.7	16.9	17.2	17.4	17.6	17.9	18.1	18.4	18.6	18.8	19.1	19.3	29
30	16.2	16.5	16.8	17.0	17.2	17.5	17.8	18.0	18.2	18.5	18.8	19.0	19.2	19.5	19.8	20.0	30
31	16.8	17.0	17.3	17.6	17.8	18.1	18.3	18.6	18.9	19.1	19.4	19.6	19.9	20.2	20.4	20.7	31
32	17.3	17.6	17.9	18.1	18.4	18.7	18.9	19.2	19.5	19.7	20.0	20.3	20.5	20.8	21.1	21.3	32
33	17.9	18.2	18.4	18.7	19.0	19.2	19.5	19.8	20.1	20.4	20.6	20.9	21.2	21.4	21.7	22.0	33
34	18.4	18.7	19.0	19.3	19.6	19.8	20.1	20.4	20.7	21.0	21.2	21.5	21.8	22.1	22.4	22.7	34
35	19.0	19.2	19.5	19.8	20.1	20.4	20.7	21.0	21.3	21.6	21.9	22.2	22.5	22.8	23.0	23.3	35
36	19.5	19.8	20.1	20.4	20.7	21.0	21.3	21.6	21.9	22.2	22.5	22.8	23.1	23.4	23.7	24.0	36
37	20.0	20.4	20.7	21.0	21.3	21.6	21.9	22.2	22.5	22.8	23.1	23.4	23.7	24.0	24.4	24.7	37
38	20.6	20.9	21.2	21.5	21.8	22.2	22.5	22.8	23.1	23.4	23.8	24.1	24.4	24.7	25.0	25.3	38
39	21.1	21.4	21.8	22.1	22.4	22.8	23.1	23.4	23.7	24.0	24.4	24.7	25.0	25.4	25.7	26.0	39
40	21.7	22.0	22.3	22.7	23.0	23.3	23.7	24.0	24.3	24.7	25.0	25.3	25.7	26.0	26.3	26.7	40
41	22.2	22.6	22.9	23.2	23.6	23.9	24.3	24.6	24.9	25.3	25.6	26.0	26.3	26.6	27.0	27.3	41
42	22.8	23.1	23.4	23.8	24.2	24.5	24.8	25.2	25.6	25.9	26.2	26.6	27.0	27.3	27.6	28.0	42
43	23.3	23.6	24.0	24.4	24.7	25.1	25.4	25.8	26.2	26.5	26.9	27.2	27.6	28.0	28.3	28.7	43
44	23.8	24.2	24.6	24.9	25.3	25.7	26.0	26.4	26.8	27.1	27.5	27.9	28.2	28.6	29.0	29.3	44
45	24.4	24.8	25.1	25.5	25.9	26.2	26.6	27.0	27.4	27.8	28.1	28.5	28.9	29.2	29.6	30.0	45
46	24.9	25.3	25.7	26.1	26.4	26.8	27.2	27.6	28.0	28.4	28.8	29.1	29.5	29.9	30.3	30.7	46
47	25.5	25.8	26.2	26.6	27.0	27.4	27.8	28.2	28.6	29.0	29.4	29.8	30.2	30.6	30.9	31.3	47
48	26.0	26.4	26.8	27.2	27.6	28.0	28.4	28.8	29.2	29.6	30.0	30.4	30.8	31.2	31.6	32.0	48
49	26.5	27.0	27.4	27.8	28.2	28.6	29.0	29.4	29.8	30.2	30.6	31.0	31.4	31.8	32.3	32.7	49
50	27.1	27.5	27.9	28.3	28.8	29.2	29.6	30.0	30.4	30.8	31.2	31.7	32.1	32.5	32.9	33.3	50
51	27.6	28.0	28.5	28.9	29.3	29.8	30.2	30.6	31.0	31.4	31.9	32.3	32.7	33.2	33.6	34.0	51
52	28.2	28.6	29.0	29.5	29.9	30.3	30.8	31.2	31.6	32.1	32.5	32.9	33.4	33.8	34.2	34.7	52
53	28.7	29.2	29.6	30.0	30.5	30.9	31.4	31.8	32.2	32.7	33.1	33.6	34.0	34.4	34.9	35.3	53
54	29.2	29.7	30.2	30.6	31.0	31.5	32.0	32.4	32.8	33.3	33.8	34.2	34.6	35.1	35.6	36.0	54
55	29.8	30.2	30.7	31.2	31.6	32.1	32.5	33.0	33.5	33.9	34.4	34.8	35.3	35.8	36.2	36.7	55
56	30.3	30.8	31.3	31.7	32.2	32.7	33.1	33.6	34.1	34.5	35.0	35.5	35.9	36.4	36.9	37.3	56
57	30.9	31.4	31.8	32.3	32.8	33.2	33.7	34.2	34.7	35.2	35.6	36.1	36.6	37.0	37.5	38.0	57
58	31.4	31.9	32.4	32.9	33.4	33.8	34.3	34.8	35.3	35.8	36.2	36.7	37.2	37.7	38.2	38.7	58
59	32.0	32.4	32.9	33.4	33.9	34.4	34.9	35.4	35.9	36.4	36.9	37.4	37.9	38.4	38.8	39.3	59
60	32.5	33.0	33.5	34.0	34.5	35.0	35.5	36.0	36.5	37.0	37.5	38.0	38.5	39.0	39.5	40.0	60

TABLE 8

Dip of the Sea Short of the Horizon

Distance	Height of eye above the sea, in feet										Distance
	5	10	15	20	25	30	35	40	45	50	
Miles	′	′	′	′	′	′	′	′	′	′	*Miles*
0.1	28.3	56.6	84.9	113.2	141.5	169.8	198.0	226.3	254.6	282.9	0.1
0.2	14.2	28.4	42.5	56.7	70.8	84.9	99.1	113.2	127.4	141.5	0.2
0.3	9.6	19.0	28.4	37.8	47.3	56.7	66.1	75.6	85.0	94.4	0.3
0.4	7.2	14.3	21.4	28.5	35.5	42.6	49.7	56.7	63.8	70.9	0.4
0.5	5.9	11.5	17.2	22.8	28.5	34.2	39.8	45.5	51.1	56.8	0.5
0.6	5.0	9.7	14.4	19.1	23.8	28.5	33.3	38.0	42.7	47.4	0.6
0.7	4.3	8.4	12.4	16.5	20.5	24.5	28.6	32.6	36.7	40.7	0.7
0.8	3.9	7.4	10.9	14.5	18.0	21.5	25.1	28.6	32.2	35.7	0.8
0.9	3.5	6.7	9.8	12.9	16.1	19.2	22.4	25.5	28.7	31.8	0.9
1.0	3.2	6.1	8.9	11.7	14.6	17.4	20.2	23.0	25.9	28.7	1.0
1.1	3.0	5.6	8.2	10.7	13.3	15.9	18.5	21.0	23.6	26.2	1.1
1.2	2.9	5.2	7.6	9.9	12.3	14.6	17.0	19.4	21.7	24.1	1.2
1.3	2.7	4.9	7.1	9.2	11.4	13.6	15.8	17.9	20.1	22.3	1.3
1.4	2.6	4.6	6.6	8.7	10.7	12.7	14.7	16.7	18.8	20.8	1.4
1.5	2.5	4.4	6.3	8.2	10.0	11.9	13.8	15.7	17.6	19.5	1.5
1.6	2.4	4.2	6.0	7.7	9.5	11.3	13.0	14.8	16.6	18.3	1.6
1.7	2.4	4.0	5.7	7.4	9.0	10.7	12.4	14.0	15.7	17.3	1.7
1.8	2.3	3.9	5.5	7.0	8.6	10.2	11.7	13.3	14.9	16.5	1.8
1.9	2.3	3.8	5.3	6.7	8.2	9.7	11.2	12.7	14.2	15.7	1.9
2.0	2.2	3.7	5.1	6.5	7.9	9.3	10.7	12.1	13.6	15.0	2.0
2.1	2.2	3.6	4.9	6.3	7.6	9.0	10.3	11.6	13.0	14.3	2.1
2.2	2.2	3.5	4.8	6.1	7.3	8.6	9.9	11.2	12.5	13.8	2.2
2.3	2.2	3.4	4.6	5.9	7.1	8.3	9.6	10.8	12.0	13.3	2.3
2.4	2.2	3.4	4.5	5.7	6.9	8.1	9.2	10.4	11.6	12.8	2.4
2.5	2.2	3.3	4.4	5.6	6.7	7.8	9.0	10.1	11.2	12.4	2.5
2.6	2.2	3.3	4.3	5.4	6.5	7.6	8.7	9.8	10.9	12.0	2.6
2.7	2.2	3.2	4.3	5.3	6.4	7.4	8.4	9.5	10.6	11.6	2.7
2.8	2.2	3.2	4.2	5.2	6.2	7.2	8.2	9.2	10.3	11.3	2.8
2.9	2.2	3.2	4.1	5.1	6.1	7.1	8.0	9.0	10.0	11.0	2.9
3.0	2.2	3.1	4.1	5.0	6.0	6.9	7.8	8.8	9.7	10.7	3.0
3.1	2.2	3.1	4.0	4.9	5.9	6.8	7.7	8.6	9.5	10.4	3.1
3.2	2.2	3.1	4.0	4.9	5.7	6.6	7.5	8.4	9.3	10.2	3.2
3.3	2.2	3.1	3.9	4.8	5.7	6.5	7.4	8.2	9.1	9.9	3.3
3.4	2.2	3.1	3.9	4.7	5.6	6.4	7.2	8.1	8.9	9.7	3.4
3.5	2.2	3.1	3.9	4.7	5.5	6.3	7.1	7.9	8.7	9.5	3.5
3.6	2.2	3.1	3.8	4.6	5.4	6.2	7.0	7.8	8.6	9.4	3.6
3.7	2.2	3.1	3.8	4.6	5.4	6.1	6.9	7.7	8.4	9.2	3.7
3.8	2.2	3.1	3.8	4.6	5.3	6.0	6.8	7.5	8.3	9.0	3.8
3.9	2.2	3.1	3.8	4.5	5.2	6.0	6.7	7.4	8.1	8.9	3.9
4.0	2.2	3.1	3.8	4.5	5.2	5.9	6.6	7.3	8.0	8.7	4.0
4.1	2.2	3.1	3.8	4.5	5.1	5.8	6.5	7.2	7.9	8.6	4.1
4.2	2.2	3.1	3.8	4.4	5.1	5.8	6.5	7.1	7.8	8.5	4.2
4.3	2.2	3.1	3.8	4.4	5.1	5.7	6.4	7.0	7.7	8.4	4.3
4.4	2.2	3.1	3.8	4.4	5.0	5.7	6.3	7.0	7.6	8.3	4.4
4.5	2.2	3.1	3.8	4.4	5.0	5.6	6.3	6.9	7.5	8.2	4.5
4.6	2.2	3.1	3.8	4.4	5.0	5.6	6.2	6.8	7.4	8.1	4.6
4.7	2.2	3.1	3.8	4.4	5.0	5.6	6.2	6.8	7.4	8.0	4.7
4.8	2.2	3.1	3.8	4.4	4.9	5.5	6.1	6.7	7.3	7.9	4.8
4.9	2.2	3.1	3.8	4.3	4.9	5.5	6.1	6.7	7.2	7.8	4.9
5.0	2.2	3.1	3.8	4.3	4.9	5.5	6.0	6.6	7.2	7.7	5.0
5.5	2.2	3.1	3.8	4.3	4.9	5.4	5.9	6.4	6.9	7.4	5.5
6.0	2.2	3.1	3.8	4.3	4.9	5.3	5.8	6.3	6.7	7.2	6.0
6.5	2.2	3.1	3.8	4.3	4.9	5.3	5.7	6.2	6.6	7.1	6.5
7.0	2.2	3.1	3.8	4.3	4.9	5.3	5.7	6.1	6.5	6.9	7.0
7.5	2.2	3.1	3.8	4.3	4.9	5.3	5.7	6.1	6.5	6.9	7.5
8.0	2.2	3.1	3.8	4.3	4.9	5.3	5.7	6.1	6.5	6.9	8.0
8.5	2.2	3.1	3.8	4.3	4.9	5.3	5.7	6.1	6.5	6.9	8.5
9.0	2.2	3.1	3.8	4.3	4.9	5.3	5.7	6.1	6.5	6.9	9.0
9.5	2.2	3.1	3.8	4.3	4.9	5.3	5.7	6.1	6.5	6.9	9.5
10.0	2.2	3.1	3.8	4.3	4.9	5.3	5.7	6.1	6.5	6.9	10.0

TABLE 8

Dip of the Sea Short of the Horizon

Distance	Height of eye above the sea, in feet										Distance
	55	60	65	70	75	80	85	90	95	100	
Miles	′	′	′	′	′	′	′	′	′	′	*Miles*
0.1	311.2	339.5	367.8	396.1	424.4	452.6	480.9	509.2	537.5	565.8	0.1
0.2	155.6	169.8	184.0	198.1	212.2	226.4	240.5	254.7	268.8	283.0	0.2
0.3	103.8	113.3	122.7	132.1	141.6	151.0	160.4	169.9	179.3	188.7	0.3
0.4	78.0	85.0	92.1	99.2	106.2	113.3	120.4	127.5	134.5	141.6	0.4
0.5	62.4	68.1	73.8	79.4	85.1	90.7	96.4	102.0	107.7	113.4	0.5
0.6	52.1	56.8	61.5	66.3	71.0	75.7	80.4	85.1	89.8	94.5	0.6
0.7	44.7	48.8	52.8	56.9	60.9	64.9	69.0	73.0	77.1	81.1	0.7
0.8	39.2	42.8	46.3	49.8	53.4	56.9	60.4	64.0	67.5	71.1	0.8
0.9	34.9	38.1	41.2	44.4	47.5	50.7	53.8	56.9	60.1	63.2	0.9
1.0	31.5	34.4	37.2	40.0	42.8	45.7	48.5	51.3	54.2	57.0	1.0
1.1	28.7	31.3	33.9	36.5	39.0	41.6	44.2	46.7	49.3	51.9	1.1
1.2	26.4	28.8	31.1	33.5	35.9	38.2	40.6	42.9	45.3	47.6	1.2
1.3	24.5	26.7	28.8	31.0	33.2	35.4	37.5	39.7	41.9	44.1	1.3
1.4	22.8	24.8	26.8	28.9	30.9	32.9	34.9	37.0	39.0	41.0	1.4
1.5	21.4	23.3	25.1	27.0	28.9	30.8	32.7	34.6	36.5	38.3	1.5
1.6	20.1	21.9	23.6	25.4	27.2	29.0	30.7	32.5	34.3	36.0	1.6
1.7	19.0	20.7	22.3	24.0	25.7	27.3	29.0	30.7	32.3	34.0	1.7
1.8	18.0	19.6	21.2	22.8	24.3	25.9	27.5	29.0	30.6	32.2	1.8
1.9	17.2	18.7	20.1	21.6	23.1	24.6	26.1	27.6	29.1	30.6	1.9
2.0	16.4	17.8	19.2	20.6	22.0	23.5	24.9	26.3	27.7	29.1	2.0
2.1	15.7	17.0	18.4	19.7	21.1	22.4	23.8	25.1	26.5	27.8	2.1
2.2	15.1	16.3	17.6	18.9	20.2	21.5	22.7	24.1	25.3	26.6	2.2
2.3	14.5	15.7	16.9	18.2	19.4	20.6	21.9	23.1	24.3	25.6	2.3
2.4	14.0	15.1	16.3	17.5	18.7	19.9	21.0	22.2	23.4	24.6	2.4
2.5	13.5	14.6	15.7	16.9	18.0	19.1	20.3	21.4	22.5	23.7	2.5
2.6	13.0	14.1	15.2	16.3	17.4	18.5	19.6	20.7	21.8	22.8	2.6
2.7	12.6	13.7	14.7	15.8	16.8	17.9	18.9	20.0	21.0	22.1	2.7
2.8	12.3	13.3	14.3	15.3	16.3	17.3	18.3	19.3	20.4	21.4	2.8
2.9	11.9	12.9	13.9	14.9	15.8	16.8	17.8	18.8	19.7	20.7	2.9
3.0	11.6	12.6	13.5	14.4	15.4	16.3	17.3	18.2	19.2	20.1	3.0
3.1	11.3	12.2	13.2	14.1	15.0	15.9	16.8	17.7	18.6	19.5	3.1
3.2	11.1	11.9	12.8	13.7	14.6	15.5	16.4	17.2	18.1	19.0	3.2
3.3	10.8	11.7	12.5	13.4	14.2	15.1	15.9	16.8	17.7	18.5	3.3
3.4	10.6	11.4	12.2	13.1	13.9	14.7	15.6	16.4	17.2	18.1	3.4
3.5	10.3	11.2	12.0	12.8	13.6	14.4	15.2	16.0	16.8	17.6	3.5
3.6	10.1	10.9	11.7	12.4	13.3	14.1	14.9	15.6	16.4	17.2	3.6
3.7	9.9	10.7	11.5	12.2	13.0	13.8	14.5	15.3	16.1	16.8	3.7
3.8	9.8	10.5	11.3	12.0	12.7	13.5	14.2	15.0	15.7	16.5	3.8
3.9	9.6	10.3	11.1	11.8	12.5	13.2	14.0	14.7	15.4	16.1	3.9
4.0	9.4	10.1	10.9	11.6	12.3	13.0	13.7	14.4	15.1	15.8	4.0
4.1	9.3	10.0	10.7	11.4	12.1	12.7	13.4	14.1	14.8	15.5	4.1
4.2	9.2	9.8	10.5	11.2	11.8	12.5	13.2	13.9	14.5	15.2	4.2
4.3	9.0	9.7	10.3	11.0	11.7	12.3	13.0	13.6	14.3	14.9	4.3
4.4	8.9	9.5	10.2	10.8	11.5	12.1	12.8	13.4	14.0	14.7	4.4
4.5	8.8	9.4	10.0	10.7	11.3	11.9	12.6	13.2	13.8	14.4	4.5
4.6	8.7	9.3	9.9	10.5	11.1	11.8	12.4	13.0	13.6	14.2	4.6
4.7	8.6	9.2	9.8	10.4	11.0	11.6	12.2	12.8	13.4	14.0	4.7
4.8	8.5	9.1	9.7	10.2	10.8	11.4	12.0	12.6	13.2	13.8	4.8
4.9	8.4	9.0	9.5	10.1	10.7	11.3	11.9	12.4	13.0	13.6	4.9
5.0	8.3	8.9	9.4	10.0	10.6	11.1	11.7	12.3	12.8	13.4	5.0
5.5	7.9	8.5	9.0	9.5	10.0	10.5	11.0	11.5	12.1	12.6	5.5
6.0	7.7	8.2	8.6	9.1	9.6	10.0	10.5	11.0	11.5	11.9	6.0
6.5	7.5	7.9	8.4	8.8	9.2	9.7	10.1	10.5	11.0	11.4	6.5
7.0	7.4	7.8	8.2	8.6	9.0	9.4	9.8	10.2	10.6	11.0	7.0
7.5	7.3	7.6	8.0	8.4	8.8	9.2	9.5	9.9	10.3	10.7	7.5
8.0	7.2	7.6	7.9	8.3	8.6	9.0	9.3	9.7	10.0	10.4	8.0
8.5	7.2	7.5	7.9	8.2	8.5	8.9	9.2	9.5	9.9	10.2	8.5
9.0	7.2	7.5	7.8	8.1	8.5	8.8	9.1	9.4	9.7	10.0	9.0
9.5	7.2	7.5	7.8	8.1	8.4	8.7	9.0	9.3	9.6	9.9	9.5
10.0	7.2	7.5	7.8	8.1	8.4	8.7	9.0	9.2	9.5	9.8	10.0

TABLE 9

Natural and Numerical Chart Scales

Natural Scale	Miles Per Inch		Inches Per Mile		Feet Per Inch
	Nautical	Statute	Nautical	Statute	
1:500	0.007	0.008	145.83	126.72	41.67
1:600	0.008	0.009	121.52	105.60	50.00
1:1,000	0.014	0.016	72.91	63.36	83.33
1:1,200	0.016	0.019	60.76	52.80	100.00
1:1,500	0.021	0.024	48.61	42.24	125.00
1:2,000	0.027	0.032	36.46	31.68	166.67
1:2,400	0.033	0.038	30.38	26.40	200.00
1:2,500	0.034	0.039	29.17	25.34	208.33
1:3,000	0.041	0.047	24.30	21.12	250.00
1:3,600	0.049	0.057	20.25	17.60	300.00
1:4,000	0.055	0.063	18.23	15.84	333.33
1:4,800	0.066	0.076	15.19	13.20	400.00
1:5,000	0.069	0.079	14.58	12.67	416.67
1:6,000	0.082	0.095	12.15	10.56	500.00
1:7,000	0.096	0.110	10.42	9.05	583.33
1:7,200	0.099	0.114	10.13	8.80	600.00
1:7,920	0.109	0.125	9.21	8.00	660.00
1:8,000	0.110	0.126	9.11	7.92	666.67
1:8,400	0.115	0.133	8.68	7.54	700.00
1:9,000	0.123	0.142	8.10	7.04	750.00
1:9,600	0.132	0.152	7.60	6.60	800.00
1:10,000	0.137	0.158	7.29	6.34	833.33
1:10,800	0.148	0.170	6.75	5.87	900.00
1:12,000	0.165	0.189	6.08	5.28	1,000.00
1:13,200	0.181	0.208	5.52	4.80	1,100.00
1:14,400	0.197	0.227	5.06	4.40	1,200.00
1:15,000	0.206	0.237	4.86	4.22	1,250.00
1:15,600	0.214	0.246	4.67	4.06	1,300.00
1:15,840	0.217	0.250	4.60	4.00	1,320.00
1:16,000	0.219	0.253	4.56	3.96	1,333.33
1:16,800	0.230	0.265	4.34	3.77	1,400.00
1:18,000	0.247	0.284	4.05	3.52	1,500.00
1:19,200	0.263	0.303	3.80	3.30	1,600.00
1:20,000	0.274	0.316	3.65	3.17	1,666.67
1:20,400	0.280	0.322	3.57	3.11	1,700.00
1:21,120	0.290	0.333	3.45	3.00	1,760.00
1:21,600	0.296	0.341	3.38	2.93	1,800.00
1:22,800	0.313	0.360	3.20	2.78	1,900.00
1:24,000	0.329	0.379	3.04	2.64	2,000.00
1:25,000	0.343	0.395	2.92	2.53	2,083.33
1:40,000	0.549	0.631	1.82	1.58	3,333.33
1:48,000	0.658	0.758	1.52	1.32	4,000.00
1:50,000	0.686	0.789	1.46	1.27	4,166.67
1:62,500	0.857	0.986	1.17	1.01	5,208.33
1:63,360	0.869	1.000	1.15	1.00	5,280.00
1:75,000	1.029	1.184	0.97	0.85	6,250.00
1:80,000	1.097	1.263	0.91	0.79	6,666.67
1:100,000	1.371	1.578	0.73	0.63	8,333.33
1:125,000	1.714	1.973	0.58	0.51	10,416.67
1:200,000	2.743	3.157	0.36	0.32	16,666.67
1:250,000	3.429	3.946	0.29	0.25	20,833.33
1:400,000	5.486	6.313	0.18	0.16	33,333.33
1:500,000	6.857	7.891	0.15	0.13	41,666.67
1:750,000	10.286	11.837	0.10	0.08	62,500.00
1:1,000,000	13.715	15.783	0.07	0.06	83,333.33
FORMULAS	$\frac{\text{SCALE}}{72{,}913.39}$	$\frac{\text{SCALE}}{63{,}360}$	$\frac{72{,}913.39}{\text{SCALE}}$	$\frac{63{,}360}{\text{SCALE}}$	$\frac{\text{SCALE}}{12}$